the New James Beard

Drawings by

Karl Stuecklen

the New James Beard

a James Beard Cookbook

Drawings by Karl Stuecklen

WINGS BOOKS
New York • Avenel, New Jersey

Copyright © 1981 by James Beard
Illustrations copyright © 1981 by Karl Stuecklen
All rights reserved.

This 1995 edition is published by Wings Books,
distributed by Random House Value Publishing, Inc.,
40 Engelhard Avenue, Avenel, New Jersey 07001,
by arrangement with Alfred A. Knopf, Inc.

Random House
New York • Toronto • London • Sydney • Auckland

Printed and bound in the United States of America

Library of Congress Cataloging-in-Publication Data
Beard, James, 1903–1985
The new James Beard.
Reprint. Originally published: New York : Knopf, 1981.
Includes index.
ISBN 0-517-68800-X
1. Cookery, American.   I. Title.
[TX715.B3717   1989]   89–33945
641.5—dc20   CIP

10   9   8   7   6   5   4   3

Contents

Introduction   vii

Appetizers   2

Soups   42

Salads   70

Vegetables   114

Fish and Shellfish   192

Eggs and Cheese   246

Pasta, Rice, Grains, and Dried Beans   272

Poultry   312

Meat   358

Breads and Cookies   466

Desserts   496

Basic Stocks and Sauces   529

Concordance   539

Index   599

Introduction

At my ripe age, I acknowledge with some pleasure that my lifelong liaison with good food has gradually been creating a new me. Only four years ago, when I published *Theory & Practice of Good Cooking*, I had planned a recipe book as its complement—a needed one, since *T & P*'s detailed explanations of basic techniques left only just room enough for the recipes I'd picked to illustrate them. For you, the two books would add up to a fairly complete kitchen guide; for me, they would be the culmination of my long cooking career. My model for the second book was to be *The James Beard Cookbook*, a fat compendium first published in 1959, somewhat updated in 1970—with all the world's cooks surging with activity and bursting with good ideas, it was sorely in need of a complete update. As I set to work, I thought of my recipe book as *The Revised Standard Beard*.

But something had been quietly happening, I came to realize: a shift straight across the whole spectrum of my cookery, all the way from menu making right down to how I now wrote recipes. Neither the form nor the content of *The James Beard Cookbook* would serve as a model. The new me had to write a new book, from scratch.

This is still a recipe compendium, as planned, and a practical guide. All the basic information you need is here—sometimes in detail, where I'm dealing with new ideas, but in brief form where the basic sauces are con-

vii

cerned—and for those see page 529. For marketing information, see the Concordance repeated from *T & P*, with helpful additions and references to both books. The recipes are detailed enough for any cook. I don't think it's fair to you to make one book depend on another, and you don't need to own *T & P* to use this. (I do commend it to anyone in search of understanding, for the whys and wherefores of the basic processes like boiling, frying, sautéing, baking, and so on.) It does have delicious recipes, it has useful reminders for even the seasoned cook, and its instructions for the food processor and the heavy-duty mixer are up to date. This book includes, as well, newer equipment like pasta machines and microwave ovens, but if you don't have any of these gadgets, both books explain hand methods.

Technique is modified by equipment, heat sources (e.g., charcoal vs. gas), and other factors, but the principles don't change. Relatively stable, technique is the warp of good cooking. Ingredients are the woof, and the takeoff point of *The New James Beard*. I've dealt with novel ingredients like green peppercorns, new fruits, whole grains, improved flours and colorful pastas. I've taken a fresh look at some of this country's resources like beef and re-evaluated them. Yogurt, which most people treat as something to be eaten on its own, is shown to be as adaptable in cooking as cream. My new style of seasoning involves less salt, more use of major ingredients that heighten each other—vegetable combinations, for instance—and more recourse to Far Eastern and South American flavor patterns. The recipes number plenty of old favorites, some modified, a few not: in every case the recipe has been newly scrutinized to see if it needed improvement. What I want to stress is a new, flexible approach to ingredients, to the way we put them together, and the way we plan a meal.

The chapters are arranged in an unorthodox order, a change in structure which corresponds to my new thinking about menus. Almost any dish in the first six chapters can be served either as an appetizer or as a main course, including most of the soups, the salads, and the vegetables. Put the emphasis where you please. Feel free.

In a number of chapters, I explore different flavor affinities, in the hope that you will adapt these suggestions in creating a dish of your own. The recipes themselves have other suggestions. Take a fresh look. My emphasis is on options, my motto is "Why not?" and my hope is to provide you with inspiration as well as practical guidance.

Take a Fresh Look

Old-fashioned cookbooks, including my early ones, used to treat recipes as formulas. But in cooking along with my friends, colleagues, and students, I came to find the formula style boring and rigid. Listening is much more useful than prescribing *what*, and everybody learns best through thinking, not just performing. More and more, in class, my students talk back and speak up, to my benefit *and to their own, too*. We finally thought up "tasting" classes as a route to real sharing. One evening, for instance, we tasted vinegars—thirty-two kinds—and made alternative versions of poulet au vinaigre. Then everyone was asked to imagine which kind of oil, what herb each vinegar "asked for" as a complement for a vinaigrette sauce. The resonances and harmonics were fascinating, useful, and highly individual. Every palate is different; every cook has a personal style. I want you to make "my" dishes your own, so nowadays my basic recipes usually suggest variations, which really amount to new dishes. In many cases, you'll find the variation offers a new way of cutting down on fats and starches—restrictions, alas, that most of us are faced with at some point in our lives.

Let the quality of your ingredients speak to you. Taste things half-done, done—and overdone, if that happens; mistakes are to learn from, not to pine over. You may decide not to cook your meat or fish at all. I love paper-thin slices of a fine raw tenderloin, or a steak tartare when I feel like a higher seasoning, or sushi or sashimi if the fish is impeccably fresh. If the beef you brought home seems underaged, lacking in texture and flavor like most beef these days, check the meat chapter for ways of stepping it up a bit. If your horsy winter carrots seem a bit blah, don't automatically head for the spice shelf or the salt; try puréing them with beets. Check the flavor charts, take off from there, but remember that you can't always predict or imagine the effect of one flavor on another. Would you believe sardines with mint? I urge you to try it.

Taste every time you cook, and take nothing for granted—not even your own palate, for it can change. Mine has. I seem to be leaning toward lighter food in general—less meat, lighter sauces, fewer items on my plate and in my menus. Fish and vegetables I always loved, and not just as carriers for sauces; but now my appreciation has evolved toward simplicity. Since doing time on a salt-free diet, I approach a plain baked potato reverently. Maybe I've been missing the truth—the nutty, delicate earthiness of a perfect baked potato. Salt only masks it. In a fancy mood, I heighten it with caviar; in a plain mood, I just give it several grinds of fresh black pepper. Again, during that diet I sometimes craved intense aromas, so this book has a new trove of recipes for root vegetables.

Feel Free

Cooking has entered a grand era of liberation, not just in how we cook, but whether we cook, and what. People are making a lot of things from scratch instead of buying them. The commercial product is sometimes disappointing, and besides, with modern equipment you can make your own sausage, pasta, bread, cookies, pastries, mayonnaise, sorbets, etc., in less time than it takes to run over to the supermarket. So this book includes recipes for what were formerly "store" items. Do try them all and vary them: my students say it's like entering another world to find that bread, for instance, isn't just a standard-brand slab to put butter on, but that every loaf has character of its own. (This book contains only my newest bread ideas, plus a basic loaf for beginners; the world of bread is so vast I gave it a book of its own, *Beard on Bread*.)

On the other hand, people nowadays feel free to serve store-bought items if they're good. I've always loved composing a picnic right on the spot in a market or delicatessen. Look in the appetizer chapter, especially, for delicious ways to use sardines and herring and pickles—not just at picnics, but at dinner parties. Serve anything you really like, any way you like, any time you like. Culinary snobbery used to stress expense and show: the filet de boeuf en bellevue, the larded saddle of venison, the pheasant en plumage. Now it's moved toward ingenuity and surprise—and incidentally, toward cheaper cuts and neglected fish. In the present gastronomic furor, restaurant chefs the world over are reaching in all directions for novelty—often with good results. We are not thinking in the same stiff categories that we used to. Meat can be a seasoning, not a prime ingredient. A main dish of grains, or a robust combination of vegetables, sufficiently anchors a meal. More and more we're composing menus by instinct rather than by rule.

In my youth, a "proper" dinner had to have something light at each end, like consommé to begin and fruit to finish—you could call the menu diamond-shaped, with a big bulge at the main course, after the fish and before the made dessert. Usually it was a roast, with something starchy and several vegetables. By the middle of the century, with hosts and hostesses doing everything themselves, the number of courses had shrunk, but the big bulge had remained: at home meals, on one big greedy overloaded plate. At restaurants you were kept as busy as a one-man band, flailing to right and to left of you at the little bread-and-butter plate (already filled up with relishes that had been passed the minute you sat down), the little oval bowl —or what were called fish bowls in a restaurant kitchen—of, say, creamed onions, and the other little bowl, which usually contained peas and carrots. If you happened to have ordered corn, a large ear was invariably crowded onto that same dinner plate. How can you really enjoy corn like that? I like to serve it all by itself. And when it's really fresh and perfect I serve it first, for emphasis.

In other words, the main course is whatever you want to star—the nicest thing, perhaps, that you are offering at that meal. For some cooks, it may well be dessert, though not for me; I'm not a great dessert man. (Nevertheless, I recommend my grand Sharlotka (page 525) and my broad array of cheesecakes to cooks who take the Viennese, or delayed-climax, point of view about menus.)

I like to express emphasis by copiousness, not elaboration. I've never had any regard for sugar roses or orange cups or lemon frills or noodle baskets—for food that imitates something else. Yes, I garnish platters with parsley, but the parsley is to eat if you like it. I do. (I even like a salad of pure parsley—see page 80.) This year for my annual celebration of the first shad roe, we had a luscious pair of sautéed roe apiece—with parsley—then very small paillards of veal with a little cucumber salad—together on the plate, so the juices would mingle, which used to be heresy—and wound up with just a taste of fresh strawberry sorbet. A wedge-shaped dinner, then. And why not? It tasted wonderful, and taste is the only rule a cook need acknowledge, in this happy time of freshness and freedom.

The culinary world was never livelier than now, restaurants were never more experimental, and great cooks were never more appreciated. Taste responds to feedback—well named, because it does nourish the imagination. The razzle-dazzle is a great stimulant. But what truly stimulates, sustains, and rewards good cooking is honor at home. It gives me joy to see so many couples cooking together these days, and to watch their children growing up where they belong, right in the kitchen, as I did long ago.

One last word: During the preparation of this book and others over the years, I have been assisted by José Wilson. Not only was she a wonderful collaborator but she was a beloved friend. Her untimely death is a great loss to me, and I consider this book a monument to her memory.

The New James Beard

Appetizers

In planning this chapter, I set my fancy free to roam across every category but soups and sweets, assembling a lively bazaar of inventive, bright-flavored dishes that whet the appetite without sating it too soon. It was happy work, for no kind of food is more fun to think about, has more variety, or lends itself to such alluring presentations and such piquant contrasts. Arranging the finished dishes for a big party is as much fun as composing them; I like the colors of a garnished tuna platter next to the soft yellow-greens of avocado stuffed with pink shrimp, and the plump shape of a big golden brioche contrasted with layers of tiny blini. The aromas hovering over a grand buffet blend so enticingly: the bracing marine waft of sizzling-hot mussels and clams, the subtleties of herbed pâtés, the comforting richness of chicken livers with scrambled eggs. I relish a mouthful in which textures combine on the tongue, like succulent, cool ripe fruit with a salty wisp of prosciutto, or the dense crumb of good dark bread with satiny smoked

salmon. It's luxurious to eat like this, choosily and at leisure, between sips of wine or a crackling-cold mineral water, trying a sliver of this or a little mound of that, experimenting here, repeating there, pausing for greetings and conversations and laughter, and gradually, as the evening passes, composing a meal as you would a mosaic.

You might turn to this chapter first, when planning a big party, but bear in mind that almost all these dishes are excellent first courses for dinner, or main courses for luncheons and light suppers. Their number includes lots of delicious, quickly made "little somethings," too, for the times when a friend is expected for a glass of champagne and a chat. And don't confine your planning to this chapter. Appetizers can be anything that is easy to serve and fun to eat, and many dishes elsewhere in this book are excellent for the purpose. Salads, for instance, or egg or cheese or vegetable dishes, or even roast meats if the occasion and the hour seem to call for something substantial. What could be more appetizing than a rosy, fine-grained slice of roast fillet on your own good bread, with plenty of herbed butter?

I have even included a couple of novel cocktail tidbits here, though the long era of the old-fashioned cocktail party ended sometime in the seventies. With it departed "appetizer" as a misnomer for a salty, soggy bit of finger food, whose rather insidious purpose was to sop up alcohol

3

while promoting a thirst for more. "Thirstifying" it was, perhaps, but appetizing, seldom. Hard liquor has lost favor, and now that people drink in a saner way, to enhance not dull the senses, they want delightful and interesting things to eat, not to snap up absent-mindedly. Small plates are called for, and forks; and I like my guests to have room to sit down before they move on again, to greet other friends—or to revisit the array of appetizers.

APPETIZERS

Anchovies with sweet
    peppers
    with peppers and tuna
    with shallots and parsley
    with eggs and tomatoes
    with tomatoes

Herring
    pickled
    marinated
    in sour cream
    Madeira
    mustard
    salad
    rollmops

Smoked salmon
    marinated
    rolls with horseradish
        cream

Smoked haddock mousse
    smoked trout mousse
    kipper mousse
    sardine mousse

Tuna
    with artichoke hearts
    with hard-boiled egg
    with tomatoes
    with tomatoes and onions
    primavera

Tuna pâté
    salmon pâté
    smoked sturgeon pâté

Pike and salmon pâté

Salmon tartare
    sturgeon tartare
    tuna tartare
    striped bass tartare

Mussels
    Hiely
    provençal
    salad
    rémoulade
    with snail butter

Clams
    au gratin
    herbed
    anchovy
    provençal
    casino

Brains gribiche

Escabeche of fish
    of tongue
    of brains
    of sweetbreads
    of beef
    of chicken
    of mackerel

Soused shrimp
    with tarragon
    soused scallops

Shrimp in sour cream with
    mushrooms
    crabmeat in sour cream
    scallops in sour cream

Shrimp Kiev

Goujonettes of sole
    in beer batter

Sardines with mint

Snails with garlic butter
    in mushroom caps

Rolled chicken pâté

Pâté of chicken livers
    and ham

Rabbit pâté

Pork liver pâté en brioche

Herbed pâté

Pork rillettes
    goose rillettes
    truffled rillettes

Brioche bohémienne

Brioches with ham

Sausage en brioche

Sausage and croissants

Chicken in lettuce leaves
    squab in lettuce leaves

Chicken hearts and livers
    en brochette
    with béarnaise sauce
    with scrambled eggs
    hearts en brochette

Anticuchos
    with chicken hearts

Prosciutto with asparagus
    with melon
    with papaya
    with figs
    with pears
    with pineapple

Crabmeat and prosciutto

Eggplant purée

Caponata
    with tuna
	Avocado stuffed with
	    shrimp
	    with crab
		Twice-baked potato skins

Mushroom pâté	with avocado and
	    Russian dressing
		Onions à la grecque
		    monégasque
		    gratin

Tapenade
    with mustard
    tomatoes stuffed with
    with hard-boiled eggs
    with avocado
    as a sauce for fish
    mayonnaise
    with seafood
	with seviche
	    with chili
	    with chicken, ham, and
	    cheese
		Asparagus Italian style
		    Dutch
		    Belgian
		    in ambush

Peppers stuffed with
    anchovies and raisins
	Baked potatoes with caviar
	new potatoes with caviar
	deep-fried new potatoes
	    with caviar
		Blini
		    buckwheat
		    carrot

Anchovies

With the exception of the herring, no other salted fish is as widely used for an hors d'oeuvre as the anchovy. Shop for the large 1- or 2-pound tins of fillets in oil from Italy, Spain, or Portugal. They vary considerably in quality, from firm to mushy, so find a good brand and stick with it. Properly wrapped in foil, the opened tin will keep in the refrigerator for 2 weeks.

Or shop for the salted anchovies which come whole in large tins or jars and are of excellent quality and flavor. You can fillet these anchovies very easily after they have been soaked in water to remove excess salt.

Sweet Peppers with Anchovies

Makes 12 servings

12 red bell peppers
½ cup olive oil
1 to 2 tablespoons wine vinegar or
    sherry wine vinegar

Salt, freshly ground black pepper
2 dozen anchovy fillets
2 tablespoons chopped parsley

Roast the peppers (see page 165); remove skins, stems, and seeds; and quarter or halve them. Arrange in a flat serving dish. Make a dressing with the oil, vinegar, salt to taste (remember the anchovies are salty), and a few grinds of pepper. Pour this over the peppers and let them marinate several hours.

Remove from marinade and combine with the anchovy fillets and parsley and serve as an appetizer. Or serve in the dish with the marinade and pass the anchovies and parsley separately.

¶**Anchovies, Peppers, and Tuna.** For a more substantial dish, arrange the peppers with anchovies around a mound of fish and sprinkle with capers.

¶**Anchovies with Shallots and Parsley.** Alternate layers of chopped shallots with layers of chopped parsley and anchovy fillets, ending with parsley. Add enough olive oil to moisten each layer. For 1 pound of anchovy fillets you will need at least 1 cup chopped parsley and 1 cup chopped shallots. If shallots are not available, thinly sliced spring onions, scallions, or green onions can be substituted.

¶**Anchovies with Eggs and Tomatoes.** Alternate, in a serving dish, layers of thinly sliced, unpeeled ripe tomatoes, sliced hard-cooked eggs, and anchovy fillets arranged in crisscross fashion. Garnish with capers, chopped parsley, and black olives, and dress the hors d'oeuvre lightly with a vinaigrette sauce.

Anchovies with Tomatoes

Makes 12 servings

12 *large ripe tomatoes, peeled, seeded, and chopped*
6 *tablespoons olive oil*
2 *teaspoons finely chopped fresh basil or 1 teaspoon dried basil*
2 *cloves garlic, finely chopped*
1 *teaspoon freshly ground black pepper*
Salt
24 *anchovy fillets*
½ *cup capers*
1 *cup black olives, the Greek or Italian ones*
GARNISH: *Chopped parsley*

Cook the tomatoes slowly in the oil with the basil, garlic, pepper, and salt. (Be sparing with the salt as the anchovies will be salty.) When the tomato mixture is thickened (it should be more the consistency of a thick cream sauce or a fondue than a purée), taste for seasoning. Allow to cool, and spoon into a serving dish. Top with anchovy fillets, capers, and black olives. Add olive oil if you want to. Garnish with chopped parsley.

Herring

Herring is one of those foods that many people forget about as an hors d'oeuvre, but it is amazingly versatile and can be prepared and served in all kinds of ways. In Sweden, for instance, you'll find it accompanied by hot new potatoes and fresh dill, a delicious combination of flavors.

Salt herring can be bought packed in brine or already soaked and pickled. If you buy it in brine, the fish must be freshened first in cold water by soaking it for 24 hours, changing the water several times. Then remove, cut off the head, slit the fish and remove the fillets from the bone with a sharp knife. Any small remaining bones can be removed with tweezers, or they will dissolve eventually in the pickle. You can skin the herring or leave the skin on, as you wish.

Pickled Herring

Makes 8 to 10 servings

8 to 10 salt herring fillets, freshened
1 large onion, sliced
1 tart apple, diced
2 bay leaves
12 peppercorns
1 lemon, sliced
1 cup wine vinegar
½ cup dry white wine
⅓ cup sugar
2 tablespoons Dijon mustard

Arrange the herring in a flat dish with the onion, apple, bay leaves, and peppercorns. Blend remaining ingredients separately in a saucepan, and bring to a boil. Cool slightly and pour over the herring. When thoroughly cooled, cover and refrigerate for several days before serving.

¶Marinated Herring. Omit mustard from recipe.

¶Herring in Sour Cream. Prepare marinated herring. Remove fillets from marinade and cut in pieces, or leave whole, as you wish. Arrange in a dish with the onions from the marinade and additional thinly sliced onion. Cover with sour cream.

¶Madeira Herring. Omit vinegar and sugar from pickled herring and cover with Madeira.

¶Mustard Herring. Arrange freshened fillets in a dish and cover with 1 onion, sliced into rings. Blend ⅔ cup Dijon mustard and ½ cup olive oil. Add a dash of Tabasco, 2 tablespoons chopped fresh dill, and ½ cup white wine. Pour over fish, cover, and refrigerate for 2 days.

¶Herring Salad. Cut 3 soaked herring fillets into bite-size pieces. Combine with 1 to 1½ cups diced cold meat (tongue, veal, or beef), 1 crisp apple (diced with the skin on), 1 cup diced cooked potatoes, and 1 cup diced beets. Toss well with mayonnaise or mayonnaise mixed with sour cream. Pack into a mold and chill. Unmold on a bed of greens and sprinkle with chopped fresh dill or parsley.

Rollmops

Makes 12 rollmops

3 fresh dill pickles, quartered lengthwise
6 salt herring, freshened and filleted
    but unskinned (12 fillets)
4 medium onions, sliced
1 cup vinegar
1 cup water

½ cup sugar
2 bay leaves
1 clove garlic
4 to 6 whole allspice berries
8 peppercorns
GARNISH: Fresh dill

Place a piece of dill pickle on each fillet, roll the fillet around it, and fasten with a toothpick. Arrange over sliced onions in a deep dish or bowl. Combine the remaining ingredients in a saucepan, stirring to dissolve the sugar, and bring to a boil. Pour over the rollmops and allow to cool. Refrigerate for 48 hours. Serve with a garnish of fresh dill.

Marinated Smoked Salmon

Use a lesser grade of smoked salmon or lox, not the most expensive imported kind, and have it sliced very thin.

Makes 4 servings

½ pound smoked salmon or lox,
    thinly sliced
1 large onion, peeled and sliced
    paper-thin
GARNISH: Parsley and dill sprigs, 1 thinly sliced unpeeled cucumber (not waxed)

6 to 8 sprigs fresh dill
¼ cup capers
1 cup mayonnaise (see page 76)
1 cup yogurt

Cut the smoked salmon into strips. In a rectangular serving dish arrange alternate layers of salmon, onion slices, sprigs of dill, and capers. Thin the mayonnaise with the yogurt (this gives it a sharp flavor) and pour the dressing over the salmon. Refrigerate for several hours before serving. To serve, garnish with the parsley and dill sprigs and arrange cucumber slices around the edge. If you can't get an unwaxed cucumber, either scrub off the coating of wax under scalding water or peel the cucumber.

Smoked Salmon Rolls with Horseradish Cream

The rich filling stretches smoked salmon for a dinner-party first course. Serve the rolls with strips of thin buttered rye-bread sandwiches or fingers of crisp hot buttered toast.

Makes 6 servings

½ cup cream cheese
½ cup sour cream
½ cup coarsely grated fresh horseradish
   or ⅓ cup drained bottled
   horseradish

6 long, very thinly cut slices of smoked
   salmon
GARNISH: *Capers, parsley sprigs, lemon
   wedges*

Beat the cream cheese and sour cream to a paste and mix in the horseradish; if you use freshly grated horseradish, save some for the garnish. Spread the cream on the smoked salmon and roll up loosely. Arrange on individual plates and garnish with capers, parsley, lemon, and reserved horseradish.

Smoked Haddock Mousse

Smoked haddock, or finnan haddie, is usually served for breakfast, but this unusual way of treating it makes it elegant enough for a dinner party. You can buy either finnan haddie fillets or the whole fish. If you buy the whole fish, fillet it before cooking.

Makes 6 servings

1 pound smoked haddock, whole fish
   or fillets
Milk
1 tablespoon butter

2 tablespoons béchamel sauce
   (see page 531)
1½ ounces gelatin
1 pint heavy cream

Poach the haddock in milk to cover with the butter for 15 minutes, or until it flakes. Drain and purée in a food processor or blender or by putting through a food mill. Mix the purée with the béchamel sauce. Soften the gelatin in ¼ cup cold water in a small saucepan, then stir over low heat until dissolved. Mix into the haddock thoroughly. Whip the cream until it is nearly thick, then mix it gradually into the haddock mixture with a wooden spatula, stirring to combine thoroughly. Pour the mixture into a 5-cup mold and chill until firm and set.

¶Smoked Trout Mousse. Instead of the haddock, use filleted, skinned smoked trout (this does not require cooking).

¶Kipper Mousse. Instead of the haddock, use canned kippered herrings.

¶Sardine Mousse. Instead of the haddock, use large boneless and skinless sardines.

Tuna

Tuna is a classic hors d'oeuvre. The best brands are those packed in oil and imported from Europe; they contain either solid-pack meat or sliced fillets. If imported tuna is not available, use tuna packed in brine or a solid-pack white meat, draining it well and anointing it with good olive oil ahead of time so that it absorbs some of the oil flavor. Serve tuna with nothing more than capers or parsley for a garnish.

¶Tuna with Artichoke Hearts. Serve with artichoke hearts, anchovy fillets, and black olives.

¶Tuna with Hard-Boiled Egg. Surround with hard-boiled egg halves, capers, and anchovy fillets. Or alternate slices of hard-boiled egg and tomato. Garnish with capers and black Niçoise olives.

Tomatoes with Tuna

Scoop seeds and pulp from ripe tomatoes and drain. Fill with flaked tuna dressed with olive oil and tossed with finely chopped garlic, capers, and parsley. Garnish with black olives and anchovy fillets.

Tomatoes with Tuna and Onions

Fill the tomato shells with flaked tuna mixed with chopped green onion, or scallion, chopped parsley, chopped garlic, and chopped fresh basil, and dressed with olive oil and lemon juice. Sprinkle tops with chopped parsley and crisscross two anchovy fillets on top. Garnish with Greek or Italian black olives.

Tomatoes Primavera

Fill the tomato shells with flaked tuna mixed with drained canned cannellini beans, chopped garlic, chopped parsley, chopped basil, dressed with a basil-flavored vinaigrette. Sprinkle tops with chopped parsley.

Tuna Pâté

Quick, inexpensive and easy, and yet another way to use this good old standby. If you want to make it a bit grander, add a truffle.

Makes about 2½ cups

6 ounces cream cheese
2 hard-boiled eggs
7-ounce can tuna in olive oil
3 to 4 tablespoons cognac

1 truffle (optional) or 12 Italian or
    Greek black olives, pitted
Freshly ground black pepper
½ cup jellied consommé

Let the cream cheese soften at room temperature. Purée the hard-boiled eggs in the blender or food processor. Add tuna, with oil, and cognac, and blend or process until smooth (in a blender, you may have to do this in batches). Chop half the truffle and slice the rest thin, or chop half the olives and cut the others in two. Combine the chopped truffle or olives with the cream cheese, working with a fork until smooth. Season to taste with pepper. Put in blender or processor with the tuna and eggs and blend until smooth. Taste for seasoning and add salt if needed. Pack the pâté into a bowl and decorate with the sliced truffle or olives. Melt the consommé, then stir in a metal bowl over ice until syrupy and about to set. Cover the pâté with a thin coating of the consommé and chill until set. Serve with strips of toast or Melba toast.

¶Salmon Pâté. Use canned salmon, drained, with skin and bones removed.

¶Smoked Sturgeon Pâté. Use canned smoked sturgeon with the juices from the can and 2 tablespoons olive oil.

Pâté of Pike and Salmon

Makes 8 to 10 slices

PIKE MOUSSE

1½ pounds fillet of pike, finely ground
    and well chilled
5 egg whites, well chilled
2 egg yolks, well chilled

1½ cups heavy cream, well chilled
3 tablespoons brandy
1 teaspoon salt

1 head romaine lettuce
1 pound fresh salmon, thinly sliced
Salt and pepper

¼ cup dry white wine
½ stick sweet butter

Prepare the mousse by combining all the first six ingredients thoroughly. Set aside. Blanch the romaine leaves in boiling salted water for 1 minute, remove and discard the stems, and use half of the romaine to line a well-buttered 2-quart pâté mold or terrine. Season the salmon slices with salt and pepper and arrange half of them over the romaine leaves. Spoon in the mousse and cover with overlapping salmon slices and remaining romaine leaves. Pour in the wine and dot the top with the remaining butter. Cover with foil and bake in a roasting pan half filled with water in a 300° oven for 1 hour, making sure that the water never boils. Chill thoroughly—at least a couple of hours. To serve, unmold and slice.

Salmon Tartare

This unusual variation on steak tartare, made with raw salmon, became the rage of Paris a few years ago, when some of the great chefs were evolving their French version of low-calorie cooking, or *cuisine minceur*, which owed more than a little to the Japanese. It is essential to buy fish that has been freshly caught because, like the Japanese sashimi and sushi, it is eaten raw. If you have a food processor, use it to chop the salmon, onion, and garlic and mix them all together.

Makes 8 servings

4 pounds very fresh salmon fillets
1 medium-large onion, very finely
    chopped
2 or 3 garlic cloves, very finely chopped,
    or more to taste
1 tablespoon Dijon mustard
2 tablespoons cognac

3 teaspoons chopped dill, or more to
    taste
2 tablespoons chopped parsley
1 to 2 tablespoons lemon juice
Salt, freshly ground black pepper
GARNISH: Greens

Remove the skin and every tiny bit of bone from the salmon (pull out any bones left behind after filleting with pincers or eyebrow tweezers). Chop the salmon quite coarse, using a very heavy chopping knife or a Chinese cleaver. Mix the onion and garlic well with the salmon, chopping it in with your knife, then mix in the mustard, cognac, dill and parsley, and add lemon juice, salt, and pepper to taste. Keep tasting as you work and add whatever seasoning you think is needed. The amounts depend on your personal taste.

Pile the salmon tartare in a serving dish, garnish with greens, and chill for 1 hour before serving. Serve with fingers of freshly made toast.

¶**Sturgeon Tartare.** Instead of salmon, use fresh sturgeon.

¶**Tuna Tartare.** Instead of salmon, use fresh tuna.

¶**Striped Bass Tartare.** Instead of salmon, use fresh striped bass, or rockfish.

Mussels Hiely

If you don't live in fresh mussel country, any of these dishes can be made with canned (preserved in brine) mussels, carefully drained and rinsed. Where mussel broth is needed, substitute fish stock or canned clam juice.

Makes 6 to 8 servings

2 to 3 quarts mussels	*Salt and pepper to taste*
1 cup dry white wine	*1 cup heavy cream*
3 to 4 pounds spinach or 2 packages	*4 egg yolks, beaten*
frozen spinach	*Pinch of saffron*
4 tablespoons olive oil	*½ cup fine bread crumbs*
3 tablespoons butter	

Place the cleaned mussels in a heavy pan with the white wine and steam until they open. Shell and debeard the mussels. Strain and reserve the liquid. If fresh spinach is used, blanch for 3 minutes in boiling water. Drain well and chop. If frozen spinach is used, thaw, drain, and chop. Heat spinach in olive oil and butter. Season with salt and pepper. Place in a gratin dish and top with the mussels.

Prepare a sauce by cooking the heavy cream, ½ cup mussel liquid, and egg yolks over low heat until thickened. Do not allow to boil. Season to taste with salt, pepper, and a pinch of saffron. Pour sauce over mussels. Sprinkle with crumbs. Glaze in a 400° oven for 5 to 10 minutes.

¶**Mussels Provençal.** Steam the mussels until they open. (Strain broth and reserve for soup or sauce.) When cool enough to handle, remove one half shell from each mussel. Blend ½ pound butter with 4 finely chopped garlic cloves, 6 finely chopped shallots, 1 teaspoon dried basil or 2 tablespoons chopped fresh basil, 6 tablespoons chopped Italian parsley, and salt and pepper to taste. Spoon the butter mixture over the mussels on the half shell and sprinkle with fine bread crumbs. Bake in a 425° oven just long enough to heat through. Serve on hot plates.

¶**Mussel Salad.** Steam mussels, remove from shells, and cool. Combine 1¼ cups mayonnaise with 1 finely chopped garlic clove, 2 tablespoons finely cut chives, 1 tablespoon finely cut dill, and 1 tablespoon chopped Italian parsley. Season to taste with lemon juice and Tabasco and spoon over the mussels. Toss the salad, arrange in a serving dish on greens or watercress, and garnish with sprigs of parsley and dill and a few capers. Serve as a first course.

¶**Mussels Rémoulade.** Steam mussels and remove one shell from each. Cool. Serve on the half shell with a spoonful of rémoulade sauce (see page 77) on top. Serve 6 or 8 mussels as a first course.

¶**Mussels with Snail Butter.** Arrange steamed mussels on the half shell, in sautéed mushroom caps, or in snail shells; top with snail butter (see page 20); and bake in a 450° oven for 8 to 10 minutes, until very hot.

Clams au Gratin

One of the simpler ways with clams, which can be varied according to your imagination and the contents of the refrigerator. To hold the clams steady during baking, put on a bed of rock salt in small aluminum-foil pie plates set on a baking sheet. Heat the plates with the salt first, then put the clams in their shells on the salt, which retains the heat and keeps the seafood hot.

Makes 6 servings

½ cup finely chopped mushrooms
½ cup finely chopped shallots or
    green onion, or scallion
¼ pound butter
2 tablespoons finely chopped parsley

2 tablespoons finely chopped
    peeled and seeded tomato
Salt, freshly ground black pepper
36 small clams on the half shell
⅓ to ½ cup fresh bread crumbs

Sauté the mushroom and shallot or onion in 6 tablespoons butter for 3 minutes. Mix in the parsley, tomato, and salt and pepper to taste. Spoon over the clams. Sprinkle with crumbs, dot with the remaining butter cut in tiny pieces, and bake in a 400° oven for 5 to 8 minutes or until clams are just heated through.

¶**Herbed Clams.** Sprinkle the clams on the half shell with chopped chives, garlic, and parsley. Top with a small piece of partially cooked bacon and bake in a 425° oven until the bacon is crisp.

¶**Anchovy Clams.** Top each clam with a spoonful of anchovy butter (cream ¼ pound butter with 1 tablespoon finely chopped anchovies and 1 tablespoon finely chopped onion), sprinkle with buttered crumbs, and bake in a 400° oven for 5 to 8 minutes, or until heated through, or put under the broiler for 3 minutes.

¶**Clams Provençal.** Top the clams with the flavored butter for Mussels Provençal (see page 13), sprinkle with bread crumbs and bake at 400° for 5 to 8 minutes.

¶**Clams Casino.** Blend ¼ pound butter with ⅓ cup finely chopped shallots or green onions, or scallions, ¼ cup finely chopped parsley, and ¼ cup finely chopped green pepper. Spoon over the clams and add a dash of lemon juice. Top with pieces of partially cooked bacon and bake in a 425° oven until bacon is crisp.

Brains Gribiche

Prepare one pair of calf's brains according to the method described on page 449. After the brains have been chilled and weighted, cut them in slices ¼ to ½ inch thick. Arrange on a bed of greens and serve with Sauce Gribiche (see page 535) spooned over them, as a first course (1 pair will serve 3 as a first course).

Sautéed Marinated Fish
(*Escabeche*)

Escabeche is the Spanish word for "pickled," and this is the kind of recipe where you start with a basic idea, then play around with your own variations, altering the flavors in the marinade as you see fit. You can have it slightly on the sweet-sour side, or acid, or bland, or hot. *Escabeche* is ideal summer food, because of the refreshing quality, whether you serve it as a first course or as a main dish with a green salad or rice salad or onion and cucumber salad.

Makes 4 to 6 servings

2 pounds firm fish fillets (sole, flounder, cod, or salmon), cut into even diagonal strips
Flour

4 tablespoons butter
2 tablespoons oil
Salt

MARINADE
½ cup olive oil
1 tablespoon wine vinegar
1 tablespoon lemon or lime juice
⅓ cup orange juice
1½ teaspoons salt
½ teaspoon (or less, to taste) Tabasco

3 tablespoons orange zest
¼ to ⅓ cup thinly sliced canned peeled mild green chilies
¼ to ⅓ cup finely chopped onion or ½ cup chopped green onion, or scallion

GARNISH: *2 peeled and thinly sliced oranges, marinated in oil and lemon or lime juice; chopped parsley; leaves of cilantro (fresh coriander) if available*

Dust the fillets lightly with flour and sauté them in the hot butter and oil in a heavy skillet until delicately browned on both sides, turning them once and salting them lightly. As the fish browns, remove to paper towels to drain and cool. Then arrange the fillets in a flat round or oblong serving dish that will look attractive on the table.

Combine the ingredients for the marinade and pour over the fish. There should be enough sauce to cover the fish; if there isn't, add more oil and orange juice. You can season and spice this marinade as you wish, perhaps adding 1 or 2 finely chopped garlic cloves, increasing the amount of mild green chilies or using a little hot chopped jalapeño or serrano chili (in which case omit the Tabasco) or some freshly ground black pepper, and maybe paper-thin slices of red onion. Let the fish marinate for 8 to 10 hours, or up to 24 hours. Serve garnished with the orange slices, parsley, and fresh coriander. If you can't get fresh coriander, you might add a touch of ground coriander to the marinade, although it hasn't the same pungency.

¶**Escabeche of Tongue.** Instead of the sautéed fish use thinly sliced cooked fresh or smoked beef tongue.

¶**Escabeche of Brains.** Use thinly sliced poached brains. Garnish with marinated lime or lemon slices.

¶**Escabeche of Sweetbreads.** Use thickly sliced poached sweetbreads with a garnish of lemon or lime slices.

¶**Escabeche of Beef.** Use thinly sliced rare roast beef and add 2 teaspoons Dijon mustard to the marinade. Garnish with orange and red onion slices. Serve with potato or rice salad.

¶**Escabeche of Chicken.** Cut poached, roast, or sautéed chicken into strips and marinate. Garnish with lemon or lime slices.

¶**Escabeche of Mackerel.** Sauté 6 mackerel fillets, cut in thin strips. Marinate in a mixture of the oil, lemon or lime juice, orange juice, 6 finely chopped green onions, or scallions, 2 crushed garlic cloves, and a dash of Tabasco. Garnish with lime quarters and black olives.

Soused Shrimp

This keeps well and is good to have on hand for cocktails, so it is worth making in quantity—if affordable. The lemon slices must be paper thin.

Makes about 20 servings

5 pounds large cooked shrimp (12 to 15 per pound), shelled and deveined

3 medium red Italian onions, thinly sliced

3 lemons, thinly sliced

1½ teaspoons dried rosemary, finely crushed, or 3 teaspoons chopped fresh rosemary

2 garlic cloves, finely chopped

Olive oil

GARNISH: Salad, greens, capers (optional)

Arrange layers of shrimp, onion, and lemon in a good-sized bowl, sprinkling each layer with rosemary. Add the garlic and pour in olive oil to cover the shrimp. Cover the bowl and let the shrimp marinate in the refrigerator for several days. Serve from the bowl, or arrange in another bowl, lined with greens, and sprinkle with capers. Thin bread-and-butter sandwiches are a good accompaniment. Serve as a first course or cocktail appetizer.

¶**Tarragon Shrimp.** Use chopped fresh tarragon or crumbled dried tarragon instead of rosemary.

¶**Soused Scallops.** Use tiny raw bay scallops in place of shrimp. (The acidity of the lemon will "cook" the flesh.)

Shrimp in Sour Cream with Mushrooms

An extremely simple recipe that works just as well with other seafood.

Makes 4 servings

1 cup sour cream

½ pound cooked shelled bay shrimp, Maine shrimp, or other tiny shrimp

3 to 4 teaspoons horseradish, drained

1 teaspoon cognac

½ cup firm white mushroom caps, cut into julienne strips

GARNISH: Lettuce leaves, chopped parsley

Mix together in a stainless steel bowl the sour cream and the shrimp. Mix in the drained horseradish (to taste) and the cognac. Add the mushrooms and mix in lightly. Serve as a first course in ramekins or scallop shells lined with lettuce leaves, and sprinkle chopped parsley on top.

¶**Crabmeat in Sour Cream with Mushrooms.** Use lump crabmeat instead of shrimp.

¶**Scallops in Sour Cream with Mushrooms.** Use lightly poached or raw bay scallops instead of shrimp.

Shrimp Kiev

This is an American takeoff on the familiar Chicken Kiev, one of the dishes Russia has contributed to our dining. You need the largest shrimp you can find in the market; smaller ones are almost impossible to shape properly.

Makes 6 first-course servings

18 raw jumbo shrimp
4 tablespoons firm butter
Optional seasoning: chopped parsley,
*   garlic, tarragon*

¾ cup flour
2 eggs, beaten
1 cup fine bread crumbs
Oil for deep frying

Shell the shrimp by cutting down the back with scissors and removing the shell, leaving the tails on. With a very sharp knife, split the shrimp on the underside (the inside curve), about three-quarters of the way to the tail. Place them, split side down, between sheets of dampened wax paper and pound very gently with the back of a heavy chef's knife or a meat pounder, being careful not to tear the flesh. You just want to flatten them.

Cut the butter in 18 very tiny sticks, no thicker than a fat toothpick. Leave it plain or season it, if you wish, by rolling the sticks in 1 to 2 tablespoons finely chopped parsley and finely chopped garlic, or finely chopped tarragon. Chill in the freezer until frozen hard. Put a stick of butter in the center of each flattened shrimp and roll or fold the shrimp around it lengthwise, re-forming the shape. Dip the shrimp in flour, then beaten egg, and roll in bread crumbs. Put on a cookie sheet lined with wax paper and put in the refrigerator, or briefly in the freezer, until they get very cold.

Just before you are ready to serve, heat oil in a deep fryer to 400°. Drop a few shrimp at a time into the hot fat and cook until brown, about 1 to 2 minutes. Drain on paper towels and serve immediately with hollandaise, béarnaise, or mustard sauce (see pages 532 and 531), and French bread.

Goujonettes of Sole

These delectable little bits of fried fish make a good first course or cocktail hors d'oeuvre, or a light luncheon entrée. The name comes from *goujons*, tiny fish fried whole, of which these are a sort of mock version.

Makes 4 servings

4 or 5 firm fillets of sole
½ to ¾ cup flour
3 eggs, lightly beaten with ¼ cup
    cream

3 cups fine fresh bread crumbs
Oil for deep frying

Cut the fillets into diagonal strips about ½ inch wide. Coat them with flour, shaking off the excess, then dip them in the egg-cream mixture and roll them in the bread crumbs, coating on all sides.

Heat the oil in a deep fryer to 370° and lower the strips into it, a few at a time, either in a frying basket or with a wire skimmer. After each batch, bring the oil back to the correct frying temperature. Cook the strips just until lightly browned, about 2 minutes. Drain on paper towels. Serve with fresh or fried parsley and tartare or rémoulade sauce (see page 77).

¶**Goujonettes in Beer Batter.** Dip the fish strips in flour, then in beer batter (see page 188) and fry a delicate brown.

Sardines with Mint

I discovered this at Le Bistrôt in Mougins, a lovely old hill town above Cannes, and asked for the recipe because it is such an unusual and delicious way to treat small fish like sardines or smelts. You could use the same stuffing in a baked whole fish, between fish steaks, or in rolled fish fillets.

Makes 4 servings

12 fresh sardines or smelts
1½ pounds spinach
¼ cup finely chopped fresh mint or
    2 tablespoons crumbled dried mint
¼ cup finely chopped Italian parsley

2 garlic cloves, finely chopped
2 shallots, finely chopped
½ cup fresh bread crumbs
Salt, freshly ground black pepper
Olive oil

Clean the fish, split, and remove backbones; this is easy to do by pulling off the head—the whole bone will come with it. Blanch the spinach in boiling water, drain well, pressing out all the water, and chop fine. Mix the spinach with the mint, parsley, garlic, shallots, and bread crumbs, and season to taste with salt and pepper. Mix well. Spread the fish flat, flesh side up, and put a little bit of the stuffing on the widest end. Roll up toward the tail and pack the rolled fish tightly together in a baking dish so they can't unroll. Brush well with oil and bake in a 425° oven for 10 minutes, basting once or twice with oil. Serve hot.

Snails with Garlic Butter

The classic escargots à la bourguignonne, one of the standby first courses of most French restaurants, are easy to make at home, at a fraction of the cost. Snails are sold already cooked, cleaned, and canned, with their sterilized shells in a separate package. For heating and serving, the snails are usually put on metal or ovenproof snail plates that have indentations for the shells, but you can also put the shells on a bed of rock salt in small baking dishes, or just coat the snails well with the snail butter and bake them without the shells. Serve snails out of the shells on fried toast, or speared with cocktail picks, as an appetizer. Another good way to serve snails is in sautéed mushroom caps, which add a complementary texture and flavor.

Makes 4 to 8 servings

4 dozen canned snails with their shells
¼ pound soft (not melted) butter
2 to 3 tablespoons finely chopped
  shallots
2 or more garlic cloves, finely chopped,
  or 2 tablespoons garlic purée
  (see page 534)

¼ cup chopped parsley
Salt, freshly ground black pepper
1 to 2 cups dry white wine

Remove the snails from the cans and rinse them well under running water. Cream the butter with the shallots, garlic (the amount depends on how much you like garlic), parsley, and salt and pepper to taste. You can change the proportions of shallots, garlic, and parsley to suit your own preference. The garlic purée gives a smoother, less strong flavor than raw garlic. Slip the snails into shells and cover them well with the garlic butter, pushing it into the shell and mounding it at the aperture. Chill in the refrigerator for a few hours so the butter penetrates and flavors the snails.

When ready to serve, arrange the shells in the hollows of snail plates and pour a teaspoon or two of white wine over each one. Put in a 450° oven for 10 minutes, until piping hot. Serve with plenty of French bread to mop up the butter, and snail tongs and forks to hold and extract the snails (or use oyster forks and protect your fingers with paper napkins while holding the hot shells). Allow half a dozen or a dozen per serving, according to your liking for snails, and the rest of the menu.

¶**Snails in Mushrooms Caps.** Sauté 4 dozen firm mushroom caps, about 1 inch across, in 6 tablespoons butter until just cooked through, but not soft. Arrange cup side up on a baking sheet or in individual baking dishes. Coat the snails well with the snail butter and put a snail in each cap. Sprinkle the tops with finely chopped walnuts and chopped parsley and heat through in a 450° oven for 10 minutes, until very hot. These may be served on rounds of fried toast.

Rolled Chicken Pâté

This is an Italian recipe, thoroughly delicious, easy to do, and a delight for spring or summer menus when a regular pâté might be too heavy.

Makes about 10 to 12 servings

8 tablespoons butter
1 medium onion, thinly sliced
1 stalk celery, cut in julienne strips
1 carrot, cut in julienne strips
1 tablespoon salt
¼ teaspoon quatre épices seasoning (see page 536)
2 large chicken breasts
1 pork chop, about 6 to 7 ounces

¾ pound sweet butter, softened
⅓ cup cognac
2 to 3 dashes Tabasco
1 tablespoon chopped fresh basil or tarragon
Freshly ground black pepper
¼ cup shelled pistachio nuts
1 pound prosciutto, sliced

Combine the 8 tablespoons butter, onion, celery, carrot, salt, and spice in a heavy saucepan. Add the chicken and pork chop. Cook, covered, over medium heat until tender. Do not overcook. Remove the chicken and pork from the saucepan and cool. Trim away skin, fat, and bone. Process the meats in a food processor or grind them with a meat grinder, using the finest blade. Beat into the softened sweet butter, adding the cognac, Tabasco, basil or tarragon, pepper to taste, and pistachio nuts as you beat. If you have one, use an electric mixer with a paddle attachment. Taste the pâté for seasoning, adding salt, pepper, and more Tabasco, if needed. Turn out on a piece of wax paper.

On 2 other pieces of wax paper or plastic wrap arrange overlapping slices of prosciutto, forming a rectangle. Divide the chicken-pork mixture and form into 2 rolls. Place 1 roll on each of the prosciutto rectangles. Roll tightly, without squeezing, so the pâté is completely enveloped by the prosciutto. Place in polyethylene bags and refrigerate for 24 hours before serving. Cut in slices about ½ inch thick and serve on greens with toast.

Pâté of Chicken Livers and Ham

This is not only a simple pâté but wonderfully economical.

Makes 10 to 12 servings

1 pound pork fat, cut in ⅛-inch-thick
    sheets (for lining the terrine)
1 pound chicken livers, trimmed
¾ cup port or Madeira

1 tablespoon salt
2 tablespoons chopped parsley
1 bay leaf
¼ teaspoon quatre épices (see page 538)

FORCEMEAT
½ pound chicken hearts, finely
    chopped
½ pound chicken gizzards, finely
    ground

½ pound cooked ham, finely ground
1 pound sausage meat
½ cup fresh bread crumbs
2 eggs, lightly beaten

Line the bottom and sides of a 2-quart terrine with the pork fat. Marinate the chicken livers in the port or Madeira with the seasonings for 30 minutes. Combine the chicken hearts, gizzards, ham, and sausage meat with the bread crumbs to make a forcemeat. Remove the chicken livers and bay leaf from the marinade. Add the marinade and lightly beaten eggs to the forcemeat and mix well. In the terrine alternate layers of forcemeat and chicken livers, ending with forcemeat. Top with a piece of pork fat and the bay leaf from the marinade. Cover the terrine with foil, and place the lid on top. Bake in a 375° oven for 1½ to 2 hours. Cool. Unmold and cut into ½-inch slices. Arrange on a platter.

Rabbit Pâté

Something rather unusual in the pâté repertoire.

Makes 10 servings

STOCK
The bones from 5- to 6-pound rabbit
1 veal knuckle, cracked
2 carrots
3 large onions
1 leek
1 cup dry white wine

1 cup water
½ teaspoon freshly ground black pepper
2 or 3 pinches of rosemary and thyme
Bouquet garni of parsley, bay leaf, and
    chervil
Salt

FORCEMEAT

Boned rabbit meat (about 2 pounds)
½ pound veal leg
¼ pound ham, chopped
¼ pound lean belly of pork, chopped
¼ pound pork fatback, chopped

½ cup brandy
2 teaspoons salt
Rosemary, thyme
1 pound pork fat, cut in ⅛-inch-thick
    sheets (for lining the terrine)

Have the rabbit boned, or bone it yourself, and use the bones for the stock. Put them in a pan with the veal knuckle, carrots, onions, leek, wine, water, pepper, rosemary, thyme, and bouquet garni. Bring to a boil, skim off the scum, reduce the heat, and simmer for 1 hour. Strain, then boil the liquid hard to reduce by half. Add salt to taste.

While the stock is cooking, chop most of the rabbit meat and the veal, leaving some large pieces of both meats. Mix the chopped rabbit and veal with the ham, pork belly, pork fatback, and brandy. Season to taste with salt and pinches of rosemary and thyme, and let marinate until the stock is done.

Line a 2-quart terrine, pâté mold, or loaf pan with the pork fat sheets, saving some to put on top. Make layers of the marinated meats and the pieces of rabbit and veal in the terrine, beginning and ending with the marinated meats. Cover with sheets of pork fat, then pour in ¼ cup of the reduced rabbit stock. Cover the top of the mold with aluminum foil, stand it in hot water in a roasting pan, and bake in a 325° oven for 2 hours. Remove and cool, then chill overnight with a weight on top, until the stock is jellied and the fat firm.

Pork Liver Pâté en Brioche

This is a very simple way of making the classic pâté en croûte, with brioche dough replacing the usual pastry. Be sure the pâté is cooled before putting it in the brioche; this prevents the dough from separating from the pâté during cooking.

Makes 8 servings

2 tablespoons butter
1½ cups chopped onion
1 clove garlic, finely chopped
¼ teaspoon crushed thyme (fresh, if
    possible)
¾ pound pork liver, finely ground
½ pound ground pork with about 30
    percent fat

1 egg
⅓ cup dry white wine
1 tablespoon salt
1 teaspoon freshly ground black pepper
1 recipe classic brioche dough,
    refrigerated (see page 477)
1 beaten egg (for egg wash)

Melt the butter in a skillet, add the onion, and sauté for 5 minutes, until limp and golden. Add the garlic and thyme and cook 1 minute, then put in a bowl with all the remaining ingredients, except the brioche dough and egg wash. Mix well.

Pour the mixture into a 2-quart round mold, such as a charlotte mold. Place the mold in a roasting pan half filled with hot water and bake in a 325° oven for 2 hours. Remove the mold from the water and, when cool enough to handle, unmold onto a platter. Drain off fat and juices and dry the pâté with paper towels. Let cool to room temperature, or refrigerate, well wrapped, until you are ready to continue.

With your hands, pat out the brioche dough on a lightly floured board so the center is about ½ inch thick and the edges about ¾ inch thick. Brush dough with egg wash and place the lukewarm or cold pâté in the center. Fold the dough so that all sides join on top of the pâté, and pleat the edges together. Press edges together firmly so they do not separate during cooking. Butter a 9-inch springform pan and place the pâté and dough in it, upside down, with pleated edges on the bottom and the thinnest part on top. This is important because the pâté will sink a little during cooking. Let the dough rise for about 30 minutes in a warm place—no longer—as the dough should just start to "work up" when it goes into the oven. Brush with egg wash. Bake in a 400° oven for about 30 minutes. Let the brioche rest about 5 minutes before unmolding. Place it on a platter lined with a towel, linen if you wish. Serve hot. This may be served with Bordelaise or mushroom sauce (see page 533).

Herbed Pâté

The close texture you find in most pâtés is greatly relieved by the lightening addition of spinach, olives, and aromatic herbs. This pâté may be served hot or cold.

Makes 10 to 12 servings

1 pound bacon, cut in strips
3 pounds spinach (or 2 packages frozen, thawed, and water removed by pressing through a sieve), chopped
3 tablespoons chopped parsley
1 medium onion, finely chopped
3 small garlic cloves, finely chopped
1 tablespoon finely chopped fresh basil or 1 teaspoon dried basil

1 cup coarsely chopped pitted small Italian or French black and green olives
1½ pounds pork (¾ lean, ¼ fat), coarsely ground
1 teaspoon salt
½ teaspoon freshly ground black pepper
2 eggs
½ teaspoon rosemary

½ teaspoon thyme
⅛ teaspoon nutmeg
⅛ teaspoon Tabasco

⅓ cup cognac
½ pound uncooked ham, sliced thin
2 large bay leaves

Line the bottom and sides of a 1½-quart terrine with the bacon strips. Cook the spinach until just wilted. (If frozen spinach is used, do not cook.) Chop the spinach very fine and combine with half the parsley, onion, garlic, basil, and olives. Combine the ground pork with salt and pepper, eggs, and the remaining half of the herbs, seasonings, and olives. Add the rosemary, thyme, nutmeg, Tabasco, and cognac, and mix well.

Place half the pork mixture in the bottom of the terrine, cover with thin slices of ham, then with half the spinach mixture. Next add a layer of half the remaining pork mixture. Add the remainder of the ham and of the spinach mixture, and finally the remaining pork mixture. Press down well and place the bay leaves on top. Cover the terrine with foil and place the lid on top. Place the terrine in a roasting pan and add enough water to the pan to reach two-thirds of the way up the sides of the mold. Bake the pâté in a 350° oven for 1½ hours.

Remove the terrine from the pan, pour out the water, and return the terrine to the pan to catch any fat that spills out. Remove the lid, leaving the foil intact, allow to cool for 15 to 30 minutes, and weight the pâté with a 3-pound weight. Refrigerate overnight. Unmold and cut into ½-inch slices. Arrange on a large platter.

Pork Rillettes

This very simple French pâté is nothing more than pork cooked down with an equal amount of pork kidney fat, then shredded and packed into pots (small pots of rillettes make excellent Christmas gifts). You will have to order the kidney fat from your butcher in advance.

Makes 8 to 12 pots

3 pounds leaf lard (pork kidney fat)
3 pounds fresh pork shoulder, loin, or
    leg, cut in small pieces

1 cup water
Salt, freshly ground black pepper, a few
    grains of cayenne

Heat the leaf lard in a large pot over low heat until it has all melted down. Add the pork and water and cook very slowly on top of the stove or in a 250° to 300° oven until the meat is so tender it almost falls apart. This will take about 4 hours.

Drain the pork, reserving the fat. Shred the meat very fine, using two forks, then season to taste with salt, pepper, and cayenne. Spoon the pork into crocks or small pots, adding some of the reserved clear fat and mashing the pork so it absorbs the fat and becomes a smooth paste—this is essential to give a smooth texture and rich flavor. When pots are almost full, ladle enough clear fat on the top to cover and form an airtight seal, then cover the pots with lids or tie aluminum foil over them and refrigerate. This will keep for weeks under refrigeration, provided the covering layer of fat is not broken. Serve as an hors d'oeuvre or first course, with thin toast or French bread.

¶**Goose Rillettes.** This is basically the same pâté, but made with goose rather than pork. Roast and cool an 8- or 9-pound goose, remove the skin, and take the meat from the bones. Reserve some of the goose fat from the roasting pan. Put the meat in a heavy pan, sprinkle with salt and add 2 to 2½ pounds rendered leaf lard, ½ cup water, 1 clove garlic, freshly ground pepper to taste and some of the reserved goose fat. Cook in a 250° to 300° oven for about 4 hours, or until the meat is thoroughly cooked down. Drain the meat, reserving the fat, and shred and pack into pots as for the pork rillettes.

¶**Truffled Rillettes.** 1 or 2 black truffles, finely chopped, may be mixed with the meat.

Brioche Bohémienne

A spectacular and lusciously rich first course that is not as difficult to prepare as it may seem. You will need about 4 rather thin slices of marrow per person. Ask the butcher to saw marrow bones into small sections or split them lengthwise through the middle so you can extract the marrow easily.

Makes 6 servings

1½ cups water
½ cup port wine
1 small onion
1 small carrot
2 sprigs parsley

Salt, freshly ground black pepper
Beef marrow bones, about 2 dozen
    1½-inch pieces, or 8 to 10 bones,
    split

PORT WINE SAUCE
3 shallots or green onions, finely
    chopped
3 tablespoons butter

1 cup red wine
10½-ounce can beef bouillon
Pinch of thyme

Salt, freshly ground black pepper
Beurre manié (see page 536)
1 tablespoon tomato purée
1 cup port wine

2 black truffles
6 large brioches (from a bakery, or
made according to directions on
page 477)

Combine the water, port wine, onion, carrot, parsley, and salt and pepper to taste in a large shallow pan and cook for 15 minutes. Remove and discard the carrot, onion, and parsley. Extract the marrow from the bones with a sharp-pointed knife, add to the liquid, and poach very gently just until softened and translucent, about 2 minutes. Do not overcook or it will become oily and liquid. Drain the marrow and cut it into small pieces.

Meanwhile, make the port wine sauce. Sauté the shallots or green onions in the butter until soft. Add the wine and bouillon and bring to a boil. Season with thyme and salt and pepper to taste, and cook down for a few minutes. Thicken the sauce with beurre manié, simmer a few moments, and strain. Add the tomato purée and port wine and simmer 10 minutes.

Cut 6 thin slices of truffle and set aside. Chop the rest. Carefully remove the tops of the brioches and take out the soft insides, leaving a shell. Reserve the tops. Heat the brioche shells for a few minutes in a 275° oven, then put some chopped truffle in each one. Mix the marrow with 1 cup of the port wine sauce and put into the brioche. Put a slice of truffle on top of each. Cover with the brioche tops and heat through for about 10 minutes in a 375° oven. Spoon more sauce over the top before serving.

Brioches with Ham

A less complicated and rich filling for brioches. You might have this with hot potato salad or a green salad for lunch instead of serving it as an hors d'oeuvre.

Makes 6 servings

6 large brioches
4 tablespoons butter
2 medium onions, finely chopped
1½ cups finely chopped cooked ham
½ cup chopped black olives, preferably
soft Italian or Greek

½ teaspoon salt
½ teaspoon Tabasco
¼ cup chopped parsley
2 egg yolks blended with ½ cup
heavy cream
Melted butter

Slice the tops from the brioches and scoop out the interior of each, leaving a shell thick enough to hold the filling. Remove some of the crumb of the topknot as well. Keep the brioches warm while you are preparing the filling.

Melt the butter in a heavy skillet and when foaming add the onions.

Sauté gently until golden. Add the ham and olives, and mix well. Season with salt and Tabasco, and add the parsley. Remove from the heat and cool slightly. Then return to very low heat and stir in the egg yolk and cream mixture. Cook gently until slightly thickened, but do not allow to boil.

Fill the brioches with this mixture and replace the tops. Place on a buttered baking sheet, brush with melted butter, and heat through in a 350° oven for about 15 minutes.

Sausage en Brioche

Makes 6 servings

THE SAUSAGES

2½ pounds pork shoulder, coarsely
    ground
½ pound pork fat, coarsely ground
4 cloves garlic, finely chopped
2 tablespoons rosemary

3 teaspoons thyme
3 teaspoons salt
1 tablespoon freshly ground black
    pepper
1 cup bourbon

Combine all ingredients in a bowl and mix well. Test by frying a small amount in a skillet, taste, and adjust seasonings if necessary.

Form into 2 sausage-shape rolls (about 7 inches long and 2 inches in diameter). Wrap the sausages in a double thickness of cheesecloth and twist ends of the cheesecloth securely. Tie the ends with string.

Poach the sausages in boiling salted water for about 20 to 25 minutes, or until the internal temperature reaches 170°. Remove and chill overnight. Before using remove cheesecloth.

BRIOCHE

1½ packages (1½ tablespoons) active
    dry yeast
2 tablespoons granulated sugar
½ cup warm water (100° to 115°,
    approximately)
1 cup melted butter

1½ teaspoons salt
4 cups all-purpose flour
4 eggs
2 egg yolks blended with 3 tablespoons
    heavy cream

Combine the yeast, sugar, and warm water, and let stand until it begins to swell. Mix the melted butter and salt. In a large bowl combine the flour, eggs, melted butter, and yeast mixture. Beat with the hand until smooth. Place in a buttered bowl, turning to butter the surface, cover, and set in a warm, draft-free place to rise until light and doubled in bulk, about 1 to 1½ hours. Punch the dough down and refrigerate for about 3 hours, covered. Remove and divide in half. Roll each half out ⅓ inch thick. Place sausage in center of dough, and make a neat package, tucking in the ends and then bringing the sides together to overlap. Place seam side down on a buttered baking sheet, and let dough rise for 5 minutes. Brush with 2 egg yolks and 3 tablespoons heavy cream beaten together. Bake at 375° till brioche is done and lightly browned—about 35 minutes.

Slice, and serve with a variety of mustards.

Sausage and Croissants

This recipe is so simple it seems silly. But it is a treasure not to be missed; the hot buttery croissant mingling with the spicy meatiness of the sausage gives not only a tantalizing bouquet but a most satisfying flavor.

12 croissants
35 to 40 slices kielbasa, cut thin on
    the diagonal

Slice each croissant, starting from the outside of the crescent and cutting not quite all the way through. Tuck 3 or 4 slices of kielbasa into each croissant. Heat them in a preheated 350° oven for 8 to 10 minutes. Cut the filled croissants in half and serve hot.

Chicken in Lettuce Leaves

This rather Westernized version of an Oriental dish is simple to make and great fun to eat. Good for a buffet party or a summer luncheon.

Makes 6 to 8 servings

3 heads iceberg lettuce
1½ cups finely chopped onion
¾ cup finely chopped green bell pepper
6 tablespoons butter
4-ounce can peeled green chilies,
    drained and chopped
1 to 2 tablespoons finely chopped
    fresh hot pepper
3 cups finely diced cooked chicken
    (or turkey)

1½ cups cooked rice
2 tablespoons chopped basil, or
    1½ teaspoons dried basil
1 teaspoon salt, or to taste
½ teaspoon freshly ground black pepper
⅓ cup cognac
½ cup chicken broth, if needed

GARNISH: ¼ cup chopped parsley, ¾ cup toasted shaved almonds

Carefully separate the lettuce leaves from the heads, leaving leaves whole. Arrange in a bowl and chill in the refrigerator.

Sauté the onion and green pepper in the butter in a large skillet until just wilted. Add the chopped canned chilies, the fresh hot pepper (remove the seeds before chopping), chicken, and rice. Toss well, cover and simmer for 4 or 5 minutes, then add the basil, salt, pepper, cognac, and broth, if needed. The mixture should not be dry, but you don't want it sloppy. Heat through and taste for seasoning. Arrange on a platter and garnish with the parsley and almonds, with the bowl of lettuce leaves next to it. Each person spoons some of the chicken mixture onto a lettuce leaf and rolls it up, to be eaten with the fingers.

¶**Squab in Lettuce Leaves.** For a more Chinese version, omit the canned chilies, fresh hot pepper, basil, cognac, and the garnish. Substitute cooked squab for the chicken and add to the mixture 2 teaspoons chopped garlic (cook with the onion), ½ to ¾ cup chopped walnuts, and 2 tablespoons dark soy sauce. Garnish with chopped fresh coriander.

Chicken Hearts and Livers en Brochette

A good way to cook these often neglected parts of the chicken is to marinate and broil them. Be sure to soak the bamboo skewers in water for several hours to prevent them from burning under the broiler.

Makes 6 servings

18 chicken hearts
12 chicken livers

¼ cup oil

MARINADE
1 cup medium-sweet sherry
½ cup olive oil
1½ teaspoons dried tarragon

1 teaspoon salt
½ teaspoon freshly ground black pepper

Trim the fat from the chicken hearts. Remove the connecting fibers in the livers and cut out any greenish or blackish spots. Combine the marinade ingredients in a bowl, add the hearts and livers and marinate for 1 hour, turning them once or twice.

Preheat the broiler. When ready to cook, remove the livers and hearts from the marinade and string them on 8 bamboo skewers, alternating the hearts and the livers. Brush them well with oil. Arrange the skewers on an oiled broiling rack and broil 2 inches from the heat, turning the skewers once, for 8 minutes, or until browned and just cooked through. To test, make a tiny incision in a liver with a small knife; it should still be pinkish inside. Do not overcook or the livers will be tough. Serve as a first course, with a mustard sauce.

¶**With Béarnaise Sauce.** Double the recipe and serve with Béarnaise sauce (see page 532) as a luncheon entrée.

¶**With Scrambled Eggs.** Serve with scrambled eggs as a breakfast or brunch dish.

¶**Hearts en Brochette.** Omit the livers and serve the hearts alone, as a cocktail appetizer.

Anticuchos
(Broiled Beef Heart on Skewers)

This interesting and fiery dish of spiced and skewered beef heart originated in Peru, where it is often served as an hors d'oeuvre at holiday time. Anticuchos makes a good appetizer for an outdoor barbecue, or with cocktails. If you serve it as a first course, accompany it with warmed tortillas or French bread. Or have it as a light main course with tortillas and an orange and onion salad, and drink beer to quench the fire.

Makes 8 to 10 servings as an appetizer,
or 6 servings as a main course

3- to 3½-pound beef heart
2 or 3 hot red peppers, seeded and cut
*   into thin strips*
3 garlic cloves, finely chopped
2 teaspoons ground cumin seed,
*   warmed in a skillet*

Salt, freshly ground black pepper
Wine vinegar to cover
¾ cup olive oil
1 to 1½ tablespoons Tabasco

Clean and trim the beef heart and cut into 1-inch cubes for appetizers, larger cubes for a main course. Put in a bowl with the hot red peppers, garlic, cumin seed, salt and pepper to taste, and wine vinegar to cover. Marinate in the refrigerator for 12 to 24 hours.

When ready to cook, thread the cubes on skewers and brush them well with olive oil. Add ½ cup olive oil and the Tabasco to the marinade. Broil the skewered meat quickly over a charcoal fire or close to the broiling unit until browned on all sides (the cubes of beef heart will be cooked through by then). Serve at once with the heated marinade as a hot dipping sauce.

¶**Anticuchos with Chicken Hearts.** Use chicken hearts instead of the cubed beef heart.

Prosciutto with Asparagus

You could make this delicious hot hors d'oeuvre with thin slices of Virginia or other country ham.

Makes 4 servings

4 large paper-thin slices of prosciutto   ⅓ cup grated Parmesan cheese
2 dozen hot cooked asparagus spears

Spread the prosciutto slices out on a board. Put 6 asparagus spears on one half of each slice. Fold the other half over the asparagus and arrange in a baking dish or on a baking sheet. Sprinkle lavishly with grated Parmesan cheese and put under a preheated broiler for just a minute or two to lightly brown but not melt the cheese and heat the ham through. Don't overcook or the ham will harden.

Prosciutto with Fruit

One of the most popular of all first courses, and for good reason. The contrast of salty ham and sweet fruit is delicious to the palate and piquant without being surfeiting. Use good imported prosciutto or Westphalian ham. If you can't get imported prosciutto (the domestic product is less satisfactory), you are better off with paper-thin slices of Virginia ham. Here are some combinations:

Prosciutto with Melon—use Cranshaw, honeydew, or cantaloupe, peeled and sliced.

Prosciutto with Papaya—use ripe papaya, peeled and sliced.

Prosciutto with Figs—use fine, ripe white or black figs, peeled.

Prosciutto with Pears—use fine, ripe Bartlett or Anjou pears, quartered.

Prosciutto with Pineapple—use fingers of ripe, fresh pineapple.

Drape the ham over the fruit and serve on a plate, with a knife and fork. Or cut larger fruit in bite-size sections, wrap in pieces of ham, and secure with a toothpick, for a cocktail appetizer. Have a peppermill at hand—freshly ground black pepper enhances the taste of both ham and fruit.

Crabmeat and Prosciutto

To the best of my knowledge, this simple, elegant dish was first served at The Coach House Restaurant in New York City. Larger portions can be served as a luncheon entrée with a good salad, and cheese and fruit for dessert.

Makes 6 servings

4 tablespoons butter
2 tablespoons finely chopped shallots
1½ to 2 cups crabmeat (preferably lump crabmeat or Dungeness crab legs)
2 tablespoons chopped parsley

3 teaspoons finely chopped fresh tarragon, or 2 teaspoons dried tarragon, crushed fine
Salt, freshly ground black pepper
6 large thin slices of prosciutto
GARNISH: Watercress or parsley

Melt the butter in a skillet. When bubbling, add the shallots and cook 2 or 3 minutes, until limp. Add crabmeat and let it merely heat through, tossing it with the shallots and butter. Remove from the heat. Toss gently with the parsley and tarragon. Taste for seasoning. Add salt, if needed, and 3 or 4 grinds of pepper. Spoon carefully onto one half of each ham slice and fold the other half over it and arrange on a baking sheet. Put under a preheated broiler just long enough to heat the ham. Serve on warm plates with a garnish of watercress or parsley, and homemade Melba toast or crisp rolls.

Eggplant Purée

This sweet-sour eggplant mixture bears some resemblance to the recipe for Caponata, which follows, but here the texture is quite different. Also good spread on French bread or fingers of toast as a cocktail hors d'oeuvre.

Makes 6 servings

1 medium eggplant
¼ cup olive oil
1 medium onion, finely chopped
¼ cup finely chopped shallots
2 garlic cloves, finely chopped

¼ cup tomato paste
Salt, freshly ground black pepper
1 tablespoon sugar
3 tablespoons lemon juice
Greens

GARNISH: Chopped hard-boiled egg whites and yolks (separate), chopped onion, chopped parsley, paper-thin slices of lemon

Blanch the eggplant in boiling water until just soft, about 10 minutes. Plunge into ice water to cool. When cool enough to handle, peel eggplant and chop the pulp fine.

Heat the olive oil in a skillet, add the onion, shallot, garlic, and eggplant pulp, and sauté until quite dry. Add the tomato paste, mix thoroughly, and simmer the mixture until it is very thick and almost sticking to the pan. Season to taste with salt and pepper, and mix in the sugar and lemon juice. Cool and chill. Serve on a bed of greens with a garnish of the egg whites and yolks (chopped separately), onion and parsley. Drizzle olive oil over the eggplant mixture and arrange the lemon slices on top.

Caponata

While this Sicilian dish is traditionally served cold as part of the antipasto course, on its own it makes a zesty, refreshing appetizer for a summer meal, or before a meat entrée such as Sicilian Veal Roll (see page 404).

Makes 6 to 8 servings

3 eggplants, cut in cubes, skin left on
Salt, freshly ground black pepper
1 celery heart, thinly sliced crosswise
½ cup olive oil
1 large onion, sliced
5 large ripe tomatoes, peeled, seeded, and quartered, or 1½ cups drained canned Italian plum tomatoes
1 or 2 pinches thyme
1 bay leaf
6 to 8 anchovies, chopped
¼ pound soft black Italian olives, pitted
3 tablespoons capers
3 tablespoons sugar
2 tablespoons vinegar
2 tablespoons chopped parsley
A little grated lemon zest (optional)

Salt the eggplant cubes and let them drain in a colander. Blanch the celery briefly in boiling water, then drain and plunge into cold water to stop it from cooking further. Drain and dry.

Heat 2 tablespoons of the oil in a saucepan, add the onion and cook slowly over medium-low heat until soft and melted down. Add the tomatoes, thyme, bay leaf, and salt and pepper to taste. Cook until the tomatoes are soft and thick. Put mixture through a sieve.

While the tomato mixture is cooking, dry the eggplant cubes and brown them in the remaining olive oil. They should just cook through. Combine them with the tomato mixture, blanched celery, anchovies, olives, and capers. Dissolve the sugar in the vinegar and stir this into the eggplant-tomato mixture. Sprinkle with the parsley and add lemon zest, if desired. Serve warm or cold.

¶**Caponata with Tuna.** For a heartier version, drain a 7-ounce can tuna in olive oil, break it up, and add to the caponata after blending in the sugar-vinegar mixture. Serve cold.

Mushroom Pâté

If the addition of baking powder seems odd to you it does make a lighter, more palatable finished dish.

Makes 3 cups

3 onions, finely chopped
3 tablespoons olive oil
1 pound mushrooms, finely chopped
20 biscottes or enough Melba toast to
　　make 2 cups, crumbled
⅔ cup water
3 bay leaves
1 teaspoon crushed thyme

3 garlic cloves, crushed
¼ cup chopped parsley
¼ pound butter
Pinch of nutmeg
Salt, freshly ground black pepper
Dash Tabasco
2 tablespoons bourbon
3 tablespoons baking powder

Sauté the onions for 10 minutes in the olive oil over medium heat. Add the mushrooms and cook over low heat for 15 minutes. Crush the biscottes in a bowl and add the water. To the mushroom mixture add the bay leaves, thyme, garlic, parsley, butter, and, lastly, the bread.

Cook for 20 minutes over low heat. Remove from heat, remove and discard the bay leaves, and add the nutmeg, salt and pepper to taste, Tabasco, bourbon, and the baking powder. Chill. Serve cooled as an hors d'oeuvre with crackers or French bread.

Tapenade

A spicy sauce from Provence that can be used to flavor a mayonnaise, as a dip for raw vegetables, as a sauce for hard-boiled eggs. Some restaurants in France used to pit olives and stuff them with this mixture.

Makes about 1½ cups

24 to 30 soft black Italian or Greek
　　olives, pitted
3 or 4 garlic cloves
1½ tablespoons capers

¼ cup or more olive oil
14 to 16 anchovy fillets
4-ounce can tuna in olive oil
1 to 2 tablespoons cognac

Put the olives, garlic, capers, and enough of the olive oil to make a paste in the container of a blender or food processor. Blend or process until smooth.

Remove to a bowl. Put anchovy fillets, tuna, and their oils plus the olive oil in the container and blend to a paste. Then blend in the first mixture and the cognac to a thick purée. Taste for seasoning. It will not need salt, because of the anchovies, but it may need more cognac, some freshly ground black pepper, a dash of Tabasco, or a touch of thyme or summer savory.

¶**Tapenade with Mustard.** Add 1 tablespoon Dijon mustard to the tapenade, with the cognac.

¶**Tomatoes Stuffed with Tapenade.** Scoop out cherry tomatoes, drain, fill with tapenade, serve as a cocktail appetizer.

¶**Tapenade Eggs.** Arrange hard-boiled eggs, halved or not, on greens. Spoon tapenade over them.

¶**Tapenade with Avocado.** Fill the cavities of halved avocados with tapenade. Garnish with fresh parsley.

¶**As a Sauce for Fish.** Spoon tapenade over broiled fish fillets.

¶**Tapenade Mayonnaise.** Mix half mayonnaise and half tapenade. Use as a sauce for fish or a dressing for vegetable salads. Also good with cold roast veal or pork.

¶**Seafood Tapenade.** Crabmeat, shrimp, or lobster is greatly enhanced by tapenade mayonnaise in lieu of rémoulade or other sauces.

Peppers Stuffed with Anchovies and Raisins

An excellent first course, piquant but not surfeiting, to have before roast lamb or beef.

Makes 8 servings

8 green bell peppers	2 garlic cloves, finely chopped
2½ cups croutons, sautéed in oil and butter until golden	2 teaspoons chopped parsley
	2 teaspoons dry vermouth
½ cup raisins	Salt and freshly ground black pepper to taste
½ cup pine nuts	
16 chopped anchovies	3 tablespoons olive oil

Parboil the peppers for 10 minutes in salted water to soften them slightly, then split in half lengthwise and remove the seeds (leave the stem ends on). Arrange in one large or two medium baking dishes. Combine the croutons, raisins, pine nuts, anchovies, garlic, parsley, and vermouth in a bowl, toss together, and season to taste—go easy on the salt as the anchovies are salty. Fill the peppers with this mixture, put a teaspoon of oil on top of each one and bake in a 350° oven for 30 minutes. Serve hot.

Avocado Stuffed with Shrimp

While this is probably the favorite American way of serving avocado as a first course, it is only one of many combinations in which the bland, buttery texture of the avocado can be contrasted with other flavors. Teaming cold avocado with hot chili is perhaps the most exciting to the palate.

Makes 6 servings

2 cloves garlic	*3 avocados*
¼ cup olive oil	*1½ pounds cold cooked shrimp*

RUSSIAN DRESSING

1 cup mayonnaise	*1½ teaspoons Dijon mustard*
1 tablespoon finely chopped onion	*1 ounce caviar*

Crush the garlic in a mortar and combine with the olive oil. Halve the avocados and remove the pits and part of the pulp. Dress each one with a little of the garlic-oil mixture and fill the centers with the shrimp. Combine the ingredients for Russian dressing and serve with the shrimp-stuffed avocados.

¶**Crab-Stuffed Avocado.** Stuff the halved avocados with crabmeat mixed with Louis dressing (see page 77).

¶**Avocado Stuffed with Avocado.** Remove the flesh of the avocado and dice. Mix with Russian dressing and return to the shell.

¶**Avocado Stuffed with Seviche.** Marinate raw bay scallops or thin strips of raw white fish in lime juice to cover for 4 hours. Drain. Combine a little of the lime juice with olive oil, chopped green onion, chopped parsley, chopped canned green chilies, chopped garlic, salt. pepper, and Tabasco to taste. Pour over the scallops or fish and toss lightly. Chill and then stuff the avocados with the mixture. Garnish with chopped cilantro (fresh coriander).

¶**Avocado with Chili.** Heap hot chili (made with ground beef, no beans) in the avocado shells; top with a spoonful of sour cream.

¶**Avocado with Chicken, Ham, and Cheese.** Slice avocados crosswise, not lengthwise, so they stand up like little bowls. Fill with coarsely shredded cooked chicken, ham, and Gruyère cheese bound with mayonnaise. Top with cucumber slices and a cherry tomato.

Baked Potatoes with Caviar

This great specialty of the S.S. *United States* is one of the most glamorous of all the stuffed-vegetable first courses, and not expensive if you use fresh red salmon caviar rather than costly beluga.

For each serving

1 *small freshly baked potato, split*	1 *to 2 tablespoons sour cream*
1 *tablespoon caviar*	*Chopped chives (optional)*

Scoop a small amount of the pulp from the freshly baked potato and replace it with the caviar and sour cream. Serve hot garnished with chives, if you wish; I think it is better without.

¶New Potatoes with Caviar. Boil small new potatoes until tender, scoop out part of the inside with a melon-ball cutter, and fill with a touch of caviar and sour cream. Serve as a cocktail appetizer (to make them stand up on the plate, slice off a little of the bottom).

¶Deep-Fried New Potatoes with Caviar. Bake tiny new potatoes in their jackets for about 25 minutes, scoop out the pulp, drop the shells in 375° deep fat for 1 minute, until crisp. Fill the shells with the potato pulp mixed with sour cream and caviar. Serve hot.

Twice-Baked Potato Skins

Bake potatoes and remove all the pulp. Use in another dish, such as Disgustingly Rich Potatoes (see page 168). With scissors cut the skins in strips about an inch wide. Put on a baking sheet; brush generously with melted butter; season with salt, freshly ground black pepper, and a little Tabasco; and put in a 475° oven or under the broiler until they get brown and quite crisp. Serve with drinks, as an appetizer. These are better than any potato chips.

Onions à la Grecque

These crunchy little onions are good to keep on hand, refrigerated in jars, for summer entertaining.

Serves 6 as an hors d'oeuvre

36 to 40 small white onions (identical
    size, if possible)
4 tablespoons olive oil
⅔ cup dry white wine
½ cup water
1 teaspoon sugar

1 teaspoon salt
Sprig of fennel, if available, or
    ¼–½ teaspoon fennel
½ teaspoon thyme
1 bay leaf
Pinch of saffron

Pour boiling water over the onions and leave for 5 minutes to loosen skins. Peel. Arrange in a large skillet with the oil, wine, water, and all seasonings, except saffron. Poach gently until tender but still crisp. Add saffron and cook about 10 minutes. Transfer the onions to a serving dish and reduce the sauce a little. Pour sauce over onions and chill. Serve as part of an hors d'oeuvre selection.

¶Onions Monégasque. Add 1 or 2 tablespoons tomato paste and 1 cup white raisins with the saffron. Cook until raisins are puffy.

¶Onions Gratin. Drain onions, put in a baking dish and cover with 1½ cups béchamel sauce (see page 531). Arrange 12 cooked asparagus tips (or canned asparagus tips) on top and sprinkle with ⅓ cup buttered crumbs. Bake in a 400° oven for 10 minutes or put under a hot broiler until the crumbs are lightly browned.

Asparagus Italian-Style

The combination of asparagus with different kinds of cooked eggs is unusual and pleasant. Here again, you can think up variations of your own.

Makes 4 servings

2 pounds asparagus
Salt
4 to 8 tablespoons olive oil, warmed
½ cup grated Parmesan cheese

¼ cup chopped parsley
4 hard-boiled eggs, sieved
3 to 4 tablespoons capers, finely
    chopped

Clean the asparagus, breaking off the tough ends. Lay the asparagus flat in a skillet, pour on boiling water to cover, season with salt, and cook uncovered until the tips are just tender, but the stalks still bitey. To test, remove a stalk from the water; the tip should just droop over a little. Drain well on a cloth, then arrange on warm plates. Spoon 1 to 2 tablespoons of the warm oil over each serving, sprinkle lavishly with Parmesan cheese and parsley, and top each serving with sieved egg. Serve with capers, to be added to taste.

¶**Dutch Asparagus.** Top each serving of asparagus with an egg fried in oil, and chopped capers.

¶**Belgian Asparagus.** Arrange cooked asparagus on plates with a halved hot hard-boiled egg and butter sauce (for sauce, cream ¼ pound sweet butter, adding lukewarm water, drop by drop, until it has the consistency of hollandaise). To eat, crush egg with a fork, blend with the butter sauce and a dash of nutmeg, and dip the asparagus into the sauce mixture.

Asparagus in Ambush

Serve these rolls as an hors d'oeuvre or even a separate course. Knives and forks are definitely called for with this dish.

Makes 8 servings

8 long French rolls
¼ pound butter
3 pounds asparagus spears

1 cup hollandaise sauce (see page 532)
Strips of pimiento

Slice the tops neatly from the French rolls and remove most of the crumb, leaving about a ⅓-inch thickness of bread and crust. Toast the rolls and the tops under the broiler until they are lightly browned. Butter them well and keep them warm. Trim the asparagus spears and cut them so they will fit easily into the hollowed-out rolls. Cook the asparagus according to directions in the preceding recipe. Arrange the cooked spears in the rolls, dress with hollandaise sauce, and decorate each one with a strip or two of pimiento. Cover with the top of the roll. Dribble additional hollandaise over the top of the roll in a crosswise pattern.

Buckwheat Blini

A sophisticated form of tiny pancake made popular by the Russians, eaten hot as a first course with quantities of melted butter, sour cream and caviar (fine California caviar or Gold caviar from the Great Lakes), smoked salmon, or herring, according to the taste of your bank account.

Makes 12 servings

1½ packages dry yeast
2½ cups lukewarm milk (110° to 115°)
1 teaspoon sugar

½ cup buckwheat flour
2 cups all-purpose flour
4 egg yolks, lightly beaten

2 tablespoons melted butter   *4 egg whites*
3 tablespoons sour cream   *½ teaspoon salt*

Sprinkle the yeast into the milk with the sugar and stir. When dissolved, combine with the buckwheat and all-purpose flours and the beaten egg yolks. Stir slowly, then beat vigorously until the batter is smooth—this can be done by hand, with an electric mixer and paddle attachment, or in the food processor. When smooth, put the batter in a bowl, cover with a towel and let rise in a warm, draft-free place for 1½ to 2 hours, until doubled in bulk. Punch down the batter; stir in the melted butter and sour cream. Beat the egg whites with the salt until stiff but not dry, and fold into the batter.

    Brush a hot griddle or heavy skillet well with melted butter and drop the batter on by spoonfuls, enough to make pancakes 3 inches in diameter. When the bottom is lightly browned and bubbles have formed on the surface, flip over and brown the second side. Keep warm in the oven, add a little melted butter to them and serve with more butter, sour cream, and caviar or smoked fish.

Carrot Blini

A different and much simpler form of blini, basically a crêpe batter with shredded carrot added.

Makes 8 servings

1 cup sifted flour   *¼ teaspoon freshly ground black pepper*
3 eggs, lightly beaten   *1 cup milk, approximately*
1 teaspoon salt   *1 cup shredded raw carrot*
3 tablespoons olive oil   *3 tablespoons butter*
ACCOMPANIMENTS: *Sour cream and red or black caviar*

Put the flour in a bowl. Stir in the eggs, salt, oil, pepper, and just enough milk to make a thick batter. Stir in the shredded carrot. Heat enough butter in a heavy skillet to cover the surface, and drop the batter in by spoonfuls, enough to make pancakes about 3 inches in diameter. Cook on both sides until lightly browned, adding more butter as needed. Serve with sour cream and caviar.

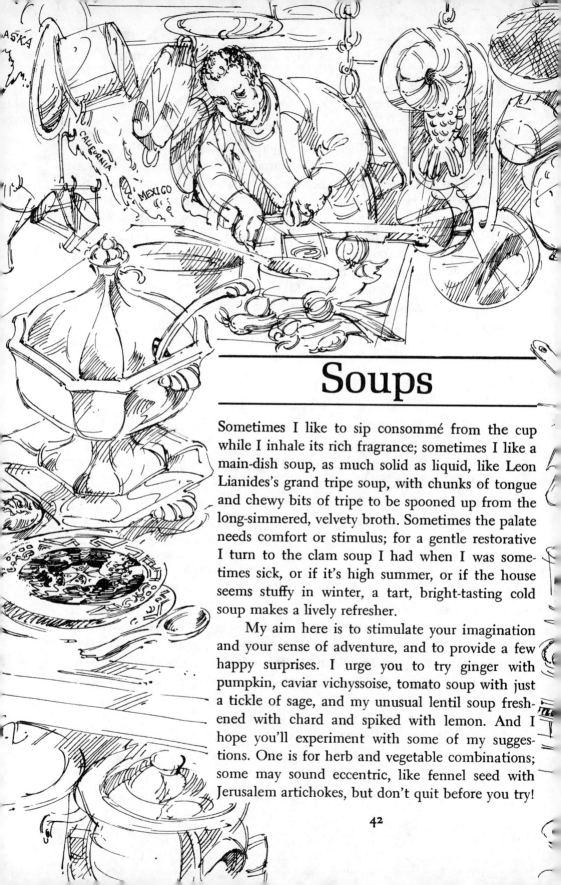

Soups

Sometimes I like to sip consommé from the cup while I inhale its rich fragrance; sometimes I like a main-dish soup, as much solid as liquid, like Leon Lianides's grand tripe soup, with chunks of tongue and chewy bits of tripe to be spooned up from the long-simmered, velvety broth. Sometimes the palate needs comfort or stimulus; for a gentle restorative I turn to the clam soup I had when I was sometimes sick, or if it's high summer, or if the house seems stuffy in winter, a tart, bright-tasting cold soup makes a lively refresher.

My aim here is to stimulate your imagination and your sense of adventure, and to provide a few happy surprises. I urge you to try ginger with pumpkin, caviar vichyssoise, tomato soup with just a tickle of sage, and my unusual lentil soup freshened with chard and spiked with lemon. And I hope you'll experiment with some of my suggestions. One is for herb and vegetable combinations; some may sound eccentric, like fennel seed with Jerusalem artichokes, but don't quit before you try!

42

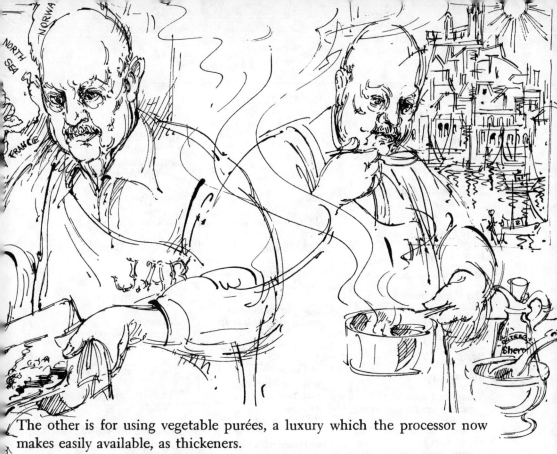

The other is for using vegetable purées, a luxury which the processor now makes easily available, as thickeners.

Speaking of techniques, soup making doesn't require many, and all are illustrated in the recipes I chose. Chowders you'll find in the fish chapter, and I've devised a master recipe for cream soups that can vary according to the vegetables in season. I hope you'll make up variants, too. For instance, use different thickeners: add puréed vegetables, for a more delicate density than flour gives; or try nuts, powdered in the blender or processor, or even crumbs, in the old French style; or stir in a luscious, classic finish of eggs and cream; or give the liquid a slightly gelatinous body, using an oxtail stock.

Not only can soup be made imaginatively by the cook, it can and should be used imaginatively in menu planning. Reasonably enough, this chapter begins with beginners, soups to precede a main course; but the main-course soups, which follow, are a wonderful resource. Like most soups, they are generally very little work, and can usually be prepared well in advance. If you're short of time, you could precede them with a simple choice of crudités or follow them with a bit of fruit. Or, if you like making elaborate desserts, why not offer a choice of two or three? I always like good home-made buttered toast or a crisp roll with any soup, and I notice that soup is a very frequent choice of good bread bakers.

SOUPS

Vegetable broth

Essence de poisson
  seafood soup

Fresh tomato soup
  purée
  with orange juice

Lady Curzon soup

Boula-boula

My clam soup that cures

Oxtail consommé

Oxtail gratin

Oxtail and vegetable soup

Borsch

Mustard green soup

Squash and corn soup
  puréed squash and corn
    soup

Sorrel soup
  with crème fraîche
  with yogurt

Basic cream vegetable soup
  artichoke soup

Cream of spinach soup
  cream of watercress soup

Vichyssoise
  caviar
  apple
  watercress
  carrot
  turnip

Cold minted pea soup

Cold beet soup

Watercress soup, Chinese
    style

Ginger-pumpkin soup
  cream of squash soup

Cold minted yogurt soup

Lentil soup
  with frankfurters
  with cream
  with ham
  split-pea soup

Lentil soup with chard
    and lemon
  with cotechino

Garbure basquaise
  garbure gratiné
  garbure with pig's
    knuckles

Marion Cunningham's
    minestrone
  with sausage
  with chickpeas or
    kidney beans
  with ham

Black bean soup

The Coach House tripe
    soup

Oyster bisque
  clam bisque

Shrimp soup
  curried scallop soup
  chili scallop soup

Castilian mussel soup

The Palace mussel soup
  billi bi

Marseilles fish soup
  rouille

Cullen skink
  Scotch vichyssoise

Gruyère soup
  Cheddar soup
  Cheddar-olive soup

Vegetable Broth

For certain vegetable soups, a delicately flavored vegetable broth is preferable to a strong, rich beef or oxtail stock. As vegetables contain their own natural sodium, season with salt after making the broth.

Makes 3 quarts

3 carrots, finely cut
3 cups finely cut celery
3 onions, finely chopped
½ pound mushrooms or mushroom
    stems, sliced

3 leeks, sliced
3 quarts water
1 bay leaf
Salt

Combine the carrots, celery, onions, mushrooms, leeks, water, and a bay leaf in a pan. Bring to a boil, reduce the heat, and simmer, covered, for 2½ hours. Strain the broth, discarding the vegetables, and season to taste with salt.

Essence de Poisson

A light, clear, refreshing soup that depends for its excellence on the flavor of the fish stock, vegetables, and herbs, concentrated by being left to infuse an hour before straining. A good palate stimulant before a heavy main course.

Makes 6 servings

4 tablespoons butter
3 tablespoons oil
½ cup finely chopped onion
½ cup finely cut scallions, or green
    onion
1 garlic clove, finely chopped
½ cup chopped fresh dill or 1½
    teaspoons dried dill weed

½ cup chopped parsley
1 green sweet pepper, chopped
1 whole hot pepper
6 cups fish broth (see page 530)
Salt
½ teaspoon Tabasco
Pinch of saffron

GARNISH: Finely chopped parsley, sour cream (optional)

Heat the butter and oil in a deep saucepan. Add the onion, scallions, garlic, fresh or dried dill, parsley, green pepper, and whole hot pepper. Sauté until wilted and well blended. Add fish broth and season with salt to taste, Tabasco, and a healthy pinch of saffron. Cook for 15 to 20 minutes, then allow to stand for 1 hour before straining through cheesecloth. Serve this clear soup with a garnish of finely chopped parsley and, if you wish, a dollop of sour cream in each cup.

¶Seafood Soup. Do not strain the soup. Add 1 cup white wine, 12 shelled clams, 12 shelled raw shrimp, and 12 bay scallops. Bring to a boil and cook for 3 minutes. Serve in cups, dividing the shellfish evenly among the cups. Garnish with additional chopped parsley, if you wish.

Fresh Tomato Soup

Sage is a difficult herb I like to use in crazy places, such as this tomato soup. The baking soda, incidentally, is there to neutralize the acid-curdling action the fresh tomatoes would have on the heavy cream. Or you could use evaporated milk, which won't curdle, instead of the cream.

Makes 4 servings

1 small onion, finely chopped
3 tablespoons unsalted butter
6 medium-large ripe tomatoes, peeled,
    seeded, and chopped
Salt, freshly ground black pepper

¼ teaspoon baking soda
¼ to ½ teaspoon dried sage
1 cup heavy cream
GARNISH: Sour cream, chopped parsley

Sauté the onion in the butter until soft and limp. Add the tomatoes, salt and pepper to taste, baking soda, and sage. Cook for 10 to 12 minutes, or until thickened and pastelike. Remove from the heat and stir in the cream. Taste for seasoning, and reheat. Serve hot, garnished with a spoonful of sour cream sprinkled with chopped parsley. Or refrigerate and serve chilled, with the same garnish.

¶**Purée of Tomato Soup.** Purée the tomato mixture and cream in a food processor for a smooth soup.

¶**Tomato Soup with Orange Juice.** Omit the sage and add ¼ to ½ teaspoon dried thyme and 3 tablespoons concentrated orange juice.

Lady Curzon Soup

There are differing stories about the origin of this soup. It is a great standard of the German cuisine, and you still see it on restaurant menus there, although we seldom see it here. Some say the soup was created by the American wife of Lord Curzon, a Viceroy of India, others that it was created in her honor. Whatever the truth of the matter, this is certainly a very elegant dinner-party soup with an unusual blend of flavors, delicate but rich and best served in small quantities.

Makes 6 servings

4 cups canned turtle soup, with turtle
    meat
2 egg yolks

⅓ cup heavy cream
½ teaspoon (or more, to taste) of good
    curry powder

¼ cup Madeira, sherry, or cognac
6 tablespoons lightly whipped cream

1 to 2 tablespoons finely chopped
parsley (optional)

Heat the soup to boiling. Beat the egg yolks with the cream and curry powder. Very gradually stir 1 cup of the hot soup into the egg mixture, then remove the soup from the heat and stir the egg mixture into it, with the Madeira, sherry, or cognac. Reheat gently, stirring, without letting the soup boil, until light and creamy (it won't thicken). Pour into hot soup cups, and float a tablespoon of whipped cream on each one. If the cups are heat-proof, put briefly under a hot broiler to glaze the cream—it should only take a second or two. Otherwise, just dust the cream with chopped parsley.

Boula-Boula

Rather similar to Lady Curzon Soup, this is an American invention, easy to make, and, again, an interesting soup for a dinner party. While you could use cooked fresh green peas for this, frozen peas do very well and are less expensive.

Makes 6 servings

3 tablespoons finely chopped onion or
    green onion
4 tablespoons unsalted butter
2 eight-ounce packages frozen peas,
    thawed
½ cup water
3 cups canned turtle broth, strained
    (reserve and dice the meat)

¼ teaspoon Tabasco
Salt
1 cup heavy cream
¼ cup dry sherry
6 tablespoons lightly salted whipped
    cream

Cook the onion in the butter until just soft. Add the peas, water, turtle broth, Tabasco, and salt to taste, and cook for 5 to 8 minutes, until peas are tender. Remove from heat. Purée the soup in a food mill, or in batches in the blender or food processor. Return to the pan and stir in the cream, reserved diced turtle meat, and sherry. Reheat. Pour the soup into heatproof soup cups or bowls and put a spoonful of whipped cream on top. Put under a hot broiler for a couple of seconds, just long enough to glaze the cream. Serve with crisp buttered crackers.

My Clam Soup That Cures

This soup of my childhood doesn't just soothe the troubled tummy, it also serves as a fine way to awaken the appetite at the start of a meal. Milk is not as rich today as it was when I was young, so I now add a little heavy cream.

Makes 4 servings

3 cups milk
2 cups minced clams (razor clams,
    if possible)
3 tablespoons butter

½ cup heavy cream
Salt, freshly ground black pepper
Chopped parsley

Heat the milk to the boiling point, being careful that it doesn't burn. Add the minced clams, butter, cream, and salt and pepper to taste, and heat until the butter is melted and the clams just hot. Serve in warmed soup bowls, garnish with parsley, and have crisp soda crackers with the soup.

Oxtail Consommé

Delicious on its own as a clear soup, this richly flavored oxtail stock can also be used like beef stock whenever it is called for in a recipe or as a base for vegetable soups. You can remove the pieces of meat from the bones and add them to make a heartier soup for a late supper or Sunday lunch.

Makes about 3 quarts

3 oxtails, cut in sections
1 veal knuckle, cracked
4 quarts water
3 carrots, cut in strips
3 leeks, well cleaned
1 onion stuck with 2 cloves

1 bay leaf
1 teaspoon rosemary
1 tablespoon salt
8 to 10 peppercorns
Beaten egg whites (optional)
Madeira

Arrange the oxtails on the rack of a broiling pan about 4 inches from the heat. Broil, turning the pieces once or twice, until they are well browned on all sides and crisp at the edges.

Remove oxtail pieces to an 8-quart pot and add the veal knuckle and water. Bring to a boil and boil rapidly for 5 minutes, removing the scum from the surface. Add the carrots, leeks, onion, bay leaf, rosemary, salt, and peppercorns. Reduce the heat, cover, and simmer for 2 to 3 hours. Taste for seasoning. Strain the stock and cool overnight. Remove the fat. If you wish, clarify with beaten egg whites before serving. Serve in soup cups with 1 tablespoon Madeira added to each cup.

Oxtail Gratin

Oxtail consommé replaces the more customary beef stock in this version of onion soup.

Makes 6 servings

3 large Spanish onions or yellow globe
   onions
6 cups oxtail consommé (page 48)
¼ teaspoon nutmeg or mace
1 garlic clove, finely chopped

Tabasco
¾ cup port
6 slices French bread, well toasted
1 cup shredded Gruyère or Parmesan
   cheese

Peel and coarsely chop the onions. Put in a 2½-quart saucepan with the consommé, nutmeg or mace, and garlic. Cover and simmer for 1 hour.

Ladle the soup into 6 ovenproof individual serving bowls and add a dash of Tabasco and 2 tablespoons port to each. Arrange on each serving 1 slice of well-toasted French bread and heap with some of the Gruyère cheese. Place the bowls on a baking sheet and heat in a 350° oven for about 15 minutes, until the cheese has melted and formed a rich crust on top of the soup. Serve at once with additional grated Gruyère or Parmesan cheese.

Oxtail and Vegetable Soup

This is the kind of easy, basic vegetable soup you can vary according to season, or the vegetables you have on hand. I very often use leeks, celery, squash, lima beans, cabbage, corn, tomatoes, parsnips, or for a heartier soup mix in drained canned chickpeas or beans. A good vegetable soup can be a meal in itself.

Makes 6 to 8 servings

3 carrots, cut in small dice
2 turnips, cut in small dice
2 medium onions, thinly sliced
4 potatoes, cut in fine dice
¼ pound green beans, cut in small
   pieces
3 garlic cloves, crushed

2 quarts oxtail consommé (page 48)
½ cup orzo (rice-shaped pasta) or
   pastina
Meat removed from oxtails
1 package frozen peas
Grated Parmesan or Romano cheese

Put the carrots, turnips, onions, potatoes, green beans, garlic, and consommé in a heavy saucepan. Bring to a boil, then reduce the heat and simmer until the vegetables are barely tender. Add the orzo or pastina and the little bits of meat removed from the oxtails. Bring to a boil once more and cook until the vegetables and pasta are done. Add the frozen peas and cook 2 minutes longer. Correct the seasoning and serve the soup in heated bowls. Pass grated Parmesan or Romano cheese and thick slices of toasted and buttered French or Italian bread.

Borsch

There are many versions of borsch. This one makes an excellent one-dish meal for supper or a winter lunch, when served with some good black bread and butter, and followed by cheese and fruit. There should be a balance of sweet and sour, so adjust the lemon juice and sugar to taste. If possible, add cooked meat from the stock for a heartier soup.

Makes 6 to 8 servings

3 quarts beef stock (see page 530) or *oxtail consommé (see page 48)*
4 or 5 small raw beets, shredded
4 potatoes, peeled and thinly sliced
2 onions, coarsely chopped

2 cups finely shredded cabbage
½ cup lemon juice
2 or 3 tablespoons sugar
2 cups beef (from the stock) or oxtail *(from the consommé), diced*

Bring the stock to a boil in a large pot, add the beets and simmer 15 minutes, then add the remaining vegetables, and cook until the potatoes and cabbage are soft and sufficiently overcooked to give the soup body. Add the lemon juice and as much sugar as needed to augment the natural sweetness of the beets, adjusting the ratio to taste. Stir in the cooked beef and serve in large heated bowls or soup plates.

Mustard Green Soup

A hearty and distinctive vegetable soup with an unusual combination of flavors that might be the main dish for a supper.

Makes 8 servings

2 pounds mustard greens
Handful of sorrel (if available) or *spinach*

3 garlic cloves, chopped
1 medium onion, chopped
8 cups vegetable broth (see page 44)

2 tablespoons soy sauce

1 tablespoon grated fresh ginger root

1 cup fine Chinese or Italian noodles
   or orzo

Blanch the mustard greens and sorrel in boiling water for 4 minutes. Drain and chop very fine. Cook the garlic and onion in the vegetable broth until tender, add the chopped greens, soy sauce, and ginger and cook for 2 minutes. Then add the noodles or orzo and cook until just tender. Correct the seasoning and serve the soup in hot bowls. The amount of pasta added is up to you—if you like a heavier soup, add more noodles or orzo.

Squash and Corn Soup

This interesting combination of squash and corn is typical of Latin America, but the touch of ginger makes it a little different.

Makes 6 servings

5 to 6 cups vegetable broth (see page 44)

1 or 2 small yellow crookneck or other summer squash, cut in ½-inch slices

1 leek, cut in ½-inch rounds

1 green pepper, cut in julienne strips

1 large garlic clove (or 2 small cloves), crushed

¼ teaspoon thyme

2 or 3 slices fresh ginger

1 ear of corn, split and cut into tiny slices

Salt

GARNISH: Grated Parmesan or Romano cheese

Put the vegetable broth, squash, leek, pepper, garlic, thyme, and fresh ginger into a saucepan. Bring to a boil, reduce the heat, and simmer for 1 hour. Add the corn. Taste and adjust seasoning. Serve sprinkled with grated Parmesan or Romano cheese.

¶Puréed Squash and Corn Soup. After cooking the vegetables, except corn, put them through the food mill or purée in a blender or food processor. Then add the pieces of corn to the soup. You can also serve this purée cold, combined with heavy or sour cream to taste. Garnish with chopped fresh dill and parsley.

Sorrel Soup

Makes 4 to 6 servings

1 pound sorrel
6 tablespoons peanut oil
3 cups chicken broth (see page 529)

1 cup heavy cream
3 egg yolks
Salt, freshly ground black pepper

Wash the sorrel well, remove the stems, and cut the leaves into thin strips. Heat the oil in a heavy 2-quart saucepan, add the sorrel, and cook for 5 to 6 minutes, or until it is wilted. Add the chicken broth and simmer for 5 to 6 minutes over moderate heat. Remove the pan from the stove and allow the soup to cool slightly. Purée the sorrel in a food processor or blender. Return to pan. Beat together the heavy cream and egg yolks and gradually stir this into the soup, and season to taste with salt and pepper. Return the pan to the stove and cook the soup over moderate heat until it thickens slightly—being sure not to let it boil. Serve hot or chill the soup and serve cold.

¶**Sorrel Soup with Crème Fraîche.** Add ½ cup crème fraîche (see page 548) to the soup after thickening with egg yolks and cream.

¶**Sorrel-Yogurt Soup.** Do not add cream and egg thickening. After chilling soup, stir in plain yogurt to taste. Serve cold.

Basic Cream Vegetable Soup

This is easy and quick because it consists of little more than puréed cooked vegetables and their cooking liquid (preferably homemade chicken stock, skimmed of all fat) mixed with cream, sour cream, half-and-half, or yogurt. If you have a food processor or blender the puréing is simplicity itself. Failing that, a food mill will serve. If you use a blender, you will have to blend the vegetables with some or all of the cooking liquid, in batches; but unless the vegetable is very dense and starchy, like potatoes or shell beans, this isn't necessary with the food processor.

The usual proportions for the soup are 1 cup of uncooked chopped or cooked puréed vegetable and 2 cups stock to 1 cup cream, but the thickness of the soup depends on the vegetable you are using. Starchy root vegetables provide their own thickening. If you are using vegetables with a high water content, such as summer squash, cucumbers, or leafy green vegetables, you need a larger quantity of the vegetable and added thickening. I find instant mashed potato, which cooks smooth and is comparatively tasteless, to be an excellent thickener. In fact, it is the best use I know for this "convenience" product. Use one of the 2-serving packages, or more if needed, and stir it into the reheated soup, cooking until you get the consistency you want.

For a more traditional and richer thickening, beat 2 egg yolks with the 1 cup cream before adding it to the soup, and cook gently, stirring, until thickened. However, I think you will find the all-vegetable thickening gives a better, purer flavor and a lighter result—with fewer calories.

The soup base of stock and puréed vegetable can be made in quantity, frozen, thawed, and reheated with the cream when you are ready to serve— and, of course, any of the soups may be served cold.

Once you start to play around with the basic recipe that follows, you can alter and adjust it to suit yourself, adding different flavoring herbs and experimenting with various vegetables and combinations of vegetables. For instance, a cut-up avocado put in the blender or food processor (not the food mill) with a zucchini, watercress, or cucumber soup will both thicken and give a lovely flavor and velvety texture.

Makes 4 servings

*2 cups strong fat-free chicken stock
  (see page 529)*
1 cup sliced or finely cut vegetable
1 small onion, finely chopped
2 tablespoons chopped parsley
*1 tablespoon chopped fresh herb of
  your choice or 1 teaspoon dried
  herb*

Salt, freshly ground black pepper
*1 cup cream (heavy, light, sour),
  half-and-half, or yogurt*
*Instant mashed potato for thickening,
  if needed*

Put the stock, vegetables, and herbs in a pan and simmer until tender but not mushy. Purée vegetables in a food mill, food processor, or blender. Return vegetables and liquid to pan and season to taste with salt and pepper, depending on how highly seasoned the stock is. Stir in the cream and reheat. If using sour cream or yogurt, be sure to keep the soup under the boiling point, or it will curdle.

If the soup needs more thickening, stir in instant mashed potatoes and cook over medium-low heat, stirring, until thickened to taste. The amount will depend on the natural thickness of the vegetable used. Serve with a garnish of chopped parsley, chives, dill, or whatever herb is appropriate, or a dash of paprika.

¶**Artichoke Soup.** Boil the artichokes until tender. Remove and purée the bottoms and scrapings from the leaves; use 1 cup of this purée.

OTHER VEGETABLE AND SEASONING COMBINATIONS

Parsnips	Cinnamon	*Salsify*	Chervil
Rutabagas	Rosemary	*Summer squash*	Dill
Pumpkin	Nutmeg	*Winter squash*	Ginger

Jerusalem artichokes   Fennel seed

Cream of Spinach Soup

This soup can be thickened two ways: with a medium béchamel sauce or with instant mashed potatoes. I find that the potato is a far more delicate thickener for a soup you are going to serve cold than the béchamel, which has a flour taste after chilling.

Makes 3 servings

½ cup spinach purée (made from
    fresh or frozen spinach)
3 tablespoons butter
1 onion, finely chopped
1 garlic clove, finely chopped
2 cups chicken broth (fresh or canned)

½ teaspoon tarragon
1 cup medium béchamel (page 531), or
    1 serving instant mashed potato
    (following package directions for
    preparing)

Cook spinach (if using frozen, 5 ounces; if fresh, 16 to 20 leaves). Remove to colander and drain, squeezing out most of the liquid. Purée in either a food processor or blender. Sauté onion and garlic in butter till soft. Add spinach purée and sauté gently 2 to 3 minutes. Add chicken broth and tarragon and simmer 3 to 4 minutes. Add the béchamel or mashed potato and heat to boiling. Serve in heated bowls.

¶Cream of Watercress Soup. Proceed as above, using ½ cup watercress purée (1 bunch, blanched in boiling water for 3 minutes, drained and puréed), 1 tablespoon chopped parsley and ½ teaspoon dill weed instead of tarragon.

Vichyssoise

Louis Diat, who created this famous soup while he was chef at the Ritz in New York, allowed me and my partner, the late William Rhode, to sell it in our shop, Hors d'Oeuvre Incorporated. It was a great hit with New Yorkers in our vicinity, who would order it to take away on weekends.

Makes 6 servings

6 leeks
1 quart rich chicken stock (see page 529)
3 medium potatoes, peeled and finely diced

1 cup sour cream or heavy cream (preferably sour cream)
Salt to taste
Freshly grated nutmeg
Finely chopped chives

Trim and wash the leeks. Cut off green tops, leaving only the white part. Slice this rather fine. Put leeks in a pan with chicken stock and finely diced potatoes. Bring to a boil and simmer, covered, for 30 minutes, or until potatoes are well cooked. Strain the broth. Purée the vegetables in a food mill, blender, or food processor. Combine broth and purée and chill 24 hours. A few minutes before serving, stir in sour cream or heavy cream. Add salt to taste and a dash of nutmeg, and chill again for a few minutes. Serve in chilled cups with finely chopped chives on top.

¶Caviar Vichyssoise. Just before serving, stir 1 tablespoon red or black caviar into each cup, then garnish with chives.

¶Apple Vichyssoise. Add ½ cup finely chopped raw apple to the soup before chilling.

¶Watercress Vichyssoise. Add 1 large bunch watercress to vegetables.

¶Carrot Vichyssoise. Use only 1 leek and add 3 large carrots, coarsely chopped, to the vegetables.

¶Turnip Vichyssoise. Use only 1 leek and add 3 sliced white turnips to the vegetables.

Cold Minted Pea Soup

This is one of my favorite summer soups, which can be made with yogurt instead of cream if you like a tarter soup with fewer calories.

Makes 8 servings

6 cups chicken stock (see page 529)
1 small onion stuck with 2 cloves
1 garlic clove
1 teaspoon tarragon

3 pounds freshly shelled peas or 3 packages frozen peas
Salt, freshly ground black pepper
3 cups heavy cream or yogurt

GARNISH: Finely chopped fresh mint

Put the chicken stock in a saucepan with the onion, garlic, tarragon, and peas. Cook until the peas are just tender. Remove and discard onion. Add salt and pepper to taste and purée in a food mill, blender, or food processor. Combine with cream or yogurt and serve well chilled with a generous sprinkling of mint.

Cold Beet Soup

The final touch of raw grated beets makes this rather different from other beet soups.

Makes 4 servings

7 small beets, washed
2 cups chicken stock (page 529)
1 large Idaho potato, peeled and
    quartered

Salt
1 tablespoon wine vinegar
1 teaspoon chopped tarragon
1 cup sour cream

Leave the roots and an inch of the tops on 6 of the beets. Boil the beets in salted water until tender. Peel, slice, and put in a pan with the chicken stock. Cook the potato very slowly in salted water until very soft. Drain, add to the beets and bring to a boil. Purée the broth, beets, and potato in a food mill, blender, or food processor (don't overcrowd the blender or food processor; it is best to do this in two batches). Reheat the soup with salt to taste, wine vinegar, and chopped tarragon. Mix in the sour cream, off the heat. Chill thoroughly. Before serving, peel and grate the remaining beet. Serve the soup in cups with the finely grated beet on top, or put a dab of sour cream on top and sprinkle with the beet, or with finely cut green onion.

Watercress Soup, Chinese Style

A very different kind of soup from the Orient, rather fun to serve.

Makes 4 servings

6 cups chicken broth, free of fat
    (page 529)
Soy sauce
2 large bunches watercress, washed and
    trimmed of coarse ends

4 poached eggs
4 tablespoons finely diced water
    chestnuts
12 thin strips Virginia ham

Heat the chicken broth to boiling point and season to taste with soy sauce (the amount depends on the seasoning in the broth). Arrange watercress in the bottom of a tureen, like a nest, and carefully lower the poached eggs onto it. Sprinkle with the water chestnuts and ham. Very carefully pour the boiling broth down the side of the tureen, so as not to upset the arrangement. Serve each person an egg and some cress, water chestnuts, ham, and broth. The tureen should be hot, the broth boiling, the watercress crisp, and the eggs firmly poached. Serve with thin buttered toast.

Ginger-Pumpkin Soup

Pumpkin is one of those vegetables that has got into a rut. You usually find only recipes for baked pumpkin or pumpkin pie, but it makes a perfectly splendid soup for a Thanksgiving or winter dinner.

Makes 6 servings

2-pound pumpkin
1 onion, stuck with 2 cloves
3 cups chicken stock (see page 529)
¼ teaspoon cinnamon
2 tablespoons finely chopped fresh
ginger

½ teaspoon freshly ground black pepper
Salt
1 cup heavy cream or yogurt

GARNISH: *Thin slivers of Smithfield ham or baked country ham (optional)*

Peel the pumpkin, remove seeds and strings, and cut into cubes. Put in a pan with the onion, chicken stock, and seasonings—except salt. Cover and cook slowly until pumpkin is soft. Remove onion and purée the soup in a food mill, blender, or food processor. Taste for seasoning, adding salt and more pepper, if needed. Return to the pan and mix in the heavy cream or yogurt. Heat through (if yogurt is used, be sure not to let it get near the boiling point). Garnish with ham, if desired.

¶**Cream of Squash Soup.** Use winter squash, such as Hubbard, acorn, or butternut, instead of the pumpkin.

Cold Minted Yogurt Soup

A tart, refreshing soup that is perfect for a summer luncheon or if you are having barbecued steak, chops, or kebabs for dinner.

Makes 8 servings

4 cups yogurt
⅓ cup heavy cream
3 tablespoons chopped fresh mint

Juice and grated zest of 2 lemons
3 cups rich chicken stock (page 529)
Salt, freshly ground black pepper

GARNISH: *Red caviar, paprika*

Combine the yogurt, cream, chopped fresh mint, lemon juice and zest, and the chicken stock. Season to taste and whisk lightly. Chill. Serve in chilled cups with a spoonful of red caviar and a sprinkling of paprika.

Lentil Soup

For a one-dish meal on a cold winter's day, nothing is quite as warming and heartening as a big pot of lentil soup, which can be stretched with the addition of sausages, ham, or smoked pork butt.

Makes 6 servings

1 ham or pork bone
1 pound lentils
2 to 3 quarts water or stock
Salt, freshly ground black pepper

1 cup finely chopped onions
2 garlic cloves, finely chopped
1 teaspoon thyme
¼ teaspoon nutmeg

GARNISH: *Chopped parsley, crisp croutons*

Put the bone and lentils in a deep pot with the water or stock and cook until lentils are very soft, about 1 hour. Put them through a sieve or food mill, or purée in a blender or food processor. Taste the puréed soup for seasoning, and add salt (not much if the meat bone was salty) and pepper to taste. Add the onions, garlic, thyme, and nutmeg and additional water or stock, if necessary, to make a good thick soup. Simmer for 30 minutes. Taste for seasoning again and serve topped with chopped parsley and crisp croutons.

¶**Lentil Soup with Frankfurters.** Add thinly sliced frankfurters or knockwurst for the last 10 minutes of cooking time.

¶**Lentil Soup with Cream.** Stir ¾ cup heavy cream into the soup for the last 5 minutes of cooking time.

¶**Lentil Soup with Ham.** Add bite-size pieces of baked ham or cooked pork butt for the last 5 minutes of cooking time.

¶**Split-Pea Soup.** Instead of lentils, use split peas, which will take about twice as long to cook.

Lentil Soup with Chard and Lemon

A rather different, Syrian version of lentil soup, tartened by lemon juice, that is also delicious served cold.

Makes 6 servings

1½ cups lentils
2½ pounds Swiss chard or spinach
½ cup olive oil
3 to 4 cloves garlic
Salt, freshly ground black pepper

¾ cup chopped onion
1 rib celery, chopped
¾ cup lemon juice
1 teaspoon flour

Put the lentils in a pot, cover with cold water, and cook, covered, until tender—between 30 and 45 minutes, depending upon processing; taste to see when done. Wash and chop the chard or spinach, and add to the lentils with 1 cup water. Cook until chard is wilted.

Meanwhile, heat the oil in a skillet. Crush the garlic with ½ teaspoon salt. Sauté the onion, garlic, and celery until soft, then add to the lentils. Mix the lemon juice and flour and stir into the soup. Simmer, stirring, until the soup thickens slightly. Taste and correct seasoning. Serve in soup bowls, with crusty French or Italian bread.

¶Lentil Soup with Cotechino. Poach a cotechino with the lentils, during the first cooking. Remove, slice, and add to the finished soup.

Garbure Basquaise

A hearty soup-stew from the Basque country which combines beans, other vegetables, and ham. It can be varied in all kinds of ways by adding leftover meat or poultry.

Makes 6 servings

1 pound white pea beans
½ pound dried peas, green or yellow
1 ham bone, with meat
3 bay leaves
1 onion, stuck with 2 cloves
3 quarts water
Salt
4 white turnips, cut in small pieces
6 potatoes, cut in small pieces

4 carrots, sliced
4 leeks, washed and sliced
6 cloves garlic, finely chopped, or
    1 tablespoon garlic purée (see
    page 534)
1 teaspoon thyme
12 small sausages
1 small cabbage, shredded
GARNISH: Grated Swiss cheese

Put the beans and peas in a pot, cover with water, and bring to a boil. Boil 2 minutes, then remove from the heat and let stand 1 hour. Drain. Put in a deep pot with the ham bone, 2 bay leaves, onion, and 3 quarts water, and cook until the beans are just tender, but not mushy, about 1 to 1½ hours, adding salt if needed (if the ham is salty, it may not be necessary). Drain beans, reserving liquid, and remove meat from the ham bone. Return the bean liquid to the pot with all the vegetables and seasonings, except for the beans and cabbage, and cook until tender. Prick sausages with a fork and cook in water to cover for 10 minutes to draw out the fat. To the soup add the shredded cabbage, beans, ham, and drained sausages. Cook until the cabbage is just done and the soup thick enough almost to hold a spoon upright. Serve in bowls or deep soup plates, sprinkled with grated Swiss cheese, with French bread.

¶**Garbure Gratiné.** Ladle the soup into ovenproof bowls, top with toast, and sprinkle the toast with grated Swiss cheese. Put under the broiler just long enough to glaze the cheese.

¶**Garbure with Pig's Knuckles.** Substitute pig's knuckles for the ham bone.

Marion Cunningham's Minestrone

Another wonderful main-course soup that is interesting enough to serve to a group of friends for supper or a buffet. Follow it with cheese and fruit.

Makes 8 servings

¾ cup Great Northern beans or
    white pea beans
Salt, freshly ground black pepper
2 tablespoons olive oil
⅛ pound salt pork, cut in fine shreds
6 sprigs parsley, chopped
1 small onion, chopped
Leaves from 1 rib celery, chopped
½ teaspoon dried thyme
3 ribs celery, chopped
2 tomatoes, peeled, seeded, and
    coarsely chopped
1 carrot, diced

1 potato, diced
12¾-ounce can beef broth or 2 cups
    beef stock
2 cups coarsely chopped cabbage
2 zucchini, coarsely chopped
A few leaves Swiss chard or spinach,
    coarsely chopped
1 teaspoon dried or 1 tablespoon fresh
    basil
1 cup cooked pasta, such as small
    macaroni (optional)
Grated Parmesan cheese

Cover the beans with water, bring to a boil, and boil 2 minutes. Remove from the heat and let stand 1 hour. Drain. Put back in the pot with 1½ quarts water and salt, and simmer until tender, from 1 to 1½ hours. Drain the beans, reserving the liquid. Purée in the blender or food processor with some of their liquid, then add enough of the remaining liquid to make a thick soup. Return to the pot.

Heat the olive oil in a skillet and sauté the salt pork, parsley, onion, celery leaves, and thyme until onion is soft. Add the celery, tomatoes, carrot, potato, beef broth, and bean soup. Simmer gently 15 minutes, then add the cabbage, zucchini, chard or spinach, and basil. If the broth seems too thick, add more bean liquid or beef broth. Cook 15 to 20 minutes. Add the cooked pasta, if used, for the last 5 minutes to reheat. Taste and correct the seasoning. Serve in bowls, sprinkled with grated cheese, and accompany with crusty hot French or Italian bread.

¶**Minestrone with Sausage.** Add slices of poached garlic sausage or Italian sausages to the soup 4 to 5 minutes before serving.

¶**Minestrone with Chickpeas or Kidney Beans.** Add drained, rinsed canned chickpeas or red kidney beans to the soup.

¶**Minestrone with Ham.** Add pieces of cooked ham to the soup.

Black Bean Soup

One of the greatest of all American soups. This version also comes from Leon Lianides, owner of The Coach House Restaurant in New York, where it is one of the specialties of the house. Black bean soup freezes well and is worth making in quantity.

Makes 12 servings

2 cups black beans	2 or 3 cloves
4 tablespoons butter	1 ham shank, split, with bone and rind
2 large onions, coarsely chopped	3 pounds beef or veal bones
2 garlic cloves, crushed	8 peppercorns
3 leeks, well washed and coarsely cut	2 tablespoons flour
1 celery rib, cleaned and coarsely cut	4 to 5 quarts water
2 bay leaves	½ cup Madeira wine

GARNISH: *Chopped parsley, 2 or 3 finely chopped hard-boiled eggs, thin slices of lemon*

Soak beans overnight in cold water to cover. Next day melt the butter in a stock pot, add the onions, garlic, leeks, celery, bay leaves, and cloves. Sauté for 3 minutes. Add the ham shank and bones and cook 3 or 4 minutes. Add the peppercorns and flour and blend well. Cook for 2 or 3 minutes, then add 4 to 5 quarts water and bring to a boil. Reduce heat, skim off scum and simmer for about 8 hours, covered except for a small air space between pot and lid.

Drain the soaked beans, add them to the pot, and simmer a further 2½ hours, stirring occasionally. If the mixture gets too thick or the beans are not completely covered with liquid, add more water. When the beans are soft, discard the bones and purée all the ingredients by putting the soup through a food mill or processing in batches in a food processor or in a blender. Reheat the puréed soup with the Madeira. Serve garnished with chopped parsley, hard-boiled egg, and lemon slices. Or put a whole hard-boiled egg in each serving, to be broken up with a spoon. Hot cornsticks are wonderful accompaniments.

The Coach House Tripe Soup

A marvelously hearty, lip-smacking soup from Leon Lianides, owner of The Coach House Restaurant. As it is rather a production, you might as well make a good batch and have soup-loving friends in to share it. One evening six of us consumed almost the whole amount, it was so good, and served in my big, round porcelain bowls, it was the main dish of the meal. You can always freeze whatever is left over. This is a soup that tastes better if made a day or two ahead, chilled, skimmed of all fat, and reheated. As the cooking times for tripe depend on how much it has been processed—some supermarket tripe may take only an hour or two to become tender, whereas tripe bought in a meat market may need four hours or more—it is as well to test a small piece of the tripe first to see how long it takes to get to the stage you like. I prefer tripe when it is still a bit chewy and gutsy, not when it is so soft all the texture has been lost. Veal tongues are best for this soup, but as they are often hard to come by you can substitute the more widely available beef tongue.

Makes about 6 quarts

5 pounds honeycomb tripe
3 pounds veal bones
3 pig's feet, split lengthwise
2 veal tongues or 1 beef tongue
6 cloves garlic, crushed
2 ribs celery, with leaves on, coarsely cut
3 large onions, coarsely chopped
2 carrots, coarsely chopped
3 leeks, well cleaned and sliced
Bouquet garni of 1 bay leaf, 4 parsley
    sprigs tied in a rib of celery

3 teaspoons thyme
3 teaspoons freshly ground black pepper
Coarse (kosher) salt to taste
½ teaspoon Tabasco
½ cup brandy
10 egg yolks
2 tablespoons potato starch
Juice of 3 lemons, or to taste
GARNISH: *Chopped parsley*

Wash the tripe, bones, and pig's feet in cold water. The tripe may need several rinsings, according to how clean it is when you buy it. Remove excess fat from the tripe and cut it into fairly large pieces, about 3 inches square. Put the bones, pig's feet, tripe, and tongues or tongue in a deep stock pot with enough water to more than cover the ingredients (about 1 gallon). Bring to a boil and boil 5 minutes, skimming off all the scum that rises to the surface. Add the garlic, celery, onions, carrots, leeks, bouquet garni, thyme, pepper, and a fair amount of salt, about 3 tablespoons. Return to boiling point, then reduce the heat, and simmer for 2½ to 3 hours, skimming off any scum that rises to the surface. The veal tongues will take about 1½ hours to cook, the beef tongue about 3 hours. Check the meats periodically, and if the veal tongues are done (test by inserting the point of a knife), remove them from the broth. Check the tripe and the beef tongue also. When any of the meats are done, they can be removed to a large platter. Skin the tongues and cut them and the tripe into strips about ½ inch wide and 1½ inches long.

When all the meats are cooked, discard the veal bones, take the meat from the pig's feet and add to the other meats and discard the pig bones. Remove and discard the bouquet garni. Chill the broth until the fat congeals on top, then remove by skimming and laying paper towels on the surface to absorb the remaining fat. Add the Tabasco and brandy. Reheat the broth and reduce by about a third by rapid boiling. Taste for seasoning, adding salt and pepper as needed.

Beat the egg yolks until light in a bowl. Mix the potato starch with 1 cup cold water and add this mixture and the lemon juice to the egg yolks. Beat in a cup of the hot broth, a little at a time, beating continuously. Return to the pot and mix well. Add the meats. Reheat the soup gently, stirring, until it comes almost to a boil and thickens. Do not let it boil. Serve the soup hot, sprinkled with parsley.

Oyster Bisque

A deliciously velvety soup that is equally good hot or cold. If you serve it chilled, garnish with chopped chives instead of parsley. Either fresh or canned oysters can be used, with liquor from fresh oysters substituting for part of the bottled clam juice.

Makes 6 servings

½ cup rice
1 quart bottled clam juice
4 tablespoons butter
18 oysters

Salt, freshly ground black pepper
¼ teaspoon Tabasco
1½ cups heavy cream
¼ cup cognac

GARNISH: *Chopped parsley*

Cook the rice in the clam juice in a pan until very soft. Add the butter. Force the mixture through a fine sieve, or whirl in the blender until smooth. Finely chop 12 of the oysters (or whirl in the blender or food processor until finely chopped; if you use the blender it will be necessary to add a little of the oyster liquor). Combine chopped oysters and rice mixture in a pan. Season to taste with salt and pepper and add the Tabasco. Stir in the heavy cream. Heat just to the boiling point. Add the 6 whole oysters and heat until they just curl at the edges. Add the cognac and cook 2 minutes. Ladle the soup into heated cups, putting a whole oyster in each cup. Garnish with chopped parsley and serve with Melba toast.

¶**Clam Bisque.** Use fresh or canned clams instead of oysters.

Shrimp Soup

A simple and delicious soup that is equally good hot or cold.

Makes 4 to 6 servings

1½ pounds shrimp
4 cups fish stock (page 530)
½ teaspoon thyme
½ teaspoon freshly ground black pepper

1 garlic clove, finely chopped
¼ cup chopped onion
3 tablespoons dry sherry
1 cup heavy cream

GARNISH: *Salted whipped cream, grated lemon rind*

Place the shrimp in the fish stock and cook for 3 minutes after the stock comes to a boil. Remove and shell the shrimp. Return the shells to the broth with the thyme, pepper, garlic, onion, and sherry. Bring to a boil, cook 10 minutes, then strain. Purée the shrimp in the blender or food processor with the cream. Combine shrimp and soup, mix well, correct the seasoning, and serve with a spoonful of salted whipped cream sprinkled with grated lemon rind in each cup.

¶**Curried Scallop Soup.** Cook 1½ pounds bay scallops in the fish stock for 5 minutes after stock comes to a boil. Remove scallops. Add and cook the thyme, pepper, garlic, and onion, but omit the sherry and instead add 1 tablespoon curry powder. Purée scallops and cream and purée the vegetables and stock. Combine the 2 mixtures. Correct seasoning and add 2 tablespoons dry sherry or Madeira, if desired. Serve hot. Or serve cold with 1 tablespoon chutney stirred into each serving and a little toasted coconut sprinkled on top.

¶Chili Scallop Soup. Instead of curry powder, use chili powder.

Castilian Mussel Soup

Mussels are another shellfish that lend themselves beautifully to puréed soups. In this case the addition of vegetables gives another, heartier dimension.

Makes 6 to 8 servings

½ cup olive oil	Salt
1 cup chopped onion	½ teaspoon freshly ground black pepper
2 cloves garlic, chopped	½ teaspoon ground coriander
2 cups chopped blanched spinach	2 quarts mussels
½ teaspoon rosemary	6 cups fish stock (see page 530)
1 tomato, peeled, seeded, and chopped	

GARNISH: Finely chopped parsley or hard-boiled egg

Heat the olive oil in a heavy skillet and sauté the chopped onion, garlic cloves, chopped blanched spinach, rosemary, and tomato. Season with salt to taste, pepper, and coriander. Wash, scrub, and beard the mussels, and steam them open in the fish stock in a heavy pan. Remove the opened mussels from the broth, take them from the shells, and strain the broth through a triple thickness of cheesecloth or a linen napkin.

Combine the mussels, the sautéed vegetables, and the broth and bring to a boil. Reduce the heat and simmer 5 minutes. Taste for seasoning. Force the mixture through a food mill or whirl in the blender. Reheat and serve with a garnish of parsley or egg.

The Palace Mussel Soup

Another type of mussel soup from New York's luxury restaurant. This one is highly refined and a lot of trouble, but worth the effort as a special beginning for a dinner party. Billi Bi is a simpler version of cream of mussel soup.

Makes 4 servings

3 pounds mussels, washed, scrubbed,
    and bearded
5 shallots, chopped
2 tablespoons diced parsley stalks
1 bay leaf
Pinch of thyme
Freshly ground black pepper
¾ cup dry white wine
½ cup water
2 cups fish stock (see page 530)
9 tablespoons butter

4 tablespoons flour
2 egg yolks
½ cup heavy cream
Salt
2 pinches saffron
½ pound raw bay scallops
⅓ cup celery, cut in julienne strips
⅓ cup carrot, cut in julienne strips
⅓ cup leeks, cut in julienne strips
1 or 2 drops lemon juice

Put the mussels in a large pot with the shallots, parsley stalks, bay leaf, thyme, 5 grinds of black pepper, ½ cup of the white wine, the water, and fish stock. Cover, bring to a boil, and cook quickly over high heat until shells open. Remove the opened mussels (discard any with closed shells) and use cold for mussel salad or mussels rémoulade (see page 14). Strain the broth through a double thickness of fine cheesecloth into an enameled pan, and boil down rapidly over high heat to about 3 cups, to concentrate the flavor.

Melt 3 tablespoons butter in a saucepan, blend in the flour and stir over low heat for 2 minutes. Mix in the hot mussel broth and cook, stirring, until it boils and thickens. Cook over low heat for 30 minutes. If the mixture gets too thick (it should be of cream-soup consistency), thin with additional fish stock. Strain through a sieve into another pan. Beat the egg yolks lightly with the heavy cream, add a little of the hot soup, then mix into the soup in the pan. Heat gently, stirring, until soup comes just to the simmer (if it boils, the egg will curdle). Season to taste with salt and pepper. Boil the saffron with the remaining ¼ cup white wine until dissolved. Add to the soup with the bay scallops, julienne vegetables, and lemon juice. Finally, enrich the soup by gradually stirring in the remaining 6 tablespoons sweet butter. Taste for seasoning and serve immediately.

¶**Billi Bi.** Cook the mussels as directed. After removing the mussels and straining the broth through cheesecloth, bring the broth to the boiling point in a large pan. Beat 2 egg yolks with 2 cups heavy cream and stir in about ½ cup of the hot broth. Remove pan from heat and stir the egg-cream mixture into the broth. Reheat, stirring, until slightly thickened, but do not allow the mixture to get near the boiling point or the eggs will curdle. Serve hot or cold. A few of the cooked mussels may be used as a garnish.

Marseilles Fish Soup

A Provençal soup with many different versions, the one constant factor being the fiery rouille that is stirred into it. This one, almost like a puréed bouillabaisse, makes a full meal.

Makes 6 to 8 servings

4 tablespoons olive oil
2 leeks, trimmed and finely sliced
2 medium onions, finely chopped
2 ripe tomatoes, peeled, seeded, and
    finely chopped
3 cloves garlic, finely chopped
Bouquet garni of fennel, bay leaf,
    parsley, and oregano
3 quarts water
2 pounds sole fillets, cut in thirds

Fish heads, scraps, and bones, tied in a
    cheesecloth bag
3 tablespoons cognac
½ pound orzo (rice-shaped pasta) or
    acini di pepe
Large pinch of saffron
Salt, freshly ground black pepper
GARNISH: Garlic croutons, grated
    Parmesan cheese
Rouille

Heat the olive oil in a large pan and sauté the leek and onion until soft, about 4 minutes. Add the tomatoes, garlic, bouquet garni, water, fish and bag of fish bones and heads. Simmer 15 to 20 minutes. Strain, reserving liquid. Discard bouquet garni and bag of fish bones and heads. Purée fish and vegetables in a blender or food processor, or by putting through a food mill. Return purée to pan with liquid (reserving ¾ cup of the liquid for the sauce). Bring to a boil and add the cognac and orzo. Pound the saffron in a mortar with a little salt and add to the soup. Season to taste with salt and pepper. Cook gently until orzo is soft. Serve in deep soup plates with the garlic croutons, cheese, and rouille. The rouille, an intensely hot sauce, is stirred into the soup at the table to taste and should be handled with caution.

ROUILLE
Pound 8 cloves garlic, 3 small dried red peppers (seeds removed), and 2 tablespoons bread crumbs in a mortar and pestle. Gradually work in ¼ cup olive oil, 2 tablespoons tomato paste, 1 teaspoon paprika, at least 1 teaspoon or more Tabasco, and ½ cup of the reserved fish stock. Or process all the ingredients in a food processor or blender until mixed to a smooth paste, adding a little more stock if necessary.

Cullen Skink

This traditional Scottish soup resembles the French peasant leek and potato soup (the inspiration for the elegant Vichyssoise on page 54) with smoked fish added, which is maybe not too surprising as the Scots and the French had so many historic links. In fact, if you purée the soup and serve it cold, you might call it Scotch Vichyssoise. It makes a beautiful cold soup, with great body, flavor, and flair.

Makes 6 servings

3 medium to large potatoes
2 or 3 leeks, well washed, and cut in
    small pieces
½ to ¾ pound finnan haddie
    (sometimes called "smoked fillet")

½ to 1 cup heavy cream (optional)
Salt, freshly ground black pepper
Grated nutmeg
4 to 5 tablespoons butter
GARNISH: Chopped parsley

Peel the potatoes and put in a pan with 3 cups of very lightly salted water (the finnan haddie is salty) with the leeks. Cook until potatoes are tender. Remove potatoes and purée by putting through a food mill or processor. Set aside. Add the finnan haddie to the pan and poach gently until soft, about 15 minutes. It should flake easily with a fork. Strain, reserving the cooking liquid, and put two-thirds of the fish through the food mill or processor, reserving the rest for garnish. Combine the puréed fish, puréed potatoes, and cooking liquid, add the cream, if desired, and bring slowly to a boil, stirring, until the potato thickens the soup. Taste for seasoning, adding salt if needed, some pepper, and a pinch of nutmeg. Stir in the butter and serve in large soup plates or cups. Just before serving, crumble the reserved fish and sprinkle on top of the soup, with chopped parsley.

¶Scotch Vichyssoise. Purée all the fish, combine with the puréed potatoes and cooking liquid and chill. Before serving, stir in heavy cream to taste and adjust the seasonings. Garnish with finely chopped chives and parsley.

Gruyère Soup

This is very close to the more usual Cheddar soup, but the flavor and texture are entirely different. Be sure to use Gruyère cheese from Switzerland, or your soup will not be a success.

Makes 6 servings

4 tablespoons melted butter

4 tablespoons flour

2 cups milk

2 cups chicken broth, blended with
   1 teaspoon or more Dijon mustard

2½ cups grated or shredded Swiss
   Gruyère cheese

Tabasco

GARNISH: Croutons, chopped parsley

Combine the melted butter and flour in a 2-quart saucepan and cook over low heat for several minutes. Stir in the milk and continue stirring until slightly thickened. Then add the chicken broth and mustard. Heat through. Very carefully stir in the grated or shredded cheese and a dash or two of Tabasco, stirring until the cheese is just melted. Correct the seasoning, adding a little salt if necessary, and serve in heated cups or soup plates, adding a few croutons to each and a bit of finely chopped parsley.

¶**Cheddar Soup.** Use grated Cheddar cheese in place of the Gruyère.

¶**Cheddar-Olive Soup.** Add ½ cup sliced ripe olives to the Cheddar soup at the last minute.

Salads

I remember in a Paris restaurant being served as a first course a most unusual combination of slaws—coleslaw with a hot dressing on one half of the plate, red cabbage dressed with vinaigrette on the other, and small squares of crisply fried duck skin scattered on top, an interesting idea that I have adapted here. At another restaurant a mound of chilled very fresh greens was topped with a little piece of toasted goat cheese and dressed with a slightly warm vinaigrette, an exciting contrast of hot and cold, and certainly a switch on the usual green salad and cheese. Also French and very *"nouvelle"* is a luxurious composition of green beans, endive, foie gras, and duck breast.

The idea of serving one of these small, decorative composed salads as a first course is very appealing, and I have a lot of suggestions here, some strikingly simple, like shrimp with papaya and avocado, some more complex, like marinated vegetables with noodles, which has variants with tomato, foie gras, and corn. A lot of the heartier salads at

the end of the chapter would make fine main dishes for lunch or a light supper, but they too can be arranged in small, attractive portions and served as appetizers. It does lend charm and a lively look to a dinner-party table, and I like to have something delicious before me when I sit down. When I was young, good restaurants almost always placed on each table a long glass dish with celery, radishes, and olives nestled on a bed of ice, and how pleasant they were to crunch on as you looked over the menu.

This custom still flourishes in many parts of the country, and may be the ancestor of the Californian practice of serving a green salad as an appetizer. Elsewhere green salads usually follow the main course, and can be delicious, particularly if you use a fine light, fruity olive oil. But I do think the *ritual* appearance of a green salad, and the idea that it is a must for every menu, can get pretty dull.

As the greatest salad eaters in the world, which Americans undoubtedly are, we ought to be getting more fun out of it. If you start by asking yourself, "What would be a nice surprise, or a happy complement?" to your main course, all sorts of tasty combinations will probably occur to you. With, or after, fish or veal I like a cucumber salad; a good coleslaw is nice with seafood or cold roast quail; and I have two special favorites for a steak dinner. One is parsley and nothing but, except for plenty of dressing and chopped garlic over the little mound of sprigs. And the other is a dish of onions, sliced paper thin and soaked in ice water in the refrigerator for several hours until crisp, then just lightly sprinkled with coarse salt, which is delicious and crunchy, or else a touch of sherry wine vinegar. Those are just a few possibilities, and I've included plenty more. In the salad department, especially, a cook's resources are enormous, and it's just foolish not to exploit their variety.

SALADS

Basic vinaigrette
   with herbs
   with shallots or green
     onions
   with garlic
   with mustard
   processor garlic-herb
     vinaigrette
   processor lemon
     vinaigrette

Dieter's yogurt dressing

Avocado-yogurt sauce or
   dressing

Mayonnaise
   blender method
   food processor method
   yogurt mayonnaise
   mustard mayonnaise
   anchovy mayonnaise
   tartare sauce
   rémoulade sauce
   Louis dressing
   green mayonnaise

Green salads and
     vegetable salads
   herbs
   onions
   beets
   cucumber
   artichoke hearts
   mushrooms
   green or red sweet
     peppers
   tomatoes
   croutons
   olives
   bacon
   anchovies
   nuts
   cheese
   capers

Spinach salad

Spinach and cucumber
   salad

Wilted spinach salad

Tom Isbel's parsley salad

Vintner's salad

Bibb lettuce and
     mushroom salad
   spinach and mushroom
     salad
   bibb lettuce and crab
     salad

Wilted celery salad

Green pea salad

Turkish cucumber salad

Spicy Szechuan salad

Vegetable and olive salad
     with mustard-yogurt
     dressing
   with blue cheese
   with Gruyère cheese

Caesar salad

Marinated mushroom and
   beet salad

A salad of marinated
     vegetables and noodles
   with tomatoes
   with foie gras
   with corn

Greek salad
   with cucumber
   with cucumbers, radishes,
     and capers

Salade beaucaire

Stuffed tomatoes with
     smothered cucumbers
   with green beans
   with chicken salad
   with crab and rice salad
   with fish salad
   with scallop salad
   with herring salad

My quick chopped
     coleslaw
   with yogurt mayonnaise
   with mustard mayonnaise
   with green onions or
     chives
   with carrots and radishes
   with carrots and peppers
   with shrimp or crabmeat,
     or tuna
   with fresh dill

Billy's coleslaw

Spicy coleslaw

Hot slaw
   with red slaw
   with red slaw and
     crisp duck skin

Pepper slaw

Sauerkraut salad
   with tomatoes
   with beans
   with knockwurst
   sauerkraut slaw

Old-fashioned Oregon
   potato salad

Potato salad with boiled
   dressing

Alexandre Dumas potato
salad

French hot potato salad

Potato and hearts of palm
salad

Basic rice salad

Fruit and rice salad

Orange and radish salad

Grapefruit and apple salad

Papaya, avocado, and
shrimp salad
papaya, shrimp, and
crab salad

Orange, onion, and shrimp
salad

Basic chicken or turkey
salad
with celery
with celery and grapes
with sweetbreads
with macadamia nuts

Chicken salad with fresh
coriander

Chicken salad with olive
sauce

Chicken and seafood salad

Chicken and rice salad

Chicken, bean, and potato
salad

Turkey and chutney salad
with foie gras

Duck and orange salad
duck and olive salad
with crisp duck skin

Tongue and spinach salad
with hot soy vinaigrette

Hearty beef salad
with tarragon vinaigrette

Hussar salad

Duck, bean, and foie gras
salad
chicken, beet, and
crabmeat

Poached salmon salad

Codfish salad

Fish salad
with yogurt dressing

Scallop salad with avocado
and chili
with sauce gribiche
with tomato and egg

Lobster salad with
mayonnaise
with potato and onion

Marinated scallop salad
with potato and onion

Lobster salad with
cucumber and egg
with chicken and celery
with avocado and onion
with tomatoes and
green onion

Crab salad with onion
and egg
with cucumber,
anchovies, and onion
with avocado and onion
with radish

Crab salad with Oriental
vegetables
with cucumber,
anchovies, and onion
with avocado, onion,
and radish
with carrot, onion, and
celery

Shrimp salad
with cucumber and
tarragon
with olives and eggs
with avocado

Tuna salad with onion,
avocado, and egg
with fennel
with olives, anchovies,
and tomatoes
with apple

Salad Dressings

Making a good vinaigrette, the basic salad dressing, is not only a matter of
using the right proportions of oil and vinegar; it also depends on the strength
of the vinegar and the type of oil. I always taste vinegar before I make a

dressing. My current favorite is a superb sherry wine vinegar that is so strong and overpowering in flavor that I have to use less than if I used a red or white wine vinegar, a Japanese rice vinegar, or a cider vinegar. My preference in oils is for a full-bodied, fruity olive oil (vegetable oils are too light and tasteless to make a decent dressing), although if I want a more delicate dressing with a slightly nutty overtone I may substitute the French walnut or hazelnut oil.

Basic Vinaigrette

While the proportions of oil to vinegar are a matter of taste, this is the balance I prefer.

Makes just over ½ cup, enough for a green salad for 4

1 teaspoon coarse (kosher) salt   *2 tablespoons wine vinegar*
½ teaspoon freshly ground black pepper   8 tablespoons fruity olive oil

Mix the salt, pepper, vinegar, and oil with a wooden spoon or a fork, then taste and add more oil, vinegar, or seasoning if you feel the dressing needs it.

This basic dressing may be flavored with chopped herbs, shallots or green onions, garlic, or Dijon mustard according to preference and the ingredients of the salad.

¶**Herb Vinaigrette.** Add 1 tablespoon chopped fresh herb or 1 teaspoon dried crushed herb to the dressing. See page 78 for choices.

¶**Shallot (or Green Onion) Vinaigrette.** Add ¼ cup finely chopped shallot or finely cut green onion to the dressing.

¶**Garlic Vinaigrette.** Unless you want a very strong garlic flavor in your salad, as in the parsley salad on page 80, don't add chopped garlic to the dressing. Instead spear a crushed garlic clove with a toothpick, put it in the dressing and remove before tossing the salad, or rub the crushed clove into the salt before adding the other ingredients.

¶**Mustard Vinaigrette.** A mustard-flavored vinaigrette is mostly used for strong-flavored greens or marinated vegetables. I like to use Dijon mustard rather than the dry hot mustard as it blends better and is more flavorful. Blend ½ teaspoon Dijon mustard with the salt, pepper, and vinegar before adding the oil. Increase the mustard for salads that need a very spicy dressing, such as Wilted Celery Salad (page 82).

¶**Processor Garlic-Herb Vinaigrette.** Put the basic vinaigrette ingredients in a food processor with 3 garlic cloves, 1 tablespoon Dijon mustard, and a handful of fresh basil leaves. Process until well blended; the machine will make a rather creamy dressing.

¶**Processor Lemon Vinaigrette.** Put the oil, salt, pepper, 3 peeled garlic cloves, and 1 small peeled lemon, with all pith and seeds removed, into the food processor. Omit vinegar. Process until smooth. This sharp, lemony dressing is excellent on crabmeat and other shellfish.

More and more these days I find that I prefer to reduce the caloric content of salads by substituting plain yogurt for some or most of the oil in a vinaigrette, which gives a lovely acidity, zest, and creaminess. Either replace half the oil with yogurt or make the following dressing. You'll be surprised how refreshing and rewarding this can be when you are dieting.

Dieter's Yogurt Dressing

Makes ½ cup

1 teaspoon salt (or to taste)   ½ cup plain yogurt
¼ teaspoon freshly ground black pepper 1 to 2 tablespoons olive oil (optional)
2 tablespoons wine vinegar

Mix the salt, pepper, and vinegar into the yogurt. Taste for seasoning. For a smoother dressing, blend in the oil. (Ingredients will blend better if you shake them in a screw-topped jar.)

Avocado-Yogurt Sauce or Dressing

This has the consistency of a thick sauce or a dip and I like to serve it on crisp romaine, Bibb, or endive leaves as a first course or as a salad after a main course. If you want a thinner mixture to use as a salad dressing, add more yogurt.

Makes 1 cup

1 large avocado, peeled and pitted   1 tablespoon olive oil
1 clove garlic, crushed   2 teaspoons lime or lemon juice
2 tablespoons yogurt

Put the avocado, garlic, yogurt, oil, and juice in a blender and blend to a smooth purée.

Mayonnaise

This is such an essential dressing, not just for salads but also for cold poached fish, other cold dishes and mayonnaise-based sauces, that I find it odd how many people resist making it and resort to the commercial jar. It really is not difficult to make by hand with a whisk, and it's a cinch if you have an electric hand mixer, a blender, or a food processor. I like to make mayonnaise with a fruity imported olive oil or half olive oil and half peanut oil, but according to how flavorful or bland you like your mayonnaise you can use any oil you like—olive, peanut, corn, safflower, cottonseed, or the light grapeseed oil imported from France.

Makes 1¾ cups

2 egg yolks (from extra-large eggs)
1 teaspoon coarse (kosher) salt
½ teaspoon Dijon mustard

1½ cups olive oil, or half olive and half
    peanut oil
1 tablespoon lemon juice

To make mayonnaise by hand, beat the egg yolks, salt, and mustard in a bowl with an electric hand mixer or wire whisk until the yolks become thick and sticky. Gradually beat in the oil, drop by drop, until the mayonnaise starts to thicken and stiffen, then beat in the remaining oil more rapidly, making sure it is incorporated before adding more. When all the oil is beaten in, beat in the lemon juice. Remove to a covered jar or bowl and refrigerate. It will keep for up to 10 days in the refrigerator.

¶Blender Mayonnaise. Put 2 whole eggs, the salt, mustard, and lemon juice in the blender and mix for just 5 seconds at the blend or high setting, then, with the machine still running, remove the cover insert and dribble the oil in very slowly until the mayonnaise starts to thicken, then add the rest of the oil more quickly. The minute the mayonnaise is thick and smooth, stop blending.

¶Food Processor Mayonnaise. Use the metal blade of the processor when making mayonnaise. Put 1 whole large egg and 1 egg yolk, the salt, mustard, and lemon juice in the beaker and process until blended, about 2 or 3 seconds. Then, with the machine still running, gradually pour in the oil, as you would if using the blender, until thick and smooth; then stop processing.

¶Yogurt Mayonnaise. Combine equal parts of mayonnaise and plain yogurt.

¶Mustard Mayonnaise. To each cup of mayonnaise add 1 tablespoon Dijon mustard.

¶**Anchovy Mayonnaise.** Mix into the mayonnaise 12 coarsely chopped anchovy fillets, 2 finely chopped garlic cloves, ¼ cup chopped parsley, ¼ cup chopped fresh basil (if available), 1 tablespoon coarsely chopped capers, and 1 tablespoon Dijon mustard.

¶**Tartare Sauce.** Mix 1½ tablespoons finely chopped onion, 2 teaspoons chopped parsley, 1 teaspoon lemon juice, and 1 tablespoon finely chopped dill pickle into 1 cup mayonnaise.

¶**Rémoulade Sauce.** Mix 1 finely chopped hard-boiled egg, 2 tablespoons finely chopped capers, 1 tablespoon finely chopped parsley, 1 teaspoon lemon juice into 1½ cups mayonnaise. Check for seasoning and add salt and pepper to taste. Or omit the salt and add ½ teaspoon anchovy paste.

¶**Louis Dressing.** Mix ⅓ cup chili sauce, 1 tablespoon grated onion, a dash of Tabasco, and ⅓ cup whipped cream into 1 cup mayonnaise.

¶**Green Mayonnaise.** Purée ½ cup very dry raw spinach in a blender or food processor, or chop by hand until it is as near as possible to purée consistency. Combine with 1½ cups mayonnaise, 2 tablespoons finely chopped parsley, 2 tablespoons finely cut chives, and 2 tablespoons chopped dill or tarragon.

Green Salads and Vegetable Salads

The secret of a good green salad is to have your greens dry, crisp, and cold and to toss them with the dressing just before serving. Nothing is as grim as a salad that has been tossed and left to stand until the leaves are limp, soggy, and *fatigué*, as the French say—tired out.

Wash the greens well, shake them dry or whirl them in a salad dryer, then wrap them in paper towels, put them in a plastic bag, and refrigerate in the crisper section until you are ready to make the salad.

These days, as I'm always watching calories, instead of tossing greens with the customary vinaigrette, I may arrange whole endive or romaine leaves in a bowl or on a plate and either give them a sprinkling of salt and pepper and a few drops of olive oil or dip them in the Dieter's Yogurt Dressing on page 75. Other greens, such as Bibb lettuce, watercress, arugula, and chicory can be eaten this way and you really taste their flavor because they haven't been dressed to death. Sometimes I add a few slices of raw mushroom to the plate and give them a squeeze of lemon juice and some salt and pepper. Or I may break iceberg lettuce into big chunks and have nothing but a little lemon juice as a dressing. Unlike many of the food snobs in this country, I happen to like the crunchiness and crispness of iceberg lettuce. You'll find a list of greens for salad in the Concordance on page 556.

While I'm on the subject of green salads, let me say that I abhor the habit of serving them on plates that have been left in the freezer or the coldest part of the refrigerator until they are so icy the dressed greens practically stick to the plate. Naturally you don't want a warm plate, unless your salad has a hot dressing, but please see that your plates are room temperature.

There are all manner of things that I like to add to salads to give them variety through different textures and flavors. You'll find a lot of the salads in this chapter include such things as herbs, crumbled cheese, olives, nuts, croutons, bacon, and anchovies. Here are some of my choices:

Herbs. Those I like best for salads are tarragon, chives, parsley, chervil, basil (especially for salads containing tomatoes), dill (for cucumber, seafood, and tomato salads), fresh coriander, and lovage (an herb with a strong, wild, celerylike flavor that should be used sparingly).

Onions. Sweet red onions, Spanish onions, green onions, and shallots, sliced or chopped.

Beets. Cooked or raw, shredded or in julienne strips. Their sweetness contrasts well with bitter or pungent greens like endive, chicory, escarole, and watercress.

Cucumber. Peeled, seeded, and cut in strips or slices. (If you don't seed them, they are watery and bitter.)

Artichoke Hearts. Cooked or canned, plain or marinated.

Mushrooms. Raw and sliced or left whole if small, and marinated. I like slices of raw mushroom in a spinach or Bibb lettuce salad.

Green or Red Sweet Peppers. Seeded and cut in strips. (I first roast and peel peppers. They are more digestible and pleasant to the bite, but this is a personal preference.)

Tomatoes. I prefer whole cherry tomatoes to wedges or slices of tomato, which have to be added at the last minute lest they make the salad watery.

Croutons. Make these freshly by browning small cubes of bread in hot oil or butter, with or without garlic, then cool and drain on paper towels. Traditional in Caesar salad but also nice in a tossed green salad.

Olives. Green or black olives are both a garnish and a flavorful addition to salads. I use the Italian, Greek, or Niçoise black olives, not the California, which have little taste and a mealy texture.

Bacon. Cook it crisp, drain, and crumble. Good with coarse, strong greens like spinach.

Anchovies. Cut down on the salt in the dressing when you use them.

Nuts. Walnuts, peanuts, macadamia nuts, toasted almonds, and toasted cashews, whole or chopped, and whole pine nuts.

Cheese. Best choices are sharp-tasting cheeses like crumbled feta and blue, or nutty Gruyère, shredded. The bland mozzarella, shredded, is surprisingly good with tomatoes.

Capers. These little pickled buds of the caper bush have an herby flavor and spiciness that perk up bland salads.

Spinach Salad

If you can, buy the loose spinach for salads; spinach that has been packaged in plastic bags is usually full of broken leaves so that often a great deal has to be discarded, and the packaging encourages spoilage.

Makes 4 servings

1 pound leaf spinach

1 sweet onion, sliced

SOY DRESSING
6 tablespoons olive oil

1 tablespoon soy sauce

2 teaspoons Dijon mustard

1½ tablespoons lemon juice

Salt and freshly ground black pepper
    to taste

Wash the spinach well, removing the heavy stems, and dry thoroughly. Put in a salad bowl with the sliced onion. Combine the dressing ingredients, blending them well, and pour over the salad just before serving. Toss thoroughly.

Spinach and Cucumber Salad

Makes 8 servings

2 pounds raw spinach, washed,
    stemmed, and dried
2 cucumbers, peeled, seeded, and diced
    (preferably the long English type;
    these need not be seeded)
1 cup finely sliced celery

½ cup minced parsley
½ cup pitted green olives, quartered
½ cup pitted ripe olives, quartered
½ cup pine nuts
1 cup vinaigrette dressing (page 74)
Pinch of oregano

Tear the spinach into pieces and combine with the remaining salad ingredients in a salad bowl. Combine the dressing and oregano and pour over the salad. Toss lightly.

Wilted Spinach Salad

A warm version of spinach salad, with a soy dressing, that makes a good first course.

Makes 4 servings

1 large or 2 small cloves garlic, finely
    chopped
4 tablespoons olive oil
2 tablespoons soy sauce
½ cup thinly sliced water chestnuts

Freshly ground pepper
2 tablespoons lemon juice
1 pound spinach, washed, stems
    removed, and dried

GARNISH: 2 hard-boiled eggs, coarsely chopped

Cook the garlic in the oil over medium heat for 2 minutes. Add the soy sauce, water chestnuts, and pepper to taste. Cook 1 minute, tossing the water chestnuts. Add the lemon juice and blend. Then add the spinach and toss as you would a salad until the spinach is just wilted. Taste and correct the seasoning, if necessary. Transfer to a salad bowl and garnish with the chopped eggs.

Tom Isbel's Parsley Salad

A departure from the usual green salad of which I heartily approve because it is light, flavorful, and stays crisp and crunchy. I like to serve parsley salad with a roast, broiled steak, or roast or broiled chicken. The green freshness and glorious pungency of the herb has a great affinity for plainly cooked meat and poultry. The salad was originally made with curly parsley, but I prefer to combine it with some of the Italian flat-leaf variety. To measure parsley, break off the little sprigs from the stalks and let them fall loosely into a measuring cup.

Makes 4 servings

5 or 6 garlic cloves, very finely chopped
8 tablespoons olive oil
1½ to 2 tablespoons sherry wine
    vinegar

Salt, freshly ground black pepper
1½ cups Italian parsley sprigs
2 cups curly parsley sprigs
½ cup freshly grated Parmesan cheese

Marinate the garlic in the oil for at least 2 hours before making the salad. Then combine it with the vinegar (sherry vinegar is very strong in flavor, so start with 1½ tablespoons, then taste and see if you need more) and salt and pepper to taste. Mix well.

Put the parsley sprigs in a bowl, pour the dressing over them and toss thoroughly. Then add the cheese and toss again.

Vintner's Salad

A good salad to serve after the main course, as it includes cheese and walnuts. The dressing is made with red wine and very little vinegar, so you may continue to drink a red wine with it—hence the name, vintner's salad.

Makes 6 servings

3 heads Bibb lettuce, washed and dried
½ head romaine, washed and dried
½ bunch watercress, washed and dried
½ cup walnut halves
½ cup shredded Gruyère cheese
    (optional)

½ cup walnut, olive, or hazelnut oil
2 tablespoons red wine
1 tablespoon red wine vinegar
1 teaspoon salt
½ teaspoon freshly ground black pepper

Tear the lettuce leaves into small pieces. Arrange in a salad bowl, and add the watercress, walnut halves, and Gruyère. Mix the oil, wine, vinegar, salt, and pepper for the dressing, pour over the salad at the last minute, and toss.

Bibb Lettuce and Mushroom Salad

Makes 4 servings or more

4 heads Bibb lettuce, washed, quartered,   2 tablespoons chopped parsley
    and dried   2 teaspoons chopped fresh basil or
½ pound firm white mushrooms,   ½ teaspoon dried basil
    stemmed and thinly sliced   ½ cup vinaigrette dressing (page 74)

Place lettuce and mushrooms in salad bowl. Sprinkle with chopped parsley and basil. Pour vinaigrette dressing over salad just before serving and toss.

¶Spinach and Mushroom Salad. Use 1 pound spinach, washed, stemmed, dried, and crisped; ½ pound sliced mushrooms; and ⅓ cup crisp bacon bits. Add vinaigrette and toss.

¶Bibb Lettuce and Crab Salad. Add 1 cup crabmeat to the salad and toss with the vinaigrette to which you have added 1 tablespoon chopped fresh dill.

Wilted Celery Salad

Make this salad 3 to 8 hours before you plan to serve it, as it needs lengthy marinating. It goes very well with all kinds of meat.

Makes 4 servings

1 stalk celery, separated into ribs and   2 tablespoons wine vinegar
    washed   8 tablespoons olive oil
2 level tablespoons Dijon mustard   1 tablespoon chopped fresh tarragon or
½ teaspoon salt   1 teaspoon dried tarragon
½ teaspoon freshly ground black pepper Crisp salad greens
    GARNISH: 2 tablespoons chopped parsley or chopped hard-boiled egg

Remove tough strings from the outer ribs of the celery, then slice the ribs rather fine. Mix the mustard, salt, pepper, vinegar, and oil well, add the tarragon, and pour over the celery. Toss extremely well, then cover with plastic wrap and leave at room temperature until ready to serve, shaking the bowl every now and then so the vinaigrette and celery mix well. Line a salad bowl with greens, put the marinated celery in the bowl and sprinkle with chopped parsley or egg.

Green Pea Salad

When peas are in season, they make an extremely pleasant and offbeat salad, either cooked or, if they are really young and tender, raw. On a summer luncheon plate with cold chicken or veal the cool, delicate green salad looks extremely refreshing and inviting.

Makes 4 servings

4 pounds very fresh young green peas
4 tablespoons olive oil
1 tablespoon wine vinegar or lemon
   juice
2 tablespoons finely chopped fresh
   shallot or sliced green onion, or
   scallion

Salt, freshly ground black pepper
Salad greens (Boston, Bibb, or romaine)
2 tablespoons chopped parsley
2 teaspoons coarsely chopped fresh
   tarragon

OPTIONAL GARNISH: 1 to 2 teaspoons finely chopped shallot
or green onion, or cut chives

Shell the peas and cook until just crisply tender in 1 quart boiling salted water, about 12 minutes. Drain and while hot toss with the oil, vinegar, shallot or onion, and salt and pepper to taste. Allow to cool, then make a bed of salad greens in a bowl, add the pea salad and toss it with the parsley and tarragon. Garnish, if you wish, with additional chopped shallot or green onion or chives (easiest to cut if you use scissors).

Turkish Cucumber Salad (Cacik)

This combination of cucumbers with yogurt and mint is typical of the Middle East. There is also a soup made with the same ingredients (see *Theory & Practice*, page 339). A refreshing salad for summer, with broiled meats, poultry, or kebabs.

Makes 4 servings

1 large cucumber, peeled and seeded
2 cloves garlic
1 teaspoon salt
1 cup yogurt
¼ cup finely cut green onions, or
   scallions

2 to 3 tablespoons chopped fresh mint
   or 1 tablespoon crushed dried mint
¼ teaspoon freshly ground black pepper
Lemon juice
Lettuce leaves

Shred the cucumber. Crush the garlic cloves to a paste with the salt and mix into the yogurt, along with the cucumber, green onions, mint, pepper, and lemon juice to taste. Taste for seasoning and serve on lettuce leaves.

Spicy Szechuan Salad

This could make an interesting first course or a main course for lunch.

Makes 6 to 8 servings

1 small head crinkly Chinese cabbage,
    sliced in long, thin strips
1 small head red or purple cabbage,
    sliced in long, thin strips

2 cups fresh bean sprouts
2 cups fresh alfalfa sprouts
1 or 2 carrots, cut in julienne strips
8 radishes, thinly sliced

SESAME OIL AND SOY DRESSING
1 clove garlic, finely chopped
2 teaspoons dried basil, pounded in a
    mortar and pestle
½ teaspoon salt
¼ teaspoon freshly ground black pepper
⅓ cup wine vinegar

⅓ cup soy sauce
⅓ cup Oriental sesame oil
1 tablespoon hot chili-flavored sesame
    oil (available in Oriental groceries
    and specialty stores)

Combine the vegetables in a good-size bowl. For the dressing, combine the garlic, basil, salt, and pepper in a small bowl. Add vinegar and soy sauce and mix the ingredients well. Slowly add the regular and the chili-flavored sesame oils. Taste for seasoning and add more hot sesame oil, if desired. Pour dressing over vegetables and toss well.

Vegetable and Olive Salad
with Mustard-Yogurt Dressing

An interesting mixture of greens, olives, and vegetables with another version of yogurt dressing. With rye bread and butter this makes a good luncheon salad, or you can serve a smaller helping as a first course.

Makes 4 to 6 servings

1 head chicory, washed, dried, and
    crisped
1 head romaine, washed, dried, and
    crisped

36 pitted soft black Italian or Greek
    olives

10 to 12 radishes
2 carrots, grated

1 bulb fennel, thinly sliced, or 1 cup
   sliced celery

MUSTARD-YOGURT DRESSING

1 teaspoon salt (optional)
A little freshly ground black pepper
1 tablespoon Dijon mustard

1 cup plain yogurt
3 tablespoons olive or vegetable oil

Break the salad greens into pieces with your fingers. Put in a bowl with the olives, radishes, carrot, and fennel or celery. Mix the salt (you can omit this, as the mustard contains salt), pepper, and mustard into the yogurt and blend in the oil until smooth. Spoon the dressing over the salad and toss well.

¶**Vegetable Salad with Olives and Blue Cheese.** Add ½ cup crumbled blue cheese.

¶**Vegetable Salad with Olives and Gruyère Cheese.** Add ½ cup grated Gruyère cheese.

Caesar Salad

When properly assembled, mixed at the last moment, and eaten right away (it must never be allowed to stand), this classic West Coast salad is deliciously crisp and flavorful. It is extremely important to coat the romaine leaves thoroughly with oil before adding the other ingredients so the salad mixes well and doesn't get soggy. This can be served as a main-course luncheon salad or, California-style, as a first course before steak or roast beef.

Makes 4 servings

10 tablespoons olive oil
4 tablespoons butter
4 slices white bread (crust removed),
   cut into ½-inch cubes
4 cloves garlic
2 heads romaine, washed, dried, and
   crisped

18 to 24 anchovy fillets, cut into pieces
2 tablespoons lemon juice or to taste
Freshly ground black pepper
Salt, if needed
1 egg, cooked in boiling water 1 minute
½ cup grated Parmesan cheese

Combine 2 tablespoons olive oil and the butter in a skillet over moderate heat. When hot, add the bread cubes and 3 of the garlic cloves, thinly sliced, and toss until the croutons are brown and crisp. Drain on paper toweling.

When ready to serve, rub the interior of a glass or pottery salad bowl with the remaining whole garlic clove, crushed or cut. Add the romaine, broken into bite-size pieces. Pour the remaining oil over the romaine, toss well, then add the croutons, the anchovies, lemon juice, and freshly ground pepper to taste. Toss again lightly and then taste for salt. Because of the anchovies, you may not need any. Break the egg over the salad, add the cheese, and toss very well.

Marinated Mushroom and Beet Salad

This combination of flavors and textures goes well with meats such as lamb, pork, and veal, either hot or cold.

Makes 4 servings

½ pound firm white mushrooms, sliced
3 tablespoons olive oil
½ teaspoon salt
½ teaspoon dried tarragon or 1 teaspoon
  chopped fresh tarragon
2 teaspoons wine vinegar

¾ cup sliced cooked or canned beets
2 tablespoons finely chopped onion
Juice of half an orange (about ¼ cup)
5 to 6 cups mixed greens—romaine,
  iceberg lettuce, and chicory
2 tablespoons chopped parsley

Put the mushrooms in a bowl and add the olive oil, salt, tarragon, and wine vinegar. Toss well, cover, and marinate for 1 hour. Put the sliced beets in another bowl with the onion and orange juice and let stand for 1 hour. When you are ready to serve break the greens into a salad bowl. Add the mushrooms and beets with their marinades and toss thoroughly. If you feel you need more dressing, you can add 1 or 2 more tablespoons oil and a few drops of vinegar or lemon juice. Sprinkle with chopped parsley and serve.

Salad of Marinated Vegetables and Noodles

Presentation is important with this rather elaborate composed salad. The various ingredients should be prepared and dressed separately and then arranged attractively on a platter or individual plates, alternating colors and shapes. It's a wonderfully decorative addition to a buffet or an outdoor barbecue.

Makes 6 servings

1 pound whole white mushrooms
1 cup vinaigrette sauce, seasoned with
  chopped garlic to taste and
  1 tablespoon chopped fresh basil
12 to 18 small baked beets (see page
  128)

Raspberry vinegar or plain yogurt
  to taste
6 red peppers, roasted and peeled
  (see page 165)
2 tablespoons vinegar
8 tablespoons olive oil

8 ounces buckwheat noodles, cooked,
    drained, and chilled
6 tablespoons Oriental sesame oil
3 tablespoons rice wine vinegar

3 tablespoons chopped green onion
2 tablespoons chopped parsley
36 small white onions Monégasque
    (see page 39)

Clean the mushrooms by wiping them with damp paper towels. Then dress them with the vinaigrette sauce. Dress the baked beets with raspberry vinegar or yogurt. Dress the peppers with vinegar and olive oil. Dress the noodles with a combination of the sesame oil, rice wine vinegar, green onion, and parsley, and toss thoroughly. Arrange these ingredients and the onions on a platter or individual plates.

¶With Tomatoes. Add to the salad a row of paper-thin slices of tomato.

¶With Foie Gras. Add a slice of foie gras to each serving.

¶With Corn. Add a mound of uncooked corn kernels, freshly removed from the cob, dressed with heavy cream and black pepper.

Greek Salad

A lovely, piquant salad for a first course or a luncheon main dish. The layers of ingredients are intended to create a pleasing contrast in color. They may also be arranged in circles on a shallow platter, with the parsley scattered on top.

Makes 4 servings

4 ripe tomatoes, peeled and thinly sliced
    (if possible, a mixture of red and
    yellow tomatoes for color)
1 onion, diced
2 green peppers, cut in slivers
½ pound feta cheese, thinly sliced

20 to 24 Greek olives, pitted
⅓ cup chopped flat-leaf parsley
Salt, freshly ground black pepper
    to taste
½ cup vinaigrette sauce (see page 74)

Make layers of the tomatoes, onion, green pepper, cheese, olives, and parsley in a bowl or serving dish, sprinkling with salt and pepper. Chill well. When ready to serve, pour the vinaigrette sauce over the layers.

¶Greek Salad with Cucumber. Use thin slices of cucumber in place of the onion. Sprinkle the salad with a little crumbled oregano.

¶Greek Salad with Cucumbers, Radishes, and Capers. Alternate layers of cucumber, sliced green onions or scallions, radishes, and a sprinkling of capers. Garnish the edges with tomato wedges and anchovy strips and the center with Greek olives. Sprinkle the salad with crumbled oregano and chopped fresh mint.

Salade Beaucaire

A hearty salad with a most unusual combination of tastes and textures.

Makes 6 to 8 servings

1 cup celery, cut in julienne strips
  (to measure, stand strips upright
  in measuring cup)
1 cup celery root, peeled, sliced, and
  cut in julienne strips
1 cup Belgian endive leaves, cut in
  julienne strips
4 tablespoons oil
1 tablespoon wine vinegar
1 teaspoon Dijon mustard
Salt, freshly ground black pepper
½ cup lean ham, cut in fine julienne
  strips

½ cup raw apple, peeled, sliced, and
  cut in julienne strips
½ cup raw mushrooms, cut in julienne
  strips
2 to 3 cups mayonnaise
Chopped parsley
Chopped fresh tarragon (if available)
3 or 4 cooked beets, peeled and thinly
  sliced
5 or more boiled new potatoes, peeled
  and thinly sliced
3 tomatoes, cut in quarters

Marinate the celery, celery root, and endive for 1 hour in the oil, wine vinegar, mustard, and salt and pepper to taste. Combine with the ham, apple, and mushrooms, and add enough of the mayonnaise to bind loosely. Arrange the mixed julienne strips in a salad bowl, and sprinkle with chopped parsley and chopped tarragon. Surround with overlapping slices of beets, make an inner circle of sliced potatoes, and garnish with tomato wedges. Serve with remaining mayonnaise.

Stuffed Tomatoes with Smothered Cucumbers

Makes 6 servings

6 large ripe tomatoes
Salt
4 medium-sized cucumbers
4 tablespoons mayonnaise

3 tablespoons yogurt
1½ teaspoons finely chopped fresh dill
  weed, or 1 teaspoon dried

GARNISH: *Finely chopped parsley and fresh dill*

Slice off the tops of the tomatoes and scoop out the seeds and most of the flesh. Salt the insides and invert on a rack or on paper towels to drain. Chill while preparing the cucumbers. Peel, halve, and seed the cucumbers, cut into 1½-inch-long thin strips, and salt well. Refrigerate for 1 hour. Drain thoroughly and run water over them; drain again and dry. Combine with the mayonnaise, yogurt, and dill, and blend thoroughly. Allow to mellow in the refrigerator for 2 hours. Just before serving, fill the tomatoes with the chilled cucumber mixture, and top with the chopped parsley and dill. Serve with poached salmon, or alone as a light first course.

¶**With Green Beans.** Fill the shells with 1 pound crisply cooked green beans that have been tossed with ½ cup finely chopped onion, 4 tablespoons oil, 1 tablespoon lemon juice, 1 teaspoon salt, and ½ teaspoon freshly ground black pepper. Top with chopped parsley. Serve with broiled chicken or steak.

¶**With Chicken Salad.** Fill each tomato shell with ½ cup Basic Chicken Salad, Chicken Salad with Celery, or Chicken Salad with Macadamia Nuts (see page 99).

¶**With Crab and Rice Salad.** Fill with ½ cup crabmeat and ½ cup Rice Salad (see page 96), omitting the chopped tomato in the salad.

¶**With Fish Salad.** Fill with ½ cup Fish Salad (see page 108).

¶**With Scallop Salad.** Fill with ½ cup Marinated Scallop Salad (see page 110).

¶**With Herring Salad.** Fill with ½ cup Herring Salad (see page 7).

Coleslaw

I love cabbage, and coleslaw is something I make very often as a change from the eternal green salad. There are so many ways to present it that it is a never-ending delight. I like it tossed with a hot sweet-and-sour dressing; with a pungent vinaigrette; with mayonnaise, either plain, mixed half-and-half with yogurt or sour cream, or spiced with Dijon mustard. Or, when I'm watching calories, I just toss the shredded cabbage with yogurt, finely chopped onion, a touch of chopped garlic, and perhaps some finely chopped red or green pepper. Frequently I will combine a basic coleslaw with other vegetables, such as shredded raw carrot or beet, sliced or shredded radish, or finely cut green onion.

Although most people make slaw with white or green cabbage, you can also use the curly-leafed savoy type, red cabbage, or Chinese cabbage.

My Quick Chopped Coleslaw

Recently I have been making coleslaw in the food processor, which is idiotically simple. I either make a mayonnaise in the processor, then add chunks of cabbage and process until it is finely chopped, or chop the cabbage and mix it with mayonnaise. If you don't have a food processor, first shred the cabbage and then chop it very fine with a large knife.

Makes 4 servings

½ head firm white cabbage, trimmed
  of limp or discolored leaves,
  stalk and hard core

1 cup mayonnaise (see page 76)
Salt, freshly ground black pepper
  (optional)

Cut the cabbage in chunks, put it in the work bowl of the processor fitted with the steel blade, and process until finely chopped, then mix with the mayonnaise. Taste for seasoning. If the mayonnaise is well seasoned, you may not need any.

¶Coleslaw with Yogurt Mayonnaise. Combine the chopped cabbage with ½ cup mayonnaise and ½ cup yogurt.

¶Coleslaw with Mustard Mayonnaise. Add 1 tablespoon Dijon mustard to the mayonnaise.

¶Coleslaw with Green Onions or Chives. Add ½ cup finely cut green onions or chives to the slaw.

¶Coleslaw with Carrots and Radishes. Add 1 cup shredded raw carrot and ½ cup thinly sliced radish to the slaw.

¶Coleslaw with Carrots and Peppers. Instead of the radish, add ½ cup roasted, peeled, and shredded red or green sweet peppers with the carrots.

¶Shrimp (or Crabmeat or Tuna) Coleslaw. Fold 1½ to 2 cups tiny shrimp, lump crabmeat, or drained, flaked tuna into the slaw.

¶Dilled Coleslaw. Add 2 tablespoons chopped fresh dill to the slaw.

Billy's Coleslaw

This is a slaw on which I was brought up. Billy was a Chinese chef, a pal of my mother's chef, Let, and his coleslaw was superb. He often mixed it

with tiny shrimp, crabmeat, or bits of lobster, which made it entirely different but equally delicious.

Makes 4 to 6 servings

½ cup olive oil   6 tablespoons sugar
2 tablespoons flour   ½ cup wine vinegar
½ teaspoon salt   1 cup heavy cream mixed with
2 teaspoons dry mustard   2 egg yolks
Dash Tabasco   1 medium cabbage

Heat the oil in a heavy skillet or sauté pan, add the flour, and blend well.
Add the salt, mustard, Tabasco, sugar, and vinegar, and stir until thickened.
Combine some of the hot oil mixture with the egg-cream mixture, and then
pour into the oil mixture. Stir over low heat until it thickens. Shred the
cabbage very thin and combine with the hot dressing. Cool and chill several
hours. If the dressing is too thick, mix with a little more heavy cream or
with a touch of mayonnaise.

Spicy Coleslaw

This version is made with shredded cabbage, which should be soaked in
salted water to crisp it, and a vinaigrette sauce. You can add any of the
vegetable variations given for My Quick Chopped Coleslaw (opposite).

Makes 4 servings

½ large head cabbage, trimmed, stalk   1 teaspoon celery seed
    and hard core removed   1 teaspoon mustard seed
⅔ cup vinaigrette sauce (see page 74)

Cut the cabbage in wedges and shred fine with a large knife. Soak in a bowl
of salted water for 1 hour, then drain well. Combine the vinaigrette and
celery and mustard seeds and toss well with the cabbage. Let stand for 1
hour to allow flavors to blend and mellow.

Hot Slaw

A hot slaw is served with meats or fish. Or use the variation—the combination of hot slaw and red slaw—as a first course, with or without the duck
skin.

Makes 6 to 8 servings

1 head firm white cabbage, weighing	1 teaspoon salt
2 to 3 pounds, trimmed	½ cup vinegar
6 tablespoons sugar	2 to 3 tablespoons heavy cream
1 teaspoon dry mustard	

Cut the cabbage into quarters, remove the hard core, and shred fine. Mix the sugar, mustard, salt, and vinegar in a skillet and heat, stirring, until the sugar melts and the ingredients are well blended. Stir the hot dressing into the cabbage with the cream and toss until wilted.

¶**Hot Slaw with Red Slaw.** Shred and soak red cabbage, as for Spicy Coleslaw (page 91), drain, and toss with vinaigrette sauce. Arrange on one half of individual serving plate with the hot slaw on the other half.

¶**Hot Slaw with Red Slaw and Crisp Duck Skin.** Top the two mixtures with small pieces of duck skin cooked in hot oil until crisp (see page 104).

Pepper Slaw

There used to be a restaurant in the Midwest that was famous for this dish. I experimented for a long time until I achieved a version that was as good— or even better.

Makes 6 servings

6 to 8 roasted, peeled, and seeded red,	2 to 3 tablespoons wine vinegar
green, or yellow peppers	1½ teaspoons salt
2 to 3 cups coarsely shredded cabbage	1 teaspoon freshly ground black pepper
½ cup finely chopped onion	1 teaspoon dry mustard
½ cup olive oil	1 teaspoon celery seeds

Cut the peppers into very fine strips and combine with the cabbage and onion. Make a vinaigrette with the oil, vinegar, and seasonings, add to the slaw, and toss well. Adjust the seasoning to taste. Let the slaw ripen for several hours before serving, tossing it every half hour or so.

Sauerkraut Salad

A rather novel salad reminiscent of coleslaw but with a strong personality— a natural partner for ham, pork, or poached sausages.

Makes 6 servings

2-pound package sauerkraut　　　*⅔ cup vinaigrette sauce (see page 74)*
⅓ cup finely cut green onions　　*2 tablespoons chopped fresh dill*

Wash the sauerkraut well in a colander under running water to remove excess salt. Drain thoroughly. Toss with the green onions, vinaigrette, and dill.

¶**Sauerkraut Salad with Tomatoes.** Add or garnish with 4 tomatoes, peeled and cut in wedges.

¶**Sauerkraut and Bean Salad.** Combine the sauerkraut with a 15-ounce can of drained and washed kidney beans, ½ cup finely cut celery, and 2 green onions, with tops, finely cut. Toss with vinaigrette.

¶**Sauerkraut Salad with Knockwurst.** Combine the sauerkraut with ½ pound cooked and thinly sliced knockwurst or frankfurters; 3 tablespoons chopped dill pickle; 1½ cups cubed cooked potatoes; 6 green onions, finely cut; 3 tablespoons chopped parsley, and 2 tablespoons chopped chives. Mix with enough mayonnaise or half mayonnaise and sour cream or yogurt to moisten. Chill well and leave for 1 to 4 hours to blend the flavors.

¶**Sauerkraut Slaw.** Omit onions and dill. Toss with vinaigrette and then with half mayonnaise and half sour cream or yogurt.

Potato Salads

Almost every country where potatoes are part of the diet includes potato salad in its culinary repertoire. The salads vary considerably. Some are hot, some cold, some tart, some sweet-and-sour, and others just bland. Here are a few of my favorites.

Old-Fashioned Oregon Potato Salad

This salad, which was very popular when I was growing up, is one I like to serve with very simple foods, such as ham, cold chicken, and other cold meats. The nasturtium leaves, a particularly Western addition, were picked from the garden and tossed into the salad bowl to add a peppery zest. If you don't grow nasturtiums, you might add a little garden cress, arugula, or watercress.

Makes 6 servings

2½ *pounds small new potatoes,*   ⅓ *cup cider vinegar*
    unpeeled   *4 or 5 nasturtium leaves (if available),*
1 large onion, finely chopped   *cut in shreds*
2 ribs celery, finely diced   *Mayonnaise (approximately ¾ cup)*
1 or 2 carrots, shredded   *Salt, freshly ground black pepper*
½ *cup chopped parsley*   *Greens*
      GARNISH: *3 hard-cooked eggs, quartered or sliced; 12 stuffed olives, sliced;*
          2 tablespoons chopped parsley; 1 tablespoon chopped chives

Boil the potatoes in their skins in salted water to cover until they can just be pierced with a fork. Drain. Peel and slice into bowl while still warm and combine with the onion, celery, carrot, and parsley. Add the vinegar and nasturtium leaves and toss to mix well. Let the salad stand at room temperature for 15 minutes. Blend with enough mayonnaise to coat the vegetables well, and season with salt and pepper to taste. Refrigerate for 2 to 3 hours. Line a deep platter with greens and unmold the chilled salad onto it. Garnish with quartered or sliced hard-cooked eggs and sliced olives. Sprinkle with chopped parsley and chives.

Potato Salad with Boiled Dressing

One of the earliest and most popular of American potato salads, this used to be standard picnic fare, especially throughout New England and the Middle West.

Makes 4 to 6 servings

6 large, firm, waxy potatoes, unpeeled

BOILED DRESSING
4 eggs   *1 teaspoon dry mustard*
5 tablespoons boiling vinegar   *1 teaspoon salt*
1 tablespoon butter   *Dash of cayenne*
½ *pint heavy cream*   ½ *teaspoon white pepper*
2 tablespoons finely chopped onion   *2 tablespoons finely chopped parsley*

Boil the potatoes in their skins in salted water to cover until tender. While they are cooking, beat together the eggs and vinegar in the top of a double boiler. Cook the mixture until it thickens slightly, and stir in the butter. Then add the cream, onion, and seasonings. Drain the potatoes. Peel and slice into a bowl while still hot. Pour the dressing over them. Mix thoroughly, sprinkle with the parsley, and chill for several hours.

Alexandre Dumas Potato Salad

The classic French potato salad with a wine-and-oil marinade. First introduced in Alexandre Dumas's *Dictionary of Cuisine*.

Makes 6 servings

6 good-size new or waxy potatoes,
    unpeeled
2 tablespoons salt
1 teaspoon freshly ground black pepper
½ cup dry white wine

8 tablespoons olive oil
1 tablespoon white wine vinegar
½ cup chopped parsley
½ cup chopped green onion or chives

Boil the potatoes in their skins in salted water to cover until just pierceable. Drain and peel while hot. Slice them into a bowl, season to taste with salt and pepper, and pour the wine and oil over them. Let them cool, then add the vinegar, parsley, and green onions or chives, and toss lightly. Serve with cold meats or chicken, or as part of a summer buffet.

French Hot Potato Salad

The classic accompaniment to hot garlic sausage or Sausage en Brioche (see page 28).

Makes 6 servings

2½ pounds small new potatoes,
    unpeeled
12 green onions, finely cut, or ⅓ cup
    finely chopped onion
⅓ cup chopped parsley

½ cup heated olive oil
1 teaspoon salt
½ teaspoon freshly ground black pepper
3 tablespoons heated vinegar
GARNISH: 1 tablespoon chopped parsley

Boil the potatoes in their skins in salted water to cover until just tender. Drain. When cool enough to handle, peel them. (If the potatoes are really new and the skins thin, this is not necessary.) Cut into halves or quarters, according to size, put in a flameproof casserole, add the onion, ⅓ cup parsley, hot oil, seasonings, and hot vinegar. Toss lightly. A few minutes before serving, heat through. Serve at once, sprinkled with the 1 tablespoon parsley.

Potato and Hearts of Palm Salad

A variation on French potato salad (page 95) that is especially popular in Brazil and other tropical countries where you find hearts of palm. I like this with small cold roast birds such as Cornish game hens, or as picnic food.

Makes 6 servings

2½ pounds small new potatoes,
    unpeeled and well scrubbed
½ cup olive oil
3 tablespoons wine vinegar, or to taste
Salt, freshly ground black pepper
2 one-pound cans hearts of palm,
    drained

¾ cup vinaigrette sauce (see page 74)
¼ cup chopped parsley
¼ cup finely cut green onion, or
    scallion
Salad greens

GARNISH: 3 hard-boiled eggs, sliced; 2 tablespoons chopped green onion

Boil the potatoes in their skins in salted water to cover until just pierceable. Cool slightly, then peel and slice thick into a bowl. Add the oil, vinegar, salt and pepper to taste, and let the potatoes cool in the marinade. They should absorb most of it.

Cut the hearts of palm into ½-inch slices. Combine the vinaigrette sauce with the parsley and green onion. When the potatoes are almost cool, combine them with the hearts of palm and the vinaigrette and toss lightly. Leave at room temperature to mellow for 2 or 3 hours before serving. Serve the salad on greens.

Garnish with the egg slices and sprinkle with the 2 tablespoons green onion.

Basic Rice Salad

Makes 4 to 6 servings

2 cups cooked rice
¼ cup finely chopped parsley
1 tablespoon chopped mint, dried or
    fresh
¼ cup chopped onion
2 tablespoons chopped green pepper

1 medium tomato, peeled, seeded, and
    chopped
3 tablespoons lemon juice
1 teaspoon salt
3 tablespoons olive oil
Freshly ground black pepper to taste

Mix all ingredients in a medium-size bowl. Chill several hours or overnight.

Fruit Salads

Fruit and Rice Salad

While I am not normally a lover of fruit salads, this one makes a very pleasant summer luncheon dish.

Makes 8 to 10 servings

4 cups hot cooked rice
2 tablespoons vegetable oil
1 cup navel-orange sections
¾ cup pineapple chunks

¾ cup sliced strawberries
8 whole strawberries
½ cup whole pecans

POPPY-SEED DRESSING
¾ cup sugar
1 teaspoon dry mustard
1 teaspoon salt
⅓ cup white wine vinegar

1½ tablespoons onion juice
1 cup vegetable oil
1½ tablespoons poppy seeds

Toss the hot rice with the 2 tablespoons vegetable oil and allow to cool. Make the poppy-seed dressing by combining the sugar, mustard, salt, vinegar, and onion juice in a bowl and beat for a few minutes with an electric beater or whirl briefly in a blender. Gradually beat or blend in the oil as for a mayonnaise. When thickened, gradually beat in the poppy seeds until the seeds and dressing are well blended. When the rice is cold, add the orange sections, pineapple, sliced strawberries, and poppy-seed dressing and toss well. Garnish with the whole strawberries and pecans.

Orange and Radish Salad

A Moroccan salad that is enchanting to look at, with its contrast of colors, and something quite different in flavor. You might have this before couscous (see page 298) or with roast duck.

Makes 4 servings

⅓ cup lemon juice
1 tablespoon sugar
¼ teaspoon salt

4 large navel oranges
1 bunch red radishes

Combine lemon juice, sugar, and salt in a bowl and stir or beat until sugar and salt dissolve. Peel oranges by cutting off the top and bottom with a sharp knife and peeling in a spiral fashion, removing the skin and pith. Cut into sections. Grate radishes coarsely. Arrange oranges and radish in a serving dish and add lemon-juice mixture, mix gently, and serve chilled.

Grapefruit and Apple Salad

The tartness of the fruit and the bitter tang of the chicory make this a good foil to rich meats like pork or ham.

Makes 6 servings

1 medium head chicory, washed, dried, and crisped
1 grapefruit, peeled and sectioned

1 large tart apple
½ cup vinaigrette sauce (see page 74)

Break the chicory into a bowl. After sectioning the grapefruit, remove the membrane from each section and let the fruit drain in a colander. Just before serving, cut the apple into very thin slices, leaving the peel on, and add the chicory with the drained grapefruit. Add the vinaigrette and toss.

Papaya, Avocado, and Shrimp Salad

A luscious combination of colors, flavors, and textures that might be, in a small serving, a first course or, in a more generous proportion, a luncheon main course.

Makes 4 servings

2 papayas
2 avocados
1 head Bibb lettuce, washed, dried, and crisped
1 pound small cooked shrimp
2 tablespoons finely chopped green onion, or scallion

½ cup peeled, seeded, and coarsely chopped ripe tomato
1 cup mustard mayonnaise (see page 76)

Peel the papayas and avocados and cut into slices. Arrange on individual salad plates on Bibb lettuce leaves. Make a mound of shrimp on top, sprinkle with green onion, and put 2 tablespoons tomato over each serving of shrimp. Serve with mustard mayonnaise.

¶**Papaya, Shrimp, and Crab Salad.** Arrange papaya slices, shrimp, and crab-meat on greens; dress with vinaigrette (see page 74).

Orange, Onion, and Shrimp Salad

Oranges and onions are a classic salad combination that teams well with shrimp.

Makes 4 servings

1 head lettuce, washed, dried, and
    crisped
1 cup red or sweet onion rings
1 cup orange sections

2 pounds cooked shrimp
½ to ¾ cup vinaigrette sauce
    (see page 74)

Arrange the lettuce in a bowl and top with the onion rings, orange sections, and shrimp. Dress with the vinaigrette.

Poultry, Meat, Fish, and Cheese Salads

Although the majority of these salads are substantial enough for a main course, some may be served in a smaller quantity as a first course, and I have indicated those that qualify. For a first course, serve about 1 cup of salad per person on a bed of greens.

Basic Chicken or Turkey Salad

Of all the main-dish salads in our culinary lexicon, chicken salad is far and away the most popular—and yet it is all too often as badly prepared as many other simple foods. The first necessity is that the salad be made with freshly poached chicken, preferably a plump roasting chicken well endowed with fat. The second is that it should be cooled at room temperature so the meat remains juicy and delicious. Use dark as well as white meat, as it adds more flavor, and cut it into fairly generous bite-size pieces. (It's amusing to note that in the old days, when chicken was expensive, many restaurants used cold veal or pork instead. You can, too, if you want to be extravagant.)

Makes 4 servings

3 cups cooled poached chicken (or
    roast or poached turkey breast),
    cut in bite-size pieces
1 cup (or to taste) homemade
    mayonnaise (page 76) or half
    mayonnaise, half sour cream or
    yogurt

Salad greens (watercress, Boston or Bibb
    lettuce, or chicory)

GARNISHES: *Halved or quartered hard-boiled eggs and chopped parsley;
    or toasted salted walnut halves and watercress; or toasted salted almonds,
    thin strips of green pepper, and finely chopped fresh chervil or parsley*

Mix the chicken and the mayonnaise and arrange on a bed of the greens. Garnish with eggs and parsley; or walnut halves and watercress sprigs; or almonds, green pepper, and finely chopped fresh chervil or parsley.

¶Chicken Salad with Celery. Add 1 cup finely chopped crisp celery to the chicken. Garnish with sliced hard-boiled eggs, capers, and black olives.

¶Chicken Salad with Celery and Grapes. Add ¾ cup peeled white grapes to the chicken and celery. Garnish with sliced toasted almonds and a few more peeled grapes.

¶Chicken Salad with Sweetbreads. Blanch and cool a pair of sweetbreads. Cut into pieces of the same size as the chicken. Combine chicken, sweetbreads, and 1 cup peeled, seeded, and finely sliced cucumber. Add 1 tablespoon finely chopped tarragon to the mayonnaise. Garnish with capers, chopped hard-boiled egg, and watercress.

¶Chicken Salad with Macadamia Nuts. Combine chicken with a mixture of half sour cream or yogurt and half mayonnaise and 1 tablespoon chopped fresh tarragon. Mix in ⅔ cup macadamia nuts. Garnish with quartered hard-boiled eggs, capers, and more mayonnaise. This salad is also good made with roast or braised veal instead of chicken.

Chicken Salad with Fresh Coriander

This Chinese salad is one of the most delicious things I have ever tasted, but it is essential that you use Chinese parsley, otherwise known as fresh coriander or cilantro, as the flavor is so distinctive and different from regular parsley. Fortunately, it is now becoming more generally available, especially in Chinese, Hispanic, Indian, and Korean markets, and is easy to grow in the garden. A small helping makes an unusual first course.

Makes 6 to 8 servings

4½- to 5-pound roasting chicken
1 tablespoon hot Chinese mustard
1 to 2 tablespoons sesame seeds
6 to 8 green onions, finely shredded
     in 1½-inch lengths
1 bunch fresh Chinese parsley

1½ teaspoons salt
⅛ teaspoon sugar
½ teaspoon monosodium glutamate
    (optional)
½ head iceberg lettuce

Roast the chicken according to directions in *Theory & Practice* (page 83). Remove from oven, cool, then strip the meat from the bones, discarding skin and bones. With your fingers, pull the meat into very fine shreds and put in a bowl. Mix with the hot mustard.

Toast the sesame seeds in a 375° oven until brown. Cool. Add to the chicken with the shredded onions and the feathery leaves of the Chinese parsley, stripped from the stalks (reserve a few sprigs for garnish). Add the salt, sugar, and monosodium glutamate, if desired. Toss well together.

Shred the lettuce very fine and line a large platter with it. Arrange the chicken salad on top and garnish with the sprigs of Chinese parsley.

Chicken Salad with Olive Sauce

Blanching the olives, which removes a good deal of the brine, gives a truer olive flavor to the sauce. You could use dried black Italian olives, but the color would not be as attractive.

Makes 4 servings

4 large chicken breasts
4 cups chicken broth, or water

OLIVE SAUCE
1 whole egg
2 egg yolks
1 tablespoon white wine vinegar
1 teaspoon salt
1½ cups fruity olive oil
Reserved skin from the poached
    chicken, roughly chopped

1 small onion
Lettuce leaves

3 small white onions, cut in half
2 cups ripe green olives, blanched for
    1 minute, drained and pitted
Dash of Tabasco
GARNISH: *Thin slices of pimiento*

Poach the chicken breasts in the broth or water with the onion for 10 to 12 minutes. Remove from the broth and cool. Remove the skin from the breasts and reserve. Bone the chicken breasts and arrange on a platter lined with lettuce leaves.

To prepare the sauce, put the whole egg and egg yolks in the beaker of the food processor with the metal blade in place. Add the vinegar and salt, and process for 2 to 3 seconds. Continue processing and gradually pour the olive oil through the feed tube, pouring slowly until the mayonnaise thickens. Add the reserved skin from the chicken, the onions, and olives. Process for about 30 seconds. Season with a dash of Tabasco.

Mask the chicken breasts with the olive sauce, and garnish with thin slices of pimiento. Serve as main dish or a substantial first course.

Chicken and Seafood Salad

You want a very crisp lettuce for this salad, preferably romaine or iceberg. A small helping makes a pleasant first course.

Makes 6 servings

1 large head romaine or iceberg lettuce
2½ cups lobster, crabmeat, or shrimp
2½ cups diced cooked chicken or turkey
1 cup finely cut celery or water chestnuts
1 small to medium onion, sliced in
    paper-thin rings
1 cup vinaigrette sauce (see page 74)
1 tablespoon Dijon mustard
GARNISH: *Sliced hard-boiled eggs, black olives, chopped parsley*

With a very sharp knife shred the lettuce into a large salad bowl. Add the lobster, crabmeat, or shrimp, chicken or turkey, celery or water chestnuts, and onion. Season the vinaigrette sauce with the Dijon mustard, blend well, and taste for seasoning. Pour vinaigrette over the salad and toss until nicely coated, adding more oil if necessary. Garnish with sliced eggs, olives, and parsley.

Chicken and Rice Salad

Salads of rice with other foods are best served as main courses. They are too filling to be first courses.

Makes 4 servings

1½ cups cold cooked rice
½ cup diced cooked chicken
½ cup diced tongue
½ cup chopped green onion, or scallion
¼ cup chopped parsley
⅔ cup vinaigrette sauce (see page 74)
GARNISH: Artichoke hearts, tarragon

Toss the rice, chicken, tongue, onion, and parsley with the vinaigrette sauce. Garnish with artichoke hearts and sprinkle with tarragon.

Chicken, Bean, and Potato Salad

A substantial salad that makes a meal in itself. Good picnic fare, but don't add the dressing until just before serving.

Makes 4 to 6 servings

1½ cups diced cooked potatoes
1½ cups diced cooked chicken
1½ cups finely cut cooked green beans
12 anchovy fillets
3 tablespoons capers

2 tablespoons chopped basil
1 cup vinaigrette sauce (see page 74),
 seasoned with ¼ teaspoon salt
Lettuce leaves

GARNISH: *4 tomatoes, quartered or thinly sliced*

Combine potatoes, chicken, beans, anchovy fillets, and capers. Sprinkle with basil. Dress with vinaigrette sauce. Arrange on lettuce leaves in a bowl and garnish with tomato.

Turkey and Chutney Salad

An interesting departure from the norm of turkey salads. A small serving could be a first course before a fish entrée.

Makes 4 servings

2½ cups diced turkey
½ cup chutney, finely chopped
¼ cup olive oil
1 tablespoon wine vinegar
4 heads Bibb lettuce or 2 heads
 Boston lettuce

½ cup toasted filberts
2 tablespoons chopped parsley
½ cup vinaigrette sauce (see page 74)

Combine the turkey, chutney, oil, and vinegar in a bowl. Toss well and chill, covered, for 1 to 2 hours. Break the lettuce into a large salad bowl in bite-sized pieces and add the turkey mixture, filberts, and parsley. Toss with the vinaigrette sauce and taste for seasoning.

¶**Turkey and Chutney Salad with Foie Gras.** Add a thin slice of foie gras to the plates when serving and sprinkle with alfalfa sprouts.

Duck and Orange Salad

The classic marriage of duck and orange translates felicitously into a salad that could be a first or a main course.

Makes 4 servings

2 cups diced cooked duck
1 large or 2 medium oranges, peeled
    and sectioned
1 large red Italian onion, thinly sliced
    and separated into rings

1 cup celery root, cut in fine julienne
    strips
1 head romaine
1 cup mayonnaise

Combine the duck, orange sections, onion, and celery root. Arrange romaine leaves in a bowl, top with the duck salad and serve with the mayonnaise.

¶Duck and Olive Salad. Combine the duck with 1 cup thinly sliced green olives and ⅔ cup toasted, salted walnuts or pecans. Toss the salad with just enough mayonnaise to bind it lightly. Serve on greens with sliced hard-boiled eggs, pimiento strips, and additional mayonnaise.

¶With Crisp Duck Skin. Garnish either of the above salads with strips of duck skin that have been cooked in 2 to 3 inches hot oil in a skillet until very crisp.

Tongue and Spinach Salad

Tongue and spinach, another classic culinary partnership, are good as a first- or main-course salad, with the horseradish adding a nice zip.

Makes 4 servings

1½ cups julienne of tongue
2½ cups spinach leaves
½ cup crisp bacon bits

⅓ cup shredded fresh horseradish or
    2 tablespoons prepared horseradish
½ cup vinaigrette sauce (see page 74)

Toss the tongue, spinach, bacon, and fresh horseradish with vinaigrette sauce (if prepared horseradish is used, mix it into the sauce).

¶Tongue and Spinach with Hot Soy Vinaigrette. Add 2 tablespoons soy sauce and 2 finely chopped garlic cloves to the vinaigrette. Combine with the salad in a skillet and toss over medium heat until spinach is just wilted. Garnish with the bacon bits.

Hearty Beef Salad

This beef salad is served as a first course in France, but I find it very satis-factory as a buffet, luncheon, or supper dish.

Makes 6 servings

2 cups boiled sliced new potatoes
1 cup finely cut green onions
2 cups coarsely chopped celery, with
   leaves
3 cups lean boiled or pot-roasted beef,
   sliced and then cut in 1-inch
   squares
12 cornichons (French sour gherkins)

1 cup cherry tomatoes or 4 peeled
   tomatoes cut in sixths
¼ cup capers
1 cucumber, peeled, seeded, and diced
½ cup roasted and peeled green pepper
   strips
Salad greens

DRESSING
6 hard-boiled eggs
1 tablespoon Dijon mustard
1 cup olive oil
1 clove garlic rubbed into 1½ teaspoons
   salt

1 teaspoon freshly ground black pepper
⅓ cup wine vinegar
Dash of Tabasco

Arrange the salad ingredients attractively on a bed of greens, either on a deep platter or in a large bowl.

To make the dressing, shell the eggs, reserving the whites. Mash the yolks with a fork and work in the mustard. Stir in the oil, garlic-flavored salt, pepper, vinegar, and Tabasco. Pour dressing over the salad and garnish with the reserved egg whites, chopped.

¶Beef with Tarragon Vinaigrette. Omit green onions and capers. Put on bed of greens the potatoes, celery, beef, tomatoes, cucumber, green pepper, and ½ pound cooked green beans. Dress with ⅔ cup vinaigrette heavily flavored with 1 tablespoon chopped fresh tarragon or 1 teaspoon dried tarragon and 2 tablespoons chopped parsley. Garnish with 6 halved hard-boiled eggs, 1 sliced red onion, and the cornichons.

Hussar Salad

A very different kind of beef salad that came to me by way of my column, from a reader of Dutch ancestry, Max Dekking. This Dutch national dish is called *Huzarensla* (Hussar Salad) because it was the favorite meal of the

Hussars when they invaded the Netherlands many centuries ago. This is the kind of salad that should be prepared well in advance and left to mellow in a bowl in the refrigerator. Unmolded on a bed of greens it is a most attractive dish for a buffet.

Makes 6 to 8 servings

3 cups very finely chopped cold rare roast beef

2 cups very finely chopped cold boiled new potatoes

1 cup very finely chopped cold cooked or canned beets

½ cup very finely chopped apple

2 large onions, very finely chopped

½ cup very finely chopped celery

1 finely chopped shallot or garlic clove

3 small Dutch sour gherkins or 1 large kosher sour dill pickle, very finely chopped

1 or more cups mustard vinaigrette sauce (see page 74)

1 to 2 tablespoons mayonnaise

Salad greens

GARNISH: *2 hard-boiled eggs, sliced; chopped parsley*

Combine all the finely chopped ingredients (and for this salad they must be *very* finely chopped) in a large bowl and mix in just enough vinaigrette sauce, plus a spoonful or two of mayonnaise, to bind. The salad must not be sloppy, but firm enough to unmold. Mix everything together well, pack into a 2½- to 3-quart mold or bowl, and leave in the refrigerator for 3 hours. When ready to serve, unmold on a bed of greens on a platter and garnish with the sliced eggs and parsley.

Duck, Bean, and Foie Gras Salad

This spectacular and substantial nouvelle cuisine first-course salad is admittedly extravagant, something you should keep for a special dinner party. Presentation is important.

FOR EACH SERVING:

8 to 10 endive leaves

8 to 10 crisply cooked green beans

4 paper-thin slices of tomato

1 slice foie gras

4 strips of cold roasted duck breast

2 tablespoons vinaigrette sauce (see page 74)

On individual plate arrange the endive leaves in a fan shape. Put the green beans on one half of the plate, the tomato slices on the other. Top with the foie gras and the strips of duck. Dress with the vinaigrette.

¶**Chicken, Beet, and Crabmeat.** Substitute chunks of cooked chicken breast for the duck and a spoonful of lump crabmeat for the foie gras. Omit the tomatoes and garnish the salad with thinly sliced cooked beets. Dress with dill mayonnaise.

Poached Salmon Salad

One of the most perfect of all summer luncheon salads, a cool, beautiful marriage of flavors and colors.

Makes 6 servings

6 salmon steaks, 1 inch thick
3 slices lemon
1 sprig fresh dill or 1 teaspoon dried dill
Greens
3 medium cucumbers, peeled, halved,
    seeded, and thinly sliced

1 cup mayonnaise
1 cup yogurt or sour cream
1 tablespoon chopped fresh dill
2 tablespoons chopped parsley

GARNISH: Watercress sprigs, cherry tomatoes

Poach the salmon in salted water with the lemon and dill sprig or dried dill, allowing just 10 minutes per measured inch of thickness. Drain, cool, then carefully remove the bone and skin, keeping the steaks intact.

Arrange the salmon on a bed of greens on a large serving platter. Combine the cucumbers, mayonnaise, yogurt or sour cream, chopped fresh dill, and 1 tablespoon chopped parsley. Toss well. Spoon some of the cucumber mixture lavishly over each salmon steak and garnish with watercress and tomatoes. Sprinkle the tops with remaining chopped parsley. Serve additional mayonnaise if you wish.

Codfish Salad

This was a specialty of the barman of the observation lounge of the S.S. *Independence,* on which I made many transatlantic crossings. He was from Trieste and loved food, and when he found kindred spirits on board he would prepare certain dishes for lunch and share them. I love the flavor of salt codfish and I always looked on this as a great treat. Don't add salt to the dressing; the fish is salty enough.

Makes 6 servings

2 pounds salt codfish, soaked, poached,
   and drained (see cooking directions
   on page 243)
6 medium waxy potatoes, unpeeled
2 large red Italian onions, sliced paper
   thin

¼ to ½ cup chopped parsley, preferably
   the Italian flat-leafed variety
⅔ cup vinaigrette dressing (see page 74)
   made with 1 to 2 tablespoons
   Dijon mustard and no salt

After cooking the codfish according to directions, let it cool. While it is cooling, boil the potatoes in their skins until just pierceable, but still firm. Cool slightly, peel, and cut into rather fine dice. Flake the cooled codfish and combine with the potatoes, onions, and parsley. Mix very well with the dressing and taste for seasoning.

Fish Salad

Any firm fish that has been poached and cooled makes a delicious first- or main-course salad. Possibilities include striped bass, halibut, trout, lemon sole, flounder, sea bass or rockfish.

Makes 4 servings

3 cups cold poached fish, flaked in
   large pieces
½ cup finely chopped celery
½ cup finely chopped onion or green
   onion
1 large cucumber, peeled, seeded, and
   thinly sliced

1 tablespoon chopped fresh tarragon or
   1 teaspoon dried tarragon
2 tablespoons chopped parsley
1½ cups vinaigrette sauce, made with
   lemon juice instead of vinegar
Watercress or romaine

GARNISH: *Sliced cucumbers and radishes*

Combine the fish, celery, onion, and cucumber. Add the tarragon and parsley to the vinaigrette sauce, pour over the salad, and toss gently. Arrange on a bed of watercress or romaine and surround with a border of sliced cucumbers and radishes.

¶**Fish Salad with Yogurt Dressing.** Instead of using vinaigrette, make a combination of mayonnaise and yogurt with 1 tablespoon either freshly chopped dill or tarragon, and pour it over the salad.

Composed Salads

Any of the following composed salads of seafood and vegetables can be either a main course or, if you halve the helping, a first course. Arrange them attractively in individual salad bowls or on plates.

Scallop Salad with Avocado and Chili

If you use bay scallops, leave them whole. Quarter or halve sea scallops.

FOR EACH SERVING:

Salad greens
1 cup cooled poached scallops (for
    poaching directions, see page 240)
¼ cup onion rings
¼ cup diced avocado

2 tablespoons chopped canned peeled
    green chilies
About 3 or 4 tablespoons vinaigrette
    sauce (see page 74)

Arrange greens in a bowl or on a plate, top with the scallops, onion rings, and avocado, and sprinkle with the chopped chilies. Dress with vinaigrette to taste.

¶Scallop Salad with Avocado and Sauce Gribiche. Instead of the vinaigrette, dress the salad with sauce Gribiche (see page 535).

¶Scallop Salad with Tomato and Egg. Omit the avocado. Add a quartered tomato or cherry tomatoes and a quartered hard-cooked egg to the salad.

Lobster Salad with Mayonnaise

Makes 4 servings

3 cups cooked lobster meat, in chunks
¼ cup chopped parsley
1 tablespoon chopped fresh tarragon or
    1 teaspoon dried tarragon

1 cup mayonnaise
Salad greens

Combine the lobster, parsley, tarragon, and mayonnaise. Arrange on greens in a salad bowl or on individual plates.

¶Lobster Salad with Potato and Onion. Add to the lobster and herbs 1½ cups thinly sliced cooked potatoes and ½ cup finely chopped onion. Mix with mustard mayonnaise (see page 76).

Marinated Scallop Salad

Tiny, delicate bay scallops retain their texture and flavor when they are merely marinated in citrus juice, which turns them opaque and "cooks" the tender flesh without heat.

Makes 4 servings

2 pounds tiny bay scallops, uncooked
1 cup lime juice

1 head lettuce
¾ cup vinaigrette sauce (see page 74)

Marinate the scallops in the lime juice for 1 hour, or until opaque and "cooked" by the acid in the juice. Drain. Wash and dry the lettuce, separate into leaves. Arrange scallops on top and dress with the vinaigrette.

¶Scallop Salad with Potato and Onion. Combine the marinated scallops with 2 or 3 small cooked potatoes, cut in cubes; 1 small onion, finely chopped, or 6 to 8 finely cut green onions; and dress with mayonnaise to taste.

Lobster Salad with Cucumber and Egg

Makes 4 servings

1 head lettuce, washed, dried, and
separated into leaves
3 cups cooked lobster, cut in chunks
1 cup peeled, seeded, and diced
cucumber

2 hard-boiled eggs, coarsely chopped
½ to ¾ cup vinaigrette sauce (see
page 74), flavored with 1 teaspoon
chopped tarragon

Arrange greens in a salad bowl. Combine lobster, cucumber, and eggs, and put on top of greens. Dress with vinaigrette.

¶Lobster-Chicken Salad with Celery. Use 2 cups lobster. Add 2 cups diced cooked chicken breast and ½ cup finely chopped celery. Omit cucumber and eggs. Dress with a plain vinaigrette and garnish with cherry tomatoes.

¶Lobster Salad with Avocado and Onion. Combine the lobster with 1 cup diced avocado and ½ cup finely chopped onion. Dress with a plain vinaigrette (if you are using meat from a freshly boiled lobster, add the tomalley and any coral to the vinaigrette).

¶**Lobster Salad with Tomatoes and Green Onion.** Combine the lobster with ½ cup thinly sliced green onion, or scallion; 1 cup peeled, seeded, and chopped tomato; and ¼ cup chopped parsley. Dress with a vinaigrette flavored with 1 tablespoon chopped fresh basil or 1 teaspoon dried basil.

Crab Salad with Onion and Egg

Makes 4 servings

1 head lettuce, washed, dried, and
    separated into leaves
3 cups cooked lump crabmeat or meat
    from crab legs
¾ cup finely cut green onion, or
    scallion

4 hard-boiled eggs, coarsely chopped
½ to ¾ cup vinaigrette sauce (see
    page 74)
2 tablespoons chopped parsley

Arrange the greens in a salad bowl. Top with the crabmeat, onion, and eggs. Mix the vinaigrette and parsley and pour over the salad. Toss lightly.

¶**Crab Salad with Cucumber, Anchovies, and Onion.** Add to the crabmeat 1 cup peeled, seeded, and chopped cucumber, 2 or 3 chopped anchovy fillets (first soaked in water to remove the salt), and ½ cup finely chopped green onion, or scallion. Dress with a vinaigrette flavored with 1 tablespoon chopped fresh basil or 1 teaspoon dried basil.

¶**Crab Salad with Avocado and Onion.** Add to the crabmeat 1 sliced avocado and ½ cup finely chopped onion. Serve with a vinaigrette flavored with a little chopped garlic.

¶**Crab Salad with Radish.** Add to the crabmeat and green onion 1 cup finely shredded red or white radish. Serve with a vinaigrette flavored with 1 tablespoon chopped fresh tarragon or 1 teaspoon dried tarragon.

Crab Salad with Oriental Vegetables

FOR EACH SERVING:
1 cup shredded Chinese cabbage
1 cup lump crabmeat
¼ cup finely cut celery
¼ cup thinly sliced water chestnuts

¼ cup bean sprouts
Vinaigrette sauce (about ¼ cup) made
    with soy sauce instead of salt
    (see page 74)

GARNISH: Watercress sprigs

Arrange the cabbage in a bowl or on a plate. Top with crab, celery, water chestnuts, and bean sprouts. Dress with soy-flavored vinaigrette. Garnish with watercress.

¶**Crab Salad with Cucumber, Anchovies, and Onion.** Arrange the crab on the Chinese cabbage. Add peeled, seeded, and chopped cucumber, chopped anchovy fillets (first soaked in water to remove the salt), and finely chopped green onion, or scallion. Dress with a basil-flavored vinaigrette.

¶**Crab Salad with Avocado, Onion, and Radish.** Arrange the crab on the Chinese cabbage. Add sliced avocado, finely chopped green onion, and finely shredded white or red radish. Serve with a garlic-flavored vinaigrette.

¶**Crab Salad with Carrot, Onion, and Celery.** Arrange the crab on the Chinese cabbage. Add shredded carrot, finely chopped celery, and finely cut green onion, or scallion. Sprinkle with chopped chives. Serve with a mustard-flavored vinaigrette.

Shrimp Salad

Any of these shrimp salads can be a first or a main course.

Makes 4 servings

1 head lettuce, washed and crisped, separated into leaves	2 tablespoons capers
	1 tablespoon finely cut chives
2 pounds cooked shrimp, shelled and deveined	1 tablespoon chopped fresh dill
	½ cup vinaigrette sauce (see page 74)

Arrange greens in a salad bowl and put the shrimp and capers on top. Mix the chopped herbs into the vinaigrette sauce and pour over the shrimp.

¶**Shrimp Salad with Cucumber and Tarragon.** Add 1 cup peeled, seeded, and cubed cucumber to the salad and 1 tablespoon chopped fresh tarragon. Omit chives and dill. Add 1 tablespoon chopped tarragon to the vinaigrette.

¶**Shrimp Salad with Olives and Eggs.** Add 4 hard-boiled eggs, quartered, and ½ cup small black olives (preferably Italian or Niçoise) to the salad. Omit the capers, chives, and dill. Sprinkle with 1 tablespoon chopped parsley and garnish with cherry tomatoes.

¶**Shrimp with Avocado.** Add 1 cup diced avocados, an additional tablespoon capers, and an additional teaspoon olives instead of the dill.

Tuna Salad with Onion, Avocado, and Egg

Makes 4 servings

*1 head lettuce, washed and dried,
    separated into leaves
2 seven-ounce cans imported oil-packed
    tuna, drained
1 cup onion rings*

*1 cup diced avocado
4 hard-boiled eggs, quartered
2 to 3 tablespoons capers
½ to ¾ cup vinaigrette sauce (see
    page 74)*

Arrange greens in a salad bowl and put the tuna, onion, avocado, eggs, and capers on top. Dress with vinaigrette sauce to taste.

¶**Tuna Salad with Fennel.** Thinly slice 1 bulb of fennel and add to the salad.

¶**Tuna Salad with Olives, Anchovies, and Tomatoes.** Add ½ cup small black olives (preferably Italian or Niçoise), 3 chopped anchovy fillets, and 12 cherry tomatoes to the salad.

¶**Tuna Salad with Apple.** Omit the avocado, eggs, and capers. Add 1 cup finely diced tart apple to the tuna and onion rings.

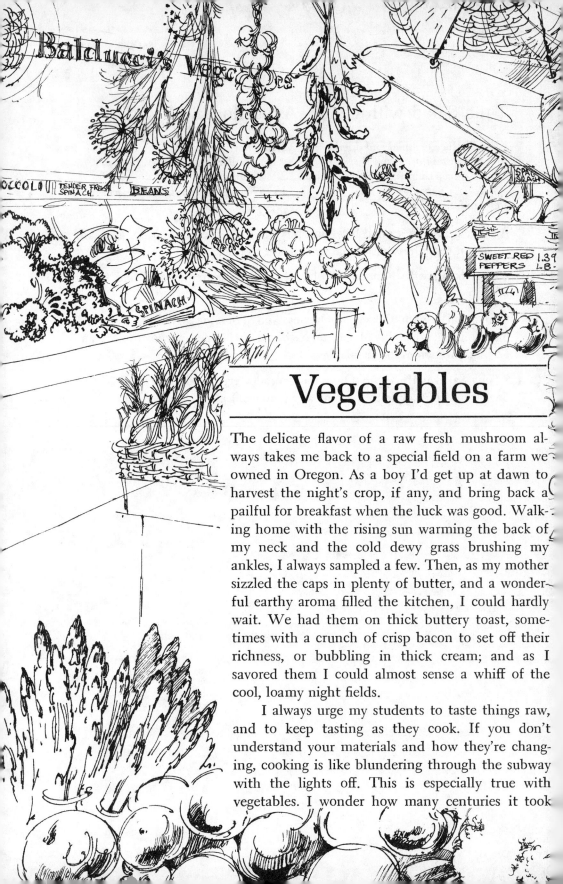

Vegetables

The delicate flavor of a raw fresh mushroom always takes me back to a special field on a farm we owned in Oregon. As a boy I'd get up at dawn to harvest the night's crop, if any, and bring back a pailful for breakfast when the luck was good. Walking home with the rising sun warming the back of my neck and the cold dewy grass brushing my ankles, I always sampled a few. Then, as my mother sizzled the caps in plenty of butter, and a wonderful earthy aroma filled the kitchen, I could hardly wait. We had them on thick buttery toast, sometimes with a crunch of crisp bacon to set off their richness, or bubbling in thick cream; and as I savored them I could almost sense a whiff of the cool, loamy night fields.

I always urge my students to taste things raw, and to keep tasting as they cook. If you don't understand your materials and how they're changing, cooking is like blundering through the subway with the lights off. This is especially true with vegetables. I wonder how many centuries it took

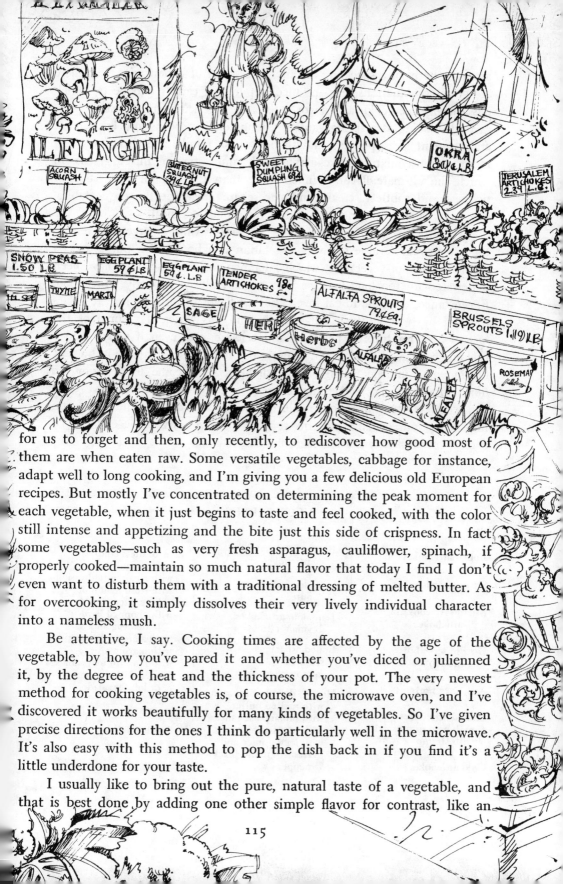

for us to forget and then, only recently, to rediscover how good most of them are when eaten raw. Some versatile vegetables, cabbage for instance, adapt well to long cooking, and I'm giving you a few delicious old European recipes. But mostly I've concentrated on determining the peak moment for each vegetable, when it just begins to taste and feel cooked, with the color still intense and appetizing and the bite just this side of crispness. In fact some vegetables—such as very fresh asparagus, cauliflower, spinach, if properly cooked—maintain so much natural flavor that today I find I don't even want to disturb them with a traditional dressing of melted butter. As for overcooking, it simply dissolves their very lively individual character into a nameless mush.

Be attentive, I say. Cooking times are affected by the age of the vegetable, by how you've pared it and whether you've diced or julienned it, by the degree of heat and the thickness of your pot. The very newest method for cooking vegetables is, of course, the microwave oven, and I've discovered it works beautifully for many kinds of vegetables. So I've given precise directions for the ones I think do particularly well in the microwave. It's also easy with this method to pop the dish back in if you find it's a little underdone for your taste.

I usually like to bring out the pure, natural taste of a vegetable, and that is best done by adding one other simple flavor for contrast, like an

115

aromatic herb, or a speckling of nuts, or a squirt of lemon juice. But there are good combinations. For instance, a purée of carrots and beets, which has a lovely deep color and flavor, or a sauté of cucumbers and snow peas, as fresh looking as a spring garden. Onions enliven beans and beets, corn and eggplant, peas, peppers, and all the squash family; and there are a few more complex mixtures, like a ratatouille and a tian of mixed greens, in which the ultimate flavor is much more than the sum of its parts. For richness and subtlety, cream and cheese are great friends to vegetables, especially when you want a main dish for a meatless meal.

I think I've provided here more, and more various, vegetable recipes than appear even in exclusively vegetarian cookbooks. I've put a special emphasis on root vegetables, which I happen to love; also, they have been underrated for too long because they weren't always properly understood. For instance, the time to eat lovely, buttery-flavored salsify is after it's been touched by frost, or even left underground all winter. Try some of the recipes here for turnips, parsnips, and celeriac, and even if you've had a lifelong prejudice I think you'll change your mind. And there are just a few, fleeting days in May when baby fiddlehead ferns come to us from the northern woods. Try everything, be receptive to new methods, give close and renewed attention to long-neglected treasures, and I do believe that you may re-jig your cooking patterns to give more priority to vegetables. To cook them brilliantly is a sure sign of a fine palate.

VEGETABLES

Boiled artichokes

Steamed artichokes

Microwave-cooked
artichokes

How to serve hot
artichokes

Artichoke bottoms

Stuffed artichokes
with ham or prosciutto
with shrimp

Cold artichokes

Buttered Jerusalem
artichokes

Jerusalem artichoke
purée

Jerusalem artichokes
vinaigrette

Boiled asparagus
steamed
microwave-cooked

How to dress hot asparagus
with melted butter
with hollandaise sauce
with mousseline sauce
with lemon juice and
freshly ground black
pepper

How to dress cold
asparagus
with vinaigrette dressing
with fresh lemon or
lime juice
with chopped hard-
boiled egg and
vinaigrette dressing
with mayonnaise
with mustard mayonnaise
topped with crabmeat
or lobster salad

Raw asparagus

Minute asparagus

Quick-boiled green beans
  with toasted almonds
  with garlic and pine nuts
  with sweet onion rings
  with fresh herbs

Cold green beans with
  walnut oil
  with mustard-flavored
    mayonnaise
  with dilled vinaigrette
  with shallots and Greek
    olives

Wax beans

Boiled shell or cranberry
  beans
  with bacon
  with vinaigrette and
    onion

Baked beets
  with onion and chopped
    tarragon
  with onion and orange
  with yogurt
  with dill
    vinaigrette

Steamed broccoli flowerets

Boiled broccoli
  with black butter
  with maltaise sauce
  with garlic and parsley
  broccoli purée
  crumbed broccoli

Steamed broccoli rabe
  broccoli rabe purée

Cold broccoli rabe

Crisp-cooked Brussels
  sprouts
  with grated Parmesan
    cheese
  with sautéed mushroom
    caps
  with chestnuts
  with shallots

Cold Brussels sprouts

Microwave-cooked Brussels
  sprouts

Steamed cabbage
  vinaigrette

Braised cabbage
  with vinegar and dill
  with heavy cream

Lemon cabbage

Whole stuffed savoy
  cabbage
  in chicken broth
  with tomato sauce

Red cabbage braised with
  apples and wine
  with raisins

Goloubtzys or choux farcis

Boiled carrots
  with fresh herbs
  glazed carrots
  with cognac or rum
  purée of carrots with
    potatoes
  with puréed parsnips
  purée of carrots and
    beets
  purée of carrots and
    parsley

Boiled cauliflower
  with Parmesan cheese
  with mornay sauce
  with cheese sauce
  with black butter and
    capers
  with olive oil and garlic
  with béarnaise sauce
  with Gruyère cheese
  with curry sauce
  with sliced ham and
    cheese sauce
  purée of cauliflower
  purée of cauliflower with
    parsley
  purée of cauliflower with
    cheese sauce
  purée of cauliflower with
    olive oil and garlic

Microwave-cooked
  cauliflower

Cold cauliflower

Celery sauté

Boiled celery root
  with cheese
  with maltaise sauce

Baked celery root and
  potatoes

Baked stuffed celery root

Skillet-boiled corn
  with butter and bacon
    crumbs
  with mustard or herb
    mayonnaise
  with rémoulade sauce
  with green pepper butter

Microwave-cooked corn

Corn off the cob
  with onion and green
    pepper
  with fresh basil

Raw corn

Corn oysters

Corn pudding
  with bacon

Poached cucumbers

Steamed cucumbers
  with herbs

Sautéed cucumbers with
  cream
  with yogurt
  with mushrooms
  with julienne of broccoli
  with snow peas

Sautéed eggplant
  with tomato sauce
  with Parmesan cheese
  in cornmeal
  with broiled or sautéed
    tomato slices
  with bacon
  with sautéed onions
  eggplant casserole

Imam Bayildi

Batter-dipped fiddlehead
  ferns

Cold fiddlehead ferns

Florence fennel

Cooking greens

Philip Brown's romaine
  soufflé

Braised mustard greens

Tian of mixed greens

Tian of mixed greens and
bacon

Steamed leeks

Microwave-cooked leeks

Braised leeks
  leeks vinaigrette
  puréed leeks

Sautéed mushrooms
  with heavy cream
  with fresh herbs and
    cream
  with sour cream or
    yogurt
  with bacon bits

Cèpes à la bordelaise

Steamed okra
  with butter and lemon
  with garlic and oil
  with garlic-anchovy
    butter
  vinaigrette

Okra and corn

Boiled onions
  buttered onions
  with nutmeg
  with cream sauce
  with cheese sauce
  with tomato sauce

Fried onions
  caramelized onions
  dieter's onions

Broiled onion slices
  with hamburgers
  with cheese

Braised onions
  with Parmesan cheese
  with pasta
  with sherry, bourbon, or
    Madeira

Boiled green onions, or
  scallions
  with hollandaise sauce
  with mornay sauce

Stuffed onions

Sautéed parsnips
  glazed parsnips

Steamed parsnips

Puréed parsnips
  parsnip patties
  with puréed potatoes

French-fried parsnips

Boiled peas
  with herbs
  with mushrooms
  with green onions
  with tiny pearl onions
  puréed

Peas with heavy cream
  with cream and herbs

To peel peppers

Peppers sautéed in olive oil
  with braised beef
  with roast chicken
  with onion rings
  with pasta

Peppers sautéed in butter
  with pork chops
  with corn kernels
  with Italian sausages

Peppers vinaigrette
  with mint
  with anchovies
  with mozzarella and
    tomatoes

Stuffed peppers
  with leftover meat
  with corn kernels

Baked potatoes
  with yogurt
  with beef drippings

Disgustingly rich potatoes

Gratin of potatoes

Mashed potatoes
  with parsley or chives
  with yellow turnips
  duchesse potatoes

German fried potatoes

Hash brown potatoes
  roesti

Potatoes sautéed in beef
  suet

Boiled salsify
  with mornay sauce
  sautéed salsify
  with shallots and lemon

Wilted spinach
  with nutmeg
  with garlic and oil
  with hard-boiled egg
  puréed spinach

Tossed spinach
  with almonds and garlic
  with bacon bits
  with tomatoes

Steamed summer squash
  with oil, herbs, and garlic

Sautéed summer squash

Sautéed zucchini
  with garlic and herbs
  with shallots
  with walnuts

Shredded zucchini
  zucchini pancake
  zucchini pancake with
    cheese

Zucchini blossoms

Deep-fried zucchini
    blossoms
  zucchini blossom omelet
  with scrambled eggs
  in cheese soufflé

Boiled spaghetti squash

Spiced winter squash
  with black walnuts
  with pecans and ginger
  with peanuts
  with raw zucchini

Winter squash soufflé

Baked Hubbard squash
  with bacon
  with brown sugar

Baked butternut squash

Baked acorn or turban
    squash
  with bacon and garlic
  with maple sugar and
    bacon

Stewed fresh tomatoes
  with basil
  with onion
  with garlic and lemon
    zest
  with chilies
  with poached eggs

Scalloped fresh tomatoes
  scalloped canned
    tomatoes

Baked tomatoes stuffed
    with mozzarella
  with corn
  Greek tomatoes

Broiled herbed tomatoes
  with pesto
  with garlic and spices

Sautéed tomatoes

Pennsylvania Dutch
  tomatoes
  fried green tomatoes
    with cream

Steamed cherry tomatoes
  steamed peeled cherry
    tomatoes

Buttered white turnips
  with mushrooms

Gratin of turnip

Buttered yellow turnips
  or rutabagas
  with yogurt
  mashed
  with Madeira or sherry
  with mashed potatoes
  with duxelles

Raw white turnips

French-fried vegetables
  beer batter
  to French-fry vegetables
    French-fried zucchini
    French-fried okra
    French-fried potatoes
    French-fried sweet
      potatoes
    French-fried parsnips

Ratatouille
  with sliced mushrooms
  with sliced fennel
  with leeks
  with poached eggs and
    cheese
  spicy ratatouille

Tian
  with rice
  with noodles

Artichokes

Globe artichokes vary in size from extremely small, 1 to 1½ inches in diameter, to those which in maturity will be 4 inches across at the widest part. They are most often cooked before eating, although I often use the very tiny artichokes as crudités, simply trimmed and eaten raw. In that case, it is merely the bottom, or the *fond*, which is eaten after the cone of pale leaves and fuzzy tiny fibers in the center, known as the choke, are removed. The larger artichokes are sometimes trimmed by cutting off about 1 inch of the tops and removing the stem and small hard leaves around the base before cooking. They may be cooked in any of the following ways:

Boiled Artichokes

Stand artichokes upright in a pan and cook in plenty of boiling, salted water with a slice of lemon and a clove or two of garlic. Boil from 25 to 40 minutes, according to size. Drain upside down on paper towels.

Steamed Artichokes

Steam over boiling water for approximately the same length of time as for boiling.

Microwave-Cooked Artichokes

Artichokes cook very successfully in a microwave oven. Stand upright in a nonmetallic dish in a small amount of water and cover with a sheet of plastic wrap, or merely wrap them individually in the plastic wrap. Steam in the oven on full power. According to size, they will take from 9 to 16 minutes.

How to Serve Hot Artichokes

1. With melted butter. If you wish, season the butter with lemon juice or a chopped fresh herb such as tarragon, rosemary, or dill.
2. With hollandaise or Béarnaise sauce (see page 532).
3. With a well-flavored vinegar, such as sherry wine vinegar, if you are dieting.

Serve as a cold appetizer, or a main dish for a luncheon, followed by a salad, such as crab, lobster, shrimp or scallop, chicken or duck salad, or a finely cut vegetable salad dressed with mayonnaise.

Cold artichokes may also be served as a first course or a very light luncheon main course with mayonnaise, vinaigrette dressing, yogurt dressing, or just with oil and vinegar as a dipping sauce for the leaves. In this case, do not remove the centers, unless you wish to serve the sauce in the artichoke.

Artichoke Bottoms

After cooling the artichokes, remove all leaves and choke, leaving only the artichoke bottoms. Use these as a base for hot dishes or to serve purées and small vegetables such as fresh peas, whole-kernel corn, or tiny sautéed mushroom caps; or chill and fill with a cold salad or seafood.

Stuffed Artichokes

Artichokes lend themselves to stuffings. Before stuffing, remove the stem and about ½ inch from the leaf tips.

Makes 4 servings

4 artichokes
1½ cups bread crumbs
¾ cup grated Parmesan cheese
½ cup chopped parsley
½ cup chopped chives

1 tablespoon grated onion
1 or 2 cloves garlic, finely chopped
¼ pound softened butter
¼ cup water or chicken broth
1 tablespoon olive oil

Trim the artichokes. Combine remaining ingredients, except water and oil, for the stuffing. Press the stuffing down among the leaves of the artichokes and across the top, then tie string around the artichokes to keep them intact. Place them in an earthenware casserole with the water or broth and dribble the olive oil over the tops. Cover with foil and bake in a 350° oven for 1 to 1½ hours.

¶Artichokes Stuffed with Ham or Prosciutto. Use 1 cup bread crumbs and add ½ cup finely chopped ham or prosciutto.

¶Artichokes Stuffed with Shrimp. Use ½ cup or more finely chopped shrimp instead of the ham.

Cold Artichokes

Cook and chill the artichokes. Remove the center leaves and the choke, leaving a hollow in the center. Fill the hollow with any type of seafood.

Jerusalem Artichokes

These are no relation at all to the globe artichoke, but a tuber belonging to the sunflower family, sometimes marketed as "sun chokes." They look like small knobby new potatoes, and I feel they are a much neglected vegetable, probably because most people have no idea what they are or how to cook them. They deserve to be much more recognized as they not only taste delicious but are extremely low in calories. Boiled in their skins until tender, like new potatoes, they may be eaten with butter or hollandaise sauce (or with nothing at all, if you are counting calories), turned into a purée, or sliced and used cold in salads. If peeled, thinly sliced, and tossed raw into a salad, they have a lovely crisp quality rather like a water chestnut. And, as you probably know, they make excellent pickles.

Buttered Jerusalem Artichokes

Makes 4 servings

1 pound Jerusalem artichokes
3 tablespoons unsalted butter
Salt, freshly ground black pepper

1 to 2 tablespoons finely chopped
parsley (optional)

Scrub the Jerusalem artichokes and toss into a bowl of cold water until ready to cook. Put in salted water to cover and boil in their skins for 8 to 10 minutes, or until just tender when tested with a knife point. Peel, slice ½ inch thick, and toss with the butter, salt and pepper to taste and, if you wish, the parsley.

Jerusalem Artichoke Purée

Makes 6 servings

2 pounds Jerusalem artichokes
4 tablespoons unsalted butter

½ cup heavy cream
Salt, freshly ground black pepper

Scrub and boil the Jerusalem artichokes as before, until tender. Peel and purée in a food processor or food mill. Beat in the butter and cream, season with salt and pepper to taste, and reheat.

Jerusalem Artichokes Vinaigrette

Makes 4 servings

8 to 10 Jerusalem artichokes
Assorted salad greens

½ cup vinaigrette sauce

As you are going to use the Jerusalem artichokes raw, you will have to peel them, using a vegetable peeler. Immediately drop them into a bowl of very cold water with a squeeze of lemon juice to prevent them from discoloring. When you are ready to make the salad, remove the Jerusalem artichokes, dry well, and slice very thin. Add them to the greens in a salad bowl and toss with the vinaigrette sauce.

Asparagus

Asparagus nowadays is in the market almost 12 months of the year. It varies a great deal in size, and sometimes comes in rather irregular-sized bunches. I find the most satisfactory way of cooking asparagus is flat in a skillet with cold water.

To peel or not to peel? In a season when the jumbo stalks are at their prime, it seems to me that peeling the lower half of the stalk is doubly advantageous: the asparagus looks more trim and you tenderize the bottom section by peeling so that more of the stalk is edible. A vegetable peeler or a small paring knife will do the job in very quick fashion. I find that with smaller stalks it's not necessary to peel; just snap off the lower part of the stalks at the point where they break easily.

Boiled Asparagus

Lay the asparagus flat in a skillet—in several layers, if necessary. Barely cover with cold water seasoned with salt. Bring to a boil, uncovered, and boil until just tender—this usually takes 6 to 8 minutes. To test, remove one stalk with a pair of tongs and shake it lightly. If the head bobs, consider the asparagus cooked. Two pounds of asparagus is supposedly enough for 4 people, but that depends on appetites.

Steamed Asparagus

Steam upright in a specially designed pot with a rack which keeps the whole stalk above water. Steaming takes a little longer. Test for doneness the same way as above.

Microwave-Cooked Asparagus

Asparagus cooks extremely well in a microwave oven. Arrange stalks in a large, rather flat nonmetallic container with about ½ cup water and cover with plastic wrap. As my taste is for crisply tender asparagus, I cook it at full power for just 5 to 6 minutes, but this is something you'll have to work out for yourself.

HOW TO DRESS HOT ASPARAGUS:

With Melted Butter

With Hollandaise Sauce—Although hollandaise is considered the classic sauce for asparagus, I find it smothers the good flavor of the vegetable and eschew it.

With Mousseline Sauce—This combination of hollandaise sauce blended with whipped cream is considered a delicacy by many people, but not by me.

With Lemon Juice and Freshly Ground Black Pepper—for dieters.

HOW TO DRESS COLD ASPARAGUS:

With Vinaigrette Dressing—(see page 74)
With Fresh Lemon or Lime Juice
With Chopped Hard-Boiled Egg and Vinaigrette Dressing—(see page 74)
With Mayonnaise—(see page 76)
With Mustard Mayonnaise—(see page 76)
Topped with Crabmeat or Lobster Salad

Raw Asparagus

Never forget that good, fresh asparagus is delicious eaten raw, either with a mayonnaise-based sauce in which to dip it or merely with salt and pepper. If young, slim, and tender, it requires no peeling.

See Appetizers and Salads for other asparagus recipes.

Minute Asparagus

Makes 4 to 6 servings

2 pounds asparagus
Salt
¼ pound unsalted butter

3 to 4 tablespoons soy sauce
1 tablespoon lemon juice
Freshly ground black pepper to taste

Wash and trim the asparagus and cut into diagonal slices no more than ¼ inch thick—thinner if possible. Place the slices in a colander or frying basket. Place enough water to cover the asparagus in a kettle large enough to accommodate the colander or frying basket, add salt to taste, and bring the water to a full, rolling boil. Meanwhile, melt the butter in a large skillet and have the soy sauce, lemon juice, and pepper close at hand.

Plunge the asparagus into the kettle of boiling water, bring the water to a second boil, and cook the asparagus for just one full minute. Drain the asparagus very well and add it to the melted butter in the skillet with the remaining ingredients. Toss well over moderate heat until the butter has browned and the asparagus is crisp and deliciously flavored.

Green Beans

The most common variety of green bean is the snap bean, formerly known as a string bean because it invariably needed stringing. This is no longer true, unless the beans are definitely overage. Buy the smallest, freshest, and crispest you can find—they should snap when you break them. You will occasionally find in specialty vegetable markets the very tiny beans called by the French name, *haricots verts*; these are expensive but well worth buying. Then there is the flat, broad Italian bean and the scarlet runners beloved of the English, which are almost never sold in markets but grown by some gardeners here for their lush vines and brilliant scarlet flowers. They must be picked and cooked when very young as they grow rapidly to tough-skinned inedibility.

There is a lot of controversy about cooking beans. It's very much a matter of taste preference. While they used to be cooked until they were thoroughly limp and soft (some people still like them that way), nowadays there is an equally unfortunate tendency to go to the other extreme and barely blanch them, so they still taste quite raw. Personally, I like green beans cooked until the raw taste disappears but they still retain a fresh taste and a crispness to the bite. The trick is to keep the cooking water boiling rapidly while adding the beans. My friend Julia Child owns an esoteric piece of equipment called a buffalo iron which is heated until fiery hot and plunged into the water to keep it boiling furiously and cook the beans faster. While it might be fun to have, I've always managed to get along without one.

Quick-Boiled Green Beans

Makes 4 servings

2 pounds green beans
¼ pound unsalted butter, cut in pieces

Salt, freshly ground black pepper

Wash the beans and trim off the ends. Bring a plentiful amount of salted water to a rapid, rolling boil in a large saucepan. Drop in the beans, a few at a time, so the water never ceases to boil. If it does, replace the cover until it returns to a boil, then take it off and boil the beans uncovered or they will lose their fresh bright color. Boil for 10 to 15 minutes, depending on age and size, tasting from time to time to see if they are done to your liking. Drain immediately. Some people advise plunging the beans into cold water to stop them cooking further, but if you have drained them while they are still bitey-crisp, this should not be necessary. Return beans to the pan and toss with the butter for 1 to 2 minutes, seasoning with salt and pepper to taste. Serve at once.

¶**Green Beans with Toasted Almonds.** Toss with the butter and ½ cup toasted sliced almonds.

¶**Green Beans with Garlic and Pine Nuts.** Toss the beans with ¼ cup olive oil, 3 to 4 finely chopped garlic cloves, and ½ cup toasted pine nuts.

¶**Green Beans with Sweet Onion Rings.** Toss the beans with ¼ cup olive oil or unsalted butter and garnish with thinly sliced raw sweet onion rings.

¶**Green Beans with Fresh Herbs.** Toss with ¼ cup melted butter or olive oil and 1½ tablespoons finely chopped herb of your choice, such as tarragon, dill, marjoram, or with chopped garlic and basil.

Cold Green Beans with Walnut Oil

Makes 4 servings

2 pounds cooked green beans, chilled
4 to 6 tablespoons walnut oil
3 tablespoons lemon juice
¼ cup finely chopped walnuts

Toss the green beans with walnut oil and lemon juice, and garnish with the finely chopped walnuts.

¶**Green Beans with Mustard-Flavored Mayonnaise.** Season a good rich mayonnaise (see page 76) with 2 to 3 tablespoons Dijon mustard. Mix with the beans. Garnish with crumbled bacon.

¶**Green Beans with Dilled Vinaigrette.** Toss the beans with ½ cup well-dilled vinaigrette sauce.

¶**Green Beans with Shallots and Greek Olives.** Toss the beans with ¼ cup olive oil, 3 to 4 tablespoons finely chopped shallots, and 4 tablespoons chopped, pitted Greek olives.

Wax Beans

Wax or yellow beans may be prepared in the same way as green beans.

Shell or Cranberry Beans

Too few people know and appreciate these delicious and very American beans, which you find in markets in the summer. The pods are dry, pink-flecked, and the beans inside are fully formed and have a shiny ivory skin speckled with red and green. The texture is mealy, like that of dried beans, but as they are younger and fresher they take less time to cook.

At one period—and even now in certain parts of the country—the beans were cooked, or rather overcooked, with smoked jowl or loin of pork, which was then cut up and served with them. If you cherish these lovely beans as I do, you'll never overcook them. Because the beans have to be shelled before cooking, count on 3 to 4 pounds unshelled beans for 4 to 6 servings.

Boiled Shell or Cranberry Beans

Makes 4 to 6 servings

3 to 4 pounds shell or cranberry beans *Salt, freshly ground black pepper*
6 tablespoons melted butter *1 tablespoon chopped parsley*
⅓ cup chopped onion

Shell the beans and bring to a boil in plenty of salted water. Reduce heat, cover, and simmer until just tender, which should take about 20 to 25 minutes, according to age. Drain well. Toss in the pan with the butter, onion, and salt and pepper to taste. Serve garnished with the parsley.

¶**Shell Beans with Bacon.** Fry 4 to 5 thick slices of bacon until crisp. Drain and crumble. Add to the cooked beans with the bacon fat, 3 to 4 finely chopped garlic cloves, ¼ cup chopped mint, 2 to 3 tablespoons red or sherry wine vinegar and salt and pepper to taste.

¶**Shell Beans with Vinaigrette and Onion.** Serve cold with ⅔ cup very garlicky vinaigrette, ½ cup chopped onion, and 2 tablespoons chopped parsley.

Beets

Baked Beets

To my mind, baking beets is a much more flavorful and effortless method of preparation than the customary boiling, and the color will not bleed as it does in water. Wash the beets, without puncturing the skin. Leave on the roots and trim off all but about 1½ inches of the tops (if the leaves are in good condition, they can be cooked separately as beet greens). Wrap each beet securely in aluminum foil, leaving about an inch of the stalk protruding from the foil. Bake on the middle rack of a preheated 450° oven, allowing 1½ hours.

¶**Beets with Onion and Chopped Tarragon.** Slice the beets and serve hot with butter, chopped onion, vinegar, and chopped tarragon.

¶**Beets with Onion and Orange.** Slice and serve hot with thinly sliced raw onion and orange sections.

¶**Beets with Yogurt.** Slice and serve hot with yogurt and freshly ground black pepper.

¶**Beets with Dill.** Cut the peeled beets into julienne strips and serve with melted butter and chopped fresh dill.

¶**Beets with Vinaigrette.** Serve cold sliced beets with a vinaigrette to which you've added ¼ cup chopped shallots and 2 to 3 tablespoons chopped fresh dill.

Broccoli

Although broccoli is colorful, versatile, and undoubtedly one of the most popular vegetables in the United States, it has never been a favorite of mine. To me it lacks the excitement that many other vegetables have. Broccoli is usually sold in bunches of approximately 2 pounds. It's wisest to pick bunches with slender stems, rather than thick woody ones. I find it preferable to remove the stems and cook them separately from the flowerets. I like to peel the stems, cut them into julienne strips, and combine them with julienne strips of white or yellow turnip, as we did in the Three-Vegetable Sauté in *Theory & Practice of Good Cooking*; other suggestions appear on page 190.

Steamed Broccoli Flowerets

Makes 4 servings

2 *pounds broccoli, stems removed*   *Salt, freshly ground black pepper*
½ *cup melted butter*

Steam the broccoli flowerets over a small amount of boiling water for approximately 10 to 12 minutes, or until crisply tender. Remove to a serving bowl, and gently toss with the melted butter. Season to taste with salt and freshly ground black pepper.

Boiled Broccoli

Makes 4 servings

2 *pounds broccoli, with stems*   *Salt, freshly ground black pepper*
½ *cup melted butter*

If you wish to serve the broccoli whole, trim off the tough, heavy ends of the stalks, peel the remaining part of the stalks, and break or cut the top part into several small bunches. Stand the broccoli upright in a rather deep pot in about 1½ inches of cold water, with the stems in the water and the flowerets above it. Bring water to a boil, cover the pot, and cook for about 12 to 15 minutes, or until crisply tender.

¶**Broccoli with Black Butter.** Melt ¼ pound unsalted butter over low heat until it turns a golden brown. Pour over the cooked broccoli.

¶**Broccoli with Maltaise Sauce.** Combine 1 tablespoon orange zest and a drop or two of orange juice with 1 cup hollandaise (see page 532). Pour over the cooked broccoli.

¶**Broccoli with Garlic and Parsley.** Combine 2 or 3 finely chopped cloves garlic with ⅓ cup olive oil. Pour over the broccoli and garnish with chopped parsley.

¶**Broccoli Purée.** Purée the cooked broccoli in a food processor or food mill. Season to taste with salt, freshly ground black pepper, and a touch of nutmeg, and mix with melted butter and either heavy cream or yogurt to taste.

¶**Crumbed Broccoli.** Melt ¼ pound unsalted butter in a skillet over moderate heat, add ½ cup dried bread crumbs and cook for 2 minutes, being careful they do not burn. Add ¼ cup freshly grated Parmesan cheese and spoon over the hot broccoli just before serving.

Steamed Broccoli Rabe

This type of broccoli, usually found in Italian markets, and also called *rape* or *broccoli rape*, is an elongated green leafy vegetable with long, thin, rather coarse stems, lots of leaves, and little clumps of yellow buds. I happen to adore the rather bitter flavor, although I have to admit it is an acquired taste. Broccoli rabe should be cooked only until crisply tender.

Makes 4 servings

2 pounds broccoli rabe
3 cloves garlic, finely chopped
⅓ cup olive oil

Salt, freshly ground black pepper
¼ cup grated Parmesan cheese

Soak the broccoli rabe well in cold water, then remove and discard about an inch of the thick bottom parts of the stems, leaving the top parts with leaves and flowers. Steam these in a very little water for just a few minutes until barely wilted down, then drain and chop. Meanwhile, heat the garlic in the oil. Pour the hot oil and garlic over the broccoli rabe, season with salt and pepper and toss well. Sprinkle with the cheese and serve at once.

¶**Broccoli Rabe Purée.** Purée the cooked broccoli rabe in a food processor or food mill, and mix with ¼ pound butter and a dash of lemon juice. Sprinkle the top with crisp bacon bits.

Cold Broccoli Rabe

Steam, but do not chop the broccoli rabe. When cold, dress with a vinaigrette sauce.

Brussels Sprouts

Although people who have been subjected to limp, soggy Brussels sprouts while traveling in England may not agree with me, I consider this one of the most delicious of our vegetables. Look for small, compact heads—not large, loose heads. Sometimes in farmers' markets now you can buy sprouts still clinging to their thick stalks. When overcooked, Brussels sprouts become mushy in texture and strong in taste, with an overpowering cabbagelike smell. They must be cooked quickly, so the centers are still rather crisp when you bite into them.

Crisp-Cooked Brussels Sprouts

Makes 6 servings

2 pints Brussels sprouts
½ cup melted unsalted butter

Salt, freshly ground black pepper

Trim outside leaves and stem ends from the Brussels sprouts and soak in salted water for 15 minutes. Put in a saucepan with a small amount of boiling salted water. Cook for about 10 minutes, or until crisply tender. Drain, toss with the melted butter, and season to taste with salt and freshly ground black pepper.

¶**Brussels Sprouts with Grated Parmesan Cheese.** Toss the Brussels sprouts with ⅓ cup olive oil, a touch of lemon juice, and a sprinkling of freshly grated Parmesan cheese.

¶**Brussels Sprouts with Sautéed Mushroom Caps.** Toss the Brussels sprouts with an equal quantity of lightly sautéed mushroom caps.

¶**Brussels Sprouts with Chestnuts.** Toss the Brussels sprouts with an equal quantity of whole cooked chestnuts which have been heated in butter.

¶**Brussels Sprouts with Shallots.** Toss with ¼ pound unsalted butter, 4 to 5 tablespoons finely chopped shallots, ½ teaspoon caraway seeds, and 1 to 2 tablespoons vinegar.

Cold Brussels Sprouts

Combine cold Brussels sprouts, cooked to the crisp-tender stage, with a brisk, tart mustard mayonnaise (see page 76) and toss thoroughly before serving.

Microwave-Cooked Brussels Sprouts

Place the Brussels sprouts in a nonmetallic dish with a small amount of water. Cover the dish with plastic wrap, venting one corner to release steam. Cook for 5 to 8 minutes on full power. Drain, and serve in any of the ways mentioned.

Cabbage

Cabbage is probably the most widely used and common vegetable next to potatoes, and an integral part of a New England boiled dinner.

We have several different varieties in the markets: white cabbage, with firm, solid heads; the young green cabbage, which is tender and not as large as the white; and the more loosely formed curly cabbage called savoy, whose flavor is more delicate, perhaps, than the others. In addition, there is red cabbage, which is best braised or used raw in some salads.

For cooking, the outer leaves should be stripped off, the cabbage quartered, the heart or core removed, and the leaves shredded or coarsely cut. Or, if you wish to serve the cabbage in pieces, cut into wedges and leave the core in to hold the leaves together. For dishes such as a gratin of cabbage, stuffed cabbage, or stuffed cabbage leaves, the whole head should be kept intact for blanching. I prefer cabbage steamed in a small amount of water rather than boiled. It should be cooked for a very short time to preserve its texture and flavor.

Steamed Cabbage

Makes 4 to 6 servings

1 medium head of cabbage, shredded   ½ cup melted butter
    or cut in wedges   Salt, freshly ground black pepper

Trim off the stalk and any discolored or limp outer leaves. Cut into wedges, remove the hard core with a sharp knife, and shred the leaves. Or cut into wedges, leaving the core in.

Put about ½ inch salted water into a heavy pot. Bring the water to a boil and, when the steam begins to rise, add the cabbage. Cover the pot tightly, reduce the heat, and steam about 4 minutes for shredded young cabbage, up to 8 minutes for an older one, and about 6 to 8 minutes for cabbage cut into wedges. When the cabbage is just crisply tender, drain it well. Toss with the melted butter, and season to taste with salt and pepper.

¶With Vinaigrette. Toss the cooked cabbage with 4 tablespoons melted bacon fat and crisp bacon bits, with the final touch of a few drops of vinegar.

Braised Cabbage

This is extremely good with pork dishes, corned beef, or boiled beef in lieu of simple steamed cabbage.

Makes 4 to 6 servings

1 medium head cabbage   1½ teaspoons salt
¼ cup unsalted butter, bacon fat, pork   ½ teaspoon freshly ground black pepper
    drippings, or goose fat   1 cup stock or dry white wine

Trim the cabbage, cut into wedges, remove the core, and either shred or cut coarsely. Melt the fat in a heavy 12-inch skillet. Add the cabbage and stir over medium heat until it wilts and turns a light brown around the edges. Add salt, pepper, and stock or white wine. Cover the skillet tightly and simmer until the cabbage is just tender, about 30 minutes.

¶Braised Cabbage with Vinegar and Dill. Braise the cabbage in ½ cup of fat until well browned. Add salt and pepper to taste. Cover the skillet and simmer for about 30 minutes, stirring occasionally. Remove from heat. Add 1 tablespoon vinegar, and 1 to 2 tablespoons chopped fresh dill. Shake the pan well and serve.

¶Braised Cabbage with Heavy Cream. Proceed as above, omitting the dill. Add ⅓ to ½ cup heavy cream. Allow the cabbage to cook down in the cream.

Lemon Cabbage

Makes 4 servings

2- to 3-pound head of cabbage
3 tablespoons unsalted butter
3 tablespoons all-purpose flour
1½ to 2 cups cabbage cooking water

Juice of 2 lemons
Salt, freshly ground black pepper
1 lemon, cut into paper-thin slices

Trim the cabbage, remove core, and shred. Bring to a boil enough salted water to cover the cabbage. Add cabbage and cook until just tender. Drain off the cooking liquid, and reserve 2 cups for the sauce.

Melt the butter in a heavy 1½-quart saucepan, mix in the flour, and cook over low heat, stirring constantly, for 2 to 3 minutes, or until the roux is well blended. Gradually stir in the reserved cabbage liquid. Cook over medium heat until the sauce is smooth, thick, and at the boiling point. Let the sauce simmer, stirring, for 3 or 4 minutes, then add the lemon juice, and season to taste with salt and pepper.

Place the cabbage in a gratin dish, pour the sauce over it, and garnish with paper-thin slices of lemon. Place in a preheated 350° oven for 10 to 15 minutes. Serve at once.

Whole Stuffed Savoy Cabbage

If you have a food processor, it can simplify the business of chopping the ham, shallots, and mushrooms for the stuffing.

Makes 8 servings

1 large savoy cabbage
¾ cup chopped shallots
6 tablespoons butter
½ cup finely chopped mushrooms
2 cups finely chopped ham

1 tablespoon chopped fresh tarragon,
    or 1½ teaspoons dried tarragon
Salt, freshly ground black pepper
1½ cups cooked rice
1 cup hollandaise sauce (see page 532)

Soak the cabbage well in cold water, then blanch in boiling salted water for about 10 to 12 minutes, or until the leaves will separate easily. Do not detach the leaves. Meanwhile sauté the shallots in the butter until they are transparent, then add the mushrooms. Combine the shallot-mushroom mixture with the ham, tarragon, salt and pepper to taste, and the cooked rice. Taste and correct the seasoning. Spoon some of this stuffing between cabbage leaves, starting with inner leaves and pushing the cabbage back into its original shape as you do so. When all the leaves have been stuffed, reshape cabbage and wrap securely in cheesecloth, tying a string around and up the sides, leaving a piece on top to act as a handle. Have ready a large pot full of boiling, salted water with a rack. Carefully place the cabbage on the rack, and simmer, covered, for 35 to 40 minutes. With the string handle, carefully remove the cabbage from the pot to drain. Remove the string and cheesecloth from the cabbage, and transfer it to a serving platter. Top with hollandaise sauce. Serve cut into wedges.

¶Stuffed Savoy Cabbage in Chicken Broth. To increase flavor and richness, substitute a good strong chicken broth for water when poaching the cabbage. The resulting liquid will make a flavorful stock for vegetable and cabbage soups, especially borsch.

¶Stuffed Savoy Cabbage with Tomato Sauce. Top with tomato sauce instead of hollandaise.

Red Cabbage Braised with Apples and Wine

A wonderfully aromatic and flavorful accompaniment to pork, duck, or goose.

Makes 4 servings

2- to 3-pound head red cabbage
3 to 4 tablespoons bacon drippings
Salt, freshly ground black pepper
    to taste

1 cup red wine
2 unpeeled tart apples, cored and diced
2 tablespoons brown sugar
1 tablespoon vinegar

Remove wilted outer leaves of the cabbage and the core. Shred fine and soak for 20 to 30 minutes in cold salted water. Drain well.

Melt the bacon drippings in a large skillet or sauté pan, add the cabbage, and sauté, stirring often, for several minutes. Season to taste with salt and pepper and add the wine. Simmer the cabbage for 5 to 6 minutes, then add the apples. Sprinkle the cabbage with brown sugar and the vinegar, mix well, cover, and simmer until cabbage and apples are tender, about 6 to 8 minutes.

¶With Raisins. Ten minutes before serving, add ¼ cup white raisins.

Goloubtzys, or Choux Farcis

Makes 6 servings

1 large head cabbage	1½ cups cooked rice
2 small onions, finely chopped	Salt, pepper, paprika
5 to 6 tablespoons butter	Butter
2 cups cooked cold beef, or other	Broth or water
leftover meat, finely chopped or	2 tablespoons flour
ground	1 cup cream

Blanch the cabbage in boiling salted water 8 to 10 minutes, or until softened. Remove 12 to 15 large leaves, cut out the large ribs, and dry the leaves on a towel.

Sauté the onion lightly in 2 tablespoons of the butter and add to the meat with the rice and salt, pepper, and paprika to taste. Mix well. Put a large spoonful of the mixture on each leaf. Fold and roll. Arrange the rolls in a buttered baking dish and surround with a little broth or water. Dot them with butter and bake in a 350° oven for about 1 hour.

While the Goloubtzys are baking prepare a sauce by combining 3 tablespoons of butter and flour and letting it color slightly over a low heat. Add the cream and continue cooking, stirring constantly, until thickened. Season with salt, pepper, and paprika to taste.

When the Goloubtzys are tender, pour the sauce over them and let it brown lightly under the broiler for a few minutes before serving.

Carrots

The time was when every restaurant in the country served forth a most boring combination of sliced carrots and fresh, frozen, or canned green peas that was one of the most grim mixtures ever conceived.

Recently, it seems to me, carrots have more than come into their own. We are no longer limited to those huge, woody, tasteless ones. Supermarkets sell plastic bags of small carrots, called finger carrots, which when cooked quickly and served with butter and/or fresh herbs are quite delicious. I also find that the young carrots which come in bunches with the tops attached are often extremely good.

Boiled Carrots

Makes 4 servings

2 pounds fairly small carrots   Salt, freshly ground black pepper
4 tablespoons (½ stick) unsalted butter   to taste

Scrape the carrots and cut into julienne strips, slice, or leave whole. Put in a pan in enough boiling salted water to cover and cook until just tender, about 7 to 20 minutes, depending on the cut (julienne strips and slices will take the least time). Drain, toss with the butter and salt and pepper to taste.

¶**Carrots with Fresh Herbs.** Toss the buttered carrots with 1 to 2 tablespoons of chopped fresh dill, marjoram, or tarragon.

¶**Glazed Carrots.** Add 1 to 2 tablespoons honey or maple syrup to the buttered carrots, and shake the pan well over low heat until the butter and syrup combine to form a glaze on the carrots. Garnish with chopped parsley.

¶**Carrots with Cognac or Rum.** Add 2 to 3 tablespoons of cognac or rum to the glazed carrots and shake the pan very well so that the vegetable and seasonings blend thoroughly.

¶**Purée of Carrots with Potatoes.** Purée the cooked carrots in a food processor or food mill, mix with the butter, then blend the carrot purée with an equal quantity of puréed potatoes, an additional 4 tablespoons butter, ½ cup heavy cream, and salt and pepper to taste.

¶**Purée of Carrots and Parsnips.** Combine carrot purée with an equal quantity of puréed parsnips. Add butter to taste.

¶**Purée of Carrots and Beets.** Combine equal quantities of puréed carrots and puréed baked beets. Add 4 tablespoons butter and ⅛ teaspoon nutmeg. This is especially good with pork.

¶**Purée of Carrots and Parsley.** Combine the puréed carrots with ½ cup chopped parsley and 2 tablespoons chopped chives. Fold in 4 to 5 tablespoons butter.

Cauliflower

Cauliflower, which used to be pretty much a winter vegetable, seems to have extended its growing cycle to year-round. When purchasing white cauliflower, look for firm, snowy heads and be sure the leaves at the base are green and not discolored. Occasionally you will find in the markets a purple cauliflower, sometimes called purple broccoli, which makes an amusing change from the white and may be cooked in exactly the same way. Cauliflower can be cooked whole or broken up into flowerets. The main thing is to avoid overcooking, for nothing is as bad as watery, mushy cauliflower.

Boiled Cauliflower

Makes 4 to 6 servings

1 medium head cauliflower
½ cup melted unsalted butter

Salt, freshly ground black pepper

Wash the cauliflower well, cut off the heavy stem end and green leaves. Cook whole, stem down, or broken into flowerets, in boiling salted water to cover. A whole cauliflower will take from 12 to 20 minutes, depending on the size. Flowerets will take about 5 to 6 minutes. Drain, pour the melted butter over, and season to taste with salt and pepper.

¶**Cauliflower with Parmesan Cheese.** Sprinkle with ¼ pound grated Parmesan cheese and freshly ground black pepper.

¶**Cauliflower with Mornay Sauce.** Pour 1 cup mornay sauce (see page 531) over the boiled cauliflower and sprinkle with grated Parmesan cheese. Place under the broiler to brown for 1 to 2 minutes.

¶**Cauliflower with Cheese Sauce.** Pour over the cauliflower a creamy cheese sauce (see page 531), using either Gruyère, Cheddar, or fontina.

¶**Cauliflower with Black Butter and Capers.** Pour ½ cup browned butter, mixed with 1 to 2 tablespoons vinegar and 1 tablespoon capers, over the cauliflower.

¶**Cauliflower with Olive Oil and Garlic.** Pour ¼ cup olive oil mixed with 2 finely chopped cloves garlic over the cauliflower, and sprinkle grated Parmesan cheese on top.

¶**Cauliflower with Béarnaise Sauce.** Pour 1 cup Béarnaise sauce (see page 532) over the cauliflower.

¶**Cauliflower with Gruyère Cheese.** Force thin fingers of Gruyère cheese into the head of a whole cooked cauliflower, return to the saucepan, and pour melted butter over the top. Cover and heat 2 minutes.

¶Cauliflower with Curry Sauce. Pour 1 cup curry sauce (see page 532) mixed with ¼ cup finely ground toasted almonds or filberts over the cauliflower.

¶Cauliflower with Sliced Ham and Cheese Sauce. Serve the cauliflower on slices of good-quality ham, and top with cheese sauce (see page 531) or well-buttered crumbs.

¶Purée of Cauliflower. Purée the cauliflower in a food processor or food mill, and blend with ½ cup unsalted butter and salt and pepper to taste.

¶Purée of Cauliflower with Parsley. Blend the purée of cauliflower with ½ cup butter and 3 to 4 tablespoons chopped parsley.

¶Purée of Cauliflower with Cheese Sauce. Blend the purée of cauliflower with 1 cup cheese sauce (see page 531).

¶Purée of Cauliflower with Olive Oil and Garlic. Blend the purée with ¼ cup olive oil, 2 or 3 finely chopped cloves garlic, and the juice of 1 lemon.

Microwave-Cooked Cauliflower

A whole head of cauliflower may be cooked in a small amount of water in a nonmetallic dish, covered with plastic wrap, on full power for about 12 to 13 minutes, depending on the size. Flowerets will take about 4 to 5 minutes. Remove the plastic wrap and drain. Serve in any of the variations given for boiled cauliflower. Cauliflower with Gruyère cheese is especially good done in the microwave oven. Pour butter over and heat for 2 minutes on full power.

Cold Cauliflower

Cold cooked cauliflower may be served as an appetizer, a vegetable, or a salad. It looks more attractive if put in a bowl on a bed of greens. Dress with any of the following:
   1. Vinaigrette with herbs such as chopped parsley, chives, or tarragon.
   2. Mayonnaise or half mayonnaise and half yogurt.
   3. Green mayonnaise (see page 77).
   4. Russian dressing (see page 37).

Celery

For me, the greatest use for celery is raw in salads (see page 82), or finely cut as an additive and flavor enhancer for stews, stuffings, vegetable combinations, and certain dishes. As a simple boiled or steamed vegetable I feel that it leaves much to be desired, although it does gain by being braised (see *Theory & Practice*, page 168) or sautéed, either alone or in a mixed sauté.

Although most people refer to a bunch or head of celery, actually it is correct to describe it as a stalk, which is made up of ribs. The small ribs in the center are known as the heart.

Celery Sauté

Makes 4 to 6 servings

1 large stalk of celery, cleaned and   *6 to 7 tablespoons unsalted butter*
trimmed   *Salt, freshly ground black pepper*

Cut the stalk into thin slices. Heat the butter in a sauté pan, add the celery slices and salt and pepper to taste. Shake the pan occasionally and cook over medium heat until the celery is fairly tender—about 5 minutes.

Celery Root or Celeriac

This deliciously flavored root vegetable has been all too little used, except for Celery Root Rémoulade (see *Theory & Practice*, page 330), which is found on the menu of every good French restaurant and has helped to awaken people to its distinctive and excellent taste. Because of this, we are beginning to use celery root in ways that were not part of our cooking pattern—boiled, puréed (see *Theory & Practice*, page 59), or baked. The rough-looking bulbs vary in diameter from 2 to 6 inches, and you may find the larger ones somewhat pithy inside. Just scrape away the soft part; there will still be enough to use. While the bulb must be peeled if it is to be used raw, there is no need to peel it first if it is going to be cooked whole.

Boiled Celery Root

Makes 6 servings

2 to 2½ pounds celery root
½ cup melted butter

Salt, freshly ground black pepper
Toasted bread crumbs

Cook the whole celery roots in boiling salted water until just tender—about 30 to 40 minutes. Drain. Peel the celery root, cut into slices and serve with melted butter, salt and pepper to taste, and toasted bread crumbs on top.

¶Celery Root with Cheese. Cook the celery root as above. Arrange the slices in a buttered baking dish, dot with butter, and sprinkle liberally with a combination of grated Parmesan and Gruyère cheeses. Place under the broiler until the cheese melts and browns nicely.

¶Celery Root with Maltaise Sauce. Arrange slices of cooked celery root in a serving dish and spoon Maltaise sauce (see page 532) over them just before serving.

Baked Celery Root and Potatoes

Arrange layers of thinly sliced raw potatoes and celery root in a well-buttered baking dish. Dot with butter and barely cover with beef or chicken stock. Bake in a preheated 350° oven until the vegetables are tender, about 45 minutes. This is especially good with game.

Baked Stuffed Celery Root

Makes 8 servings

4 celery roots, peeled and halved
6 tablespoons butter
⅓ cup chopped shallots
1 cup chopped mushrooms
½ cup tomato paste

½ cup finely chopped cooked tongue
Salt, freshly ground black pepper,
    dried thyme
Buttered crumbs
Chopped parsley

Blanch the celery roots in boiling salted water for 10 minutes. Drain, scoop out the centers, and trim neatly. (Scooped-out centers may be reserved for a purée.) Preheat the oven to 325°.

Melt 4 tablespoons butter in a skillet and sauté the shallots and mushrooms until soft. Mix in the tomato paste, tongue, salt and pepper to taste, and a good pinch of thyme. Fill the celery root centers with this mixture, dot the tops with the remaining butter, cut in pieces, and arrange in a baking dish. Bake in a 325° oven for 45 minutes. Sprinkle the tops with buttered crumbs and chopped parsley, and serve. These are excellent with roast beef and wild duck.

Corn

Corn is certainly one of our most popular vegetables. It's been much spurned by most Europeans, probably because it has never been a standard item of their diet. However, I well remember a delightful bistro in Paris where during corn season it was not unusual to find delicious corn from Alsace presented in a most intelligent way. The corn on the cob was cooked in half milk and half water and served as an hors d'oeuvre, which to me makes great sense. At the beginning of a meal it is delicious, refreshing, and most satisfying, and you are not chewing on an ear while other things on your plate get cold.

Naturally, the best way to prepare corn is to rush it from your garden to a pot of boiling water and eat it at once. Few of us can do that anymore.

Skillet-Boiled Corn

Everyone has his own opinion as to how corn should be cooked. This is my preferred method. Shuck the ears and put them flat in a skillet with cold water. Bring to a boil over rather high heat and remove the corn when the water reaches a full, rolling boil. Serve the corn at once with plenty of melted butter, salt, and a peppermill.

¶**Corn with Butter and Bacon Crumbs.** Roll the cooked corn in melted butter and then in crisp bacon crumbs.

¶**Corn with Mustard or Herb Mayonnaise.** Serve the corn hot with herb or mustard mayonnaise (see page 76).

¶**Corn with Rémoulade Sauce.** Use rémoulade sauce (see page 77) instead of the mayonnaise.

¶**Corn with Green Pepper Butter.** Combine butter with finely chopped skinned green pepper.

Microwave-Cooked Corn

Cook in the husks in a microwave oven for about 3 minutes on full power.

Corn off the Cob

Makes 6 servings

6 to 8 ears corn
¼ pound unsalted butter

Salt, freshly ground black pepper
½ to ¾ cup heavy cream

With a sharp knife, remove the kernels from the corn. Melt the butter in a heavy saucepan or skillet over medium heat. Add the corn and shake the pan for about 1 minute, just to heat it through. Add salt, pepper, and the heavy cream and heat. Then serve at once.

¶Corn with Onion and Green Pepper. Sauté 4 tablespoons chopped onion and ½ cup finely chopped green or red pepper (preferably skinned) in ¼ pound butter. Add the corn kernels and sauté in this mixture till just heated through.

¶Corn with Fresh Basil. Mix 1 to 2 tablespoons chopped fresh basil leaves into the corn just before serving. This felicitous combination of flavors is Chilean.

Raw Corn

Young corn is good just cut from the cob and blended with lightly whipped heavy cream seasoned with salt and freshly ground black pepper. Serve with cold fish or meat.

Corn Oysters

Makes 6 servings

12 ears corn
3 tablespoons heavy cream
2 tablespoons sifted flour

1 tablespoon melted butter
1 well-beaten egg

Shuck and clean the corn very well, and with a sharp knife make a cut lengthwise in the center of each row of kernels. Scrape with the back of the knife to push all of the pulp out. Blend with the cream and flour, then the butter and egg. Drop the batter by spoonfuls on a well-buttered griddle or skillet. Cook until delicately browned on both sides.

Corn Pudding

Makes 4 servings

10 ears corn
3 well-beaten eggs
1 cup milk
½ cup cream

1 tablespoon melted butter
½ teaspoon salt
1 teaspoon freshly ground black pepper
5 or 6 dashes Tabasco

Shuck, clean, and scrape the corn as in preceding recipe, being certain to scrape the cobs well after removing the corn in order to get all of the milk. Combine with the beaten eggs, milk, cream, butter, and seasonings. Pour the mixture into a 1½-quart baking dish and bake in a 350° oven for 45 to 50 minutes, or until just firm to the touch.

¶**Corn Pudding with Bacon.** Place crisp rashers of bacon atop the pudding just before serving.

Cucumbers

We now have two types of cucumber, the regular fat, heavily seeded kind that is very watery and all too often waxed, and a long, thinner, practically seedless one, sometimes called a Chinese or English cucumber, that is more expensive but of better quality. You can also find in summer and fall cucumbers that are sold for pickles. These are often cheaper and better flavored than the regular kind. While the cucumber is primarily one of our most reliable salad vegetables, it can also be quite delicious if lightly poached, steamed, or sautéed, dressed with butter and herbs, and served as an accompaniment to fish.

Poached Cucumbers

Makes 4 servings

Peel, split, and seed 3 cucumbers of average size and cut them into oval lozenges (the small pieces left over after the ovals are shaped may be finely chopped and added to cold soups or used for sandwich fillings). Poach lightly in boiling, salted water for just a few minutes, until they turn pale and translucent. Drain and toss with melted butter and a few grinds of pepper.

Steamed Cucumbers

Prepare in the same way as poached cucumbers, but steam over boiling water in a steam basket or colander just until translucent.

¶Steamed Cucumbers with Herbs. Toss with butter and finely chopped fresh dill, tarragon, chives, parsley, or mint.

Sautéed Cucumbers with Cream

Makes 4 servings

3 cucumbers, peeled, split, seeded, and
   sliced ¼ inch thick, or cut into
   oval lozenges as for Poached
   Cucumbers, above
2 tablespoons unsalted butter

Salt, freshly ground black pepper
1 tablespoon finely chopped tarragon
   or dill
¼ cup heavy cream

Blanch the cucumber pieces for 3 minutes in boiling water to remove the bitter juices. Drain well. Melt the butter in a skillet, add the cucumbers, and toss briefly until heated through but still crisp. Sprinkle with salt, pepper, tarragon or dill, and add the cream. Let it cook down for a minute and serve.

¶Sautéed Cucumbers with Yogurt. Use 2 tablespoons plain yogurt instead of the cream. Just heat through with the cucumbers; it must not boil or it will curdle.

¶Sautéed Cucumbers with Mushrooms. Toss 1 cup tiny sautéed mushroom caps (if caps are large, halve or quarter them) with the cucumbers before adding the cream.

¶**Cucumbers Sautéed with Julienne of Broccoli.** Peel broccoli stalks, cut in julienne strips, and blanch with the cucumbers. Toss vegetables in butter and sprinkle with chopped herb of your choice. Omit cream.

¶**Cucumbers Sautéed with Snow Peas.** Trim and string 1 pound snow peas. Sauté in skillet with blanched cucumbers and butter over high heat, tossing constantly, until snow peas turn bright green. Sprinkle with finely chopped herb of your choice—tarragon, mint, basil, or fresh coriander. Omit cream.

Eggplant

This beautiful, versatile vegetable can be found in markets most of the year and deserves to be used more frequently and imaginatively than is usually the case here. Oriental, Middle Eastern, Greek, Italian, Spanish, and Provençal recipes for eggplant are legion, but apart from ratatouille (see page 190), we seem to have adopted very few of them. This may be because we mostly grow the large bell-shaped purple eggplants that tend to be full of seeds, with a coarse texture and bitter flavor. The elongated purple eggplants about 4 to 6 inches long sold in Italian markets and some supermarkets or the round white Oriental eggplant, still rare but occasionally to be found in specialty vegetable stores and farmers' markets, have an infinitely better texture and a more delicate flavor. When you buy eggplants pick out those that are firm, smooth, and shiny, with unblemished, unwrinkled skin.

If you are going to cook eggplant for a short time, slice and salt it, peeled or unpeeled, according to the recipe, and let it drain to draw out the bitter juices. This is not necessary if you are going to cook it for a long time, as the liquid will evaporate naturally.

Sautéed Eggplant

Makes 4 servings

1½ *pounds eggplant*
Flour seasoned with salt and freshly
  ground black pepper

⅓ *cup olive oil*
4 *tablespoons unsalted butter*

Trim off ends of eggplant and cut into ½-inch slices. Salt and drain the slices, if you wish, but this is not necessary; if you do, pat dry before proceeding.

To cook, dip the slices into the seasoned flour. Heat the olive oil and butter in a 12-inch skillet and sauté the eggplant slices until tender and nicely browned on both sides. Be sure not to crowd the pan. It's best to sauté a few slices at a time, drain them on paper towels, and remove them to a heated serving dish to keep warm in a low oven.

¶Sautéed Eggplant with Tomato Sauce. Serve the eggplant slices with hot tomato sauce (see page 534).

¶Sautéed Eggplant with Parmesan Cheese. Sprinkle the sautéed slices with freshly grated Parmesan cheese and place under the broiler for 2 to 3 minutes.

¶Sautéed Eggplant in Cornmeal. Use fine cornmeal instead of flour.

¶Sautéed Eggplant with Broiled or Sautéed Tomato Slices. Top the sautéed eggplant with lightly broiled or sautéed tomato slices.

¶Sautéed Eggplant with Bacon. Add rashers of crisply cooked bacon cut into small pieces to the eggplant.

¶Sautéed Eggplant and Onions. Top the slices with sautéed onions.

¶Eggplant Casserole. Sauté the eggplant slices, but do not cook them through, as they will have further cooking. Arrange the slices in a well-oiled casserole, alternating them with layers of sliced onion, peeled and sliced green pepper, and peeled, seeded, and sliced tomato. Dribble a little olive oil on each layer and season with salt, freshly ground black pepper, and 2 or 3 finely chopped garlic cloves. Top with a mixture of buttered crumbs and grated Parmesan cheese. Bake in a 350° oven for 30 to 45 minutes, or until vegetables are just tender.

Imam Bayildi

This Turkish stuffed eggplant is said to have been given its name, which translates as "the imam fainted," when the imam, or priest, tasted the dish and swooned with pleasure. Whether you believe that or not, there's no denying that this is an utterly delicious way of preparing eggplant. It may be served hot or cold, alone as a luncheon dish or first course, or with roasted or broiled meat.

3 large eggplants
Salt and freshly ground black pepper
10 tablespoons olive oil
3 large onions, finely chopped
1 clove garlic, peeled and crushed
2 medium tomatoes, peeled, seeded,
    and chopped

½ teaspoon ground cinnamon
1 teaspoon sugar
1 tablespoon chopped parsley
1 tablespoon finely chopped pine nuts
    (optional)

Cut the green ends from the eggplants, wash them, and put them in a large saucepan. Add boiling water to cover, put a lid on the pan, and cook for about 10 minutes. Drain the eggplants well, plunge them into cold water, and leave for 5 minutes. Cut them in half lengthwise and scoop out most of the flesh, leaving a ½-inch-thick shell. Set aside the scooped-out flesh. Arrange the shells in a buttered baking dish and sprinkle with a little salt and pepper. Pour 4 teaspoons olive oil into each shell and cook the shells, uncovered, in the center of a preheated 350° oven for 30 minutes.

While the shells are cooking, heat remaining olive oil in a skillet, add the onions and garlic, and sauté gently for 5 minutes, then add the tomatoes, cinnamon, sugar, and parsley. Season to taste with salt and pepper. Continue simmering this mixture until the liquid has reduced by half, about 20 minutes. Chop the eggplant flesh and add it to the skillet with the chopped pine nuts, if used, and cook for 10 minutes more. Remove the shells from the oven and stuff them with the tomato mixture.

Fiddlehead Ferns

Fiddlehead ferns are young ferns which are edible when the tightly curled fronds pop out of the soil in the spring. These tenderly delicious morsels can occasionally be found fresh in markets. Cook them very briefly in boiling salted water and serve with melted butter or with olive oil, a bit of chopped garlic, and a touch of vinegar. Frozen and canned fiddleheads are also available.

Batter-Dipped Fiddlehead Ferns

Dip into beer batter (see page 188) and deep-fry in 365° fat for about 2 minutes. Drain on absorbent paper. These are especially good with broiled birds.

Cold Fiddlehead Ferns

They are also delicious blanched, chilled, and served with an herbed vinaigrette.

Florence Fennel

Florence fennel is a cultivated bulbous vegetable that has the same crisp texture as celery, but a very strong flavor of anise. It may be sliced and eaten raw as part of a tray of crudités or prepared like celery. Cultivated fennel should not be confused with wild fennel, which grows along the roads in California, Oregon, and other parts of the country. The dried stalks of wild fennel are often used when cooking fish, or run through loin of pork (see page 419). My preferred way of cooking cultivated fennel is braised (see *Theory & Practice*, page 167), but it is also good blanched, separated, and French-fried (see page 187) or served with an anise-flavored sauce. Cold, it is nice poached à la Grecque (*Theory & Practice*, page 60), or used raw, like celery, in salads and vegetable hors d'oeuvre.

Greens

Each year over 240 million pounds of greens are eaten in the United States, and that isn't counting the wild greens, like pokeweed, gathered in various parts of the country. The range of greens in our markets is impressive and includes beet greens, collards, kale, mustard greens, turnip greens, spinach, Swiss chard, and dandelion greens. There is almost no leafy green that can't be cooked and that goes for salad greens such as lettuce, delicious braised (see *Theory & Practice*, page 168), escarole, chicory, watercress, and the Italian arugula. Recently, at a Moroccan meal, I had a combination of spinach, watercress, and arugula that had been lightly cooked, blended with a little olive oil and a good deal of lemon juice. Served as a salad, it made an extraordinarily refreshing contrast to the food.

Traditionally, wild and cultivated greens were cooked for two or three hours with salt pork, ham hocks, or smoked hog jowl until they collapsed. I think a short cooking time and a variety of seasonings make greens more palatable and flavorful, although you might like to try the traditional method and see which you prefer.

Cooking Greens

Allow 1 pound greens for 2 servings. Wash the greens thoroughly in several changes of water, discarding discolored leaves and trimming off tough stems, if necessary. The water clinging to the greens after the final washing is usually enough for cooking. If it evaporates too fast, add a little boiling water to the pan.

My preferred method of cooking greens is to put them in a heavy pan after washing, sprinkle them with a little salt, cover, and let them wilt over moderate heat, turning them once or twice with a wooden spoon so they cook evenly. Cooking times vary according to the type, sturdiness, and age of the greens. Chicory, watercress, and lettuce leaves will take about 15 minutes, escarole a little longer. Turnip, beet, and mustard greens vary as to age and size. Count on a minimum cooking time of 5 minutes, a maximum of 15 for turnip and beet greens, and cook mustard greens until the stems are tender, from 10 to 25 minutes. Kale, a coarse green, takes about 20 minutes, collards 15 to 20 minutes. When cooking Swiss chard, cut off the leaves and cook the white stems separately, like asparagus, in boiling salted water to cover until just tender. The leaves will take about 10 to 15 minutes.

When the greens are tender, drain them well, chop them if you like, and dress them with melted butter, olive oil and garlic, or ham or bacon fat (¼ cup for each 2 pounds of cooked greens). A dash of vinegar or lemon juice will heighten the flavor.

Certain greens, such as spinach, mustard greens, lettuce, and kale, cooked and chopped, are delicious in soufflés and timbales (see page 262).

Philip Brown's Romaine Soufflé

This new and different way to cook crunchy romaine was originated by my friend Philip Brown at one of his California cooking classes. The soufflé has an unusual flavor and the little bits of chopped romaine give a pleasant crunchiness. Serve it with roast lamb or beef or a chicken casserole and you will need no green vegetable, starch, or salad to complete the meal, it stands in for all three. Another nice thing about this dish is that you can make the base and fold in the egg whites an hour before you need to bake it, then leave it in the refrigerator until it is time to pop it into the oven.

Makes 6 servings

1 large head of romaine
4 tablespoons butter
3 scallions or green onion, chopped
3 tablespoons flour
1 cup milk, heated
4 eggs, separated

1 cup shredded Cheddar cheese
1 teaspoon salt
½ teaspoon Worcestershire sauce
Tabasco to taste
Grated Parmesan cheese

Cut off the coarse bottom of the romaine stalk. Wash romaine thoroughly and chop coarse. Put in a heavy pan with a little water and cook until wilted. Drain well and chop fine. Melt 1 tablespoon butter in a skillet and cook scallions, or green onions, including green tops, until soft but not brown. Add romaine and cook, stirring, until moisture evaporates. Melt remaining butter in a saucepan, blend in flour, and cook for 2 to 3 minutes, stirring. Mix in milk and cook until thickened. Beat egg yolks into sauce, one at a time, then add Cheddar cheese and cook until smooth. Stir in romaine mixture until well blended. Season with salt, Worcestershire, and Tabasco. Lavishly butter a 1½-quart soufflé dish, sprinkle with Parmesan cheese, coating bottom and sides. Shake out excess. Beat egg whites until stiff but not dry; fold one-third into the romaine mixture, blending thoroughly. Fold in remaining whites lightly. Pour into soufflé dish, sprinkle with a little grated Parmesan and put in a preheated 400° oven. Immediately reduce heat to 375° and bake 25 to 35 minutes, according to how you like your soufflé. At 25 minutes it will be still a little runny in the center.

Braised Mustard Greens

Makes 4 to 6 servings

2 pounds mustard greens
6 to 7 tablespoons olive oil
1 or 2 cloves garlic, finely chopped

Salt, freshly ground black pepper
Lemon juice or vinegar

Wash the mustard greens. Heat the olive oil in a 10-inch skillet and add the garlic, the greens, and a tiny bit of water, if needed. Cover and steam the greens for 15 to 20 minutes. Add salt and pepper and toss well with a fork and spoon several times during the cooking period. Serve very hot with a little lemon juice or vinegar.

Tian of Mixed Greens

Makes 6 servings

1 pound each dandelion greens, collards,
   and mustard greens
1 cup chopped green onion, or scallions
1 cup chopped smoked ham

1 tablespoon lemon juice or vinegar
Salt, freshly ground black pepper
Chopped hard-boiled egg (1 or 2)

Cook the greens until tender, about 25 minutes, following basic recipe for cooking greens. Drain well and chop coarse. Add the onion, smoked ham, lemon juice or vinegar, and salt and pepper to taste. Toss well and serve with a garnish of chopped hard-boiled egg.

Tian of Mixed Greens and Bacon

Makes 6 servings

1 pound each dandelion greens, mustard
   greens, and escarole
½ pound thick-cut bacon, cut into
   cubes and partially cooked
   (not crisp)

2 or 3 cloves garlic, finely chopped
2 to 3 tablespoons wine vinegar, or
   to taste
1 to 2 tablespoons chopped fresh mint,
   or 2 teaspoons dried and crumbled

Cook the greens until tender, about 25 minutes, following basic recipe for cooking greens. Drain well, and chop coarse.

Combine the greens in a 12-inch skillet with the bacon, garlic, and vinegar. Toss over medium heat, until thoroughly heated, and add the fresh mint just before serving. Correct the seasoning and serve at once.

Leeks

Although leeks have been grown in this country for two centuries, until rather recently they were generally used only as a flavoring vegetable for soups and stews. The French and the Italians have always been partial to leeks and cooked them in various ways, and I think it must have been after the introduction here of vichyssoise, the soup invented by the famous chef Louis Diat, that they joined the American vegetable repertoire.

Leeks are a nuisance to clean because of the sand and dirt that get trapped between the tight layers of leaves. First trim off the root end and all but an inch or so of the green top and rinse well under cold water, spreading the leaves as much as possible. You'll probably find it necessary to make a slit in the top with a sharp knife in order to separate them. Very small or large leeks are best cut in small pieces before cooking. I love leeks and my preferred cooking method is to steam them.

Steamed Leeks

Allow 2 or 3 average-sized leeks per serving. Steam them in a small amount of boiling salted water until just tender, which should take from 15 to 18 minutes.

Microwave-Cooked Leeks

Put the leeks in a heatproof glass baking dish with a small amount of water, and cover with plastic wrap. Cook about 10 to 12 minutes at full power. Drain the leeks well and serve them hot with melted butter or with hollandaise sauce (see page 532), or chill them and serve with a vinaigrette dressing.

Braised Leeks

Makes 4 to 6 servings

12 average-sized leeks, trimmed and
    cleaned
3 tablespoons olive oil
1 teaspoon salt
1 teaspoon freshly ground black pepper
Sprig of fresh thyme, finely chopped, or
    ½ teaspoon dried thyme, crumbled

½ cup chicken or beef broth
⅓ cup cognac
Lemon juice
Chopped parsley

Brown the leeks in a heavy skillet in the olive oil and season them with salt, pepper, and thyme. Add broth, bring to a boil, reduce the heat, cover and simmer the leeks until they are just tender, about 15 minutes. Add the cognac, let the liquid come to a boil again, and simmer for 2 to 3 more minutes. Sprinkle with a few drops of lemon juice and garnish with chopped parsley.

¶**Leeks Vinaigrette.** Poach 12 to 14 leeks in chicken or beef broth to cover until just tender. Drain and cool the leeks and reserve the broth for soup. Arrange the leeks in a serving dish and cover with a sauce vinaigrette. Chill for several hours before serving. Garnish with chopped hard-boiled eggs, olives, or onion rings.

¶**Puréed Leeks.** Cut leeks into small pieces and poach in chicken broth, beef stock, or water to cover until very tender. Drain well, purée in a food processor, dress with butter and salt and pepper, and serve with a dusting of finely chopped fresh parsley.

Mushrooms

Although there are scores of varieties of wild mushrooms, they're not available (unless you are an adventurous mushroom hunter) and we must resort to the cultivated variety. They are available at all times of the year, have a good flavor and reliable texture, and need no cleaning—just a wipe with a damp towel to remove any surface dirt. Never peel mushrooms or you will lose most of the flavor. Very often mushrooms are boiled or sautéed without the stems, in which case the stems may be chopped and used for making duxelles (see page 535) or tossed into soups or stews for extra flavor. If mushrooms are used purely as a garnish, they should not take on color; simply poach them in acidulated water barely to cover for 5 minutes over medium heat, shaking the pan occasionally. If they are not to be used immediately, they may be held over hot water.

NOTE: Any of the recipes that follow would also apply to sautéed fresh chanterelles and other edible wild mushrooms, such as oyster mushrooms (except for cèpes, which need special preparation) or to the large Black Forest or the shiitake mushrooms that are now being sold fresh in specialty markets.

Sautéed Mushrooms

Makes 4 servings

1 pound mushrooms
5 tablespoons unsalted butter

2 tablespoons oil
Salt, freshly ground black pepper

Remove mushroom stems and wipe caps well with a damp towel. Heat the butter and oil in a 10-inch skillet. When quite hot add the mushroom caps and sauté very quickly, for 5 to 7 minutes, shaking the pan frequently so the mushrooms move about and do not burn. Sprinkle with salt and pepper as they sauté.

¶Sautéed Mushrooms with Heavy Cream. Add ½ to ¾ cup heavy cream to the mushrooms and cook down slightly. Sprinkle with chopped parsley before serving.

¶Sautéed Mushrooms with Fresh Herbs and Cream. Add 2 tablespoons finely chopped fresh tarragon, some chopped chives, and ½ cup heavy cream to the mushrooms and let this cook down for a few minutes.

¶Sautéed Mushrooms with Sour Cream or Yogurt. Add ¼ cup chopped parsley and 2 to 3 tablespoons chopped fresh dill to the mushrooms. Remove the skillet from the heat and stir in 1 cup sour cream or yogurt. Return the pan to the heat and shake it as the sauce heats through. Do not allow sour cream or yogurt to come to a boil, or it will curdle.

¶Sautéed Mushrooms with Bacon Bits. Add ¼ cup chopped parsley, a dash or two of lemon juice, and ½ cup crisp bacon bits to the sautéed mushrooms, or sauté the mushrooms in bacon fat and garnish with fried bacon slices.

Cèpes à la Bordelaise

If you are a mushroom hunter or can obtain these delicious fall mushrooms, the *Boletus edulis*, this is the best way I know of preparing them. I like to serve them with chicken, squab, or game.

Makes 4 servings

1 pound fresh cèpes (wood mushrooms) *Salt, freshly ground black pepper*
8 to 10 tablespoons olive oil *Chopped parsley*
3 to 4 cloves garlic, finely chopped

Clean the cèpes well, separate caps from stems, and inspect carefully to make sure there are no worms residing inside. Slice the caps about ⅛ inch thick, and chop the stems rather coarsely. Use 2 skillets for cooking the cèpes. In the first skillet heat 4 to 5 tablespoons very fruity olive oil. Add the sliced caps and sauté very gently, turning them once or twice, until they turn rather brown and are crispy around the edges. Heat 4 to 5 tablespoons olive oil in the second skillet, add 3 or 4 finely chopped cloves garlic and the chopped mushroom stems. Sauté very quickly, shaking the pan as you do so to blend the mixture. Season with salt and freshly ground black pepper. When the stem pieces are cooked, combine them with the cooked caps and toss together well. Sprinkle with chopped parsley, taste, and correct the seasonings.

Okra

Okra, a vegetable that is enormously popular in the South and with Hispanic people, is the basis of many Southern and Creole dishes, notably gumbos. Usually it is deep-fried, steamed, rolled in cornmeal and sautéed or fried. Sometimes it is dipped in a batter and fried (see page 189). The rather slimy texture of okra offends some palates but delights others. Always buy young and tender okra—it should be very green and fresh-looking, not browned at the edges—and don't ever overcook it.

Steamed Okra

Makes 4 servings

Cook 1 pound okra in a small amount of boiling salted water for about 8 to 10 minutes, or until barely tender. Drain very well.

¶Okra with Butter and Lemon. Dress the cooked okra with a good amount of melted butter and a teaspoon or two of lemon juice.

¶Okra with Garlic and Oil. Dress the okra with a small amount of olive oil and some finely chopped garlic.

¶Okra with Garlic-Anchovy Butter. Serve the okra with butter which has been blended with mashed anchovies or anchovy paste and finely chopped garlic.

¶Okra Vinaigrette. Chill the okra well and serve with vinaigrette.

Okra and Corn

An old Southern dish with an interesting combination of vegetable flavors that is very good with pork dishes and with fried chicken.

Makes 6 servings

1 *large onion, finely chopped*
2 *garlic cloves, finely chopped*
6 *tablespoons butter*
1 *large green or red bell pepper,*
    skinned, seeded, and finely chopped
2 *cups Italian plum tomatoes*

6 to 8 *small okra, tops removed and*
    thinly sliced
Salt, freshly ground black pepper
    to taste
2 to 2½ *cups corn kernels, cut from*
    the cob

Sauté the onion and garlic in the butter and add the pepper. When they are just beginning to soften, add the tomatoes and simmer for 25 to 30 minutes, until well blended and smooth. Add the okra, seasonings, and corn and cook for 4 to 5 minutes more. Taste and correct the seasoning.

Onions

The onion family includes large sweet globe onions; sweet red Italian onions, which are ideal for salads; slim-bulbed white onions, both large and small, which are used mainly for cooking; and the ordinary, run-of-the-mill small brown onions, which are highly unpredictable—sometimes sweet and delicious, and sometimes almost uncompromisingly hot and disagreeable. For further details, see the Concordance, page 576. Then there are the green—or spring—onions, usually called "scallions" and sometimes "seed onions." They are usually served raw in plates of crudités or cut up in salads, but they can also be very good boiled or braised whole.

When peeling onions, it is best not to remove the root end completely, otherwise the onion might break apart and lose its shape. Brown onion skins, incidentally, can be used in soups and stocks for color and flavor. If you are not using all of a large onion in a recipe, wrap the unused part tightly in plastic wrap and refrigerate.

Boiled Onions

This is the most basic (and in my opinion the least interesting) of all onion preparations, but it lends itself to embellishment. If you use the small white onions, the easiest way to peel them is to cover them with boiling water and let them stand 3 to 4 minutes; the blanching loosens the skins.

Makes 4 servings

Cook 1 pound peeled onions whole or sliced in just enough salted water to cover. Tiny onions will take 15 to 20 minutes of cooking time, large ones will take 30 to 35 minutes, and sliced onions will take somewhat less time. Drain the onions very well.

¶**Buttered Onions.** Serve with butter and freshly ground black pepper.

¶**Buttered Onions with Nutmeg.** Add a small amount of nutmeg or mace to the buttered onions.

¶**Onions with Cream Sauce.** The traditional Thanksgiving way of serving onions is in a rich cream sauce, which I find is much improved by adding 1 or 2 finely chopped cloves garlic and a dash of nutmeg.

¶**Onions with Cheese Sauce.** Add shredded or grated Gruyère, Cheddar, or Monterey jack cheese to the cream sauce.

¶**Onions with Tomato Sauce.** Serve the onions with tomato sauce which has been well seasoned with freshly ground black pepper, skinned sautéed green or red peppers (see page 166), and finely chopped garlic.

Fried Onions

Makes 4 to 6 servings

6 tablespoons butter or good beef
    drippings

3 to 4 large onions, sliced very thin
Salt, freshly ground black pepper

Melt the butter or, if possible, beef drippings, which give an extraordinarily good flavor, in a heavy skillet. Add the onions and cook over rather brisk heat until they begin to color, turning them often with a spatula. Reduce the heat and let them cook down, tossing them well, until almost caramelized (sprinkling with a teaspoon or two of granulated sugar will aid in coloring and glazing the onions). Sprinkle with salt and pepper, and serve on steak, hamburgers, or other meat dishes, or just enjoy them as they are.

¶**Caramelized Onions.** Let the onions cook until completely caramelized and sort of crispy. Use as a garnish for various meats, such as steak, broiled liver, or pork chops.

¶**Dieter's Onions.** Brown the sliced onions very carefully in a heavy skillet over low heat without any fat. Turn them often and watch to make sure they don't burn. They will soften and turn color very nicely. You can also add them to dishes prepared without fat.

Broiled Onion Slices

These make a delicious garnish for hamburgers, steaks, and chops. They do not become as softly tender as boiled onions, but retain a pleasing crispness.

Makes 4 to 6 servings

Slice 1 to 1½ pounds large onions ⅜ to ½ inch thick. Place on the rack of a broiling pan, brush well with melted butter, and season with salt and freshly ground black pepper. Broil until they turn a rather delicate brown. Be careful that they don't burn, and brush with more butter, if necessary. When cooked on one side, turn the slices with a spatula, brush with melted butter, sprinkle with salt and freshly ground black pepper, and broil until delicately colored.

¶Broiled Onions with Hamburgers. Place a broiled hamburger on top of each slice of broiled onion.

¶Broiled Onions with Cheese. Heap shredded Gruyère or Cheddar cheese onto the broiled slices. Return to the oven just long enough to melt the cheese. Serve at once.

Braised Onions

Makes 4 servings

6 to 8 tablespoons butter or oil, or a
   combination of the two
20 small white onions or onion slices

½ cup chicken or beef stock
Salt, freshly grated black pepper

Heat the fat in a heavy skillet or sauté pan with a lid, and sauté the onions until lightly browned. Add the stock and salt and pepper to taste, cover the pan, and cook the onions until crisp-tender—about 20 to 30 minutes for small white onions, and somewhat less for slices.

¶Braised Onions with Parmesan Cheese. Just before serving, sprinkle the onions liberally with freshly grated Parmesan cheese.

¶Braised Onions with Pasta. Use these braised onions as a sauce for pasta, and sprinkle with Parmesan cheese.

¶Braised Onions with Sherry, Bourbon, or Madeira. Add ¼ cup medium-dry sherry, bourbon, or Madeira to cooked onions and let liquid cook down very quickly for about 3 to 5 minutes. These go well with game, turkey, chicken, or veal.

Boiled Green Onions, or Scallions
Makes 4 to 6 servings

Trim 5 to 8 bunches of green onions, or scallions, and cook in boiling, salted water to cover until crisply tender, about 8 to 10 minutes. With a slotted spoon or pancake turner lift the onions very carefully to a serving platter, making sure they are well drained. Serve with melted butter, salt, and freshly ground black pepper.

¶**Boiled Green Onions with Hollandaise Sauce.** Serve, like asparagus, with hollandaise sauce (see page 532).

¶**Boiled Green Onions with Mornay Sauce.** Serve the onions with a rich cream sauce (see page 531) enhanced with grated Gruyère or Cheddar cheese.

Stuffed Onions

With a baked potato these make a delicious luncheon or supper.

Makes 6 servings

6 medium-large onions
1 to 1½ pounds well-seasoned sausage
    meat

2 tablespoons bread crumbs
8 to 9 slices bacon

Cook the onions in boiling salted water until they are tender but not so soft they collapse. Run cold water over them. When cool enough to handle, remove the center rings, leaving a cup in each onion. Stuff the onions with the sausage meat and sprinkle with a few bread crumbs. Place the bacon slices on the bottom of a baking dish and arrange the stuffed onions on top. Bake in a 375° oven for 25 to 30 minutes until the sausage meat is just cooked through. Do not overcook.

Parsnips

For the life of me, I cannot understand why so many people dislike parsnips, which are one of our most delicious winter vegetables, if properly treated. They have a sweetness that is particularly suited to sautéing and glazing, and they make a most delectable purée. There is a good deal of waste on parsnips, because the cores tend to be quite woody. Look for those that are fat around the top, not the long skinny ones, and count on about 2½ to 3 pounds parsnips for 4 servings. They aren't the easiest of vegetables to peel, either, so if I am boiling or blanching them I cook them in the skins and peel them afterward.

Sautéed Parsnips

Makes 4 servings

2½ to 3 pounds parsnips, unpeeled   6 to 8 tablespoons butter
Salt, freshly ground black pepper

Cook the parsnips in a good amount of boiling salted water for from 20 to 45 minutes, depending on the age and size of the vegetables. They are done when easily pierceable with a skewer or the point of a small knife. Plunge the cooked parsnips into cold water and, when cool enough to handle, peel, discarding the tough ends. Slice the parsnips very thin, sauté in butter, 5 to 6 minutes, and season to taste with salt and freshly ground black pepper.

¶Glazed Parsnips. While the parsnips are sautéing, sprinkle lightly with a small amount of granulated sugar and let them glaze. Serve at once.

Steamed Parsnips

Steam parsnips until tender in a small amount of boiling salted water, peel, and slice in julienne strips. Dress with butter and season to taste with salt and freshly ground black pepper.

Puréed Parsnips

One of my favorite ways with parsnips is to purée them with Madeira and serve with turkey, pork, or beef.

Makes 6 to 8 servings

3 pounds parsnips, cooked
1 teaspoon salt
1 teaspoon sugar
½ to ¾ cup butter, melted
3 to 4 tablespoons heavy cream

¼ cup Madeira, or to taste
Additional butter
2 tablespoons bread crumbs or finely
    chopped nuts (for topping)

Peel cooked parsnips and purée them in a food processor or by putting them through a food mill. Combine the purée with the salt, sugar, melted butter, cream, and Madeira, and whip together well with a spatula or whisk. Spoon the purée into a 1-quart baking dish, dot with butter, and sprinkle with the crumbs or chopped nuts. Bake in a 350° oven for 20 to 30 minutes.

¶**Parsnip Patties.** Form above mixture into small patties, roll lightly in flour, and sauté in 4 to 6 tablespoons butter, turning once, until browned nicely on both sides.

¶**Puréed Parsnips and Potatoes.** Combine puréed parsnips with an equal amount of puréed potatoes and prepare in either of the above fashions.

French-Fried Parsnips

Makes 4 servings

8 cooked parsnips, cut into fingers
    2 inches by ¼ inch
All-purpose flour

2 eggs, lightly beaten
Fresh bread crumbs
Peanut or vegetable oil for frying

Dip the parsnip fingers in flour, then in beaten egg, and roll in fresh bread crumbs. Fry in deep hot oil (380°) for 3 to 5 minutes. Drain on absorbent paper. Serve at once.

Peas

We have become so used to the frozen pea that the idea of buying fresh garden peas and shelling them has become almost forgotten. However, in summer you will find in various sections of the country locally grown and freshly picked peas that are in the markets for a short season. Make the most of them. When you're buying them, be sure to snitch a couple, open the pods and bite into a pea to check on their juiciness and sweetness before you buy. Sometimes they may look okay, but the peas inside the pod are overage and starchy.

It takes 3 to 4 pounds of peas in the pod, depending on size, to yield enough for 4 persons. Fresh garden peas should be shelled just before cooking and never washed. While a little sugar will enhance their flavor, I find it is best not to salt them until after cooking. Fresh peas, cooked until just crisply tender, make a delicious salad (see page 83), as do raw peas, if they are really young and tender.

In the last couple of years a new variety of pea has appeared, called the sugar snap, an edible-pod type of great flavor and distinction. It is different from the flat Chinese snow pea because the peas are fully formed inside the sweet, crunchy, edible pod. All you have to do is remove the stem end and little strings, and then eat the whole thing, either raw or cooked very simply—blanched and tossed with butter or sautéed or stir-fried until the shells just turn green.

Boiled Peas

Makes 4 servings

3 to 4 pounds peas in the pod　　　　　*Butter*
1 teaspoon sugar　　　　　　　　　　　*Salt, freshly ground black pepper*

Shell the peas just before they are to be cooked. Cook them gently in a small amount of unsalted boiling water with the sugar for about 10 to 15 minutes, according to size, or until just tender. Drain well and toss in the pan with an ample amount of butter, salt, and freshly ground black pepper.

¶**Buttered Peas with Herbs.** Sprinkle the buttered peas with fresh chopped parsley, tarragon, or mint.

¶**Buttered Peas with Mushrooms.** Combine the buttered peas with an equal quantity of sautéed sliced mushrooms and 1 tablespoon chopped fresh tarragon.

¶**Buttered Peas with Green Onions.** Thinly slice green onions, or scallions, heat through in a little butter, and toss with the peas.

¶**Buttered Peas with Tiny Pearl Onions.** The tiny pickling onions are hard to get these days. If you can find them, parboil them in salted boiling water, then cook with the peas.

¶**Puréed Peas.** Boil the peas until tender, then purée in a food mill, using the fine blade, or a food processor. For a finer texture, force the puréed peas through a tamis or a very fine sieve. Mix with 4 to 6 tablespoons butter, salt and freshly ground black pepper to taste, and, if you like, 1 or 2 tablespoons heavy cream.

Peas with Heavy Cream

Makes 4 servings

3 to 4 pounds peas in the pod   *1 cup heavy cream (approximately)*
6 tablespoons butter   *Salt, freshly ground black pepper*

Shell the peas. Melt the butter in a heavy saucepan and add the peas. Cover with heavy cream and cook gently until the peas are tender, 6 to 8 minutes. Just before serving, add salt and freshly ground black pepper to taste.

¶**Peas with Cream and Herbs.** Add finely chopped parsley or a little chopped mint, or both, to the preceding if you wish.

Peppers

In my kitchen, no pepper is used until it has first been peeled. If the peppers are to be stuffed, I may decide just to blanch them in boiling water to retain the shape, but that is the only time I make an exception. I consider the flavor of the peeled pepper more distinguished and delicious, and the vegetable lies more gently on the stomach when there is no tough skin to digest.

There are always plenty of green bell peppers in the markets, more of the red than formerly, and occasionally some yellow peppers, but not often. Red and yellow peppers are much more decorative to serve than green and have a richer flavor, but green will suffice if there is nothing else. If you can stand the heat, hot peppers can be treated in the same ways as sweet bell peppers.

To Roast and Peel Peppers

If you have a gas range, impale the pepper on a fork and turn over the flame until the skin blisters and pops. Or put on a pan under the broiler, and broil, turning the peppers frequently, until the skins turn black. After that the peeling process is easy. Let the peppers cool slightly, then pinch and pull the skin away with your fingers, using the point of a knife on stubborn spots. Sometimes it helps to put the peppers in a paper bag or wrap them in damp paper towels before peeling, as the steam they give off helps to loosen the skins. Remove the seeds after the pepper has been peeled and, unless you are going to stuff them, cut the peppers in half.

Peppers Sautéed in Olive Oil

A nice change of pace with pork, veal, or chicken dishes.

Makes 4 servings

4 large or 8 small peppers, peeled, seeded, and cut in ½-inch strips
4 to 5 tablespoons olive oil
2 cloves garlic, finely chopped
Salt, freshly ground black pepper

1 to 2 tablespoons shredded fresh basil leaves
1 tablespoon wine vinegar, or more to taste
Grated Parmesan cheese

Sauté pepper strips a few minutes in olive oil with the chopped garlic and salt and freshly ground black pepper to taste. Add the shredded basil and vinegar and mix thoroughly. Sprinkle lightly with grated Parmesan cheese.

¶**Sautéed Peppers with Braised Beef.** Omit the Parmesan cheese and vinegar and add the sautéed peppers to the sauce for a braised beef or beef stew.

¶**Sautéed Peppers with Roast Chicken.** Double the recipe and smother a good-sized roast chicken with the sautéed peppers.

¶**Sautéed Peppers with Onion Rings.** Combine the sautéed peppers with an equal quantity of sautéed onion rings and serve with steak or hamburgers.

¶**Sautéed Peppers with Pasta.** Add an extra clove garlic, finely chopped, and a good amount of fresh basil, cut into thin strips, as you sauté the peppers. Use as a sauce for 1 pound pasta, cooked to your taste and thoroughly drained. Serve with freshly grated Parmesan or Romano cheese.

Peppers Sautéed in Butter

Makes 4 servings

4 large or 8 small peppers, peeled,   *Salt, freshly ground black pepper*
* seeded, and cut in ½-inch strips*   *2 teaspoons lemon or lime juice*
4 tablespoons butter

Very gently sauté the peppers in the butter until just heated through. Season to taste with salt and freshly ground black pepper and add the lemon or lime juice.

¶**Sautéed Peppers with Pork Chops.** Heap the sautéed pepper slices on 4 grilled pork chops.

¶**Sautéed Peppers with Corn Kernels.** Combine the sautéed peppers with 2 to 2½ cups cooked corn kernels, freshly cut from the cob. Omit the lemon or lime juice, add 4 tablespoons extra butter and an additional grind or two of black pepper, and heat thoroughly.

¶**Sautéed Peppers with Italian Sausages.** Cook the pepper slices with 1 or 2 finely chopped cloves garlic and combine with 4 to 8 Italian sausages (depending on size), briefly poached in water and then broiled until delicately browned. Heat through and serve at once, or use the pepper-sausage mixture as a sauce for your favorite pasta, and serve with freshly grated Parmesan cheese.

Peppers Vinaigrette

Makes 6 to 8 servings

6 to 8 large peeled red, yellow, or   *1 to 2 tablespoons sherry wine vinegar,*
* green peppers, or a combination*   * or other wine vinegar*
3 to 4 tablespoons olive oil   *Salt to taste*
1 to 2 cloves garlic, finely chopped

Cut the peeled peppers into ½-inch strips. Combine the oil, garlic, and vinegar, and pour over the pepper strips. These may be served warm or cold and will hold in the refrigerator, covered, for several days.

¶**Peppers Vinaigrette with Mint.** Add to the vinaigrette mixture 1 table-spoon or more finely chopped fresh mint or parsley.

¶**Peppers Vinaigrette with Anchovies.** Serve the peppers flanked with anchovy fillets.

¶**Peppers Vinaigrette with Mozzarella and Tomatoes.** Top slices of mozzarella cheese with sliced tomatoes, strips of pepper vinaigrette, and anchovy fillets.

Stuffed Peppers

Stuffed peppers are a great American tradition. Blanch or peel them, then stuff with various savory mixtures or leftover chopped meat, and bake with a little broth.

Makes 8 servings

8 *rather small peppers*　　　　　　　*1 cup stock*
2 *pounds well-seasoned sausage meat*

Remove the tops, seeds, and membranes from the peppers and blanch them for 3 to 4 minutes. Drain the peppers well and make a few small holes in the bottom of each with the point of a small knife. Stuff the peppers with the sausage meat. Arrange in a baking dish, add the stock, and bake for about 25 to 30 minutes in a 375° oven. Serve the stuffed peppers with scrambled eggs, poached eggs on toast, or shirred eggs (see page 251).

¶**Peppers Stuffed with Leftover Meat.** Instead of sausage meat, use cooked chopped beef, pork, or chicken mixed with finely chopped onion, garlic, and bread crumbs and highly seasoned.

¶**Peppers Stuffed with Corn Kernels.** Fill the peppers with whole-kernel corn, add a dab or two of butter and a spoonful of heavy cream and bake for 15 to 20 minutes. Buttered crumbs may be placed on top if you like.

Potatoes

Buy your potatoes according to the way you are going to use them. The waxy types, such as California long whites and new potatoes, are best for boiling and slicing, for potato salads (see pages 93–96), hash browns (see page 170), and the various hashes. I like to cook the small round new potatoes whole, either boiled, steamed, or quickly baked in their jackets in a 425° oven for 20 to 30 minutes. They can also be cut into chunks with the skin on and deep-fried (see *Theory & Practice*, page 230).

Our greatest baking potato, of course, is the brown-skinned Idaho, which is grown in soil with a high lava content like the soil in Peru, where potatoes originated.

Baked Potatoes

Allow 1 potato per serving, or half a potato if they are extra large. Scrub them well and prick the skins a little to allow an escape route for the steam so the potato doesn't burst. Place on the rack of a preheated 425° oven and bake for about 1 to 1½ hours, or until soft to the touch when squeezed. Split and serve at once.

I so love the earthy flavor of good baked potatoes that I put nothing on them but coarsely ground black pepper, but others may prefer them with salt, pepper, and a good dollop of butter. The standard recipe of sour cream and chives is not something I am particularly fond of, as I feel it detracts from the flavor.

¶**Baked Potatoes with Yogurt.** Split the potato, add a dollop of yogurt and freshly ground black pepper.

¶**Baked Potatoes with Beef Drippings.** If you are serving the potato with roast beef or a broiled steak, moisten it with a little of the tasty pan drippings, and season with salt and pepper.

Disgustingly Rich Potatoes

I gleaned from Mildred Knopf a great idea for using the skins of baked potatoes after the pulp has been scooped out for this dish and serving them with cocktails. See Twice-Baked Potato Skins (page 38).

Makes 6 servings

6 large Idaho potatoes	1 cup heavy cream
¾ cup butter	4 tablespoons butter
2 teaspoons salt	Gruyère or Cheddar cheese, shredded
1 teaspoon freshly ground black pepper	

Bake the potatoes until soft, split lengthwise and scoop the pulp into a mixing bowl, scraping the shells well. Add the ¾ cup butter, salt, pepper, and cream, mix lightly, and transfer to a flat baking dish. Dot with the 4 tablespoons butter and sprinkle with shredded cheese. Bake in a 375° oven for 15 minutes.

Gratin of Potatoes

Makes 6 servings

2 pounds Idaho potatoes, peeled and
    cut in ¼-inch slices
¾ pound Gruyère cheese, cut in tiny
    cubes
2 eggs

2 cups milk
1 teaspoon salt
½ teaspoon freshly ground black pepper
⅛ teaspoon freshly ground nutmeg

Arrange in a well-buttered baking dish layers of potato slices alternating with cubes of cheese. Beat the eggs, milk, salt, pepper, and nutmeg and pour over the potatoes. Bake in a 350° oven for 1¼ to 1½ hours, or until liquid is absorbed and potatoes soft.

Mashed Potatoes

This most basic of American methods of serving potatoes can be turned into something as elegant as Duchesse Potatoes.

Makes 6 servings

8 medium potatoes
¾ stick (6 tablespoons) butter
Salt to taste

½ cup heavy cream, heated
Freshly ground black pepper

Peel the potatoes and boil until they are tender. Drain well, return to the pan, and toss them quickly over moderate heat to dry them. Mash the potatoes with a masher, add the butter and salt, and mash again. Add the hot cream, and whip the potatoes with a spatula or a whisk until they are light and fluffy. Place the potatoes in a heated serving dish with an extra pat of butter in the center, and dust them with freshly ground black pepper. If the potatoes are exceptionally dry, you may add more cream.

¶Mashed Potatoes with Parsley or Chives. Whip in a little chopped parsley or chopped chives, or both.

¶**Mashed Potatoes and Yellow Turnips.** Whip together equal quantities of whipped potatoes and yellow turnips that have been mashed with butter.

¶**Duchesse Potatoes.** After adding the cream, add 2 or 3 egg yolks and whip potatoes vigorously. This mixture is usually forced through a pastry bag with a rosette tube to form small medallions on a buttered baking sheet, or to make a border on a planked dish. Brown the medallions lightly in a 375° oven before serving.

German Fried Potatoes

Makes 4 servings

4 to 6 medium-sized firm, waxy potatoes   *Salt, freshly ground black pepper*
5 tablespoons butter   *to taste*

Peel the potatoes and slice ⅛ inch thick. Heat the butter in a large skillet, add the potato slices, and sauté over fairly intense heat until crisp and brown, turning them often with a spatula and seasoning them as they cook with salt and pepper.

Hash Brown Potatoes

For this use the best boiling potatoes you can find. They should be firm and waxy. New potatoes or medium-size potatoes that are not too floury are good. Once cooked, they need not be fried right away; they can be left overnight.

Makes 6 servings

6 to 8 potatoes   *Salt, freshly ground black pepper*
8 tablespoons butter

Boil the potatoes in their skins in a small amount of salted water, covered, until just barely pierceable—for hash browns it is better if they are not completely cooked. Drain, peel, and chop fairly coarse. Melt 6 tablespoons butter in a black iron or Teflon-lined skillet (you may add a tablespoon of oil if you like). When hot, add potatoes and press down well. Cook over fairly brisk heat until a brown crust forms on the bottom. Invert the pan onto a plate and slide out the potato cake. Return pan to heat, add rest of butter to pan, slide potatoes back, unbrowned side down, and brown the second side. Salt and pepper on both sides during cooking. Slide the potatoes out onto a hot plate and serve at once.

¶**Roesti.** Boil potatoes for about 10 minutes, or until they are half cooked. Peel and shred. Cook as for hash brown potatoes, pressing the shreds into a cake with a spatula.

Potatoes Sautéed in Beef Suet

The rich flavor that the beef suet and the crisp cracklings impart to the potatoes makes them taste like poor man's steak.

Makes 4 servings

3 tablespoons rendered beef suet with   Salt, freshly ground black pepper
    cracklings
4 medium potatoes, boiled, peeled, and
    sliced about ¼ inch thick

When rendering the beef suet in the skillet, leave the crisp cracklings in the pan. Add the potatoes to the hot fat and sauté in batches over medium-high heat until nicely browned and crisp around the edges, sprinkling them with salt and pepper as they cook.

Salsify

At one time there was a great vogue for salsify, sometimes called oyster plant because people believed it had a flavor reminiscent of oysters (vegetarians even made mock-oyster soup with salsify), although I have never been able to detect any similarity. It then dropped into virtual oblivion and is now hard to find and correspondingly expensive. This long skinny root, rather like a parsnip, varies in color from light brown to very dark. Before cooking, scrape the roots, remove any little tendrils, and toss the salsify into a bowl of cold acidulated water, to prevent its discoloring, until ready to cook.

Boiled Salsify

Makes 4 servings

2 to 3 pounds salsify, whole or cut in   Salt, freshly ground black pepper
    3-inch lengths   Chopped parsley
6 to 8 tablespoons butter

Cook the salsify in boiling salted water until just tender—about 15 minutes. Remove from the heat, drain well, and serve with butter, salt and pepper to taste, and chopped fresh parsley.

¶**Salsify with Mornay Sauce.** Arrange the cooked salsify in a baking dish, cover with a rich mornay sauce (page 531), sprinkle with buttered crumbs and freshly grated Parmesan cheese, and heat in a 350° oven for about 20 minutes, or until bubbling hot.

¶**Sautéed Salsify.** Melt 6 to 8 tablespoons butter in a heavy skillet, add the cooked, well-drained salsify, and cook over moderate heat, shaking the pan often, until delicately browned. Sprinkle with salt, pepper, and 2 tablespoons chopped fresh parsley.

¶**Salsify with Shallots and Lemon.** Sauté ½ cup finely chopped shallots in the butter before the final sautéing of the salsify. Just before serving, add about 2 teaspoons lemon juice and shake the pan well.

Spinach

Spinach is certainly one of our most versatile vegetables. Delicious by itself, either as leaf spinach, chopped, or as a purée, it also combines magnificently well with various other foods, notably with fish, eggs, and cheese, and in the south of France it emerges as a dessert, combined with sugar, a custardy sauce, and apricots. I am happy to think that the days are over when children loathed spinach because they were forced to eat something that was supposedly good for them.

Wilted Spinach

Makes 4 servings

2 pounds fresh spinach   *Salt, freshly ground black pepper*
⅓ cup melted butter   *A little lemon juice or vinegar*

Wash the spinach extremely well, drain it, and transfer it to a heavy pot, with no water other than that which clings to the leaves. Let it wilt, covered, over medium to high heat, making sure to toss it once or twice during the wilting process. This should take just minutes. When wilted, drain at once, and if you are serving it *en branche* toss it with butter, salt and pepper to taste, and lemon juice or vinegar.

¶**Spinach with Nutmeg.** Toss the cooked spinach with melted butter and finely ground nutmeg to taste.

¶**Spinach with Garlic and Oil.** While the spinach is cooking, sauté 2 to 3 finely chopped cloves garlic in 4 tablespoons olive oil. Season spinach with salt and freshly ground black pepper to taste, and toss well with the garlic and oil to blend the flavors. Add a touch of vinegar, if you wish.

¶**Spinach with Hard-Boiled Egg.** Toss the wilted spinach with 4 to 5 tablespoons olive oil and a touch of nutmeg. Transfer to a serving dish and garnish with 1 or 2 hard-boiled eggs, quartered or coarsely chopped.

¶**Puréed Spinach.** Drain the wilted spinach extremely well. Purée in a food processor or chop it extremely fine by hand and add 4 to 6 tablespoons melted butter, 2 tablespoons heavy cream, and a dash of nutmeg. Blend very well. Serve topped with buttered crumbs.

Tossed Spinach

Makes 4 servings

2 pounds fresh spinach
6 tablespoons olive oil
1 teaspoon freshly ground black pepper

2 or 3 finely chopped shallots
3 tablespoons soy sauce

Wash and dry the spinach thoroughly. Heat the olive oil in a very large skillet or sauté pan over medium heat. Add the pepper, shallots, soy sauce, and spinach. With a wooden fork and spoon toss the spinach as if you were tossing a salad. Be patient and keep tossing. Eat as soon as it is wilted.

¶**Spinach with Almonds and Garlic.** Substitute garlic cloves for the shallots, add about ½ cup coarsely chopped toasted almonds while you toss the spinach, and finish it off with a good dash of Tabasco.

¶**Spinach with Bacon Bits.** Toss the spinach with shallots and soy, as above, and just before serving add a good ½ cup crisp bacon bits.

¶**Spinach with Tomatoes.** Sauté ⅔ cup chopped onion in 6 tablespoons olive oil. Add the uncooked spinach; 3 tomatoes, peeled, seeded, and chopped; and a dash of nutmeg. Cook until the spinach is just wilted, tossing well. Just before serving add ½ cup finely grated Parmesan cheese.

Summer Squash

Summer squash have become much more a part of our vegetable lives since we have learned that they should be cooked fast so they don't disintegrate to an unappetizing mushiness. Look for the youngest, smallest, and firmest squash you can find and don't on any account peel them. My favorite method of cooking zucchini, the little yellow straightnecks and crooknecks, and the tiny pattypans or scalloped squash is to steam them briefly and serve them with plenty of butter, or to slice and sauté them.

Steamed Summer Squash

Makes 6 servings

1½ pounds summer squash
6 to 7 tablespoons melted butter

Salt, freshly ground black pepper
Lemon juice

Trim off ends of squash and leave whole, if they are really small. Otherwise, cut into 1-inch pieces. Cook in a small amount of boiling salted water in a heavy saucepan until just crisply tender, about 8 minutes. Dress with melted butter, salt and pepper to taste, and a dash of lemon juice.

¶**Summer Squash with Oil, Herbs, and Garlic.** Toss the cooked squash with 6 tablespoons olive oil, 2 or 3 finely chopped garlic cloves, 1 tablespoon finely chopped parsley, and 1 tablespoon finely chopped dill (if available). Serve at once.

Sautéed Summer Squash

Makes 6 servings

1½ pounds summer squash
6 tablespoons butter or olive oil or a
*   combination of the two*
4 or 5 green onions, or scallions,
*   finely chopped*

Salt, freshly ground black pepper
2 tablespoons chopped parsley
Lemon juice

Trim the squash and slice thin or cut in long fingers (for zucchini or crooknecks). Heat the fat in a heavy skillet and sauté the green onions until just translucent. Add the squash and sauté very quickly, tossing well, and seasoning with salt and pepper to taste. Just before serving, add the parsley and a dash of lemon juice.

Sautéed Zucchini

Makes 6 servings

1½ pounds small, firm zucchini
6 tablespoons butter or olive oil or a
    combination of the two

Salt, freshly ground black pepper

Trim ends from the zucchini and slice coin-thin (the food processor slicing attachment is good for this). Heat the butter or oil in a heavy skillet, add the zucchini and sauté for 4 to 5 minutes over medium to high heat, tossing well. Season with salt and pepper to taste as they cook. Serve at once.

¶Zucchini Sautéed with Garlic and Herbs. Add 2 or 3 finely chopped garlic cloves when sautéing the zucchini. Just before serving add 2 tablespoons chopped parsley and 1 tablespoon chopped fresh basil.

¶Zucchini Sautéed with Shallots. Sauté ½ cup finely chopped shallots in the butter or oil until just translucent, then add the zucchini. Season with salt and pepper to taste.

¶Zucchini Sautéed with Walnuts. Add ½ cup shelled, coarsely chopped walnuts to the zucchini and sauté as before, shaking the pan until the zucchini is crisply tender and the walnuts heated through. Serve garnished with 2 tablespoons finely chopped parsley and a few more walnuts.

Shredded Zucchini

Makes 6 servings

6 to 7 small, firm zucchini
6 tablespoons butter

Salt, freshly ground black pepper
1 to 2 tablespoons chopped parsley

Trim the zucchini and shred, either on a grater by hand or with the shredding attachment of the food processor. Put shreds in a heavy dish towel, bring ends together and twist towel, squeezing the shreds to remove all the excess liquid. Melt the butter in a heavy skillet. When hot, add the zucchini and toss very quickly until the shreds are just crisply tender and delicately browned. Season with salt and pepper and sprinkle with parsley.

¶Zucchini Pancake. Heat 4 tablespoons butter or olive oil or a combination of the two in a very heavy skillet. Add the shredded zucchini and press down into a flat cake with a spatula. Sprinkle with salt and freshly ground black pepper. Shake the pan gently so the cake does not stick.

When brown on underside, invert a plate over the pan and turn out the zucchini cake. Add 2 tablespoons more butter to skillet, and when hot, slip zucchini cake back into pan, uncooked side down, and cook until crisp and brown. Slide onto a plate and serve cut in wedges.

¶**Zucchini Pancake with Cheese.** This slightly different version of the zucchini pancake is mixed with eggs and cheese. Cook the shredded zucchini and 1 or 2 finely chopped garlic cloves in 2 tablespoons butter and 2 tablespoons olive oil, tossing well, until lightly browned. Remove to a bowl and mix with 1 egg and ½ cup grated Parmesan cheese. Reheat the pan, add more butter and oil if needed, return zucchini to pan and press down into a flat cake. Brown on one side, then either flip the cake over as you would a flapjack or, if you are not that dextrous, invert onto a plate, slide back into pan, uncooked side down, and cook until brown and crisp.

Zucchini Blossoms

The flowers of the zucchini are absolutely delicious deep-fried or sautéed. If you are gathering them from your own garden, pick only the male blossoms that grow on thin stems (the females have a small zucchini forming at the base of the flower) or you'll have no zucchini crop. Zucchini blossoms can be found in Italian markets in summer, sold in bunches.

Deep-Fried Zucchini Blossoms

Allow 6 blossoms per serving. Gently wash and dry the blossoms, trim off stalks, and dip in beer batter (see page 188). Deep fry in 360° oil until crisply brown, about 4 to 5 minutes, drain on absorbent paper, sprinkle with salt and freshly ground black pepper.

¶**Zucchini Blossom Omelet.** Use the deep-fried blossoms as an omelet filling, adding 2 or 3 tablespoons grated Parmesan cheese.

¶**Zucchini Blossoms with Scrambled Eggs.** Incorporate the sautéed blossoms into the eggs about midway in the cooking, allowing 2 blossoms per serving.

¶Cheese Soufflé with Zucchini Blossoms. Incorporate the sautéed blossoms into the sauce base for a Parmesan cheese soufflé, before mixing with the egg whites.

Winter Squash

The most common of the so-called winter squashes, some of which are no longer confined to the winter months but in markets for most of the year, are the acorn, butternut, banana, turban, and Hubbard. In the fall, you can usually buy the huge Hubbards and the banana squash cut in pieces with the hard skin left on, ready to cook. Acorn, turban, and butternut are sold whole, though some markets peel the butternut and sell it in plastic bags. I find it keeps better in the skin. A new type of hard-shell squash that has become very popular with dieters who long for a pasta substitute is spaghetti squash, the stringy inside of which is like strands of spaghetti. If you grow this squash in your garden, it may be picked when small and immature and treated like summer squash.

Boiled Spaghetti Squash

Boil the whole hard-shell squash in water to cover for 20 to 30 minutes, according to size, then split, drain, and remove the seeds. With a fork, scrape out the spaghetti-like strands of the flesh and serve with any light, delicate pasta sauce (see pages 279–285).

Spiced Winter Squash

Makes 4 servings

2 pounds Hubbard, banana, or butternut
    squash, cut in pieces, seeds removed
6 tablespoons butter

1 teaspoon salt, or to taste
½ teaspoon allspice
½ teaspoon mace

Put the squash on a rack or in a steam basket over simmering water and steam until the flesh is just tender, which will depend on the size and age of the squash. Do not overcook. Scrape the pulp from the shell and beat well with a fork or whisk, adding the butter, salt, and spices, until light and fluffy. Serve in a heated dish dotted with more butter.

¶**Winter Squash with Black Walnuts.** Omit spices. Add ½ cup coarsely chopped black walnuts to the purée. Season with salt and freshly ground black pepper.

¶**Winter Squash with Pecans and Ginger.** Beat the steamed squash with the butter and add ½ cup chopped pecans, ¼ cup finely chopped candied ginger, and ⅓ cup dry sherry. Put in a deep 9-inch baking dish, dot with butter, and bake in a 350° oven until butter is melted and squash hot.

¶**Winter Squash with Peanuts.** Use ½ cup coarsely chopped salted peanuts instead of black walnuts.

¶**Puréed Winter Squash with Raw Zucchini.** Omit spices. Mix ½ cup shredded raw zucchini into the hot purée for a lovely color, flavor, and texture contrast. Season with salt and freshly ground black pepper.

Winter Squash Soufflé

Makes 6 servings

1½ cups puréed steamed winter squash   6 tablespoons butter
1 teaspoon salt   5 egg yolks
½ teaspoon freshly ground black pepper   7 egg whites
½ teaspoon nutmeg

Combine squash with the seasonings and butter and beat lightly. Mix in the egg yolks, one at a time, beating well after each addition. Beat the egg whites until stiff but not dry. Fold one-quarter of the whites into the purée, incorporating thoroughly. Lightly fold in the remaining whites. Pour mixture into a well-buttered 1½-quart soufflé dish, stand dish in a roasting pan half filled with hot water, and place on top of the stove over medium heat for 5 minutes. (This will help to stabilize the soufflé and quicken the rising process.) Preheat the oven to 375°. Remove dish from the water to the oven and bake for 25 to 30 minutes.

Baked Hubbard Squash

Because of the hard, thick skin, Hubbard squash is impossible to peel and practically has to be chopped into pieces with a hatchet; fortunately markets sell the squash cut up and ready for steaming or baking. There is something particularly appetizing about having a big square of the crinkly-skinned, orange-fleshed Hubbard, adrip with butter and delicately brown around the edges, on a plate with roast pork, chicken or turkey, or corned beef. Use one 4- to 5-inch square of Hubbard squash per person. Spread with 2 tablespoons of soft butter and sprinkle generously with salt and pepper. Place the squash in a baking pan and bake in a 350° oven for 45 to 60 minutes, or until tender.

¶**Baked Hubbard Squash with Bacon.** Place a slice or two of bacon on the squash instead of spreading with the butter.

¶**Baked Hubbard Squash with Brown Sugar.** Prepare as for Baked Hubbard Squash, and sprinkle the squash lightly with brown sugar.

Baked Butternut Squash

While butternut is delicious peeled, cubed, steamed, and mashed with salt, pepper, and either butter, sour cream, or yogurt, or treated like Spiced Winter Squash, the hard but thin skin becomes completely soft and edible when baked. Try it this way sometime. The squash retains more flavor, stays firm, and is highly economical, as you can eat it all.

Makes 4 servings

2 small butternut squash
Unsalted butter
2 small white onions, finely sliced or
   chopped
Salt, freshly ground black pepper or
   aromatic pepper (see note)

2 tablespoons butter mixed with
   1 teaspoon chopped parsley and
   chives or parsley and dill, or
   2 tablespoons green peppercorn
   butter (see page 318)

Wash squash and cut in half lengthwise, removing strings and seeds. Slice in long strips about ½ inch thick, skin and all. Well butter a large glass casserole or baking dish (you can use other flavorful fats instead of the butter, such as goose or duck fat) and scatter the onion over the bottom. Arrange squash on onion, skin side down, sprinkle with salt and pepper or aromatic pepper, and dot with the herb or green peppercorn butter, cut in small pieces. Cover casserole with aluminum foil and bake in a 400° oven for 40 minutes, or until squash and skin are soft enough to eat, but not mushy. Remove foil once or twice during baking and brush surface of squash with the melted butter.

NOTE: To make aromatic pepper, grind a mixture of 3 parts black peppercorns, 2 parts white peppercorns, and 1 part allspice berries.

Baked Acorn or Turban Squash

Makes 6 servings

3 good-sized acorn or turban squash   Salt, freshly ground black pepper
6 tablespoons unsalted butter

Split the squash crosswise, remove seeds and strings, fill cavities with a tablespoon of butter, add salt and pepper. Bake in a 350° oven until tender, about 45 to 50 minutes.

¶Acorn or Turban Squash with Bacon and Garlic. Omit butter. Put 1 slice of bacon, cut in pieces, and just a touch of finely chopped garlic in each cavity, season, and bake until squash is tender and bacon crisp.

¶Acorn or Turban Squash with Maple Sugar and Bacon. Sprinkle the cavity with 1 teaspoon maple sugar before adding the bacon. Omit garlic.

Tomatoes

When tomatoes are perfect, ripe and luscious, they are perhaps the most admirable of all our vegetable-fruits. Unfortunately, it's hard to find them that way. So-called advances in vegetable culture designed to give tomatoes greater shelf life have all but ruined them. Florida tomatoes are gassed to give them color, at the expense of flavor and texture—and resemble pink flannel. In the West we do get good tomatoes from Mexico and some from California, but in the East we are forced to wait until the local tomatoes are in season and can be enjoyed to the hilt. Out of season it is much better to cook with good-quality canned tomatoes, such as the small Italian plum tomatoes from California, Italy, and other places. There are many good brands of canned tomatoes on the market and it pays to shop around until you find one you like. I recently came across a brand from California, canned in tomato purée, that was delicious.

Stewed Fresh Tomatoes

One of my favorite ways of preparing fresh, ripe seasonal tomatoes is to stew them. I often eat this most satisfying dish for lunch, varying the seasonings and occasionally adding a poached egg. Good canned tomatoes can be substituted (use about 1½ cups as the equivalent of 1 pound fresh tomatoes).

Makes 4 servings

4 pounds ripe tomatoes   *Salt, freshly ground black pepper*
4 tablespoons butter

Scald the tomatoes in boiling water and run them under cold water. Cut out the cores and peel the tomatoes, using your fingers to remove the skin. Cut the tomatoes into large chunks and place in a heavy saucepan with the butter. Cover and cook slowly over medium heat until they begin to break down. Add salt and pepper to taste and continue cooking until well blended, 8 to 10 minutes or slightly longer. Correct the seasonings and serve the tomatoes with an additional dab of butter, if you wish.

¶**Stewed Tomatoes with Basil.** Add 2 tablespoons finely cut basil leaves and 4 additional tablespoons butter to the stewed tomatoes.

¶**Stewed Tomatoes with Onion.** Cut 1 medium-size onion in thin slices and sauté in 3 tablespoons butter until just translucent. Add to the tomatoes and cook until well blended and soft.

¶**Stewed Tomatoes with Garlic and Lemon Zest.** Add to the stewed tomatoes 1 finely chopped garlic clove. Just before serving, add 1 to 2 tablespoons freshly grated lemon zest and 2 additional tablespoons butter.

¶**Stewed Tomatoes with Chilies.** Add to the stewed tomatoes 3 finely chopped canned peeled green chilies and 1 chopped garlic clove.

¶**Stewed Tomatoes with Poached Eggs.** Drop poached eggs into individual bowls of stewed tomatoes at the last minute, along with little dabs of butter.

Scalloped Fresh Tomatoes

These have always been a great American standby.

Makes 4 servings

8 to 10 medium-size ripe tomatoes,   *1 teaspoon salt*
    peeled and seeded   *½ teaspoon freshly ground black pepper*
1 to 1½ cups fresh bread crumbs
1 to 1½ sticks butter, cut in small
    pieces

Butter a deep baking dish and alternate layers of tomato slices, crumbs, dots of butter, and salt and pepper, finishing with a top layer of crumbs. Salt and pepper the crumbs and dot with butter. Bake in a 350° oven for about 20 to 25 minutes and serve bubbling hot.

¶**Scalloped Canned Tomatoes.** Line a baking dish with crumbs and add a 32-ounce can of Italian plum tomatoes, salt, freshly ground black pepper, and ¼ cup finely chopped onion or shallot. Cover liberally with additional crumbs, dot with butter, and bake in a 350° oven for 35 to 40 minutes.

Baked Tomatoes Stuffed with Mozzarella

A versatile and attractive little dish I like to serve as a first course, with veal scaloppine, or as a light luncheon entrée. Dieters who live in parts of the country where fresh mozzarella is made should look out for the cheese made with skim milk and no salt.

Makes 4 to 6 servings

4 to 6 large, ripe, firm tomatoes
2 to 3 tablespoons olive oil
Salt, freshly ground black pepper
3 tablespoons olive oil
¼ to ½ pound mozzarella cheese
(amount depends on size of
tomatoes)

2 tablespoons minced fresh basil, or
2 teaspoons dried basil

Cut a slice from the top of each tomato. Using a teaspoon, scoop out the pulp and seeds. Turn the tomato shells upside down on a platter and allow them to drain for about 15 minutes. Use some of the oil to brush a baking dish just large enough to hold the tomatoes. Place them in the dish. Season each tomato cavity with salt and pepper, and drizzle 1 teaspoon olive oil into each one. Chop the mozzarella fine and mix it with the basil. Stuff the tomatoes with this mixture. With a pastry brush, brush the outside skin of the tomatoes with the remaining olive oil. Bake in a preheated 375° oven for about 20 minutes, or until the mozzarella has melted. Serve hot.

¶**Baked Tomatoes Stuffed with Corn.** Blend a little of the chopped tomato pulp with 2 cups corn kernels, 2 tablespoons finely chopped onion, 2 tablespoons chopped parsley or basil, 1 teaspoon salt, ½ teaspoon freshly ground black pepper, and 6 tablespoons melted butter. Stuff tomato shells, cover tops with bread crumbs, dot with butter, and bake for 25 to 30 minutes.

¶**Greek Tomatoes.** Sauté 1 finely chopped small onion and 2 chopped garlic cloves in 6 tablespoons butter until limp. Mix in 2½ cups cooked rice, ½ cup ground cooked lamb, ¼ cup pine nuts, 1 teaspoon salt, 1 teaspoon freshly ground black pepper, and 1 teaspoon dried oregano or basil. Stuff tomato shells and arrange in a baking dish. Combine ½ cup olive oil, ¼ cup tomato purée, and 1 tablespoon lemon juice. Pour over tomatoes and bake in a 350° oven for 30 minutes, basting now and then with the sauce. Serve hot as a light main course or cold as a first course with a touch of wine vinegar to add zip.

Broiled Herbed Tomatoes

If the tomatoes are very large, cut them in half. If small, merely cut off a generous portion of the top.

Makes 6 servings

3 large tomatoes, halved, or 6 smaller tomatoes, tops cut off
6 tablespoons fresh bread crumbs
4 tablespoons chopped parsley
4 tablespoons chopped basil (optional)
1 tablespoon finely chopped garlic
2 tablespoons butter or olive oil

Sprinkle the tops of the tomatoes with a mixture of the crumbs, herbs, and garlic. Dot tops with butter or dribble olive oil on them. Place under a preheated broiler, about 4 to 5 inches from the heat, and broil for about 10 minutes, or until tomatoes are heated through and crumbs nicely browned, watching carefully to make sure the crumbs do not burn.

¶**Broiled Tomatoes with Pesto.** Sprinkle the tops of the tomatoes with bread crumbs and spread each one with 1 to 2 teaspoons pesto. Broil about 5 inches from the heat.

¶**Broiled Tomatoes with Garlic and Spices.** Remove tops from 6 large ripe but firm tomatoes, squeeze lightly to loosen the pulp and drain upside down on paper towels. Combine ½ cup olive oil, 3 finely chopped garlic cloves, ½ teaspoon cinnamon, a touch of nutmeg, and ½ cup bread crumbs and spread this over the tops of the tomatoes. Brush lightly with olive oil, sprinkle with salt and freshly ground black pepper, and broil about 5 inches from the heat for 12 to 15 minutes.

Sautéed Tomatoes

Good for breakfast with bacon or ham, or with hamburger or roast chicken.

Makes 4 servings

4 small to medium tomatoes
½ cup flour
Salt, freshly ground black pepper

3 tablespoons butter
3 tablespoons olive oil

Slice the tomatoes rather thick. Season the flour with salt and pepper to taste and dip the tomato slices in the flour, lightly coating both sides. Heat the butter and oil in a skillet and sauté the slices rather quickly until lightly browned on both sides and heated through.

Pennsylvania Dutch Tomatoes

Makes 6 servings

Flour
6 rather firm tomatoes, cut in thick
    slices
5 tablespoons butter

2 tablespoons oil
⅔ cup (approximately) firmly packed
    brown sugar
1½ cups heavy cream

Flour the tomato slices very well on both sides. Melt the butter and oil in a heavy skillet and add the tomato slices. While they're cooking sprinkle the tops generously with brown sugar. Turn the slices and again sprinkle them with brown sugar. Allow the slices to caramelize, then turn them so the other side can caramelize as well. Add the heavy cream to the pan and allow the slices to simmer in it for 3 to 4 minutes. Remove the tomato slices to a hot platter and serve them with plenty of crisp bacon and buttered toast.

¶Fried Green Tomatoes with Cream. Green tomatoes may be sliced thick, floured, and treated in exactly the same fashion.

Steamed Cherry Tomatoes

Makes 6 servings

4 tablespoons butter
2 pint baskets cherry tomatoes
1 teaspoon salt

½ teaspoon freshly ground black pepper
1 teaspoon, or more, chopped fresh dill,
    basil, or tarragon

Melt the butter in the upper part of a double boiler. Wash and dry the tomatoes and add them to the butter. Add the salt, freshly ground black pepper, and herb of your choice. Cover and cook over boiling water until they are just tender.

¶Steamed Peeled Cherry Tomatoes. Pour boiling water over the cherry tomatoes and let them stand for 1 minute, then plunge them into cold water. Carefully peel the tomatoes and place them in the top of a double boiler. Add ⅔ cup melted butter, 1 teaspoon salt, 1 teaspoon chopped chives, 1 tablespoon cut fresh basil or tarragon. Heat over boiling water until just heated through. Do not overcook. Sprinkle with chopped parsley.

Turnips

This is a plea for greater appreciation of the turnip, one of our most maligned and least understood vegetables. Although it is widely used by the Chinese, the Scandinavians, the French, the British, and the Germans, here it is a social outcast. I can't understand why, as I'm terribly fond of turnips; perhaps no one has bothered to taste turnips lately. But as they are with us most of the year, I think it is high time we learned how to make the most of them. Start slowly. Carve turnips into small lozenges about as long as an olive, the way the French do, then add to stews and sautés to enrich the flavor of the sauce or gravy. You can place the lozenges under a roast to brown in the fat along with roast potatoes, or add them to a New England boiled dinner or a pot-au-feu. They may also be lightly browned in butter first with a touch of sugar to glaze them (see *Theory & Practice*, page 211). Glazed turnips have a natural affinity for game. Before long you will find yourself quite infatuated with this peppery vegetable.

These days we have a good variety of turnips, mainly the big yellow turnips, also called rutabagas, and the white globe turnips with a little band of purple around the top and greens that are delicious when cooked (see page 150). There are also tiny white turnips and, at times, you may see in specialty markets a dwarf variety, known as *rapinata*, which have a very delicate flavor and tender little greens.

Buttered White Turnips

1½ pounds white turnips, peeled and
    sliced

2 to 3 tablespoons unsalted butter
Salt, freshly ground black pepper

Cook the sliced turnips in a small amount of boiling salted water until just tender, about 15 minutes, according to size and age. Drain. Toss with the butter and salt and pepper to taste.

¶Buttered Turnips with Mushrooms. Combine the buttered turnips with an equal quantity of lightly sautéed mushrooms.

Gratin of Turnip

4 medium or 6 small turnips, peeled
    and sliced
Salt, freshly ground black pepper
2 cups cooked rice

4 to 5 tablespoons butter
1 cup shredded Gruyère cheese
1 tablespoon chopped parsley

Cook the turnips in boiling salted water until tender. Drain. Add salt and pepper to taste. Arrange the turnips with alternating layers of rice in a gratin or baking dish and dot with butter. Bake in a 350° oven for 15 minutes. Remove from oven, sprinkle with the cheese and parsley, and return to the oven until the cheese has melted. Serve with lamb, beef, or chicken dishes.

Buttered Yellow Turnips or Rutabagas

1 large rutabaga, weighing about
    1½ pounds, peeled and diced

2 to 3 tablespoons butter
Freshly ground black pepper

Cook the diced turnip in a small amount of boiling salted water until just tender, about 15 minutes. Drain well. Toss with the butter and plenty of pepper.

¶With Yogurt. If you are watching calories, stir in cold yogurt and omit the butter.

¶Mashed Rutabagas. Mash the cooked rutabagas, season to taste with salt and freshly ground black pepper, and beat in 6 tablespoons melted butter.

¶**With Madeira or Sherry.** Flavor the mashed rutabaga with a tablespoon of Madeira or sherry, turn into a casserole, sprinkle the top heavily with bread crumbs, and place in a 350° oven until the top is browned.

¶**With Mashed Potatoes.** Combine the mashed rutabagas with an equal quantity of mashed potatoes, a generous amount of butter, and heavy cream to taste. (This is what I call a contagious dish; once you've been exposed to it you'll use it often.)

¶**With Duxelles.** Combine the mashed rutabagas with about ½ cup duxelles (see page 535), lacing it in for a marbleized effect. This is a startlingly good flavor combination. You might think the strong peppery taste of the turnips would wipe out the delicate mushroom quality but, oddly enough, they meet on equal ground.

Raw White Turnips

Cut peeled raw white turnips into thin round slices or julienne strips and serve as crudités or toss in a salad. Or shred the turnips and combine with other shredded vegetables such as carrots, beets, and cabbage, and toss with vinaigrette sauce or a yogurt dressing.

French-Fried Vegetables

Far too often French-fried vegetables are ruined by the wrong batter and poor frying, but when properly prepared they can be tender and delicious.

I greatly favor a beer batter for vegetables because the yeast in the beer gives a lightness and crispness to the batter. Vegetables that lend themselves to being dipped in batter and fried are artichoke hearts, artichoke bottoms, asparagus, green beans, wax beans, cauliflower flowerets, broccoli flowerets, small Brussels sprouts (if large, cut in half), eggplant fingers or slices (soaked first in salted water, then pressed to release the bitter juices and dried well), mushrooms, green and red pepper rings or strips, snow peas, sugar snap peas, spinach leaves, fiddlehead ferns, salsify, green onions, and strips of cabbage leaves. Onion rings are much better if dipped in a buttermilk batter (see *Theory & Practice*, page 222), and okra and zucchini should be floured and rolled in crumbs or cornmeal for deep-frying.

Beer Batter

Enough for approximately 2 pounds vegetables

¾ cup flour
2 eggs, separated
1½ teaspoons salt

2 tablespoons salad oil
¾ cup beer at room temperature
Freshly ground black pepper

Place the flour in a mixing bowl and add the egg yolks, salt, oil, beer, and a grind or two of pepper. Stir the batter clockwise with a wire whisk until thoroughly mixed. Cover the bowl with plastic wrap and allow it to rest for anywhere from 2 to 24 hours. Stir the batter well. In a separate bowl beat the 2 egg whites with a wire whisk until stiff but not dry. Gently fold the whites into the batter.

NOTE: The same batter may be used for deep-frying edible flowers, such as elderberry blossoms, white acacia blossoms. Wash, dry, and dip the bunches of blossoms in the batter.

To French-Fry Vegetables

Select the vegetables you wish to cook; see that they are trimmed, washed, and well dried; and dust lightly with flour. Dip into the batter and lower into the deep-fryer, in which the oil has been heated to 360°. Do not fry too many pieces at a time or it will lower the temperature of the oil. Cook until just golden brown, allowing a little more cooking time for the denser vegetables, less for the thin or leafy ones. Remove and drain on absorbent paper and keep warm in a 250° oven until all are fried. Serve immediately.

¶French-Fried Zucchini. Slice the zucchini in rounds about ½ inch thick. Dust lightly with flour, then roll in fine bread crumbs. Deep-fry in 370° fat until golden brown.

¶French-Fried Okra. Trim the ends of the okra pods, dust with flour, roll in fine cornmeal and deep-fry in 370° fat until golden.

¶French-Fried Potatoes. I like to use rendered beef suet for French-frying potatoes; it gives great flavor but you can use oil or the solidified vegetable fat if you prefer. Peel potatoes and cut into long strips ¼ to ½ inch wide and thick, or in round or long slices, cut ⅛ inch thick (these may be peeled or left unpeeled, as you wish). Dry well, then deep-fry in 325° fat until flabby but not colored, for about 5 or 6 minutes. Remove and drain on absorbent paper. Leave at room temperature for 1 or more hours, then complete the frying by plunging the potatoes into 375° fat. Fry until crisp and brown, about 2 or 3 minutes.

¶**French-Fried Sweet Potatoes.** Cook as for French-Fried Potatoes.

¶**French-Fried Parsnips.** Cut small parsnips into julienne strips, as for French-Fried Potatoes, and cook in the same way. Large parsnips should first be blanched in boiling water until just tender, peeled, and cut into rounds or strips. They may also be dipped in flour or in batter before frying.

Mixed Vegetable Sautés

Mixed vegetable sautés can be prepared with practically any vegetables that are currently available. In order to make a good sauté, it is important to gauge the different cooking times for the various vegetables you plan to use; start with the vegetable that requires the longest cooking time—for example, small peeled white onions. Melt 4 to 6 tablespoons butter along with 3 or 4 unpeeled garlic cloves in a heavy pan over fairly low heat. Add the onions, cover the pan, and let them simmer for about 10 minutes. Then, while the onions are cooking, shred either a head of cabbage or a head of lettuce (a solid head such as romaine or iceberg), and add to the cooking onions; this will create steam and liquid in which to cook the other vegetables. Now add the next-longest-cooking vegetable, let us say carrots and perhaps turnips, cut in rather large chunks. Cover the pan again and continue cooking for about 20 to 25 minutes; test the vegetables for tenderness—they should be nearly done but not quite. After this you might add cauliflower flowerets, perhaps a bit of zucchini, either sliced rather thick or, if they're very small, leave them whole. Let these cook for another 5 to 10 minutes, covered, and finally add any green vegetables you prefer: shredded spinach, finely cut green beans, shelled green peas, or asparagus tips. Give these another 4 to 5 minutes. Remove the cover and test the vegetables again for tenderness. Stir in additional butter to taste; add salt and freshly ground black pepper and any herb you may desire. Toss the vegetables thoroughly and remove them immediately to a serving dish.

For an interesting sauté, you'll want to have at least 3 vegetables in addition to the bed of greens and onions. Choose what is in season, and the amounts will be determined by the number of people you're serving.

Here's a partial list of other vegetables that would work for a good sauté:

Artichoke bottoms or baby artichokes	*Edible-podded peas or sugar snap peas*
Mushrooms	*Salsify (oyster plant)*
Eggplant	*Broccoli flowerets and broccoli stems*
Tiny new potatoes	*(these take different cooking times)*
Leeks (carefully washed and trimmed)	*Kohlrabi*
Green or red peppers, peeled	*Brussels sprouts*
Small tomatoes	*Tiny radishes*
Chayote	

And practically any other vegetable of your choice. The secrets of a really good sauté are: don't overcook the vegetables, use plenty of seasoning, and be careful of your timing.

Ratatouille

This has become an all-time favorite with roast lamb or beef.

Makes 4 to 6 servings

1 or 2 large onions, sliced	*8 to 10 very ripe tomatoes, peeled,*
4 large garlic cloves, finely chopped	*seeded, and chopped, or 2 to 3*
½ cup olive oil	*cups canned Italian plum tomatoes*
2 green peppers, peeled and slivered	*1 tablespoon shredded fresh basil or*
1 large eggplant, diced	*1 teaspoon dried*
4 or 5 small zucchini, cut into ¼-inch	*1½ teaspoons salt*
slices	*Freshly ground black pepper*

Sauté the onions and garlic in the oil in a deep saucepan with a heavy bottom. When the onions are just translucent, add the peppers, eggplant, and zucchini, and mix together well. Reduce the heat, cover the pan tightly, and simmer for 10 minutes, shaking the pan or tossing the vegetables 2 or 3 times so they cook evenly. Add the tomatoes and the seasonings and continue simmering for another 10 or 12 minutes. Uncover the pan and allow the mixture to cook down and the liquid to reduce, stirring frequently. The vegetables should be somewhat intact, well mixed and blended but not mushy and liquid. Taste and correct the seasoning.

¶**Ratatouille with Sliced Mushrooms.** Add ½ pound sliced mushrooms to the ratatouille 5 minutes before the end of the cooking time.

¶**Ratatouille with Sliced Fennel.** Add 1 large bulb of fennel, thinly sliced, with the eggplant, peppers, and zucchini.

¶**Ratatouille with Leeks.** Add 2 sliced leeks with the eggplant.

¶**Ratatouille with Poached Eggs and Cheese.** Serve the ratatouille in small individual ramekins or baking dishes topped with a poached egg and covered with shredded Gruyère cheese. Run under the broiler or place in a 450° oven just long enough to melt the cheese. Serve as a first course for dinner or a luncheon main dish.

¶**Spicy Ratatouille.** In place of 1 cup fresh or canned tomatoes, use 1 cup Mexican canned tomatoes and hot green chilies.

Tian

This dish is as good served cold as hot.

Makes 6 to 8 servings

Olive oil
2 pounds raw spinach, coarsely chopped
2 pounds raw Swiss chard, coarsely
    chopped
6 to 8 finger-size zucchini, cut in
    small dice
2 medium onions, coarsely chopped, or
    3 bunches of scallions, finely cut
3 cloves garlic, finely chopped

½ cup finely chopped basil leaves or
    2 tablespoons dried basil
Salt to taste
1½ teaspoons freshly ground black
    pepper
6 eggs, lightly beaten
1½ cups grated Parmesan cheese
Fresh bread crumbs

Cover the bottom of a large skillet with olive oil and add the spinach and Swiss chard. Cook until just wilted. Remove and drain. Press out all liquid. Add the zucchini, onion, and garlic to the skillet, adding more oil if needed, and repeat cooking procedure.

Combine the vegetables, the fresh or dried basil, salt, and pepper, and place in a lightly oiled heavy earthenware casserole or tian. Pour the eggs over the vegetables and top with the cheese and bread crumbs. Bake in a 350° oven until the eggs are just set and the cheese is melted.

¶**Tian with Rice.** Add 2 cups cooked rice and spoon the vegetables over.

¶**Tian with Noodles.** Mix 2 cups cooked fine noodles with the vegetables.

Fish and Shellfish

When I go back to Oregon I always stop in at my favorite fish store. Out back, a brisk and hearty bunch of women in rubber aprons are working at top speed, shaking the meat from crab shells. Up front, there's a big clean counter with a glistening display of the day's catch bedded on chopped ice, as well as such attractions as smoked sturgeon, kippered salmon, and smoked oysters, all of which were prepared in the smokehouse in the back yard. If an order from the hinterlands for fresh salmon has just been filled, there's bound to be a whole slew of chopped-off heads around, from which are plucked those legendary salmon cheeks—some of the best eating ever. (I have a recipe just in case you might happen upon such good fortune.)

I realize that not everyone has such a fish market, and I've always felt that I was very lucky to have grown up on a bountiful seacoast. Today, however, Air Express makes it possible for fresh fish to circulate around the country, and restaurateurs whose reputations are built on using the

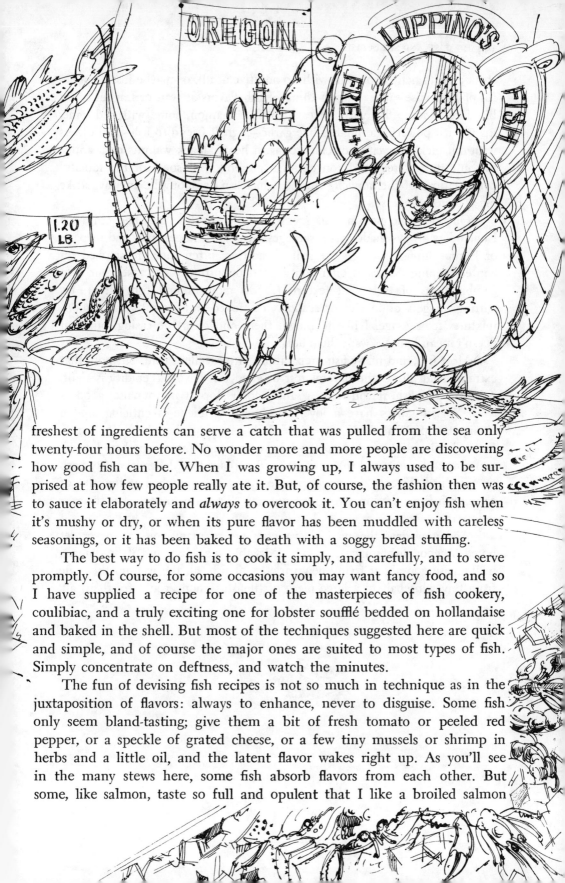

freshest of ingredients can serve a catch that was pulled from the sea only twenty-four hours before. No wonder more and more people are discovering how good fish can be. When I was growing up, I always used to be surprised at how few people really ate it. But, of course, the fashion then was to sauce it elaborately and *always* to overcook it. You can't enjoy fish when it's mushy or dry, or when its pure flavor has been muddled with careless seasonings, or it has been baked to death with a soggy bread stuffing.

The best way to do fish is to cook it simply, and carefully, and to serve promptly. Of course, for some occasions you may want fancy food, and so I have supplied a recipe for one of the masterpieces of fish cookery, coulibiac, and a truly exciting one for lobster soufflé bedded on hollandaise and baked in the shell. But most of the techniques suggested here are quick and simple, and of course the major ones are suited to most types of fish. Simply concentrate on deftness, and watch the minutes.

The fun of devising fish recipes is not so much in technique as in the juxtaposition of flavors: always to enhance, never to disguise. Some fish only seem bland-tasting; give them a bit of fresh tomato or peeled red pepper, or a speckle of grated cheese, or a few tiny mussels or shrimp in herbs and a little oil, and the latent flavor wakes right up. As you'll see in the many stews here, some fish absorb flavors from each other. But some, like salmon, taste so full and opulent that I like a broiled salmon steak and its rich crispy skin with no additive at all, or maybe just a spoonful of Béarnaise sauce. I never think of fish flavors as wan or fragile: not a bit. I cook some fish with spices such as cinnamon, some with red wine, many with powerful aromatics like garlic—a great friend to fish—and others with dill pickles or curry or cider, or with hearty black walnuts or peanuts, not just the discreet and conventional almond. But some of the fanciful combinations of the nouvelle cuisine, which isn't so nouvelle anyway, strike me as merely perverse.

One nouvelle notion, fish sausages, isn't novel at all. The old New Englanders always made oyster sausages, hearty with beef suet, and in parts of Europe fin-fish sausages are still a tradition; often they are smoked for winter keeping. Sausages offer you a good opportunity to make your own combinations of taste and texture (as do mousses and fish pâtés); try stirring nuggets of lobster or scallop or smoked salmon into the smooth mixtures for sausage. I like to brown them and crisp the casing, but that doesn't mean I always want them hot.

Most fish, and many fish preparations, are excellent cold, but note that extreme cold blunts the natural zest of good fish flavors. Tepidity is right. And for cold fish, if you want a sauce, don't stop at mayonnaise, good as it is. Yogurt sauces have a lovely freshness. Gribiche is enticing, and a vinaigrette, particularly if you mince in tarragon or chervil, or, for a full-flavored fish, mint or sage. Often I bake or poach more fish than I need, planning to have it cold the next day, and perhaps in a delicious crusty hash on the third. Twenty years ago, people would have laughed at the idea of eating fish three days in a row, but not now. To learn to cook it is to learn to love it.

And nowadays the available varieties are so many you can never get bored. A good fishmonger is a knowledgeable specialist, and if he's smart, he'll advise you about trying new varieties of fish, all the way up the scale from tiny whitebait to a large piece of tilefish. I hope you'll try them all.

FISH AND SHELLFISH

Broiled fish fillets
  with almonds
  with peanuts
  with lemon butter
  with herbed butter
  with white wine and
    herbs
  with cheese
  with white wine and
    garlic
  with bread crumbs
  with bacon and green
    onion
  provençal
  leftover marinated

Sautéed fish fillets

Walnut-breaded sole

Sautéed sole fillets with
  curry sauce

Poached whole fish

Poached pike with white
    butter sauce
  with white wine sauce
  with egg sauce
  with parsley or dill sauce
  with green mayonnaise
  with yogurt-herb sauce

Poached fish fillets with
  garlic mayonnaise
  (bourride)

Sole poached in vermouth
  in whisky with caviar

Turban of sole mousseline
  with shrimp mousseline
  individual turbans of sole

Fish hash

Broiled swordfish steak
  with pepper
  with rosemary
  with garlic and olives
  marinated

Baked swordfish steak

Baked halibut steak niçoise

Baked stuffed shad

Shad roe poached in butter

Flemish green eel

Matelote of eel, from
  Normandy

Mrs. Rockey's shad roe

Broiled trout

Sautéed trout in crêpes

Fried smelts or sardines
  with garlic and parsley
  skewered

Baked spiced smelts or
  sardines

Coulibiac of salmon
  with rice

Scalloped salmon

Salmon cheeks

Salmon tart

French seafood sausages
  with shrimp
  with crab

Seafood en brochette

Cocotte of seafood
  manzanilla

Hellenic seafood stew

Bouillabaisse

Solianka
  with dill

Cioppino
  with mussels
  with oysters

Cotriade

Seafood à l'américaine

Mussels marinière
  with garlic
  with cream
  with tomatoes
  clams marinière

Curried seafood with rice
  pilaf

Tuna tart

Clam hash

Sauté of clams
  with white wine
  with tarragon
  with mustard and
    Worcestershire sauce

Scalloped clams

Clam pie

Baked oysters on the half
  shell with shrimp
  sauce

Stuffed oysters

Fried oysters
  oyster loaves

Oyster sausages

Shrimp jambalaya
  with crabmeat

Shrimp on a stick

Shrimp with curry butter
  with dill butter

Shrimp floridian en
  papillote

Chuck's baked shrimp

Shrimp loaf

Stuffed baked lobster

Lobster napoule

Lobster soufflé

Crab soufflé

Crab parisienne

Deviled crab
  deviled clams

Broiled soft-shell crabs

Sautéed scallops
  provençal

Poached scallops
  with heavy cream and
    tarragon

Lo-cal coquilles St. Jacques

Sautéed frogs' legs	Deep-fried frogs' legs	Codfish cakes
fines herbes	batter-fried	with ginger
provençal		with onion
niçoise		codfish balls
Italian style		**Brandade of cod**
deviled	Poached codfish	codfish portugaise
southern-fried	codfish béchamel	brandade fritters
southern-fried with	codfish au gratin	brandade tart
Madeira sauce	codfish mornay	**Raïto**

Fish Fillets

I'm starting this chapter with fillets because that is the way fish is mostly sold across the country these days, although the types you find in your markets will vary according to where you live. They include sole, flounder, cod, haddock, ocean perch, trout, red snapper, sea bass, striped bass, bluefish, mackerel, salmon, whitefish, and that great Eastern delicacy, shad.

According to the size of the fish and whether it is flat, like flounder, or round, like cod, the thickness of the fillets will vary from about ⅓ inch up to 1½ inches or even more. No matter what the thickness, there is one simple, reliable rule for broiling, sautéing, or poaching fillets or, for that matter, steaks or whole fish, that I have followed successfully for years. Measure the depth of the fillet at the thickest point (from underside to top side) and cook for 10 minutes per inch or fraction thereof. If the fillets are thicker in the center than at the ends, cut down a little on the cooking time, or the ends will be overdone. Fish, like eggs or meat, goes on cooking with its own internal heat, so the thick part will be cooked through by the time it is served. Never overcook fillets, or they will be dry, flaky, and flavorless. Frozen fillets are best cooked from the frozen state, in which case you should double the cooking time.

Broiled Fish Fillets

This is really my favorite way of cooking fillets. The quick-cooking process seems to retain all the natural flavor and goodness, and lends itself to all kinds of interesting flavor variations. I discussed broiling fillets at some length in *Theory & Practice,* so I'm just going to give a brief summary of the main points and the basic method, then give you some flavoring suggestions. I like to allow ⅓ to ½ pound fillets per serving.

Unless the fillets are very thick (¾ inch or more), they are best broiled on one side only, without turning. Thick fillets should be turned halfway through the cooking time. Turning and lifting is a rather tricky process, especially with thin fillets, which break easily. I find the best solution is to broil the fish on a long piece of aluminum foil laid the length of the broiler rack, with overlapping ends for handles. Then all you have to do, with the aid of the foil, is slide the cooked fillets onto a serving platter or plates. Brush the foil well with oil to prevent the fish from sticking (if you are broiling thin fillets, heat the broiler rack first, while you are preheating the broiler, which helps to cook the underside of the fish), then arrange the fillets on the foil in a single layer.

Makes 4 servings

2 *pounds fish fillets*
½ *cup unsalted butter or vegetable oil*
  (*or a combination of the two*)
1 *teaspoon salt*
¼ *teaspoon freshly ground black pepper*
1 *to 2 tablespoons lemon juice*
Chopped parsley (optional)

Preheat the broiler. Arrange the fillets on a long piece of oiled aluminum foil on the broiler rack. Melt the butter or warm the oil in a small pan and add the salt, pepper, and lemon juice to make a basting mixture. Brush the fillets well with this mixture, then broil 3 inches from the preheated broiler, allowing 10 minutes per measured inch of thickness, or fraction thereof, and turning once with a broad-bladed spatula or turner if the fillets are thick. Baste well as they cook. When done, slide the fillets onto hot plates or a heated platter and pour over them any of the basting mixture left on the foil or in the pan. If you wish, sprinkle the fish with chopped parsley. Serve with lemon wedges, small new potatoes dressed with melted butter and chopped parsley, and a green vegetable or salad.

¶**Broiled Fish Fillets with Almonds.** Just before the fillets are done, sprinkle them with thinly sliced or slivered almonds and baste well with the butter mixture, making sure the almonds do not scorch or burn.

¶**Broiled Fish Fillets with Peanuts.** Combine finely chopped peanuts and melted butter and spoon over the fillets just before they are done.

¶**Broiled Fish Fillets with Lemon Butter.** Increase the lemon juice to 4 tablespoons and add 2 tablespoons grated lemon zest. Use to baste the fillets.

¶**Broiled Fish Fillets with Herbed Butter.** Omit the lemon juice and combine the melted butter with 2 tablespoons chopped fresh herb (dill, basil, chives, or parsley). If you use dried herbs, use 2 teaspoons and soak in dry white wine for 15 minutes before using.

¶**Broiled Fish Fillets with White Wine and Herbs.** Use dry white wine instead of lemon juice, and add 2 teaspoons chopped chives or parsley.

¶**Broiled Fish Fillets with Cheese.** Three minutes before the fillets are done, sprinkle each one with 1 to 2 teaspoons grated Parmesan or Romano cheese, and add a grind or two of pepper.

¶**Broiled Fish Fillets with White Wine and Garlic.** Combine butter with ¼ cup white wine (omit lemon juice) and 2 finely chopped or crushed garlic cloves.

¶**Broiled Fish Fillets with Bread Crumbs.** Three minutes before the fillets are done, sprinkle each one with 1 tablespoon buttered crumbs and baste well.

¶**Broiled Fish Fillets with Bacon and Green Onion.** Sauté 3 slices finely chopped bacon for 3 to 4 minutes, drain well, and combine with 3 table-spoons finely chopped green onion, or scallion, and 1 peeled, seeded, and finely chopped tomato. Baste the fillets with butter and lemon juice, spoon the bacon mixture over them, and broil as before, without further basting.

¶**Broiled Fish Fillets, Provençal.** Sauté 3 finely chopped shallots in 4 tablespoons olive oil until soft. Add 3 peeled, seeded, and coarsely chopped tomatoes, 1 finely chopped garlic clove, 1 teaspoon basil, 1 teaspoon salt, ½ teaspoon freshly ground black pepper, and 2 tablespoons chopped parsley. Arrange fillets on foil and brush well with olive oil. Broil for half the cooking time, spoon tomato mixture over them, and continue broiling until done. Serve with saffron rice.

¶**Leftover Marinated Fish Fillets.** Arrange any leftover cold broiled fillets in a baking dish in a single layer. Top with thin slices of onion, green pepper rings, and slices of peeled orange or lemon. Add olive oil barely to cover. Sprinkle with your favorite herb (dill, tarragon, basil, or thyme) and season with salt and pepper to taste. Cover with plastic wrap or foil and refrigerate 24 hours or overnight. Serve with a rice salad or a green salad.

Sautéed Fish Fillets

The classic method of sautéing fish, which I gave in *Theory & Practice*, is the sauté meunière. The fish is lightly floured; cooked quickly in clarified butter (see page 543) or a mixture of butter and oil, which can be heated to a fairly high temperature without burning; turned once; seasoned and served with the butter from the pan, lemon, and chopped parsley. The following recipes are a little more unusual.

Walnut-Breaded Sole

The walnuts, especially if you can get black walnuts, lend a satisfying crunchiness and flavor to the fish. Serve the fillets with boiled or steamed potatoes and perhaps a cucumber salad.

Makes 6 servings

6 large fillets of sole, flounder, or other white fish
Flour
2 eggs
3 tablespoons heavy cream
1 cup fresh bread crumbs
1½ cups coarsely chopped walnuts, preferably black walnuts

6 tablespoons clarified unsalted butter, or 3 tablespoons unsalted butter and 3 tablespoons oil
Salt, freshly ground black pepper
Lemon wedges

Flour the fillets lightly. Lightly beat the eggs and mix in the cream. Dip the fillets in the egg-cream mixture, then into the crumbs and then the nuts. Arrange on cookie sheets lined with wax paper for a few minutes to set the coating. Heat the clarified butter, or butter and oil, until hot but not smoking, add the fillets, 2 or 3 at a time (do not crowd the pan), and sauté until lightly browned on one side, then turn, using a broad-bladed spatula, and sauté the second side. Sprinkle with salt and pepper to taste and serve at once, with lemon wedges.

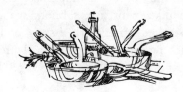

Sautéed Sole Fillets with Curry Sauce

Makes 6 servings

2 pounds ripe tomatoes, peeled, seeded
    and chopped, or 4 cups canned
    Italian plum tomatoes, drained
    and chopped
3 onions, finely chopped
1 tablespoon butter
1 tablespoon curry powder, or more to
    taste

Salt, freshly ground pepper
6 tablespoons clarified unsalted butter
6 large or 12 small sole or flounder
    fillets
Flour
Chopped parsley
½ cup heavy cream

Combine the tomatoes and the onions, and let them cook down over low heat for 1 to 1½ hours. The mixture should be well concentrated. Melt the 1 tablespoon butter in a pan and cook the curry powder gently in the butter for 3 or 4 minutes, to remove the raw taste. Add to the tomato-onion mixture, season to taste with salt and pepper, and continue cooking while sautéing the fish.

Melt the clarified butter in a large skillet. Dip the fillets in flour and sauté them quickly until nicely browned on both sides, being careful not to break them when you turn them. Salt and pepper to taste, and sprinkle with chopped parsley. Arrange on a hot platter.

Combine the cream with the sauce and let it heat just to the boiling point. Pour the sauce over the fish and serve at once.

Poached Whole Fish

It never ceases to surprise me how many good cooks overlook the possibilities of poached fish. Not only is this the most satisfactory way of cooking the delicate flesh, but a whole fish makes a most attractive presentation for a dinner party or buffet, either hot with a white butter or white wine sauce, or cold with a green mayonnaise or an herbed yogurt sauce.

According to the part of the country you live in, you can usually find large fish weighing 5 pounds or more that make excellent candidates for poaching, among them pike, whitefish, salmon, striped bass, red snapper, and sea bass. Although salted water with a sprig or two of parsley is perfectly adequate for poaching large, flavorful fish, I prefer to make a simple *court bouillon* of water and wine with aromatic vegetables and herbs, which gives the fish a richer flavor. The court bouillon can then be reduced and strained if you wish to make a white wine sauce.

The timing for poaching whole fish, whether they are large or as small as trout, is the same. Measure the fish at the thickest point—its depth, not across the fish—and cook exactly 10 minutes per inch. Start timing after the fish has been lowered into the poaching liquid and the liquid has returned to a simmer. Remember that fish will continue to cook by its own internal heat after it is removed from the liquid, so remove and drain it immediately.

Whether I'm using the traditional fish poacher or just a large pot for poaching fish, I find it's a good idea to lay the fish on a double thickness of heavy-duty aluminum foil long enough so the ends can act as handles for lowering the fish into the liquid and taking it out. Leave the head and tail on the fish, which keeps it intact and makes it look more attractive on the platter. I've never been able to understand people who shudder at the sight of a fish with its head on.

Poached Pike with White Butter Sauce

Makes 8 to 10 servings

1 pike, weighing 5 pounds or more
    (or substitute other large fish
    suitable for poaching)

White-wine court bouillon (see page
    203)

WHITE BUTTER SAUCE (BEURRE BLANC)
¼ cup dry white wine
¼ cup white wine vinegar
¼ cup finely chopped shallot
¼ teaspoon salt

Freshly ground black pepper
12 ounces (3 sticks) unsalted butter,
    well chilled

Put the fish in a fish poacher or cooking pot large enough for it to lie flat, and add sufficient water and wine (from recipe for court bouillon), half and half, barely to cover the fish. Remove fish. Add other court bouillon ingredients to the liquid, bring to a boil, reduce the heat, and simmer 10 to 15 minutes.

Measure the fish at the thickest point, lay it on a double thickness of aluminum foil, and lower it carefully into the simmering liquid. Start timing when the liquid returns to a simmer, allowing 10 minutes per inch. Immediately remove fish from the liquid with the aid of the foil, drain, and arrange on a warm serving platter.

While the fish is poaching, prepare the beurre blanc, or white butter sauce. This is a tricky sauce as the butter must not melt but remain a creamy emulsion. I prefer to use a small, heavy enameled cast-iron saucepan. Put the wine, wine vinegar, shallot, salt, and a grind of pepper into the pan and reduce over brisk heat to about 1 to 2 tablespoons. There should be just a mushy glaze in the bottom of the pan. While the liquid is reducing, cut the chilled butter into 24 slices, keeping them cold. Remove the pan from the heat to cool a little, and quickly beat in 2 pieces of butter with a wire whisk until creamy, then beat in the remaining butter, piece by piece, over the lowest possible heat, until the sauce has the consistency of very heavy cream. Lift the pan off the heat any time it seems to be getting too hot and do not add more butter until each piece has been incorporated. Serve the sauce immediately with the fish; it can't wait. I like to serve poached fish with tiny new peas, buttered and flavored with a touch of tarragon, and steamed or boiled new potatoes.

¶**Poached Fish with White Wine Sauce.** Serve the fish with white wine sauce (see page 534), using 1 cup of the reduced, strained cooking liquid.

¶**Poached Fish with Egg Sauce.** Serve the fish with a béchamel sauce (see page 531) to which you have added 2 peeled and sliced hard-boiled eggs. (This is the traditional sauce for poached salmon on the Fourth of July in New England.)

¶**Poached Fish with Parsley or Dill Sauce.** Serve the fish with béchamel sauce into which you have stirred ¼ cup chopped fresh parsley or 1 tablespoon finely chopped fresh dill and a few drops of lemon juice.

¶**Poached Fish with Green Mayonnaise.** Serve the poached fish cold, but not refrigerated, with green mayonnaise (see page 77).

¶**Poached Fish with Yogurt-Herb Sauce.** Serve the fish cold with a sauce of 1½ cups plain yogurt mixed with 1 tablespoon chopped fresh chives, tarragon, or dill, 1 finely chopped garlic clove, 1 tablespoon Dijon mustard, and horseradish to taste.

Poached Fish Fillets with Garlic Mayonnaise (Bourride)

Garlic is the very breath of Provence, and in this recipe, which came from my friend Elizabeth David, the poaching liquid is thickened with aïoli, the headily garlicky Provençal mayonnaise, which does something quite wonderful for bland white fish fillets. The traditional way to make aïoli is to pound the garlic and egg yolks in a huge marble mortar with a pestle and then gradually work in the olive oil until the mayonnaise is very stiff. I find this arduous, time-consuming process can be considerably simplified if you use a food processor or blender.

Makes 8 servings

WHITE-WINE COURT BOUILLON
2 quarts water
2 cups dry white wine
1 onion, stuck with 2 cloves
1 rib celery
1 clove garlic

1 tablespoon salt
1 strip lemon peel
2 sprigs parsley
4 pounds fillets or white fish (bass, sole, flounder, haddock)

AÏOLI
4 large garlic cloves
3 large egg yolks
2½ cups fruity olive oil

½ teaspoon salt
1 tablespoon lemon juice

4 or 5 large egg yolks, beaten

8 slices toast

Combine the court bouillon ingredients in a fish poacher or a large sauté pan, bring to a boil, reduce heat, and simmer 20 minutes. Add the fish fillets and poach gently for 10 minutes for each measured inch of thickness. Remove fish to a hot platter and keep warm. Strain the court bouillon.

To make the aïoli, put the garlic cloves and 3 egg yolks in a blender and blend at high speed until combined, about 30 seconds. If you use a food processor, process the garlic and 3 egg yolks for about 2 to 3 seconds, just until blended, using the metal blade. With the machine running, very slowly pour in the olive oil, in a thin trickle at first until the mayonnaise starts to thicken, then more rapidly. When stiff, season with salt and lemon juice.

Combine the aïoli and the 4 or 5 egg yolks, and stir in 2½ to 3 cups of the strained court bouillon, whisking over low heat until the sauce is thick, creamy, and foamy. Arrange the fish on pieces of toast in soup plates and spoon the sauce over them.

Sole Poached in Vermouth

In certain French recipes, instead of being poached in court bouillon or wine and water, fish fillets are poached in undiluted wine, dry vermouth, or sometimes spirits. The aromatic cooking liquid becomes the basis for a rich and flavorful sauce.

Makes 6 servings

6 large fillets of sole
1¼ cups dry vermouth
4 egg yolks

¼ pound butter, cut in small pieces
3 tablespoons heavy cream
Salt

Measure the thickness of the fillets, then arrange them in a large skillet in one layer. Add the vermouth, which should just cover them, bring to the boiling point, reduce the heat, and poach, allowing 10 minutes per measured inch, until just cooked through. Remove the fillets with a spatula to a large baking dish and keep warm. Increase the heat to high and reduce the cooking liquid until it is practically a glaze.

Put the egg yolks and pieces of butter in the top of a double boiler over hot water. Beat with a wire whisk or electric hand beater until smooth and thickened, then beat in the cream, reduced cooking liquid, and salt to taste. Don't let the water boil at any time or the eggs will curdle. Pour the sauce over the fillets and brown the top quickly under a hot broiler.

¶**Sole Poached in Whisky with Caviar.** Poach sole in Scotch whisky to cover. Remove fish to a hot platter. Blend 1 cup heavy cream and 4 egg yolks, add a little of the poaching liquid to warm the yolks, then stir gradually into poaching liquid in pan. Stir and cook over low heat until slightly thickened. Do not allow to boil. Add 1 teaspoon black or red caviar and salt to taste. Arrange the fish on serving plates, put a small dab of caviar on each one, and spoon the sauce around it.

Turban of Sole Mousseline

Makes 6 to 8 servings

1¼ pounds raw salmon
3 egg whites
1½ cups heavy cream
½ teaspoon salt

¼ teaspoon freshly ground black pepper
¼ teaspoon nutmeg
A dash or two of Tabasco
6 to 8 sole fillets

WHITE WINE SAUCE
3 tablespoons unsalted butter
3 tablespoons flour
1 cup strong fish stock (see page 530)

Salt, freshly ground black pepper
½ cup heavy cream
2 egg yolks

If you have a food processor, you may prepare the mousseline by placing the salmon and egg whites in the beaker of the food processor. Process for 30 seconds to make a smooth paste. With the machine on, gradually pour the cream into the paste until absorbed, then blend in the seasonings.

Otherwise, grind the salmon two or three times, using the finest blade of the meat grinder. Pound in a mortar, or work with a heavy spoon, to a very smooth paste. Place the salmon in a bowl over cracked ice and gradually beat in the egg whites, using a wooden spoon or whisk, until the mixture is smooth and all liquid is absorbed. Gradually beat in the cream until the mixture is stiff and the cream absorbed. Season to taste with salt and pepper, nutmeg, and Tabasco. Beat a few seconds longer and let the mixture stand over ice for an hour until very firm.

Arrange the sole fillets in a heavily buttered 9-inch ring mold, with the darker sides facing inward, draping them so that they overlap slightly and the ends of the fillets hang over the edges of the mold.

Carefully spoon the fish mousseline into the ring mold and fold the ends of the fillets over the top of it. Stand the mold in a roasting pan, add boiling water to come halfway up the mold, and bake in a 375° oven for 35 to 40 minutes.

While the mousseline is in the oven, make the white wine sauce. Melt the butter in a pan, stir in the flour, and cook until the roux is bubbling and golden. Gradually stir in the fish stock, and cook over medium heat, stirring, until the sauce is smooth and thickened. Simmer 3 or 4 minutes, then season to taste with salt and pepper. Blend the cream and egg yolks, stir a little of the hot sauce into them, then return to the remainder in the pan. Cook over medium-low heat, stirring, until smooth and thick, but do not let sauce boil or the eggs will curdle.

Unmold the mousseline onto a round platter and serve with the white wine sauce.

¶**Turban of Sole with Shrimp Mousseline.** Instead of the raw salmon, use 1 pound raw shelled shrimp for the mousseline. Process or grind and prepare in the same way. Season the mousseline with salt, pepper, nutmeg, and ½ teaspoon finely chopped fresh dill.

¶**Individual Turbans of Sole.** Cut the sole fillets into largish pieces and use to line 6 buttered custard cups. Divide the mousseline among the cups and cover tops with pieces of sole. Stand the custard cups in a baking pan of hot water and cook in a 425° oven for 10 to 15 minutes. To serve, unmold each Turban onto a dinner plate and spoon over white wine sauce.

Fish Hash

This is an excellent way to recycle leftover cooked fish fillets. Serve with a tossed salad as a luncheon dish, or with tomato relish or chili sauce and toasted muffins for breakfast.

Makes 6 servings

1½ cups coarsely chopped onion
3 tablespoons bacon fat or butter
3 cups diced cooked potatoes
2 to 2½ cups flaked cooked fish fillets
2 teaspoons salt
1 teaspoon freshly ground black pepper

2 teaspoons Worcestershire sauce
¼ teaspoon Tabasco
½ cup heavy cream
2 tablespoons chopped cilantro or
　　parsley

Sauté the onion in the bacon fat or butter over medium-high heat until just delicately colored and limp. Add the potatoes and toss well with the onions. Cook over medium heat for 4 to 5 minutes. Add the flaked fillets, blend well, and add the seasonings. Press down in the pan with a spatula. Add the cream and let it cook down with the hash. Add the cilantro or parsley. Cook until the hash is crusty on the bottom then turn it out onto a serving plate.

Broiled Fish Steaks

I'm a great lover of broiled fish steaks. They hold their juices and their shape and any leftovers are delicious cold with a little mayonnaise or yogurt mixed with chopped fresh herbs. Good candidates for broiling are swordfish, halibut, salmon, cod, haddock, tilefish, bluefish, striped bass (known as rockfish below the Mason-Dixon line), sea bass, redfish, sablefish, carp, sturgeon, fresh tuna or albacore, and mako shark.

Whenever possible, I like fish steaks cut at least 1 inch thick, or up to 2 inches for large fish such as swordfish or halibut—a thin steak never has quite the juiciness of a thick one. Follow the same rule of timing, 10 minutes per measured inch, as you would for fillets or whole fish to determine cooking time. I find oil preferable to butter for brushing and basting fish steaks; it seeps into the flesh better. For flavoring, fresh or dried herbs go well with fish and I also happen to believe that garlic is a friend of fish at all times. Try it in the variations for broiled swordfish steak and you'll see what I mean.

Broiled Swordfish Steak with Pepper

The firm, dense flesh of swordfish tends to dry out if not well lubricated, so it should be brushed frequently with oil during the broiling.

Makes 4 servings

1 large or 2 smaller swordfish steaks
  (about 2 pounds), cut 1½ inches
  thick

2 teaspoons coarsely ground black
  pepper
¼ cup olive oil

Preheat the broiler. Put a piece of heavy-duty aluminum foil on the broiler rack and brush with oil. Press the pepper into both sides of the fish with the heel of your hand. Brush top side with oil and arrange fish on the foil. Broil about 2 inches from the heat for 6 to 7 minutes a side, turning once and brushing with more oil during the broiling.

¶**Broiled Swordfish with Rosemary.** Substitute dried rosemary for the pepper.

¶**Broiled Swordfish with Garlic and Olives.** Omit the pepper. Broil the swordfish on one side, turn, broil 3 minutes, then top with a mixture of 1 teaspoon finely chopped garlic, ½ cup coarsely chopped Italian or Greek black olives, and 2 teaspoons lemon juice, and broil 4 minutes longer.

¶**Broiled Marinated Swordfish.** Before broiling, marinate the fish for 15 minutes, turning once or twice, in a mixture of ⅓ cup lemon juice, 2 tablespoons olive oil, 1 teaspoon finely chopped fresh mint or crumbled dried mint, salt and freshly ground black pepper to taste. Broil, basting with the marinade, but cut the broiling time to 5 to 6 minutes a side as the lemon juice will have penetrated and partially "cooked" the fish.

Baked Swordfish Steak

Press pepper or rosemary into the flesh of the fish, as in the previous recipe, and brush with oil. Arrange in an oiled baking dish and bake in a preheated 450° oven for 15 minutes, without turning.

Baked Halibut Steak Niçoise

An excellent way to treat this white-fleshed, rather bland-flavored fish, which takes kindly to strong flavoring. Cod, haddock, or tilefish may be treated the same way. Serve with steamed rice.

Makes 4 servings

2 shallots, finely chopped
1 green bell pepper, seeded and finely chopped
½ red bell pepper, seeded and finely chopped
2 large or 4 small halibut steaks, 1 to 1½ inches thick
Salt, freshly ground black pepper
2 ripe tomatoes, peeled, seeded, and chopped

1 lemon, halved and thinly sliced, blanched in boiling water 1 minute
½ cup dry white wine
2 tablespoons dry vermouth
½ cup strong fish stock (see page 530) or bottled clam juice
4 tablespoons cold butter
2 tablespoons chopped parsley
2 tablespoons chopped chives

Make a bed of the shallots and peppers in a buttered baking dish large enough to hold the steaks. Arrange steaks on top, sprinkle with salt and pepper, and cover with the chopped tomatoes and the lemon slices. Combine the wine, vermouth, and fish stock, pour over the fish, and bring slowly to a simmer over low heat. Transfer the dish to a 400° oven and bake for 10 to 15 minutes, just until the fish is done.

Drain the cooking liquid into a small, heavy pan and boil down over high heat to 2 to 3 tablespoons. Remove from heat and beat in the cold butter with a whisk, to make a creamy sauce. Add the chopped herbs, correct the seasoning, pour over the fish, and serve.

Baked Stuffed Shad

This superb fish is in season on the Atlantic Coast from early in January, when the first catch arrives from the South, to May, when the northern supply is at its peak. Because of its intricate bone structure, which makes filleting a highly paid art, most shad is sold boned and may be broiled or sautéed like other fish fillets. It is also excellent baked. In the old days, people baked shad for hours in the mistaken belief that this would dissolve the bones (a French recipe for shad stuffed with sorrel specified 10 hours' baking time). All it did was ruin the fish.

Makes 4 servings

1 shad, split and boned

STUFFING

2 large onions, sliced thin
4 tablespoons unsalted butter
1 cup bread crumbs
¼ cup chopped parsley
½ teaspoon dried thyme

2 tablespoons finely chopped celery
leaves
1 teaspoon salt
1 egg, beaten

Sauté the onions in the butter until soft. Combine with the other stuffing ingredients, mixing well. Stuff the shad and either sew it up or tie it with string. Place in an oiled baking dish and bake in a 450° oven, allowing 10 minutes per inch of thickness, measured at the thickest point. Serve with boiled potatoes and a green vegetable.

Shad Roe Poached in Butter

Shad roe is so delicate that it needs little more than a gentle simmering in plenty of butter. I find this much preferable to broiling, which hardens and dries out the roe. Crisp bacon and little boiled potatoes go well with shad roe.

Makes 2 servings

6 ounces unsalted butter
2 pairs shad roe
Salt, freshly ground black pepper

Lemon wedges
1 tablespoon chopped parsley (optional)

Melt the butter in a heavy skillet with a cover. When warm, but not hot, add the roe, coating them well with the butter, cover and cook very gently over low heat for about 12 to 15 minutes, turning once. Season to taste with salt and pepper, and serve with the pan juices poured over them and lemon wedges. You can sprinkle them with parsley if you like, but I think the butter and lemon are all they need.

Eel

I think of eels as fascinating and rather romantic fish. Both the European and American varieties breed in the deep Sargasso Sea (ranging in size from 1½ to 7 feet; see Concordance) and then, by some ancient instinct, swim east or west to live in the freshwater streams where we catch them.

I don't know why so many people shun eel. I love its sweet, delicate flesh and gelatinous quality, whether it is broiled, sautéed, poached, baked, cooked in wine with chopped herbs and left to chill in the rich green jelled juices, or made into a matelote, the traditional eel stew of Normandy. If you have never tried eel, start with smoked eel and you'll find how good that succulent flesh can be.

Most good fish markets will skin and clean eel. If they don't, first remove the skin by cutting it around the head and peeling it back in one piece, like a glove (pliers will help you get a good grip on the skin). Then remove the innards, wash the fish and cut it into pieces about 3 inches long.

Flemish Green Eel

A marvelous cold dish that can be served as a first course or for a summer buffet.

Makes 6 servings

3 tablespoons butter
3 tablespoons oil
3 pounds eels, skinned, cleaned, and
    cut in 3-inch pieces
¼ pound finely chopped sorrel or
    spinach
½ cup finely chopped parsley
1 tablespoon chopped fresh tarragon
    or 1 teaspoon dried tarragon

A good pinch each of savory, rosemary,
    sage, thyme
Salt, freshly ground black pepper
White wine to cover
4 egg yolks
1½ teaspoons lemon juice

Heat the butter and oil in a large skillet with a cover. Add the eels and brown on all sides. When just colored, add the sorrel or spinach and the herbs. Season to taste with salt and pepper and mix well. Add enough white wine to cover. Cover skillet and simmer gently until the eel is just tender, about 20 minutes. Remove the fish with a slotted spoon to a large serving dish. Lightly beat the egg yolks, add a little of the hot pan juices to them, and mix well. Stir them into the juices in the pan and stir until lightly thickened, taking care the liquid does not come near the boiling point. Taste and adjust the seasoning, add the lemon juice, and pour over the eel. Chill and serve cold.

Matelote of Eel, from Normandy

For this stew, the eel is cooked, Normandy style, in dry cider from that region of apples, cider, and Calvados. Don't on any account use sweet cider or you'll ruin the dish. You can buy imported dry cider from Europe in most liquor stores, or in a pinch substitute white wine.

Makes 6 servings

3 onions, cut in fine julienne strips
2 carrots, cut in fine julienne strips
3 ribs celery, cut in fine julienne strips
2 to 3 pounds eel, skinned, cleaned, and
    cut in 3-inch pieces
Salt, pepper, thyme, tarragon
1½ cups dry cider

24 small white onions, peeled
3 tablespoons butter
3 tablespoons flour
2 egg yolks
½ cup heavy cream
A handful of chopped fresh sorrel,
    if available, or lemon juice

GARNISH: 12 small bread croutons, fried in butter

Put the finely cut vegetables in the bottom of a saucepan and arrange the pieces of eel on top. Season with salt, pepper, and herbs to taste and pour the cider over the mixture. Bring to a boil, reduce the heat, and simmer until the eel is tender, about 20 minutes. Meanwhile, cook the whole onions in salted water until tender.

Remove the cooked eel to a hot serving dish. Strain the broth and reduce to 1 cup. Melt the butter in a saucepan, blend in the flour, and slowly mix in the broth, stirring until thickened. Mix the egg yolks and cream and stir a little of the hot sauce into them. Stir this into the sauce in the pan and continue cooking and stirring over low heat until smooth and well blended. Do not allow it to boil. Add the chopped sorrel, if available. If not, substitute lemon juice to taste. Garnish with croutons.

Mrs. Rockey's Shad Roe

Makes 6 servings

2 pairs shad roe
1 teaspoon Worcestershire sauce
½ cup bouillon
1 cup buttered bread crumbs
6 hard-boiled egg yolks, mashed

1 teaspoon lemon juice
1 teaspoon anchovy paste
1 tablespoon chopped parsley
Salt and freshly ground black pepper
    to taste

Blanch the shad roe for 1 minute. Remove the membrane and gently break the roe up and place in a 2-quart casserole. Mix and add the remaining ingredients, reserving some of the bread crumbs to sprinkle over the top. Bake in a 350° oven for 20 minutes. Serve at once.

Broiled Trout

An old recipe from the fabled Poodle Dog Restaurant in San Francisco, which opened in the days of the Gold Rush. This is a variation of the fisherman's method of cooking freshly caught trout by rolling them in cornmeal and sautéing them over the campfire.

Makes 6 servings

6 brook trout
1 cup melted butter
1 cup cornmeal
Salt, freshly ground black pepper

¼ cup lime juice
¼ cup chopped chives
¼ cup chopped parsley or chervil

Dip the trout in some of the melted butter, reserving ½ cup or more for the sauce. Roll the trout in cornmeal and broil about 3 to 4 inches from the heat, allowing 10 minutes per measured inch of thickness, turning once. Be careful not to let the coating scorch. If necessary, lower the rack so the fish is farther from the heat. Season to taste with salt and pepper. Heat the remaining melted butter and combine with the lime juice and chopped herbs. Serve as a sauce for the trout.

Sautéed Trout in Crêpes

A different and effective way to prepare trout or other small fish. Serve with asparagus or a salad.

Makes 6 servings

½ pound mushrooms, finely chopped
10 tablespoons unsalted butter
Salt, freshly ground black pepper
½ cup or more flour
4 tablespoons heavy cream

6 brook trout
⅔ cup clarified unsalted butter
  (see page 543)
6 savory crêpes (see page 265)
Juice of ½ lemon

Sauté the mushrooms in 4 tablespoons butter until soft. Sprinkle with ½ teaspoon salt, ¼ teaspoon pepper, and 2 tablespoons flour. Stir until the flour is absorbed by the mushroom juices and cooked through, then add the cream and stir until the mixture is thick.

Sprinkle the trout with salt and pepper and dust both sides with flour. Melt the clarified butter in a 12-inch heavy skillet or sauté pan until bubbling but not browned. Measure the thickness of the trout, add to the pan and sauté for 10 minutes per measured inch, turning once, until nicely browned on both sides.

Spread each crêpe with some of the mushroom mixture, place a trout on top and roll the crêpe so the head and tail of the trout stick out at either end. Arrange the trout in an oval baking dish. Discard the butter in the pan, rub out the pan with paper towels, and add the remaining 6 table-spoons butter. Heat until lightly browned, but not burned, and pour over the crêpes and trout. Sprinkle with lemon juice and put in a 375° oven for a few minutes to reheat. Serve at once.

Fried Smelts or Sardines

Inexpensive smelts and sardines are ideal candidates for deep-frying because the backbones are soft and easily removed. If the fish market has not already cleaned the little fish, slit them along the belly and pull out the entrails. Then loosen the bone at the tail end with your fingers and pull it away from the flesh. Remove the heads but leave the tails on. Flour the fish, dip them in beaten egg and then in bread crumbs or cornmeal until well coated.

Heat deep fat to 370°, drop in the fish and fry for 2 or 3 minutes, until brown and crisp. Drain on paper towels. Salt and pepper them well and serve with rémoulade or tartare sauce (see page 77). Half a dozen of these little fish makes a good hearty serving.

¶Fried Smelts with Garlic and Parsley. Add finely chopped garlic and parsley to the crumbs or cornmeal. Serve with a well-seasoned tomato sauce.

¶Skewered Smelts. Arrange the boned fish on small metal skewers, about 3 to a skewer, dip in flour, egg, and crumbs and deep-fry. Drain, sprinkle with salt and pepper, and serve on the skewers. You can, if you wish, add a few drops of Tabasco to the egg mixture to make them a little zestier. Alternatively, after boning the smelts or sardines, flatten them and string them on the skewers, placing 2 skewers through each one lengthwise.

Baked Spiced Smelts or Sardines

These pickled fish should be served very cold, with potato salad, pickled beets, rye bread, and beer.

Makes 6 to 8 servings

36 to 48 smelts or sardines
2 large onions, thinly sliced
2 carrots, chopped
3 cloves garlic, finely chopped
2 bay leaves
6 peppercorns
5 slices lemon
½ cup olive oil

½ cup wine vinegar
1 tablespoon salt
1 teaspoon allspice
1 teaspoon whole cloves
2-inch piece cinnamon stick
2 cups water
1 cup dry white wine

Clean the fish and arrange in a large baking dish. Put all the other ingredients in a pan and bring to a boil. Simmer 15 minutes, then pour the hot mixture over the fish and bake in a 400° oven for 12 minutes. Let the smelts cool in the liquid.

Coulibiac of Salmon

This famous Russian specialty is perfect for a buffet as it looks spectacular, slices well, is easy to eat with a fork, and will serve up to 10 guests. With a spinach salad, it makes a complete meal.

Makes 10 servings

¼ pound butter
2 pounds salmon fillets, cut in small
    strips (sturgeon or fresh tuna may
    be substituted)
½ pound sole fillets, cut in small strips
Salt, freshly ground black pepper
6 shallots, finely chopped
½ pound mushrooms, sliced
1 teaspoon paprika
¼ cup chives

½ cup buckwheat groats (kasha)
1 egg, lightly beaten
2 cups boiling water
Double recipe brioche dough (see page
    477), refrigerated overnight
3 tablespoons melted unsalted butter
3 hard-boiled eggs, sliced
1 beaten egg (egg wash) for brushing
    the brioche

ACCOMPANIMENTS: Hollandaise sauce (page 532) or melted butter
                and chopped parsley

Melt 4 tablespoons of the butter in a skillet and sauté the fish strips lightly for about 2 minutes, until just firm. Season with salt and pepper to taste.

Melt the remaining 4 tablespoons butter in a second skillet and sauté the shallots and mushrooms until soft, and season with salt and pepper, paprika, and chives. Mix the buckwheat with the lightly beaten egg and stir in a third skillet over medium heat until each kernel is separate. Add boiling water, cover tightly, and steam for 20 minutes over very low heat.

Roll out the brioche dough to a rectangle 14 by 20 inches and ½ inch thick. Roll it onto a rolling pin and unroll onto a lightly floured cloth or a piece of heavy aluminum. Brush the surface of the dough with melted butter. Put in the center layers of the fish, buckwheat, shallots and mushrooms, and sliced eggs, ending with the remainder of the buckwheat. Fold the ends and sides of the dough over the filling so that it is completely covered, and seal by pressing the edges of the dough together well. Butter a baking sheet large enough to hold the coulibiac, invert it onto the coulibiac and, with the aid of the cloth or foil, turn the whole thing over so the smooth side is uppermost. Let rise on the baking sheet in a warm place for 20 to 30 minutes. Preheat the oven to 375°. Brush the surface of the brioche with beaten egg. Cut a center vent in the top for the steam to escape.

Bake for 30 to 40 minutes, or until the brioche is nicely browned and cooked through. Slice, and serve with hollandaise sauce, or use melted butter as a sauce and accompany it with a bowl of chopped parsley.

¶**Coulibiac of Salmon with Rice.** Use 1½ cups boiled rice in place of the buckwheat groats and mix it with 2 tablespoons chopped parsley and ¼ cup melted butter before putting it into the coulibiac. Accompany with hollandaise sauce (page 532).

Scalloped Salmon

Makes 4 servings

16-ounce can salmon
2 tablespoons lemon juice
2 tablespoons chopped onion
1½ cups coarse cracker crumbs
½ cup melted butter

½ teaspoon salt
½ teaspoon freshly ground black pepper
1 cup milk or other liquid
Butter

Combine the salmon, lemon juice, and onion. Blend the crumbs, melted butter, and seasonings. Pile in alternate layers in a buttered baking dish and add just enough milk (or fish broth or tomato juice) to moisten the crumbs. Dot with butter and bake in a 350° oven for about 30 minutes or until nicely browned.

Salmon Cheeks

Salmon cheeks are best lightly sautéed.

Makes 4 servings

2 dozen salmon cheeks
All-purpose flour
4 tablespoons butter

½ teaspoon salt
½ teaspoon freshly ground black pepper
1 lemon cut into wedges

Dredge the cheeks lightly with flour and sauté very quickly in butter. Cook for approximately 3 to 4 minutes. Turn once and season with salt and pepper. Serve with wedges of lemon.

Salmon Tart

A pleasant and unusual first course or light luncheon entrée for summer. Serve it hot or cold with thin slices of dill pickles.

Makes 8 servings

CREAM CHEESE PASTRY
½ pound cream cheese
½ pound unsalted butter

½ cup heavy cream
2½ cups flour

SALMON FILLING
2 pounds fresh salmon (or halibut,
    swordfish, or fresh tuna)
1 cup white wine
1 onion stuck with 3 cloves
1 tablespoon dried dill weed
2 bay leaves
1 teaspoon Tabasco

2 cloves garlic, peeled
Salt, freshly ground black pepper
1 teaspoon chopped fresh dill
2 tablespoons chopped parsley
3 egg yolks
⅔ cup sour cream
Egg wash

The pastry should be chilled 2 to 3 hours. Overnight is even better. Blend the cream cheese, butter, heavy cream, and flour in an electric mixer or by hand. Form into a ball, wrap in wax paper, and chill.

Put the fish in a large pan, add the white wine and enough water to cover the fish. Remove fish. Add to the pan the onion, dried dill, bay leaves, Tabasco, garlic, 1 tablespoon salt, and 1 teaspoon freshly ground black pepper. Bring to a boil. Simmer 20 minutes, then add fish and poach gently, allowing 10 minutes per measured inch of thickness. Do not overcook.

Remove the fish. When it is cool enough to handle, remove the skin and bones and flake the fish. Blend with dill, parsley, egg yolks, sour cream, and a teaspoon each of salt and black pepper.

Remove the pastry from the refrigerator and divide in half. Roll out one half on a floured board in a circle large enough to fit a 9-inch pie pan. Roll out the other half to fit the top. Line pan with first piece of dough and chill lined pan and top dough thoroughly for about 30 minutes. Remove from refrigerator and fill the pastry-lined pan with fish mixture. Cover with top layer of dough and cut a vent to allow the steam to escape. Brush top with egg wash and bake in a 400° oven for 30 to 35 minutes, or until crust is nicely browned and filling hot and bubbly.

Mixed Seafood and Seafood Stews

French Seafood Sausages
(Cervelas aux Fruits de Mer)

An elegant, haute cuisine version of seafood sausage, made with a mousseline of fish studded with pieces of lobster, scallops, and salmon. Serve this as a first course for a special dinner party with a velouté or Nantua sauce.

Makes 8 servings

¾ pound sole or pike fillets
1 egg white
⅔ cup heavy cream
½ teaspoon salt
⅛ teaspoon pepper
Dash of paprika
3 drops Tabasco
¼ cup finely chopped parsley

¼ cup finely chopped mushrooms
¼ cup finely chopped scallops
2 tablespoons finely chopped salmon
    (smoked salmon may be used)
Meat from a 1¼- to 1½-pound lobster,
    finely chopped
2 to 3 feet of sausage casings
3 tablespoons vegetable oil

Put the fish through the fine blade of a meat grinder. Transfer to a large bowl over a bowl of ice cubes or ice water. Beat in the egg white until smooth and absorbed. Gradually beat in the cream, a teaspoon at a time, until the mixture is smooth, thick, and stiff. Season with salt, pepper, paprika, and Tabasco. Stir in the parsley, mushrooms, scallops, salmon, and lobster meat. Using a sausage stuffer or funnel, stuff the mixture into well-rinsed casings, twisting and tying the casing at intervals until you have 8 sausages. Try to eliminate air bubbles. Prick the casings with a fork and poach sausages gently in salted water to cover for 1½ hours. Drain and brown quickly in hot oil.

FOOD PROCESSOR METHOD: Make the fish mousse by processing the sole or pike, cut in pieces, with 1 *whole* egg (not egg white) to a smooth paste. Gradually pour in the cream, with the motor running, then the seasonings. Process just until thick and liquid absorbed. Combine with the other ingredients.

¶**Seafood Sausages with Shrimp.** Use ⅓ cup finely chopped shrimp instead of lobster.

¶**Seafood Sausages with Crab.** Use ⅓ cup finely chopped crabmeat instead of lobster.

Seafood en Brochette

Makes 4 servings

1½ pounds halibut, sturgeon, or other firm white fish cut 1½ inches thick	⅓ cup lemon juice
12 sea scallops	1 teaspoon salt and freshly ground black pepper
8 to 10 mushroom caps	2 to 3 tablespoons chopped parsley
½ cup peanut or olive oil	Beurre blanc (see page 201)

Cut the fish in 1½-inch cubes. Using 4 to 6 skewers, alternate the fish and scallops, using a mushroom cap at each end of the skewer.

Combine oil, lemon juice, salt, pepper, and parsley in a bowl. Brush the fish on the skewers well with the mixture. Arrange skewers on a broiling rack, and broil 3 inches from the heat for 5 minutes on each side, brushing several times with lemon juice and oil. Remove from the broiler and either slide the fish off the skewers with a fork onto hot plates or leave on the skewers. Serve with a beurre blanc.

Cocotte of Seafood Manzanilla

A breakaway from the usual method of serving seafood mixtures in a creamy sauce. The combination of flavors is different and delicious. You could use any combination of seafood and/or cold cooked fish. The flavor of a *good* dry sherry makes a world of difference in this dish.

Makes 6 to 8 servings

¾ pound softened butter	2 shallots, finely chopped
3 cloves garlic, finely chopped	2 tablespoons chopped parsley

1 tablespoon minced fresh dill or
  1 teaspoon dried dill weed
1 tablespoon chopped fresh tarragon
  or 1 teaspoon dried tarragon
1 teaspoon salt
½ teaspoon freshly ground black pepper
Dash of nutmeg

1 cup soft bread crumbs
⅔ cup dry sherry
1 pound shrimp, cooked and deveined
½ pound bay scallops, uncooked
½ pound crabmeat
1 cup buttered crumbs
GARNISH: Lemon slices, chopped parsley

Cream the butter, garlic, shallots, and seasonings and mix with the soft crumbs. Add enough of the sherry to flavor. Combine seafood and divide among 6 or 8 ramekins or individual baking dishes, sprinkle with remaining sherry, cover with the butter mixture, and top with buttered crumbs. Bake in a 400° oven for 10 to 15 minutes. Serve as a first course with lemon slices and chopped parsley.

Hellenic Seafood Stew

This is one of the many delicious soup-stews found around the Mediterranean shores, each offering basically the same ingredients, but varied by different seasonings and techniques. Long a favorite of mine, this stew is quick to make and can be stretched or reduced according to the number of guests.

Makes 6 servings

6 frozen lobster tails, thawed
½ cup good fruity olive oil
4 garlic cloves, peeled and finely
  chopped
2½ cups canned Italian plum tomatoes
2 bay leaves
1 teaspoon oregano

1 cup dry white wine
18 small clams, well washed and
  scrubbed
18 raw shrimp, shelled but with the
  tails left on
1 cup finely chopped parsley

Cut the thawed lobster tails in thirds crosswise and snip through the underside of the shell with kitchen shears (the lobster is cooked in its shell to retain the tenderness and flavor, and removed with a fork by the diner). Heat the oil in a large, heavy sauté pan or skillet, add the lobster tail pieces and garlic, and sauté over medium-high heat for 3 or 4 minutes. Add the canned tomatoes, bay leaves, oregano, and wine, and bring to a boil. Add the clams, arranging them around the sides of the pan, hinged side down, cover the pan, and cook over medium heat for 4 to 5 minutes, or until the clam shells have been steamed open. If any are not opened, steam 5 minutes longer. Add the shrimp, cover the pan, and cook another 3 minutes, or until they are pink. At this point, discard any clams that have not opened and the bay leaves. Add the parsley to the soup and serve immediately in heated soup bowls or plates, with toasted French bread.

Bouillabaisse

Although this specialty of the South of France is basically simple, its excellence lies in the fact that the taste and texture of each fish comes through. Timing is all, or you will end up with a mess of overcooked fish. Although we cannot find here the same fish that are used in France, it is perfectly possible to make substitutions. On the Atlantic Coast you have a choice of halibut, striped bass (rockfish), cod, or even swordfish for the firmer fish; flounder, snapper, or sole for the less firm; mussels, clams, and lobsters for the shellfish. On the West Coast you might use halibut, black cod, or sablefish for the firm-textured types; sand dabs, snapper, or rex sole for the softer, and crabs instead of lobster.

Makes 10 servings

5 pounds fish, firm and softer types
    from those listed above
½ cup good olive oil
5 or 6 garlic cloves, finely chopped
2 large onions, finely chopped
4 or 5 ripe tomatoes, peeled, seeded, and
    chopped, or 2 cups canned Italian
    plum tomatoes
1 stalk dried fennel or 2 teaspoons
    fennel seeds

Pinch of saffron
2 tablespoons salt
1½ teaspoons freshly ground black
    pepper
2 lobsters or 4 crabs, cut or broken into
    bite size pieces
1 quart mussels or 24 small clams
1 loaf French bread, sliced and lightly
    toasted

ROUILLE

4 or 5 dried hot red chili peppers,
    soaked for several hours in hot
    water
3 garlic cloves, peeled

¼ teaspoon salt
4 to 5 tablespoons olive oil
1 cup bouillabaisse broth
1 tablespoon hot paprika (optional)

For the bouillabaisse, clean all the fish and cut in slices about 1 inch thick. If heads are available, cut them in half. Separate firm fish from soft.

Heat the oil in a wide braising pan or kettle large enough to hold all the seafood. Add the garlic, onion, tomatoes, fennel, a good pinch of saffron, salt, pepper, firm fish, fish heads, lobster or crabs, and enough boiling water to more than cover the seafood. Boil briskly for 7 to 8 minutes (this makes the oil and water combine, giving a richer broth). Add the soft fish and cook for 5 to 6 minutes, but at not so high a heat. Be careful not to over-cook the fish. Meanwhile, in a separate kettle cook the well-scrubbed and bearded mussels or the clams with 1½ cups water over high heat, covered, until the shells open (discard any with closed shells). Strain the broth through cheesecloth into the bouillabaisse.

Transfer the fish and shellfish, discarding the fish heads, to a hot serving dish and keep warm while reducing the broth over high heat for several minutes. Correct the seasoning.

Prepare the rouille. Drain the soaked peppers and pound to a paste in a mortar. Work in the garlic, salt, and oil until the mixture is smooth and well blended. Stir in the broth and the hot paprika, if desired.

Line a soup tureen or large bowl with some of the sliced toasted bread, add the fish and mussels or clams. Cut the lobsters or crabs into serving pieces with shells on, discarding inedible parts, and add to the tureen. Pour the broth over the top. Serve the bouillabaisse in bowls or soup plates with the rest of the bread and the rouille, to stir into the bouillabaisse to taste.

Solianka

This fish stew, introduced to the Pacific Northwest by Russian immigrants, became very popular in Oregon and Washington, where it is made with salmon from the Columbia River.

Makes 4 servings

2 pounds fish bones and heads, or
    2-pound bony fish, with head
1½ quarts water
Salt, freshly ground black pepper
3 large ripe tomatoes, peeled, seeded,
    and chopped
7 tablespoons unsalted butter

1½ pounds salmon, cut in strips
2 onions, finely chopped
1 tablespoon each of chopped black
    olives and chopped green olives
4 dill pickles, finely chopped
2 teaspoons capers
1 bay leaf

GARNISH: Additional chopped green or black olives,
chopped parsley, lemon slices

Simmer the fish bones and heads in the water, well seasoned with salt and pepper, for 1½ hours. Strain the broth and reserve. Simmer the tomatoes in 3 tablespoons butter for 15 minutes. Season to taste. Arrange the salmon strips in a deep pot with the onions, olives, pickles, tomatoes, and capers. Cover with the fish broth, add the bay leaf, and simmer 12 to 15 minutes. Add the remaining 4 tablespoons butter. Serve in bowls, garnished with the chopped olives, parsley, and lemon slices.

¶**Solianka with Dill.** Add 1 to 2 tablespoons chopped fresh dill or 2 teaspoons dried dill weed to the soup before serving.

Cioppino

This marvelous fish soup-stew originated among the Italian and Portuguese fishermen of the California coast. Serve it in deep plates or bowls with forks and spoons and lots of French or Italian bread.

Makes 6 servings

1 quart clams
1 cup dry white or red wine
½ cup olive oil
1 large onion, chopped
2 cloves garlic, chopped
1 green pepper, chopped
¼ pound dried mushrooms, soaked in
    water and drained
4 ripe tomatoes, peeled, seeded, and
    chopped
4 tablespoons Italian tomato paste
2 cups red wine, such as Pinot Noir or
    Zinfandel

2 teaspoons salt
1 teaspoon freshly ground black pepper
2 tablespoons finely chopped fresh basil
    or 1 teaspoon dried basil
1 sea bass or striped bass, about 3
    pounds, cut into serving pieces, or
    3 pounds thick fish fillets, cut
    into serving pieces
1 pound crabmeat
1 pound raw shrimp, shelled
3 tablespoons chopped parsley

Steam the clams in the 1 cup white or red wine until they open—discard any that do not open. Strain the broth through two thicknesses of cheesecloth and reserve.

Heat the olive oil in a deep 8-quart pot and cook the onion, garlic, pepper, and mushrooms for 3 minutes. Add the tomatoes and cook 4 minutes. Add the strained clam broth, tomato paste, and 2 cups red wine. Season with salt and pepper and simmer for about 20 minutes. Taste and correct seasoning. Add the basil and the fish, and just cook the fish through about 3 to 5 minutes. Finally, add the steamed clams, crabmeat, and shrimp. Heat just until shrimp are cooked. Do not overcook. Sprinkle with parsley and serve.

¶**Cioppino with Mussels.** Substitute mussels for clams.

¶**Cioppino with Oysters.** Substitute oysters for the clams.

Cotriade

Another good fish stew is the Breton bouillabaisse, cotriade.

Makes 6 servings

4 large potatoes, peeled and quartered
4 large onions, peeled and quartered
2 or 3 fish heads
Bouquet garni of thyme, bay leaf,
    rosemary, and parsley tied in
    cheesecloth

Salt
3 pounds fish (mackerel, mullet, cod,
    eel, fresh sardines), cut in serving-
    size pieces

Put the potatoes, onions, fish heads, and bouquet garni in a pot with salt to taste, and cover with water, allowing about 1 pint per serving. Bring to a boil, reduce the heat, and simmer for 20 minutes. Remove the fish heads and the cheesecloth pouch of bouquet garni and add the fish. Cook until the potatoes are tender and the fish cooked through, about 15 minutes. Serve the broth in one bowl, the fish and vegetables in another.

Seafood à l'Américaine

Makes 2 cups

SAUCE À L'AMÉRICAINE
3 tablespoons butter
1 small onion, finely chopped
6 shallots, finely chopped
2 cups canned tomatoes
1 clove garlic, peeled and chopped
3 tablespoons chopped parsley

1 tablespoon chopped fresh tarragon
    or 1 teaspoon dried tarragon
1½ teaspoons thyme
½ bay leaf
3 tablespoons tomato paste

Makes 6 servings

2- to 2½-pound lobster
6 tablespoons olive oil
12 raw shrimp
4 to 6 tablespoons butter
4 fillets of sole

4 fillets of tilefish (or substitute
    haddock or flounder)
12 scallops
Flour
Salt, freshly ground black pepper

Prepare the Sauce à l'Américaine: Melt the butter in a skillet, add the onion, and cook for a few minutes without letting it brown. Add the shallots, tomato, garlic, and herbs, and simmer for 1 hour, or until the water from the tomatoes has cooked away. Add the tomato paste.

Split the lobster down the back from the head to the tail and remove the tomalley and coral. Sear the lobster in 4 tablespoons of the olive oil, turning until the shell has become brilliant red. Remove the lobster to absorbent paper. Remove the pieces of lobster from the shells and keep hot in the sauce.

Shell and devein the shrimp. Melt the butter and the remaining oil in one large or two small skillets. Dust the fillets, scallops, and shrimp with flour and sauté until delicately browned and just cooked through, about 5 minutes. Salt and pepper to taste.

Arrange the fish, scallops, shrimp, and lobster in a deep serving dish and cover with the sauce. Serve with rice.

Mussels Marinière

This is far and away the most popular of all the mussel dishes served in French restaurants in this country, yet surprisingly few people make it at home, considering how easy it is. Maybe they are daunted by the thought of having to scrub and beard the mussels, but the result is well worth the time and effort. All you need with this is plenty of hot crusty French bread to sop up all the goodness.

Makes 4 servings

2 quarts mussels
1 large onion, finely chopped
⅓ cup chopped parsley
⅛ teaspoon thyme

8 tablespoons unsalted butter
Freshly ground black pepper
1 to 1½ cups white wine

Scrub the mussels well with a scouring pad and scrape off any encrustations on the shells. Wash them thoroughly in several changes of water and pull or snip off the beard—the stringy black thread attached to the shells.

Put the mussels in a deep, heavy pan with the onion, ¼ cup of the parsley, the thyme, 4 tablespoons butter, a couple of grinds of pepper, and the wine—no salt; the mussel liquid will be salty enough. Cover and steam over medium-low heat just until the shells open, about 8 or 10 minutes. Remove the opened mussels, in their shells, to a big tureen, add the remaining butter and parsley to the pan to heat, and taste for salt as you do so. Pour the liquid over the mussels. To serve, ladle the mussels and their broth into deep soup plates.

¶**Mussels Marinière with Garlic.** Instead of onion, use 4 or 5 finely chopped garlic cloves.

¶**Mussels Marinière with Cream.** Stir ⅔ cup heavy cream into the liquid after removing the mussels, and bring to a boil.

¶**Mussels Marinière with Tomatoes.** Add 1 cup canned Italian plum tomatoes to the broth with the remaining parsley and omit the butter.

¶**Clams Marinière.** Substitute hard-shell clams for mussels in any of the above recipes.

Curried Seafood with Rice Pilaf

Makes 6 servings

THE RICE PILAF

1 onion, chopped
6 tablespoons butter
1½ cups long-grain rice
3 cups fish stock or 1½ cups bottled
    clam juice and 1½ cups water

½ teaspoon freshly ground pepper
½ teaspoon crumbled tarragon
Salt (you probably won't need this if
    you have used bottled clam juice)
Chopped parsley

3 cups dry white wine
1 cup water
½ cup chopped scallions, or green
    onions, including the green tops
1 carrot, finely chopped
A handful of parsley
1 teaspoon thyme
1 bay leaf
¾ pound fresh shrimp
Salt and freshly ground black pepper
    to taste
4 tablespoons butter
4 tablespoons flour

1 tablespoon curry powder
1 quart (about 30) hardshell clams,
    scrubbed and soaked in several
    changes of cold water
1 quart (about 30) mussels, scrubbed,
    debearded, and soaked in several
    changes of cold water
1 pound cod fillets, cut into strips about
    1 inch wide and 2 inches long
8 large mushrooms, quartered and
    sautéed in 2 tablespoons butter
Chopped cilantro or parsley

Prepare the rice pilaf. Sauté the onion in the butter until soft. Add the rice and cook, stirring constantly, until the grains become translucent—3 to 5 minutes. Add the fish stock and seasonings and put the mixture into a 1½-quart casserole. Cover and bake at 375° for about 45 minutes, or until all liquid is absorbed. Sprinkle parsley on top.

Meanwhile, shell the shrimp and set aside, reserving both shrimp and shells.

About 15 minutes before the rice will have finished cooking, prepare the seafood. In a deep saucepan, bring the wine, water, vegetables, herbs, shrimp shells, ½ teaspoon salt, and a few grindings of fresh pepper to a rapid boil. Cook for about 3 minutes to evaporate the alcohol, then set aside. Melt the butter in a heavy medium-size saucepan. Add the flour and curry powder and cook the mixture gently for 2 minutes, without browning. Immediately set the bottom of the pan in cold water to stop the cooking and prevent the curry powder from burning. Set aside.

Bring the seasoned cooking liquid back to a boil and add the clams. Cover the pot and steam for 3 minutes. Then uncover the pot and add the mussels. Cover and steam for 3 minutes longer, or until the shells are open. Remove the clams and mussels to a warm bowl, baste them with a few spoonfuls of the cooking liquid, and cover them loosely with foil. Strain the cooking liquid through several thicknesses of cheesecloth. Proceed immediately to the sauce.

Bring the roux back to bubbling over medium heat and whisk in the strained liquid. Bring the sauce to a simmer, and gently fold in the cod fillets and shrimp. Poach them in the sauce for about 3 minutes, until the shrimp have turned from their grayish raw color to a pale pink. Add the mushrooms.

Remove the rice from the oven and fluff it with a fork. Make a circle of the rice on the heated serving platter, sprinkle with parsley, and fill the center of the dish with the hot curried seafood. Arrange the clams and mussels around the rice, and sprinkle the platter generously with chopped parsley or cilantro.

Tuna Tart

Makes 6 to 8 servings

Cream cheese pastry (see page 216)
7-ounce can white-meat tuna
½ pound shrimp, cooked and shelled
¾ cup tiny green olives or anchovy-
*   stuffed cocktail olives*
¼ cup heavy cream

1 teaspoon paprika
½ teaspoon freshly ground black pepper
¼ teaspoon Tabasco
2 cups rich béchamel sauce (see page
*   531)*

Line an 8-inch tart mold that has a removable bottom with pastry, rolled a little thicker than usual. Place a piece of foil over the pastry and weight it down by filling with dry beans. Bake in a 400° oven for 15 to 20 minutes, or until the shell is nicely browned and done. Remove from the oven and take out the beans and foil. Keep the tart shell warm until ready to use.

Flake the tuna quite fine. Cut the shrimp into rather small pieces, reserving a few whole shrimp for garnish. In a saucepan, mix the seafood with the olives, reserving a few for garnish. Add the cream and seasonings and enough hot béchamel sauce to fill the shell. Heat to the boiling point. Fill the shell with the mixture and decorate with the whole shrimp and the olives. Serve the remaining béchamel sauce separately.

Clam Hash

I've been a clam lover ever since my childhood in Oregon, when we used to dig for clams at the beach and cook them in every way imaginable. This hash was a family favorite.

Makes 4 to 6 servings

6 tablespoons butter
½ cup finely chopped onion
1½ cups minced steamed clams (see
    steaming directions on page 222)
    or drained canned clams (reserve
    clam liquid)

1½ cups finely diced cooked potatoes
Salt, freshly ground black pepper
1 tablespoon Worcestershire sauce
3 eggs
½ cup grated Parmesan cheese
3 tablespoons chopped parsley

Melt the butter in a heavy skillet, preferably cast iron. Add the onion and sauté until just transparent. Add the drained clams and potatoes and press down with a spatula. Salt and pepper lightly and add the Worcestershire sauce. Cook about 10 minutes over medium heat, stirring occasionally with a fork or spatula and mixing in some of the crust from the bottom. Press down again. Beat the eggs with ¼ cup of the reserved clam liquid (this intensifies the clam flavor), combine with the cheese and pour over the hash. Cover tightly until the egg is set, about 6 to 8 minutes. Sprinkle with chopped parsley and serve.

Sauté of Clams

A simple way to cook clams that keeps them plump and juicy. You can think up your own variations on the basic recipe. Serve them on hot buttered toast.

Makes 4 to 6 servings

4 cups shucked and drained hardshell
    clams
¼ pound unsalted butter

Salt, freshly ground black pepper
1 tablespoon chopped parsley
1 tablespoon finely cut chives

Trim the tough necks from the clams. Heat the butter in a large, heavy skillet, add the clams, and cook just until the edges curl and they are plump and heated through. Season to taste with salt and pepper and sprinkle with the chopped herbs.

¶**Sauté of Clams with White Wine.** After the clams are plumped, add ½ cup white wine to the pan juices and let them cook down for 1 minute.

¶**Sauté of Clams with Tarragon.** Sprinkle the clams as they cook with 1 tablespoon chopped fresh tarragon or 1 teaspoon dried tarragon. Omit the parsley and chives.

¶**Sauté of Clams with Mustard and Worcestershire Sauce.** Stir 2 teaspoons Dijon mustard and 1 tablespoon Worcestershire sauce into the pan juices. Omit the herbs.

Scalloped Clams

Makes 4 servings

3 tablespoons grated onion
2 cups minced drained clams
¼ cup finely chopped parsley
1 teaspoon salt
Dash of Tabasco

½ cup bread crumbs
1 cup coarsely crushed cracker crumbs
½ cup melted butter
Additional butter
½ cup heavy cream

Combine the onion, clams, parsley, salt, and a dash of Tabasco in a mixing bowl. Mix thoroughly the bread crumbs and cracker crumbs with the melted butter. Set aside one-third of the mixture. Combine the remaining two-thirds with clam mixture and put in a buttered baking dish. Top with remaining crumbs, dot with butter, and pour the heavy cream over the top. Bake for 25 minutes in a 375° oven or until top is browned and crisp.

Clam Pie

Makes 6 to 8 servings

1 carrot, cut in julienne strips
1 onion, cut in julienne strips
1 bay leaf
Salt, freshly ground black pepper
2 cups dry white wine
2 quarts clams in shell, well scrubbed

1 pound mushrooms
5 tablespoons butter
2 cups white wine sauce (see page 534)
3 tablespoons sherry or Madeira
Lard Pie Crust (see page 509)
1 egg, beaten with a little water

Combine the carrot, onion, bay leaf, 1 teaspoon pepper, and white wine in a large kettle. Add the clams. Cover and steam over medium heat until the shells open. Remove the clams from the shells and strain the broth through a linen cloth to remove the sand. Reserve for other uses, or use to make the white wine sauce.

Clean and slice the mushrooms and sauté quickly in the butter, seasoning to taste with salt and pepper. Mix the mushrooms and clams with the sauce and the sherry or Madeira. Taste for seasoning.

Pour into a deep baking dish or pie dish and cool. Roll out pie crust to ¼-inch thickness. Place a support such as a metal or porcelain cup in the center of the dish to hold up the crust and top the pie with the pastry. Brush with egg mixture and bake in a 450° oven for 15 minutes. Reduce the heat to 350° and continue baking until the crust is nicely browned, about 20 minutes.

Oysters

Baked Oysters on the Half Shell with Shrimp Sauce

Makes 4 servings

½ pound medium raw shrimp
6 tablespoons butter
2 dozen fresh oysters, shucked (reserve the deeper half of the shell plus all oyster liquor)
½ to 1 cup milk
2 tablespoons dry white wine

3 tablespoons all-purpose flour
1 egg yolk
1 teaspoon salt
¼ teaspoon freshly ground black pepper
¼ cup soft fresh bread crumbs
½ cup freshly grated Gruyère or Emmenthaler cheese

Preheat the oven to 450°. Shell and devein the shrimp, then chop fine. Melt 2 tablespoons butter in a small skillet, drop in the shrimp, and cook over moderate heat, stirring constantly, until they turn pink. Set aside.

Pour the oyster liquor into a large measuring cup and add enough milk to make 1¾ cups. Stir in the wine. In a skillet melt remaining 4 tablespoons butter over moderate heat, stir in the flour, and cook, stirring, until golden and bubbly. Gradually pour in the milk-oyster-liquid-wine mixture, stirring constantly with a whisk, and cook over high heat until the sauce thickens slightly. Reduce the heat to low and simmer for about 3 minutes. Then beat the egg yolk lightly in a bowl, add about ¼ cup of the sauce, and whisk the egg yolk mixture into the sauce in the pan. Add the salt and pepper and taste for seasoning. Remove the pan from the heat and stir in the shrimp.

Fill a large shallow baking dish to a depth of about ¼ inch with rock or coarse salt. Spoon 1 tablespoon of the shrimp sauce into each oyster shell, top with an oyster, and blanket the oyster with a second tablespoon of the shrimp sauce. Arrange the filled shells side by side in the salt-lined baking dish. Bake in the top third of the oven for about 8 minutes, or until the sauce has barely begun to bubble. Sprinkle the oysters evenly with the bread crumbs and the cheese. Return to the oven for another 4 minutes, until the cheese melts and the crumbs brown lightly. You may then slide them under the broiler, about 3 inches from the heat, for a few minutes to brown the tops even further. Serve at once.

Stuffed Oysters

Makes 2 servings

6 shallots, finely chopped
½ cup chopped parsley
¼ cup chopped chervil

3 ounces butter, softened
12 oysters on the half shell

Blend the shallots, parsley, and chervil well with the butter. Spoon the herbed butter onto the oysters in their shells. Arrange the oysters in a large pan and place them under the broiler until the butter is melted and the edges begin to curl.

Or, if you have flat casseroles of sufficient size, you may fill them with rock salt and heat them. Arrange the oysters on the beds of rock salt and place them in a 500° oven for a few minutes or run them under the broiler.

Fried Oysters

Makes 4 servings

Unsalted butter or butter and oil
3 eggs
3 tablespoons heavy cream
1 quart freshly opened oysters of
   medium size

3 to 4 cups freshly rolled cracker crumbs
Salt, freshly ground black pepper
Lemon wedges or tartare sauce
   (see page 77)

Heat enough butter or mixed butter and oil in a heavy 12-inch skillet, preferably iron, to a depth of half an inch. Lightly beat the eggs and mix in the cream. Dip the oysters in the egg-cream mixture, then roll them in the cracker crumbs. Arrange on cookie sheets lined with waxed paper. Let them stand several minutes for the coating to set. Drop them into the hot fat, a few at a time so as not to crowd the skillet, and fry just long enough to brown the coating and heat them through, no more than a minute or two. Remove, sprinkle with salt and pepper, and serve on hot plates with lemon wedges or tartare sauce. Allow 6 or more oysters, according to appetite.

¶Oyster Loaves. For each serving, use a small loaf of unsliced white or French bread. Cut off the top crust about 1 inch down from the top and remove nearly all the crumb. Butter well. Place in a 350° oven to toast. Fill each loaf with fried oysters and replace the toasted top. Serve with lemon wedges and chili sauce.

Oyster Sausages

In the fishing communities of New England, there are many versions of seafood-and-suet sausages. They make excellent breakfast fare with scrambled eggs, or you could serve them for lunch on a bed of rice with a green vegetable or a salad.

Makes 4 servings

2 cups minced raw oysters
1⅓ cups finely chopped or shredded
    beef suet
1 cup fresh white bread crumbs
1½ teaspoons lemon juice
2 eggs

⅛ teaspoon allspice
⅛ teaspoon nutmeg
⅛ teaspoon freshly ground black pepper
Salt to taste
2 tablespoons butter
1 tablespoon oil

LEMON-PARSLEY BUTTER
½ cup melted butter
Lemon juice to taste

2 tablespoons chopped parsley

Combine the oysters, suet, bread crumbs, lemon juice, eggs, and seasonings in a bowl. Mix well. Stuff the mixture into well-rinsed sausage casings, using a small sausage stuffer. Tie one end of the casing and force the mixture in, making small, fat links of sausage about 5 inches long. Twist the casing and tie tightly with string. Continue until you have 8 or 10 sausages. Prick the sausages with a fork and poach in salted water in a skillet for 10 to 15 minutes, until just firm. Drain. When ready to eat the sausages, brown them quickly on both sides in the butter and oil. Combine the ingredients for lemon-parsley butter and serve with the sausages.

Shrimp

Shrimp Jambalaya

Makes 6 servings

5 tablespoons bacon fat or butter
3 tablespoons flour
1 large onion, chopped
2 cloves garlic, chopped
2½ cups canned Italian plum tomatoes
      (reserve the juice)
¾ cup cubed country ham
2 teaspoons crushed dried basil, or
      2 tablespoons chopped fresh basil

Salt, freshly ground black pepper
      to taste
2 dried red peppers, crushed
2 cups long-grain white rice
3 cups chicken or fish stock, boiling
2 pounds medium shrimp, shelled,
      deveined, and well rinsed

Melt the fat and stir in the flour. Cook, stirring, over low heat for 2 to 3 minutes. Add the onion and garlic and continue cooking over medium heat for a few minutes. Add the tomatoes and ham and cook for a few minutes more. Add the basil, salt, pepper, dried red peppers, and the rice. Pour the boiling stock over to cover by more than 2 inches. Cover the pan tightly and simmer the mixture over low heat for 20 to 30 minutes, or until the rice is almost tender. If the mixture should become too dry, add additional stock or some of the reserved tomato juice. Just before serving, add the shrimp. They should not cook for more than about 8 minutes with the mixture or they will toughen. If you prefer, cook the shrimp separately and add them to the pot at the last minute before serving.

¶Crabmeat Jambalaya. Use 1½ pounds crabmeat in place of the shrimp. Merely heat the crabmeat through before serving, lest you overcook it.

Shrimp on a Stick

Makes 8 servings

2 pounds raw jumbo shrimp or prawns
      (16 to 24)
2 cups dry white wine
6 cups water
¼ cup white wine vinegar
1 onion, sliced

1 carrot, sliced
1 tablespoon salt
2 whole cloves
1 stalk celery, sliced
Bouquet garni (bay leaf, parsley, thyme)

DILL BUTTER
½ pound soft butter
1 tablespoon minced fresh dill or
   2 teaspoons dried dill weed

1 teaspoon lemon juice
Dash of Tabasco

Thread each shrimp on a long, thin bamboo skewer. Insert the point of the skewer at the tail of the shrimp and impale its full length, so that the point of the skewer just shows at the head end of the shrimp. Refrigerate until cooking time.

Make a court bouillon of the wine, water, wine vinegar, onion, carrot, salt, cloves, celery, and bouquet garni. Bring to a boil, reduce to a simmer, and cook for ½ hour. Strain.

Cream the butter with the fresh or dried dill, lemon juice, and Tabasco. Divide mixture among 8 small dishes, one for each guest.

When guests have assembled, bring the court bouillon to a boil, pour into an electric frying pan or other table cooker which has been placed on the cocktail table. Bring on the skewered shrimps, attractively arranged on a platter, and give each guest a napkin, a dish of prepared dill butter, and a small tray or plate. When the court bouillon is bubbling, add one skewer of shrimp for each guest, allowing the handles to stick out, but completely immersing the shellfish. Cook for about 5 minutes, or until they have lost their translucent look. Serve one to each guest, to be dipped in the dill butter and eaten right from the skewer. Cook the remaining shrimp in 1 or 2 batches.

Shrimp with Curry Butter

An easy, quick party dish, especially if you arrange the shrimp on the skewers and make the curry butter ahead of time. Serve with rice and a green salad.

Makes 6 servings

2 pounds large shelled raw shrimp

½ pound lean bacon

CURRY BUTTER
2 shallots or 1 very small onion,
   finely chopped
2 tablespoons butter
2 to 3 teaspoons good curry powder

1 tablespoon chopped chutney
¼ pound softened butter
GARNISH: Chopped parsley

Arrange the shrimp on 6 skewers, lacing the bacon strips in between them. Set aside until ready to broil.

To make the curry butter, sauté the shallot or onion in the 2 tablespoons butter until limp, then blend in the curry powder and cook 2 to 3 minutes. Mix in the chopped chutney and let the mixture cool slightly before blending it with the soft butter. Form into balls and chill well in the refrigerator.

Preheat the broiler. Put the skewers of shrimp under the broiler and broil for 5 to 7 minutes, according to thickness, turning once, until the shrimp are cooked through and the bacon is slightly crisp. Serve on hot plates and put a ball or two of curry butter on each one. Sprinkle with parsley and serve.

¶**Shrimp with Dill Butter.** Blend ¼ pound butter with 2 tablespoons chopped fresh dill and a squeeze of lemon juice.

Shrimp Floridian en Papillote

Makes 4 servings

½ pound blue cheese
8-ounce package cream cheese
1 tablespoon chopped chives
1 tablespoon chopped parsley
1 clove garlic, finely chopped

¾ cup dry white wine
2 pounds raw shrimp, shelled and
  deveined
4 slices lemon

Blend the blue cheese with the cream cheese and the chives, parsley, and garlic. Thin the mixture with the wine.

Take 4 large squares aluminum foil and heap one-quarter of the cheese mixture on each. Top with a quarter of the shrimp and a slice of lemon. Bring the edges of the foil up over the shrimp and fold them together. Fold up the ends of the foil to make a tight package. Arrange the packages on a baking sheet and bake in a 400° oven for 20 minutes.

Chuck's Baked Shrimp

My friend Chuck Williams is a past master at turning out a good dinner in next to no time. His baked shrimp are easy and quick and can be prepared well in advance, except for the final anointment of oil. Serve them with rice and a green salad.

Makes 4 servings

2 pounds medium-size shrimp, in the
   shell
2 tablespoons chopped fresh tarragon,
   or 1½ teaspoons dried tarragon
   soaked in 1 tablespoon dry white
   wine

Salt, freshly ground black pepper
⅓ cup melted butter or olive oil

Split the shrimp down the back with scissors so they can almost be spread flat, butterfly fashion. Peel off the body shell, but leave the tail shell on. Arrange the shrimp, tails up, in a lightly buttered round oven-to-table baking dish, and sprinkle with the tarragon, salt and pepper to taste, and enough butter or oil to moisten them. Bake in a 350° oven for 10 minutes, or until just cooked through.

Shrimp Loaf

Makes 2 servings

1 pound shrimp, shelled, deveined,
   and cooked
1 tablespoon olive oil
1 tablespoon butter
½ cup chili sauce

¼ cup cream
½ cup bread crumbs
2 teaspoons Worcestershire sauce
½ teaspoon Tabasco

Combine all ingredients and place in a buttered casserole. Bake in a 350° oven for 20 minutes. Serve at once.

Lobster

Stuffed Baked Lobster

One of my long-time favorite lobster recipes, because of its earthy Provençal combination of flavors. Serve it with shoestring potatoes and a green salad.

Makes 4 servings

Four 1½-pound lobsters, boiled and
   cooled
4 cloves garlic, finely chopped
¾ cup olive oil
½ cup chopped parsley

¼ cup lemon juice
Salt, freshly ground black pepper
2 to 3 tablespoons butter
½ cup buttered bread crumbs

Split the lobsters lengthwise and crack the claws. Remove the body and claw meat, the tomalley and the coral, if there is any. Clean and reserve the shells. Chop the meat quite fine and blend with the garlic, oil, parsley, lemon juice, and salt and pepper to taste. Mix in the tomalley and the coral. Generously butter the lobster shells and stuff them with the mixture. Sprinkle with buttered crumbs, dot with butter, and arrange on a rack in a shallow baking pan. Bake in a 350° oven for 20 to 30 minutes, or until stuffing is well heated and crumbs delicately browned.

Lobster Napoule

This dish of lobster and vegetables à la Grecque, which I first ate in Nice many years ago, looks perfectly ravishing on a summer buffet table. Use all your artistic talents to make the arrangements spectacular. Serve with crisp rolls and a cucumber salad.

Makes 8 or more servings

FOR THE VEGETABLES À LA GRECQUE
2 cups water
1 cup white wine
⅔ cup olive oil
½ cup white-wine vinegar
2 garlic cloves, crushed
2 tablespoons chopped parsley
1½ teaspoons salt
1 teaspoon thyme
1 bay leaf
16 peppercorns

8 small zucchini, all the same size
36 very tiny pearl onions, or 12 to 18
    very small white onions
Pinch of saffron
1 tablespoon tomato paste
6 boiled lobsters, cooled
2 cups mayonnaise, made with lemon
    juice and olive oil (see page 76)
Watercress or leaf lettuce
GARNISH: Black olives, hard-boiled eggs

Put the water, wine, oil, vinegar, garlic, parsley, salt, thyme, bay leaf, and peppercorns in a large skillet. Add the zucchini and bring slowly to a boil. Reduce the heat to a simmer and poach the zucchini until just crisply tender when tested with a knife point. Remove and cool. Add onions and saffron to the poaching liquid and poach until crisply tender, stirring in the tomato paste for the last 5 minutes of cooking time. Remove and cool.

Crack the lobster claws and remove the meat in one piece (if necessary, split the claws down the side with lobster shears or scissors). Remove the meat from the tail in one piece. Remove the tomalley and coral, if any, pound in a mortar until smooth, and mix into the mayonnaise, along with any bits of meat from the body shell.

Make a bed of greens on a large serving platter. Arrange the zucchini on it like the spokes of a wheel, with lobster meat in between, curved sides up. Pile onions in the center. Decorate the platter with the lobster claw meat, olives, and halved hard-boiled eggs. Serve with a bowl of the mayonnaise.

Lobster Soufflé

Makes 6 servings

Three 2-pound live lobsters or 6 rock lobster tails

SAUCE À L'AMÉRICAINE
3 tablespoons butter
1 small onion, finely chopped
6 shallots, finely chopped
2 cups canned tomatoes
1 clove garlic, peeled and chopped
3 tablespoons chopped parsley

*1 tablespoon chopped fresh tarragon
    or 1 teaspoon dried tarragon*
1½ teaspoons thyme
½ bay leaf
3 tablespoons tomato paste

¾ pound mushrooms
3 tablespoons butter
1 ounce cognac

½ cup cream
4 egg yolks
5 egg whites

Prepare the Sauce à l'Américaine as in the recipe on page 223. Do not cut the lobsters in pieces; rather, split them in half. Remove the meat from the shell halves, and reserve the shells.

Cut the mushrooms in slices. Sauté them in the butter with a little cognac added when they have cooked lightly. Cut the lobster meat into scallops and remove the meat from the claws. Add lobster meat to the mushrooms with half the Sauce à l'Américaine and the cream. Let it cook about 3 minutes: the mixture should be nicely thickened.

Spread a little of the Sauce à l'Américaine in the bottom of each lobster shell. Fill the shells with the lobster mixture. Arrange in a deep baking dish. Add 4 well-beaten egg yolks to the remaining sauce à l'Américaine.

Beat the egg whites very stiff and fold the yolk mixture into them. Spread this over the lobsters, about ½ inch deep. Bake in a 425° oven until it is delicately browned and puffy, approximately 20 minutes; do not overcook. The top should be set and the rest rather runny. Serve at once.

Crab

Crab Soufflé

The tomato sauce makes this very different from the usual crab soufflé.

Makes 4 servings

1 pound crabmeat
1½ cups fresh tomato sauce (see
    page 534)
3 tablespoons unsalted butter

3 tablespoons flour
4 egg yolks
½ cup Parmesan cheese
5 egg whites

Arrange the crabmeat in the bottom of a 2½-quart soufflé dish. Pour ½ cup of the tomato sauce over the crab.

Melt the butter in a saucepan, blend in the flour, and cook, stirring, until golden and bubbling. Mix in the remaining tomato sauce. Stir until well blended and thickened. Remove from the heat and mix in the egg yolks. Stir in the cheese. Beat the egg whites until stiff but not dry, and fold them into the sauce mixture, as for any soufflé. Cover the crab with the soufflé mixture and bake in a 375° oven for 35 to 40 minutes, until risen and brown on top.

Crab Parisienne

Makes 4 servings

4 slices bacon
2 onions, chopped
1 clove garlic, finely chopped
2 ripe tomatoes, peeled, seeded, and
    chopped
1 teaspoon basil
Salt, freshly ground black pepper

3 tablespoons tomato purée
1 pound crabmeat
¼ cup cognac
1 cup dry white wine
2 tablespoons chopped parsley
Pinch of sugar

Sauté the bacon until crisp. Remove the slices, break into bits, and set aside. Sauté the onion and garlic in the fat until just soft. Add the tomatoes, sprinkle with the basil and salt and pepper to taste, and cook down over low heat until well blended. Stir in the tomato purée, add the crabmeat, pour the cognac over all and blaze. When the flame dies down add the white wine, parsley, and sugar. Cook and stir until well blended and hot through. Garnish with the crumbled bacon. Serve with rice.

Deviled Crab

This is far and away my favorite of the many versions of this most traditional of American dishes. I often serve a small helping as a first course before broiled or roast meats.

Makes 4 to 6 servings

1 cup finely chopped celery
1 large green pepper, finely chopped
1 cup finely sliced green onions
½ cup chopped parsley
2 pounds crabmeat
2½ cups coarsely crushed cracker
    crumbs

1 teaspoon salt
1½ teaspoons dry mustard
Dash of Tabasco
½ cup heavy cream
1 cup melted butter

Combine the vegetables, parsley, crabmeat, 1½ cups crumbs, seasonings, cream, and butter, and toss lightly. Spoon into a buttered baking dish, top with remaining cup of crumbs and bake in a 350° oven for 25 to 30 minutes, or until the top is delicately browned. Serve at once.

¶**Deviled Clams.** Substitute 2 cups steamed minced clams or drained chopped canned clams for the crabmeat.

Broiled Soft-Shell Crabs

Soft-shelled crabs, a specialty of the East Coast, are not a variety of crab, but merely blue crabs caught after they have molted or busted out of their old shells (hence, they are often known locally as "buster crabs"), before the brand-new shell has had a chance to harden. The soft-shell crabs sold in the market are usually sold cleaned and ready to cook. Sautéing (see *Theory & Practice*, page 200) and broiling are the simplest and best ways to cook these delicious morsels. The smaller crabs are the most desirable for eating. Allow 2 or 3 per serving.

Makes 4 servings

8 to 12 soft-shell crabs, cleaned
Flour
½ to ¾ cups unsalted butter

½ cup chopped parsley
2 teaspoons paprika
1 teaspoon salt

According to size, allow 2 or 3 crabs per serving. Dust crabs lightly with flour and arrange on the broiler pan, lined with foil, or in a flat broiling dish. Preheat the broiler. Cream the butter with the parsley, paprika, and salt. Dot the crabs liberally with the butter mixture. Broil about 3 inches from the heat, basting with melted butter in the pan. Turn once during the cooking (they will take from 5 to 8 minutes' total cooking time, depending on size) and dab second side with more of the butter mixture. Serve with the pan juices poured over them.

Scallops

Sautéed Scallops

If you use the little bay scallops, they need to be cooked very briefly or they will toughen. The larger sea scallops will take slightly longer. I like to sauté scallops in a Teflon-lined pan, to prevent them from sticking.

Makes 4 servings

Flour
1½ pounds scallops, well dried
6 tablespoons unsalted butter
Salt, freshly ground black pepper

3 tablespoons chopped parsley
1 teaspoon each chopped fresh tarragon
    and chives (optional)
Lemon wedges

Lightly flour the scallops. Heat the butter in a skillet until foaming. Add the scallops and sauté very quickly, tossing them in the pan, until lightly browned and just cooked through. Bay scallops will take about 2 to 3 minutes, sea scallops 3 to 4 minutes. Sprinkle with salt, pepper, parsley, additional herbs, if you like, and serve with lemon wedges.

¶Scallops Provençal. Finely chop 2 or 3 garlic cloves and mix with ¼ cup finely chopped parsley. Sauté the scallops in hot oil, adding the garlic-parsley mixture and tossing until they are well coated. Season with salt and pepper and serve.

Poached Scallops

Makes 4 servings

1 cup dry white wine
1 cup water
Bouquet garni (parsley, thyme, celery
    leaf)

6 shallots, finely chopped
2 pounds scallops
¼ cup chopped parsley
Lemon wedges

Put the wine, water, bouquet garni, and shallots in a saucepan and bring to a boil. Reduce heat, add the scallops, and simmer until just cooked through, about 2 minutes for bay scallops, 3 or 4 minutes for sea scallops. Drain and serve sprinkled with parsley and accompanied by lemon wedges.

¶Scallops with Heavy Cream and Tarragon. After draining scallops, strain and reduce the cooking liquid by two-thirds over brisk heat. Combine with ½ cup heavy cream blended with 2 egg yolks and stir over medium heat until sauce starts to thicken; do not let it boil. Stir to thicken and add scallops, 1 teaspoon tarragon, and 1 tablespoon chopped parsley.

Lo-Cal Coquilles St. Jacques

A dieter's version of this classic dish, without the rich sauce. I find you can really taste the delicate scallops done this way.

Makes 4 servings

1 cup dry white wine
5 tablespoons unsalted butter or
    margarine
1 small onion, chopped
3 sprigs parsley with stems
½ teaspoon thyme

1 bay leaf
1 tablespoon fresh lemon juice, strained
1½ pounds sea scallops
1 teaspoon cornstarch mixed with
    3 tablespoons cold water
1½ teaspoons grated Parmesan cheese

Bring the wine, butter, onion, herbs, and lemon juice to a boil. Reduce the heat, add the scallops, and simmer them until tender—about 5 minutes. Remove the scallops with a slotted spoon and set aside. Boil the liquid for about 5 minutes, reduce to a simmer, add the cornstarch-water mixture, and stir this sauce until it thickens. Remove from the heat and strain. Place the scallops in ovenproof shells or a baking dish. Top with sauce, sprinkle with cheese, and run under the broiler until nicely browned.

Frogs' Legs

Sautéed Frogs' Legs

Tender, meaty frogs' legs are delicate morsels and, like fish, low in calories. They come in various sizes, of which the smallest are the best. They should be soaked in milk for 1 hour before cooking. Sautéing is the most usual way of cooking frogs' legs, but as they have a tendency to stick, you must shake the pan as they cook so they move around, and keep turning them with a spatula. Fast cooking is also essential.

Makes 4 servings

12 pairs frogs' legs	*6 tablespoons butter*
Milk	*6 tablespoons olive oil*
½ cup flour	*Salt, freshly ground black pepper*

GARNISH: *Lemon wedges*

Soak the frogs' legs in milk to cover for 1 hour. Drain, dry well, and roll in the flour. Heat the butter and oil in a heavy skillet or sauté pan, add the frogs' legs and sauté quickly, turning them often and shaking the pan, until nicely browned on both sides. They should take only about 5 minutes to cook. Season with salt and pepper and serve with lemon wedges.

¶**Sautéed Frogs' Legs Fines Herbes.** Mix 1 cup bread crumbs with 2 tablespoons each chopped parsley, chives, and tarragon. Add to sautéed frogs' legs and mix well before seasoning with salt and pepper.

¶**Frogs' Legs Provençal.** Add 2 finely chopped garlic cloves and ¼ cup chopped parsley to sautéed frogs' legs before seasoning.

¶**Sautéed Frogs' Legs Niçoise.** Peel, seed, and finely chop 4 tomatoes and cook down to a paste in 2 tablespoons butter. Add a spoonful of paste to each serving.

¶**Sautéed Frogs' Legs Italian Style.** Add 1 finely chopped onion and ¼ pound chopped mushrooms to the pan with the frogs' legs. Season and serve with parsley.

¶**Deviled Frogs' Legs.** After rolling in flour, dip in beaten egg, and roll in bread crumbs. Sauté frogs' legs as before. Remove from pan. Add to the pan salt and pepper to taste, 1 tablespoon lemon juice, 1 tablespoon Dijon mustard, 1 tablespoon Worcestershire sauce, and 1 tablespoon brandy. Swirl around and mix well, then pour over frogs' legs.

¶**Southern-Fried Frogs' Legs.** Roll legs in flour, dip in milk, then roll in dry bread or cracker crumbs. Sauté as before. Remove frogs' legs. Pour off all but 4 tablespoons fat from pan. Mix in 4 tablespoons flour and 1½ cups light cream; stir and cook until thickened. Season and pour over legs.

¶**Southern-Fried Frogs' Legs with Madeira Sauce.** Add 3 tablespoons Madeira to sauce in preceding variation before pouring over legs.

Deep-Fried Frogs' Legs

Soak frogs' legs in milk. Dry, roll in flour, dip in a mixture of beaten egg and milk, then roll in bread crumbs. Deep-fry in 370° fat for 2 minutes, or until brown. Drain on paper towels, sprinkle with salt and pepper, and serve with lemon wedges or tartare sauce.

❡Batter-Fried Frogs' Legs. Make a beer batter by combining ¾ cup flour, 2 egg yolks, 1½ teaspoons salt, 2 tablespoons salad oil, ¾ cup room-temperature beer, and a few grinds of pepper. Cover and leave for 1 to 2 hours. Just before using, stir in 2 stiffly beaten egg whites. Dip frogs' legs in batter and deep-fry in 375° fat for 3 or 4 minutes, until brown and crisp. Serve with tartare or rémoulade sauce (page 77).

Salt Cod

I have always been a lover of salt cod, an important part of our food heritage that has been almost forgotten, except perhaps in New England, where codfish cakes and codfish balls are still much in favor. In the cooking of France, Italy, Spain, and Portugal you will find infinite variations on the salt-cod theme—Portugal alone is said to have a recipe for almost every day of the year. When using salt cod, it is essential to soak it well, changing the water once or twice, to get rid of the salt, after which it is usually poached, although it may also be sautéed or fried.

Poached Codfish

Makes 4 servings

Soak 1 pound codfish in cold water for several hours or overnight, changing the water once or twice. Rinse well, put in a skillet or saucepan with fresh cold water to cover, and bring to a boil. Reduce heat and simmer for 10 to 15 minutes. Drain and arrange on a hot platter. Surround with boiled potatoes sprinkled with parsley, and serve with either melted butter or a sauce, such as egg sauce (see page 531), parsley sauce (see page 531), or hollandaise sauce (see page 532).

¶**Codfish Béchamel.** Flake the poached codfish and combine with 2 cups béchamel sauce (see page 531). Serve hot on toast fried in olive oil, and sprinkle with parsley.

¶**Codfish au Gratin.** Put the Codfish Béchamel in a baking dish, sprinkle with buttered crumbs and grated Gruyère cheese, and put under the broiler for a few minutes to melt the cheese.

¶**Codfish Mornay.** Stir 1 cup grated Cheddar, Gruyère, or Swiss cheese into the béchamel sauce before combining with the codfish. Put in a baking dish, sprinkle with grated Parmesan cheese, and put under the broiler until the cheese melts.

Codfish Cakes

Makes 4 servings

2 cups flaked poached codfish
2 cups potatoes mashed with
    3 tablespoons butter
1 egg

1 egg yolk
½ teaspoon freshly ground black pepper
4 tablespoons butter
GARNISH: Chopped parsley

Combine the codfish, potatoes, egg, egg yolk, and pepper, mix well, and form into cakes about 3 inches across and 1 inch thick. Melt the butter in a heavy skillet and sauté the cakes until crisply brown on both sides, adding more butter if needed. Garnish with parsley and serve with toast. You can accompany these with strips of bacon or fried salt pork if you wish.

¶**Codfish Cakes with Ginger.** Add 1 teaspoon ground ginger or 1½ to 2 teaspoons grated fresh ginger to the codfish mixture.

¶**Codfish Cakes with Onion.** Add 2 tablespoons finely chopped green onion to the codfish mixture.

¶**Codfish Balls.** Form the mixture into balls, roll in flour, beaten egg, and bread crumbs, and deep-fry in 370° fat for about 3 minutes, until browned.

Brandade of Cod

A specialty of Nîmes in Provence, this gloriously garlicky, creamy paste is without doubt one of the greatest and most exciting of all salt-cod dishes. Serve it warm in a mound and eat with fried toast as a first or main course.

1 pound poached salt cod, finely flaked *2 cloves garlic, crushed*
⅔ cup olive oil *½ teaspoon freshly ground black pepper*
⅓ cup heavy cream

Remove any bits of bone from the flaked codfish. Heat the oil and cream separately in small saucepans. Pound or work the fish and garlic to a paste, either with a mortar and pestle, a blender, a food processor or a mixer with paddle attachment, adding the warm oil and cream alternately by the spoonful as you do so. When the oil and cream are completely absorbed and the mixture has the consistency of mashed potatoes, season with the pepper and heap in a serving dish. Serve warm, surrounded with triangles of fried toast (bread fried in olive oil).

¶**Codfish Portugaise.** Beat 2 cups mashed potatoes into the brandade. Turn into a buttered baking dish, sprinkle the top with ½ cup buttered crumbs, and bake in a 350° oven until very hot, about 35 minutes.

¶**Brandade Fritters.** Drop the brandade mixture by teaspoons into deep fat heated to 365°. Fry until lightly browned, about 2 to 3 minutes.

¶**Brandade Tart.** Turn the brandade into a partially baked 9-inch pie shell. Bake in a 350° oven for 20 minutes.

Raïto

2½ pounds salt codfish *1½ cups boiling water*
1 large onion, chopped *1 sprig parsley, chopped*
3 cloves garlic, chopped *½ teaspoon thyme*
Olive oil *2 or 3 slices lemon*
Flour *2 tablespoons tomato paste*
1¾ cups red wine

Soak the cod for several hours or overnight, changing the water once or twice. Rinse and drain.

Sauté the onion and garlic in 6 tablespoons olive oil until nicely browned. Stir in 2 tablespoons flour and cook 3 minutes. Add the liquids, herbs, lemon slices, and tomato paste and simmer until well reduced. Correct the seasoning and strain the sauce. Return to the pan.

Cut the cod into serving pieces, roll in flour and brown well in olive oil. Remove the browned pieces to the sauce and simmer for 10 to 15 minutes. Serve at once.

Eggs and Cheese

Eggs are more than a breakfast food. When the refrigerator is bare or when nothing else seems to excite my appetite, to me an egg is always the answer. Boiled, poached, scrambled just right, eggs are delicious and satisfying. The important thing is never to overcook eggs and always to serve them promptly, since their internal heat is still at work when you take them off the range or out of the oven.

Cheese is a natural partner to eggs: a senior partner in dishes like Welsh Rarebit, for which you use the pronounced flavor of Cheddar. It is what I'd call a cheese dish enhanced by eggs (as a binder and an enrichment). When the eggs are the senior partner, I like cheeses which have good melting qualities and great delicacy, like Switzerland Emmenthaler and Gruyère, Italian or Swedish fontina, and fresh mozzarella, sometimes with grated Parmesan, which is almost a seasoning in

246

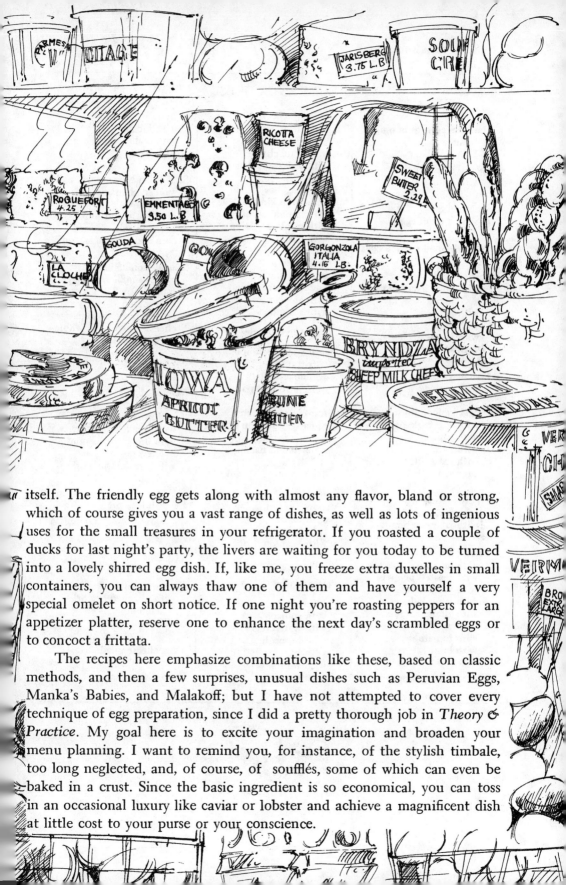

itself. The friendly egg gets along with almost any flavor, bland or strong, which of course gives you a vast range of dishes, as well as lots of ingenious uses for the small treasures in your refrigerator. If you roasted a couple of ducks for last night's party, the livers are waiting for you today to be turned into a lovely shirred egg dish. If, like me, you freeze extra duxelles in small containers, you can always thaw one of them and have yourself a very special omelet on short notice. If one night you're roasting peppers for an appetizer platter, reserve one to enhance the next day's scrambled eggs or to concoct a frittata.

The recipes here emphasize combinations like these, based on classic methods, and then a few surprises, unusual dishes such as Peruvian Eggs, Manka's Babies, and Malakoff; but I have not attempted to cover every technique of egg preparation, since I did a pretty thorough job in *Theory & Practice.* My goal here is to excite your imagination and broaden your menu planning. I want to remind you, for instance, of the stylish timbale, too long neglected, and, of course, of soufflés, some of which can even be baked in a crust. Since the basic ingredient is so economical, you can toss in an occasional luxury like caviar or lobster and achieve a magnificent dish at little cost to your purse or your conscience.

EGGS AND CHEESE

Hard-boiled eggs in onion
  sauce

Special stuffed eggs
  with sardines

Scotch eggs
  Scotch quail eggs

Old-fashioned pickled eggs

Shirred eggs
  with duck livers and
    Madeira
  with pesto
  with ham
  with Gruyère cheese
  with spinach purée

Poached eggs
  with sausage
  eggs benedict
  eggs benedictine
  with vegetable purée
  with spinach
  with pâté
  with roast fillet
  eggs meurette

Huevos rancheros
  with tortillas
  with jalapeño peppers

Scrambled eggs
  with mozzarella cheese
  with roasted peppers
  with prosciutto
  with lamb kidneys
  with alfalfa sprouts
  in a tart shell
  with tomatoes
  with brains

Pipérade basquaise

Basic omelet
  with fresh tomatoes
  with spinach
  with asparagus
  with chili
  with duxelles
  with lamb kidney
  with finnan haddie
  with smoked salmon
  with caviar and sour
    cream
  with cheese
  farmer's omelet
  omelette savoyarde
  with chicken and curry
  with shrimp

Cold layered omelet

Onion and zucchini
    frittata
  artichoke frittata
  prosciutto frittata
  ham and potato frittata
  frankfurter frittata
  tomato and onion frittata
  spinach frittata
  spinach and bacon
    frittata
  bean sprout and pork
    frittata

Vanessi special
  with ham
  with spinach
  with beans and rice

Minina

Peruvian eggs

Lettuce timbales
  with spinach
  with watercress
  with broccoli
  with ham
  with shrimp
  with chicken

  with lobster
  with crabmeat
  with basil

Salmon and sour cream roll
  minced clam and sour
    cream roll
  mushroom and sour
    cream roll
  corn and sour cream roll

Marrow soufflé in pastry
  cheese soufflé in pastry
  spinach soufflé in pastry
  ham soufflé in pastry
  crabmeat soufflé in pastry
  cheese soufflé with whole
    eggs in pastry

Savory crêpes

Manka's babies
  with ham
  with roast beef
  with spinach and cheese
  with broccoli rabe and
    cheese
  with strawberries and
    yogurt

Flemish leek pie

Gougères

Malakoff

Welsh rarebit
  with poached egg or
    hamburger
  with tomato juice

Swiss cheese salad

Deep-dish pizza

Hard-Boiled Eggs in Onion Sauce
(Les Oeufs à la Tripe)

I have never been able to discover the origin of the name of this traditional and exquisitely simple French dish, which I like to serve for breakfast, brunch, a light lunch, or a late supper.

Makes 2 to 3 servings

1 medium-size onion, finely chopped
4 tablespoons butter
3 tablespoons flour
1 teaspoon salt
½ teaspoon freshly ground black pepper

A few gratings of nutmeg
1¼ cups light cream
4 or 5 hard-boiled eggs, cut in ½-inch
    slices

Sauté the onion in butter until soft and delicately golden. Stir in the flour and cook for 2 or 3 minutes to remove the raw taste of the flour. Add salt, freshly ground black pepper, and nutmeg, then gradually stir in the light cream, stirring until the sauce thickens. Let it simmer gently for 3 or 4 minutes to get a good flavor. If you wish, add a small pat of butter to enrich the sauce. Taste for seasoning, then carefully fold in the sliced eggs. Heat through quickly and serve on toast or small croutons of fried bread.

Special Stuffed Eggs

These are not the usual picnic eggs. They are very elegant, decorative, and tasty, and may be served as a salad, on a bed of greens.

Makes 24 eggs

2 dozen hard-boiled eggs, shelled
1 can mousse de foie gras or 1 cup
    homemade liver pâté
1 tablespoon sour cream
2 tablespoons chopped parsley

1 truffle, finely chopped
Salt, freshly ground black pepper
Cognac
24 truffle slices

Cut a thin slice from the broad end of each of the hard-boiled eggs to enable them to stand upright on the serving dish. Slice off enough of the small ends of the eggs so that you can remove the yolks. Mash the yolks well and mix with the mousse de foie gras or pâté, sour cream, parsley, chopped truffle, and salt and pepper to taste. Add enough cognac to make a good paste. Using the rosette point of a pastry bag, pipe the yolk mixture back into the eggs and finish off the top of each egg with a decorative swirl. Top each with a slice of truffle and chill well. You may also glaze the eggs with aspic, if you so desire.

¶**Stuffed Eggs with Sardines.** Mash the yolks with 3 tablespoons mayonnaise, then add 1 can boneless and skinless sardines, mashed, ½ cup finely chopped chives, ¼ teaspoon Tabasco, 1 teaspoon lemon juice, and salt and freshly ground black pepper to taste. Mix thoroughly and pipe filling into the eggs. Top with chopped chives or parsley.

Scotch Eggs

These are one of the great British pub foods and something I just adore, either hot or cold. The spicy sausage meat is such a great contrast to the egg hidden within.

Makes 6 servings

6 hard-boiled eggs, shelled
Flour
1 pound well-seasoned sausage meat

2 eggs, lightly beaten
Bread crumbs
Oil for deep-frying

Lightly flour the eggs. Divide the sausage meat into 6 equal portions and flatten. With floured hands, wrap the sausage meat around the eggs, making a firm covering. The eggs should be completely encased. Dust with flour, dip in beaten egg and roll in crumbs. Deep-fry until the meat is nicely browned and cooked through. Drain on absorbent paper. Serve hot for lunch or a snack, cold as picnic food.

¶**Scotch Quail Eggs.** Use quail eggs in the same way and serve as cocktail food.

Old-Fashioned Pickled Eggs

Makes 24 eggs

2 dozen hard-boiled eggs, shelled
2 cups cooked beet slices
2 large onions, sliced very thin
1 teaspoon salt

2 tablespoons sugar
1 bay leaf
Mild vinegar, such as cider vinegar

Place the hard-boiled eggs in a large jar or bowl, and add the sliced beets, onions, salt, sugar, and bay leaf. Add just enough vinegar to cover all the ingredients and cap the jar or cover the bowl with plastic wrap. Allow to marinate in the refrigerator for at least 24 hours.

To serve, arrange drained eggs, beets, and onions in a large bowl, moisten with some of the vinegar mixture, and serve as an accompaniment to meat salads, cold meats, and cheese. If you prefer, arrange the eggs in one bowl and the beets and onions in another.

Shirred Eggs

Achieving perfect shirred eggs, with a delicate white and a yolk that is still liquid, can be something of an art. They must be rushed from oven to table lest they continue to cook and become hard.

Makes 6 servings

½ pint heavy cream, approximately   *Salt, freshly ground black pepper*
6 eggs

Pour a small amount of heavy cream in the bottoms of 6 ramekins. Carefully break 1 egg into each ramekin, add a little more heavy cream, and sprinkle with salt and pepper. Bake in a preheated 350° oven for about 8 minutes, or until the eggs have barely set.

¶**Shirred Eggs with Duck Livers and Madeira.** Oil the ramekin dishes, omitting the heavy cream. Add the eggs and place about 1 tablespoon finely chopped duck liver, sautéed briefly with finely chopped shallots and Madeira, on top of each. Season and bake as above.

¶**Shirred Eggs with Pesto.** Oil the ramekin dishes, omitting the heavy cream. Place about 1 tablespoon peeled, seeded, and finely chopped tomato and ½ teaspoon pesto on each egg. Season and bake as above.

¶**Shirred Eggs with Ham.** Oil the ramekin dishes, omitting the heavy cream and the salt. Top each egg with about 1 tablespoon finely chopped ham or frizzled Virginia ham, and season and bake as above.

¶**Shirred Eggs with Gruyère Cheese.** Pour a small amount of heavy cream on each egg and sprinkle with grated Gruyère cheese. Season and bake as above.

¶**Shirred Eggs with Spinach Purée.** Oil the ramekin dishes, omitting the heavy cream. Place 1 tablespoon spinach purée on top of each egg, and season and bake as above.

Poached Eggs

Poached eggs are more than breakfast food. I like to serve them as a first course or light luncheon dish on a bed of vegetable purée or brandade, on thin slices of pâté or meat, or Burgundy-style in a red wine sauce.

To poach eggs, put 2 or 3 inches of water, ½ teaspoon salt, and ½ teaspoon vinegar in a skillet and bring to a slow boil. Break each egg into a tiny cup, such as a Japanese tea cup, lower it into the water, and quickly tip out the egg. Don't do more eggs than can be handled easily, about 2 or 3 at a time, depending on the size of the skillet. When the eggs are in the water, remove the pan from the heat and let the eggs poach gently in the hot water for 3 to 4 minutes, basting the tops with hot water, if necessary, until the whites are set and the yolks are filmed with white. Remove the eggs with a perforated skimmer to paper towels to drain. If you need to warm them again before serving, slip into simmering water for 30 seconds.

¶**Poached Eggs with Sausage.** Top hot sausage cakes with poached eggs and cover with freshly made hollandaise sauce (see page 532) or creamy cheese sauce (see page 531).

¶**Eggs Benedict.** Put a slice of sautéed ham or Canadian bacon on half a buttered toasted English muffin, top with a poached egg, cover with freshly made hollandaise sauce, and garnish with a sliver of black truffle.

¶**Eggs Benedictine.** Serve poached eggs on a bed of Brandade of Cod (see page 244).

¶**Poached Eggs with Vegetable Purée.** Serve the eggs on a bed of puréed vegetables. Good choices are asparagus, spinach, mustard greens, broccoli, rabe, tarragon-flavored beets, a blend of beets and carrots, or yellow turnips, then, if you like, top each egg with a strip of bacon.

¶**Poached Eggs with Spinach.** Serve the eggs on a slice of ham covered with a bed of spinach. Top with mornay sauce (page 531).

¶**Poached Eggs with Pâté.** Arrange thin slices of pâté or pâté de foie gras on toast; top with a poached egg.

¶**Poached Eggs with Roast Fillet.** Put thin slices of rare roast fillet on slices of toast or toasted halved English muffins. Serve with a sauce made from the pan juices reduced with shallots.

¶**Eggs Meurette.** For 6 eggs, combine in a skillet 1 bottle red wine, ¼ cup chopped shallots, 1 teaspoon thyme, and ½ teaspoon freshly ground black pepper, bring to a boil, and poach the eggs as before. Remove and drain the eggs. Boil the wine sauce down until reduced by half. Pour the sauce over the eggs and serve with triangles of toast for dipping.

Huevos Rancheros

Poached eggs with a spicy Mexican flavor.

Makes 6 servings

2 medium-size onions, finely chopped	½ teaspoon freshly ground black pepper
2 cloves garlic, finely chopped	2½ teaspoons chili powder
⅓ cup olive oil	1 tablespoon fresh basil, shredded, or
2 cups peeled, seeded, and chopped	½ teaspoon dried basil, crumbled
tomatoes	6 poached eggs
1 teaspoon salt	Grated Parmesan cheese

In a heavy skillet, preferably cast iron, sauté the onions and garlic in the olive oil until transparent. Add the tomatoes, salt, pepper, chili powder, and basil, and simmer, covered, until well blended and slightly thickened. Pour the sauce over the poached eggs and sprinkle with Parmesan cheese. Serve at once.

¶**Huevos Rancheros with Tortillas.** Serve each egg on top of a soft corn tortilla heated briefly in olive oil or a combination of olive oil and butter. Top with sauce and cheese, as above. The tortillas may be homemade, canned, or the kind sold in plastic packages in supermarkets.

¶**Huevos Rancheros with Jalapeño Peppers.** Sprinkle finely chopped or shredded jalapeño peppers on top of each egg—if you can stand the heat!

Scrambled Eggs

Although universally popular, scrambled eggs are far too often overcooked until they form hard, unappetizing little lumps. As I pointed out in *Theory & Practice* (see page 202), the main point when scrambling eggs is to know when to stop, as they continue cooking with their own internal heat after being removed from the stove. Like omelets and frittatas, scrambled eggs take gracefully to a variety of seasonings and flavorings.

Makes 1 serving

2 eggs   1 teaspoon to 1 tablespoon water
Salt, freshly ground black pepper   2 tablespoons butter
Tabasco

Beat the eggs lightly in a bowl with salt and pepper to taste and a dash
or two of Tabasco, beating in the water if you like lighter, less "eggy"
scrambled eggs. Melt the butter in a skillet (I prefer to use a Teflon-lined
skillet) over medium-high heat. When hot but not sizzling, pour in the
eggs and scramble with a wooden spatula; if you're new at this, check the
detailed directions given in *Theory & Practice*. When soft but not too
runny, transfer the eggs to a plate.

¶**Scrambled Eggs with Mozzarella Cheese.** Just before the eggs are done
to your taste, add 2 tablespoons chopped mozzarella cheese and proceed as
above.

¶**Scrambled Eggs with Roasted Peppers.** When the eggs are just beginning to thicken, add 2 to 3 tablespoons finely chopped roasted peppers.

¶**Scrambled Eggs with Prosciutto.** When the eggs start to thicken, toss
in 2 to 3 tablespoons prosciutto strips or cubes.

¶**Scrambled Eggs with Lamb Kidneys.** For each serving, sauté a lamb
kidney lightly in butter, then purée in a food processor or chop very fine
and stir into the eggs as they are beginning to set.

¶**Scrambled Eggs with Alfalfa Sprouts.** Top the eggs with 2 tablespoons
fresh alfalfa sprouts.

¶**Scrambled Eggs in a Tart Shell.** Spread the bottom of a baked 9-inch
tart shell with Dijon mustard. Heap with 4 or more servings of scrambled
eggs into which you have folded ½ cup warm duxelles (see page 535) and
sprinkle chopped parsley or crisp crumbled bacon on the top.

¶**Scrambled Eggs with Tomatoes.** Peel, seed, and roughly chop tomatoes,
mix with chopped fresh basil, and add 2 to 3 tablespoons of the mixture
to the eggs just before they are done.

¶**Scrambled Eggs with Brains.** Parboil and cool brains according to directions on page 449. Cool until firm, then cut into small dice. Heat butter
for the eggs, add brains, and toss in the hot butter for a few seconds, then
add the eggs and scramble together. Serve garnished with watercress. This
may also be served in large or small patty shells that have been heated
in the oven.

Pipérade Basquaise

A Basque version of eggs scrambled with sautéed vegetables.

Makes 4 servings

4 tablespoons olive oil
3 red or green bell peppers, roasted
    and cut into strips
1 large onion, coarsely chopped
1 clove garlic, finely chopped
4 medium-size tomatoes, peeled, seeded,
    and coarsely chopped

½ teaspoon Tabasco
½ teaspoon thyme
Salt, freshly ground black pepper
6 eggs
5 tablespoons butter
2 tablespoons chopped parsley

Heat the oil in a skillet, add the peppers, onion, garlic, tomatoes, Tabasco, thyme, and salt and pepper to taste. Cook over medium heat, stirring, until lightly sautéed and soft, but not cooked down to a purée. Lightly beat the eggs. Heat the butter in a Teflon-lined skillet, add the eggs, spoon in the vegetable mixture, and stir over medium heat, as for scrambled eggs, until soft curds form. Serve immediately, sprinkled with chopped parsley.

Basic Omelet

I discussed in detail the making of a perfect omelet in *Theory & Practice* (see page 203), so I'm not going to repeat all the steps here. Once you have the technique down pat, it is one of the fastest, easiest, most versatile and economical of all light egg dishes, and the range of fillings is enormous. One omelet restaurant in New York City lists over a thousand on its menu, many of them just variations of mixtures of the same ingredients, others quite unusual.

For 1 individual omelet

2 large eggs
½ teaspoon salt
Pinch of freshly ground black pepper

Dash of Tabasco
1 tablespoon water
1 tablespoon butter

Beat the eggs lightly with a fork, adding the seasonings and water, just enough to blend the yolks and whites. Heat a 9-inch omelet pan, preferably Teflon-lined, over high heat. Add the butter and swirl it around until melted and foaming. Quickly pour in the eggs and stir them lightly with the back of a fork, meanwhile shaking the pan over the burner with your other hand. When the eggs are set to the degree you like, add any desired filling. Then roll the omelet with the fork or a spatula, starting at the handle end of the pan. Tip omelet out onto the plate in a neat roll, edges underneath, and serve at once. Spoon any excess filling over the omelet before serving.

¶**Fresh Tomato Omelet.** Season ⅓ cup peeled, seeded, and coarsely chopped ripe tomatoes with salt, pepper, and some fresh basil, chopped. Add to the omelet when it has set, just before you roll it.

¶**Spinach Omelet.** Add ⅓ cup cooked, drained, chopped, and buttered spinach.

¶**Asparagus Omelet.** Add ⅓ cup crisply cooked hot buttered asparagus tips.

¶**Chili Omelet.** Add ⅓ cup reheated leftover chili (see page 380).

¶**With Duxelles.** Add ⅓ cup duxelles (see page 535) to the omelet just as it is starting to set.

¶**Lamb Kidney Omelet.** Add ⅓ cup sautéed lamb kidneys, cut in small pieces and seasoned with a little prepared mustard and a tablespoon of sautéed onion.

¶**Finnan Haddie Omelet.** Add ⅓ cup creamed finnan haddie (smoked haddock).

¶**Smoked Salmon Omelet.** Add ⅓ cup smoked salmon, cut in strips and lightly tossed in butter.

¶**Caviar and Sour Cream Omelet.** Roll the basic omelet, make a slit in the top, and spoon in 2 tablespoons red or black caviar and 2 tablespoons sour cream.

¶**Cheese Omelet.** Add grated Parmesan, Cheddar, or Swiss, shredded mozzarella, crumbled feta, or Roquefort to the eggs just before they set, so the cheese can melt. Allow 2 to 3 tablespoons of cheese per omelet.

¶**Farmer's Omelet.** Sauté cubed ham, diced cooked potato, and chopped onion in butter. Add ⅓ to each omelet.

¶**Omelette Savoyarde.** Make the omelet as directed, but do not roll it. Slip it, pancake fashion, onto a slice of broiled or fried ham, sprinkle liberally with grated Cheddar, Emmenthaler, or Gruyère cheese, and put under the broiler until the cheese melts.

¶Chicken and Curry Omelet. Sauté ⅓ cup chopped onion in 4 tablespoons butter with 1 tablespoon curry powder, or to taste. Add 1 tablespoon chutney, 2 teaspoons potato starch, 1 cup heavy cream, 2 teaspoons salt, and a dash of Tabasco. When sauce has thickened, add 1 cup chopped cooked or canned chicken.

¶Shrimp Omelet. Combine 1 cup chopped cooked shrimp (canned may be used) with 2 tablespoons chopped parsley, 2 teaspoons dried tarragon or 1 tablespoon chopped fresh tarragon, ¼ cup vegetable oil, and 2 teaspoons wine vinegar.

For other filling suggestions, see *Theory & Practice*, page 205.

Cold Layered Omelet

Makes 6 to 8 servings

1 tablespoon vegetable oil	¼ teaspoon Tabasco
18 large or extra-large eggs	¼ cup cold water
1 teaspoon salt	Butter
½ teaspoon freshly ground black pepper	Omelet filling (see page 256)

FOR THE SAUCE

3 tablespoons butter	½ cup grated Parmesan cheese
1 small onion, chopped	½ teaspoon salt
3 tablespoons all-purpose flour	Freshly ground black pepper
1½ cups chicken broth	2 tablespoons chopped parsley
⅛ teaspoon nutmeg	1 tablespoon chopped chives
1 cup heavy cream	1 teaspoon lemon juice
1 egg yolk	

Lightly oil a 2- to 2½-quart glass bowl. Beat the eggs lightly with a fork, just enough to blend the yolks and whites, and add the seasonings and water. Follow the instructions for Basic Omelet (see page 255), using ½ cup of egg mixture for each omelet; don't roll the omelets—just slip them out of the pan. Line the bowl with the omelets, covering the bottom and sides. Place ¼ cup of one of the suggested omelet fillings (page 256) in the center of the omelet at the bottom of the bowl. Add another omelet and another filling of your choice. Continue until the last omelet is used up—it should be on top.

For the sauce, melt the butter in a saucepan and sauté the onion until lightly colored but not brown. Stir in the flour and cook for 1 to 2 minutes. Add the chicken broth, nutmeg, heavy cream beaten with the egg yolk, and cook until quite thick; do not allow the sauce to boil. Add the Parmesan cheese, salt and pepper, parsley, chives, and lemon juice. Blend thoroughly and pour over the omelets, allowing the sauce to run down the sides by pulling the omelets gently away from the sides of the bowl as you pour the sauce. Cool and refrigerate to chill thoroughly. When ready to serve, remove from refrigerator and unmold onto a plate.

Frittata

The Italian frittata is not something you make in seconds, like a French omelet, but a substantial combination of ingredients and flavorings bound by eggs and cheese that needs slow top-of-the-stove cooking and a final setting in the oven. It is served cut into wedges and usually hot, although I think it is even more delicious at room temperature, tepid—even cold. I can remember when a cold zucchini and prosciutto frittata was in much demand at Balilla on Bleecker Street, one of the best small Italian restaurants New York City ever had. Practically anything goes into a frittata. It's a chance to improvise with whatever is in the refrigerator. If you are having guests, you can make two or three different frittatas and let them sample each one. All you need add to complete the meal is a salad, good bread, and seasonal fruit.

You'll find variations on the frittata in different countries, such as the Spanish flat omelet or tortilla (not to be confused with the Mexican tortilla), the Omelette Savoyarde (see page 256), and some of the Middle Eastern egg dishes, such as Minina (see page 261).

Onion and Zucchini Frittata

Makes 6 servings

1 cup thinly sliced onion
⅓ cup olive oil
3 tiny zucchini, sliced paper thin
6 extra-large eggs
½ teaspoon salt
½ teaspoon finely ground black pepper

5 tablespoons freshly grated Parmesan
    cheese
4 tablespoons butter
1 tablespoon finely chopped parsley
1 or 2 basil leaves, cut into thin strips

Cook the onion in olive oil until transparent. Add the zucchini and brown lightly. Reduce heat and let onion and zucchini cook down for 4 to 5 minutes, then season with salt and pepper, drain off oil and excess liquid, and cool slightly.

Beat the eggs in a bowl with salt and pepper. Add the zucchini and onion mixture and 4 tablespoons freshly grated Parmesan cheese. Heat the butter over medium-low heat in a heavy 10-inch skillet, preferably black iron, until it foams and begins to bubble. Pour the mixture into the pan, add the finely chopped parsley and basil leaves. Keeping the heat very low, cook only until the eggs have set, about 20 minutes. The top should still be a little runny. Sprinkle with the remaining tablespoon grated Parmesan cheese, and put under a hot broiler for not less than 30 seconds nor more than a minute, until barely set on top, but not brown. Run a sharp knife or thin spatula around the edges of the frittata to loosen it from the pan, slide it out onto a plate, and cool to room temperature. Serve cut in wedges with a good salad. This is equally good if it is chilled.

¶**Artichoke Frittata.** Thinly slice 3 large cooked artichoke bottoms or 12 canned or thawed frozen artichoke hearts. Sauté 3 finely chopped garlic cloves in 2 to 3 tablespoons olive oil until soft, add the artichokes, and sauté 4 minutes. Season lightly with salt. Drain off oil and slightly cool the artichokes. Add the artichokes and Parmesan cheese in place of the zucchini to the egg mixture and cook as before.

¶**Prosciutto Frittata.** Add shredded prosciutto to the onion and zucchini frittata.

¶**Ham and Potato Frittata.** Use cubed cooked ham and potato instead of the zucchini.

¶**Frankfurter Frittata.** Instead of zucchini, cook ½ roasted green pepper, chopped fine, with the onion. Add 4 to 5 frankfurters, cut in shreds, and cook about 5 minutes, until heated through and delicately brown. Combine with the egg mixture and cook as before. Use 2 tablespoons chopped fresh parsley and omit the basil. You may use salami or knockwurst instead of frankfurters, if you wish.

¶**Tomato and Onion Frittata.** Cook the onion and 1 cup peeled, seeded, and finely chopped tomato (instead of zucchini) in the oil for 10 minutes. Drain off the oil and excess liquid, add to the egg mixture, and cook as before.

¶**Spinach Frittata.** Instead of zucchini, use 2 cups chopped raw spinach combined with 2 finely chopped garlic cloves sautéed with the onion.

¶**Spinach and Bacon Frittata.** Add crisply cooked pieces of bacon to the spinach and egg mixture.

¶**Bean Sprout and Pork Frittata.** To the egg mixture add 1½ cups bean sprouts and 1 cup shredded roast pork. Just before putting the frittata under the broiler, top with Chinese noodles, fried until crisp.

Vanessi Special

One of the old Italian restaurants in San Francisco is noted for this hearty dish, yet another frittata variation. I have often sat at the counter and watched it being prepared.

Makes 6 servings

1 pound fresh spinach, or 10-ounce package frozen spinach
1 medium-size onion, finely chopped
3 cloves garlic, finely chopped
⅓ cup olive oil

1 pound ground beef, preferably chuck
6 extra-large eggs
1 teaspoon salt
½ teaspoon freshly ground black pepper

Wilt the fresh spinach, with just the water clinging to the leaves after washing, in a heavy saucepan over low heat, covered, until limp. Remove from the heat, squeeze all the moisture out of the spinach, and finely chop it. If using frozen spinach, do not wilt; simply thaw it and proceed as above.

In a 10-inch skillet (preferably cast iron), cook the onion and garlic in olive oil until transparent. Add the ground beef and brown lightly. Beat the eggs in a bowl with the salt and pepper. Pour the eggs over the meat and onion mixture, and cook over low heat until they are barely set. Scatter the chopped spinach over the eggs, and place the skillet under the broiler until lightly browned. Run a sharp knife or thin spatula around the edges of the frittata to loosen it from the pan, slide it out onto a plate, and cut into wedges. Or you may serve it from the skillet, cut into wedges.

¶**Ham Frittata.** Use ½ pound finely chopped ham in place of the ground beef. Omit the spinach, garlic, and salt, and proceed as above.

¶**Spinach Frittata.** Omit the ground beef and use 2 pounds fresh spinach, wilted, or 2 ten-ounce packages frozen spinach, thawed, all moisture squeezed out and finely chopped. Proceed as above.

¶**Frittata with Beans and Rice.** Omit the ground beef, substituting 2 cups cooked or canned red kidney beans and 1 cup cooked rice, and proceed as above.

Minina

The countries of the Middle East have evolved some delicious ways of combining eggs and other foods. This one is hearty enough for a luncheon main course.

Makes 8 servings

½ pound calves' brains
Juice of ½ lemon
Salt, freshly ground black pepper
1 pound chicken breast
9 eggs

3 hard-boiled eggs, finely chopped
⅛ teaspoon nutmeg
4 tablespoons peanut oil
Lemon wedges

Clean the brains according to directions on page 449. Put them into a pan of cold water with the lemon juice and ½ teaspoon salt, slowly bring to a boil, reduce heat, and simmer for 5 to 7 minutes, no longer, as they will have further cooking. Drain, dry well, and cut into dice.

Put chicken breast in a skillet, add water to cover and ½ teaspoon salt, bring to a boil, skim, reduce heat, and simmer just until firm, about 12 minutes. Drain, saving stock, and when cool enough to handle, remove skin and bones and cut meat into strips 1 inch long and ½ inch wide. Preheat oven to 350°.

Beat uncooked eggs until well mixed. Add brains, chicken, and hard-boiled eggs. Mix gently. Season with nutmeg and salt and pepper to taste. Heat oil in a deep metal skillet, such as a cast-iron skillet, that can go into the oven. When oil is very hot, add egg mixture and bake for 15 minutes, or until a knife inserted in the center comes out clean. Loosen around edges with a knife and invert onto a plate. Sprinkle with about 4 tablespoons of the reserved chicken stock and surround with lemon wedges. Serve cut in wedges.

Peruvian Eggs

A most unusual egg dish that makes a nice change from pasta as a first course or a light luncheon. Credit for this goes to a young Peruvian chef, Felipe Rojas-Lombardi, who at one point in his career helped me with my cooking classes.

Makes 8 servings

12 *large eggs*
4 *tablespoons grated Parmesan cheese*
3 *tablespoons crushed soda crackers or*
    English water biscuits
¼ *cup milk*
½ *teaspoon basil*

Dash of Tabasco
2 *teaspoons salt*
1 *teaspoon freshly ground black pepper*
Tomato sauce (see page 534) or butter
Grated Parmesan or Romano cheese

Put the eggs into a mixing bowl and whisk lightly. Add the cheese, crackers, milk, basil, Tabasco, salt, and pepper, and mix well. Spoon 2 tablespoons of the mixture into a well-heated and buttered omelet pan, 8 to 10 inches in diameter, and spread around the pan to about ⅛-inch thickness. When lightly browned on one side, turn and brown the other. Remove to a plate. Continue with remaining mixture and stack omelets on the plate. Roll each one up and cut as you would noodles. Heat the strips in tomato sauce well seasoned with basil and garlic, or just in butter. In either case, serve with freshly grated Parmesan or Romano cheese.

Lettuce Timbales

It is rather amusing when you think that timbales, which once graced the tables of house-proud hostesses, are having a great renaissance with followers of nouvelle cuisine. I like to serve vegetable timbales as a light accompaniment to certain roast meats and broiled or poached fish, and others with a sauce as a light luncheon dish.

Makes 4 to 6 servings

1½ *pounds (approximately 4 heads)*
    Boston lettuce
1 *cup heavy cream*

4 *eggs*
Salt, pepper, nutmeg, to taste
Butter

Pick over and wash the lettuce leaves. Parboil for 3 to 4 minutes after the water returns to a boil, drain, refresh in cold running water, and squeeze the lettuce of excess moisture. Finely chop the lettuce and reserve.

Whisk the cream, eggs, and seasonings together in a bowl and add the finely chopped lettuce. Butter well six 2½-inch custard cups or a large charlotte mold, line the bottoms with parchment cooking paper and butter that also. Pour in mixture. Place the timbales in a large baking pan and pour in just enough water to come halfway up the sides. Place in a 375° oven and bake for 20 to 25 minutes for the small timbale molds, or for 45 to 50 minutes for the charlotte mold. Run a knife around the edges, unmold, then lift off and discard the parchment. Serve either plain or with the juices from a roast. As a course apart, you may serve it with a light tomato sauce or with a hollandaise or, if you like, sauce mousseline.

¶Spinach Timbales. Use 1½ pounds spinach instead of the lettuce.

¶Watercress Timbales. Use 1½ pounds watercress instead of lettuce.

¶Broccoli Timbales. Use 1 pound broccoli flowerets, fresh or frozen, blanched in boiling water for 1 minute, squeezed dry of all moisture, and finely chopped.

¶Ham Timbales. Use ¼ pound cooked ham, finely chopped, and proceed as above, omitting the salt.

¶Shrimp Timbales. Use ¼ pound cooked shrimp, finely chopped, and proceed as above.

¶Chicken Timbales. Use ¼ pound cooked chicken, finely chopped, and proceed as above.

¶Lobster Timbales. Use ¼ pound fresh, frozen, or canned lobster meat, finely chopped, and proceed as above.

¶Crabmeat Timbales. Use ¼ pound fresh, frozen, or canned crabmeat, finely chopped, and proceed as above.

¶Basil Timbales. Use ¼ cup finely chopped fresh basil, and proceed as above.

Salmon and Sour Cream Roll

A different way of baking and serving a soufflé, which we described in *Theory & Practice* (page 250). A rolled soufflé makes a great light luncheon dish, and the fillings are limited only by your imagination.

Makes 4 to 6 servings

4 tablespoons butter	1 tablespoon cognac
8 tablespoons flour	½ pint sour cream
2 cups hot milk	3 eggs, separated
1 teaspoon salt	4 to 6 finely chopped green onions
⅛ teaspoon cayenne pepper or Tabasco	½ pound smoked salmon, cut in slivers

Melt the butter in a heavy saucepan, blend in the flour, and cook until golden. Gradually stir in the hot milk, stirring constantly to prevent the sauce from lumping. Return to the heat and cook, stirring, until thick. Mix in the salt, pepper, cognac, and 2 tablespoons sour cream. Lightly beat the egg yolks and mix in, off the heat. Preheat the oven to 325°. Butter a 10-by-15-by-1-inch jelly-roll pan, line with wax paper, and butter the paper well.

Beat the egg whites until they stand in soft peaks, as for a soufflé. Fold about one-third of the whites into the sauce, incorporating them completely; pour sauce mixture onto whites in the bowl, then lightly fold in the whites. Spread in the prepared pan, evening the top with a rubber spatula. Bake for 40 minutes, or until golden and firm to the touch.

Remove the pan from the oven and invert onto large sheets of wax paper. Loosen the paper from the roll, and carefully peel it off. Trim the edges of the roll with a large sharp knife. Spread the roll with the remaining sour cream and sprinkle with the green onions and smoked salmon. Use the long side of the wax paper to roll it up like a jelly roll and slide it onto a board or heated platter.

¶**Minced Clam and Sour Cream Roll.** Spread the roll with sour cream or yogurt, and top with about 2 cups minced clams, barely heated through in their own juice and drained. Sprinkle with chopped parsley.

¶**Mushroom and Sour Cream Roll.** Spread the roll with sour cream or yogurt. Add a purée of mushrooms that have been sautéed in butter with salt and freshly ground black pepper.

¶**Corn and Sour Cream Roll.** Spread the roll with sour cream or yogurt. Top with 2½ to 3 cups corn kernels, freshly cut from the cob, that have been heated in butter and seasoned with finely chopped green peppercorns.

Marrow Soufflé in Pastry

Another good variation on the theme of the soufflé, which we covered in *Theory & Practice* (pages 245–256), is to bake it in a pastry shell.

Makes 6 servings

RICH TART PASTRY
2 cups unsifted flour
¾ cup (6 ounces) butter
3 hard-boiled egg yolks, mashed

2 raw egg yolks
½ teaspoon salt

Put the flour on a board or in a bowl and make a well in the center. Put all the other ingredients in the well and work to a paste with the fingertips, gradually incorporating the flour to make a firm, smooth ball of dough. Work quickly to prevent the butter from becoming greasy. When the dough leaves the board or the sides of the bowl, wrap in wax paper, and chill until firm. Roll out and use to line a 9-inch pie pan. Prick the crust well with a fork. Bake in a 425° oven for 12 minutes.

SOUFFLÉ MIXTURE

3 tablespoons butter
3 tablespoons flour
1 cup scalded milk
Salt to taste

2 tablespoons chopped fresh fines herbes
4 egg yolks
Poached or baked marrow from 6 bones
5 egg whites

Melt the butter and blend in the flour. Remove the pan from the heat and gradually stir in the milk, blending until smooth. Return to the heat and cook, stirring, until thick and smooth. Cool slightly and season with salt. Mix in the chopped herbs and egg yolks. Remove the marrow from the bones, cut it into small pieces, and add. Beat the egg whites until stiff but not dry. Fold half the egg whites into the sauce mixture fairly well, then lightly fold in the remainder. Pour the soufflé mixture into prebaked pastry shell and put in a 400° oven until just puffed and brown, about 20 to 25 minutes. Serve at once.

¶Cheese Soufflé in Pastry. Fill shell with cheese soufflé mixture (see *Theory & Practice*, page 247) instead of the marrow soufflé.

¶Spinach Soufflé in Pastry. Fill shell with spinach soufflé.

¶Ham Soufflé in Pastry. Fill shell with ham soufflé.

¶Crabmeat Soufflé in Pastry. Put a layer of crabmeat in the pastry shell, then add the basic soufflé mixture, omitting marrow. Use finely chopped dill instead of the fines herbes.

¶Cheese Soufflé with Whole Eggs in Pastry. Half fill shell with cheese soufflé mixture, then space 6 eggs around the edge. Cover with remaining mixture and bake.

Savory Crêpes

Makes about 16 six-inch crêpes

3 eggs
⅛ teaspoon salt
1 to 1¼ cups milk or beer
⅞ cup (1 cup less 2 tablespoons)
    all-purpose flour

4 to 5 tablespoons unsalted butter,
    melted

Beat the eggs in a bowl with a wire whisk until smooth. Mix in the salt and 1 cup of the milk or beer (beer makes the crêpes lighter). Blend well, then stir in the flour with the whisk and add 2 tablespoons of the melted butter. Beat until batter is smooth, free of lumps, and the consistency of heavy cream. You may need to add more liquid, but do not add until the flour has been mixed in. If you have a blender or food processor, the ingredients may be added all at one time and blended or processed until smooth.

Cover the bowl with plastic wrap and leave at room temperature for 2 to 3 hours (or up to 12 hours in the refrigerator). When ready to make the crêpes, check the consistency of the batter and beat it with the whisk as the flour will have settled. If the batter is thicker than heavy cream, add a little extra liquid.

Heat an iron crêpe pan or Teflon-lined pan with a 6-inch bottom diameter over medium heat until good and hot. Brush with a light film of melted butter, then scoop up about 3 tablespoons of the batter with a ladle or ¼ cup dry measure and pour into the pan. Raise pan from heat and tilt so the batter runs over the bottom of the pan, covering it with a thin layer. Replace pan on heat and cook just until surface is set. Run a spatula around the edges of the crêpe to loosen it and then flip it over. Bake the second side and then turn the crêpe out onto a plate by inverting the pan. Continue to make crêpes until batter is used, brushing pan with more melted butter as needed.

If you are using the crêpes right away, simply stack them on a plate. If you wish to keep them for later use, put wax paper between the crêpes as you stack them, then cover with plastic wrap and refrigerate. If you wish to freeze them, remove from the plate when cool, wrap tightly in aluminum foil, label, and freeze.

Manka's Babies

Many years ago I encountered this lovely batter pudding, which is kin to a German pancake or an English Yorkshire pudding, at an old-style Czech restaurant in Seattle called Manka, hence the name. Recently I tried out one of the puddings one day for lunch and have been eating them, with savory or sweet fillings, ever since, and using them in demonstrations. They are fun, easy, inexpensive, and lend themselves to infinite flavor variations. I often serve fruit on them and flambé them. You can also make individual versions in small metal skillets that can be put in the oven.

Makes 6 servings

⅓ cup unsalted butter   1 cup milk
4 eggs   1 cup all-purpose flour

Preheat oven to 425°. Melt the butter in a 9- to 10-inch skillet in the oven. Put the eggs, milk, and flour in the beaker of a food processor and blend until smooth. Remove the gratin pan from the oven and pour in the batter. Bake for 15 to 20 minutes until puffed and nicely browned. Serve rolled and sliced, or cut in wedges, with syrup, fresh fruit, or hot fruit.

¶**Manka's Babies with Ham.** Serve with broiled or sautéed ham slices.

¶**Manka's Babies with Roast Beef.** Use beef drippings in place of butter. Serve with roast beef.

¶**Manka's Babies with Spinach and Cheese.** Top baked pudding with finely chopped cooked spinach, sprinkle with grated Parmesan cheese, roll, and serve.

¶**Manka's Babies with Broccoli Rabe and Cheese.** Top with a purée of broccoli rabe (see page 130), sprinkle with grated Parmesan cheese, and roll.

¶**Manka's Babies with Strawberries and Yogurt.** Serve with sugared strawberries and plain yogurt.

Flemish Leek Pie

Makes 1 nine-inch pie

2 pounds leeks   Few pieces of finely cut ham (optional)
4 to 5 tablespoons butter   3 egg yolks plus 1 whole egg
Salt   ½ to ⅔ cup heavy cream
Freshly ground black pepper   Grating of nutmeg
Chilled unbaked shell for a 2-crust
    9-inch pie

Clean and finely slice the leeks (be sure to wash them well, as leeks always have sand and dirt between the leaves) and sauté in butter over medium-low heat—they should just melt down, not brown. When soft and limp, salt and pepper them to taste and spread them in the chilled pastry shell. (While not traditional, I find that a few pieces of finely cut ham are a very good addition.) Beat the egg yolks and whole egg with heavy cream and pour over the leeks and ham. Give it a grating of nutmeg, roll out the remaining pastry, fit it over the filling as a top crust, and cut a ½-inch hole in the center. Bake at 450° for 10 minutes, then reduce the heat to 350°, and continue cooking until the custard is set and the pastry nicely browned, about 30 minutes. Serve warm or cooled.

Gougères

These wonderfully cheesy little puffs of pâte à choux—cream puff pastry— are easy to make and terribly popular at a party—so make lots!

Makes 26 to 30 puffs

1 cup water
½ cup (1 stick) unsalted butter
½ teaspoon salt
¼ teaspoon ground pepper
1 cup all-purpose flour
4 medium-size eggs

¾ to 1 cup grated Gruyère cheese
1 teaspoon dry mustard
Pinch of cayenne pepper
Grated Parmesan or Gruyère cheese or
  small cubes of Gruyère for garnish

Combine water, butter, salt, and pepper in a medium-size saucepan and cook over medium heat until the butter melts. Add the flour all at once and stir the mixture vigorously and constantly, still over medium heat, with a wooden spoon or spatula until it is very firm and pulls away from the sides of the pan. Off the heat, add the eggs, one at a time, beating vigorously after each addition until completely incorporated. The dough should be smooth and glossy. Add the ¾ to 1 cup grated cheese, mustard, and cayenne, and blend thoroughly. Drop the mixture by small spoonfuls onto a lightly buttered baking sheet, or if you want to be a little fancier, pipe small puffs of the mixture through a plain-tipped pastry bag. Sprinkle the tops with additional grated Gruyère or Parmesan cheese or place 2 or 3 small pieces of Gruyère on top of each puff. Bake the gougères in a preheated 375° oven for 30 to 40 minutes, or until puffed and golden brown. Remove from the oven and make a crosswise slash in the bottom of each to allow excess steam to escape. Return the gougères to the warm oven for a few minutes to dry them. Serve hot or at room temperature.

Malakoff

I first had these glorious, puffy cheese concoctions at a small Swiss country restaurant on the shores of Lake Geneva, where they are the house specialty. With cornichons, pickled onions, a green salad, and a light young white wine they make a whole meal—so addictive you can't stop eating them. Or serve as a first course or cocktail food. The un-Swiss name, incidentally, honors a famous Russian general, like the dessert charlotte Malakoff.

Makes 6 to 8 servings

½ pound Gruyère cheese, grated
1 clove garlic, finely chopped
3 eggs, separated
¼ teaspoon freshly ground black pepper
Pinch of nutmeg, or more, to taste

¼ cup milk
1 tablespoon flour
⅓ cup kirsch
Oil for frying

Mix the cheese, garlic, egg yolks, pepper, and nutmeg. Stir in the milk, flour, and kirsch, and mix well. Beat the egg whites until stiff but not dry, and fold them gently into the cheese mixture. Refrigerate until ready to use.

Cut French bread or other white bread into thick rounds or rectangles, and spread the cheese mixture on one side of the bread twice, rounding over the second layer. Set aside for 1 hour to mellow.

Heat oil to 365°. Place a few cheese rounds at a time in the oil, cheese side down, and fry until golden brown. Turn and fry the second side. Drain on paper towels and serve with above suggestions.

Welsh Rarebit

Makes 4 servings

3 tablespoons unsalted butter
2 egg yolks
⅔ cup dark beer
1 tablespoon Dijon mustard

2 teaspoons Worcestershire sauce
¼ to ½ teaspoon Tabasco
8 ounces aged Cheddar cheese,
    shredded

Melt the butter in a heavy saucepan or in the top of a double boiler. Beat together the egg yolks, beer, and seasonings. Add to the pan and cook until quite hot but not boiling. Gradually add handfuls of shredded cheese, stirring with a wooden spoon—always in the same direction—until the cheese is entirely melted and the resulting rarebit is smooth and velvety. Serve on buttered toast.

¶Welsh Rarebit with Poached Egg or Hamburger. Serve the Welsh Rarebit spooned over a poached egg on toast or a freshly cooked hamburger on a bun.

¶Welsh Rarebit with Tomato Juice. Use tomato juice instead of beer and the rarebit becomes a Blushing Bunny.

Swiss Cheese Salad

An unusual and satisfying main-course salad from a country that produces superb cheeses and uses them in every way imaginable. I like the spicy contrast of the mustard and horseradish with the nutty flavor of the cheese.

Makes 6 servings

½ pound Swiss Emmenthaler cheese,
    cut in 1-inch cubes
6 hard-boiled eggs, finely chopped
1½ teaspoons dry mustard
1 teaspoon grated horseradish or
    drained bottled horseradish

½ teaspoon salt
½ teaspoon freshly ground black pepper
⅛ teaspoon cumin seed
½ cup sour cream or yogurt
Salad greens

Combine the cheese and chopped eggs and season with the mustard, horseradish, salt, pepper, and cumin seed. Toss lightly with the sour cream or yogurt and serve on a bed of greens.

Deep-Dish Pizza

Makes 6 servings

PIZZA DOUGH
1 package active dry yeast
Pinch of sugar
1¼ cups warm water (100° to 115°,
    approximately)

1 teaspoon salt
2 tablespoons olive oil
3 cups flour, preferably hard-wheat

FILLING
1 cup reduced basic tomato sauce
    (see page 534)
2 tablespoons tomato paste
¾ pound mozzarella cheese, cut into
    julienne strips
½ pound fontina, cut into julienne
    strips

2 cups sliced pepperoni, kielbasa, salami,
    or sweet Italian sausages previously
    poached
½ cup pitted black Italian olives,
    halved
¾ cup grated Parmesan cheese

In a mixing bowl combine the yeast, sugar, and ½ cup of the water, and allow the yeast to dissolve. Add the rest of the warm water to the yeast mixture along with the salt and the olive oil. Stir in the flour and beat with a wooden spoon or with your hands to make a stiff, sticky dough. Turn the dough out on a well-floured board and knead until velvety smooth and elastic but firm, about 10 minutes. Oil a large bowl, add the dough, and turn to coat thoroughly with the oil. Place in a warm, draft-free spot to rise until about doubled in bulk, 1 to 1½ hours.

While the dough is rising, make the tomato sauce. Purée the sauce in a food processor or blender, add the tomato paste and reduce to 1 cup very thick sauce.

Punch the dough down, turn out on a lightly floured board, and roll out dough ⅛ inch thick. Fit it into a 10-inch iron skillet, patting it over the bottom and sides. Cover with half the sliced cheese, then half the tomato sauce and sausage. Cover with the remaining cheese, tomato sauce, sausage, and black olives. Sprinkle with Parmesan and bake in a 450° oven for 10 minutes. Reduce the heat to 400° and bake the pizza for an additional 5 to 7 minutes.

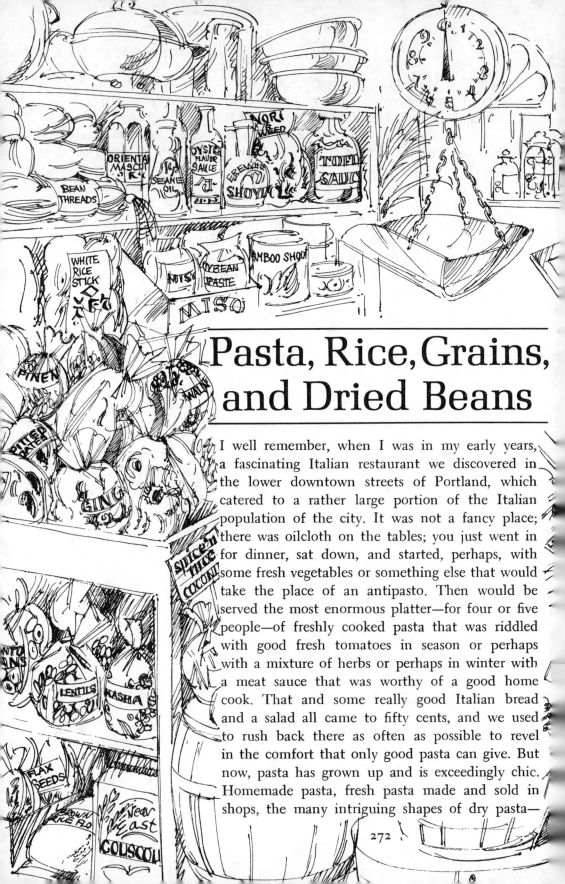

Pasta, Rice, Grains, and Dried Beans

I well remember, when I was in my early years, a fascinating Italian restaurant we discovered in the lower downtown streets of Portland, which catered to a rather large portion of the Italian population of the city. It was not a fancy place; there was oilcloth on the tables; you just went in for dinner, sat down, and started, perhaps, with some fresh vegetables or something else that would take the place of an antipasto. Then would be served the most enormous platter—for four or five people—of freshly cooked pasta that was riddled with good fresh tomatoes in season or perhaps with a mixture of herbs or perhaps in winter with a meat sauce that was worthy of a good home cook. That and some really good Italian bread and a salad all came to fifty cents, and we used to rush back there as often as possible to revel in the comfort that only good pasta can give. But now, pasta has grown up and is exceedingly chic. Homemade pasta, fresh pasta made and sold in shops, the many intriguing shapes of dry pasta—

272

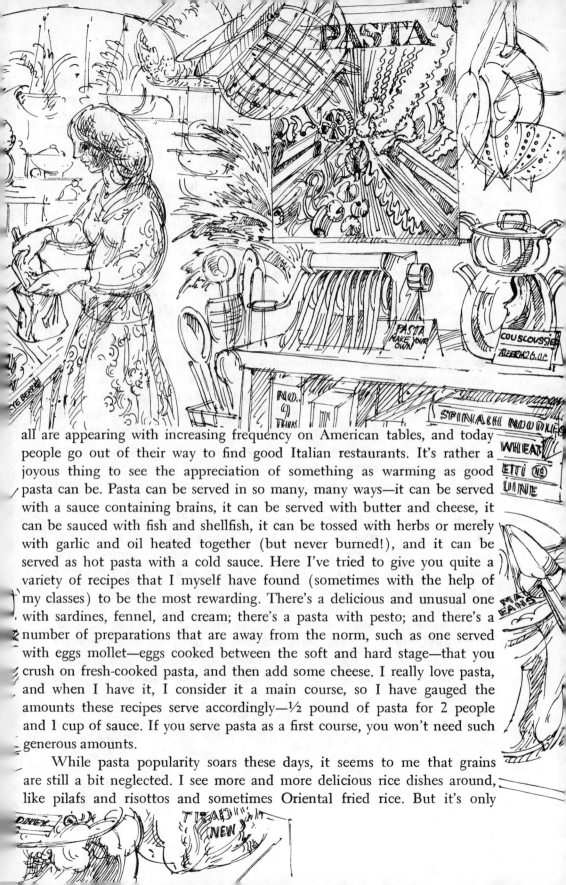

all are appearing with increasing frequency on American tables, and today people go out of their way to find good Italian restaurants. It's rather a joyous thing to see the appreciation of something as warming as good pasta can be. Pasta can be served in so many, many ways—it can be served with a sauce containing brains, it can be served with butter and cheese, it can be sauced with fish and shellfish, it can be tossed with herbs or merely with garlic and oil heated together (but never burned!), and it can be served as hot pasta with a cold sauce. Here I've tried to give you quite a variety of recipes that I myself have found (sometimes with the help of my classes) to be the most rewarding. There's a delicious and unusual one with sardines, fennel, and cream; there's a pasta with pesto; and there's a number of preparations that are away from the norm, such as one served with eggs mollet—eggs cooked between the soft and hard stage—that you crush on fresh-cooked pasta, and then add some cheese. I really love pasta, and when I have it, I consider it a main course, so I have gauged the amounts these recipes serve accordingly—½ pound of pasta for 2 people and 1 cup of sauce. If you serve pasta as a first course, you won't need such generous amounts.

While pasta popularity soars these days, it seems to me that grains are still a bit neglected. I see more and more delicious rice dishes around, like pilafs and risottos and sometimes Oriental fried rice. But it's only lately that people have begun to take an interest in polenta and couscous and kasha. Barley, especially, which used to turn up only in soup, has a different bite from the other grains, and lends itself to wonderful casserole dishes, with almonds or mushrooms, for instance, that I have always liked to serve with meat or fish. Cornmeal, and its Italian and Rumanian cousins, polenta and mamaliga, have a hearty consistency that lends itself to molding, slicing, and saucing, or to forming in little cakes to be crisped and browned in butter—lovely with grilled chicken—and the flavor is a natural for plenty of butter and cream and cheese. Buckwheat, or kasha, we've always known as a flour for pancakes and muffins; but the cracked grains have a fine rich color and a nutty flavor that takes well to mushrooms or to cheese or to whatever sauce accompanies your meat.

Somehow I always think of the wide world of dried beans along with grains, yet beans have a somewhat more velvety quality—perhaps due to their higher protein content. I delight in all kinds of beans and often lunch on sautéed lentils with onions and parsley, perhaps with a bit of thyme or another herb, and then just a salad. We can cook beans in far more ways than just baking them Boston-style with molasses. Giant limas, for instance, make an untraditional but excellent cassoulet; white kidney beans are good in a salad as well as in hot dishes—I like them with cognac perfuming their full flavor. Black beans aren't just for soup; they make a first-rate casserole, which you serve piping hot with very cold sour cream, along with sausages or a steak. Chickpeas are becoming a standard item at do-it-yourself salad bars, but I don't like their leathery skins. Instead I purée them (as I do many other beans), give them a whiff of Madeira, and serve them as a smooth, savory dish that intrigues guests. There is something both earthy and exotic about the various bean flavors, and they're so nourishing and satisfying that people seem to be turning toward them, more and more, as important in menu planning, often for the most substantial part of a good meal.

All along I've intended this chapter as my contribution to what I see as a sensible and promising change in our cooking and eating patterns. I love meat and poultry and fish, but their former place as centerpieces ought to be shared by the delicious, economical, healthy dishes I'm giving you here; and this broadening of our culinary minds seems to me the coming thing.

PASTA, RICE, GRAINS, AND DRIED BEANS

Homemade pasta
  hand method
  food-processor method
  spinach pasta
  tomato pasta
  rich egg pasta
  rolling and cutting pasta
  cooking homemade pasta

Cooking commercial dry
  pastas

Curried beef and tomato
  sauce

Virginia ham, spinach, and
  rosemary sauce

Braised onion sauce

Sardine and fennel sauce

Raisin and pine nut sauce
  with anchovies
  with dry figs

Pesto
  with walnuts
  with parsley

Diet pesto

Light tomato sauce

Mussel and tomato sauce
  clam and tomato sauce

Ham and tomato sauce
  with beef or veal
  with chicken or turkey
  with brains

Fresh tomato and duxelles
  sauce

Brain sauce
  with meat
  with lasagne

Prosciutto, peas, and cream
  sauce

Pasta with eggs mollet

Pasta with spinach and
  mushrooms
  with Parmesan cheese

Pasta with beans

Pasta asciutta rustica

Spätzle
  with heavy cream

Rice with cheese
  green rice
  with herbs
  with nuts
  saffron-flavored rice

Rice with onions and
  pine nuts

Oriental fried rice

Rice pilaf
  with nuts and raisins
  with peas
  with green chilies

Risotto
  alla milanese
  with white truffles
  with shellfish
  with raw shrimp
  with chicken
  with asparagus
  with green beans or peas
  with cherry tomatoes

Paella

Basic wild rice
  with green onions and
    pine nuts
  with duck or goose fat
    and mushrooms
  with ham
  with walnuts
  with bacon and onion
  with duxelles

Barley and mushroom
  casserole
  with almonds
  with celery and water
    chestnuts
  with chicken gizzards

Kasha
  with mushrooms
  with sautéed giblets

Sautéed hominy with cream

Hominy casserole

Couscous
  sauce piquante

Cornmeal

Polenta with sausages
  with fontina cheese
  with spinach
  with salt cod
  polenta cakes

Cornmeal gnocchi

Cornmeal soufflé
  with Parmesan cheese
  with whole-kernel corn

Corn-chili soufflé

White beans with cognac
  with ham and sausage

White bean purée
  puréed cannellini with
    Madeira

Cassoulet

Cassoulet with limas
  with cooked lamb
  with roasted duck legs
  with cooked pork and
    lamb

Cassoulet with codfish

Kidney beans with sausages

Black beans with sour cream with cheese and bacon	Chickpea purée with Madeira	Buttered lentils sautéed herbed puréed
Nevada chili beans cowpuncher beans	Lentils	Braised lentils with lamb

Pasta

If I could afford the calories, I'm sure I could eat pasta three times a day. Give me a plate of fettuccine with nothing more than sweet butter, grated Parmesan cheese, and a grind of black pepper, or a little olive oil and garlic, and I'm happy. I happen not to be a great lover of baked pasta dishes. I'll leave lasagne to those who like it. To me it is an overcooked and messy dish.

After years of making pasta by arduous hand rolling or with a hand-cranked pasta machine, my life was completely revolutionized by the advent of the electric pasta machine, a joy and a boon to anyone who loves pasta as I do, because it makes the whole process a breeze and is fun to operate. I make the dough in the food processor, then roll and cut it with the pasta machine, and I can have fresh, tender pasta on the table in a miraculous thirty minutes.

I also find it great fun to make colored pasta, using spinach, tomato paste, and egg yolks, and then mix the cooked pastas in different color combinations.

Homemade Pasta

Makes 2 servings

1½ cups all-purpose flour
½ teaspoon salt
2 whole eggs

1 tablespoon olive oil
(for food processor method)

HAND METHOD: Put the flour on a wooden board or counter top, add the salt, make a well in the center, and break the eggs into it. Do not add any oil. With a fork work the flour into the eggs until well amalgamated, then knead by hand until you have a smooth ball of dough.

Follow the procedure given below for the food processor method for dividing, flattening, and shaping.

FOOD PROCESSOR METHOD: Put the metal chopping blade in place in the food processor beaker. Add the flour, salt, and oil to the beaker and process for 8 to 10 seconds. Add the eggs and process about 15 seconds, or until the dough is pliable but not damp or sticky. If it seems too sticky, sprinkle with 1 or 2 tablespoons flour and process for an additional 6 to 8 seconds. If it feels too dry, sprinkle with a few drops of water and process to blend well.

Turn out onto a lightly floured surface. Knead with the heel of your hand for 3 to 5 minutes until it forms a smooth, compact ball of dough. Divide the dough into two equal pieces and cover one with a dish towel to keep it soft and pliable until needed. Flatten and shape the second piece of dough into a compact disk, ready for rolling, see below.

¶Spinach Pasta, Using Processor. To the flour, salt, and olive oil in the beaker add ½ pound fresh spinach, blanched 2 minutes, drained, and squeezed dry. Process about 2 minutes, until well blended. Add 1 whole egg and process an additional 8 to 10 seconds, until desired texture is reached.

¶Spinach Pasta, Hand Method. Follow directions for basic pasta starting with 1 cup of flour. Add ½ pound fresh spinach, wilted, squeezed dry, and finely chopped. Work more flour in as needed until you have a smooth ball of dough.

¶Tomato Pasta, Using Processor. To the flour, salt, and olive oil in the beaker add 2 tablespoons tomato paste. Process 8 to 10 seconds. Then add enough beaten whole egg (about 1½ eggs) to bind the dough, and process until desired texture is reached.

¶Rich Egg Pasta, Using Processor. This recipe from my good friend Jim Nassikas, director of the Stanford Court Hotel in San Francisco, makes a very tender pasta with a deep yellow color. Process the flour, salt, and oil for 8 to 10 seconds, as before. Then add 6 egg yolks and process about 15 seconds, or until dough is of desired consistency. If it seems too sticky, sprinkle with 1 or 2 tablespoons flour and process for an additional 6 to 8 seconds.

Rolling and Cutting Pasta

Start running the flattened piece of dough through the kneading rollers, set at number 6. Do this about half a dozen times, each time folding over the strip that emerges before putting it through again, so it gets a thorough kneading. As the strip gets longer and thinner, fold it over two or three times and keep on rolling until it looks and feels silky and supple.

Now lower the gauge for each successive rolling, from 6 to 5, 4, 3, and finally 2 or 1, until you achieve the thinness you like. The final setting will give the dough an almost translucent paper thinness. I usually like 2 as the last setting for my pasta. The thinner the pasta, the tenderer it will be. You will find that as the pasta gets thinner and thinner it gets longer and longer, so you will have to cut it in half when it gets too long to put through the machine easily. When you have finished rolling, keep the pasta strips moist on a damp towel while you change over to the cutting rollers. There are two. One cuts the pasta into fettuccine ¼ inch wide, the other cuts it ⅛ inch wide for very fine fettuccine. Use the thickness you prefer, according to the sauce you are going to use. I find the wider size better for heavier sauces, the thinner for very light ones.

As you feed the pasta strip into the cutting roller, put your hand on the other side to catch the long strings and toss them lightly with flour so they won't stick together. Either cook the pasta right away or, after flouring, drape the strings over a broom handle supported between two chair backs, or lay them flat on a lightly floured board and leave to dry for 5 minutes.

Cooking Homemade Pasta

If you are going to cook the pasta without drying, the water should be boiling before you start cutting the dough. Put 4 quarts water in an 8-quart pot, season with 3 tablespoons coarse salt, cover the pot, and bring the water to a rapid, rolling boil. Uncover, drop in the pasta, cover until the water returns to a rolling boil, then remove the cover and cook the pasta until it is firm to the bite (al dente). Start testing by removing a strand and tasting after 10 seconds. The cooking time depends on whether the pasta is fresh or dried, but it will be less than 2 minutes. Never overcook pasta. The minute it is done, drain it in a colander, and either return it to the pan and toss it with the hot sauce of your choice or put it on serving plates, add the sauce, and toss. For a selection of sauces, see pages 279–285.

Sauces for Pasta

Any of the following sauces can be used with homemade or commercial pasta and will be sufficient for 4 servings, or 1 pound uncooked dry pasta, unless otherwise noted.

Cooking Commercial Dry Pastas

For commercial pasta, follow the cooking method given above, but start testing after the pasta has boiled for 6 minutes. According to the brand, type, and thickness, commercial dry pastas will need different cooking times, and you can only tell when the pasta is done to your liking by testing and tasting. Do not overcook. Pasta should always be served al dente. I like to toss pasta and sauce with two forks. I find the strands stay separate and are more evenly coated.

Curried Beef and Tomato Sauce

I'm not usually fond of tomato sauce on pasta, but this is an exception. With the ground beef and spicy flavors, the sauce should be thick.

Makes 4 servings

¼ pound (1 stick) unsalted butter
3½ cups (1-pound 12-ounce can) tomato purée
3½ cups (1-pound 12-ounce can) whole-pack tomatoes
1 large yellow onion, peeled and roughly sliced

2 whole dried hot red peppers
1 whole garlic clove, peeled
2½ tablespoons curry powder
1 tablespoon turmeric
2 tablespoons peanut oil
1 pound lean ground beef

Melt the butter in a deep, heavy saucepan. Add the tomato purée, whole tomatoes, sliced onion, red peppers, garlic, curry powder, and turmeric. Simmer uncovered for about 1 hour, stirring occasionally. Remove the peppers.

Heat the oil until hot in a large, heavy skillet. Add the ground beef and sauté over medium-high heat until the meat loses its raw color and is lightly browned. Then stir the meat into the hot tomato sauce and remove from the heat.

Cook and drain 12 ounces spinach pasta (see page 277) or other pasta of your choice. Return to the hot cooking pot, add the sauce, and toss with 2 forks. Serve at once.

Virginia Ham, Spinach, and Rosemary Sauce

Makes 4 servings

½ pound Virginia ham, cut into 1½-inch cubes
½ pound fresh spinach, blanched and squeezed dry

2 tablespoons fresh rosemary
¼ teaspoon freshly grated nutmeg
1 tablespoon Dijon mustard
¼ cup chicken stock, as needed

Put the cubed ham, wilted spinach, rosemary, nutmeg, and mustard into the work bowl of a food processor, with the metal blade in place. Process for about 30 seconds, turning the processor on and off, until the mixture is coarsely chopped. Scrape down the bowl with a rubber spatula and continue to process the mixture into a thick, smooth paste. With the motor running, add chicken stock through the feed tube until the mixture becomes a thick sauce. (This may be made in a blender, if you don't have a food processor.)

Put drained cooked tomato pasta or plain pasta (see page 276) into a heated serving bowl, top with the sauce, and toss with 2 forks. Serve at once.

Braised Onion Sauce

Makes 4 servings

½ cup butter
1½ pounds yellow onions, peeled and
    sliced ⅜ inch thick

1 tablespoon sugar
¼ cup Madeira
Parmesan cheese

Melt the butter in a skillet, add the onion, and cook, covered, over medium heat until soft and transparent. Uncover, stir in the sugar, reduce the heat, and cook gently until brown, about 1 hour. Stir in the Madeira and cook 2 minutes.

Toss the sauce with drained cooked pasta, preferably tomato pasta (see page 277), spaghetti, or macaroni. Serve at once with grated Parmesan cheese.

Sardine and Fennel Sauce

Makes 4 servings

1 tablespoon butter
2 tablespoons olive oil
2 garlic cloves, chopped
2 heads of fennel, cut into julienne
    strips

Salt, freshly ground black pepper
¼ cup chopped fennel tops
½ cup chopped Italian parsley
2 cans large French sardines, packed in
    oil, coarsely chopped

Heat the butter and oil in a sauté pan. Add the garlic and fennel strips and sauté until lightly brown. Cover. Simmer for 3 to 4 minutes. Remove cover and add salt, pepper, fennel tops, and parsley. Toss well. Add the chopped sardines and heat through.

Raisin and Pine Nut Sauce

Makes 4 servings

4 garlic cloves, finely chopped
¾ cup olive oil
½ cup pine nuts

½ cup raisins
Freshly ground black pepper, to taste
⅓ cup chopped Italian parsley

Heat the garlic in the olive oil over low heat. When warm, pour the oil over cooked, drained pasta, add the pine nuts and raisins, and toss well. Add pepper to taste and sprinkle with the parsley. Toss again and serve at once.

¶Raisin and Pine Nut Sauce with Anchovies. Add 10 finely chopped anchovy fillets to the pasta and proceed as above.

¶Raisin and Pine Nut Sauce with Dry Figs. Instead of anchovies add coarsely chopped dry figs to the pasta and proceed as above.

Pesto

A sensational and highly popular pasta sauce that requires quantities of fresh basil. Make it in summer when this great herb flourishes and huge bunches can be bought for next to nothing in Italian markets. Pesto will keep well in the refrigerator in an airtight container if you pour about ½ inch of olive oil on top as a seal. It can also be frozen in meal-size batches, about ½ cup for each pound of pasta. You don't have to confine pesto to pasta, either. Stir it into a risotto (see page 291) or cooked rice; use it on gnocchi, potatoes, sautéed shrimp; in tomato sauce, minestrone, a vinaigrette for tomatoes; or mix it into shredded sautéed zucchini. It is one of the most blissful ways to use basil ever invented. Originally pesto was made the hard way, in a mortar and pestle, but I find a food processor or blender (the latter gives a finer consistency) ideal instruments.

Makes 4 servings

4 cups fresh basil leaves
3 cloves garlic, coarsely chopped
½ cup pine nuts
½ cup Italian parsley

½ to 1 cup olive oil
1 teaspoon salt
½ cup grated Pecorino or Parmesan
   cheese (or a mixture of the two)

Put the basil, garlic, pine nuts, parsley, ½ cup oil, and salt in a blender or food processor, and process or blend the mixture, adding more oil if necessary, to make a smooth paste. Then add the cheese and process or blend again. (If you are going to freeze the pesto, don't add the nuts or cheese; they should be blended with the pesto just before you use it.) Allow ½ cup pesto for 4 servings of pasta—1 pound. Dilute it with about 2 tablespoons of the hot water in which the pasta was cooked before tossing with the cooked pasta.

¶**Pesto with Walnuts.** Use ½ cup walnuts instead of the pine nuts. Omit the cheese.

¶**Pesto with Parsley.** When fresh basil is unavailable, use 3 cups Italian parsley with the garlic, nuts, cheese, and oil. Mix as before.

NOTE: To keep basil, gather the leaves in season, process with just enough oil to make an unctuous paste, then freeze it to add to a dressing for tomatoes, pasta sauces, or any dish where you crave the flavor of fresh basil.

Diet Pesto

This is a version of pesto that I worked out when I was put on a low-calorie, salt-free diet and therefore always experimenting with ways to make more palatable dishes. While it is not the normal mixture of basil, parsley, pine nuts, garlic, oil, salt, and cheese, it was most satisfying to the palate, proving that if the seasonings are right, you don't miss the salt.

Makes 2 servings

2 cups fresh basil leaves
4 large garlic cloves, coarsely chopped
1 tablespoon lemon juice

½ teaspoon freshly ground black pepper
3 tablespoons unsalted margarine

Put the basil, garlic, lemon juice, and pepper in a food processor or blender, and process or blend until the leaves are quite finely chopped, then add the margarine and blend to a smooth paste. Allow ½ cup diet pesto for 4 servings of pasta.

Light Tomato Sauce

For pasta, I like a very simple, fresh-tasting tomato sauce that is cooked very quickly, rather than a heavy sauce that smothers the texture and taste of delicate pasta. This tomato sauce can be used alone, just with grated cheese, or in any of the following recipes.

Makes 4 servings

28-ounce can whole Redpack tomatoes
   in thick purée
2 small onions, sliced
Salt, freshly ground black pepper
   to taste

1 teaspoon dried basil (optional)
4 tablespoons butter

Cook the tomatoes, onions, and seasonings over medium-high heat for 20 minutes, stirring frequently and breaking up the tomatoes, until liquid is reduced. Stir in the butter. Strain. Or purée the sauce in a food processor or blender, in which case you will have 3 *cups* of sauce. Ladle on top of each serving of pasta.

Mussel and Tomato Sauce

Makes 4 servings

1½ cups finely chopped steamed
   mussels
2 garlic cloves, chopped fine
1½ cups light tomato sauce (see
   preceding recipe)

3 tablespoons chopped Italian parsley
2 tablespoons olive oil

Combine the mussels, garlic, tomato sauce, and parsley, and heat through. Save ¼ cup cooking water from the cooked pasta. Put the pasta in a skillet with the oil, the mussel sauce, and 3 or 4 tablespoons of the cooking water. Stir gently with 2 forks over medium heat for 4 minutes, until well blended.

¶Clam and Tomato Sauce. Substitute chopped steamed clams or chopped canned clams for the mussels.

Ham and Tomato Sauce

Makes about 4 to 5 servings

1 cup ground cooked country ham
1½ cups light tomato sauce (see
   page 282)

¼ cup grated Romano cheese

Combine the ham and tomato sauce and heat through. Add cooked pasta and toss. Add cheese and cook over very low heat for 2 minutes. Serve with additional grated cheese.

¶**Beef (or Veal) and Tomato Sauce.** Substitute cooked ground beef (or veal) for the ham.

¶**Chicken (or Turkey) and Tomato Sauce.** Substitute cooked ground chicken (or turkey) for the ham.

¶**Brains and Tomato Sauce.** Blanch and clean 1 pair brains (see directions on page 449). Purée brains in a food processor, blender, or food mill. Combine with 2 cups light tomato sauce (see page 282) and heat through. Add cooked pasta, toss, and cook in sauce for 1 minute. Serve with grated Parmesan cheese.

Fresh Tomato and Duxelles Sauce

Makes 4 servings

*2½ pounds fresh ripe tomatoes, peeled,
   seeded, and coarsely chopped
4 tablespoons butter*

*2 tablespoons duxelles (see page 535)
1 cup coarsely cut green onions,
   with tops included*

Sauté the tomatoes quickly in the butter until just heated through. Stir in the duxelles and cook 1 minute. Spoon the sauce over cooked pasta, preferably fettuccine or rich egg pasta. Toss. Sprinkle with the green onions. Serve with grated Parmesan cheese.

Brain Sauce

The puréed brains give this pasta sauce a lovely velvety texture. If you have a food processor, use it to purée the brains and grind the meat. Otherwise purée the brains by rubbing them through a sieve or whirling in a blender and put the meat through the meat grinder.

Makes 4 servings

*1 pair brains, blanched and cleaned,
   then puréed
2 cups tomato sauce (see page 534)*

*Salt, freshly ground black pepper
1 pound freshly cooked pasta
Parmesan cheese*

After blanching and cleaning the brains according to directions on page 449, purée them, either by putting them in a food processor or blender or by putting through a food mill. Combine with the tomato sauce and heat through in a large pan, adjust seasoning, and add the drained hot pasta. Cook the pasta with the sauce for about 1 minute before serving with a bowl of grated Parmesan cheese.

¶**With Meat.** Add ¾ cup ground cold meat to the sauce. This may be veal, beef, chicken, or turkey.

¶**Lasagne with Brain Sauce.** Use 1 pound cooked lasagne and spread brain sauce between layers. Top with mozzarella.

Prosciutto, Peas, and Cream Sauce

Makes 4 to 5 servings

1¼ cups heavy cream
½ pound prosciutto, thinly sliced and
    cut in 1-inch strips
1 cup frozen peas, thawed in boiling
    water

2 egg yolks, lightly beaten
Grated Gruyère cheese

Cook the cream over low heat in a flameproof serving dish or shallow enameled cast-iron gratin pan until slightly reduced. Add the prosciutto and peas. Stir until mixture is warm and cream thickened. Turn heat to low, add 12 ounces freshly cooked fettuccine or similar pasta and toss. Add egg yolks and toss until pasta is coated with the sauce. Serve with grated Gruyère cheese.

Pasta with Eggs Mollet

For this you need the very fine fettuccine, ⅛ inch thick. Both this and the eggs mollet should be cooked at the same time, so they are very hot.

Makes 4 servings

8 large eggs
12 ounces freshly cooked fine fettuccine
2 tablespoons butter
¾ cup grated Parmesan cheese

2 tablespoons finely chopped Italian
    parsley
Freshly ground black pepper

Prick the rounded ends of the eggs, bring them to a boil in water to cover, and boil for exactly 3½ minutes (the yolks must remain soft and runny, but the whites should be firm enough to be peeled). Immediately plunge eggs into cold water and peel them carefully, keeping them whole.

Toss the fettuccine with the butter and divide among 4 individual serving plates. Sprinkle each serving with 3 tablespoons grated cheese and top with 2 hot shelled eggs. Sprinkle with a little chopped parsley. Each diner should break the eggs and mix with his own pasta at table. Add freshly ground pepper to taste.

Pasta with Spinach and Mushrooms

This is an exception to my negative feeling about baked pasta dishes, perhaps because it is light and delicate and no more than heated through.

Makes 4 servings

2 pounds spinach, cooked, puréed, and
    mixed with butter and cream
    (see page 173)
1 pound mushroom caps
7 tablespoons butter

Salt, freshly ground black pepper
½ pound pasta
1 tablespoon fresh tarragon, or
    2 teaspoons dried

Prepare the spinach purée and season it well. Sauté the mushrooms in 6 tablespoons of the butter and add salt and freshly ground black pepper to taste. Boil the pasta until just tender. Drain well and arrange in a well-buttered casserole. Top with the puréed spinach, dot with the remaining tablespoon of butter, and cover with the sautéed mushrooms, sprinkled with tarragon. Cover the casserole with a sheet of foil and bake in a 350° oven for 15 to 20 minutes, or until thoroughly heated through. Remove foil and let brown on top a few minutes.

¶Pasta with Spinach, Mushrooms, and Parmesan Cheese. Slice and sauté the mushrooms. Toss the cooked, drained noodles with 3 to 4 tablespoons olive oil, and place in the casserole. Cover with the spinach purée, sprinkle with freshly grated Parmesan cheese, top with the sautéed mushrooms, and sprinkle with buttered crumbs and additional Parmesan. Cover with foil and bake as above, then brown on top.

Pasta with Beans

Makes 8 servings

3 cloves garlic, chopped
2 large onions, finely chopped
2 medium-size carrots, finely chopped
¼ pound bacon, finely chopped
2 tablespoons dried basil leaves
1 cup parsley, chopped
1 teaspoon oregano
¼ cup olive oil
3 large tomatoes, peeled, seeded,
    and chopped
½ cup chicken or beef broth

1 tablespoon salt
1 teaspoon freshly ground black pepper
4 cups cooked or canned cannellini
    beans or cooked pea beans (use
    1 cup dried beans and cook accord-
    ing to directions on page 303)
1 pound elbow macaroni
4 tablespoons butter
Grated Parmesan cheese
Chopped parsley

Sauté the garlic, onion, carrot, bacon, basil leaves, parsley, and oregano in the olive oil in a large pot until limp. Add the tomatoes, broth, salt, and pepper. Cover the pot, and simmer the mixture slowly, stirring, for about 10 minutes, or until all the vegetables are tender. Add the cooked or canned beans, and simmer very slowly for another 20 to 30 minutes.

Cook the macaroni in plenty of boiling salted water to the al dente stage. Melt the butter, add the drained pasta, and toss lightly with ½ cup grated Parmesan cheese. Combine with the bean mixture and serve sprinkled liberally with parsley. Pass additional grated cheese.

Pasta Asciutta Rustica

This recipe is one I took from an Italian magazine some twenty years ago and have always loved for its hearty, stick-to-the-ribs quality.

Makes 6 to 8 servings

½ pound pancetta (Italian bacon),
    salt pork, or smoked bacon
2 pounds sweet Italian sausages
5 tablespoons olive oil
5 cloves garlic, finely chopped
1 medium onion, finely chopped
1 leek, cut in small dice
¼ cup chopped parsley
1 carrot, cut in thin rounds
1 turnip, diced
2 teaspoons basil

Salt, freshly ground black pepper to
    taste
20-ounce can Italian plum tomatoes
2 zucchini, cut in thin slices
4 tablespoons butter
12-ounce can red or white kidney beans,
    drained and rinsed
½ medium-size cabbage, shredded
1 pound rigatoni
½ cup freshly grated Parmesan cheese
    (more if desired)

Cut the pancetta, salt pork, or smoked bacon into small pieces and cook in a small skillet until the fat is rendered. Remove to absorbent paper towels. Prick the sausages, put in a skillet, and cover with water. Bring to a boil. Pour off the water and either broil the sausages or cook them slowly in the skillet over medium-low heat until nicely browned. Remove to absorbent paper towels. Heat the olive oil in a large skillet. Add the chopped garlic, onion, leek, and parsley, and sauté until limp. Add the carrot, turnip, basil, and seasoning. Sauté gently for 3 to 4 minutes. Add tomatoes, zucchini, and butter, and continue to simmer. Add the sausages, kidney beans, and bacon bits, and taste for seasoning. Add the shredded cabbage. Cover and sauté gently for about 5 minutes, or until the cabbage is tender. Meanwhile, cook rigatoni in boiling salted water until tender. Drain and arrange in a flat baking dish. Pour the sauce over all. Sprinkle with Parmesan cheese and run under the broiler to brown lightly.

Spätzle

These little free-form bits of dough are a Central European form of pasta that have been in the American cooking repertoire for about two hundred years. Although they have never been as common or as popular as noodles, they are a nice change of pace as a starch to serve with pot roast or a stew, sauced with the gravy. Most cookware shops, especially those specializing in Central European foods and equipment, sell a special tool called a "spätzle sieve." If you don't have one of these large-meshed sieves, you can use a colander. The batter can also be spread on a plate or board, pushed to the edge, and then small pieces chopped off with a sharp wet knife and dropped into boiling salted water. Any method that works is acceptable.

Makes 6 servings

2 cups flour
1 teaspoon salt
Pinch of nutmeg
Freshly ground black pepper

2 eggs, lightly beaten
⅔ cup milk
1 to 1½ sticks butter, melted

Mix the flour, salt, nutmeg, ¼ teaspoon pepper, and eggs together, then add enough milk to make a rather stiff batter. Beat well and let the batter stand 1 hour before cooking.

Bring a large pot of salted water to a boil and force the batter through the spätzle sieve or colander into the water (it helps if you place wax paper on top of the batter to help push it through the colander). Boil the spätzle 6 to 8 minutes, until just tender but still firm. Drain and run hot or cold water over them. To serve, reheat in the melted butter and add a goodly amount of freshly ground black pepper.

¶**Spätzle with Heavy Cream.** Drain the spätzle and add them to about 1 cup heavy cream, reduced, and butter seasoned with a pinch of nutmeg and grated cheese to taste. Garnish with chopped parsley.

Rice

Rice has the unique ability of being able to enter into every course of a meal, from soup through dessert, although I personally am no lover of rice pudding or other rice desserts. Too many people look on rice as a substitute for potatoes, which it isn't. It's a bed that needs to be blanketed with flavor. I would never serve plain boiled rice with steaks, chops, or roast meats, although a good pilaf or rice sautéed with pine nuts and onion is another story. Boiled rice needs savory additions, like butter and cheese, fresh herbs, or the sauce from a stew or ragout, before it can be admitted to the company of meat. You'll find detailed basic recipes for boiled long-grain rice and steamed converted rice in *Theory & Practice*, page 46.

Rice with Cheese

Makes 4 to 6 servings

1½ *cups long-grain Carolina rice*
4 *quarts water*
1 *tablespoon salt*
¼ *cup melted butter*

½ *cup freshly grated Parmesan cheese*
¼ *cup grated Cheddar or Gruyère*
  cheese (optional)

To cook the rice, bring to a rapid boil 4 quarts water seasoned with 1 tablespoon salt. Throw in the rice in small handfuls, making sure the water continues to boil. Boil rapidly for 15 minutes, uncovered, then drain. Do not overcook. The rice should be fluffy but firm to the bite. This will give you about 4½ cups cooked rice. Toss with the butter and cheeses.

¶**Green Rice.** Boil and drain the rice as above. Combine it with ¼ cup melted butter or olive oil, ½ cup finely chopped parsley, and ½ cup chopped chives or green onions (scallions).

¶**Rice with Herbs.** For the chives or onions in the Green Rice, substitute ¼ cup chopped tarragon, basil, or coriander.

¶**Rice with Nuts.** Combine the cooked rice with ½ to 1 cup toasted and coarsely chopped nuts (almonds, walnuts, filberts, or pecans) and ½ cup melted butter.

¶**Saffron-Flavored Rice.** Crush ¼ teaspoon saffron fronds in a mortar and pestle. Blend with a tablespoon of water or dry white wine, and add to the pot while the rice is cooking. Toss lightly with a fork.

Rice with Onions and Pine Nuts

This piquant Middle East version of rice is something I like to serve with roast or broiled butterflied leg of lamb or roast or broiled chicken.

Makes 6 servings

½ cup olive oil
1 cup finely chopped onion
1 cup pine nuts
1 teaspoon paprika
¼ teaspoon Tabasco

4½ cups hot cooked rice
About 1 teaspoon salt, ½ teaspoon
    freshly ground black pepper
¼ cup chopped parsley
3 pimientos, chopped

Heat the oil in a saucepan, add the onion, pine nuts, paprika, and Tabasco, and sauté lightly for 6 to 8 minutes, being careful not to let the onion brown. Add the hot rice and toss thoroughly with 2 forks. Season to taste with salt and pepper. Garnish with the parsley and pimiento.

Oriental Fried Rice

Makes 6 servings

2 to 4 tablespoons peanut or corn oil
4 cups cooked rice
4 tablespoons shredded green onion,
    or scallions
¼ cup chopped sautéed mushrooms

½ to ¾ cup shredded Virginia or
    country ham, or small pieces of
    roast pork or chicken
2 tablespoons soy sauce
2 eggs

GARNISH: *Shredded green onions, or scallions, slivered toasted*
almonds, or fresh coriander leaves

Heat the oil in a skillet, add the rice, and cook about 5 minutes, shaking the pan and tossing the rice with a fork until heated through. Add the green onion, mushrooms and meat, and toss with the fork. Combine the soy sauce and the eggs and stir into the rice, off the heat, tossing with the fork until the eggs are set. Remove to a hot serving dish and garnish with green onions, almonds or fresh coriander.

Rice Pilaf

The Middle Eastern pilaf, usually served here with kebabs or chicken, is a more flavorful version of rice, as it is first cooked in butter with onion. Vary the liquid according to the food the pilaf will accompany—chicken stock for poultry, beef stock for beef shashlik, fish stock for fish—or just use plain water. Bulghur (cracked wheat) may be cooked in the same way (see *Theory & Practice*, page 49).

Makes 4 servings

4 tablespoons butter or olive oil, or a
    mixture of the two
¼ cup finely chopped onion
1 cup long-grain rice, preferably
    Carolina

2 cups boiling stock or water
Salt, freshly ground black pepper
2 tablespoons melted butter
1 tablespoon chopped parsley

Heat the butter or oil in a heavy 1½-quart casserole, preferably enameled cast iron, which retains the heat well. Add the onion and cook, stirring, until soft and translucent. Add the rice and cook over low heat, stirring, until the grains are lightly coated with oil and have lost their raw color, about 3 minutes. Add stock or water, stir, and season to taste. The amount of salt and pepper depends on the liquid you use and the seasoning in the stock. Bring to a boil, cover, and bake in a 350° oven until all the liquid is absorbed and the rice tender, about 20 to 25 minutes, or cook on top of the stove over very low heat. Remove from the heat, fluff up the rice with 2 forks, mix with melted butter, and sprinkle with parsley.

¶Rice Pilaf with Nuts and Raisins. Top the cooked rice with ¾ cup toasted almonds and ½ cup raisins plumped in ½ cup dry white wine. Replace the parsley with a little chopped fresh mint or coriander. Serve with roast lamb or kebabs.

¶Rice Pilaf with Peas. Toss 2 cups small fresh, or frozen and thawed, green peas in 3 tablespoons butter until heated through. Season to taste and toss well with the rice, using 2 forks. A little chopped fresh mint may be sprinkled on top instead of parsley. Serve with veal, chicken, or lamb.

¶Rice Pilaf with Green Chilies. Mix ½ cup chopped canned green chilies into the pilaf. Sprinkle with chopped fresh coriander.

Risotto

There is almost no limit to what can be done with risotto, the Italian rice dish for which you will find a more detailed recipe in *Theory & Practice* (pages 47–49). Vegetables add a pleasing crunchiness to the creamy rice, a spoonful or two of pesto gives a lovely flavor and color, and any kind or combination of shellfish is heaven. Or you can stir raw ingredients such as slivers of chicken breast, tiny shrimp, or cut-up shrimp, garden peas, or asparagus tips into the rice during the final cooking stage. The heat will be sufficient to cook them through. Risotto heaped with chicken livers sautéed gently in butter, seasoned, and flavored with a little Madeira or

Marsala, is a great favorite with some people, but not with me; chicken livers are one of the few foods I really dislike.

Makes 4 servings

6 tablespoons butter

1 small onion, finely chopped

1½ cups short-grain Italian Arborio rice or long-grain Carolina rice

3 to 4 cups simmering homemade chicken or beef stock

½ cup freshly grated Parmesan cheese

Melt 2 tablespoons butter in a heavy skillet, add the onion, and sauté, stirring, until soft and golden. Add 2 more tablespoons butter and, when melted, mix in the rice, stirring until the grains are well coated. Add 1 cup hot stock, stir in well, and let it cook down over medium heat. Continue to add stock, cup by cup, letting it cook away after each addition and stirring now and then to prevent the rice from sticking to the pan. Add only as much stock as the rice can absorb. It should be creamy and tender, but still firm to the bite. Cooking time should be between 25 and 30 minutes. Stir well during the final cooking. Stir the remaining butter and cheese into the cooked rice and serve immediately.

¶**Risotto alla Milanese.** Use beef stock for the cooking liquid and add ½ teaspoon saffron, dissolved in 1 cup of the hot stock, during the last 15 minutes of cooking time. About 2 minutes before the risotto is done, mix in 4 to 5 tablespoons lightly poached beef marrow. This is the traditional accompaniment to Ossi Buchi (see page 416).

¶**Risotto with White Truffles.** Garnish the top of the cooked risotto with thin shavings of fresh white truffles. (These are in season late in the year and are madly expensive, but worth the splurge.)

¶**Risotto with Shellfish.** Cook 1 chopped garlic clove with the onion, and use fish stock (see page 530) as the cooking liquid. Heat 2 cups cooked shellfish (steamed clams or mussels, poached bay scallops, shrimp, or lobster, alone or in any combination of your choice) in 4 tablespoons butter. Season to taste and mix into the cooked risotto with 3 tablespoons chopped parsley. Omit the cheese.

¶**Risotto with Raw Shrimp.** Use fish stock as the cooking liquid. Stir 2 cups tiny raw peeled shrimp (or larger shrimp, cut in pieces) into the risotto 5 minutes before the end of the cooking time. Add 3 tablespoons chopped parsley. Omit the cheese.

¶**Risotto with Chicken.** Cut enough skinned and boned raw chicken breasts into strips about 2 inches long and ¼ inch wide to make 1½ cups. Stir into the risotto (made with chicken broth) 10 minutes before the end of the cooking time.

¶**Risotto with Asparagus.** Briefly cook 2 pounds asparagus (it should still be crisp) and cut off the tips (the remaining asparagus can be puréed for soup). Stir the asparagus tips into the risotto 3 to 4 minutes before the end of the cooking time. Add ½ cup additional melted butter.

¶**Risotto with Green Beans or Peas.** Stir 1½ cups quickly cooked and buttered crisp green beans, cut in pieces, or 2 cups buttered cooked green peas (if very young and fresh, they may be left raw) into the cooked risotto. Or use a combination of the two.

¶**Risotto with Cherry Tomatoes.** When cooking the onion, add 1 chopped garlic clove. Stir 1½ cups steamed, peeled cherry tomatoes (see page 185) into the cooked risotto, along with a few leaves of fresh basil, chopped, if available.

Paella

I find meaty, inexpensive chicken legs are excellent for paella. Chorizo, the smoked and dried hot Spanish sausage, is traditional in this dish, but if you can't find it you can substitute Italian pepperoni or the hot Italian pork sausages, poached for 5 minutes in water to cover to draw out the fat.

Makes 4 servings

½ cup flour
8 chicken legs, separated into thighs
    and drumsticks
6 tablespoons peanut oil
24 clams, well scrubbed
24 mussels, well scrubbed
1 cup dry white wine
2 garlic cloves, unpeeled
1 large or 2 medium-size onions,
    chopped fine
3 cloves garlic, chopped fine
3 cups long-grain or converted rice
1 generous pinch of saffron soaked in
    2 tablespoons dry white wine
Salt, freshly ground black pepper

Chicken broth or water, heated to
    boiling
3 chorizo or pepperoni sausages, or
    4 or 5 poached hot Italian
    sausages, sliced ½ inch thick
1 cup peeled, seeded, and chopped
    fresh tomatoes, or drained and
    chopped canned Italian plum
    tomatoes
12 raw shrimp, unpeeled
½ package frozen peas, thawed in
    boiling water and drained
4-ounce jar pimientos, drained, sliced,
    and warmed

Lightly flour the chicken drumsticks and thighs. Heat the oil in a large, heavy skillet. Add the chicken pieces and brown on all sides, then reduce the heat and continue to cook until the chicken is tender, about 20 minutes. Remove to a platter and keep warm.

In separate pans, steam the clams and mussels in white wine with the garlic cloves just until the shells open, being sure to discard any that do not. Drain the clams and mussels, reserving the broth.

Add the onions and garlic, chopped fine, to the pan in which the chicken was cooked, and sauté, stirring, until soft and golden. Add the rice and cook, stirring, until it turns translucent. Add the saffron and the reserved clam and mussel broths to the rice, and season to taste with salt and pepper. Bring to a boil, then reduce the heat, and simmer the rice until the liquid has been absorbed and the rice is almost done, adding chicken stock or water if the liquid cooks away too fast. Add the sausages and tomatoes and mix into the rice. Cook another 5 minutes. Add the shrimp to the rice and cook 3–4 minutes, or until they turn pink. Add the peas, stirring them into the rice, then arrange the chicken pieces and the opened clams and mussels on top of the rice. Garnish with warmed pimiento strips and serve immediately.

Wild Rice

Because this grain of an aquatic grass that grows wild in shallow water has to be harvested by hand from a canoe, it has always been a scarce luxury item. Fortunately, because of cultivation processes developed over the last twenty-five or thirty years, there are now wild rice paddies throughout the Great Lakes area, and the grain is more widely available. I find the cultivated wild rice to be an excellent product, with grains of a regular size and good flavor. While many people are at a loss as to how to cook wild rice, it is a simple process, but remember that if you are going to use the cooked rice in a stuffing or casserole it will require less cooking time.

Basic Wild Rice

Makes 4 servings

1 cup raw wild rice
3 cups water

Salt, freshly ground black pepper
⅓ to ½ cup melted butter

First, wash the rice in running water until the water runs clear. Bring 3 cups water to a rapid boil in a saucepan, and add salt to taste. Add the wild rice, and bring the water back to a full boil. Stir the rice with a fork, reduce the heat to a low simmer, cover the pan, and cook the rice until the grains puff open and the white interiors show, about 20 minutes. I like it slightly al dente, with a bite to it. Drain the rice, add the melted butter, and toss well with a fork. Season to taste with salt and pepper.

¶Wild Rice with Green Onions and Pine Nuts. After seasoning, toss the rice with ½ cup finely sliced green onion, or scallion, and ½ cup toasted pine nuts and sprinkle with 1 tablespoon chopped parsley.

¶Wild Rice with Duck or Goose Fat and Mushrooms. If you are serving the wild rice with roast duck or goose, use the rendered fat instead of butter, and mix in 1 cup sautéed sliced mushrooms.

¶Wild Rice with Ham. Add about ½ cup finely diced country or Virginia ham, with the ham fat, instead of butter. Just before serving, add freshly chopped parsley or chives.

¶Wild Rice with Walnuts. Add ½ cup finely chopped walnuts or black walnuts to the cooked rice.

¶Wild Rice with Bacon and Onion. Toss with the melted butter, ½ cup crisp bacon, crumbled, and ½ cup sautéed onion.

¶Wild Rice with Duxelles. Add ½ cup duxelles (see page 535) when tossing the wild rice.

Barley and Mushroom Casserole

I'm very fond of the nutty quality of barley, a much-neglected grain, and often serve it with poultry or game instead of the much more expensive wild rice.

Makes 6 servings

¾ cup (12 tablespoons) butter
½ pound firm white mushrooms,
    cleaned and sliced
2 medium-size onions, coarsely chopped

1½ cups pearl barley
3 cups chicken stock (approximately)
Salt

Melt 4 tablespoons of the butter in a skillet and sauté the mushrooms for 4 minutes. Remove from the pan and set aside. Melt the remaining butter and sauté the onions until they are soft and wilted. Add the barley and stir over medium heat until the barley becomes beautifully brown—this is important as it improves the flavor and texture. Return the mushrooms to the pan, mix well with the barley, place the mixture in a 2-quart casserole, and add 1½ cups chicken stock. Cover and cook in a 350° oven for 30 minutes. Add the remaining 1½ cups stock and cook 30 minutes longer, adding salt if necessary (this will depend on the seasoning of the stock). If the mixture seems too dry, add a little more stock. The barley should be tender but not mushy.

¶**Barley Casserole with Almonds.** Add ½ cup finely slivered almonds toasted in butter to the barley just before serving.

¶**Barley Casserole with Celery and Water Chestnuts.** Add ¼ cup finely chopped celery and ¼ cup thinly sliced water chestnuts to the barley mixture for the last 2 minutes of cooking, and season the broth with a dash of soy sauce. Serve topped with chopped parsley. This is good with broiled teriyaki chicken (see *Theory & Practice*, page 115), or steak.

¶**Barley Casserole with Chicken Gizzards.** Cook 4 chicken gizzards in part of the stock you will use for the casserole. Slice the gizzards thin and stir them into the barley just before serving.

Kasha (Buckwheat Groats)

Every once in a while I get a craving for kasha. The crunchiness of the groats makes a nice contrast to foods with a very soft texture, like chicken breasts in a creamy sauce.

Makes 4 servings

1 cup buckwheat groats	*Salt*
1 egg	*4 tablespoons butter or rendered*
2 cups boiling beef stock	*chicken fat*

Put the buckwheat groats in a preheated frying pan or an electric skillet. Add an egg and stir vigorously over high heat. When each grain is separate, add the stock and salt to taste. Cover the pan, lower the heat, and steam the groats for 30 minutes, then stir in the butter or chicken fat.

¶**Kasha with Mushrooms.** Mix ½ cup sautéed sliced mushrooms into the cooked kasha.

¶**Kasha with Sautéed Giblets.** Mix ½ cup sautéed chopped chicken gizzards, hearts, and livers into the cooked kasha.

Hominy

Hominy, corn steamed with lye to remove the seed germ and swell the kernels, is one of those traditional American foods I remember with much nostalgia from my childhood. The hominy vendor used to come down our street twice a week with big tins of whole fresh hominy. Whole fresh hominy is difficult to find these days, but you can buy hominy in cans, and that's what I use when I get a craving for it with my fried chicken, roast pork, duck, or turkey.

Sautéed Hominy with Cream

Makes 4 to 6 servings

Two 1-pound 12-ounce cans whole
*   hominy*
6 tablespoons butter

Salt, freshly ground black pepper
⅓ to ½ cup heavy cream
1 tablespoon chopped parsley

Drain the hominy and rinse it well. Melt the butter in a saucepan, add the hominy, and heat it through, shaking the pan and tossing the kernels gently so they don't break up. Season well with salt and plenty of pepper— pepper greatly enhances hominy. When heated through, add the cream and let it just cook down and blend. Taste for seasoning, adding more pepper, if necessary. Put the hominy in a serving dish and sprinkle it with parsley.

Hominy Casserole

I adore this combination of hominy, chilies, and sour cream, and serve it with barbecued or broiled meats.

Makes 4 to 6 servings

Two 1-pound 12-ounce cans hominy,
*   drained and rinsed*
Salt, freshly ground black pepper to
*   taste*
1 cup sour cream

1 cup peeled green chilies, finely
*   chopped*
2 tablespoons butter
¼ cup grated Parmesan cheese

Butter a deep casserole and arrange a layer of hominy in the bottom, sprinkling it liberally with salt and pepper. Cover with some of the sour cream and sprinkle with chilies. Repeat this process, sprinkling each layer of hominy with salt and pepper, until the hominy, sour cream, and chilies are used, making sure that the top layer is hominy.

Dot with butter and sprinkle with Parmesan cheese. Bake in a preheated 350° oven for 20 to 25 minutes.

Couscous

Couscous, the national dish of Morocco, Algeria, and Tunisia, is great party food. Arranged on a big platter, it looks inviting, feeds a lot of people economically, and is fun to eat. There isn't much meat in the dish, which is usually only part of a North African meal, so I like to serve it with chicken cooked in the Moroccan style, with pickled lemons and olives (see page 322), or spiced lamb kebabs (see *Theory & Practice*, page 123).

The traditional cooker for couscous is a couscousier, a piece of equipment with a deep bottom and a perforated top in which the couscous, a tiny semolina grain, steams over spicy, aromatic broth. (You can substitute an 8-quart cooking pot over which a colander will fit.)

Couscous grain is sold in Middle Eastern and specialty food shops. Be careful not to buy the instant variety; you need the regular, long-cooking type.

Makes 8 servings

COUSCOUS

2 pounds neck or shoulder of lamb, cut into 1½-inch cubes
2 large onions, thinly sliced
1 teaspoon ground ginger
1 teaspoon turmeric
2 teaspoons freshly ground black pepper
¾ cup vegetable oil
8 tablespoons butter
Pinch of saffron
1½ pounds (4 cups) long-cooking couscous

6 carrots, scraped and quartered
4 turnips, peeled and quartered
4 potatoes, peeled and quartered
3 teaspoons salt
3 medium-size zucchini, cut in thick slices
20-ounce can chickpeas, drained and rinsed, or about 2 cups
¼ cup raisins

Start the couscous about 2 hours before serving time. Put the lamb, onions, ginger, turmeric, pepper, ½ cup oil, 4 tablespoons butter, and saffron in the bottom of a couscousier or an 8-quart pot and add enough water to come 2 inches above the ingredients. Bring to a rapid boil.

Line the steamer top of the couscousier or the colander with a triple thickness of cheesecloth (this prevents the tiny grains from falling through), put in the couscous, place over the boiling mixture, and either cover with the lid of the couscousier or wrap aluminum foil tightly over the colander and the edges of the pot to keep the steam from escaping. Steam for 1 hour, then remove the steamer section and run cold water over the puffed-up couscous for 2 or 3 minutes, breaking up the lumps with your fingers. Set aside to drain.

Add to the bottom of the pot the carrots, turnips, and potatoes. Cover and cook 20 minutes. Meanwhile, turn the drained couscous into a big bowl and mix in the remaining ¼ cup oil and the salt with your fingers. Replace the couscous in the cheesecloth-lined steamer. Add the zucchini, chickpeas, and raisins to the stew in the bottom of the pot, replace the steamer over the stew and steam for another 15 to 20 minutes. Then transfer the hot couscous to a bowl and mix in the remaining 4 tablespoons butter.

To serve, mound the couscous on a very large platter. Make a well in the center and put about 2 cups of the drained lamb and vegetables into it. Serve the rest of the meat and vegetables in another dish, the broth from the stew in a large bowl, and sauce piquante in a small bowl. The accompanying chicken or kebabs should be served separately.

SAUCE PIQUANTE (*Red Pepper Sauce*)

2 or 3 hot red chili peppers	1 teaspoon Tabasco
3 tablespoons olive oil	¼ cup finely ground walnuts
1 garlic clove, crushed	

Combine all the above ingredients in a blender or food processor and blend to a paste.

NOTE: Leftover couscous may be resteamed and served like pilaf, with any of the additions given for pilaf (see pages 290–291), or with chopped, cooked prunes and sautéed apple slices. Or serve it cold as a salad, mixed like tabbouleh (see *Theory & Practice*, page 337), with chopped green onions or scallions, chopped parsley, mint, lemon juice, oil, salt, and chopped tomato.

Cornmeal

To my mind, the greatest derivative of corn is cornmeal, a grain that is too often overlooked, except in the South, where it is practically a way of life. The finest, most flavorful cornmeal is the water-ground, which can be bought in health-food stores or specialty food shops or ordered by mail from small mills across the country.

I have always loved cornmeal mush cooled in a pan, sliced, and sautéed in butter or bacon fat and eaten for breakfast with maple syrup or preserves. I remember when I first went to Europe I discovered that Italian polenta was like cornmeal mush, although in Italy it is made rather differently, in a heavy pot, with the cornmeal added to simmering water in a thin, continuous stream and stirred constantly. I have my own way of making it, which I find much simpler. The earthiness of polenta gives it a great affinity for simple, tasty foods like sausages and salt cod.

Polenta with Sausages

Makes 6 servings

1½ cups cornmeal
4½ cups cold water
1 teaspoon salt
4 tablespoons unsalted butter

¾ cup grated Parmesan cheese
1½ pounds hot Italian sausages
2 cups tomato sauce (see page 534)

Put the cornmeal and 1 cup water in the top part of a double boiler and mix well. Bring the rest of the water to a boil in a saucepan, stir it into the cornmeal, and cook over direct, very low heat, stirring constantly, until the mixture comes to a boil. Add the salt. Put enough water in the bottom of the double boiler to come just below the top part. Cover the top of the double boiler, place it over the water simmering in the bottom, and steam the cornmeal for 1 hour. Stir in the butter and ½ cup of the grated cheese.

Prick the sausages, place them in a skillet with water to cover, and bring the water to a boil. Lower the heat and simmer the sausages for 12 minutes. Drain them thoroughly, then brown them slowly on all sides over medium-low heat.

Oil a baking dish and pour in the cooked cornmeal or polenta. Top with the sausages. Bake in a 375° oven for 15 minutes, then spoon ¾ cup tomato sauce over the top and sprinkle with the remaining ¼ cup grated Parmesan cheese. Serve with the remaining tomato sauce and additional grated cheese.

¶Polenta with Fontina Cheese. Pour the polenta into an oiled baking dish, top with 1 cup shredded fontina cheese, and place under a hot broiler until the cheese is melted.

¶Polenta with Spinach. Cook 2 packages frozen spinach or 2 pounds fresh, drain well, chop fine, and blend with 1 chopped garlic clove, the juice of ½ lemon, 4 tablespoons olive oil, and salt to taste. Place in the bottom of an oiled baking dish, top with the polenta, dot with butter, sprinkle with grated Parmesan cheese and bake in a 375° oven for 15 to 20 minutes, or until delicately browned. A great accompaniment to roast beef, pork, or veal.

¶**Polenta with Salt Cod.** Cook 2 pounds salt cod according to directions for poached codfish (see page 243). Pour the polenta into an oiled baking dish or casserole and top with the codfish. Cover with 3 cups thick tomato sauce, sprinkle with grated Parmesan cheese, and glaze the top under a hot broiler.

¶**Polenta Cakes.** Pour the polenta mixture into a buttered dish and spread out 1½ inches thick. Cut into 3-inch squares and dredge in grated Parmesan or Gruyère cheese. Put in a buttered baking dish and bake in a 375° oven until polenta is delicately brown and cheese is melted. Serve with roast veal, pork, or other types of roasts.

Cornmeal Gnocchi

These gnocchi are, I admit, somewhat fattening, but I adore their soul-satisfying flavor and texture. Here I use the Italian method of making the basic polenta, but instead of water I prefer milk, which gives a more delicate result.

Makes 6 servings

5 cups milk or water (or a combination of water and evaporated milk)
1¼ cups coarse cornmeal
1 teaspoon salt

½ cup melted butter
¼ cup freshly grated Parmesan or Romano cheese

Bring the milk or other liquid to a boil in a heavy pan, taking care not to let it scorch. While it is boiling, gradually cascade the cornmeal into the liquid in a thin stream, stirring constantly until the polenta thickens, heaves, and bubbles. Stir well to make sure there are no lurking lumps. Remove from the heat, stir in the salt, then pour into a jelly-roll pan, and leave until cold. Cut into rounds with a 1½- to 2-inch cutter, and arrange the rounds in a baking dish, with the edges overlapping slightly. Pour the melted butter over them, sprinkle with cheese, and bake in a 350° oven for 10 to 15 minutes, or until they are hot, soaked with butter, and slightly browned on top. Serve as a first course or as an accompaniment to meat.

Cornmeal Soufflé

This soufflé is a good accompaniment to braised dishes or roasts.

Makes 4 to 6 servings

1 cup milk
¾ cup cornmeal
2 tablespoons butter

1 teaspoon salt
4 eggs, separated

Put the milk in a saucepan and bring to a simmer. Gradually add the cornmeal and cook, stirring constantly, until thickened. Add the butter and salt and mix well. Stir in the egg yolks and set aside. Whisk the egg whites until they reach the soft-peak stage. Stir a good spoonful of the egg whites into the cornmeal mixture to soften it slightly, then fold in the remaining egg whites. Pour the soufflé mixture into a buttered 2-quart soufflé dish and bake in a preheated 400° oven for 25 minutes. Serve with melted butter or a sauce.

¶Cornmeal Soufflé with Parmesan Cheese. Omit the salt and add ½ cup grated Parmesan cheese to the cornmeal mixture.

¶Cornmeal Soufflé with Whole-Kernel Corn. Add ½ cup whole-kernel corn to the cornmeal mixture.

Corn-Chili Soufflé

This is one of my all-time favorite cornmeal dishes. The whole-kernel corn gives it an interesting texture, and the spicy ingredients complement the flavors. I like to serve this with pork dishes.

Makes 6 servings

1 cup cornmeal
17-ounce can whole-kernel corn, drained
1 cup milk
6 eggs, separated
1½ teaspoons chili powder
1 teaspoon salt

1 teaspoon freshly ground black pepper
2 teaspoons baking powder
1 cup stuffed olives, chopped
1 green chili, finely chopped
1½ cups crisp bacon pieces
¾ cup grated Parmesan cheese

Soak the cornmeal and the corn in the milk, then heat the mixture until it's at the thickening stage (just about at the boiling point), stirring it very well with a heavy whisk. Off the heat, stir in the egg yolks, seasonings, baking powder, olives, and green chili, mixing thoroughly. Add the bacon pieces and cheese. Stir well until thoroughly integrated. Preheat the oven to 375°.

Beat the egg whites until stiff but not dry. Fold about one-fourth the whites into the corn mixture very thoroughly. Add the remaining whites and stir and fold until no white shows. Pour into a well-buttered 2-quart baking dish or soufflé dish. Bake for about 35 minutes.

White Beans with Cognac

Makes 6 servings

1 pound (2 cups) dry white beans (pea, navy, or Great Northern)
1 garlic clove
1 onion, stuck with 2 cloves
1 bay leaf
1 sprig fresh thyme or ¼ teaspoon dried

4 tablespoons unsalted butter
1 small onion, chopped
2 cups tomato purée
¼ cup finely chopped parsley
2 teaspoons salt
⅓ cup cognac

Cover the beans with cold water, bring to a boil, cook 2 minutes, then remove from the heat and let stand, covered, 1 hour. Add the garlic, whole onion, bay leaf, and thyme. Bring to a boil, cover, reduce the heat, and simmer until tender, about 2 hours. Drain, reserving the liquid. Discard the onion, bay leaf, and thyme sprig (the garlic will have disintegrated).

Melt the butter in a large skillet and sauté the chopped onion until soft. Add the tomato purée, parsley, salt, cognac, and 1 cup liquid from the beans. Simmer 30 minutes, then mix with the beans, correct seasoning, and reheat in a casserole. Serve with lamb or almost any broiled meat.

¶White Beans with Ham and Sausage. Add 1 cup diced cooked ham and 1 pound cooked sausages to the beans and sauce. Correct the seasoning. Bake in a casserole in a 325° oven until just bubbling. Serve as a hearty main dish.

White Bean Purée

Makes 6 servings

1 pound (2 cups) dry white beans (pea, navy, Great Northern, or cannellini)
4 garlic cloves
1 onion, stuck with 2 cloves

1 bay leaf
Salt, freshly ground black pepper
4 tablespoons unsalted butter
¾ cup heavy cream
Chopped parsley for garnish

Cook the beans with the garlic, onion, bay leaf, and 1 teaspoon pepper according to directions for White Beans with Cognac (see preceding recipe). Drain. Discard the bay leaf and cloves. Purée the beans with the onion and garlic, then beat in the butter, cream, and salt and pepper to taste. Reheat and garnish with chopped parsley. Serve with roast lamb or other roast or broiled meats.

¶**Puréed Cannellini with Madeira.** Use 4 twenty-ounce cans of cannellini beans, drained and rinsed, instead of cooked beans. Purée the cannellini, then combine with ½ cup butter, ⅔ cup heavy cream, ½ cup Madeira, and salt, pepper, and nutmeg to taste. Heat, stirring constantly, in a heavy saucepan.

Cassoulet

There are many versions of cassoulet, all monumentally substantial. This version, one of the best I've ever eaten, was originated by a fine cook of an independent turn of mind, a Frenchwoman who had lived for many years in this country and adapted the recipes of her native land to the local ingredients. You can vary this recipe by adding roast or preserved goose or crisp roast duck, or you can make it with just lamb and sausages, omitting the pork, or leave out the tomato paste and add more garlic.

Makes 10 to 12 servings

2 pounds dry white beans	*2 cups red wine*
1 onion, stuck with 2 cloves	*1 saucisson à l'ail (garlic sausage),*
8 to 10 garlic cloves	*cotechino, or kielbasa*
1 bay leaf	*1½ teaspoons crumbled thyme*
1 pig's foot, split	*2 tablespoons tomato paste*
Salt, freshly ground black pepper	*6 strips salt pork, cut thin*
½ leg of lamb (about 3½ pounds)	*1 cup bread crumbs*
3 pounds pork loin or shoulder	

Soak and then cook the beans with the onion, 4 garlic cloves, bay leaf, and pig's foot according to directions for White Beans with Cognac (see page 303), adding 1 tablespoon salt halfway through the cooking.

While the beans are cooking, salt and pepper the lamb and pork and roast in a 325° oven for 1½ hours, basting from time to time with 1½ cups of the red wine. Let the meats cool and chill in the roasting pan until the fat congeals on the pan juices and can be skimmed off. Reserve the juices. Cut the meats into 2-inch cubes and reserve.

Poach the sausage in water to cover for 35 to 40 minutes, then drain and slice ½ inch thick. Finely chop the remaining garlic cloves and mix with the thyme and 1 teaspoon pepper.

When the beans are cooked, drain them, reserving the liquid. Remove the bay leaf, onion, and pig's foot. Cut the skin and meat from the pig's foot and reserve. Put a layer of the beans in a large earthenware or enameled cast-iron casserole and sprinkle with some of the garlic mixture, cubed meats, meat from the pig's foot, and sausages. Continue making layers until all these ingredients are used, ending with beans. Combine the reserved pan juices with the bean liquid, ½ cup red wine, and the tomato paste. Pour enough of this liquid over the cassoulet to reach almost to the top layer of beans. Top the cassoulet with salt pork slices and cover tightly with foil. Bake in a 350° oven for 1 hour, then remove the foil and sprinkle bread crumbs on top. Bake 1 hour more, or until the liquid is absorbed, the top is glazed and the crumbs browned. If too much liquid is absorbed during the first hour of cooking, add more. Serve the cassoulet with crusty bread and a hearty red wine.

Cassoulet with Limas

Makes 6 servings

1 pound large dry lima beans
1 onion stuck with 2 cloves
2 teaspoons salt
8 cloves garlic
4 or 5 slices salt pork or bacon cut
   ⅜ inch thick
1 cup chopped onion
1 pound Italian sausage (sweet or hot),
   poached for 2 minutes and drained

¼ cup chopped fresh basil or 2
   teaspoons dry basil
¼ cup chopped parsley
2 hot red peppers or ½ teaspoon
   Tabasco
¾ cup fresh bread crumbs (preferably
   pumpernickel or whole wheat)

Put the beans, onion stuck with cloves, salt, and 5 cloves garlic in a 4-quart saucepan. Cover with water by 1 inch and bring to a boil. Boil for 10 minutes. Turn off the heat and let rest for 1 hour. Cook until tender. Drain and reserve the liquid.

Fry the salt pork or bacon until crisp. Remove and cut into cubes. Sauté 3 cloves garlic and the chopped onion in the bacon fat until translucent.

In a 2-quart baking dish arrange layers of beans, salt pork, onion and garlic mixture, sausage, herbs, and red peppers or Tabasco. Add reserved liquid from the beans to come two-thirds the way up. Cover. Bake at 350°

for 1 to 1½ hours. If the liquid evaporates, add more. Remove cover and for the last 15 minutes of cooking sprinkle with bread crumbs. Serve at once, or it may be reheated and served the following day.

¶**Cassoulet with Limas and Cooked Lamb.** Instead of salt pork add 1½ cups diced cooked lamb and use ⅔ cup sliced kielbasa sausage.

¶**Cassoulet with Limas and Roasted Duck Legs.** Use roast duck legs and thighs and sliced garlic sausage.

¶**Cassoulet with Limas and Cooked Pork and Lamb.** Use 1 cup each cooked diced pork and lamb. A few slices of sausage may be added as well.

Cassoulet with Codfish

Makes 4 to 6 servings

1 pound dry lima beans
4 ounces salt pork with the skin,
    in 1 piece
½ cup finely chopped onion
3 cloves garlic, finely chopped
2 tablespoons tomato paste
1 cup peeled, seeded, chopped,
    squeezed-dry tomatoes
4 cups chicken or veal stock
1 ham hock
1 bay leaf
1 whole clove

1 dried red pepper
¼ teaspoon nutmeg
1 tablespoon honey
¾ pound salt cod, soaked in cold water
    overnight, skinned and boned
8 Finn Crisp crackers
4 sprigs marjoram or ½ teaspoon dry
    marjoram
4 sprigs thyme or ½ teaspoon dry
    thyme
3 tablespoons unsalted butter

Soak the beans overnight in cold water to generously cover; drain.

Score the salt pork on the fat side but leave in one piece. Place in a large saucepan, skin side up, over low heat. When about half the fat has rendered, add the onion and garlic. Sauté until transparent. Add the tomato paste and stir until well blended. Stir in the drained beans, chopped tomato, and stock, and add the ham hock. Add the bay leaf, clove, dried pepper, nutmeg, and honey.

Bring the liquid to a boil, lower the heat, and cover tightly. Cook very slowly until the beans are soft, about 1½ hours. Discard the salt pork and red pepper.

Poach the codfish in water for about 5 minutes, or until flaky. Drain. Pull the fish apart with your fingers or 2 forks. Stir the fish into the beans. Mix well and pour into a 12-inch baking dish.

Break up the crackers with your fingers or rolling pin so you have coarse pieces. Mix with the marjoram and thyme. Spread over the bean mixture and dot with butter. Bake in a preheated 350° oven for 45 minutes or until the top is crusty.

Kidney Beans with Sausages

Makes 6 servings

1 pound (2 cups) dry kidney beans
2 kielbasa (Polish garlic sausage)
2 cups red wine
1 cup finely chopped onion

Salt, freshly ground black pepper
6 strips of bacon
Chopped parsley

Cover the beans with water, bring to a boil, and cook 2 minutes. Remove from the heat and let stand, covered, 1 hour. Then simmer them until tender, about 45 minutes to 1 hour. Drain.

While the beans are cooking, combine the sausages, wine, and onion in a skillet and poach the sausages in this mixture for 25 to 30 minutes, seasoning to taste with salt and pepper (do not season heavily, as the wine will be reduced and this intensifies the seasoning). Remove the sausages and cut into 1½-inch slices. Reduce the wine and onion mixture by two-thirds over high heat.

Arrange layers of beans and sausages in a baking dish, ending with beans. Pour the reduced wine over them. Cover the top with bacon and bake in a 350° oven until the bacon is crisp and the bean mixture bubbly, about 20 minutes. Remove from the oven and serve sprinkled with chopped parsley.

Black Beans with Sour Cream

Makes 12 to 16 servings

2 pounds dry black beans
1 onion, sliced
1 bay leaf
Sprig of thyme
2 ribs celery
3 or 4 sprigs parsley
1 ham bone, ¼ cup diced salt pork,
*   ¼ cup olive oil, or ¼ cup*
*   bacon fat*

Salt
Dash of Tabasco
½ cup Jamaica rum
Sour cream

Put the beans in a pan with water to cover by 1 inch, bring to a boil, boil 2 minutes, remove from heat, and let stand, covered, 1 hour. Add the onion, bay leaf, thyme, celery, parsley. Add ham bone, if you have one. Otherwise use salt pork, olive oil, or bacon fat. Cook until the beans are tender, about 1½ hours; add salt to taste and a dash of Tabasco. Fish out and discard bay leaf, vegetables, and ham bone. Put the beans and their liquid in a casserole, add the rum, correct seasoning, and bake at 350° until well heated, about 20 minutes. Serve with cold sour cream. This dish goes extremely well with charcoal-grilled ham steak or with grilled sausages.

¶**Black Beans with Cheese and Bacon.** Sprinkle the finished dish with grated cheese and strips of bacon.

Nevada Chili Beans

This spicy Southwestern dish is made with the pale pink, brown-speckled pinto beans common to the Western states and Mexico (they were dubbed "pinto," Spanish for "paint," because of the coloring). Pinto beans grow in a very dry climate and so take longer to cook than some of the other dried legumes. They may be substituted in bean casseroles in place of white beans or red kidney beans.

Makes 8 servings

1 pound (2 cups) dry pinto beans	*Pinch of ground cumin*
¼ pound salt pork, cut in small pieces	*2 cups tomato purée*
2 cups chopped onion	*3 tablespoons chili powder*
3 cloves garlic, chopped fine	*Salt, freshly ground black pepper*
½ teaspoon oregano	

Put the beans in a saucepan, cover with water, bring to a boil, boil 2 minutes, remove from heat, and let stand, covered, 1 hour. Return to the heat and simmer very slowly until they are not quite cooked, still a bit bitey, approximately 1 to 1½ hours.

Cook the salt pork in a large skillet until fat is rendered and pork crisp. Add the onion and garlic and sauté until soft, then add the oregano, a healthy pinch of cumin, tomato purée, and chili powder. Season to taste with salt and pepper and bring to a boil. Add the beans with their liquid, reduce heat, and simmer for 45 minutes. Taste for seasoning, adding more chili powder or salt if you want it spicier or saltier. Serve with old-fashioned soda crackers or tortillas and beer.

¶**Cowpuncher Beans.** Add 1 pound diced cooked pork and 1 pound diced cooked beef to the finished dish.

Chickpea Purée

To me a chickpea needs to be puréed. I do not find the tough skins particularly pleasing to the bite or the palate. Puréed, they have a smooth, mealy texture that lends itself to a variety of flavorings. A chickpea purée makes a welcome change from the usual starch or grain with pork and various other meats and poultry, including the Thanksgiving turkey and especially game birds. If you don't want to go to the trouble of cooking dried chickpeas, the canned serve very well.

Makes 8 servings

*3 one-pound cans chickpeas or 6 cups
    cooked chickpeas (see page 546)
6 tablespoons butter*

*2 cloves garlic, finely chopped
Salt, freshly ground black pepper
½ cup (approximately) heavy cream*

If using canned chickpeas, drain them and rinse well under running water. Purée in a blender, food mill, or food processor. Put the purée in a heavy pan with the butter, garlic, salt and pepper to taste, and heat through, adding enough heavy cream to give a consistency like mashed potatoes. Stir constantly to make sure it does not stick.

¶**Chickpea Purée with Madeira.** Omit the garlic. Season with ¼ teaspoon mace and add ¼ cup Madeira.

Lentils

Lentils are a highly nutritious, satisfying, and economical legume with a flavor that I find more distinctive than that of many of the beans. There are several different kinds of lentils and they vary in size and color from the tiny red Egyptian lentils and the very small green ones from the Auvergne, in France, to the larger brown ones from Oregon or Washington, which are what you find packaged in supermarkets. They require no presoaking and are processed for quick cooking.

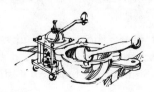

Buttered Lentils

Makes 6 servings

3 cups quick-cooking lentils
1 onion, stuck with 2 cloves
1 bay leaf
1 tablespoon salt

½ cup melted butter
¼ teaspoon mace
¼ teaspoon ground ginger

Put the lentils in a pan, cover with water, add the onion and bay leaf and simmer until just tender, about 25 to 30 minutes, adding the salt after the lentils have cooked for 15 minutes. Drain well. Remove bay leaf and onion. Toss the lentils with the butter and spices and correct seasoning. Serve with roast pork, chicken, duck, or game.

¶Sautéed Lentils. Sauté quickly in ⅓ cup olive oil and 4 tablespoons bacon fat with 1 cup finely cut green onions, 1 cup crisp bacon bits, and ½ cup chopped parsley, tossing everything well together.

¶Herbed Lentils. Add 2 finely chopped garlic cloves, 4 tablespoons fruity olive oil, ¼ cup chopped parsley, ½ teaspoon thyme and fresh chervil to taste.

¶Puréed Lentils. Remove the cloves from the onion and discard. Purée the lentils with the onions and stir in the butter, ½ cup heavy cream, and spices and correct seasoning. Reheat. If you wish a fine purée you may put the purée through a fine sieve.

Braised Lentils with Lamb

Makes 6 servings

1 pound lentils
1 onion stuck with 2 cloves
1 bay leaf
Salt
1 shoulder of lamb about 4 to 4½
    pounds, boned and tied after most
    of the fat is removed (lamb shanks
    may be used)

2 garlic cloves
Freshly ground black pepper
3 medium onions, peeled and thinly
    sliced
1 teaspoon rosemary
1 cup dry red wine
¼ cup chopped parsley

Soak the lentils overnight, unless they are the quick-cooking variety, in which case follow the directions on the package. Add the onion, bay leaf, and salt, and bring to a boil. Simmer till tender but still on the firm side—they will be recooked later. Pique the lamb shoulder with slivers of garlic, and rub it well with pepper. Place the lamb on a broiling pan and brown on all sides under the broiler until it has a nice golden color. Remove from the broiler and put the meat and the fat from the broiling pan into a braising pan, add the onions and rosemary and let them cook with the meat for 4 or 5 minutes over rather brisk heat. Reduce the heat, cover the pan, and cook about 4 minutes. Add the wine, cover, and simmer 1 hour. Add the lentils and a little of their liquid or add additional red wine. Continue slow cooking until the lamb is tender—½ to 1 hour. Salt to taste. The meat should not be brown and stringy but should still have a faint touch of pink in it.

Transfer the lamb to a hot platter. Drain the lentils, reserving the pan juices. Arrange the lentils around the lamb and sprinkle generously with chopped parsley. Serve the pan juices apart. A brisk salad and a bottle of Cabernet Sauvignon would go well with this dish.

Poultry

I could eat poultry every day of the year without repeating a single dish, and without getting the least bit bored. Chicken alone I could happily eat four or five times a week, partly because it's so much fun to cook, and there are so many ways to cook it apart from the standard methods of roasting, poaching, and frying. If you get a really fine bird, you may find, as I do, that the true, full, old-fashioned chicken flavor needs no additives. Nothing can beat the plump, fine-grained chicken breasts served by a good new restaurant in my neighborhood, La Gauloise, just simply grilled, with those appetizing crossbars lightly charred on the crackling golden skin. But you can also liven chicken up with puckery tastes or the nutty flavors of ham or bacon, sweeten it with onions, or deepen it with garlic. Marinated in yogurt, or in oil and spices, Moroccan style, or with a soy-centered teriyaki, the flesh readily absorbs flavor. Basic dishes like Southern-fried chicken can be varied with herbs and spices. And as for sautés!

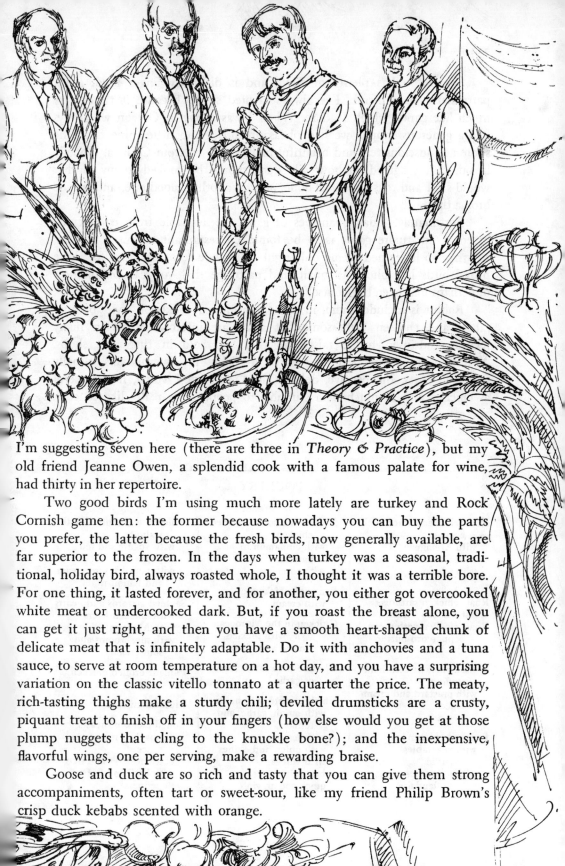

I'm suggesting seven here (there are three in *Theory & Practice*), but my old friend Jeanne Owen, a splendid cook with a famous palate for wine, had thirty in her repertoire.

Two good birds I'm using much more lately are turkey and Rock Cornish game hen: the former because nowadays you can buy the parts you prefer, the latter because the fresh birds, now generally available, are far superior to the frozen. In the days when turkey was a seasonal, traditional, holiday bird, always roasted whole, I thought it was a terrible bore. For one thing, it lasted forever, and for another, you either got overcooked white meat or undercooked dark. But, if you roast the breast alone, you can get it just right, and then you have a smooth heart-shaped chunk of delicate meat that is infinitely adaptable. Do it with anchovies and a tuna sauce, to serve at room temperature on a hot day, and you have a surprising variation on the classic vitello tonnato at a quarter the price. The meaty, rich-tasting thighs make a sturdy chili; deviled drumsticks are a crusty, piquant treat to finish off in your fingers (how else would you get at those plump nuggets that cling to the knuckle bone?); and the inexpensive, flavorful wings, one per serving, make a rewarding braise.

Goose and duck are so rich and tasty that you can give them strong accompaniments, often tart or sweet-sour, like my friend Philip Brown's crisp duck kebabs scented with orange.

Squab too has plenty of flavor and is distinctly finger food, a joy particularly on a picnic. I've always favored squab because it tastes very much like game, which I adore. When I was a boy in Oregon we always had a generous supply; we had pheasant and plump little snipe from the shore and luscious teal and beautiful mallards down from Canada. Nobody in our family agreed on how wild duck should be cooked so my mother would stuff and roast one well-done, and do another blood-rare, and maybe broil a third.

Fortunately, today quantities of game are available from commercial breeders, and more game is to be found on restaurant menus across the country. So it seemed to me only right to include several recipes for those prized birds like pheasant, quail, and partridge that you can obtain now or perhaps may even bag yourself.

Rabbit is included here, in the old-fashioned cookbook style, because rabbit and chicken taste somewhat alike, are interchangeable in many recipes, and used to be raised together and sold in the same shops. Nowadays, rabbit is becoming easily available in supermarkets, usually frozen in parts. Inexpensive, delicate, lean, and fine-flavored, it's as useful as chicken and as much of a stimulus to people who really like to cook and eat.

POULTRY

Roast chicken flamed with
cognac
 with Armagnac
 with Calvados
 with whisky

Roast chicken sarthoise
Roast chicken Picasso
Roast chicken with green
peppercorn butter

Braised chicken with ham
stuffing
 with mustard and cream
 sauce

Poached chicken
 with vegetables
 with garlic
 with onion-rice sauce
 with hollandaise

My favorite southern-fried
chicken
 with cinnamon or
 paprika
 with rosemary

Pan-fried chicken
 with cream

Chicken in the Moroccan
style, with pickled
lemons and olives

Chicken with forty cloves
of garlic

Chicken sauté with herbs
 with onion, garlic, and
 tomato
 with lemon
 with onion and chilies
 with vinegar
 basquaise
 quick coq au vin

Chicken legs sautéed with
walnuts
 with yogurt and red
 peppers
 with paprika, sour cream,
 and lemon rind

Sautéed gizzards and hearts
 with chicken livers
 with Madeira
 with mushrooms and
 sour cream

Piquant broiled chicken
halves

Mustard chicken

Boned chicken breasts
poached in tomato
sauce
chicken strips and rice
 with basil and hot
 peppers

Chicken in yogurt

Roast turkey breast
hot: 4 variations
cold: 3 variations

Turkey breast pappagallo

Turkey saltimbocca

Turkey divan
with endive
with asparagus
with spinach

Hot turkey salad

Turkey tonnato

Turkey casserole

Turkey chili

Deviled turkey drumsticks

Braised turkey wings
provençal
piquant

Roast cornish hens with
tarragon
with rice stuffing
with herb stuffing
with garlic stuffing

Broiled rock cornish hens
with tarragon butter
with rosemary butter
with garlic-parsley butter

Poached rock cornish hens

Sautéed squab with bacon
squab à la crème
spatchcocked squab

Roast duck with cherries
with green olives

Duck in white wine

Duck kebabs
flamed duck kebabs

Roast goose with apple and
apricot stuffing
with sauerkraut

Rare roast wild duck
with juniper berries
with olives

A favorite Oregon wild
duck

Spitted wild duck
flamed

Roast stuffed wild duck
southern-french-style
wild ducks

Broiled wild duck
with soy sauce
flambé
teriyaki

Salmi of wild duck

Roast wild goose

Wild goose gumbo

Roast partridge
with orange sauce

Braised partridge with
cabbage and sausage

Roast quail
stuffed with oysters
with tarragon
with duxelles
in vine leaves
on scrapple
with mustard

Sautéed quail
with juniper berries
with shallots and
mushrooms

Braised quail with white
wine

Roast pheasant pompadour

Fricassee of pheasant

Braised pheasant with
sauerkraut

Sautéed pheasant
with white wine and
tarragon

Sautéed pheasant with
calvados and apples

Broiled pheasant
with tarragon butter

Rabbit provençal

Mustard rabbit with
turnips

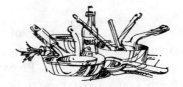

Roast Chicken Flamed with Cognac

Simply roasting a chicken is described in *Theory & Practice* as a most satisfactory way of preparing a bird. These pleasant variations show how one may vary the basic flavor by changes and additives.

Makes 4 servings

4- to 5-pound roasting chicken
½ lemon
¼ pound softened butter
1½ teaspoons salt
1 teaspoon freshly ground black pepper

⅓ cup cognac
½ cup chicken broth or dry white wine
1½ cups heavy cream
4 egg yolks
GARNISH: *Chopped parsley*

Preheat the oven to 425°. Rub the inside of the chicken with the cut lemon and then with some of the butter. Truss the chicken securely and arrange on its side on a rack in a shallow roasting pan. Rub the uppermost side with butter. Roast the chicken for 20 minutes, then turn it to the other side and brush that side with butter. Roast another 20 minutes, then turn the chicken on its back and baste well with the pan juices. Sprinkle with the salt and pepper and continue roasting another 20 minutes or until done. This may take an extra 15 minutes. Test after 1 hour of cooking by puncturing the skin at the thigh joint; there should still be a tinge of pink in the juices. After 1 hour insert a meat thermometer into the thickest part of the thigh (not touching the bone). If done, the temperature should register 160°.

When the chicken is done, remove to a hot platter. Pour the juices from the roasting pan into a saucepan, return the chicken to the roasting pan, and flame it with the cognac, warmed so it will ignite. The flavor of the cognac will be noticeable in the chicken and prominent in the sauce. Return the chicken to the platter, sprinkle with chopped parsley, and keep warm in the turned-off oven while you make the sauce.

Skim excess fat from the pan juices in the saucepan. Rinse the roasting pan with the chicken broth or white wine and add to the saucepan. Blend the cream and egg yolks. Heat the pan juices (do not boil) and stir a couple of tablespoons into the egg mixture, then stir this into the saucepan and stir over medium heat until the sauce thickens—do not let it boil or it will curdle. Adjust the seasoning and pour into a sauce boat to serve with the chicken.

¶**Chicken Flamed with Armagnac.** Add a sprig of rosemary to the cavity of the chicken and rub the skin with a mixture of rosemary and butter. After roasting, flame with ⅓ cup Armagnac. Prepare the sauce as before and serve the chicken with sautéed potatoes and a salad. The Armagnac and rosemary make a most interesting flavor combination.

¶**Chicken Flamed with Calvados.** Baste the chicken as it roasts with a mixture of ⅓ cup melted butter and ⅔ cup white wine. After roasting, flame with ⅓ cup Calvados. Prepare the sauce as before, flavoring it with 2 tablespoons Calvados. Serve the chicken with thinly sliced apple rings sautéed in butter, sprinkled with sugar, and glazed under the broiler. If Calvados is not available, you may use applejack or apple brandy.

¶Chicken Flamed with Whisky. Rub the chicken inside and out with softened butter and dried tarragon. Put 1 or 2 sprigs fresh tarragon or 1 teaspoon dried tarragon inside the bird. Baste chicken as it roasts with ⅓ cup melted butter and ½ cup chicken broth. After roasting, flame with ⅓ cup Scotch whisky. Make a sauce by combining pan juices, skimmed of excess fat, with 1 cup brown sauce (you may use the Quick Brown Sauce on page 533) and additional tarragon to taste. Reduce slightly over high heat and serve with the chicken and boiled new potatoes.

Roast Chicken Sarthoise

Roast chicken as directed opposite. Do not flame. Meanwhile, prepare Belgian endive. Trim 6 heads and cut in half lengthwise. Put in a buttered casserole, add the juice of 2 lemons and heat to the boiling point. Cover with buttered wax paper and bake in a 350° oven for 15 to 20 minutes, or until tender. Season with salt and pepper. Cut roast chicken in quarters with poultry shears. Remove breast bone. Arrange pieces on a flat oven-proof dish and top each piece with a thin slice of boiled or baked ham. Arrange endive on top. Pour juices from roasting pan over chicken, sprinkle with ¼ cup grated Gruyère cheese and heat in a 475° oven or under the broiler until the cheese melts.

Roast Chicken Picasso

Roast chicken as directed opposite. Do not flame. Meanwhile, prepare the sauce. Heat 2 tablespoons olive oil and 1 tablespoon butter in a pan. Add 1 seeded and diced green bell pepper; 1 seeded and diced red bell pepper; ⅓ cup pitted green olives, coarsely chopped; ⅓ cup pitted black olives, coarsely chopped; ¼ cup diced baked ham; 4 ripe tomatoes, peeled, seeded, and quartered; salt and pepper to taste; and a pinch of saffron. Cover and simmer gently until tomatoes are soft. Remove cover, increase heat, and simmer until most of liquid has been reduced. Cut chicken in quarters and serve topped with sauce.

Roast Chicken with Green Peppercorn Butter

Crush 1 tablespoon drained canned green peppercorns with 3 slivers garlic and ¾ teaspoon ground cinnamon in a mortar with a pestle. Work in ½ cup soft unsalted butter until well blended, and season with ½ teaspoon salt. Lift the skin of the uncooked chicken and with your hand rub the spiced butter over the flesh, making a few gashes in the drumsticks with the point of a small, sharp knife so the spices will penetrate. Put remaining spiced butter inside the bird. Leave 1 hour before roasting to allow flavors to permeate chicken. Roast chicken as directed on page 316, basting with pan juices. Serve with saffron rice. This is particularly delicious served cold.

Braised Chicken with Ham Stuffing

A pleasant change from roast chicken; the braising process makes the bird extremely succulent and flavorful. Serve with rice or crisp French bread and a green salad.

Makes 6 servings

2 cups baked ham, cut into thin julienne strips, with fat
3 or 4 cloves garlic, chopped
2 medium-size onions, thinly sliced
4- to 5-pound roasting chicken
3 stalks celery, cut into julienne strips

2 leeks, well washed and cut into julienne strips
Several sprigs parsley
2 tablespoons butter
Salt, freshly ground black pepper
¾ cup dry sherry

Combine the ham, garlic, and onion and stuff the bird with this mixture. Close the vent with a piece of foil and truss the bird. In the bottom of a braising pot make a bed of the celery, leeks, and parsley. Place the bird on top and rub it well with butter, salt, and pepper. Pour sherry over and cover pot with aluminum foil, then the lid. Cook the chicken in a 375° oven for 1¾ hours, removing the foil and lid for the last ½ hour.

Remove the chicken to a hot platter and surround it with the vegetables. Reduce the pan juices one half by rapid boiling and serve separately.

¶**Ham-Stuffed Chicken with Mustard and Cream Sauce.** After removing chicken and vegetables, skim fat from the pan juices and cook down to half. Stir in 1 tablespoon Dijon mustard. Add some of the hot juices to ½ cup heavy cream blended with 2 egg yolks, then stir into remainder of sauce and cook gently, stirring, until thickened. Do not boil. Adjust seasoning and serve with chicken.

Poached Chicken

To poach a chicken sounds deceptively simple—and that may be the reason so many birds are cooked too long or at too high heat until the flesh is dry, grainy, stringy, and flavorless. For moist, succulent poached chicken the liquid should be kept at the gentlest simmer and the bird removed when the breast is firm to the touch and the legs barely wiggle when moved. On no account should it be cooked until the skin shrinks and breaks and the flesh starts to fall from the bone. Good accompaniments are boiled or mashed potatoes, steamed rice, or buttered noodles. If you want a creamy sauce, whisk 3 egg yolks with 1 cup heavy cream and add to 1 cup béchamel (see page 531). Season to taste with chopped tarragon. Reheat, but do not allow to boil. For a green vegetable, you might have tiny buttered green peas or green peas and little pearl onions. If you want to use the chicken for cold dishes, such as chicken salad, it will yield about 4 to 4½ cups meat.

Makes 4 servings

4- to 5-pound roasting chicken
1 onion, stuck with 1 clove
1 bay leaf
1 to 2 sprigs parsley
2 to 3 garlic cloves

1 thin sliver lemon rind (without the
    white pith)
½ teaspoon freshly ground black pepper
Water or chicken stock
1 tablespoon salt

Put the chicken in a deep pot with the onion, bay leaf, parsley, garlic, lemon rind, and pepper. Add water or chicken stock barely to cover. Bring to a boil, skim off the scum, reduce the heat, add the salt, cover, and cook at the gentlest simmer (the water should not bubble, but merely move) for 50 minutes to 1¼ hours, or until breast is firm but still moist and the legs can be wiggled. Transfer chicken to a hot platter and strain the broth. Carve chicken into serving pieces.

¶Poached Chicken with Vegetables. Add thinly sliced carrots and tiny white onions to the pot for the last 30 minutes' cooking time. Serve with the chicken, some of the broth, and boiled potatoes.

¶Poached Chicken with Garlic. Simmer 15 to 20 unpeeled large garlic cloves with the chicken. Serve these with the chicken, to be squeezed from the husks and spread on thin slices of French bread.

¶**Poached Chicken with Onion-Rice Sauce.** Cook 2 large onions, each stuck with 1 clove, with the chicken. Remove cloves from cooked onions. Cook ½ cup rice in 1 cup strained chicken stock until very soft. Purée onions, rub rice through a fine sieve, and combine the two with enough hot heavy cream to make a smooth sauce for the chicken. If desired, you may add 1 cup grated Parmesan or ½ cup shredded Gruyère cheese to the sauce before serving. Garnish with parsley.

¶**Poached Chicken with Hollandaise.** Before poaching chicken, put 2 slices lemon and a few rosemary leaves in the cavity. Serve with hollandaise sauce (see page 532) and rice cooked in some of the strained, defatted chicken broth.

Chicken Parts

Nowadays, most of the chicken sold in supermarkets is cut into parts and packaged—whole or halved breasts, legs, thighs, drumsticks, and wings, backs and necks (perfect for the stock pot), gizzards, hearts, and livers. This is a great boon to people like me who love dark meat and find little occasion for using white meat.

Often you'll find low-cost specials on family-size packages of combinations of the different parts—perhaps three breasts, three legs and thighs, and some wings. Take advantage of these, for there are many ways to prepare parts and you can often get two or three meals from one package. The meaty little thighs are excellent sautéed, the breasts may be sautéed, baked, broiled, or poached, the drumsticks broiled, and the wings sautéed or deep-fried.

However, I prefer to buy a whole chicken for a sauté or fried chicken and cut it into pieces myself. Supermarkets hack poultry, instead of disjointing it carefully, and you are apt to find nasty little splinters of bone. This way, too, you can save and freeze the giblets and backs for the stock pot, or the gizzards and hearts for a quick sauté.

My Favorite Southern-Fried Chicken

This is perhaps the most famous version of fried chicken, and it can be extraordinarily good, especially when fried in lard as it should be. Good, well-rendered lard is as delicate as butter, and it does wonderful things not only for fried chicken but also for pastry (see page 509).

In this recipe you are frying, not pan-frying or sautéing, so you need enough fat in the pan to cover rather more than half of each chicken piece, and they need constant attention if they are to be uniformly brown, crisp, and tender. As the dark meat takes longer to cook than the white, if I'm cooking more than one chicken, I fry the white meat in one pan, the dark in another. If you do cook them together, after browning the pieces put the white meat on top of the dark for the final cooking so it stays warm without overcooking in the fat. I'm a dark meat man, myself, so often I fry only legs and thighs. I also adore picking the neck and back of a chicken and getting the oyster and all those tasty bits, so I often fry those, too.

Everyone has a different idea of how long fried chicken should be cooked. I like it moist and juicy all through with perhaps a bit of pink remaining in the dark meat, so I cook it for the minimum time, 20 minutes for dark meat, 15 minutes for white.

Makes 8 servings

1 to 1½ cups flour
1½ teaspoons salt
¾ teaspoon freshly ground black pepper
Two 2½- to 3-pound frying chickens,
    cut into 4 drumsticks, 4 thighs,
    4 halves of breast (sever wings
    from breasts if you wish), 2 backs
    and 2 necks

Lard for frying (or substitute peanut or
    corn oil if you prefer)
GARNISH: Watercress

Mix the flour and seasonings in a plastic bag, add the chicken pieces, and shake well, then remove and rub in the flour so the chicken is well coated. Let the pieces stand on a board for 30 minutes before frying.

In 2 large heavy skillets melt enough lard to come 1½ inches up in the pan (or use the same amount of oil). When hot, fit in the chicken pieces without crowding, otherwise you won't get an even color. Start the pan of white meat 5 minutes after the dark. Add necks and backs to pan of white meat after 5 minutes. Cook at a rather high heat, being careful the flour doesn't burn, until brown on one side. Lift frequently with tongs to check browning. Turn and brown other side, then reduce the heat to cook the chicken more slowly, and keep turning. You don't want the chicken to stew in the fat but cook to a delicious crispness. Total cooking time, according to how you like your meat done, is 20 to 25 minutes for dark meat, 15 to 20 minutes for white meat, and 10 to 15 minutes for necks and backs. Gauge your timing carefully.

Remove cooked chicken to paper towels to drain briefly, then arrange on a hot platter with watercress. If you want to eat the chicken cold, cover with paper towels to absorb surplus fat, and don't refrigerate, if possible, as fried chicken tastes better tepid or close to room temperature.

¶**Southern-Fried Chicken with Cinnamon or Paprika.** Add ¼ teaspoon cinnamon or paprika to the seasoned flour.

¶**Southern-Fried Chicken with Rosemary.** Add ¼ teaspoon crushed rosemary to the seasoned flour.

Pan-Fried Chicken

Dredge chicken pieces with flour. For this method, melt lard to a depth of ½ or ¾ inch in skillets and brown the chicken quickly on all sides. Reduce heat, cover pans, and cook 20 to 25 minutes for dark meat, 15 to 20 minutes for white.

¶**Pan-Fried Chicken with Cream.** After cooking chicken, pour off all but 1 tablespoon fat from each skillet and flame each pan of chicken with 4 tablespoons brandy. Remove chicken to a hot platter. Combine pan juices in one skillet. Blend 2 cups heavy cream with 4 egg yolks, stir into pan juices, and cook over low heat, stirring, until just thickened. Do not let it come near the boiling point or the eggs will curdle. Taste for seasoning. Serve over the chicken.

Chicken in the Moroccan Style, with Pickled Lemons and Olives

Makes 8 servings

2 three-pound chickens, cut in serving pieces	1 cup vegetable oil
2 tablespoons coarse salt	2 teaspoons ginger
7 garlic cloves	1 teaspoon turmeric
	1 teaspoon black pepper

Pinch of saffron
3 large onions, grated
4 tablespoons butter
2 cups chicken broth

1 cup soft ripe olives, preferably the
    Greek Kalamata
8 slices pickled lemon (see below)

Rub the chicken pieces well with a mixture of the salt and 4 of the garlic cloves, finely chopped. Let stand 1 hour for flavors to penetrate, then wipe off the garlic salt. Mix the oil, ginger, turmeric, pepper, and saffron, and rub the chicken pieces with this mixture. Put them in a large bowl with any remaining oil mixture and marinate, covered and refrigerated, for 8 hours or overnight.

To cook, put the chicken pieces in a large pot with the onion, remaining garlic, coarsely chopped, butter, chicken broth, and 2 cups water. Simmer until tender, about 40 to 45 minutes. Remove chicken and rapidly boil the liquid down to a thick, rich sauce, stirring frequently. Add the olives and pickled lemon slices, replace chicken, and reheat in the sauce. Serve with couscous (see page 298) or rice pilaf (see page 290), and a bowl of extra pickled lemons.

PICKLED LEMONS: These keep for months in the refrigerator and are worth making in quantity.

6 lemons
Coarse salt

Vegetable oil

Slice the lemons about ¼ inch thick, peel and all, put in a colander, sprinkle heavily with salt. Cover with plastic wrap and drain over a bowl for 24 hours, until limp, with most of the juice drawn out. Wash off salt. Pack the lemon slices into a 1-quart jar, sprinkling them with about 2 tablespoons more salt. Fill the jar with vegetable oil. Cover jar with lid and let the lemons stand from 1 to 3 weeks, by which time they will be soft, mellow, and not at all bitter.

Chicken with Forty Cloves of Garlic

A Provençal recipe I taught for years in my classes—and which never failed to astonish the students. They couldn't believe we would use forty garlic cloves, but the slow braising softens the garlic to a lovely buttery consistency and delicate flavor, like the garlic purée on page 534.

Makes 8 servings

⅔ cup oil
8 chicken drumsticks and thighs (or
    use 16 drumsticks or 16 thighs)
4 ribs celery, cut in long strips
2 medium-size onions, chopped
6 sprigs parsley
1 tablespoon chopped fresh tarragon
    (or 1 teaspoon dried)

½ cup dry vermouth
2½ teaspoons salt
¼ teaspoon freshly ground black pepper
Grated nutmeg
40 cloves garlic, unpeeled

Put the oil in a shallow dish, add the chicken pieces, and turn them to coat all sides evenly with the oil. Cover the bottom of a heavy 6-quart casserole with a mixture of the celery and onion, add the parsley and tarragon, and lay the chicken pieces on top. Pour the vermouth over them, sprinkle with the salt, pepper, and a dash or two of nutmeg, and tuck the garlic cloves around and between the chicken pieces. Cover the top of the casserole tightly with aluminum foil and then the lid (this creates an airtight seal so the steam does not escape). Bake in a 375° oven for 1½ hours, without removing the cover.

Serve the chicken, pan juices, and whole garlic cloves with thin slices of heated French bread or hot toast. The garlic should be squeezed from the root end of its papery husk onto the bread or toast, spread like butter, and eaten with the chicken.

Chicken Sauté with Herbs

Makes 4 servings

6 tablespoons unsalted butter
2 frying chickens, 2 to 2½ pounds
    each, quartered
Salt, freshly ground black pepper

½ cup dry white wine
3 tablespoons finely chopped parsley,
    chives, and dill, mixed
A few drops of lemon juice

Melt the butter in a large, heavy skillet or sauté pan with a tight-fitting cover. Add chicken pieces and brown on all sides. Lower heat, season to taste with salt and pepper, cover, and cook very gently for 5 to 8 minutes. Add ¼ cup wine and cook 10 minutes more. Then move pieces of white meat to the top, leaving the dark meat, which takes longer to cook, on the bottom. Sprinkle chicken with the chopped herbs, cover, and cook until just tender but still juicy, about 5 to 10 minutes. Check after 5 minutes.

Remove chicken to a hot platter. Add remaining wine and the lemon juice to pan and turn up the heat. Boil, scraping up the brown glaze from the bottom of the pan. When juices have reduced by half, pour them over the chicken and serve.

You can use other mixtures of herbs, such as tarragon and parsley; tarragon, parsley, and chives; parsley and rosemary; parsley and chervil.

¶**Chicken Sauté with Onion, Garlic, and Tomato.** After browning and seasoning the chicken, add 3 tablespoons finely chopped onion and 1 finely chopped garlic clove. Cook as before. When moving white meat to the top, add to the pan 3 medium tomatoes, peeled, seeded, and coarsely chopped. Cover and cook until done. Remove chicken, add 1 tablespoon chopped parsley and let the sauce cook down for 2 minutes before pouring it over the chicken.

¶**Chicken Sauté with Lemon.** Omit the wine. Just before removing the cooked chicken, pour over it the juice of 2 lemons and the grated rind of 1 lemon. Remove chicken. Add 1 tablespoon chopped parsley to the pan juices and lemon and cook down for 1 minute. Pour over the chicken.

¶**Chicken Sauté with Onion and Chilies.** After browning and seasoning the chicken, add to the pan 2 tablespoons chopped onion, 1 finely chopped garlic clove, and 3 canned green chilies, cut in strips. Add ⅔ cup dry white wine and cook until tender. Serve with polenta.

¶**Chicken Sauté with Vinegar.** After browning and seasoning chicken, add ⅓ cup water and simmer 15 minutes. Add 2 finely chopped green onions, or scallions, and 1 tablespoon chopped parsley when moving chicken pieces, cover, and cook until tender. Remove chicken and add ¼ cup wine vinegar to the pan. Boil, scraping up brown glaze, until vinegar has cooked down to a bubbly consistency, then add ¼ cup water and mix until smooth. Add ¼ cup chopped parsley and pour pan juices over the chicken.

¶**Chicken Sauté Basquaise.** Sauté the chicken, omitting the herbs. While it is cooking, make the sauce. Heat 3 tablespoons olive oil in a pan. Add 1 finely chopped onion; 2 green bell peppers, peeled, seeded, and cut in large squares; 1 small hot pepper, seeded and finely chopped (or 2 chopped canned green chilies). Cook until soft. Add 1½ cups drained Italian plum tomatoes, ¼ cup cognac, ½ cup dry white wine, and a pinch of saffron. Simmer, uncovered, until sauce is reduced and thick. Add 4 ounces diced Virginia ham. Season to taste. Pour sauce over chicken and sprinkle with chopped parsley. Serve with saffron-flavored rice.

¶**Quick Coq au Vin.** Prepare the chicken sauté, omitting herbs and using ¼ cup red wine to simmer the chicken. While it is cooking, prepare the sauce bourguignon, onions, mushrooms, and salt pork as for Instant Beef Bourguignon (see page 370). Add these to the cooked chicken and heat through, then sprinkle with chopped parsley and serve with boiled new potatoes.

Chicken Legs Sautéed with Walnuts

Makes 6 servings

6 chicken legs (drumsticks and thighs),
    in one piece
3 tablespoons oil
3 tablespoons butter
Salt, freshly ground black pepper

1 small onion, finely chopped
1 cup finely chopped walnuts
1 cup strong chicken broth
4 tablespoons chopped parsley
¼ cup toasted walnut halves

Sauté the chicken legs in the oil and butter until browned on all sides. Season to taste with salt and pepper and add the onion, chopped walnuts, and broth. Simmer 20 to 25 minutes, or until tender, turning once or twice. Sprinkle with parsley and serve garnished with toasted walnuts.

¶Chicken Legs with Yogurt and Red Peppers. Omit onion and walnuts. After browning chicken, add broth and simmer until tender. Remove chicken to serving platter. Boil pan juices down until reduced by half. Remove from heat and mix in ½ cup yogurt. When smooth, reheat but do not let it boil. Add 2 roasted, peeled, and seeded red bell peppers, cut in ½-inch strips; correct seasoning and pour over chicken.

¶Chicken Legs with Paprika, Sour Cream, and Lemon Rind. Omit walnuts. After browning chicken, remove from pan, add 1½ cups chopped onion and sauté until golden. Mix in 1 tablespoon paprika, and cook, stirring, for 1 to 2 minutes. Replace chicken, add broth, and simmer until tender. Remove chicken to serving platter. Off the heat, stir 1 cup sour cream into the pan. Reheat but do not let the sauce boil. Pour sauce over chicken and sprinkle with 1 tablespoon grated lemon rind.

Sautéed Gizzards and Hearts

Makes 4 servings

1½ pounds chicken gizzards and hearts
4 tablespoons butter
3 tablespoons oil
Salt, freshly ground black pepper

2 tablespoons chopped onion
1 tablespoon cut chives
1 tablespoon chopped parsley
¼ cup dry white wine or dry sherry

Clean and trim the gizzards and hearts. Slice the gizzards thin. Melt 3 tablespoons butter and the oil in a heavy skillet, add the giblets, and sauté quickly over high heat, shaking the pan well, until browned. Season to taste with salt and pepper. Add the onion, chives, and parsley, and sauté, stirring, until onion is golden. Add wine, reduce the heat, and simmer 4 to 5 minutes. Swirl in the remaining tablespoon butter and serve with rice or buttered noodles.

¶Sautéed Gizzards, Hearts, and Livers. Add 4 chicken livers to the sauté.

¶Sautéed Gizzards and Hearts with Madeira. Use Madeira instead of dry white wine or sherry.

¶Sautéed Gizzards and Hearts with Mushrooms and Sour Cream. After cooking the gizzards and hearts, add ½ pound sautéed sliced mushrooms. Omit last tablespoon of butter. Off heat, stir 1 cup sour cream into the pan juices, reheat, but do not allow to boil.

Piquant Broiled Chicken Halves

Makes 6 servings

1 cup ground walnuts	Tabasco
6 shallots, finely chopped	Three 2½-pound broiling chickens,
4 tablespoons butter	split, with backbone and neck
1 teaspoon salt	removed
¼ cup chopped parsley	⅔ cup melted butter
1 teaspoon dry mustard	1 teaspoon paprika

Combine the nuts, shallots, 4 tablespoons butter, salt, parsley, dry mustard, and ½ teaspoon Tabasco to a smooth paste. Loosen the skin on the chicken breasts by sliding your hand between skin and flesh and stuff the paste under the skin. Combine the melted butter, paprika, and 3 dashes Tabasco.

Arrange chicken bone side up on the broiler rack and brush with the melted butter mixture. Broil 4 inches from the heat for 12 to 14 minutes, basting once or twice with the butter, then turn, brush skin side with butter, and broil for 12 to 14 minutes, basting again.

Mustard Chicken

A mustard coating on chicken or on rabbit (see page 357) gives the bland meat unusual and intriguing flavor, and helps to thicken the cream as it bakes.

Makes 4 servings

4 half chicken breasts	½ cup finely chopped mushrooms
Flour	2 tablespoons chopped parsley
4 tablespoons butter	Salt and freshly ground black pepper
2 tablespoons oil	to taste
¾ to 1 cup Dijon or herbed mustard	1 cup heavy cream
1 medium-size onion, finely chopped	1 teaspoon lemon juice

Dust the chicken breasts lightly with flour and sauté in the butter and oil until nicely browned on all sides. Remove, cool a little, then spread each piece liberally with mustard and put in a shallow baking dish.

Cook the onion in the fat remaining in the pan until golden, add the mushrooms, and cook with the onion until soft. Add the parsley and salt and pepper to taste—you won't need much seasoning because of the mustard. Blend in the cream and let it just heat through. Pour the mixture over the chicken and bake in a 350° oven for 30 to 35 minutes, or until chicken is tender when tested with a fork. Taste to see if the sauce needs more seasoning and add the lemon juice. Serve with plain rice.

Boned Chicken Breasts Poached in Tomato Sauce

Makes 4 servings

2 whole chicken breasts
4 to 5 cups homemade light tomato
    sauce, heated (page 282)

Grated Parmesan cheese

Skin and bone the breasts and cut in half. Put halves between sheets of wax paper and pound until no more than ⅜ inch thick. (For technique see *Theory & Practice*, pages 185–187.)

Lay chicken breasts flat in 2 large skillets (or cook in 2 batches, as 1 skillet will only hold 2 pounded breasts) and pour over them just enough tomato sauce to cover. Simmer very gently until just cooked through, about 3 minutes, turning once if necessary to cook the top side.

Serve with cooked rice or pasta. Pour the poaching sauce over the chicken and rice or pasta and sprinkle with grated Parmesan cheese to taste.

¶**Chicken Strips and Rice.** After cooking the breasts, cut them into thin strips and stir into hot cooked rice or risotto with some of the tomato sauce.

¶**Chicken in Tomato Sauce with Basil and Hot Peppers.** Add to the sauce 1 tablespoon dried basil and 2 dried hot red peppers, crumbled. Poach chicken, taste sauce for seasoning, and add a dash of Tabasco, if desired.

Chicken in Yogurt

Makes 6 servings

1½ to 2 cups yogurt (the larger amount
    if you use only chicken legs)
1 garlic clove, crushed
½ teaspoon ground ginger
Salt, freshly ground black pepper

1 frying chicken, cut up (or 8 chicken
    legs, cut into drumstick and thigh
    pieces)
Flour or cornmeal or crushed cornflakes

Combine the yogurt with the crushed garlic clove, ground ginger, and salt and pepper to taste in a large flat dish. Lay the chicken pieces in the yogurt and marinate for at least 2 hours, turning the pieces once during that time.

Remove the chicken; roll the pieces in either flour or cornmeal or crushed cornflakes, and arrange in a lightly oiled baking pan or the bottom of the broiler pan. Bake in a preheated 350° oven for 1 hour, until the chicken is tender and the coating crisp and delicately browned. The pan juices are delicious, but don't pour them over the chicken because you want to keep that crispness; pour them around it. Serve with a good salad and a bottle of wine. You may also serve the chicken on a bed of rice or buttered noodles if you like.

Turkey Parts

Turkey parts have certainly altered our cooking lives. Now that we can buy the drumsticks, thighs, wings, and breasts separately, there need be no more squabbles over light and dark meat—everyone can have his choice. Because there is a large proportion of meat to bone, turkey parts are a really economical buy, especially the meaty breasts. These you can roast and use both hot and cold, for turkey salad, turkey hash, turkey in lettuce leaves (see page 29), turkey sauce for pasta, or what you will. While it is also possible now to buy turkey cutlets, thin slices cut from the breast, you are really better off buying the whole breast. If it is still partially frozen, it will be easy to slice thin. Cooked quickly and sauced like veal scaloppine, turkey cutlets are hard to distinguish from the best-quality expensive veal.

To thaw frozen turkey thighs, wings, or drumsticks, allow about 1 day in the refrigerator, or 2 or more hours in cold water, wrapped. A whole turkey breast will take 36 hours or more in the refrigerator, or about 6 hours in cold water.

Roast Turkey Breast

Makes 8 to 12 or more servings

*1 whole turkey breast, about 8 to 9
   pounds*
⅓ cup melted butter

Salt, freshly ground black pepper
¼ cup dry white wine

Brush the turkey breast with 2 tablespoons melted butter and sprinkle with salt and pepper. Arrange on a rack in a roasting pan and roast in a 350° oven, allowing about 20 minutes a pound, or until the internal temperature, tested by inserting a meat thermometer into the thickest part of the breast, reaches 160° to 165°. Baste during the roasting with the remains of the melted butter mixed with the white wine. Slice and serve in any of the following ways:

HOT

1. With Béarnaise sauce (see page 532), sautéed potatoes, and broccoli with brown butter.

2. Place a slice of turkey on a slice of baked country ham. Serve with sauce Madeira (page 533) and polenta.

3. With velouté sauce heavily flavored with chopped fresh tarragon. Serve with rice, and broiled eggplant slices.

4. For Deviled Turkey, let breast cool, then slice, dip in beaten egg and then in bread crumbs. Sauté in hot butter until lightly browned. Serve with sauce diable (see page 533).

COLD

1. With potato salad and homemade mayonnaise.

2. With sliced tomatoes, baby zucchini à la Grecque or vinaigrette, and vinaigrette sauce.

3. With a rice salad and a mixture of half mayonnaise and half sour cream flavored with chopped tarragon, parsley, and chives.

Turkey Breast Pappagallo

This is one way to use turkey cutlets. (For other ideas, see recipes for veal scallops on pages 406 to 408.) Either use the ready-cut packaged cutlets or cut slices about ⅜ inch thick from a partially thawed turkey breast (it should not be hard, but still firm enough to slice easily). These cutlets are good with sautéed potatoes and chopped spinach dressed with oil and a little garlic and nutmeg.

Makes 6 servings

12 turkey cutlets, about ⅜ inch thick
½ cup flour
12 tablespoons (1½ sticks) butter
6 tablespoons oil
Salt, freshly ground black pepper

12 thin slices ham
1 cup sautéed sliced mushrooms
½ cup grated Parmesan cheese
½ cup chicken or turkey broth
Chopped parsley

Pound the cutlets lightly between sheets of wax paper until thin, as for veal scaloppine. Flour the slices lightly.

Use 2 skillets for sautéing so the pan will not be overcrowded. Melt half the butter with half the oil in each skillet. When hot, add the turkey slices and sauté quickly, turning them once and seasoning with salt and pepper as they cook. You will probably have to do this in 2 or 3 batches. Do not overcook. Put a slice of ham on each cutlet and spoon some of the mushrooms on top. Sprinkle with the Parmesan cheese, add the broth, cover, and simmer about 5 minutes, or until the cheese has melted.

Arrange turkey on a hot platter and spoon the pan juices over the top. Sprinkle with chopped parsley.

Turkey Saltimbocca

Makes 6 to 8 servings

12 to 16 small thin slices turkey breast
4 shallots, finely chopped
6 tablespoons butter
½ cup duxelles (see page 535)
Salt, freshly ground black pepper
2 tablespoons chopped fresh tarragon
    or 2 teaspoons dried tarragon
6 tablespoons grated Parmesan cheese
All-purpose flour

2 eggs, lightly beaten
Fresh bread crumbs
2 tablespoons vegetable oil
Dry white wine or chicken broth
    (see page 529)
½ cup sour cream or yogurt
1 tablespoon chopped parsley or
    fresh tarragon

Pound the turkey breast slices until they are round in shape and about 2½ inches in diameter. Sauté the shallots in 2 tablespoons butter until limp, mix in the duxelles, and season to taste with salt and freshly ground black pepper. Remove from heat. Stir in the tarragon and Parmesan cheese. Spread 1½ to 2 tablespoons of the mixture on one piece of turkey, cover with a second piece, and press edges well together. Dust with flour, dip in beaten egg and then in bread crumbs, and put on a baking sheet covered with wax paper. Refrigerate for 30 minutes to set coating. Melt the remaining 4 tablespoons butter and the vegetable oil in a heavy skillet and sauté the saltimbocca on each side until golden brown, about 2 minutes a side. Remove and keep warm. Rinse the pan with white wine or chicken stock and let it reduce and cook down. Stir in the sour cream or yogurt, off the heat, add the chopped parsley or fresh tarragon, and pour over the saltimbocca.

Turkey Divan

Cover the bottom of a large baking dish with cooked broccoli, arrange slices of roast turkey breast on top, and cover with sauce mornay (see page 531). Sprinkle with grated Parmesan cheese and put under the broiler until cheese melts and glazes.

¶Turkey Divan with Endive. Arrange the turkey on lightly braised halves of endive. Cover with sauce mornay and proceed as above.

¶Turkey Divan with Asparagus. Arrange cooked asparagus spears in a gratin dish. Top with turkey slices and sauce mornay. Sprinkle with Parmesan cheese and proceed as above.

¶Turkey Divan with Spinach. Place slices of turkey breast on a bed of chopped drained cooked spinach lightly flavored with tarragon. Top with sauce mornay and proceed as above.

Hot Turkey Salad

For a change, hot rather than cold turkey for a salad is different and delicious. The mayonnaise helps to hold the heat. Cut hot roasted turkey breast into bite-size pieces, combine with chopped celery, sliced green onions, black olives, and mayonnaise to taste. The mayonnaise should be made with lemon juice and spiced with green peppercorns, Tabasco, Szechuan pepper, or hot paprika.

Turkey Tonnato

Before roasting, loosen the skin on the turkey breast and slip 5 or 6 anchovy fillets under the skin on each side. Make incisions in the meat with a small knife and stud with a few slivers of garlic. After roasting, cool and serve the breast carved into thin slices with the following sauce: blend with 2 cups homemade mayonnaise (page 76), 1 cup finely flaked dark tuna with its oil (canned is all right and the chunk style is usually darker), 1 finely chopped garlic clove, 2 tablespoons chopped parsley, and the cooked anchovy fillets, finely chopped. Arrange turkey slices on a platter, spoon the sauce over them, and garnish with quartered hard-boiled eggs, capers, and cherry tomatoes. Serve with a rice salad.

Turkey Casserole

Makes 4 servings

2 shallots or green onions (scallions),
  chopped
2 tablespoons butter
½ cup dry vermouth
½ cup pitted ripe olives
2 cups diced cooked turkey breast
⅛ teaspoon thyme

⅛ teaspoon crushed rosemary
1 cup brown sauce (see page 533) or
  gravy
Salt, freshly ground black pepper
Lemon juice
1 package frozen peas, thawed

Sauté the shallot or green onion in the butter until limp. Remove from heat. Combine with the vermouth, olives, turkey, thyme, rosemary, brown sauce, salt and pepper to taste, a squeeze or two of lemon juice, and the peas. Pour into a casserole and bake in a 350° oven for 35 to 40 minutes.

Turkey Chili

This is not a traditional chili, but an experiment that turned out rather well. It makes an excellent dish for a buffet party. Serve with homemade tortillas and rice or polenta. A radish and cucumber salad is good with this.

Makes 8 to 10 servings

5 to 6 pounds turkey thighs
1 onion, stuck with 2 cloves
2 ribs celery
2 sprigs parsley
2 small dried hot peppers
Salt
2 tablespoons chili powder
4-ounce can peeled green chilies,
  finely chopped

1 cup ground almonds
½ cup ground peanuts
1 large onion, finely chopped
3 cloves garlic, finely chopped
4 tablespoons olive oil
1 cup small green olives
½ cup blanched almonds

Put the turkey thighs in a pot with the onion, celery, parsley, hot peppers, and water to cover. Bring to a boil, skim off the scum, reduce heat, and simmer until meat is tender, but not falling from the bones, about 45 minutes to 1 hour. Remove turkey from broth, and when cool enough to handle, remove meat from bones in good-size pieces. Strain and degrease the broth and reduce over high heat to about 4 cups. Add salt to taste. Mix in the chili powder, green chilies, and ground nuts, and simmer until the sauce is thickened, smooth, and well blended in flavor—then taste. You may find you need more chili powder or some Tabasco.

Sauté the onion and garlic in the oil until limp. Add to the sauce and cook 5 minutes. Add the turkey meat and heat thoroughly, then add the olives and almonds and heat for 3 minutes.

Deviled Turkey Drumsticks

Makes 4 servings

4 turkey drumsticks	*2 or 3 sprigs parsley*
1 large onion, stuck with 2 cloves	*1 tablespoon salt*
1 carrot	*1 cup melted butter*
1 bay leaf	*2 to 3 cups bread crumbs*
1 rib of celery	

Put the drumsticks in a pot with the onion, carrot, bay leaf, celery, parsley, salt, and water to cover. Bring to a boil, reduce heat, cover, and simmer until tender, about 45 minutes. Remove drumsticks, drain, and dry. Dip the drumsticks in the melted butter, then roll them in the crumbs, pressing the crumbs in well. Arrange on the broiling rack or in a foil broiling pan, and broil about 6 to 7 inches from the heat, turning them until the crumbs are brown and crisp on all sides, about 15 to 20 minutes. Serve with sauce diable (see page 533).

Braised Turkey Wings

Braising is excellent for turkey wings, which are not the tenderest or most toothsome parts of the bird. Be sure to remove the cover toward the end of the cooking time so they brown nicely.

Makes 4 servings

3 tablespoons butter	*6 garlic cloves, unpeeled*
1 large onion, sliced	*1 cup dry white wine*
2 carrots, cut in julienne strips	*4 turkey wings*
2 ribs celery, cut in julienne strips	*Salt, freshly ground black pepper*
2 or 3 sprigs parsley	

Heat the butter in a braising pan or flameproof casserole, add the onion, carrot, celery, and parsley, and let them wilt down in the fat. Toss in the garlic cloves, add the wine, arrange the turkey wings on top, and sprinkle

them well with salt and pepper. Cover and braise in a 350° oven for 1 to
1½ hours, or until tender, removing the cover for the last 20 minutes. Serve
with a potato purée and a cucumber and watercress salad.

¶**Turkey Wings Provençal.** Add 4 or 5 additional garlic cloves, 1 teaspoon
rosemary, and a cup or more tomato sauce—homemade, naturally! (see
page 534)—and proceed as above. Serve with polenta.

¶**Turkey Wings Piquant.** Proceed as in basic recipe, but add 4 ounces
canned green chilies, seeded and chopped, and chili powder to taste.

Rock Cornish Hens

Roast Cornish Hens with Tarragon

If you can, use the fresh Rock Cornish hens that are now appearing in our
markets. They are infinitely better than the frozen variety. Serve these little
birds with tiny green peas and little new potatoes, tossed with butter and
chopped parsley.

Makes 6 servings

6 Rock Cornish hens
½ lemon
Fresh tarragon

½ pound (2 sticks) butter
Salt, freshly ground black pepper

Rub the birds inside and out with the cut lemon. Put a couple of sprigs of
fresh tarragon in each cavity and chop enough tarragon leaves to make
¼ cup. Cream ¼ pound butter and mix in the chopped tarragon. Rub the
birds well with this mixture (if there is any left, put it in the cavities) and
sprinkle them with salt and pepper. Melt the remaining butter for basting.
Preheat the oven to 400°.

Arrange the birds on their sides on a rack in a roasting pan and roast
for 15 minutes, then turn on the other side, baste well with the pan juices
and melted butter, and roast a further 15 minutes. Then turn on their
backs and roast breast up for 10 to 15 minutes, until just tender but not
overcooked. Test for doneness by wiggling the legs and puncturing the joint
between body and thigh with a paring knife—juices should be faintly tinged
with pink.

¶**Rock Cornish Hens with Rice Stuffing.** Stuff cavities of hens with 2 cups
cooked rice mixed with 1 cup duxelles (see page 535) and a few pistachio
nuts. Truss and roast.

¶**Rock Cornish Hens with Herb Stuffing.** Stuff cavities of hens with mixture of 3 cups freshly made bread crumbs, ½ cup finely chopped shallots, 10 tablespoons melted butter, ⅓ cup each fresh chopped tarragon, chives, and parsley, and salt and pepper to taste.

¶**Rock Cornish Hens with Garlic Stuffing.** Stuff cavities of hens with a mixture of 3 cups bread crumbs, ¼ cup finely chopped garlic, ½ cup olive oil, lots of basil (you want a strong basil flavor), and salt and pepper.

Broiled Rock Cornish Hens with Tarragon Butter

Makes 6 servings

Split 6 Rock Cornish hens in two for broiling. Slip your hand between the skin and flesh and rub tarragon butter (see preceding recipe) lavishly over the thighs and breast; rub, also, a thin layer of butter on the skin of the breast. Arrange on the rack of a broiler pan, bone side up, and rub the bone with tarragon butter. Broil 4 inches from the heat for 8 to 9 minutes, then turn with tongs, brush the skin side with melted tarragon butter, and broil for another 8 to 9 minutes, basting once or twice with the melted butter. Serve with sautéed potatoes and a salad.

¶**Rock Cornish Hens Broiled with Rosemary Butter.** Combine ½ cup butter with 1 teaspoon dried rosemary, crushed in a mortar and pestle, and proceed as above.

¶**Rock Cornish Hens Broiled with Garlic-Parsley Butter.** Combine ½ cup butter with 6 or 7 finely chopped cloves garlic and ½ cup chopped parsley. Stuff this under the skin and broil as above.

Poached Rock Cornish Hens

Makes 6 servings

Poach 6 hens as for poached chicken (see page 319), but give these little birds barely 20 minutes' poaching time. They should not be overcooked. Cool, cut into serving pieces, and cover with a mixture of half mayonnaise and half yogurt. Garnish with lemon slices and black olives. Serve cold with a rice salad (see page 96).

Squab

Sautéed Squab with Bacon

This recipe can be made with young pigeons (squab), with the tiny squab chickens weighing about 1 pound, or with fresh Rock Cornish game hens. Allow 1 of the tiny birds per serving; the Rock Cornish hens might do for two.

Makes 2 servings

6 to 8 slices bacon
2 squab or other small birds, split
    lengthwise

Salt, freshly ground black pepper
1 tablespoon chopped parsley

Cook the bacon until crisp. Drain on paper towels and keep warm while cooking the squab. Heat bacon fat in pan until hot, add the squab, and sauté over medium heat for 15 to 20 minutes, turning to color all sides. Season to taste with salt and pepper. Serve, sprinkled with parsley, with the bacon.

¶**Squab à la Crème.** Sauté the squab. Pour off all but 2 tablespoons fat from the pan. Beat 2 egg yolks lightly with 1 cup heavy cream, add the hot fat, then stir into the skillet and cook over low heat, stirring, until just thickened. Do not let it get near the boiling point. Mix in 1 teaspoon paprika, salt and pepper to taste. Serve the sauce separately; shoestring potatoes and sautéed zucchini go well with the squab.

¶**Spatchcocked Squab.** "Spatchcocked" is an old English term for splitting and grilling a bird, and it was considered in the countryside the favorite method of preparation. Split each squab down the back lengthwise. Put breast side up and, with a blow of your fist, flatten it, cracking the breast bone so it lies flat. Brush well with oil, chopped garlic, and rosemary, and grill 4 inches from the heat, allowing about 8 minutes per side, or until done to your taste. Baste well with oil during the grilling time. Serve with sautéed potatoes.

Duck

Roast Duck

Recently I have learned, after discussing it with one of my favorite chefs, Seppi Renggli of the Four Seasons Restaurant in New York City, a different way of roasting duck, which turns out to be most satisfactory way of roasting duck. The ducks are placed in a 350° oven and roasted for two hours without opening the oven door. This gives a moist duck and drains off most of the fat, and if you wish to remove the skin it comes off very easily. It is an excellent way to deal with this rather fatty bird.

If you want an extremely crisp duck skin, remove it from the duck, cut it into thin strips, and deep-fry in oil at 360° for 3 to 4 minutes, then drain on absorbent paper.

Roast Duck with Cherries

The Long Island ducklings that are sold frozen (or occasionally fresh) in our markets are rather undistinguished birds, and an interesting sauce or accompaniment can improve them greatly. These ducks, which are very fat with little meat on their bones, should be roasted at a low temperature to draw out the fat without overcooking the meat, and it is advisable to prick the skin well to let the fat drain. If you like a crisp skin on your duck, raise the temperature to 500° for the last 15 minutes, but be sure to remove most of the fat from the pan first or you'll have a very messy oven.

Makes 4 servings

2 four-to-five pound ducklings, fresh
* or frozen, thawed and well dried*
½ lemon
Coarse salt

¼ cup kirsch
1½ cups brown sauce (see page 533)
1 cup tart seeded cherries (preferably
* Montmorency)*

Wipe the ducks well, remove giblets and neck, and save for stock. Remove the loose fat from the cavity and around the neck. Rub cavity and skin with the cut lemon, then with coarse salt. Truss ducks and arrange on a rack in a shallow roasting pan. Preheat the oven to 350° and roast the ducks for 1 hour (for rare), 1½ hours for medium rare, 2 hours for medium, according to how you like your duck. After the first 30 minutes' roasting time, prick the skin well with a fork and prick once or twice more during the time the duck is in the oven. Remove excess fat from pan and save for cooking—there should be only about a cup of fat in the pan at all times. For a crisper skin, 15 minutes before the duck is done raise heat to 500°. Remove cooked ducks to a hot platter and keep warm.

Skim fat from the roasting pan and rinse with the kirsch. Add this to the brown sauce in a small saucepan, bring to a boil, and cook down over high heat for 2 to 3 minutes. Add the cherries and heat to the boiling point. Taste and correct seasoning, and serve sauce with the duck and a rice pilaf (see pages 290–291). To serve cut duck into halves or quarters with poultry shears.

¶Duck with Green Olives. Put 12 to 15 crushed juniper berries in the duck cavity. After roasting, remove ducks to a heatproof platter and flame with ⅓ cup gin. Add ⅔ cup small green olives to the brown sauce and skimmed pan juices and simmer for 4 to 5 minutes. Serve with saffron rice.

Duck in White Wine

This is an unusually light and delicious duck recipe, in which the bird is first roasted and then finished in white wine. Serve surrounded with sautéed potatoes.

Makes 4 servings

2 four- to five-pound ducks
Coarse salt
½ teaspoon ground ginger
¼ teaspoon ground cloves
⅓ cup cognac
2 cups Muscadet or similar very dry
    white wine

2 or 3 small onions, each stuck with
    1 clove
2 or 3 small carrots
⅔ cup white raisins
2 tablespoons beurre manié
    (see page 536)

Rub the ducks well inside and out with salt, ginger, and cloves. Truss and roast on a rack as for Roast Duck with Cherries (see page 338) for 1 hour at 350°, but do not increase heat to crisp skin. Remove ducks from oven and place in a deep braising pan. Warm the cognac and flame the ducks. This aids in burning off excess fat. Add the wine, onions, and carrots. Place the pan in the oven for 30 to 45 minutes, basting the ducks occasionally with the liquid. Strain the sauce, discarding vegetables, and return to the pan with the ducks and raisins. Cook for a further 10 to 15 minutes, basting once. Remove ducks to a hot platter. Thicken the sauce to taste, if you wish, with beurre manié. Pour some of the sauce around the ducks and serve the rest separately.

Duck Kebabs

This unusual recipe was the invention of Philip Brown, a friend with whom I have cooked a great deal, professionally and personally. Serve these delicious kebabs with risotto (see pages 291–293), or spinach and mushrooms and buttered noodles.

Makes 6 servings

2 ducks
½ cup olive oil
½ cup orange juice
1 tablespoon grated orange zest
3 to 4 tablespoons grated onion

1 garlic clove, crushed
6 oranges
Pitted green olives (optional)
Salt, freshly ground black pepper

Remove breast and thigh meat from the ducks, leaving the skin and fat on the meat. Combine the oil, orange juice and zest, onion, and garlic in a bowl. Cut duck meat into strips about 2 inches by 1 inch and marinate in the mixture for 2 hours.

Blanch the oranges in boiling water for 3 minutes, drain, and cut in wedges of about 1 inch, leaving the peel on. Thread duck and orange wedges on skewers, adding a few green olives, if you wish. Salt and pepper the duck and broil, skin side up, about 4 inches from the broiling unit, for 10 minutes. Turn and broil 5 minutes on the meat side. The skin should be crisp and the meat pink.

¶**Flamed Duck Kebabs.** Warm ¼ cup cognac and 1 tablespoon Grand Marnier or other orange-flavored liqueur. Arrange broiled duck kebabs on a heatproof platter and flame with the cognac-liqueur mixture.

Goose

Roast Goose with Apple and Apricot Stuffing

Unfortunately, it is almost impossible to buy freshly killed geese, except in markets in certain ethnic neighborhoods around holiday time. But it is always possible to find the frozen ones. These should be thawed in their wrappings before roasting. I prefer a fruit stuffing with roast goose, and I find mashed potatoes and sauerkraut excellent accompaniments.

Makes 8 servings

8- to 10-pound goose, thawed if frozen

FRUIT STUFFING

¼ *cup butter*	*2 teaspoons salt*
½ *cup chopped celery*	½ *teaspoon freshly ground black pepper*
½ *cup chopped onion*	*2 cups peeled chopped apples*
6 cups day-old bread cubes	*1 cup chopped dried apricots*
½ *teaspoon thyme*	

To make the stuffing, melt the butter in a skillet and sauté the celery and onion until limp and golden. Combine with the bread cubes, thyme, 1 teaspoon salt and the pepper, apples and apricots and toss lightly until well mixed.

Remove giblets and neck from goose and excess fat from the cavity (this is excellent rendered to use for cooking). Stuff the goose about three-quarters full (any leftover stuffing can be baked separately), truss the bird, and sew or skewer the vent.

Rub the skin with the remaining salt and arrange goose, breast up, on a rack in a roasting pan. Roast for 1 hour in a 400° oven, then prick the skin well with a fork to release the fat, reduce the heat to 350° and continue roasting for another hour, removing excess fat from the pan as it accumulates. Then test to see how near to done it is by pressing the leg meat (it should feel soft) and pricking the thickest part of the thigh (the juices should run clear, with a faint tinge of pink). A goose of this size will take from 2 to 2½ hours. If more time is needed, reduce the heat to 325°. Remove to a hot platter and allow to rest 15 minutes before carving.

¶**Roast Goose with Sauerkraut.** Truss, but do not stuff the goose; roast it plain. Lightly sauté ½ cup sliced onion in 2 tablespoons of the goose fat. Wash 3 pounds fresh sauerkraut well under running water in a colander. Put the onion in a deep pot, add the sauerkraut, 2 whole peeled garlic cloves, 10 juniper berries tied in cheesecloth, and a 1-pound piece of bacon or blanched salt pork. Season lightly with salt and more heavily with freshly ground black pepper, and add 2 cups dry white wine and 1 cup chicken stock or water. Cover and cook slowly for 2 hours, adding 6 to 8 frankfurters during the last 20 minutes' cooking time. Arrange cooked sauerkraut on a large platter (remove bag of juniper berries); slice bacon and carve roast goose and arrange on the sauerkraut. Surround with the frankfurters and plain boiled new potatoes.

Wild Duck

There are many varieties of wild duck in this country, of which the most common are the mallard, the canvasback, and the smaller teal. One duck is often just enough for a serving, although a larger one will serve 2. With the smaller teal, you will probably need 2 per serving, and you should allow less cooking time. Game birds are a gamble. One is never quite sure of their age or previous athletic activities. Sometimes they will seem perfect and one anticipates a tender morsel, but I'm afraid 90 percent of the time they are a risk. Many people like to hang ducks for 5 to 7 days to mature and somewhat tenderize them before roasting.

Wild duck is seldom stuffed unless it is to be roasted for a long time, but I like to place some seasonings in the cavity for flavor, such as herbs, an onion, a piece of orange or orange rind, a rib of celery, a garlic clove, a few juniper berries. Opinions vary considerably as to how long wild ducks should be roasted. Some like them rare and bloody, which is my preference, others better done. This is something you must decide for yourself.

Rare Roast Wild Duck

Allow 1 duck per serving. Rub the cavities with a cut lemon. Place a piece of celery, a piece of onion, and a piece of orange in each cavity. Rub the breasts well with butter or oil and arrange the birds on a rack in a shallow roasting pan. Roast ducks in a 450° oven for 17 to 18 minutes, basting them every 5 minutes with melted butter or a mixture of butter and red wine. Remove from the oven, sprinkle with salt and freshly ground pepper, and serve cut into halves or quarters with poultry shears. A barley casserole with mushrooms (see page 295) and an orange and onion salad with a rosemary-flavored vinaigrette sauce go well with the ducks.

¶Roast Wild Duck with Juniper Berries. Put crushed juniper berries and a piece of orange rind in the cavities. Baste with melted butter only. Remove ducks from oven and flame with gin.

¶Roast Wild Duck with Olives. Roast ducks, basting with a mixture of melted butter and dry white wine. Five minutes before ducks are done, add 1 cup of the white wine and 1 cup small green olives to the roasting pan. Remove ducks from oven and flame with ½ cup cognac. Cook pan juices down for a minute or two, then mix in 1 cup brown sauce (you may use the Quick Brown Sauce, page 533), blend well, and heat through. Serve with the ducks.

A Favorite Oregon Wild Duck

This recipe gives you a well-flavored but rather well-done duck. Stuff the cavities of the ducks with onion quarters and sections of tart apples. Cover the breasts with bacon or salt pork and roast in a 400° oven for 45 minutes, basting well with melted butter and white wine.

For the sauce, sauté 1 onion and 1 apple, both chopped, with the chopped duck hearts and gizzards in 3 tablespoons butter. Add 2 cups rich stock (duck, if you have some, otherwise chicken) and simmer for about 1 hour. Add the drippings from the roasting pan and thicken the sauce with beurre manié (page 536), if desired.

Spitted Wild Duck

Charcoaling ducks on a spit is a traditional way of roasting them. Brush the ducks with oil, arrange them on a spit, and balance them. Roast over fairly hot coals for 18 to 20 minutes for rare to medium rare.

¶Flamed Spitted Wild Duck. I like to flame the ducks with cognac or Armagnac after they have roasted. This seems to give them a nice glaze and certainly adds to the flavor.

Roasted Stuffed Wild Duck

Serve fresh cornbread, a purée of fresh turnips, and an orange and onion salad with a rosemary-hinted vinaigrette.

Makes 2 servings

STUFFING

½ cup thinly cut celery	½ teaspoon freshly ground black pepper
1 medium-size onion, finely chopped	¼ cup chopped parsley
¼ cup (½ stick) butter	2 cups bread crumbs
1 teaspoon thyme	¼ cup (½ stick) melted butter
1 teaspoon salt	1 egg, slightly beaten

THE DUCKS

2 ducks	*⅓ cup red wine, Port, Marsala, or*
4 tablespoons butter	*Madeira*
Salt, freshly ground black pepper	*The duck giblets*
⅓ cup melted butter	

Sauté celery and onion in the ¼ cup butter until just beginning to soften. Combine with the thyme, salt, pepper, parsley, bread crumbs, and ¼ cup melted butter, then mix in the egg. Stuff the ducks with the mixture, tie and truss them, and place on a rack in a shallow roasting pan.

Rub the ducks with 2 tablespoons butter and sprinkle them with salt and pepper. Roast in a 350° oven, basting every 10 minutes with a mixture of the melted butter and wine, for about 45 minutes to 1 hour, depending on how well done you like your ducks.

While the ducks are roasting, sauté the giblets in 2 tablespoons butter, chop fine, and season to taste.

Remove the ducks from the oven to a hot platter. Blend the pan juices with the giblets and serve as a sauce for the ducks. To serve, split the ducks in half lengthwise with poultry shears.

¶**Southern-French-Style Wild Ducks.** Sauté 1 thinly sliced medium-size onion, ¾ cup finely cut celery, ¼ cup finely chopped parsley, 18 to 20 pitted soft black olives, and 1 minced garlic clove in ½ stick butter. Stir in 1 cup fresh bread crumbs, 1 teaspoon pepper, ¾ teaspoon salt, and ¼ cup Armagnac. Stuff 2 ducks with this mixture, truss, and rub with butter. Roast as above, basting every few minutes with a mixture of ½ cup red wine and ½ cup hot stock. Split ducks and serve with a purée of broccoli.

Broiled Wild Duck

Allow 1 duck per serving. Halve ducks with poultry shears, cutting from the vent at the tail along the side of the breastbone and then down the center of the back. Rub bone and skin sides with a cut lemon. Then rub both sides with 1 tablespoon softened butter per duck and sprinkle with salt and pepper. Melt 4 tablespoons butter for basting.

Preheat the broiler. Arrange ducks, bone side down, on the greased rack of the broiler pan. Broil 4 inches from the heat for 11 to 12 minutes, basting once or twice with butter. Turn, brush bone side with butter and broil for 6 minutes. A total broiling time of 18 minutes is sufficient for wild duck, which should never be overcooked. Serve with sautéed turnips and mushrooms.

¶**Broiled Wild Duck with Soy Sauce.** Rub ducks well with soy sauce and crushed rosemary or tarragon. Baste during broiling with a mixture of soy sauce and butter.

¶**Broiled Wild Ducks Flambé.** Rub ducks with crushed garlic and rosemary. After broiling, flame with ¼ cup warmed gin.

¶**Wild Ducks Teriyaki.** Marinate split ducks for 6 to 8 hours in a teriyaki marinade of ½ cup soy sauce, ½ cup oil, ¼ cup dry sherry, 2 finely chopped garlic cloves, 2 tablespoons grated fresh ginger root, 1 tablespoon grated tangerine or orange rind. Turn frequently. Baste with marinade during broiling.

Salmi of Wild Duck

A salmi is a traditional English way of using up leftover game and a good dish to make if you have roasted more ducks than you needed. To make stock, which is essential to this dish, be sure you've saved the carcasses and other bones from your ducks. Serve with noodles or rice, or on squares of fried polenta.

Makes 2 to 4 servings

Carcasses from several ducks	4 cups beef stock
1 small onion, stuck with 2 cloves	4 tablespoons butter
1 teaspoon thyme	5 tablespoons flour
1 teaspoon salt	2 to 3 cups cold roasted wild duck meat
½ teaspoon freshly ground black pepper	½ cup port
2 tablespoons Worcestershire sauce	1 tablespoon grated orange rind
1 tablespoon soy sauce	1 cup small green olives

Combine bones from the ducks, plus any extra you may have in the freezer, with the onion, thyme, salt, pepper, Worcestershire sauce, soy sauce, and beef stock. Bring to a boil, reduce heat, and simmer 2 hours. Strain broth and cook down to 2 cups. Taste and correct seasoning. Melt the butter in a pan, blend in the flour, and cook 5 to 6 minutes, until lightly colored. Stir in the 2 cups duck broth and cook, stirring, until thickened. Add the duck meat, and simmer 25 to 30 minutes. Add port and orange rind and heat through. Blanch olives in boiling water for 5 minutes and add all but 6 or 8 to the sauce. Serve the salmi on a bed of rice or noodles, or on polenta squares, and garnish with the remaining olives.

Wild Goose

Roast Wild Goose

A young and tender wild goose may be roasted like wild duck. Baste it well with a mixture of melted butter and wine and roast in a 400° to 425° oven for 35 to 40 minutes. You might put crushed juniper berries in the cavity for flavor. According to size, 1 goose will serve 2 to 4. Red cabbage, braised in red wine with apples, and sautéed polenta are good accompaniments.

Wild Goose Gumbo

Makes 6 servings

1 wild goose	1 cup chopped onion
1½ teaspoons salt	4 cloves garlic, finely chopped
1 teaspoon freshly ground black pepper	4 to 5 tablespoons oil
½ teaspoon Tabasco	2 quarts water
2 tablespoons butter	2 dozen oysters and liquor
2 tablespoons flour	Cooked rice

Cut the goose into serving-size pieces and season with salt, pepper, and Tabasco. Melt the butter and add the flour, and cook slowly until it becomes a dark roux. Add the onion and garlic, and cook, stirring, until the onions soften.

Meanwhile brown the pieces of goose in the oil. Combine with the onion roux and add the water. Bring to a boil and simmer until the goose is tender. Remove meat from the bones and add to pot. Add the oysters and oyster liquor and simmer 15 minutes longer. Correct the seasoning. Serve in bowls with rice.

Partridge

Roast Partridge

Partridge has been a popular game bird for centuries. The opening of the partridge season in France is a major event, and people feast on the first birds of the season as they do on the first asparagus or raspberries. Domesticated partridge raised on game farms can be obtained most of the year, either from the farms, from specialty meat markets, or from companies that ship frozen game by mail. When roasting partridge, a bird that tends to be dry, be sure to bard the breasts well with fat and don't overcook. Traditional accompaniments for partridge are chip or shoestring potatoes and a bowl of plain watercress, green peas, or turnips, but braised celery or endive is also good.

FOR EACH SERVING

1 young partridge, 1 to 1¼ pounds,
    well cleaned and skin singed to
    remove any hairs
6 tablespoons butter
A sheet of fresh pork fat or salt pork,
    pounded thin, large enough to
    fit over the breast of the bird

Salt, freshly ground black pepper
2 slices firm white bread
Giblets from the bird
2 tablespoons Madeira

Preheat the oven to 450°. Rub each bird all over with a tablespoon of butter, then bard the breast with the fat, tying it on securely. Put each bird on its side on a rack in a shallow roasting pan. Roast at 450° for 5 minutes, turn onto the other side, roast another 5 minutes, then repeat the process once more, so each side has had 10 minutes in all. Reduce heat to 375°, turn birds breast side up, and roast for 20 to 25 minutes, depending on size. Test for doneness by wiggling the legs and piercing the thigh joint. The juices should run pinkish red or the bird will be overcooked. Season with salt and pepper.

While the birds are roasting, sauté the bread in a skillet on both sides in hot butter (about 3 tablespoons for each 2 slices) until crisp and golden. Chop the giblets and sauté them quickly in the remaining 2 tablespoons butter until cooked through, season with salt and pepper and add the Madeira. Spread this mixture on the sautéed bread and serve the partridge on top, with the barding pork still on the breast. It will be brown and crisp and a delicious contrast to the bird.

¶Roast Partridge with Orange Sauce. Roast 4 partridges. Sauté 1 tablespoon chopped shallot or green onion in 2 tablespoons butter with 1 teaspoon dried tarragon. Add 1 cup game or beef stock and cook down to ⅓ cup. Add ¼ cup Grand Marnier, ½ cup orange juice, and the grated rind of 1 orange. Cook the sauce down for a few minutes, season to taste, and add ½ cup orange sections. Remove barding pork from roast birds, arrange them on toast, and pour sauce over them. Serve with risotto and green beans, see page 293, garnished with almonds.

Braised Partridge with Cabbage and Sausage

Braising is the best way to deal with older partridge—not grandfathers but those past their tender prime. Serve with boiled potatoes or rice.

Makes 6 to 8 servings

2 mature partridges
½ lemon
8 juniper berries
2 medium-size savoy cabbages (curly type) or good-size white cabbages
¼ cup oil
4 tablespoons butter
2-pound piece salt pork
3 tablespoons goose fat, lard, or butter (for greasing pan)

4 slices salt pork, cut in 2-inch pieces
6 whole carrots, scraped
3 whole onions, peeled
2 cloves
Salt, freshly ground black pepper
1½ teaspoons dried thyme
2 cups broth (beef, veal, or chicken)
2 large sausages (Italian cotechino, Polish kielbasa, or French garlic sausage)

Rub cavities of birds well with the cut lemon. Put 4 crushed juniper berries in each cavity. Blanch the whole cabbages in boiling salted water for 10 minutes, until leaves separate easily. Drain well, upside down, then leave until cool enough to handle. Cut out cores and carefully separate leaves.

Meanwhile, heat the oil and butter in a heavy skillet and brown the birds well on all sides. Blanch the piece of salt pork in boiling water for 4 minutes. Grease an 8-quart braising pan with the goose fat or lard. Arrange some of the larger cabbage leaves overlapping on the bottom and up the sides of the pan (if you like, roll the bottom leaves), making a nest of cabbage several layers thick. Place a few of the 2-inch pieces of salt pork on the cabbage. Nestle the partridges on top of the pork. Cover with the carrots and onions (stick cloves in 1 onion), the whole piece of salt pork, and more cabbage leaves. (You may also chop the cabbage cores coarse and add.) Season with salt and pepper and the thyme. Pour in the broth; cover the pot tightly with foil and then with the lid. Braise in a 350° oven for 40 minutes. Lay sausages on top of the cabbage, cover, and cook another 40 minutes.

Remove sausages to a hot platter, cover tightly with foil and keep warm. Test partridges for tenderness (insert a knife point into the thigh). If not tender, continue cooking for another 15 minutes, or until tender.

Return the sausages to the braising pan. Carve each bird into 5 pieces—each leg in 1 piece, the breast in 2 pieces, and the back in 1 piece. Remove and slice the large piece of salt pork and the sausages. Arrange cabbage on a large serving dish and ring with the sausage slices. Place the partridges and sliced salt pork on the cabbage and garnish with the carrots and onions (remove clove). Skim excess grease off and serve the pan juices separately. Season with salt and pepper.

Quail

Roast Quail

Tiny white-meated quail are probably the most plentiful of all our game birds. They are also raised in vast numbers on game farms, so you will have no difficulty finding them in your local markets or ordering them by mail. These delicate little birds weigh only about ⅔ to ¾ pound and can't take much cooking, so roast them fast at a high temperature, and bard or baste them well. One quail is usually considered a serving, but true quail lovers can easily polish off two or three at a sitting. Serve roast quail with shoestring potatoes, watercress, and, if they come with giblets, a sauce made from the livers and pan juices. Cold roast quail are delicious with a rice salad (see page 96), and mayonnaise or a rémoulade sauce (see pages 76, 77).

Makes 2 to 4 servings

4 quail, fresh, or frozen and thawed
4 tablespoons butter
4 sprigs parsley
4 sheets of barding fat, pounded until
      thin and cut to fit over the breasts
      of the birds

Salt, freshly ground black pepper

THE SAUCE
3 tablespoons butter
Livers from the quail

1 cup chicken stock

Preheat the oven to 450°. Wipe the quail with a damp cloth and put 1 tablespoon butter and 1 sprig parsley in each cavity. Tie barding fat around the breast. Arrange birds on a rack in a shallow roasting pan. Roast for 15 minutes, then remove the barding fat and baste the birds well with the fat and juices in the pan, adding melted butter if there is not enough fat. Sprinkle the birds with salt and pepper, roast for another 5 or 6 minutes, and baste again. During the final roasting time, about 5 minutes, melt the 3 tablespoons butter in a small heavy skillet and sauté the livers very quickly over high heat, just until firm. Chop fine. Transfer the quail to a hot platter and keep warm while you make the sauce. Add livers and stock to the roasting pan, bring the liquid to a boil, then reduce over high heat for

5 minutes, stirring to scrape up the brown bits from the bottom of the pan. Season to taste with salt and pepper. Spoon the sauce under the birds before serving.

¶**Quail Stuffed with Oysters.** Put in the cavity of each quail 4 to 6 oysters, depending on size, 2 tablespoons butter, a slice of lemon. Roast as before. Serve each bird on an oval of hot buttered toast, slightly larger than the quail. Garnish with fried parsley. Serve with shoestring potatoes and steamed cucumbers (see page 145) or a cucumber salad.

¶**Quail with Tarragon.** Rub quail breasts with tarragon butter before barding. Put a few tarragon leaves in each cavity. Roast as before. Serve with shoestring potatoes and sautéed zucchini (see page 175).

¶**Quail with Duxelles.** Place a spoonful of duxelles (see page 535) in each cavity. Roast as before. Serve with creamed mushrooms and turnips, and shoestring potatoes.

¶**Quail in Vine Leaves.** Rub quail with butter, salt, and pepper. Put 2 or 3 crushed juniper berries in each cavity. Wrap with barding pork and then in vine leaves, tying securely. Roast as before, but do not remove the vine leaves and barding fat or baste during the roasting. Remove twine before arranging quail on a hot platter. Skim fat from pan juices, add enough dry white wine to deglaze the pan and 1 cup seedless grapes. Cook 4 minutes over fairly high heat. Serve the leaf-wrapped quail on fried toast, with the sauce poured over them. Accompany with fried hominy grits or polenta (see page 300).

¶**Quail on Scrapple.** Rub quail with salt and pepper. Put 1 small onion and 1 celery rib in each cavity. Roast as before. Fry slices of scrapple (fresh or canned) and arrange a quail on each slice. Pour pan juices over quail.

¶**Quail with Mustard.** Split quail down the back and flatten out. Brush breasts and legs with a heavy coat of Dijon mustard. Tuck bacon slices over breast and legs. Arrange the quail flat on rack of broiler pan and roast for 20 minutes only. Serve with shoestring potatoes and salad, or a purée of carrots and turnips. Also good halved as finger food for a cocktail buffet.

Sautéed Quail

Split birds and dust lightly with flour. Sauté in butter and oil until delicately browned on all sides, turning frequently, then reduce heat and continue cooking until tender, about 12 to 18 minutes. Season with salt and pepper and serve on fried toast. If giblets came with birds, sauté in butter, chop fine, and put on toast before adding quail.

¶Quail Sautéed with Juniper Berries. After browning quail, add 8 crushed juniper berries to the pan, reduce heat, cover and cook 5 minutes. Flame birds with ⅓ cup warmed gin and cook gently until done, basting with pan juices. Season with salt and pepper and serve on toast.

¶Quail Sautéed with Shallots and Mushrooms. Sauté 8 chopped shallots and ½ pound finely chopped mushrooms in 8 tablespoons butter, reduce heat, and cook down slowly for 25 minutes, stirring occasionally. Add 1 teaspoon salt, ½ teaspoon pepper, 1 teaspoon Worcestershire sauce, and a dash of Tabasco. Cook 5 minutes. Sauté quail with 1 finely chopped garlic clove. Flame with ⅓ cup cognac, add mushroom-shallot mixture, reduce heat, and simmer until quail are tender and flavors blended (if too dry, add a little chicken broth). Serve with polenta (see page 300), sliced and sautéed in butter.

Braised Quail with White Wine

Makes 3 to 6 servings

2 teaspoons chopped shallots
11 tablespoons butter
8 mushrooms, finely chopped
1 tablespoon chopped parsley
1 cup dry bread crumbs
Salt, freshly ground black pepper,
    nutmeg

1 tablespoon chopped fresh tarragon or
    1 teaspoon dried tarragon
¼ cup sliced blanched almonds
1⅓ cups dry white wine
6 quail
Fried toast

Sauté the shallots in 3 tablespoons of the butter, then mix in the mushrooms, parsley, and bread crumbs. Season with salt and pepper to taste, a dash of nutmeg and the tarragon. Add the almonds and ⅓ cup wine. Mix well.

Stuff the quail with this mixture. Melt the remaining butter in a heavy casserole and brown the birds very quickly on all sides. Turn breast side down, add the remaining wine, cover, and cook in a 350° oven for 20 minutes. Uncover, arrange breast up, increase heat to 450°, and cook for 5 minutes more, basting frequently. Season with salt and pepper and serve on fried toast with the pan juices as a sauce.

Pheasant

Although wild pheasant are fairly plentiful, the hunting season is very short. Most of the pheasants we eat come from game farms that supply markets and restaurants. While these lack the rich, gamy flavor of the wild birds, they are perfectly palatable and young and tender enough for roasting, broiling, or sautéing. Older birds are best braised or made into fricassees or pies. One pheasant will serve 2 or 3, depending on size and the menu.

Roast Pheasant Pompadour

Pheasant is a dry bird that needs plenty of lubrication. It should be barded and basted frequently during roasting. This recipe is a French version of roast pheasant, named for the gracious and beautiful Madame Pompadour. Serve with a cornmeal soufflé (see page 302) and a purée of spinach with mushrooms.

Makes 4 to 6 servings

Two 2½- to 3-pound pheasants
¾ cup butter
2 sheets of fresh pork fat or salt pork,
    for barding
½ teaspoon thyme
1 onion, sliced

2 carrots, sliced
½ cup red wine
¼ cup capers
1½ cups small green olives
GARNISH: Chopped parsley

Put 2 tablespoons butter in the cavity of each bird, and melt the rest. Pound the sheets of fat until thin and tie them over the breasts of the pheasants. Rub with thyme. Scatter the onion and carrot in the bottom of a roasting pan and arrange the pheasants on a rack in the pan, on their sides. Roast in a 375° oven for 15 minutes, basting every few minutes with melted butter; turn on the other side and roast another 15 minutes, basting well with melted butter mixed with red wine. Turn breast side up, cut the string that holds the fat so it hangs loosely, and roast another 15 minutes, basting frequently. Test for doneness by piercing the joint between thigh and body. If the juices run pale pink, the bird is done but still moist and juicy. If not, remove barding fat and roast until done, basting well. Strain pan juices, skim off excess fat, and add capers and olives. Heat through. Pour this sauce over the pheasants. Garnish with parsley.

Fricassee of Pheasant

Long, slow simmering tenderizes the flesh of older birds. Serve the fricassee on a platter with a mound of rice in the center, and pass the sauce separately. I find braised baby carrots are a nice addition.

Makes 4 to 6 servings

½ cup flour
2 mature pheasants, cut in serving
    pieces
6 tablespoons butter
1½ cups chicken broth
1 onion, stuck with cloves
1½ teaspoons salt

½ teaspoon freshly ground black pepper
1 teaspoon thyme
1 bay leaf
Beurre manié (see page 536)
1 cup heavy cream
¼ cup sherry or Madeira

Flour the pheasant pieces lightly and sauté in butter until just delicately colored. Do not brown. Add broth, onion, and seasonings and bring to a boil. Cover the pan, lower the heat and simmer slowly for 45 minutes to 1¼ hours, or until the pheasant is tender. Do not overcook.

Remove the pheasant to a hot platter. Correct the seasoning and remove the onion and bay leaf. Thicken the broth with beurre manié and finally stir in the heavy cream and sherry or Madeira. Simmer until the sauce is the right consistency. You may return the pheasant pieces to the sauce in order to reheat them for a few minutes, if you like.

Braised Pheasant with Sauerkraut

One of the more delightful marriages of flavor is pheasant with sauerkraut. Mature pheasants are ideal for this.

Makes 6 servings

6 pounds fresh sauerkraut
½ pound salt pork, thinly sliced
2 garlic cloves, peeled and finely
    chopped
Freshly ground black pepper
18 juniper berries
2 mature pheasants
½ lemon

2 onions, each stuck with 2 cloves
4 sprigs parsley
4 tablespoons butter
5 tablespoons oil
2½ cups chicken or veal stock
2 garlic sausages or 1 Italian cotechino
    sausage, sliced

Wash the sauerkraut well under cold running water in a colander. Drain, squeezing out the excess water. Line a deep 8-quart braising pan with the salt pork slices, and arrange a layer of the sauerkraut on top. Add the garlic, 1 teaspoon freshly ground pepper, and 12 juniper berries.

Rub the insides of the pheasants with a cut lemon and in each cavity put a clove-stuck onion and 2 sprigs of parsley. Truss the birds. Heat the butter and oil in a 12-inch skillet and brown the birds on all sides until nicely colored. Transfer to the braising pan and cover with the rest of the sauerkraut. Add the remaining juniper berries, another grind or two of pepper, and the stock. Bring the mixture to a boil over rather high heat, cover the pan tightly, transfer to a 300° oven, and cook for 1½ hours, or until birds are tender. Add the sausage for the last 45 minutes' cooking time. If additional stock is needed, add it at the same time.

To serve, heap the sauerkraut in a mound on a large, hot platter, cut the pheasants into serving pieces and arrange on top. Garnish the platter with the sliced sausages.

Sautéed Pheasant

Young tender pheasant is delicious sautéed and served with a creamy sauce. If you are cooking two pheasants, put the meat in two skillets, the white meat in one and the dark meat, which takes longer to cook, in the other. For one pheasant, arrange the white meat on top of the dark for the final cooking, as you do when sautéing chicken. Serve with a potato purée and buttered green beans.

Makes 4 to 6 servings

2 pheasants, cut in quarters	8 slices good bacon
¾ cup flour	6 tablespoons butter
Salt, freshly ground black pepper	1¼ cups heavy cream
¼ teaspoon thyme	3 tablespoons cognac

Put the pheasant pieces in a plastic bag with all but 3 tablespoons of the flour, 1 teaspoon salt, ½ teaspoon pepper, and thyme. Shake until coated, remove, and shake off excess flour. Divide the bacon between two 10-inch skillets and cook until just starting to get crisp. Remove bacon, drain on paper towels, and keep warm. Add 3 tablespoons butter to one pan and heat. When sizzling, add the dark-meat pieces, skin side down, and sauté until brown; turn and sauté on second side. Five minutes after putting the dark meat in the pan, repeat procedure in second pan with white meat.

Reduce heat under both skillets and continue to cook pheasant until just tender, about 15 to 20 minutes. Cover the pan containing the dark meat so the steam will tenderize it.

Remove pheasant to a hot platter. Pour off all but 3 tablespoons fat from pan in which the dark meat cooked, and blend in the remaining 3 tablespoons flour. Scrape the pan to loosen the brown particles, then gradually stir in the cream, and cook, stirring, until thickened. Season to taste with salt and pepper. Add the cognac, simmer for 5 minutes, and serve with the pheasant. Garnish the pheasant with the bacon strips.

¶**Pheasant with White Wine and Tarragon.** After pouring off fat, do not add flour. Deglaze pan with ½ cup dry white wine or chicken stock. Let this reduce by one-third, add 2 tablespoons chopped tarragon, and pour over the pheasant.

Sautéed Pheasant with Calvados and Apples

For this dish, it is preferable to use only the pheasant breasts, although you may, if you wish, cook the dark meat in another skillet as a second helping for guests with hearty appetites. Serve with steamed buttered rice garnished with pistachio nuts.

Makes 4 servings

Breasts of 2 young pheasants	*6 apples, cored and thinly sliced*
12 tablespoons (1½ sticks) butter	*2 teaspoons sugar*
⅓ cup Calvados or applejack	*1 cup heavy cream*
Salt, freshly ground black pepper	*3 egg yolks*
½ cup dry white wine	

Cut breasts in two, removing the breastbone. Sauté gently in 6 tablespoons butter until a rich ivory color—do not brown, this is a blond sauté. Flame the breasts with ¼ cup Calvados or applejack, sprinkle with salt and pepper, add the white wine, cover, and simmer for 8 to 10 minutes, or until just tender. Do not overcook. Remove to a hot platter.

In the same skillet sauté the apple slices in the remaining butter, sprinkling with the sugar so they glaze. Garnish the platter with the apple slices.

Add remaining Calvados to the pan. Beat the cream and egg yolks lightly, add a little of the hot pan juices, then stir into the pan, keeping the heat low, and cook, stirring constantly, until smooth and thickened. Do not allow to boil. Serve in a bowl.

Broiled Pheasant

Young pheasants may be broiled like chicken. Split the birds, rub them well with butter, and broil, bone side up, about 6 inches from the heat, for 12 to 15 minutes, depending on size. Turn, brush well with butter, and sprinkle with salt and freshly ground black pepper. Broil for 12 to 15 minutes on the skin side, according to size. Be careful the skin does not become too brown—you may have to lower the rack so the pheasant is farther from the heat. Serve with crisp fried potatoes and either asparagus or broccoli.

¶**Broiled Pheasant with Tarragon Butter.** Cream ½ cup (1 stick) butter and mix with 1½ tablespoons chopped fresh tarragon or 1½ teaspoons dried tarragon. Loosen the skin over the breasts of 2 split pheasants and push a quarter of the tarragon butter under the skin of each half breast. Brush the birds well with butter and broil as before.

Rabbit

Rabbit Provençal

The combination of rabbit and anchovies is unusual and extremely good. Try to get the salted anchovies, which are much better than the canned fillets. Serve this typically Provençal dish with rice or noodles.

Makes 4 servings

2 dozen anchovies in salt (available in
*   Italian markets)*
Flour
1 rabbit, cut in serving pieces
4 tablespoons butter
4 tablespoons oil
Salt, freshly ground black pepper
¼ cup cognac

2 tablespoons chopped fresh basil or
*   1 teaspoon dried basil*
4 garlic cloves, finely chopped
2 cups tomato purée
½ cup dry white wine
4 tablespoons freshly grated Parmesan
*   cheese*
GARNISH: *Chopped parsley*

Soak the salted anchovies in water for 36 hours, then remove the skin and backbones. Reserve 6 anchovies and coarsely chop the remainder.

Lightly flour the rabbit and brown on all sides in the butter and oil in a heavy skillet, sprinkling them with salt and pepper during the cooking. Flame the pieces with the warmed cognac and transfer them to a casserole. Add the chopped anchovies, basil, garlic, tomato purée, and white wine.

Cover and cook in a 350° oven for 1 hour, or until rabbit is tender. Add the Parmesan cheese, arrange the reserved anchovy fillets on top, and sprinkle with parsley. Serve from the casserole.

Mustard Rabbit with Turnips

Domestic rabbit, fresh or frozen, may be used for this dish, but use wild rabbit if you can get it—it has more flavor. Fresh rabbit should be cut into serving pieces—the 2 hind legs, the 2 front legs, the rib and loin sections, which may be cut in 2 crosswise. Frozen rabbit comes already cut up and packaged. It requires less cooking time, as a rule.

Makes 4 servings

1 rabbit, cut in serving pieces	*Salt, freshly ground black pepper*
8-ounce jar Dijon mustard	*1 teaspoon thyme*
1 onion, stuck with 2 cloves	*1 bay leaf*
Red wine	*6 to 8 small white turnips*
7 tablespoons butter	*2 teaspoons sugar*
3 tablespoons olive oil	*Beurre manié (optional, see page 536)*

GARNISH: *Chopped parsley and tarragon*

Spread the rabbit pieces liberally with the mustard and place them in a deep glass or earthenware bowl with the onion and enough red wine to cover. Marinate in the refrigerator for 24 to 36 hours.

Melt 3 tablespoons butter and the oil in a heavy skillet, drain and dry the rabbit pieces, and brown them on all sides in the fat. Remove them to a 6-quart casserole and season with salt and pepper to taste, the thyme, and the bay leaf. Strain and add the wine from the marinade. Bring the liquid to a boil, then put the casserole in a 350° oven and cook for 1 to 1½ hours, or until tender. The time will depend on the age and size and whether the rabbit is domestic or wild.

Meanwhile, peel the turnips and brown them all over in a skillet in the remaining 4 tablespoons butter. Sprinkle with the sugar and shake the pan until they are caramelized. Cover the pan and steam the turnips gently over very low heat until just tender, adding more butter or a little stock if necessary to keep them from drying out and burning.

To serve, arrange the rabbit on a hot platter and surround with the turnips. Strain the sauce, add ½ cup red wine, bring to a boil, and let it boil until reduced by half, or thicken it, if you wish, with beurre manié. Taste, correct seasoning, and pour some of the sauce over the rabbit. Sprinkle liberally with chopped parsley and tarragon. Serve the rest of the sauce in a bowl. Serve with boiled or steamed potatoes.

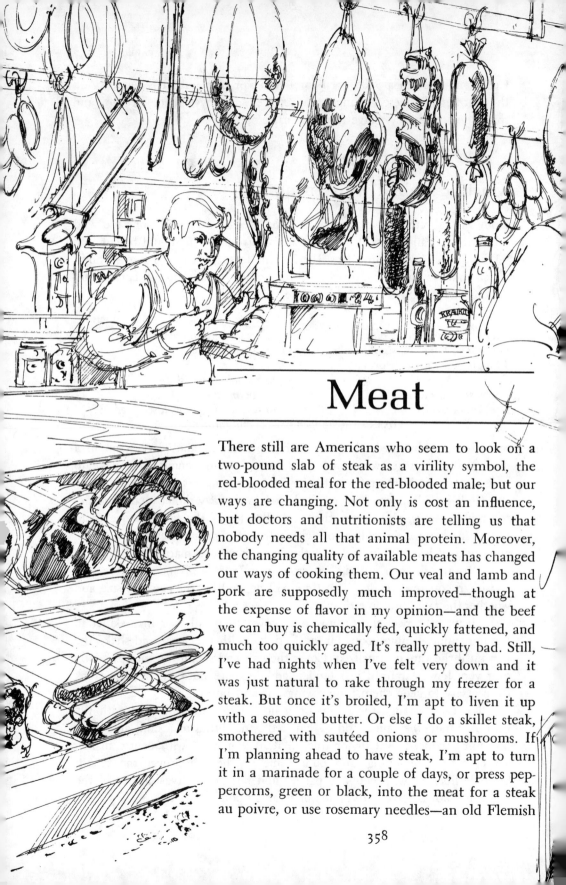

Meat

There still are Americans who seem to look on a
two-pound slab of steak as a virility symbol, the
red-blooded meal for the red-blooded male; but our
ways are changing. Not only is cost an influence,
but doctors and nutritionists are telling us that
nobody needs all that animal protein. Moreover,
the changing quality of available meats has changed
our ways of cooking them. Our veal and lamb and
pork are supposedly much improved—though at
the expense of flavor in my opinion—and the beef
we can buy is chemically fed, quickly fattened, and
much too quickly aged. It's really pretty bad. Still,
I've had nights when I've felt very down and it
was just natural to rake through my freezer for a
steak. But once it's broiled, I'm apt to liven it up
with a seasoned butter. Or else I do a skillet steak,
smothered with sautéed onions or mushrooms. If
I'm planning ahead to have steak, I'm apt to turn
it in a marinade for a couple of days, or press peppercorns, green or black, into the meat for a steak
au poivre, or use rosemary needles—an old Flemish

358

trick my friend Mary Meerson discovered when she was working on a great silent film about a Renaissance fair in Flanders, *La Kermesse Héroïque*.

In turning to other cuisines for ways of preparing meat, we seem to be borrowing good counsel from them. Good meat belongs in our lives, but it does not play the tremendous role it once did. It's less often the main dish by itself than a part of it—or, as in some of the South American recipes here, part of a one-dish meal. In Chinese and Japanese cooking, several meat-flavored dishes are often served together, yet the total amount of meat is very little; the small scraps are present as accents, overtones in a complex harmony of taste and texture. But, even when a fine cut of meat is the main point, it's not the whole one. Servings nowadays are smaller, and their accompaniments are more unusual and more savory than they used to be. Nowadays when I roast a side of pork spareribs, I use no barbe-cue sauce, but just salt and pepper. I roast them on a rack until they're quite well done, with a golden, crunchy crust. The dish is exciting and satisfying, because it brings forth the natural flavor of the pork.

I also love the rich flavor of calves' feet and pigs' feet, and the way their gelatinous juices stick to your lips. Oxtails and pigs' tails have that quality too. And then there's offal: sweetbreads, brains, liver, tongue—each uniquely delicate of texture, an invitation to imaginative cookery. Tripe I have always adored. One of the prizes here is an extraordinary dish of well-seasoned tripe with chicken gizzards—two chewy but different textures, white meat contrasted with black. It is delicious, and of course very economical: to me it is a perfect example of the modern approach to meat. Of course, the old-fashioned meat loaf was always, at its best, a study in shrewd combining and contrasting. I've never stopped experimenting with it, and have a new baking technique to suggest. Look in the Appetizers chapter for pâtés, which are meat loaf's first cousin.

And do, if you haven't already, acquire a taste for game, when you want a lusty flavor that beef no longer supplies. Wild boar is too scarce for me to give a recipe, but venison isn't, I'm glad to say. I have given recipes for (fairly) elderly game and for tougher cuts, as well as young, well-hung deer.

MEAT

BEEF

Roast fillet of beef, shell roast, eye of the rib roast

Roast fillet of beef flambé
  spiced roast fillet
  fillet with truffle and chicken liver stuffing

Marinated fillet of beef
  glazed fillet of beef

Elizabeth David's stuffed fillet of beef

Tournedos bordelaise
  tournedos with béarnaise sauce
  tournedos Argentina
  marinated tournedos
  tournedos with onions
  tournedos with sherry

Beef in red burgundy

Beef on a string

Instant beef bourguignon

Beef scallops bluegrass beef stroganoff

Bollito misto

Beef birds
  with ham and onion stuffing

Pot roast of beef
  with Madeira and turnips
  marinated
  with tomatoes
  Flemish
  Mexican
  anchovied
  leftover with ratatouille

Daube Aixoise
  daube provençale
  daube provençale with tripe
  daube niçoise

Braised short ribs of beef
  with onions
  with tomatoes
  with chilies

Chili con carne

Beef and pork chili
  with olives
  with nuts
  with beer

Basic sautéed hamburgers
  au poivre
  with onions
  with cheese
  with garlic and pine nuts
  with eggplant
  with onion and cream
  with herbs
  with chili
  with red wine
  flambé

Old-fashioned meat loaf
  with ham
  with beef liver
  with minced clams
  with olives
  with hard-boiled eggs
  chilied

LAMB

Roast rack of lamb
  persillé
  quo vadis

Crown roast of lamb
  4 stuffing variations

Roast leg of lamb,
  provençal style
  provençal no. 2
  with shallots
  Swedish
  weeping
  weeping with anchovies
  mock venison

Spoon leg of lamb

Lamb on a string

Roast shoulder of lamb
  with cream
  with eggplant and
    tomato

Braised stuffed lamb breast

Lamb en daube

Navarin

Blanquette of lamb
  blanquette of veal

Kadjemoula

Roast saddle of mutton

Lamb shanks with beans
  with ratatouille
  with onions and beer

VEAL

Roast veal with roquefort-
  butter stuffing

Veal with tuna sauce
  with yogurt and
    mayonnaise
  pork loin tonnato

Sicilian veal roll
  with omelet stuffing
  cold veal roll

Roulade of veal
  Ile-de-France
  roulade with duxelles

Veal scallops with lemon
  with lemon and
    Parmesan cheese
  with sherry
  with port
with Marsala

  with white wine
  with cognac
  with herbs
  with cream
  with almonds
  smitaine
  Lafayette
  piquant

Saltimbocca
  veal scallops with
    mozzarella cheese

Veal birds with olive-
  anchovy stuffing
  with ham
  with turkey and pork
  with tongue and
    horseradish
  provençal
  Oregon

"Minced" veal with cream
  veal strips with onion
    and mushrooms
  with mustard sauce

Sautéed veal chops with
  cream
  with onion sauce
  with hearts of palm
  with mushrooms

Broiled veal chops

Paillard of veal

Roast breast of veal

Veal en daube

Braised veal shanks with
  tomatoes and sausages

Veal ragout

Ossi buchi
  with prosciutto and
    black olives

PORK

Roast loin of pork
  with garlic
  flambé
  with rosemary
  marinated oriental style
  marinated and glazed
  orange-glazed

  with green peppercorn
    butter
  with coriander and
    fennel
  prune-stuffed
  prune-stuffed with
    potatoes and onions

Crown roast of pork
  7 stuffing variations

Roast smoked loin of pork

Roast pork leg with
  Burgundian mustard
  roast leg, Norman style

drunken pork
pork to taste like wild
    boar
Italian boned stuffed
    pork

Roast shoulder of pork
    with apples and onions

Roast suckling pig with
    pistachio-rice stuffing
    with aïoli

Pork chops, sautéed with
    onions
    with mushrooms
    Mexican style
    charcutière
    with sauerkraut

Stuffed pork chops
    with onion and herbs
    with pork and onion

Pork and sauerkraut
    goulash
    pork and veal goulash

Baked spareribs with
    sauerkraut, apples,
    and potatoes
    with onions
    with dill
    plain roasted spareribs

Pigs' feet St. Menehould
    pickled pigs' feet
    jellied pigs' feet
    jellied pigs' feet and
    hocks

Head cheese

Roast spareribs with
    sautéed lentils
    glazed spareribs

Cecilia Chiang's red-
    cooked pork shoulder

Braised pigs' hocks
    pigs' hocks with
    sauerkraut
    marinated pigs' hocks

Italian sausage
    old-fashioned sausage
    hot sausage
    pork and veal sausage

Link sausages

Sausage cakes

Broiled sausage balls

Sausage en brioche
    with mustard

HAM

Baked ham en croûte

Braised ham Chablisienne
    ham braised in Madeira

Boiled ham and cabbage

Leftover ham

Broiled ham slice
    glazed with honey and
    mustard
    barbecued
    glazed with maple syrup
    with soy and mustard

Baked ham slice in red
    wine
    in champagne
    Floridian
    arthoise

Fried ham slice with
    red-eye gravy

VENISON

Marinade for venison

Marinated roast leg of
    venison

Roast saddle of venison

Helmut Ripperberger's
    roast loin of venison

Broiled venison steaks
    with seasoned butter
    sautéed
    peppered

Venison kebabs

Venison pot roast

Venison hamburgers
    flambé
    herbed
    with garlic and chives

Venison chili

OFFAL

Parboiled or poached
    brains

Sautéed brains
    marinated
    au beurre noir

Broiled brains

Fried brains

Sautéed liver with bacon
    with onions

    with shallots and
    Madeira
    with avocado
    with mustard sauce
    deviled

Liver Venetian style
  julienne

Roast whole liver

Kidneys "on the half shell"
  flambé
  with mushrooms

Lamb kidneys en brochette
  and sweetbreads
  and sweetbreads flambé
  and mushrooms
  and mushrooms, and
    bacon
  with herb butter
  broiled deviled

Kidney sauté flambé
  deviled kidney sauté

Braised veal hearts
  braised lamb hearts

Beef tongue with provençal
  tomato sauce
Philip Brown's tongue
  with chicken liver
  sauce
  with Madeira sauce
  with spinach
  tongue pot-au-feu

Lambs' tongues poulette
  lambs' tongues with
    tomato sauce
  lambs' tongues
    vinaigrette
  pickled lambs' tongues

Tripes à la mode de Caen
  with red wine

Tripe niçoise

Menudo

Tablier de sapeur

Cecilia Chiang's tripe with
  gizzards

Sweetbreads Albert

Sweetbreads panné
  with cream
  with mustard

Broiled sweetbreads
  milanese
  herbed

Sweetbreads, kidneys, and
  sausages

Beef

Modern American beef is very tender, but too bland to suit me: a result partly of modern ranching practices, and partly of modern storage and marketing. "Normally," says *The Meat Board Meat Book*, "it takes from six to ten days to move fresh meat from packer to kitchen. . . . The customer who prefers additional aging must be prepared to pay a premium price to a meat dealer who carries specially aged meat."

Aging, which must be done under carefully controlled conditions of temperature and humidity, can't be tried safely at home. It is worth it to me to deal with a butcher who hangs beef for 3 to 6 weeks. His prices are high, reflecting the cost to him, not only of storage space, but of the shrinkage that occurs, and of surface spoilage. Well-aged beef usually develops a thick green mold on the surface fat: perfectly harmless, since it's easily trimmed off. The meat sometimes darkens slightly in color, which is harmless too. It develops a rich flavor, which some consider too gamy, and I consider exquisite.

It isn't worthwhile for most butchers to age any but the finest cuts of the finest-quality beef. So, for most beef cookery, be inventive and imaginative with seasonings—even for expensive cuts—and with marinades for tenderizing as well. For a good broiled steak, you don't have to buy sirloin or porterhouse. You can do remarkable things with lesser cuts, for example the rib eye, the rump, the chuck, the flank, the skirt, and the hanging tenderloin. True tenderloin, or fillet, steaks are better sautéed than grilled, in my opinion, and I feel the same way about hamburgers, as well as some other steaks.

Broiled steak got very thorough coverage in *Theory & Practice*, and I won't repeat myself here. But I have worked out an easier formula than the general rule given there for timing a broiled steak according to its thickness, and based on that, its distance from the broiler. Further experiments have proved to me that the following even more general rule works for any steak. It lightly chars the meat on the outside, leaving a big, red, rare heart inside—for me, the ideal.

Per measured inch of thickness, 10 minutes' broiling, 2 inches from the heat source, which must be preheated until red hot. If the steak is more than 4 inches thick, after a quick searing lower the broiling rack to mid-oven for the final cooking. (This rule is for gas or electric oven broiling only; charcoal is too variable in delivery of heat.)

Other than this, I have no recipes here for broiled beef. And only a third of my recipes involve expensive cuts. I have given the others special attention, and as a result you will find some surprises. Meat loaf, for instance: don't bake it the old way in a loaf pan. Do it free-form, protected with fat, and you'll get a better texture and a loaf that will slice perfectly for sandwiches the next day.

And speaking of the next day, party-givers who like to cook in advance should note that many of the braised or stewed dishes are actually better when made the day before, since this enables you to skim off all the fat, and since the flavors are deeper.

Roast Fillet of Beef, Shell Roast, Eye of the Rib Roast

Although expensive, these are good roasts for a dinner party, as they are boneless, very tender, cook quickly, carve easily, and have no waste. Unlike a prime rib roast, they lend themselves to a variety of presentations. The fillet, or tenderloin, weighs from 4 to 6 pounds and should be trimmed of all fat and membrane. Remove the fillet mignon, the tapering piece at the end of the fillet, which is too thin for roasting, and use it for recipes based on beef tenderloin slices or cubes, such as scallops or beef Stroganoff (see page 372) and beef shashlik (see *Theory & Practice*, page 124).

The shell roast is the top loin section boned out, with the tenderloin removed. It costs less than the fillet, can often be found on special at supermarkets, and may be prepared in any of the same ways. I like to roast the shell at 475°, allowing 11 to 12 minutes a pound (45 minutes for a 4-pound shell, 50 minutes for a 6-pound), then turn off the heat and let the roast rest in the turned-off oven for 10 minutes. The internal temperature should be the same as for a fillet—120° for very rare, 125° for rare.

The eye of the rib roast, which is the boned-out center of the rib roast with the less tender meat removed, weighs about 5 pounds. It can also be prepared like a fillet, but because it is a thicker piece of meat it needs a longer roasting time—50 minutes at 500°—to an internal temperature of 120° to 125°.

Roast Fillet of Beef Flambé

Makes 10 to 12 servings

5- to 6-pound fillet of beef, trimmed
Olive oil
1½ teaspoons salt

1 teaspoon freshly ground black pepper
⅓ cup cognac
GARNISH: Chopped parsley

Rub the fillet well with oil, salt, and pepper. Put on an oiled rack in a shallow roasting pan and roast in a 500° oven for 25 minutes or until the internal temperature reaches 120° to 125° (a fillet must always be rare). Brush frequently with oil during roasting, as a fillet has no fat of its own. Remove to a heatproof platter and flame with the warmed cognac. Let it rest for 5 minutes before carving. Sprinkle with chopped parsley and carve in ½-inch-thick slices. Serve with sauce Béarnaise (see page 532), broiled tomatoes, and watercress or, if you prefer potatoes with your beef, Potatoes Anna (*Theory & Practice*, page 238).

¶Spiced Roast Fillet. Stud the fillet with slivers of garlic and rub meat with a mixture of ½ cup olive oil, 1 tablespoon salt, 2 tablespoons chili powder, and 1 tablespoon ground cumin.

¶Fillet with Truffle and Chicken Liver Stuffing. Sauté 8 chicken livers in 3 tablespoons butter until firm, about 3 minutes. Season with salt and pepper and flame with 3 tablespoons cognac. Reserve pan juices. Make an opening the length of the fillet with a larding needle (or have the butcher do it when you buy the fillet) and stuff alternately with the chicken livers and 6 canned black truffles (reserve liquid from can). Rub meat well with butter, rosemary, salt, and pepper, and roast as in basic recipe, basting often with melted butter. Remove meat to a hot platter and flame with ⅓ cup cognac. Combine juices from roasting pan with chicken-liver pan juices, truffle juice, ½ cup Madeira, and 1½ cups brown sauce (see page 533). Simmer 2 or 3 minutes; correct seasoning. Garnish fillet with watercress, serve with sauce.

NOTE: If you can afford them, fresh truffles may be used. They will impart a heavenly bouquet and a delightful flavor to the beef. Consult your pocketbook!

Marinated Fillet of Beef

A teriyaki-marinated fillet is delicious either hot or tepid and ideal for a buffet party or a substantial cocktail buffet. Food accompaniments for a dinner would be rice mixed with toasted filberts and sautéed mushrooms, and sautéed snow peas.

Makes 10 servings

5-pound fillet of beef, trimmed

1 tablespoon peanut oil

TERIYAKI MARINADE
½ cup olive oil
½ cup Japanese or Chinese soy sauce
½ cup dry sherry or Madeira
1 tablespoon grated fresh ginger (or well-washed preserved ginger, finely chopped)

1 tablespoon grated orange or tangerine rind
1 teaspoon freshly ground black pepper

Marinate the fillet in a mixture of the olive oil, soy, sherry or Madeira, ginger, orange or tangerine rind, and pepper for 8 to 12 hours, turning often. When ready to roast, remove from marinade and dry well.

Rub fillet with the tablespoon of peanut oil and place on a rack in a roasting pan. Roast at 500° for 10 minutes, then brush well with the marinade. Reduce heat to 400°, and roast another 10 minutes. Brush again with marinade, reduce heat to 350°, and roast a further 10 minutes, or until meat registers 120° on a meat thermometer. Remove to a hot platter and allow to rest for 5 to 10 minutes before carving.

¶Glazed Fillet of Beef. Marinate the fillet as above. After removing meat from the marinade, combine 1 cup of the marinade with 1 cup honey, ¼ cup lemon juice, 1 tablespoon ground cumin, and 2 tablespoons turmeric. Brush the fillet with this glaze as it roasts.

Elizabeth David's Stuffed Fillet of Beef

This stuffed fillet needs slightly longer cooking at a lower temperature to allow the meat to become permeated with the flavors of the stuffing. Serve with sauce Bordelaise (see page 533) and tiny buttered new potatoes.

Makes 10 to 12 servings

4 to 5 medium-size onions, thinly sliced
3 tablespoons butter
3 tablespoons oil
¼ pound thinly sliced ham, preferably
    Smithfield, cut in julienne strips
10 anchovy fillets, coarsely cut
1 garlic clove, finely chopped
16 to 18 soft black olives, pitted and
    coarsely chopped

1 teaspoon thyme
½ teaspoon rosemary
¼ cup chopped parsley
2 eggs
Salt, freshly ground black pepper
5- to 6-pound fillet of beef, trimmed
2 to 3 tablespoons melted butter

Sauté the onion in the butter and oil until just limp. Add the ham, anchovies, garlic, olives, thyme, rosemary, and parsley, and mix well. Remove from heat, quickly stir in the eggs, return to heat, and stir until mixture thickens, about 3 minutes. Season with 1 teaspoon pepper and a very little salt, as the anchovies are salty.

Cut the fillet about ⅔ of the way down in thick slices, about an inch apart, and spoon the stuffing between the slices. Reshape and tie securely with string, or run a trussing needle threaded with string through the center of the fillet and tie. Brush well with melted butter, place on a rack in a roasting pan, and roast in a 350° oven for 40 to 50 minutes.

Tournedos Bordelaise

Tournedos are steaks cut from the fillet, 1 inch thick, then barded with fat and tied. These tender little morsels should be very rare and are best sautéed rather than broiled. Tournedos lend themselves to various preparations and rich or spicy sauces. They are considered excellent party fare.

Makes 4 servings

2 tablespoons salad oil
2 tablespoons butter
4 tournedos, barded and tied
Salt, freshly ground black pepper

4 slices poached beef marrow
    (see page 533)
½ cup Bordelaise sauce (see page 533)

Heat the oil and butter in a skillet or sauté pan until sizzling but not smoking. Sauté the tournedos for 3 minutes on a side, then sprinkle them with salt and pepper, remove to a hot platter, and top each with a slice of marrow. Spoon the Bordelaise sauce over them and serve.

¶**Tournedos with Béarnaise Sauce.** Do not use marrow. Serve with Béarnaise sauce (see page 532).

¶**Tournedos Argentina.** Sauté tournedos and arrange on fried toast the same size as the steaks, top each with a slice of sautéed pineapple, surround with sauce diable (see page 533).

¶**Marinated Tournedos.** Marinate tournedos in teriyaki marinade (see page 366) for 30 minutes before sautéing.

¶**Tournedos with Onions.** Top each tournedo with a 1-inch-thick slice of onion that has been braised in butter and Madeira. Serve on fried toast.

¶**Tournedos with Sherry.** Serve tournedos on a platter surrounded by sautéed mushroom caps. Heat ½ cup dry sherry and pour over tournedos.

Beef in Red Burgundy

Boeuf bourguignon, or beef in red Burgundy, is probably one of the most universally favored of all braised beef dishes, but it is also one that is often ruined by poor cooking and overseasoning. The usual method is to cut the beef into cubes, and they invariably become boiled-tasting and stringy. A much more successful way is to cook the meat like a pot roast, in one piece, so that you can lard it, thus providing natural basting of fat as it cooks. For a short-cut version of this classic preparation, try the Instant Beef Bourguignon on page 370.

Makes 10 servings (or 6 with meat left over)

5-pound piece bottom round of beef
6 to 8 lardoons, soaked for 1 hour in
*   cognac (see page 375)*
Flour
10 tablespoons butter
12 mushrooms, trimmed
3 garlic cloves
2 leeks, trimmed and washed
Salt, freshly ground black pepper
2 cups beef broth

3 cups good red Burgundy
1 bay leaf
1 teaspoon dried thyme or a sprig of
*   fresh thyme*
3 or 4 sprigs parsley
24 small white onions, peeled
1 teaspoon sugar
4 slices salt pork, ½ inch thick
Beurre manié (optional, see page 536)
¼ cup chopped parsley

Lard the beef as for pot roast (see page 375). Brown the larded meat on all sides under the broiler. Sprinkle lightly with flour, and turn so the flour browns lightly.

Melt 6 tablespoons butter in a large braising pan, add the mushrooms, garlic, and leeks, and sauté lightly. Remove and reserve the mushrooms. Add the beef to the pan, salt and pepper well, then add the broth, wine, bay leaf, thyme, and parsley. Bring to a boil, reduce heat, put a piece of buttered wax paper on top of the meat, cover pan, and simmer for 1 hour.

Meanwhile, brown the onions in a skillet in 2 tablespoons butter, sprinkle with the sugar, and shake until lightly glazed. Set aside. Melt remaining butter in the skillet, cut the salt pork into small strips, and cook them in the butter until browned and slightly crisp. Remove and reserve salt pork and onions.

Test beef for tenderness. If it seems fairly tender, add onions and cook until just tender, about 50 to 60 minutes. Remove from heat, uncover, and let stand 15 minutes for fat to settle. Skim off excess fat, add mushrooms and salt pork to the pan and simmer for 10 minutes. Transfer beef to a hot platter and arrange onions, mushrooms, and salt pork around it. If desired, thicken sauce with beurre manié. Taste and correct the seasoning. Spoon some of the sauce into the platter with the vegetables and sprinkle them with parsley. Serve with boiled potatoes.

NOTE: The beef is *much better* if made in advance, skimmed of all fat, and reheated the next day. In this case, prepare mushrooms, onions, and salt pork, and add to beef when reheated.

Beef on a String
(Beef à la Ficelle)

This most unusual way of cooking beef is quite different from boiled beef. Although it is simmered in stock, the end result is rare and deliciously tender. The *ficelle* of the name refers to the string by which the meat is suspended. Serve the same kinds of vegetables you would have with boiled beef—boiled potatoes, carrots, leeks, turnips—and a horseradish and sour cream sauce.

Makes 6 servings

2½-pound piece of eye-of-the-rib,
    strip sirloin, or fillet
3 pounds beef marrow bones
1 bay leaf
2 crushed garlic cloves

1 tablespoon dried thyme
1 tablespoon freshly ground black
    pepper
2 tablespoons salt

Tie the beef securely with string, crosswise and lengthwise, leaving at each end a piece long enough to suspend the meat in the pan. Put in a deep pan or stock pot enough cold water to almost cover the meat; add the marrow bones and all the seasonings. This is for a broth in which the beef will cook. The meat should not be added until later. Bring the liquid to a boil, skim off the scum, reduce the heat, cover, and simmer for 1 hour. Then remove the bones and skim the fat off the top of the broth.

Suspend the meat in the broth (it should not touch the bottom of the pot) by tying the ends of the string to the handles of the pan. Bring the broth to a boil (the shock of heat seals the surface of the meat and keeps the juices in), then reduce the heat to a simmer, cover the pot tightly with foil and the lid so no steam escapes, and simmer the meat for approximately 15 minutes a pound, about 35 minutes in all, testing the internal temperature by inserting a meat thermometer after 25 minutes. The temperature should be 125° to 135°, depending on how rare you like your beef. Remove the beef to a carving board, let it rest for 5 minutes, then remove the strings and carve crosswise with a very sharp knife into fairly thick slices, about ½ inch. Save the stock; strain and use for bouillon or as the base for vegetable soups.

Instant Beef Bourguignon

This quick version of the classic Beef Bourguignon, which you'll find on page 368, is to my mind infinitely better, as the beef does not get dry from long cooking and it remains rare in the center. For this you must have very tender beef fillet or sirloin. Serve with boiled potatoes or steamed rice, a green salad, and French bread.

Makes 6 servings

2½ cups brown sauce (see page 533)
1½ cups red wine, preferably Burgundy
   or Pinot Noir
1 bay leaf
½ teaspoon thyme
Salt, freshly ground black pepper
1 slice of lemon
A small piece of orange rind
14 tablespoons unsalted butter

12 to 18 small white onions, peeled
2 teaspoons sugar
¼ cup chicken or beef broth
12 to 18 firm white mushroom caps
4 thick slices of salt pork, cut into
   small dice
2½ pounds beef fillet or very tender
   sirloin, cut in 1¼-inch cubes

GARNISH: 1 tablespoon chopped parsley

Have your brown sauce in one pan. In another pan, bring the wine, bay leaf, thyme, 1 teaspoon salt, 1 teaspoon pepper, lemon slice, and orange rind to a boil, then reduce the heat and simmer until reduced to 1 cup. Strain this into the brown sauce, bring to a boil, and simmer gently for 30 to 45 minutes. This is your sauce bourguignon. Taste, and correct the seasoning, then cover surface of sauce with buttered wax paper and set aside until ready to complete the dish.

While the sauce simmers, heat 4 tablespoons butter in a skillet, add the onions and sauté over medium-high heat, sprinkling with the sugar so they glaze and brown. Add the broth, cover, and steam until just crisply tender. In another skillet, melt 3 tablespoons butter, add the mushrooms, and sauté over medium-high heat until lightly colored. Remove mushrooms, add 2 tablespoons butter to the skillet, and sauté the salt pork until crisply browned. Remove, drain, combine with onions and mushrooms, and set aside, covered with foil.

About 10 minutes before you are ready to serve, heat 5 tablespoons butter in a heavy sauté pan. Add the beef cubes, a few at a time, and sauté over high heat until well seared and browned on all sides. Add brown sauce, let it just come to a boil, add the onions, mushrooms, and salt pork, and simmer until just heated through—not long enough to overcook the beef. This has to be a very fast operation. Garnish with chopped parsley and serve.

Beef Scallops Bluegrass

Makes 4 servings

3 tablespoons oil (or a mixture of oil and butter)
12 slices beef tenderloin, ⅜ inch thick
Salt
4 tablespoons bourbon

3 tablespoons chopped green onion, or shallot
½ cup beef broth or red wine
Tabasco and Worcestershire sauce
Freshly ground black pepper

GARNISH: 2 tablespoons chopped parsley

In a heavy skillet, heat the oil, or oil and butter. When very hot, quickly sear the slices of beef tenderloin on both sides. Do this in batches, according to the size of your pan. The slices should not be crowded. As the scallops cook, salt them lightly. Put them all back in the skillet, heat the bourbon in a small pan, ignite, and pour flaming over the beef. Shake skillet until the flames die down, then remove beef to a hot serving dish and add to the skillet the green onion or shallot. Sauté for 1 minute. Add the beef broth or red wine, a dash each of Tabasco and Worcestershire sauce, and a few grinds of black pepper. Let the sauce boil up, then pour it over the beef, and garnish with chopped parsley. Serve with tiny new potatoes.

¶**Beef Stroganoff.** This differs from the above in that the sauce is an accompaniment, not part of the dish itself. A much more subtle approach. Sear the beef tenderloin slices. Do not flame with bourbon. Remove to a hot serving dish. Add the shallots or green onions to the pan and sauté. Mix in 1 tablespoon tomato paste, 1 tablespoon Worcestershire sauce, ¼ teaspoon Tabasco, ½ teaspoon dried tarragon or 1 tablespoon chopped fresh tarragon, and a few grinds of pepper. Blend thoroughly. Remove pan from heat and stir in 1 to 1½ cups sour cream or yogurt. Return to heat and let sauce just heat through; it must not boil or it will curdle. Spoon the sauce over the beef and garnish with chopped parsley. Serve with sautéed mushrooms (see page 154) and rounds of fried toast.

Bollito Misto
(Boiled Meats and Vegetables)

Bollito misto (mixed boil) is roughly the Italian equivalent of the French pot-au-feu, or the American boiled dinner on a larger scale. The true bollito misto encompasses several different meats, so it should always be planned for a large number of guests, twelve being ideal. The usual display might be chicken or capon, pork, veal, beef, tongue, and sausages, with vegetables and sauces. The choice is flexible, but there must be variety.

Makes 12 servings

4 pounds beef brisket
3 onions, peeled, 1 stuck with 2 cloves
3 carrots, scraped
3 or 4 leeks, well washed and trimmed
2 cloves garlic, peeled
1 tablespoon salt

1 bay leaf
½ teaspoon freshly ground black pepper
1 teaspoon thyme
2 veal tongues
4-pound roasting chicken or capon
1 or 2 Italian cotechino sausages

ACCOMPANYING VEGETABLES
12 medium-size potatoes, peeled
12 carrots, scraped

12 leeks, well washed and trimmed
12 small white onions, peeled

GREEN SAUCE
¾ cup olive oil
¼ cup wine vinegar
1 teaspoon salt
1 teaspoon freshly ground black pepper
3 tablespoons chopped Italian parsley

2 tablespoons chopped chives
Other chopped herbs, such as mint,
    thyme, rosemary, to taste
Finely chopped garlic to taste

Combine in a 10-quart pot the beef, flavoring vegetables, garlic, salt, bay leaf, pepper, thyme, and water to cover. Bring to a boil, skim off the scum, then reduce the heat, cover, and simmer for 1½ hours. Add the veal tongues and cook for another 1½ hours, adding more water if necessary to keep the meats covered. After 3 hours, add the chicken and sausages. Continue cooking until the meats and chicken are tender, about another hour. After 45 minutes, test to see if the chicken is cooked. If tender, remove it to a hot platter, cover with foil, and keep warm. Continue cooking the other meats until tender when pierced with the point of a knife—4 hours should be sufficient. Taste the broth and correct the seasoning.

While the bollito misto is cooking, boil the potatoes, carrots, leeks, and onions separately in salted water to cover, timing them so they are done at the same time.

Also, make the sauce. Combine the oil, vinegar, salt, pepper, and chopped herbs and garlic—the sauce should be really thick and green with fresh herbs.

When the meats and vegetables are cooked, arrange them on a large hot platter and have a carving board beside it. Carve meats and serve some of each, with a potato and other vegetables. Serve some of the rich broth in cups. Other accompaniments for a bollito misto are coarse salt, freshly grated horseradish or horseradish sauce, and mustard fruits (sold in cans or jars in Italian groceries or specialty shops).

¶**Variation.** You may use other meats in a *bollito misto*, such as pork loin or veal shoulder, boned and tied, instead of beef; a 6-pound turkey instead of the chicken; a fresh beef tongue in place of the veal tongues. Cooking times will vary according to the tenderness of the meats.

Beef Birds

Another variation on the braised beef theme, these little rolls of stuffed beef freeze well and can be kept on hand against one of those culinary emergencies people talk about more often than they really face. When freezing them, be sure they are completely covered by the sauce to prevent them from drying out. Any of the stuffings given for veal birds (see pages 409–410) can be used for beef birds. Good accompaniments are rice or orzo (rice-shaped pasta) and a green salad.

Makes 8 servings

8 slices round steak, cut 6 to 8 inches
    long and ½ inch thick
¾ pound ground pork (about 30
    percent fat)
2 cloves garlic, finely chopped
1 teaspoon salt
1 teaspoon freshly ground black pepper
¼ teaspoon dried sage
1¼ teaspoons dried thyme
1 tablespoon chopped parsley
1 egg

6 to 8 paper-thin slices of barding pork
    (fatback)
5 tablespoons butter
1 onion, finely sliced
1 carrot, finely sliced
¼ cup dry white wine
1½ cups beef broth
2 tablespoons tomato paste
1 sprig parsley
1 bay leaf
Beurre manié (optional, see page 536)

Put the slices of round steak between sheets of wax paper and flatten with a meat pounder until they are half the original thickness. Trim each slice into a perfect square or rectangle. Cut the trimmings into thin strips and reserve.

Combine in a bowl the ground pork, garlic, salt, pepper, sage, and ¼ teaspoon of the thyme. Blend the mixture well, add the chopped parsley and egg and mix this stuffing well with your hands. Place 2 or 3 tablespoons of the stuffing on each piece of beef and roll it up. Wrap each roll in a piece of barding pork and tie at each end with fine string.

Melt the butter in a heavy skillet, add the sliced onion and carrot and the beef trimmings and sauté lightly. Add the beef rolls and sauté gently, covered, turning them once or twice, until lightly browned. Add the white wine and reduce quickly over high heat. Add the broth and tomato paste, cover, bring to a boil, reduce heat, add parsley sprig, bay leaf, and remaining 1 teaspoon thyme, and simmer, covered, for about 1 hour, or until the beef rolls are tender when tested with the point of a small sharp knife.

Remove strings and barding and transfer the rolls to a hot platter. Strain the sauce and skim off the fat. Reheat the sauce and, if desired, thicken with a little beurre manié. Taste, and correct the seasoning. Serve the rolls with the sauce.

¶**Beef Birds with Ham and Onion Stuffing.** Make the stuffing with ½ cup onion sautéed in butter, ½ pound ground leftover ham, 1 cup fresh bread crumbs, salt, pepper, and summer savory. Bind with 1 egg and mix in 2 tablespoons chopped parsley.

Pot Roast of Beef

The braised beef dish we know as pot roast, one of the most popular foods in this country, is far too often served overcooked and dry. This is mainly the result of using the wrong cuts of beef or from a lack of fat—either in the beef or in the cooking. The best choice for a pot roast is a piece of well-marbled beef rump or chuck. You may, if you wish, further lubricate it with cognac-soaked lardoons, small strips of fatback inserted with a larding needle. While not strictly necessary for well-marbled beef, this does add a very pleasant flavor and looks attractive when sliced. Surround the sliced pot roast with cooked noodles sprinkled with grated Parmesan cheese, and have a salad or braised celery as the vegetable.

Makes 10 servings (or 6 with leftover meat)

5-pound piece of beef rump or chuck
¼ pound fresh white pork fatback or
    lardoons cut in 6 or 8 strips
¼ cup cognac
Salt, freshly ground black pepper
2 tablespoons dried basil
4 tablespoons butter (optional)
4 tablespoons oil (optional)
1 bay leaf

4 to 6 garlic cloves, crushed
2 leeks, trimmed and washed
2 carrots
1 large onion stuck with 2 cloves
1½ cups beef broth
1 cup canned Italian plum tomatoes
3 tablespoons tomato paste
1 tablespoon lemon juice

The strips of fatback, known as lardoons, should be rather longer than the depth of the piece of beef and just wide enough to fit into the groove of a long, wooden-handled larding needle. Soak these lardoons in the cognac for 3 or 4 hours before larding the beef. Push the grooved blade of the needle through the meat, turning it to make a hole, withdraw, and insert a strip of fatback into the groove of the needle. Then insert the blade into the hole, pushing the top of the lardoon with your thumb so it stays inside the meat. Withdraw the needle, leaving the fat behind. Repeat this with all the lardoons, and trim off any overhanging ends level with the meat. Rub the meat well with salt, pepper, and 1 teaspoon basil.

    You can either brown the meat in the butter and oil in a skillet or pan on top of the stove or put it on the broiler rack and pan under the broiler, about 7 to 8 inches from the heat, turning to brown on all sides. Browning under the broiler is preferable if you are watching calories.

    Transfer the browned beef to a deep braising pan and pour over it the fat in which it browned, or the drippings from the broiler pan. Add the bay leaf, garlic, leeks, carrots, onion, remaining basil, and beef broth. Bring to a boil, cover the meat with a piece of oiled wax paper, cover pan, and reduce heat. Simmer on top of the stove or in a 325° oven for 1 hour. Then remove the cover and add the tomatoes. Cover and continue cooking until meat is just tender when tested with the point of a knife, 1½ to 2 hours. Do not make the common mistake of cooking the beef until it is grainy and coarse. The difference is slight but important.

Remove meat and keep warm on a hot platter. Skim excess fat from the sauce and strain it into a saucepan through a sieve, pushing through any bits of vegetable to make the sauce thicker. Add the tomato paste and lemon juice, taste, and correct the seasoning. Bring the sauce to a boil and simmer 3 to 4 minutes to blend the flavors. Serve sauce separately.

¶**Pot Roast with Madeira and Turnips.** Rub the larded beef with salt, pepper, and thyme. Brown in fat or under the broiler. Put beef in braising pan and flame with ¼ cup warm cognac. Add a clove-stuck onion, 1 carrot, 1 celery rib, 1 garlic clove, 1 teaspoon thyme, 1 bay leaf, 1½ cups beef broth, and 1 split pig's foot. Cover as above and simmer for 1 hour, then add ¼ cup Madeira and continue to cook until tender. Meanwhile, cook 12 small white turnips in boiling water until just tender, drain, and keep hot. Remove pig's foot from pan, take off meat and serve with the pot roast. Transfer beef to a hot platter. Skim and strain the sauce, and bring to a boil with ¼ cup Madeira. If you wish, thicken with beurre manié (see page 536). Add turnips and heat through. Surround the pot roast with the turnips and serve the sauce separately. Boiled or baked potatoes are a good accompaniment.

¶**Marinated Pot Roast.** Rub the larded beef with salt, pepper, and nutmeg. Marinate for 8 hours in red wine to cover with 1 teaspoon thyme, 1 onion stuck with 2 cloves, and ¼ cup cognac, turning several times. Remove beef from marinade and brown on all sides in butter or beef fat in a large, heavy pan. Add marinade and 2 split pigs' feet. Cover and simmer until tender. Remove meat and pigs' feet. Skim fat from pan juices. Thicken, if desired, with beurre manié. Serve with baby carrots, steamed in butter, and boiled potatoes.

¶**Pot Roast with Tomatoes.** Put the browned beef in a pan with 1 veal knuckle, 2 cloves garlic, 1 clove-stuck onion, 1 teaspoon thyme, 1 teaspoon dried basil or 1 tablespoon chopped fresh basil, ¼ teaspoon Tabasco, 2 teaspoons salt, 1 teaspoon freshly ground black pepper, 2 cups canned Italian plum tomatoes, and ½ cup red wine. Cover and simmer until almost tender, then add 2 tablespoons tomato paste and continue cooking until tender. Remove and discard veal knuckle. Skim fat from sauce before serving with meat and macaroni or noodles.

¶**Flemish Pot Roast.** Sauté 6 large onions, sliced, in 5 tablespoons butter until limp and golden. Season with salt and pepper. Put in a deep pan with the browned beef, 1 teaspoon thyme, 1 bay leaf, and 1 pint beer. Cover and simmer until tender. Remove meat, adjust seasoning in sauce, and serve over the sliced beef. Serve with parsleyed potatoes.

¶**Mexican Pot Roast.** Stud the beef with slivers of garlic (do not lard). Sauté 4 sliced onions in rendered beef suet or beef fat, put in a braising pan with the browned beef, 1 teaspoon oregano, ½ teaspoon cumin seed, ½ teaspoon ground coriander, 2 tablespoons chili powder, salt to taste, ¼ teaspoon Tabasco, 1 cup beef broth, and ½ cup tomato purée. Cover and simmer until tender, turning meat several times in sauce. If sauce becomes too reduced, add more broth or tomato purée. Serve the meat sliced, with the sauce, skimmed of all fat. Garnish with chopped coriander or Italian parsley, and serve with pinto beans and tortillas.

¶**Anchovied Pot Roast.** Stud the beef with garlic slivers and anchovy fillets (do not lard). Brown beef and put in a pan with 1 bay leaf, 1 rib celery, 3 carrots cut in small pieces, 1 tablespoon basil, 1½ cups canned Italian plum tomatoes, and freshly ground black pepper to taste. Cover and simmer until tender, turning once and adding a little water or tomato juice if liquid reduces too much. Add 1 cup soft black Greek or Italian olives for the last 15 minutes' cooking time. Serve meat sliced, with the sauce, buttered macaroni, and a green salad.

¶**Leftover Pot Roast with Ratatouille.** A good way to recycle what's left of the pot roast for tomorrow's dinner. Arrange a layer of ratatouille (see page 190) in a casserole, cover with slices of cold pot roast, and another layer of ratatouille. Bake in a 350° oven for 30 to 35 minutes, until beef is thoroughly heated through. Sprinkle grated Gruyère cheese on top for the last 10 minutes' baking time.

Daube Aixoise

The daubes, or wine-flavored stews, of Provence derive their matchless flavor from long, slow cooking, traditionally in a daubière, a round, covered earthenware pot, that stood all night over a charcoal fire or on a metal disk set into the fireplace. A heavy enameled cast-iron pot serves the same purpose of holding the heat. When I lived in Provence I encountered many different daubes from Aix, Avignon, Nice, Marseilles, mostly made with beef, sometimes lamb (see page 394), often with a pig's or calf's foot added for thickening. Sometimes the meat was left in one piece, sometimes it was cut up, but invariably it was marinated or cooked in wine, without browning. Macaronade, macaroni mixed with the luscious sauce, is the usual Provençal accompaniment to a daube, although other pastas or rice might also be used. Daube, like other braised beef dishes, improves in flavor if made a day ahead.

Makes 6 to 8 servings

⅓ cup olive oil
3 slices thick bacon, cut in small cubes
5 onions, peeled and quartered
3 carrots, scraped and cut in 3-inch
 pieces
5 cloves garlic
1 leek, well washed
Peel of ¼ orange
2 cloves
1 bay leaf

1 teaspoon thyme or rosemary
 (or ½ teaspoon each)
1 tablespoon salt
1 teaspoon freshly ground black pepper
2 tablespoons tomato paste
3 pounds boneless beef, shin or round,
 cut in large pieces
1 pig's foot
Red wine to cover

Put the oil and bacon in the bottom of a large, heavy braising pan, preferably of enameled cast iron, and add the onions, carrots, garlic, leek, orange peel, cloves, bay leaf, thyme or rosemary, salt, pepper, and tomato paste. Lay the beef pieces and pig's foot on top and add enough red wine to cover. Cover tightly with the lid, bring to a simmer on the stove, and cook gently over the lowest possible heat or in a 275° oven, for 4 to 4½ hours. When the meat is tender, remove it to a hot platter, skim the fat from the sauce, and strain. Remove meat from pig's foot and add it to the sauce. Pour this sauce over cooked macaroni and toss well. Serve with the beef.

¶**Daube Provençale.** Put beef cubes in a pottery or glass bowl with 1 bottle red wine, ½ cup wine vinegar, and about 12 grinds pepper. Marinate overnight. To cook, render 3 slices salt pork, cut in small dice, in a heavy braising pot until brown and crisp. Add 1 cup diced ham, 10 carrots, halved, 10 cloves garlic, 16 small white onions, 5 sliced leeks, 2 cloves, 1 bay leaf, 1 teaspoon thyme, 2 pieces orange rind, the beef cubes, marinade, and 1 tablespoon salt. Cover, bring to a simmer, then transfer to a 275° oven and cook 4 hours, adding more wine or beef broth if necessary to cover the beef. Remove pot from oven and strain sauce. Reduce over fairly high heat to 3 cups, stir in 1 cup tomato purée, pour sauce over beef and return to oven to cook for 35 minutes. Taste for seasoning. Serve with macaroni or rice.

¶**Daube Provençale with Tripe.** Substitute 1½ pounds tripe, cut in squares, for 1 pound of the beef.

¶**Daube Niçoise.** Rub 3 pounds beef shin or chuck (in one piece) and 2 pig's feet with coarse salt. Combine 6 cloves garlic; 1 sliced onion; a pinch each rosemary, thyme, and basil; 6 peppercorns; and 1 bottle red wine in a pan, bring to a boil, and cook 10 minutes. Cool slightly, pour over meat, and let stand 12 to 24 hours in refrigerator. Put meat and marinade in a heavy braising pan, bring slowly to a boil, reduce heat, and simmer very gently over lowest possible heat or in a 275° oven for 3½ hours, or until almost tender. Add 3 to 4 ripe tomatoes, peeled, seeded, and chopped, or 2 cups canned Italian plum tomatoes, drained and chopped, and cook 45 minutes. Remove meat and slice thick. Skim excess fat from sauce; remove meat from pig's feet and add to sauce. Replace sliced meat and cook 15 minutes; add 1 cup pitted soft black olives and ½ cup chopped parsley. Taste and correct seasoning.

Braised Short Ribs of Beef

Although short ribs have a lot of fat and bone, when braised their texture and flavor are quite delicious. Buy the leanest ribs you can and count on 1 pound per serving. As with other braised meats, they are best browned under the broiler, which draws out a lot of the fat. Served with noodles or potatoes, boiled or baked in their jackets, short ribs make a hearty and economical meal.

Makes 6 servings

6 pounds lean beef short ribs	2 tablespoons butter
1 teaspoon thyme	2 tablespoons oil
1 teaspoon crushed rosemary	2 medium-size onions, finely chopped
3 cloves garlic, finely chopped	4 carrots, peeled and halved
Salt, freshly ground black pepper	1 cup beef stock (see page 530)

Arrange the short ribs on their sides on a broiler rack and pan, and sprinkle with half the herbs and garlic. Broil 6 inches from the heat until brown and crisp, turn, sprinkle with the remaining herbs and garlic and brown on the second side. Sprinkle with salt and pepper.

Meanwhile, heat the butter and oil in a braising pan and sauté the chopped onion and the carrots. Drain the browned short ribs on paper towels, then add to the braising pan. Spoon 2 to 3 tablespoons of the drippings from the broiling pan over them and add the broth. Bring to a boil, cover tightly, reduce the heat, and simmer on top of the stove, or braise in a 300° oven, until the meat is very tender. This will take about

2 hours, depending on the quality of the meat. Skim fat from the pan juices and serve the meat with the vegetables and the juices.

¶**Braised Short Ribs with Onions.** After sautéing the onion and carrot, add 12 small white onions, cover, and cook over low heat until barely tender, then add the ribs and cook as before.

¶**Braised Short Ribs with Tomatoes.** Add 2 cups drained Italian plum tomatoes instead of broth and season highly with basil. Cook as before. Add chopped parsley.

¶**Braised Short Ribs with Chilies.** Proceed as for Braised Short Ribs with Tomatoes but add 1 4-ounce can peeled green chilies and 1 jalapeño pepper, all finely chopped. Proceed as before and serve with polenta (see page 300).

Chili con Carne

A famous dish, Texan by adoption, that probably arouses more heated controversy about the proper style of preparation than anything I know. Some chop the beef into cubes, others grind it. Some like tomatoes, others abhor them. Almost everyone agrees that a true chili con carne is without beans, although it is perfectly all right to serve kidney beans with the chili.

Makes 6 servings

4 tablespoons beef fat
2 large onions, chopped
½ pound beef kidney fat (suet),
    finely chopped
3 pounds top round or rump, cut into
    small dice or ground
2 cloves garlic

1 tablespoon salt
3 tablespoons chili powder, or more
    to taste
1 tablespoon cumin seeds
Dash of Tabasco
2 quarts beef broth, or boiling water
    mixed with bouillon cubes

Melt beef fat in a large skillet and sauté onions for 5 minutes until translucent. Add beef kidney fat. Let this cook slowly until the suet is all rendered and the onion practically melted into the fat. Add beef, garlic, and salt. Let the meat brown well and blend with the fat and the onion. Add chili powder, cumin, and Tabasco. Cover with boiling beef stock (or boiling water mixed with bouillon cubes). Simmer over low flame, covered, for about 2½ hours, stirring occasionally. Taste for seasoning—add more salt or chili powder if necessary. Serve in bowls with chopped onion, chopped cilantro (fresh coriander), and refried beans.

Beef and Pork Chili

A completely different chili, not the Texas type but something more akin to the Mexican mole, which also contains bitter chocolate. It's very rich and hearty and makes an excellent buffet dish. Black beans topped with sour cream are good with this.

Makes 6 to 8 servings

2 pounds beef chuck, cut into 1½-inch
    cubes
1½ pounds pork loin, cut into
    1½-inch cubes
Flour
2 large onions, chopped
3 tablespoons butter
3 tablespoons olive oil
5 cloves garlic, finely chopped
1 to 2 teaspoons salt

3 tablespoons chili powder, or more
    to taste
½ teaspoon oregano
½ teaspoon ground cumin
1 cup tomato purée (preferably
    homemade)
1 cup dry white wine
2 cups beef or chicken broth
2 tablespoons sesame seeds
½ ounce unsweetened chocolate

GARNISH: Chopped cilantro or Italian parsley

Dredge the meat lightly in flour. Sauté onion in butter and olive oil until golden. Add the chopped garlic and cook 3 or 4 minutes. Push the onion and garlic to one side of the pan and quickly sear the beef cubes. When browned, remove from the pan and brown the pork thoroughly. Return the beef to the pan and add salt, chili powder, oregano, cumin, tomato purée, wine, and broth. Cover and simmer, or cook in a 300° oven, for 1½ hours. Uncover and test the meat. If it is not tender, cook another 20 minutes, or until quite tender, then add the sesame seeds and unsweetened chocolate. Stir in well and simmer another 30 minutes. (The chocolate acts as a liaison that pulls the flavors together, and is a slight thickener.) Taste before serving and correct the salt and chili powder content. Garnish with cilantro or Italian parsley.

¶Chili with Olives. Add 18 pitted or chopped olives with the sesame seeds and chocolate.

¶Chili with Nuts. Add ¾ cup finely chopped toasted almonds or filberts and 3 to 4 chopped green chilies.

¶Chili with Beer. Substitute 1½ cups beer for the white wine. This gives a completely different flavor overtone.

Basic Sautéed Hamburgers

The all-American favorite, hamburger, is not to be scorned, provided the meat is good and properly cooked. Ground chuck and top round are the usual choices, but lately I have been experimenting with meat that has a minimum of fat and I find that flank steak, though expensive, is excellent for hamburger because of its delicate, tender texture. So is the similar and less costly skirt steak. If you have a food processor, you can grind the meat yourself to the degree of coarseness you prefer. I find that sautéing is a better cooking method than broiling. There is less chance the meat will dry out, and it is easy to make all kinds of little sauces for your hamburger with the pan juices. If you have a good fan system over your stove, you might use one of the ridged iron pans that sauté without fat—this method creates a lot of smoke but does an excellent job.

Makes 4 servings

2 pounds ground top round, top sirloin, or other beef with 20 to 25 percent fat
Salt, freshly ground black pepper

2 tablespoons peanut oil, or 1 tablespoon oil and 1 tablespoon butter

Divide the meat in 4 and season to taste with salt and pepper. Gently form into patties—round or oval, thick or fairly flat—according to choice. Heat the fat in a heavy skillet until hot but not smoking. Add the patties and cook over fairly high heat for about 4 minutes a side. Reduce heat and continue cooking until done as you like them, about 2 minutes a side for rare, longer for medium.

¶Hamburgers au Poivre. Season meat with salt only. Press coarsely crushed or ground black peppercorns into the surface and sauté. Rinse the pan with ⅓ cup cognac or ½ cup dry vermouth and pour over the patties.

¶Hamburgers with Onions. Steam 4 large sliced onions in 4 tablespoons butter or beef fat in a covered skillet until soft and lightly browned. Heap on top of the sautéed patties.

¶Hamburgers with Cheese. Mix the ground beef with 1 cup grated sharp Cheddar or Gruyère cheese or crumbled blue cheese, 1 teaspoon salt, 2 finely chopped garlic cloves, 2 tablespoons Worcestershire sauce, and a dash or two of Tabasco. Form into patties and sauté.

¶Hamburgers with Garlic and Pine Nuts. Mix the beef with salt and pepper to taste, ½ cup pine nuts, and 2 finely chopped garlic cloves. Form into patties and sauté. Serve on slices of sautéed or broiled eggplant, and top with tomato slices.

¶Hamburgers with Eggplant. Serve the patties sandwich style between slices of lightly sautéed or broiled eggplant, topped with tomato sauce.

¶Hamburgers with Onion and Cream. Mix 3 tablespoons grated onion and 2 tablespoons heavy cream with the beef; add salt and pepper to taste. Sauté. Serve with sautéed potatoes and a tomato and onion salad.

¶Hamburgers with Herbs. Mix the beef with salt, pepper, 1 teaspoon tarragon, and 3 tablespoons each chopped parsley and chopped chives. Sauté patties, remove from pan, and add 3 tablespoons butter and ½ cup dry white wine or vermouth. Bring to a boil, add 1 tablespoon chopped fresh tarragon, and pour over patties.

¶Hamburgers with Chili. Form the seasoned beef into 6-ounce patties; sauté. Serve in split, toasted, and buttered buns. Cover patty with chili (made with ground meat) and chopped raw onions.

¶Hamburgers with Red Wine. Sauté patties. Remove to a platter. Pour into pan 1 cup red wine and stir to deglaze; reduce by rapid boiling, or thicken with beurre manié (see page 536). Pour sauce over meat.

¶Hamburgers Flambé. Sauté patties, remove to a heatproof platter, top with a dab of rosemary butter (see page 537), and flambé with ½ cup heated cognac.

NOTE: Any of these may be served on toasted buns, French bread, or English muffins, or in heated, split pita bread. Pickles, olives, French fries, or homemade potato chips go well.

Old-Fashioned Meat Loaf

To my mind the most delicious meat loaves are made with a combination of ground beef, veal, and pork. The veal adds a gelatinous quality and the pork richness and fat, which keep the meat loaf juicy. (If you have a food processor, you can grind the meats yourself.) This simple recipe can be varied to taste by using different seasonings and combinations of ingredients. It should not be baked in a loaf pan, incidentally. A meat loaf if molded and baked free form on a bed of bacon or salt pork sheds excess fat and makes a more firmly textured loaf, whereas, if baked in a loaf pan, it becomes much too moist and is sometimes not easily sliced. Hot meat loaf may be served with rice or mashed potatoes and a good homemade tomato sauce, brown sauce with mushrooms, or onion sauce. Cold meat loaf is good with a potato or rice salad (see pages 93–96), some pickles and relishes, or just a sharp horseradish sauce.

Makes 6 to 8 servings

2 pounds beef (top round, chuck, or rump), ground twice
1 pound pork shoulder, ground twice
1 pound veal shoulder, ground twice
1 large onion, grated
2 carrots, finely shredded
4 to 6 garlic cloves, finely chopped
2 teaspoons salt
2 teaspoons Dijon mustard

1 teaspoon freshly ground black pepper
1 teaspoon crushed rosemary
¼ teaspoon nutmeg
½ teaspoon Tabasco
3 eggs, slightly beaten
¾ cup fresh bread crumbs soaked in ½ cup cream
12 strips bacon or salt pork

Combine the meats, grated onion and carrot, and seasonings and blend well. Mix in the eggs and soaked crumbs, combining thoroughly. Make a bed of bacon or salt pork strips in a shallow baking pan, reserving 4 or 5 for the top of the loaf. Form the meat mixture into a firm loaf with your hands and place it on the bed of bacon or salt pork. Put remaining strips across the top.

Bake in a 350° oven for 1½ to 2 hours, depending on how thick you have made the loaf, and baste several times with the pan juices. If you want to serve the meat loaf cold, wrap it tightly in foil and weight it as it cools, until firm. It will taste rather like a French country pâté.

¶Meat Loaf with Ham. Use 1 pound ham in place of the pork—or use ½ pound pork and ½ pound ham—and reduce the salt to 1 teaspoon.

¶Meat Loaf with Beef Liver. Use 1 pound ground beef or pork liver in place of 1 pound of beef. Baste with the pan juices and red wine.

¶Meat Loaf with Minced Clams. Add a 7-ounce can of minced clams to the basic mixture.

¶Meat Loaf with Olives. Combine the ground meats with 4 garlic cloves ground with 1 large onion, 1 cup whole stuffed olives, ½ cup tomato paste, 2 teaspoons basil, 2 teaspoons salt, 1½ teaspoons pepper, ½ cup chopped parsley, 3 eggs, and 1 cup bread crumbs soaked in red wine. Form and bake as before, basting with red wine and pan juices.

¶Meat Loaf with Hard-Boiled Eggs. When forming the loaf, put a line of 4 whole hard-boiled eggs in the middle.

¶**Chilied Meat Loaf.** Add 2 tablespoons chili powder and 4 finely chopped canned peeled green chilies to the meat mixture.

Lamb

People who think they don't like lamb aren't talking about the same delicious meat as I am. What they mean, it always turns out, is the traditional, terrible, tallowy-tasting haunch of dry, grayish, animal matter, trimmed all wrong, roasted for hours, and served up with the final insult of a sweet mint sauce or jelly.

With understanding comes appreciation. Nowadays, butchers usually trim off the fell and some of the fat, but you should go further. Trim the fat to an absolute minimum, leaving just a few streaks here and there for lubrication, and you'll get rid of the tallowy taste and produce a good crusty exterior on your roast. Except for one classic French dish, the "spoon leg," which is first roasted, then braised for hours to a melting softness, roast lamb is best enjoyed a bit underdone, nice and pink inside, especially the expensive cuts like leg and rack.

Speaking of roasting, I've included one recipe for mutton: the roast saddle, which is the glory of English cooking. Lamb becomes yearling when the animal reaches one year of age; after that it becomes mutton—the meat darker in color, richer in flavor, with more fat. It's not always easy to get, and it is not usually cheaper than lamb.

Lamb chops are not discussed here, since *Theory & Practice* goes deeply into the subject. After the roasts, my recipes are for the less expensive cuts, best suited to stews. Since these are not so easy to trim as roasting cuts, I usually make the dish the day before, cool it overnight, then remove the congealed fat from the top before reheating and serving. If you don't have time to do this, at least let the stew stand until the fat rises to the surface and skim off as much as possible, blotting up what is left with paper towels.

Roast Rack of Lamb

The rack of lamb has come into increasing favor in restaurants, and now people are beginning to appreciate its utter simplicity of preparation in their own homes. The rack consists of one side of the ribs. In young lamb, or baby lamb, when the ribs have been well trimmed, all excess fat removed, and the fat scraped from the bones (or, in the butcher's term, "frenched"), the rack will consist of 6 to 7 delicate small chops, a perfect piece of meat for 2 people.

Ask the butcher to cut through the chine bone so that you can carve right through the chops without having to struggle with the bones. If you want to put little paper frills on the rib ends after the rack is cooked, protect the bone ends by twisting pieces of aluminum foil around each one before roasting. A rack of lamb should always be roasted at a high temperature and served rare.

Makes 2 to 3 servings

1 rack of lamb, 6 to 7 chops, trimmed
of all but about ⅓ inch of fat,
with the bones "frenched"
1 clove garlic, peeled and crushed

1 teaspoon dried rosemary or thyme,
crushed in a mortar
Salt, freshly ground black pepper

Preheat the oven to 450°. Rub the rack of lamb well with the garlic and rosemary or thyme. Twist pieces of aluminum foil around the bone ends.

Put the roast, fat side down, on a rack in a roasting pan. Roast at 450° for 15 minutes, then turn it over so the bone side is down. Reduce the heat to 400° and roast 5 minutes more. Test the meat by pressing it lightly with your fingers, protecting them with paper towels. The meat should feel firmly springy to the touch. If it seems to need more cooking time, return to the oven for a further 5 to 7 minutes. It should take 20 to 27 minutes for rare lamb. The internal temperature, tested with a meat thermometer, should be 125° to 130°.

Remove the cooked meat to a carving board; substitute paper frills for the foil (if you like to gnaw the little bones, this prevents your fingers from getting greasy). Let it stand 3 minutes, then carve. There are two ways to carve rack of lamb. The more usual is to separate the chops by cutting between the bones and serving 2 or 3 chops to each person, according to appetite. The other way is to carve the meat in long, thin slices parallel to the bone. If you serve the rack that way, serve each person 1 or 2 of the tiny bones to gnaw on. A nice contrasting accompaniment to rack of lamb would be broiled tomatoes (providing you can get firm, ripe tomatoes; see page 183) or baked cherry tomatoes, and broiled or sautéed mushrooms (see page 154).

¶**Rack of Lamb Persillé.** While the lamb is roasting, melt 4 tablespoons butter in a skillet until hot and foaming. Add 1 cup fine fresh bread crumbs and toss until lightly browned. Remove from heat and combine with ½ cup chopped parsley. After taking lamb from the oven, turn off oven and preheat broiler. Press crumb mixture firmly over the fleshy top of the lamb. Put the lamb, crumb side up, under the hot broiler, about 4 inches from the heat, just until crust is lightly browned.

¶**Rack of Lamb Quo Vadis.** Trim rack of lamb, wrap ends of bones with foil. Rub meat with butter, sprinkle with freshly ground black pepper. Spread the bottom of a shallow roasting pan with 2 small carrots and 1 medium onion, all finely chopped. Dot with 1 tablespoon butter and lay lamb, fat side down, on vegetables. Roast at 500° for 10 minutes, reduce heat to 400°, turn lamb over, and add ½ cup lamb or chicken stock to pan. Roast 10 to 15 minutes, then press bread crumbs and parsley into the fat side of lamb, as in preceding variation, and put under a hot broiler until lightly browned. Transfer to a hot platter. Add another ½ cup lamb or chicken stock to pan, heat through, then purée the mixture in a blender or food processor, correct seasoning, and serve as a sauce with the lamb.

Crown Roast of Lamb

Makes 6 to 8 servings

A crown roast of lamb, 2 or 3 racks sewn together in a crown shape, makes a very attractive roast. Allow 2 chops per serving. Rub the roast well with salt, freshly ground black pepper, and tarragon, cover the rib ends with foil to prevent them from charring, and put a thick cushion of foil in the center to hold the shape.

Place the crown on a rack in a 325° oven, allowing 13 to 15 minutes per pound for pink lamb. Because of the shape of the crown roast, it is difficult to test the internal temperature with a meat thermometer, so one must use one's judgment.

Remove roast from the oven, take the foil from the rib ends (replacing them with paper frills, if desired) and take the cushion of foil from the center. Fill the center with a combination of tiny green peas and tiny white onions, cooked together and well buttered. Sprinkle with chopped parsley.

Cut the roast into chops and serve with the filling, anchovy flavored hollandaise sauce or Béarnaise sauce (see page 532), and a salad of Bibb lettuce tossed with diced cooked beets or julienne slices of cooked beet.

¶**Variations.** Fill the center of the roast with any one of the following complementary mixtures:

Rice pilaf mixed with finely sliced, sautéed lamb kidneys.

A pilaf of cracked wheat blended with pine nuts.

Sautéed mushroom caps sprinkled with chopped tarragon, parsley, and chives.

A purée of chestnuts, with braised whole chestnuts as a garnish.

Roast Leg of Lamb, Provençal Style

Few roasts are as delicious as a properly cooked leg of lamb, which should be rare or pink, never medium or, perish the thought, well done. Over-cooked lamb is about as palatable as a piece of chewed string. Lamb is another meat that lends itself to all kinds of flavor variations—with garlic in the forefront. In this Provençal version, anchovies supplement the garlic, adding an interesting salty accent. Traditional accompaniments are cooked white beans, blended with the pan juices and a bit of peeled, seeded, and chopped tomato, or ratatouille (see page 190).

If you have a well-insulated oven—preferably self-cleaning—you may roast the lamb at a high temperature (425° to 450°) until the meat reaches 125° to 130° on the meat thermometer. Or you may start the lamb at high temperature and reduce the heat to 350° after 25 minutes.

Makes 8 or more servings

5- to 6-pound leg of lamb	*1 to 2 tablespoons oil*
6 cloves garlic, peeled and cut in slivers	*Crumbled rosemary*
8 anchovy fillets, halved	*Salt, freshly ground black pepper*

Remove the fell (papery tissue covering the fat) and most of the fat from the leg. Make incisions in the meat with a sharp paring knife and insert the garlic slivers and pieces of anchovy. Rub the meat with oil, rosemary, salt (sparingly, as the anchovies are salty) and pepper. Put on a rack in a shallow roasting pan and roast in a 350° oven for about 1½ hours, until the internal temperature registers 125° to 130° (for pink) on a meat thermometer. As legs vary in thickness, test after 1 hour to see how much more cooking time it will need, then recheck after 15 minutes. When the lamb is cooked, remove to a hot platter and allow to stand for 10 to 15 minutes before carving.

¶**Roast Leg of Lamb Provençal No. 2.** Stud the leg with garlic, anchovies, and pistachio nuts. Rub with summer savory or thyme, salt, and pepper, and roast.

¶**Roast Leg of Lamb with Shallots.** Insert slivers of shallot instead of garlic. Rub with summer savory, salt, and pepper.

¶**Swedish Leg of Lamb.** Rub with salt, pepper, and thyme. Roast for ½ hour, then baste lamb with 1 breakfast cup hot coffee with cream and sugar. Baste occasionally with coffee until done. Skim fat from coffee-flavored pan juices, correct seasoning, and serve with the lamb.

¶**Weeping Leg of Lamb.** Stud lamb with slivers of garlic and rub with salt, pepper, and rosemary. Arrange layers of sliced potatoes in a heavily buttered baking dish that is slightly larger than the lamb, sprinkling the layers with salt and pepper and dotting them with butter. After the second layer of potatoes, put in a layer of thinly sliced onion. Pour in 1 cup beef stock (see page 530). Put the dish on the lower rack of the oven with the lamb on the rack directly above it, or arrange the lamb on the potatoes. Roast until lamb is done and potatoes tender and browned. If potatoes are done first, remove and keep warm, transferring lamb to a baking sheet. Reheat potatoes for 10 minutes in the oven while the lamb rests before being carved. If you wish, sprinkle potatoes with ½ cup grated Gruyère or Parmesan cheese and leave in oven until cheese melts.

¶**Weeping Leg of Lamb with Anchovies.** Stud with garlic and anchovies, and add 12 to 14 anchovy fillets to the potatoes. Omit salt from seasoning for lamb and potatoes.

¶**Mock Venison.** Stud lamb with garlic. Marinate in a deep bowl in a mixture of ½ cup olive oil, 2 cups red wine, 2 thickly sliced onions, 1 sliced carrot, 2 teaspoons thyme, 2 teaspoons salt, 2 sprigs parsley, and ¼ teaspoon allspice. Leave in marinade at least 24 hours, turning frequently, then remove, dry, and roast in a 400° oven, basting every 20 minutes with the heated marinade, until the internal temperature is 130° to 135°. Remove meat to a hot platter. Add 1 cup marinade to the pan juices, bring to a boil, and boil until reduced by one-third. Strain, season, and serve with the lamb.

Spoon Leg of Lamb

One of the most famous of the lamb dishes in the French repertoire is *gigot de sept heures*, or boned leg of lamb slowly cooked for 7 hours until it is so soft and tender it can almost be served with a spoon—from which comes its Anglicized name, Spoon Leg of Lamb. This is one case where leg of lamb is not served rare—far from it.

5- to 6-pound leg of lamb, boned and
  tied (ask for the bones and have
  them sawed into short pieces)
Salt, freshly ground black pepper
3 medium-size onions, each stuck with
  2 cloves
3 carrots, split lengthwise
6 or 7 cloves garlic

½ cup olive oil
1 teaspoon dried thyme
1 bay leaf
1 sprig parsley
4 or 5 ripe tomatoes, peeled, seeded,
  and coarsely chopped
1 cup red wine
GARNISH: *Chopped parsley*

Rub the leg with salt and pepper and arrange on a rack in a roasting pan. Surround with the bones, onions, carrots, and 4 or 5 garlic cloves. Pour the oil over the bones and vegetables and roast the lamb in a 400° oven for 30 minutes, then reduce the heat to 350°, and roast 30 minutes more. Reduce the oven heat to 200°.

Transfer the lamb to a braising pan or casserole and add the remaining 2 garlic cloves, 1 teaspoon each of salt and pepper, the thyme, bay leaf, parsley, tomatoes, and the bones and vegetables from the roasting pan. Rinse the pan with red wine; pour over the lamb. Cover the pan tightly and cook in a 200° oven for 6 hours, by which time the meat should be meltingly tender. Transfer it to a hot platter and remove the strings. Discard bones and bay leaf, and skim excess fat from the pan juices. Remove cloves from the onions, and purée or blend all the vegetables. Combine with the pan juices; sprinkle the sauce with chopped parsley. Serve the meat with sauce and cooked white beans, seasoned with salt, pepper, a touch of garlic, and a little basil. Spoon some of the sauce over them before serving and sprinkle with parsley.

Lamb on a String
(Lamb à la Ficelle)

This is a variation on the classic Beef à la Ficelle (Beef on a String), made with a boned leg of lamb. (Unless you are very skilled at boning, ask the butcher to do it for you.) In this case, you need a rather spicier broth, to flavor the lamb and then to make the anchovy sauce that goes with it. Serve with boiled potatoes and zucchini sautéed with garlic.

5-pound leg of lamb, boned and tied
  (use bones for the stock)

5 cloves garlic, peeled
1 bay leaf

1 tablespoon dried tarragon
4 tablespoons freshly ground black
    pepper or more

3 dried red peppers
2 tablespoons salt

ANCHOVY SAUCE

1 clove garlic, peeled and finely chopped
12 anchovy fillets, drained and finely
    chopped
12 black Italian or Greek olives,
    pitted and chopped
1 or 2 small fresh hot peppers, finely
    chopped

2 tablespoons olive oil
1 teaspoon lemon juice
1 teaspoon grated lemon rind
½ cup broth from the lamb

First, make a note of the boned weight of the lamb, to estimate cooking time. Cut 1 garlic clove into slivers, make deep incisions in the lamb with the point of a paring knife, and push in the garlic. Roll the lamb in a linen towel and tie it securely lengthwise and crosswise, leaving long pieces of string at both ends.

In a deep 8-quart pan, put enough water to cover the lamb, with the lamb bones, 4 crushed garlic cloves, and the seasonings. Bring to a boil and simmer, covered, for 1 hour over medium heat. Remove cover and tie the ends of string to the handles of the pan, as for Beef à la Ficelle (see page 369). Bring the broth to a boil once more, then reduce the heat, and cook the lamb at a simmer, covered, allowing approximately 15 minutes per pound boned weight for rare lamb—which this must be. Check the internal temperature with a meat thermometer after 30 minutes, and if the temperature is near 135°, watch carefully to prevent overcooking.

When the lamb reaches 135°, remove it from the broth, take off the string and cloth and let it rest on a hot platter for 10 minutes before slicing. Meanwhile, make the sauce. Combine all the ingredients and cook, stirring, over medium heat, until smooth and heated through. Correct the seasoning. It should be very hot and spicy, with a pronounced anchovy flavor. If it isn't hot enough for your taste, add a dash of Tabasco.

Carve the meat in thickish slices and serve with the sauce. A gratin of potatoes (see page 169) is excellent, for it absorbs the delicious sauce.

Roast Shoulder of Lamb

Lamb shoulder is not as much appreciated in this country as it might be. In France, when the young lamb is in, you can find in the markets tiny shoulders which, when boned and tied securely and simply roasted, make a delicious dinner for two or three people. Here, where they may be bought boned and rolled—much heavier, to be sure—shoulders are treated with a certain neglect. In my opinion shoulder of young spring lamb is as thoroughly good and tender as the leg, but it must be young.

Serve with steamed new potatoes, the pan juices, and tiny new peas in butter sprinkled with finely minced shallots and parsley.

Makes 6 to 8 servings

Shoulder of young lamb, boned, about 3 to 4 pounds after boning and trimming
2 to 3 cloves garlic, cut into thin slivers (optional)

3 teaspoons dried tarragon, crushed
½ pound unsalted butter
½ cup dry white wine or dry vermouth
Salt, freshly ground black pepper
GARNISH: *Watercress*

Trim the shoulder of lamb well of fat, roll it compactly, and tie it. If you wish, pierce the lamb with the tip of a knife and insert slivers of garlic, then rub with 1 teaspoon tarragon.

Put lamb on a rack in a shallow roasting pan and roast in a 425° oven for 30 minutes. Reduce heat to 350° and continue cooking for 40 to 50 minutes more. Melt the butter, combine with the wine or vermouth and remaining 2 teaspoons tarragon and baste lamb with this mixture every 12 to 15 minutes. When the internal temperature reaches 130° (test by inserting meat thermometer into the thickest part), sprinkle well with salt and pepper, transfer to a hot platter, and leave for 10 minutes in a warm place. Remove the strings that tie the roast, slice, and garnish with watercress.

¶**Roast Lamb with Cream.** After roasting the lamb, skim the excess fat from the pan juices and add 1 cup heavy cream, blend well, and cook down for a minute or two to reduce the sauce slightly. Serve the lamb with this sauce, braised lettuce, and potatoes Anna.

¶**Roast Lamb with Eggplant and Tomato.** After inserting garlic, rub the shoulder with olive oil, salt, and pepper. Roast for 20 minutes, then add to the pan 1 finely cut garlic clove, 2 cups diced eggplant, 2 thinly sliced medium-size onions, 2 cups peeled, seeded, and chopped tomato or tomato purée, and 1 cup red wine. Roast as before, basting with the liquid every 15 minutes. A few minutes before the roast is done, add 1 cup ripe olives to the pan. Remove the lamb to a hot platter and surround with the vegetable mixture, sprinkled lavishly with chopped parsley. Serve with a rice pilaf (see page 290), an endive salad, and crisp French bread or rolls to mop up the juices.

Braised Stuffed Lamb Breast

Breast of lamb is a cut that braises very well. Most recipes require a pocket to be cut in the breast for stuffing, but in this case the stuffing is put between two breasts, which are then tied together. Breast of lamb is economical if not too fatty. If the lamb seems very fatty, pre-roast it on a rack in a shallow roasting pan in a 400° oven for 20 minutes to render some of the fat. I buy the leanest I can find. Because of the many bones, allow 1 pound lamb breast per serving.

Makes 6 servings

2 three-pound lamb breasts, of identical
    size and shape
6 tablespoons butter
½ cup finely chopped shallots
3 cloves garlic, finely chopped
2 teaspoons dried tarragon
¾ cup dried currants, soaked until
    plump in Madeira to barely cover

5 cups fresh bread crumbs
Salt, freshly ground black pepper
6 tablespoons vegetable oil
3 carrots, peeled and sliced
2 onions, peeled and sliced
1 rib celery, sliced
2 cups red wine
Beurre manié (optional; see page 536)

When you buy the lamb breasts, have the end bones removed. You may either have the rib bones removed as well or leave them intact.

Prepare a stuffing for the breasts. Melt the butter in a skillet; add the shallots and garlic and sauté until just limp. Remove from the heat and mix in the tarragon, currants, bread crumbs, 1½ teaspoons salt, and ½ teaspoon pepper. Mix well together and add more melted butter if the stuffing seems too dry—it should not be sloppy, but have a moist yet firm quality.

Lay one breast flat and put the stuffing on it—don't put stuffing too near the edges or it will ooze out during cooking. Put the other breast on top and tie them securely together with fine string both crosswise and lengthwise.

Heat the oil in a heavy skillet large enough to hold the breasts, add the stuffed breasts and brown thoroughly on both sides over medium-high heat, being careful not to let them burn.

Arrange the carrot, onion, and celery in the bottom of a braising pan. Put the lamb on top and sprinkle well with salt. Pour in the red wine, cover, and cook in a 325° oven for 2 hours. Test the lamb for tenderness. If tender, remove to a hot platter and keep warm. Skim excess fat from the sauce in the pan and then strain sauce through a fine sieve. Thicken, if you wish, with beurre manié, taste, and correct the seasoning.

To serve, remove the strings from the breasts and cut the breasts into serving pieces, slicing down between the ribs so you serve 2 pieces of meat with stuffing in between. (If the ribs were removed, slice ¾ inch to 1 inch thick.) Spoon some of the sauce over each serving.

Lamb en Daube

This version of daube is one of the most famous dishes around the Rhône district of Avignon and Arles. Ideally, it should be made a day in advance and allowed to cool thoroughly. The fat may then be easily removed before the daube is reheated. Plain boiled potatoes with a sprinkling of parsley or mint seem to be the most successful accompaniment. A crisp, tart salad could follow it quite satisfactorily, and you might drink a Châteauneuf du Pape.

Makes 6 to 8 servings

Leg of lamb, boned
1 onion stuck with 2 cloves
2 sprigs parsley
8 cloves garlic
Salt
Strips of larding pork, soaked in cognac
    and rolled in chopped parsley
2 onions, sliced
1 carrot, sliced

¼ cup olive oil
1 teaspoon thyme
1 bay leaf
Red wine
6 large onions, coarsely chopped
1 pig's foot, split in two
3 to 4 slices salt pork, diced
1 piece orange rind

Save the bones from the lamb and ask the butcher for a couple of more lamb bones. Place the bones in a pot with the onion stuck with cloves, 1 parsley sprig, and 2 garlic cloves. Add 2 quarts water and cook down to a good broth. Season with salt to taste. Strain and chill. Next day remove the fat from the top.

Cut the lamb in good-size pieces. Lard each piece with a portion of the larding pork. Combine the sliced onion and carrot, olive oil, thyme, bay leaf, remaining parsley, 3 crushed garlic cloves, and red wine almost to cover. Marinate the lamb for several hours or overnight in this marinade.

Make a bed of half the chopped onion in a deep casserole. Add half the pig's foot, then half the marinated meat, the remaining onion, the salt pork, the remaining meat and the rest of the pig's foot. Add the orange rind. Strain the marinade and add along with the seasonings, onion, carrot, and garlic from it, and the remaining 3 garlic cloves. Add enough of the lamb broth to cover. Put aluminum foil over the casserole, cover tightly with the lid and cook very slowly on top of the stove or in a 275° oven for 3½ to 4 hours. Remove the meat and pig's foot, skim off excess fat from the sauce, and reduce it for a few minutes over high heat. Cut the meat from the pig's foot and add it to the sauce. Arrange the lamb in a deep serving dish and pour the sauce over it.

Navarin
(French Lamb Ragout)

This is very different from the usual pedestrian American lamb stew, but economical because it uses the flavorful, cheaper bony cuts. I prefer to brown the meat under the broiler, rather than in butter, the customary way. Broiling draws out a lot of the fat and the ragout has a better flavor.

Makes 6 servings

4½ to 5 pounds lean shoulder or
    breast of lamb
Salt, freshly ground black pepper
2 to 3 cups beef broth (see page 530)
    or water
12 small white turnips, peeled and
    halved
12 small white onions, peeled

4 tablespoons butter
2 tablespoons sugar
2 garlic cloves
4 carrots, peeled and cut in strips
1 or 2 leeks, well washed and trimmed
12 small new potatoes, unpeeled
1 package frozen peas

Cut the meat in serving-size pieces. Put on the broiler rack and brown on all sides under a preheated broiler. As meat browns, remove it to a 6-quart braising pan or heatproof casserole, sprinkle with salt and pepper to taste, and add enough broth or water to half cover the meat. Cover and simmer gently for 45 minutes. Meanwhile, brown the turnips and onions in the butter in a sauté pan, then turn the heat down and let them cook gently, shaking the pan from time to time so they cook evenly and sprinkling them with the sugar so they get a nice glaze.

Skim as much fat as possible from the liquid in which the meat was cooked, and then strain the liquid into a bowl through a sieve lined with a piece of linen toweling wrung out in cold water, which will trap any remaining fat and scum from the liquid. Return the strained broth to the pan or casserole containing the meat and add the turnips, onions, garlic, carrots, leeks, and potatoes. Add more broth, if there is not enough liquid to cook the vegetables. Cover and cook in a 350° oven for 1 hour. Add the frozen peas 10 minutes before the end of the cooking time. The broth should have reduced in the oven. If you wish it thicker, strain off the broth and either thicken with beurre manié (see page 536) or reduce by rapid boiling to the desired consistency. Return to the pan and serve.

Blanquette of Lamb

Just about everyone knows blanquette of veal, the white stew thickened with béchamel sauce, cream, and egg yolks, but I prefer the less familiar version made with lamb, which has a gutsier flavor and texture. There have always been two methods of preparation for blanquettes—the straight poaching method and the one in which the meat is first seared and then simmered. I find the second method superior, and I like to brown the lamb under the broiler rather than in fat. When you have the lamb shoulder boned, ask for the bones to make stock. Rice or orzo (rice-shaped pasta) goes well with this blanquette.

Makes 6 to 8 servings

5- to 6-pound shoulder of lamb, boned
    and cut into 1½-inch pieces
    (Note: Lamb shoulder has such
    great bone content, it's not too
    much.)

1 to 1½ pounds lamb neck, boned
    and cut into smallish pieces

STOCK

Bones from the shoulder
1 veal knuckle plus bones from the
    lamb neck
1 onion stuck with 2 cloves

1 quart water
1 teaspoon salt
1 teaspoon rosemary
2 cloves garlic

THE STEW

1 teaspoon rosemary
Salt, freshly ground black pepper
2 cloves garlic, finely chopped
1 cup Madeira
8 tablespoons butter
12 small white onions

1 teaspoon sugar
12 mushroom caps
Juice of 1 lemon
5 tablespoons flour
½ cup heavy cream
2 egg yolks

GARNISH: Chopped parsley

Put the lamb bones and veal knuckle and lamb neck on the rack of the broiler pan and brown under the broiler for 10 to 15 minutes, turning once or twice, or roast in a 450° oven for 15 minutes. Put the browned bones in a large pot with the onion, 1 quart water, salt, rosemary, and garlic. Bring to a boil, skim off any scum, reduce heat, and simmer for 1½ to 2 hours. Strain the broth and discard the bones, onion, and garlic. Cool broth until the fat rises to the top and can be removed. Measure out 2 cups of the broth.

Arrange the lamb pieces on the broiling rack, sprinkle lightly with rosemary, salt, pepper, and chopped garlic. Brown under the broiler, turning the pieces once or twice, until nicely colored and slightly crispy at the edges. Remove to a large sauté pan, add the Madeira, and simmer, covered, for 45 minutes.

Meanwhile, heat 4 tablespoons butter in a skillet and brown the onions on all sides, sprinkling them with the sugar so they caramelize a little. Add ½ cup of the cooled lamb broth, cover and simmer until tender. Add the mushroom caps and lemon juice for the last 5 minutes.

Melt the remaining 4 tablespoons butter in a saucepan, stir in the flour and cook until golden and frothy, stirring constantly, then mix in the 1½ cups lamb broth, and cook, stirring, until smooth and thickened. When the lamb is tender, pour off the liquid in the pan, add to the sauce, and simmer for 10 minutes. Correct the seasoning. Combine the cream with the beaten egg yolks, add some of the hot sauce, then stir into the remainder of the sauce, and cook gently until thickened; do not let it boil or the sauce will curdle.

Arrange the lamb on a serving dish with the onions and mushrooms and pour the sauce over everything. Garnish with chopped parsley.

¶**Blanquette of Veal.** Substitute boned veal shoulder for the lamb. Use the veal bones and veal knuckle for the broth. Sear veal under the broiler. Put in a pan with water to cover, 1½ teaspoons salt, ½ teaspoon freshly ground black pepper, 1 carrot, 1 onion stuck with 2 cloves. Simmer covered until tender but not stringy, about 1 to 1¼ hours. Omit the Madeira and use the veal broth for the sauce.

Kadjemoula

This North African dish of braised lamb and beef, with its typical blend of meat, spices, and dried fruits, is a wonderful buffet dish. Serve it with steamed rice or burghul (cracked wheat) and a lightly chilled young red wine or rosé wine.

Makes 6 to 8 servings

*2 pounds lamb shoulder, cut into
    1½-inch cubes
2 pounds beef chuck, cut into
    1½-inch cubes
½ cup flour
2 tablespoons butter
2 tablespoons olive oil
1 teaspoon salt
¼ teaspoon ground cinnamon
¼ teaspoon ground ginger*

*½ teaspoon freshly ground black pepper
2 medium-size onions, peeled and
    sliced
4 carrots, peeled and quartered
2 medium-size turnips, peeled and diced
3 cloves garlic, peeled and chopped
⅔ cup dried apricots
⅔ cup dried pitted prunes
3 to 4 cups beef broth (see page 530)*

GARNISH: *Quince paste or quince preserves*

Trim all fat from the lamb and beef cubes and flour them lightly. Heat the butter and oil in a braising pan. Add the meat cubes, a few at a time, and brown them quickly on all sides over fairly high heat. Remove as cooked. Put all the browned meat back in the pan and sprinkle it with the salt, cinnamon, ginger, and pepper. Then add the vegetables and dried fruits, pour in enough broth to cover the meat, and bring to a boil. Lower the heat to a simmer; cover and simmer gently for 2 hours, or until tender. The vegetables and fruits should have blended into a thick sauce. Remove the stew to a hot platter and surround it with mounds of rice pilaf, couscous (see pages 290 and 298), or cracked wheat. Garnish the edges with slices of quince paste (available canned in specialty food shops) or with quince preserves.

Roast Saddle of Mutton

If you have a butcher who can order a well-aged saddle of mutton for you, it makes a roast appropriate for the most elegant of dinners. The fat should be trimmed to a minimum, the remainder nicely scored. Serve with a purée of potatoes and rutabagas (see page 186), Béarnaise sauce and a bowl of watercress, without dressing.

Makes 6 to 8 servings

*Saddle of mutton
Juice of 1 lemon
1 clove garlic, cut in half
1 teaspoon dried thyme
Salt, freshly ground black pepper
12 to 16 lamb kidneys, split in half
    lengthwise, cleaned, and core
    removed (soak in milk for an hour
    for better flavor)*

*6 tablespoons melted butter
Béarnaise sauce (see page 532)*

Rub both sides of the saddle with a little lemon juice, the garlic, and thyme. Put on a rack in a shallow roasting pan and roast in a 400° oven for 45 minutes, or until a meat thermometer inserted in the thickest part, but not touching the bone, registers 135° to 140°. Remove the saddle from the oven, sprinkle with salt and pepper, and let it stand in a warm place for 10 minutes.

While the saddle is resting, thread the kidneys on skewers, brush with melted butter, and broil 5 to 6 minutes, turning once.

Transfer saddle to a very hot platter. Garnish the roast with the broiled kidneys. Carve the saddle into long slices parallel to the backbone. Serve each person a long slice with a kidney and a spoonful of Béarnaise sauce.

When you have carved the first round, turn the saddle over and carve out the tenderloins. Serve each guest a small slice or two of tenderloin, with an additional dollop of Béarnaise.

Lamb Shanks with Beans

A part of the lamb that is often overlooked, the ends of the legs are wonderfully flavorful and take well to long, slow cooking. Combined with white beans they are excellent and economical eating. A salad of crisp greens tossed with grated carrot and chopped onion would go well with this substantial dish.

Makes 6 servings

2 cups Great Northern or pea beans
1 onion, stuck with 2 cloves
1 bay leaf
12 cloves garlic
Salt, freshly ground black pepper
6 meaty lamb shanks
2 teaspoons rosemary, crushed
5 tablespoons butter

6 tablespoons oil
1 cup red wine
1½ cups water or beef broth
   (see page 530)
2 large onions, thinly sliced
6 thick slices bacon
½ cup fresh bread crumbs

Put the beans in a saucepan with water to cover. Bring to a boil, boil 5 minutes, then remove pan from heat. Let the beans cool, covered, in the cooking water for 1 hour only—no longer or they will be too soft. Add more water to cover, if needed, plus the clove-stuck onion, bay leaf, 7 of the garlic cloves and 1 tablespoon salt. Bring to a boil, reduce heat, cover, and simmer until just tender to the bite—do not overcook or the resulting dish will be mushy.

While the beans are cooking, cut 2 garlic cloves into slivers, make incisions in the lamb shanks and stuff the garlic into them. Rub shanks with 1½ teaspoons rosemary and 1 teaspoon salt. Heat 3 tablespoons butter and 3 tablespoons oil in a deep heavy skillet or sauté pan. Brown the lamb shanks on all sides, turning with tongs and sprinkling with salt and pepper as they cook. Add the remaining rosemary and the wine and water or broth. Bring to a boil, reduce the heat, cover, and simmer for 1 hour.

Sauté the sliced onions in the remaining 3 tablespoons oil until lightly browned. Cover and cook over low heat until soft.

Drain the beans, reserving the liquid. Put a layer of half the beans in an 8-quart braising pan or casserole and top with a layer of the onions and the remaining garlic cloves, finely chopped. Put the lamb shanks on top, add the remaining beans and the broth from the pan in which the shanks cooked. If there is not enough liquid (there should be enough to cover the shanks), add some of the reserved bean liquid. Lay the bacon slices on top and cook in a 350° oven for 1 hour, adding more of the bean liquid if the mixture cooks down too much and the beans seem dry. Melt the remaining butter, toss the bread crumbs in it, and sprinkle them over the top of the dish. Bake 20 minutes longer, or until crumbs are golden. Serve from the pan or casserole.

¶**Lamb Shanks with Ratatouille.** Brown the shanks in butter and oil, add 1 bay leaf, ½ teaspoon rosemary or thyme, and 2½ cups beef broth. Cover and simmer 1 hour. Arrange ratatouille (see page 190) in a casserole, put the shanks on top, and pour the pan juices over them. Cover and bake in a 350° oven for 45 minutes, then remove cover and bake until meat is tender, about 30 minutes.

¶**Lamb Shanks with Onions and Beer.** Rub the lamb shanks all over with salt, pepper, and rosemary, and brown on all sides, either in butter and oil or under the broiler. Meanwhile, sauté 6 sliced large onions in 6 table-spoons butter until limp and golden. Season with salt and pepper to taste. Transfer to a heavy casserole, lay the lamb shanks on top, add 2 teaspoons thyme, 1 bay leaf, and 2½ cups beer. Cook, covered, in a 350° oven until the meat is tender, 2 to 2½ hours. If you wish, the sauce may be thickened with beurre manié (see page 536).

Veal

Top-quality veal has ivory-colored flesh, just barely flushed with pink, and a specially delicate, dense texture. For years it was almost unobtainable in this country; moreover, few butchers knew how to cut it properly. However, today veal is much in fashion despite the fact that it is wildly expensive.

Its price is not surprising. To produce pure white meat, farmers have had to resort to the "Dutch process," whereby calves are weaned very early and fed a scientifically designed diet, with no minerals or iron to color the meat. The feed costs a lot, and a good deal of expensive human attention is required for a period of 3 to 4 months. (The old-fashioned way was to leave the unweaned calf with the cow for 6 weeks, then butcher it; but the carcasses were too small for the growing market.)

You can get Dutch-process veal from selective butchers, or from mail-order businesses which ship it frozen; and it's what I choose for luxury dishes. But you can manage, even for scallops, with the pinker, premium veal (3 to 4 months old, brought up on a more or less normal diet), which is now quite regularly available, even in the supermarkets. However, don't buy scallops unless they have been cut correctly—and, alas, most places don't do this. Scallops must be deftly cut from a certain muscle in the leg—and this is what you should insist on.

And for a veal ragout, a veal Marengo, or other long-cooked dish, you can even use baby beef, from calves old enough to be called adolescent, up to 9 months old. It's quite pink, but the color doesn't matter too much since you cook the meat in a sauce, and for these dishes you don't need the ultimate in tenderness.

In other words, for any meat but for veal in particular, shop for a quality that is sufficient for the dish you plan and the method it requires.

Roast Veal

Roast Veal with Roquefort-Butter Stuffing

Although veal, a rather dry meat, is usually better braised than roasted, this recipe is an exception. The stuffing adds both moisture and a glorious flavor. Serve this with sautéed potatoes and baked apples.

CRÈME FRAÎCHE
1½ cups heavy cream

4 tablespoons buttermilk

Thin sheets of barding pork
3-pound boneless veal loin roast
¾ pound walnuts, finely chopped
1 cup plus 2 tablespoons unsalted butter
¾ pound Roquefort cheese

6 baking apples
6 tablespoons brown sugar
Vanilla
⅓ cup cognac
Salt, freshly ground black pepper

First, make the crème fraîche for the sauce ahead of time. Combine the cream and buttermilk in a screw-topped jar, cover, and shake steadily for 2 minutes, as if you were shaking a cocktail. Let the jar stand at room temperature for 8 hours or overnight, until the cream has thickened. Refrigerate until ready to use.

When you are ready to roast the meat, tie the barding pork around the veal. Arrange on a rack in a shallow roasting pan and roast in a 400° oven for 45 minutes. Make a paste of the walnuts, ¾ cup butter, and Roquefort cheese in a food processor or blender or by mashing well with a fork.

Core the baking apples. Fill the cavities with 1 tablespoon each butter and brown sugar, and a dash of vanilla.

After the veal has roasted for 45 minutes, reduce the oven heat to 325°. Remove the veal from the oven and cut it downward into thick slices, but not all the way through. Put the Roquefort butter between the slices and tie the roast back in shape lengthwise. Arrange the apples around the meat. Return to the oven and roast the meat 30 to 35 minutes longer. If necessary, continue baking apples until tender.

Remove the veal from the pan to a hot serving platter and take off the barding pork. Deglaze the pan with the cognac, then stir in the crème fraîche over medium-low heat, stirring until well blended. Taste and correct seasoning, adding salt and pepper as needed. Surround the veal with sautéed potatoes and the baked apples and serve the sauce separately.

Veal with Tuna Sauce
(Vitello Tonnato)

There are many ways of preparing this famous Italian specialty, one of the best hot-weather dishes I know. It bears a lovely piquant quality that arouses the appetite and pleases the nose. Some people slice cold roast veal and serve it with tuna mayonnaise, but I think it tastes better if the veal is braised and the sauce made with the pan juices. More time consuming, but worth the extra trouble. Serve with a rice salad or sliced tomatoes.

Makes 6 to 8 servings

3-pound veal leg or loin roast, boned
      and tied
3 cloves garlic, cut in thin slivers
6 anchovy fillets
1 teaspoon dried basil, or
      2 tablespoons fresh
5 to 6 tablespoons olive oil
3 onions, peeled and thinly sliced

1 carrot, scraped
1 leek, trimmed and washed clean
2 or 3 sprigs parsley
2 pig's feet or 1 veal knuckle, split
1½ cups dry white wine
1 cup water or veal stock
1 teaspoon freshly ground black pepper
½ teaspoon salt

TUNA SAUCE
1½ cups veal stock that has jellied
7-ounce can tuna

2 cloves garlic, crushed
4 anchovy fillets

GARNISH: *Capers, chopped parsley, chopped fresh basil*

Make incisions in the veal with the point of a sharp paring knife. Stuff the garlic slivers into the holes, then insert anchovy fillets, pushing them in very deeply with the garlic. Rub the meat with the dried basil and brown it on all sides in the oil in a deep 8-quart pot. Add the onions, carrot, leek, and parsley, and cook the vegetables a little in the oil. Then add the pig's feet, wine, water or stock, pepper, and salt. Bring the liquid to a boil, reduce the heat, cover, and simmer the meat on top of the stove or in a 300° oven for 1½ hours, or until tender when tested with a fork, but not soft and mushy. Remove the meat from the pan to a platter, cover with foil, and refrigerate overnight.

To make the sauce: Strain the pan juices into a bowl and chill overnight. Next day, skim the fat from the juices and put 1½ cups jellied juices into a blender or food processor with the tuna and its oil, crushed garlic cloves and anchovy fillets. Whirl until well blended and thick.

Remove the veal from the refrigerator and slice thin. Arrange on a platter and spoon the tuna sauce over it. Return to the refrigerator until ready to serve, so the veal absorbs the flavor of the sauce. To serve, garnish with capers, chopped parsley, and chopped basil.

¶**Veal with Tuna Sauce, Yogurt, and Mayonnaise.** Combine the tuna-anchovy purée with 1 cup each of yogurt and mayonnaise. Add additional capers and finely cut green onions. Spoon sauce over the veal and chill.

¶**Pork Loin Tonnato.** Use slices of cold roast loin of pork.

Sicilian Veal Roll

For a veal roll, *rollatine* in Italian or *roulade* in French, you need a cut from the leg—either a slice cut right across at the broadest point, with the bone in, or three slices cut across half the leg, each of which may be split in half almost to the edge and then folded back to make one long slice. In the first case, the bone is removed after cutting. In either case, the meat should be well pounded to flatten it to a thickness of about ¼ inch. Veal rolls may be served hot or cold and look extremely attractive when sliced, preferably on the diagonal. Green noodles with butter and freshly grated Parmesan cheese are good with this Sicilian version of a veal roll.

Makes 8 servings

3 to 4 veal cutlets, sliced very thin
    across the leg, with bone
¼ pound thinly sliced prosciutto or
    Virginia ham
¼ pound thinly sliced mortadella or
    a good bologna
¼ pound thinly sliced Genoa soft
    salami
⅓ cup fine fresh bread crumbs
4 cloves garlic, minced

2 tablespoons chopped parsley
2 tablespoons chopped fresh basil or
    2 teaspoons dried basil
Salt, freshly ground black pepper
5 or 6 hard-boiled eggs, shelled
Olive oil
5 or 6 slices bacon
2 to 2½ cups tomato sauce
    (see page 534)

Leave each slice of veal in one piece, but carefully cut out the bone. Pound the slices between sheets of wax paper until very thin. Arrange the slices, long sides overlapping about ½ inch, on a sheet of waxed paper. Pound overlapping areas lightly but thoroughly to be sure they adhere to each other. Starting about 1 inch in from the edge farthest from you, arrange overlapping slices of prosciutto the length of the veal, then slices of mortadella about 1 inch closer to you, and finally the salami, so that the surface of the veal is covered with 3 layers of the meats.

Mix the bread crumbs, three-fourths of the minced garlic, the parsley, and half the basil, and season lightly with salt and pepper. Sprinkle the surface with this mixture. Arrange a row of eggs down the center. Sprinkle with olive oil, salt, and pepper. Roll one long side of the rectangle carefully over the eggs, as for a jelly roll, and continue rolling, making sure the eggs stay in place, until you have a neat, firm roll. Lift carefully, using two long spatulas, into a 9-by-20-inch oval or rectangular baking dish, seam side down. Cover the top of the roll with bacon slices. Pour the tomato sauce around—not over—the roll and sprinkle it with the remaining garlic, basil, and ½ teaspoon salt. Bake in a 350° oven for about 1 hour, basting occasionally with the sauce. Remove to a hot platter and cut the roll into thick diagonal slices, spooning some of the tomato sauce over the slices. Or serve directly from the baking dish.

¶**Veal Roll with Omelet Stuffing.** Instead of the hard-boiled eggs, put a rolled fines herbes omelet in the center of the roll.

¶**Cold Veal Roll.** Remove veal from baking dish, remove bacon strips, wrap in foil, and chill. Slice and arrange on a serving platter. Garnish with watercress. Serve with thinly sliced ripe tomatoes dressed with vinaigrette sauce and finely chopped fresh basil, and a rice salad (see page 96).

Roulade of Veal Île-de-France

A French version of veal roll that can be served hot with sautéed potatoes (see page 171) and a purée of green peas (see page 164) with a touch of chopped mint, or cold, with anchovy mayonnaise and a salad of white beans with chopped fresh herbs and a garlic-seasoned vinaigrette sauce.

Makes 8 servings

3 or 4 veal cutlets, sliced as for Sicilian Veal Roll (see preceding recipe)
⅔ to ¾ pound thinly sliced Smithfield or Westphalian ham
6 eggs
Salt, freshly ground black pepper

6 to 7 tablespoons butter
1 pound spinach or sorrel, or a combination
1 tablespoon heavy cream
⅛ teaspoon nutmeg

Prepare the veal as for the Sicilian Veal Roll and cover the surface with overlapping slices of ham. Beat the eggs with 2 tablespoons water, 1 teaspoon salt, and ½ teaspoon pepper, then scramble them lightly in 2 tablespoons butter. Spread the eggs on top of the ham. Blanch the spinach or sorrel or wilt down in the water clinging to the well-washed leaves. Drain well, pressing out all moisture, chop, and mix with 3 tablespoons butter, the cream, and the nutmeg. Put on top of the eggs. Roll the veal as before and put in the baking dish. Butter the top of the roll well and sprinkle with salt and pepper. Bake in a 350° oven for 45 minutes to 1 hour.

¶**Roulade with Duxelles.** Spread the ham with a layer of duxelles (see page 535), add spinach or sorrel and ⅓ teaspoon nutmeg, and roll as above.

Veal Scallops

Probably the most versatile and universally popular of all cuts of veal are the small slices cut from the leg and pounded until very thin, known variously as *scallops* in English, *escalopes* in French, and *scaloppine* in Italian. These little morsels cook very fast and lend themselves to all manner of flavorings. Speed is essential when cooking scallops. They should be sautéed very quickly in a mixture of butter and oil (the oil prevents the butter from burning at a high temperature) until just cooked through and lightly browned. After cooking, add desired flavoring and serve at once. Two or three scallops, according to size, should be enough for a serving, or 1½ pounds for 4 to 6 persons. Veal scallops may be served with rice, noodles, gnocchi, or sautéed potatoes, or simply with a green vegetable or a salad.

Veal Scallops with Lemon

I find that many people—just because flour in cooking is so out of fashion today—object to flouring veal scallops before cooking. I consider the flour as optional, though it does enable the meat to brown better. You'll find it more convenient to use two skillets for sautéing the scallops, as that way you can serve them all at once, hot from the pan.

Makes 4 servings

8 large or 12 medium-size veal scallops, pounded until thin	Salt, freshly ground black pepper
½ to ¾ cup flour	¼ cup lemon juice
6 tablespoons unsalted butter, preferably clarified	8 or 12 thin slices of lemon
3 tablespoons olive oil	2 tablespoons chopped parsley (preferably Italian parsley)

Lightly flour the scallops, shaking off any excess. Heat the butter and oil in a large heavy skillet until it stops foaming, then add the scallops, a few at a time (do not crowd the pan). Sauté them quickly, about 1 minute on a side, until lightly browned, seasoning with salt and pepper. Add the lemon juice, lemon slices, and chopped parsley. Remove scallops to a hot platter and pour the pan juices over them.

¶**Veal Scallops with Lemon and Parmesan Cheese.** After flouring scallops, dip them in lemon juice and then in flour mixed with 2 tablespoons grated lemon zest, 2 tablespoons grated Parmesan cheese, 1 teaspoon pepper, and 1 teaspoon salt. Cook as before, but do not season.

¶Veal Scallops with Sherry. Deglaze the pan with ⅔ cup oloroso sherry. Return scallops to pan to heat through. Serve with sauce poured over them. Sprinkle with chopped parsley.

¶Veal Scallops with Port. Substitute tawny port for the sherry.

¶Veal Scallops with Marsala. Substitute Marsala for the sherry.

¶Veal Scallops with White Wine. Substitute white wine for the sherry. Add 1 tablespoon chopped tarragon or chives to the sauce. Or omit herb and add 1 tablespoon capers.

¶Veal Scallops with Cognac. Substitute cognac for the sherry. If desired, instead of returning scallops to sauce, blaze cognac in the pan and pour over the scallops.

¶Veal Scallops with Herbs. Remove the scallops and keep warm. Add to the pan 2 tablespoons chopped parsley, 2 tablespoons chopped chives, 1 tablespoon chopped fresh tarragon or 1 teaspoon dried tarragon, and ⅔ cup white wine. Bring to a boil, cook 2 minutes, and pour over the scallops.

¶Veal Scallops with Cream. Remove scallops. Add ⅔ cup heavy cream to the pan and cook down for 2 or 3 minutes. Pour over the scallops.

¶Veal Scallops with Almonds. Sauté ½ cup slivered almonds in 4 tablespoons butter until golden and crisp. Toss the cooked scallops in the pan with the almonds. Serve sprinkled with chopped parsley.

¶Veal Scallops Smitaine. Remove the scallops to a platter and keep warm. Add 1 tablespoon finely chopped shallots or green onions to the pan. Sauté quickly until limp. Mix in 2 tablespoons tomato purée, season to taste, blend in ⅔ cup sour cream, off the heat. Return to heat and let sauce warm through, but not boil. Pour over the scallops.

¶Veal Scallops Lafayette. Make the following garnish for the scallops: Arrange vertical rows of peeled, sliced tomato and crosswise slices of peeled avocado on a baking sheet and sprinkle lightly with salt, pepper, then liberally with Parmesan cheese. Put under a hot broiler until cheese is barely colored. Arrange cooked veal scallops in a single layer on a heatproof serving platter and arrange a row of garnish on each one, transferring it with a long metal spatula. Sprinkle with more Parmesan cheese and put under the broiler until garnish is lightly browned. Drain fat from skillet and rinse with 1 cup tawny port and ¼ cup veal or chicken stock. Boil until reduced to ⅔ cup, then quickly stir in 2 tablespoons butter, swirling it around in the pan. Pour around scallops and serve.

¶**Veal Scallops Piquant.** Mix 1 cup toasted bread crumbs with 1 tablespoon finely chopped garlic, 2 tablespoons chopped parsley, 1 teaspoon dry mustard, ¼ cup grated Parmesan cheese, and a dash of cayenne pepper or Tabasco. Dip scallops in flour, then in white wine, and then in crumb mixture, coating well. Sauté, turning carefully. Remove scallops to a platter, add to the pan ½ cup white wine, a dash of Worcestershire sauce, and a dash of Tabasco. Cook and blend 1 minute then pour over scallops.

Saltimbocca

Makes 4 servings

8 small veal scallops	*2 tablespoons olive oil*
3 slices prosciutto	*Salt, freshly ground black pepper*
1 sprig fresh rosemary or 4 leaves sage	*½ cup Marsala*
4 tablespoons unsalted butter	GARNISH: *Chopped parsley*

Pound each veal scallop to a round shape, about 2 to 2½ inches in diameter. Trim ragged edges. Cut the prosciutto slightly smaller than the scallops and lay a piece on each piece of veal. Add several needles of fresh rosemary or a leaf of sage, top each with another piece of veal, and fasten edges together with toothpicks. Sauté in butter and oil until cooked through. Season to taste with salt and pepper and remove to a hot platter. Deglaze the pan with Marsala and pour over the saltimbocca. Garnish with chopped parsley.

¶**Veal Scallops with Mozzarella Cheese.** Pound and trim scallops as before. Spread half the scallops with a little fresh ricotta, add a slice of mozzarella cheese, a piece of prosciutto and a leaf of sage. Top with a second scallop, making a sandwich. Pound edges with a meat pounder to seal, dust lightly with flour and sauté in olive oil, turning carefully. When cooked through, season to taste with salt and pepper and remove to a platter. Deglaze pan with ½ cup dry vermouth and let it cook down for 1 minute. Pour over the saltimbocca.

Veal Birds with Olive-Anchovy Stuffing

Practically every country in Europe, as well as various regions of the United States, has a different recipe for veal birds, which are thin slices of veal cut from the leg, pounded, rolled with a stuffing, tied and braised, like small, individual versions of the veal roll. Buttered noodles or rice goes well with these stuffed rolls.

Makes 6 servings

1 onion, finely chopped
1 clove garlic, finely chopped
8 tablespoons olive oil
½ cup olives, pitted and finely chopped
12 anchovy fillets, finely chopped
¾ cup bread crumbs

¼ teaspoon salt
½ teaspoon freshly ground pepper
1 teaspoon basil
6 veal slices, 4 by 6 inches, cut from
    the leg and pounded ⅜ inch thick
⅔ cup red wine or more

GARNISH: Chopped parsley

Sauté the onion and garlic in 3 tablespoons olive oil until translucent. Add the olives, anchovies, crumbs, and seasonings, and blend thoroughly. Correct the seasoning and remove from heat. Place a small amount of the filling on each piece of veal. Roll and tie with string about ½ inch from each end. Heat 5 tablespoons oil and brown the birds, turning often to give an even color. Reduce the heat. Add the red wine, cover, and simmer the birds for about 30 to 35 minutes, or until just tender. Transfer to a hot platter and remove the string. If the sauce has cooked down too much, you may need to add another ½ cup wine to the pan. Allow the sauce to cook for several minutes, then pour over the birds and sprinkle with chopped parsley.

¶Veal Birds with Ham. For stuffing, combine 1 cup ground ham with ¼ cup chopped parsley, 1 teaspoon rosemary, a grating of nutmeg, and salt and pepper to taste. Brown the stuffed rolls in oil, then add 1 bay leaf and ⅔ cup white wine and simmer until tender.

¶Veal Birds with Turkey and Pork. For stuffing, combine 1 cup ground raw turkey breast and ½ cup ground raw pork. Season with 1 tablespoon chopped fresh dill or 1 teaspoon dried dill, and salt and pepper to taste. Sear rolls in oil, then simmer in dry white wine and serve sprinkled with dill.

¶Veal Birds with Tongue and Horseradish. Spread each slice of veal with horseradish blended with softened butter and top with a paper-thin slice of smoked tongue. Brown the rolls, add 1 teaspoon thyme and ⅔ cup veal or chicken stock. Simmer until tender. Remove rolls to a hot platter, add ¼ cup Madeira or sherry to the pan, and reduce over high heat. Pour over the veal birds and sprinkle with parsley.

¶**Veal Birds Provençal.** For stuffing, mix ½ pound well-seasoned sausage meat with ½ cup fresh bread crumbs, 2 finely chopped garlic cloves, salt and pepper, ½ teaspoon thyme, 1 egg, and 1 tablespoon cognac. Stuff rolls and brown in hot oil. Season. Add to pan 2 garlic cloves, 1 sliced onion, ½ teaspoon thyme, a sprig of parsley, and 1½ cups dry white wine. Cover and simmer until tender. Transfer rolls to a hot dish. Add to pan juices 2 tablespoons tomato purée, ¼ cup finely chopped onion, and 1 finely chopped garlic clove. Cook sauce down for 5 minutes, then add 30 pitted soft Italian black olives and ¼ cup chopped parsley. Return birds to pan and reheat in sauce. Serve birds around a platter of macaroni, and sprinkle with chopped parsley and Parmesan cheese.

¶**Veal Birds Oregon.** Sauté ½ cup chopped shallots in 6 tablespoons butter. Add 2 cups fresh bread crumbs, 2 tablespoons fresh dill, and salt and freshly ground black pepper to taste. Add additional butter, if needed. Stuff the veal with this mixture, adding a slim finger of dill pickle with each roll. Cook as above. Deglaze the pan with ⅓ cup vodka and add ½ cup heavy cream.

"Minced" Veal with Cream

Another way of treating veal, popular in Switzerland, is to cut it into thin julienne strips and sauté: an easy quick dish when you don't have much time to prepare dinner. It's called *émincé*, which means "minced"—even though the meat is not chopped. Serve with sautéed or roesti potatoes (see page 171) or with rice.

Makes 4 servings

1 pound boneless veal cutlet, cut in
    strips 1 inch wide and 2 inches
    long
Flour

4 tablespoons clarified butter
Salt, freshly ground black pepper
¼ cup dry white wine
⅔ cup cream, sour cream or yogurt

Roll the veal strips in flour, and sauté in the butter over rather high heat till just cooked through, about 2 to 3 minutes. Season the meat with salt and pepper to taste and remove to a hot platter. Add the wine to the pan and deglaze over high heat, then stir in the cream and let it cook down for a minute or two. If using sour cream or yogurt, be certain not to let the sauce boil. Return veal to sauce just long enough to heat through and serve immediately.

¶Veal Strips with Onion and Mushrooms. Separately sauté 1 chopped medium-size onion and 6 sliced mushrooms in butter. Add to the sauce and heat through with the veal.

¶Veal Strips with Mustard Sauce. After deglazing the pan, stir 1 tablespoon Dijon mustard into the pan juices before adding the cream. Serve with a sprinkling of capers.

Sautéed Veal Chops with Cream

Young, tender loin veal chops cut ¾ to 1 inch thick can be sautéed as well as broiled. They take the same length of time—5 minutes a side. The meat will be moist and flavorful, with just a slight pinkness inside.

Makes 4 servings

4 veal chops, ¾ to 1 inch thick
½ cup flour
4 tablespoons unsalted butter
Salt, freshly ground black pepper
Sautéed potatoes (see page 171)

4 steamed leeks (see page 153)
¼ cup dry sherry
1 cup heavy cream
2 egg yolks

Dip the chops in flour, brushing off any excess. Heat the butter in a heavy skillet, preferably iron, large enough to accommodate the chops in one layer. When bubbling, add the chops and brown quickly on each side over high heat. Reduce the heat and continue cooking until done, about 5 minutes a side for the total cooking time. Season with salt and pepper and arrange the sautéed chops on a bed of crisp, golden sautéed potatoes on a hot platter. Top each chop with a steamed leek.

Deglaze the skillet with the sherry, then beat the cream and egg yolks together and stir into the pan juices. Cook over medium-low heat, stirring, until the sauce thickens, but do not let it come to a boil or the eggs will curdle. Season to taste with salt and pepper and pour over the chops.

¶Veal Chops with Onion Sauce. Before sautéing the chops, heat 6 tablespoons unsalted butter in a skillet, add 1½ cups finely chopped onion, cover, and steam over low heat until soft and juicy. Strain 3 tablespoons of the butter-onion liquid into a saucepan. Blend in 3 tablespoons flour, and cook, stirring, to make a roux. Mix in ⅔ cup heavy cream, cook until thick, then set aside. Purée the steamed onions and their liquid in a blender or a food processor, or by putting them through a food mill. Mix into the sauce in the pan, and cook over medium heat until well mixed and thickened. Add ⅔ cup grated Gruyère cheese and stir until melted into the sauce. Season with salt, pepper, and a dash of nutmeg. Sauté chops and put in a baking dish, pour the onion sauce over them, sprinkle the top with a little grated Gruyère cheese, and put under a preheated broiler until the cheese is melted and the top is glazed.

¶**Veal Chops with Hearts of Palm.** While the chops are being sautéed, heat 4 canned hearts of palm in 3 tablespoons unsalted butter over low heat. Remove the cooked chops to a heated platter. Rinse the skillet with 2 tablespoons dark rum and ½ cup port, then gradually add ½ cup heavy cream and cook until the sauce is reduced a little. Turn off the heat and whisk in 1 tablespoon unsalted butter, 3 tablespoons purée of foie gras or liver pâté, and salt and pepper to taste. Serve the chops covered with the sauce, and garnish each one with a heart of palm.

¶**Veal Chops with Mushrooms.** Follow the preceding recipe, but use sliced mushroom caps, sautéed in butter, instead of hearts of palm, and rinse the pan with ½ cup dry white wine and 1 tablespoon cognac.

Broiled Veal Chops

Veal chops can be broiled, provided they are lubricated with olive oil and not overcooked. They should be pleasantly brown on the outside, but still juicily pink inside. I usually leave them at room temperature for an hour before cooking.

Makes 6 servings

6 loin veal chops, cut ¾ to 1 inch thick   *1 tablespoon crumbled dried tarragon*
2 tablespoons olive oil   *Salt, freshly ground black pepper*

Brush the chops on one side with oil and rub them with a little tarragon. Arrange them on the rack of a broiling pan and broil, about 3 inches from the heat, for 5 minutes, then brush with a little more oil. Turn the chops, brush the second side with oil, sprinkle with tarragon, and broil for an additional 5 minutes. Season the chops with salt and pepper to taste.

Paillard of Veal

A paillard is a slice cut from the leg, like scaloppine, but instead of being sautéed, after pounding it is quickly broiled close to the heat. It won't brown, but it will become pleasantly crisp around the edges. This has become the dieter's delight, as it has no fat and needs no seasoning apart from a squeeze of lemon juice. The veal must be of excellent quality and carefully cut, with no tendons to make it curl up, so seek out a good butcher. When fresh asparagus is in season, I like a mound of cooked asparagus to munch on with my paillard.

Makes 4 servings

4 slices veal from the leg, about 2
*   inches in size, pounded until*
*   4 to 5 inches in diameter*

About ¼ cup melted butter
Lemon

Brush the slices lightly with butter, arrange on the broiler rack, and broil about 3 inches from the heat, brushing frequently with butter and turning twice, for no more than 3 minutes' total cooking time. Serve with lemon, to be squeezed on the meat.

Roast Breast of Veal

Most people stuff and braise breast of veal, but I've found that it is absolutely delicious roasted until crisp and carved like a flank steak, with the little bones reserved for munching. If you want to flavor it with an herb, tarragon would be my choice, but frankly I think good veal needs no seasoning other than a little garlic.

Makes 6 servings

5- to 6-pound breast of veal
2 to 3 tablespoons olive oil
2 cloves garlic, finely chopped

1 teaspoon crushed dried tarragon
*   (optional)*
Salt, freshly ground black pepper

Rub the veal with the oil, then with the chopped garlic and the tarragon (if desired). Place veal on the rack of a broiling pan, and broil approximately 4 inches from the heat until veal is nicely browned—about 20 to 22 minutes. Drape foil over the pan and roast in a 400° oven for about 30 minutes. Season with salt and pepper, and carve the meat from the bones on the diagonal in medium-thick slices, removing only the top meat. Cut the bones apart and serve with the sliced meat.

Veal en Daube

Although in Provence a daube is usually made with beef or lamb, there is in the region of the Dordogne a delicious daube made with veal. Serve with a purée of chestnuts or celery root and potato, and a salad of endive and julienne beets.

Makes 6 to 8 servings

3- to 3½-pound shoulder of veal
4 cloves garlic, cut in slivers
6 tablespoons goose fat or olive oil
1 cup dry white wine
½ cup cognac
2 pig's feet, split lengthwise
1 teaspoon sugar
12 small white onions
2 tomatoes, peeled and seeded
3 shallots

4 carrots, thinly sliced
4 tablespoons butter
1 sprig parsley
1 teaspoon thyme
1 rib celery
1 cup veal or chicken broth
Salt, freshly ground black pepper
Beurre manié (optional; see page 536)
GARNISH: *Chopped parsley*

Make incisions in the veal with the point of a small knife and insert the garlic slivers. Brown the meat on all sides in the goose fat or oil in a deep braising pan. Add the wine, cognac, and pig's feet. Sprinkle the veal with the sugar and add the onions, tomatoes, and shallots. Sauté the carrots in the butter for a few minutes, then add to the veal with the parsley, thyme, celery, and broth. Season well with salt and pepper and simmer, covered, over low heat for 3 hours, or until veal is tender. Transfer veal to a hot platter. Reduce the sauce over high heat. If you wish, thicken it further with beurre manié. Correct the seasoning. Slice the veal, surround with the vegetables and sauce and garnish with parsley.

Braised Veal Shanks with Tomatoes and Sausages

Known in France as *ronchys de veau,* this is an old dish, seldom seen nowadays, that is somewhat reminiscent of the popular Italian ossi buchi. Both are made with pieces of the veal shank with bone and marrow left in. Serve with rice and a good sprinkling of Parmesan cheese.

Makes 6 servings

12 *pieces of veal shank, cut about 2*
   to 2½ inches long
Salt, freshly ground black pepper
3 *tablespoons butter*
2 *tablespoons oil*
6 *very large ripe tomatoes, peeled,*
   halved, and seeded

2 *cups dry white wine*
½ *cup chopped parsley*
2 *tablespoons chopped fresh basil or*
   1½ *teaspoons dry basil*
3 *tablespoons tomato paste (optional)*
24 *small pork sausages*

Season the veal shanks well with salt and pepper and sauté in the butter and oil until browned on all sides. Stand shanks upright in pan, top each one with half a tomato and add the white wine. Simmer, covered, for 10 minutes, then add the parsley and basil. Simmer over very low heat, covered, for 1½ to 2 hours, or until the meat is very tender and the sauce well blended. If the tomatoes used are not very ripe, add the tomato paste for the last 20 minutes of cooking time to give a rich flavor. Poach the sausages in water to cover until they reach the boiling point. Simmer for 5 minutes, drain well, and add to the veal shanks for the last 10 minutes of cooking time.

Veal Ragout

A simple veal ragout or stew is a great delicacy unless subjected to over-cooking, a common habit of many stew makers. Somehow the idea took root that if long cooking is good, longer cooking must be better. This is not the case with a delicate meat like veal. Even the less tender sections are not tough enough to warrant very lengthy cooking. Noodles or rice go well with veal stew.

Makes 6 servings

2½ *to 3 pounds veal leg or shoulder*
   cut in 1½-inch cubes (or riblets
   cut from the breast)
4 *tablespoons butter*
2 *tablespoons oil*
1½ *teaspoons salt*
½ *teaspoon freshly ground black pepper*
2 *medium-size onions, thinly sliced*
2 *cloves garlic, finely chopped*

1 *to 1½ cups canned Italian plum*
   tomatoes
2 *green peppers, broiled, peeled,*
   seeded, and cut in strips
¾ *cup dry white wine*
2 *tablespoons chopped fresh basil or*
   1½ *teaspoons dried basil*
¾ *cup pitted soft black Italian olives*
GARNISH: *Finely chopped parsley*

Brown the veal in the butter and oil, season with salt and pepper, and add the onion, garlic, plum tomatoes, green pepper strips, white wine, and basil. Simmer, covered, for 1 to 1½ hours, or until tender (supermarket veal may need another 30 minutes), then add the olives and let the sauce reduce, uncovered, for 3 to 4 minutes. Correct the seasoning, remove meat to a platter, and reduce the sauce over brisk heat for 4 to 5 minutes. Pour over the veal and sprinkle with chopped parsley.

Ossi Buchi

Makes 4 servings

8 veal shanks with marrow
6 tablespoons butter
1½ cups dry white wine
1½ cups tomatoes (either chopped
fresh or canned Italian plum
tomatoes)

1½ cups stock
Salt, freshly ground black pepper

GREMOLATA
2 to 4 cloves garlic, chopped
⅔ cup chopped parsley

1 lemon

Tie each veal shank with string so as to keep the marrow intact. Melt the butter and sauté the shanks, turning once. Stand them upright in the pan. Add the white wine and cook for 10 minutes. Then add the tomatoes, stock, and salt and pepper to taste. Cover the pan and simmer the shanks for 1½ to 2 hours, or until tender.

Chop the garlic and parsley together well. Grate the zest of the lemon and combine well with the parsley mixture.

Place the veal shanks on a serving platter, spoon the sauce over them, and sprinkle with the gremolata. Serve with risotto (see page 291).

¶**Ossi Buchi with Prosciutto and Black Olives.** After cooling the shanks, add 1 cup julienne-cut prosciutto and 1 cup soft black olives, and heat through. Serve shanks with the sauce and sprinkle with gremolata.

Pork

Pork happens to be my favorite meat. I like every cut, from the fancy loin to the humble hock, and I like to make my own sausage: an easy job with the processor, and fun, because there are so many ways to vary it. The basic recipe here has three variations, and can be used for either link or country sausage. But note that I don't scorn store sausage. It turns up as an additive all around in this book, and in the Appetizer chapter I've given a recipe that is delightful for big parties. Pork in any form, I have always felt, belongs at more parties. Maybe because it's relatively inexpensive, people didn't use to think it was fancy enough. But now that the cook's taste and skill have chased "conspicuous consumption" right off the stage, pork is coming into its own.

I'm giving you recipes for the old favorites I love, but many, like the roast loin, have some pretty sophisticated variations and flavor surprises. Variety is the charm of pork cookery, for the meat is good hot or at room temperature, has a good dense texture which responds to many methods, and its rich but mellow and unassertive flavor takes well to a wonderful range of combinations, pickley, nutty, aromatic, fruity, winy, and more. And it isn't "heavy" in the least; actually a fine pork loin is no richer than a beef loin. Pork fat is exquisite anyway, and so delicate that it's the choicest kind for enriching other meats. (Use fresh pork fat in thin slices for barding, or in matchstick shapes for larding; if you can't get it and must use bacon or salt pork, blanch it first.) I love cured pork, either salted or smoked, and there's a recipe here for smoked loin and several for ham (with a dissertation on country hams in the Concordance); but I urge you to try a pork leg fresh as well as cured. The recipe has many variations, serves lots of people, and is excellent cold. Not too cold.

And speaking of temperature, the most important thing I have to say about pork is this: cook it to 160° or 170° of interior temperature, and thus have it ivory-pale, not gray, and juicy, not stringy. The old insistence on 185° to 190° was due to the fear of the trichinae sometimes (rarely nowadays) found in pork; but it has been conclusively proven that they are killed off at 150°, so it is absolutely ridiculous to cremate this good meat.

Roast Loin of Pork

Makes 6 servings

5-pound pork loin, trimmed and tied
Salt, freshly ground black pepper
1 teaspoon dried thyme

1 cup chicken (see page 529) or
    veal stock

Rub the loin well with salt, pepper, and thyme. Place fat side up on a rack in a roasting pan and roast in a 325° oven for 25 to 30 minutes a pound, until the internal temperature registers 160° on a meat thermometer. Remove from the oven and let rest for 10 minutes before carving. Skim off excess fat from the roasting pan, add 1 cup hot chicken or veal stock and let the mixture come to a boil. Simmer for a few minutes and serve with the pork. A potato purée and sautéed apple slices are good with pork.

¶**Roast Pork Loin with Garlic.** Insert 2 or 3 slivered garlic cloves in the meat before rubbing it with seasonings. Halfway through the roasting, baste with red wine and continue basting until cooked. Serve with sautéed onions and tiny new potatoes.

¶**Roast Pork Loin Flambé.** Roast as for Roast Pork Loin with Garlic. When cooked, remove to a hot platter and flame with ¼ cup warmed cognac. Skim excess fat from pan juices and serve as a sauce.

¶**Roast Pork Loin with Rosemary.** Rub the loin with garlic, salt, and rosemary, pressing the seasoning well into the meat. Put a few rosemary leaves or sprigs in the roasting pan. When the roast is done, remove it to a hot platter and skim the excess fat from the pan juices. Add ¼ cup dry white wine and ½ cup heavy cream, and season to taste with salt and pepper. Cook and blend for a few minutes and serve with the roast. With this have roast potatoes and spinach dressed with oil and lemon juice, or a purée of spinach.

¶**Roast Pork Loin Marinated Oriental Style.** Rub the loin with garlic. In a bowl, make a marinade with ⅔ cup Japanese soy sauce, ⅔ cup dry sherry, 2 or 3 finely chopped garlic cloves, and 2 tablespoons chopped fresh ginger. Turn roast in the marinade and marinate for 3 to 4 hours, turning frequently. During roasting, baste frequently with the marinade. Serve with broiled pineapple and a barley casserole (see page 295).

¶**Roast Marinated and Glazed Pork Loin.** Have the loin boned and tied. Rub well with dry mustard and thyme. Marinate as above, and roast. Melt 8 ounces of apple or currant jelly and add a tablespoon of soy sauce and 2 tablespoons dry sherry. Cook down for a minute or two, stirring contantly. When the loin is done, remove it from the oven and spoon this glaze over it. Cool at room temperature. Serve cool, but not chilled, with applesauce mixed with horseradish to taste, and a rice salad (see page 96).

¶**Orange-Glazed Roast Pork Loin.** Insert garlic slivers in the loin and rub with salt and crushed rosemary; roast. Halfway through the roasting time, baste with thawed, undiluted concentrated orange juice. Roast 30 minutes more and then spread the pork with bitter-orange marmalade. Roast 30 minutes, baste again with concentrated orange juice, and spread with more marmalade. Roast until done. Transfer the pork to a serving platter, skim fat from the pan juices, and combine with 1 cup orange sections and ½ cup fresh orange juice. Season to taste. Serve the roast loin with this orange sauce, a purée of yams or parsnips and a chicory or endive salad.

¶**Pork Loin Roasted with Green Peppercorn Butter.** Have the loin of pork boned and tied. Crush 1⅓ tablespoons fresh green peppercorns in a mortar and pestle with 1 garlic clove and 1 teaspoon ground cinnamon. Work in ½ cup sweet butter and, when thoroughly mixed, a scant teaspoon salt. With your fingers push this green peppercorn butter into the spaces where the meat is tied together, and spread a thin layer of the butter over the top of the roast. After roasting, remove from the pan and spread more butter on top. Leave at room temperature until tepid. Serve at this temperature with a French potato salad dressed with oil and vinegar.

¶**Pork Loin Roasted with Coriander and Fennel.** Rub the loin with ground sage, ground coriander, allspice, and freshly ground black pepper, and run a dried fennel stalk through the length of the meat (pierce a hole first with a larding needle or heavy skewer). When roasted, remove from the pan, add 4 tablespoons flour to make a roux and cook over medium heat, gradually stirring in 1 cup veal or chicken stock until thickened. Add ½ to 1 cup heavy cream and season to taste with salt and pepper. If available, add a little chopped fresh coriander to the sauce. Serve with roesti potatoes (see page 171).

¶**Prune-Stuffed Roast Pork Loin.** Soak 2 pounds large pitted prunes in 1 cup dry sherry for 12 hours. Make 2 long incisions in the fleshiest part of the meat, almost to the bone. Stuff incisions with prunes, pressing them in with the handle of a wooden spoon. Reshape roast and tie with string. Rub with salt and roast, basting occasionally with pan juices mixed with sherry from soaked prunes. Serve with buttered noodles and a sauerkraut salad (see page 92).

¶**Prune-Stuffed Roast Pork Loin with Potatoes and Onions.** Roast as above, adding parboiled small white onions and potatoes to the pan for the last hour of cooking time. Skim fat from pan juices. Thicken juices with flour and stir in heavy cream to make a sauce.

Crown Roast of Pork

A spectacular and festive roast for the holidays or a dinner party. The crown is made with 2 rib ends of the loin, tied together, or with the center cuts or the entire loin, according to how many people you wish to serve.

Two chops from the crown roast are an ample serving. When the butcher ties the loin, he will scrape the ends of the bones (keep the scraps; they can be used for stock). Cover the exposed rib ends with aluminum foil to prevent them from charring.

Rub the meat well with sage, thyme, and garlic, or with pepper and rosemary. Fill the center of the roast with crumpled foil. Roast on a rack in a large pan in a 325° oven, allowing 25 minutes per pound, until the internal temperature reaches 150° to 155° (test by inserting a meat thermometer in the thickest part of the meat, not touching the bone). Baste frequently with the pan juices and dry white wine or wine and melted butter.

When the meat is cooked, replace the foil on the bone ends with paper frills, if you wish. Remove the foil from the center and fill with sauerkraut, cooked for 1 hour in dry white wine or chicken stock with juniper berries and freshly ground black pepper. Garnish with thin slices of poached garlic sausage.

Carve the roast into chops and serve 1 or 2 to a person, with some of the stuffing from the center. A salad of Bibb lettuce or endive with julienne strips of beet is good with this and, if the stuffing is not a starchy one, boiled parsleyed potatoes or a purée of potatoes or potatoes and celery root.

¶**Variations.** Fill the center of the crown roast with any of the following combinations:

Buttered homemade noodles, mixed with sliced, sautéed mushrooms.
Rice mixed with peas and parsley.
Braised Brussels sprouts, with or without chestnuts.
Sautéed lentils with onion, crisp pieces of bacon, and chopped parsley.
Sautéed mushroom caps.
Sautéed apple slices.
Chestnut purée with melted butter, seasoned with ground ginger and nutmeg.

Roast Smoked Loin of Pork

Smoked pork loin is a great delicacy. When buying, ask how much cooking it needs. Some types require 30 minutes a pound in a 300° oven, while others, which are hot smoked and more fully cooked, require little more than reheating, about 12 to 15 minutes a pound at most. Baste a smoked pork loin during roasting with dry white wine or sherry, and serve it with buttered new potatoes and sauerkraut.

Individual chops or double chops may be braised or broiled and served forth with braised red cabbage or sauerkraut. The thick chops may be pocketed and stuffed with any favorite stuffing.

Roast Pork Leg or Fresh Ham
with Burgundian Mustard

The pork leg or fresh ham is another versatile pork cut that can be cooked either boned or bone in. A whole ham, which can run from 8 to 16 pounds or more, is an excellent roast for a holiday dinner or a large dinner party. For a smaller roast, buy a half ham. If you can find a butcher who will leave the skin on and score it, you'll have an extra treat with the lovely crisp crackling to chew on. Slow cooking at 300° to 325° is best for this large piece of meat. If the skin is left on, crispen it by increasing the heat to 425° for the last 20 minutes, basting it well with the pan drippings. Like the loin, the roast leg is wonderful cold, but not ice cold. Take it from the refrigerator an hour or two before serving.

Makes 12 or more servings

12-pound leg of pork

Salt, freshly ground black pepper

Crushed herb (sage, thyme, or summer savory)

Crushed garlic

BURGUNDIAN MUSTARD

1 cup Dijon mustard

2 tablespoons finely chopped sour pickle

1 tablespoon finely chopped sweet pickle

1 teaspoon cognac

Rub the meat well with the herb, salt, pepper, and garlic. Place on a rack in a shallow roasting pan and roast in a 300° to 325° oven for about 25 minutes a pound, or until the internal temperature reaches 150° to 155° on a meat thermometer. Unless the skin has been left on the ham, there is no need to baste, as the layer of fat provides sufficient lubrication. Remove the roast to a hot platter and let rest 15 minutes before carving in fairly thin slices.

For the Burgundian mustard, blend ingredients thoroughly. Serve with the ham. A potato purée and sautéed apple slices are good with roast leg.

¶**Roast Pork Leg, Norman Style.** Rub the meat with nutmeg, salt, pepper, and a touch of ground ginger. Roast, basting with warmed sweet cider for flavor. Remove the cooked leg to a heatproof platter and flame with ⅓ cup warmed Calvados or applejack. Skim excess fat from pan juices, and thicken over low heat with 4 egg yolks beaten with 1 cup heavy cream (do not allow to boil). Correct seasoning and serve with the pork, buttered noodles, and horseradish applesauce, prepared by combining ⅔ cup freshly grated horseradish, or to taste, with 3 cups applesauce.

¶**Drunken Pork.** Have the leg boned and tied. Put in a deep bowl with the following marinade: 4 crushed garlic cloves, 3 small chopped onions, 1 teaspoon basil, and red wine to cover. Leave for 5 to 6 days, turning once a day. Remove meat and dry. Make several gashes in the pork and stud with pine nuts and slivers of garlic. Rub with salt, and roast. Reduce strained marinade to 1½ cups by rapid boiling. Thicken with brown sauce or beurre manié. Rice pilaf or polenta and braised onion slices are good accompaniments.

¶**Pork to Taste Like Wild Boar.** Rub the pork with a mixture of 3 finely chopped garlic cloves, 12 crushed peppercorns, ½ teaspoon ground nutmeg, and a pinch of cloves. Place in a deep bowl with 1 teaspoon thyme, 1 bay leaf, 2 strips orange zest, and red wine to cover. Marinate 5 to 6 days, turning each day. Remove and dry meat and rub with oil. Put in a roasting pan (not on a rack) and roast, basting with the strained marinade. Remove pork to a hot platter. Skim excess fat from pan juices. Add juices to remaining marinade and cook down to 2 cups. Thicken with beurre manié. Serve as a sauce for the pork, with the same accompaniments as Drunken Pork.

¶**Italian Boned Stuffed Pork.** Stuff the ham cavity with Italian parsley, 3 or 4 chopped cloves of garlic, chopped fresh or dried basil, and a touch of sage or thyme. Tie firmly. Rub with salt and pepper. Roast on a rack in a shallow pan, basting with warmed dry white wine every 30 minutes. Remove cooked pork to a hot platter. Skim fat from the pan juices, add 1 cup dry white wine, and bring to a boil. Reduce slightly, then add chopped chives and parsley, and serve as a sauce for the pork with puréed potatoes and broccoli sprinkled with Parmesan cheese.

Roast Shoulder of Pork with Apples and Onions

A boned shoulder of pork makes a pleasant roast that slices easily. This coriander-flavored pork is wonderful cold. Serve with vegetables vinaigrette and French bread.

Makes 8 servings

4- to 5-pound boned, tied shoulder
   of pork
1 teaspoon ground coriander
½ teaspoon thyme
6 to 8 medium-size onions, peeled
   and parboiled
8 cooking apples, cored
½ cup raisins

¼ cup chopped walnuts
8 tablespoons sugar
8 tablespoons butter
½ cup melted butter mixed with
   3 tablespoons sugar
Salt, freshly ground black pepper
1 cup heavy cream

Rub the shoulder well with coriander and thyme. Arrange on a rack in a roasting pan and roast in a 325° oven, allowing 25 to 30 minutes per pound. After 1¼ hours, add the onions to the pan and baste with the pan juices. Test the temperature frequently until it reaches 150° to 155°.

Remove a center band of skin from each of the cored apples. Stuff apples with the mixed raisins, nuts, sugar, and butter. Put them in a baking dish, add ½ cup water, and bake in the oven with the pork until they are just tender, basting occasionally with the melted-butter-sugar mixture.

Salt and pepper the pork well and remove it from the oven when done to 150° to 155°. Allow to rest on a hot platter for 10 minutes before carving. Drain the onions and arrange them around the meat. Serve the apples separately. Skim the excess fat from the juices in the roasting pan and combine the juices and cream. Bring to the boiling point and cook down for several minutes. Season to taste and serve with the pork.

Roast Suckling Pig with Pistachio-Rice Stuffing

A spectacular roast for a holiday party. Suckling pigs may be bought most easily around Christmas, but if you order far enough ahead you can get them during the summer months and spit-roast them over charcoal.

Try to get the smallest pig possible, about 12 to 14 pounds. Take out your tape measure and see whether it will fit into the oven—this is vital. If you can't get a pig of a size to fit your oven, forget it! For oven roasting, the pig should rest on a rack in a fairly shallow pan. It is nice to stuff the pig, but since the meat is so rich, the stuffing must not be too rich.

I've been battling for a long time about the way roast suckling pig is usually served. I'm against the rather pagan way people have of decorating them. I feel that a roast suckling pig can be a beautiful sight without the silly embellishments. There is nothing wrong with simply garnishing it with masses of parsley or watercress or with roasted apples and onions. One really needn't make a caricature of the poor beast.

Makes 12 to 14 servings

STUFFING

¼ *pound unsalted butter*
1 *cup chopped shallots*
6 *cups cooked rice*
½ *cup pistachio nuts*

½ *cup finely chopped parsley*
2 *teaspoons salt*
1 *teaspoon freshly ground black pepper*

12- *to 14-pound suckling pig, cleaned*   *Olive oil*
     (reserve liver, heart, and kidneys)

SAUCE

2 *to 3 cups chicken broth*
¼ *cup finely chopped shallots*
4 *tablespoons unsalted butter*

3 *tablespoons flour*
1 *cup heavy cream*
Salt, freshly ground black pepper

GARNISH: *Watercress, parsley, or roasted apples and onions*

To prepare this stuffing, melt butter in a large heavy skillet and sauté shallots until limp. Add rice, pistachios, and parsley. Toss well to mix. Season with salt and pepper. If mixture seems dry, melt 4 to 6 tablespoons butter and mix in to moisten. Taste the stuffing and correct the seasoning, if necessary.

Stuff the pig rather loosely and sew the cavity up or clamp it securely. Arrange pig on a rack in a roasting pan and rub well with olive oil. Roast in a 350° oven, basting or brushing occasionally with olive oil, for about 3½ to 4 hours, or to an internal temperature of 155° to 160° (insert meat thermometer into thickest part of leg and loin, not touching the bone).

While the pig is roasting, cook the liver, heart, and kidneys in chicken broth to cover, over medium heat, until just tender. Remove and chop fine; reserve broth. Sauté shallots in butter, add flour, and blend well. Gradually stir in the reserved broth and simmer the mixture for 10 minutes. Add heavy cream and chopped innards, and season to taste with salt and pepper. Simmer sauce over very low heat for 10 minutes.

Remove the pig to a carving board and garnish with watercress or parsley or roasted apples and onions. To carve, first remove and slice the small hams, then cut down the backbone and remove the head. Carve the rib and loin sections into chops. Serve some of each kind of meat with the stuffing, sauce, the apples and onions. If you do not serve the apple and onion garnish, an orange and onion salad would be good.

¶**Roast Suckling Pig with Aïoli.** In Spain, especially in Barcelona, roast suckling pig is served with an aïoli (see page 203), which, of course, gives it an entirely new dimension, and I find I like it very much.

Pork Chops

The loin and rib chops are the best cuts, and of these the loin chops, with a bit of the tenderloin included, are the choicest. Broiling is not very successful, as it tends to dry out and toughen the meat. Chops sautéed or baked in any of the following ways are much more succulent and delicious. Allow 1 large or 2 small chops per serving.

Sautéed Pork Chops with Onions

Makes 4 servings

4 loin or rib chops, 1 to 1½ inches
   thick
4 tablespoons butter
2 tablespoons oil

Salt, freshly ground black pepper
3 large onions, thinly sliced
⅓ cup Madeira or dry sherry

Brown the chops well on both sides in a large, heavy skillet in 2 tablespoons butter and the oil, cooking them for 3 to 4 minutes a side. Season with salt and pepper, remove to a hot platter, and keep warm. Add the rest of the butter to the pan and brown the onions lightly, turning them often so they don't stick or burn. Return the chops to the pan and arrange the onions on top of them. Reduce the heat, cover, and simmer for 10 minutes, then add the wine and simmer another 10 minutes, or until chops are tender.

¶Sautéed Pork Chops with Mushrooms. Lightly flour the chops and brown on both sides in butter and oil. Season with salt and pepper, add ½ cup dry white wine, cover, and simmer 20 minutes, or until tender, turning once. Meanwhile, sauté 1 pound small mushroom caps in 4 table-spoons butter in another skillet. Season with salt, pepper, and a dash of Worcestershire sauce, sprinkle with 1 tablespoon flour, stir in ¾ cup heavy cream, and cook, stirring, until lightly thickened. Transfer the chops to a hot platter and spoon the mushrooms over them.

¶Pork Chops Mexican Style. Brown the chops in oil. Pour off excess fat, reduce heat, add 1 chopped medium-size onion and 2 finely chopped garlic cloves, and sauté until soft. Season with 1 teaspoon oregano, 1 teaspoon ground cumin, and 1½ teaspoons salt. Add 1 cup tomato sauce, cover, and simmer 10 minutes. Uncover, add 2 tablespoons chili powder, turn the chops, and simmer uncovered 10 minutes, or until tender.

Transfer chops to a hot platter. Bring sauce to a boil and pour over chops. Garnish with chopped canned peeled green chilies and chopped cilantro or parsley.

¶**Pork Chops Charcutière.** Brown the chops in butter. Season with salt and pepper, cover, and cook 10 minutes over low heat. Remove to a hot platter. Pour off all but 2 tablespoons fat from the pan, sauté 1 finely chopped onion and 1 finely chopped garlic clove until soft. Add ½ cup dry white wine and cook down to ¼ cup. Mix in 1 tablespoon Dijon mustard, 2 tablespoons tomato purée or tomato sauce, and ½ cup brown sauce (you may use the Quick Brown Sauce, page 533). Correct seasoning, add the chops, and simmer 10 minutes, or until tender. Add ¼ cup thinly sliced cornichons and heat through. Transfer chops to a serving platter and spoon sauce over them. Sprinkle with chopped parsley.

¶**Sautéed Pork Chops with Sauerkraut.** In a good-size skillet fry 4 rather thick slices bacon. Remove to absorbent paper to drain. Brown 4 thick pork chops in 2 tablespoons of the bacon drippings. Return the bacon to the skillet, add 1 medium-size onion, thinly sliced, and 1½ pounds washed sauerkraut, being sure the chops are well covered with the kraut. Add 1 teaspoon freshly ground black pepper, and enough beer barely to cover all. Cover the skillet, bring to a boil, lower heat, and simmer for 30 minutes. Serve with boiled potatoes.

To add an unusual touch, sprinkle the chops and sauerkraut with ¾ cup shredded Gruyère cheese during the last 10 minutes of cooking.

Stuffed Pork Chops

I think stuffed pork chops must be American in origin, for I have never encountered them in any other country. And delicious they are! Savory and satisfying.

For stuffing, you need loin or rib chops 2 inches thick, with a deep pocket cut in the fat edge, toward the bone.

Makes 6 servings

6 pork chops, 2 inches thick

STUFFING
1 medium-size onion, finely chopped   *1 celery rib, finely chopped*
4 tablespoons butter   *2 cloves garlic, finely chopped*

¼ cup finely chopped mushrooms
1 teaspoon thyme or rosemary,
    crumbled or pounded in a small
    mortar

1¼ cups dry bread crumbs
¼ cup chopped parsley
1 teaspoon salt
½ teaspoon freshly ground black pepper

FOR SAUTÉING AND SAUCE
3 tablespoons oil

1 cup heavy cream

With a sharp knife, cut a pocket in the fat edge of each chop, about 1½ inches long and deep enough to touch the bone.

To make the stuffing, sauté the onion in butter until limp, add the celery, garlic, mushrooms, and herb, and cook until the vegetables are soft, about 5 minutes. Stir in the bread crumbs, parsley, salt, and pepper, and blend thoroughly. Taste for seasoning. The mixture should be fairly dry. Stuff the pocket of each chop with the mixture, and fasten the openings with small skewers or toothpicks.

Heat the oil in a heavy skillet with a tight-fitting lid, large enough to hold the chops in one layer. Brown chops on both sides. Add just enough boiling water to cover the bottom of the pan, cover skillet, lower heat, and simmer gently for 25 minutes, then turn the chops, replace the lid, and simmer 10 to 20 minutes longer, until tender but not dry. If the skillet has an ovenproof handle, the chops can be cooked in a 350° oven for the same length of time. When done, transfer chops to a hot platter and keep warm.

Skim excess fat from pan juices, add the cream, and let it cook down to thicken slightly. Taste and correct seasoning if necessary, then spoon sauce over the chops.

NOTE: Dry white wine or stock may be used instead of water.

¶Onion and Herb Stuffing. Blend 2½ cups finely chopped onion, ½ cup bread crumbs, ¼ cup chopped parsley, 1 teaspoon dried tarragon, ¼ cup melted butter, 1 egg, salt and pepper to taste.

¶Pork and Onion Stuffing. Sauté ½ cup ground pork and ½ cup ground onion in 4 tablespoons butter until cooked through. Mix with ½ cup bread crumbs and 1 teaspoon oregano, salt and pepper to taste.

Pork and Sauerkraut Goulash

This very different version of the classic Middle European goulash combines pork and sauerkraut. Buttered noodles or spätzle (see page 288) go well with this.

Makes 6 servings

3 pounds lean pork shoulder, cut in
    1½-inch cubes
4 tablespoons rendered pork fat or
    olive oil
3 large onions, chopped
1 tablespoon Hungarian rose paprika
2 green peppers, peeled, seeded, and
    cut in thin strips

½ bay leaf
1 cup water or stock (veal or chicken)
1½ cups canned Italian plum tomatoes
2 pounds sauerkraut, well rinsed and
    drained
Salt, freshly ground black pepper
1 cup sour cream or yogurt

Sauté the meat in a heavy skillet in the pork fat until lightly browned. Add the onions and paprika and sauté until the onions are limp, then add the green peppers, bay leaf, water or stock, tomatoes, and sauerkraut. Cover and simmer for 1 hour or until the meat is tender. Season to taste (with the sauerkraut you will not need much salt, if any). Serve very hot with sour cream or yogurt spooned over the goulash.

¶**Pork and Veal Goulash.** Use half pork, half shoulder of veal.

Sometimes sour cream or yogurt is folded into the goulash and it is heated through without allowing it to boil.

NOTE: A few caraway seeds may be added to the goulash.

Baked Spareribs with Sauerkraut, Apples, and Potatoes

While spareribs have a lot of bone (count on at least 1 pound per serving), they are an inexpensive cut and go further if cooked or served with other ingredients. For this dish, buy the country spareribs, or back ribs, which have more meat on them than the regular kind.

Makes 4 to 6 servings

2 sides (4 pounds) country spareribs
3 to 4 pounds sauerkraut, well rinsed
    and drained
2 tart apples, peeled, cored, and sliced

3 medium potatoes, peeled and thinly
    sliced
1 to 2 teaspoons caraway seeds
1 teaspoon freshly ground black pepper

Place one side of spareribs in a lightly buttered baking pan, fat side down. Layer sauerkraut, apples, and potatoes on top, sprinkling the layers with caraway seeds. Season with pepper. Top with second side of ribs and press down onto sauerkraut mixture. Cover pan with aluminum foil and bake in a 350° oven for 1 hour, then remove foil and bake 1 hour more, or until brown and tender.

¶**With Onions.** Slice 2 large onions and layer with sauerkraut, apples, and potatoes.

¶**With Dill.** Substitute 3 tablespoons chopped fresh dill for the caraway seeds.

¶**Plain Roasted Spareribs.** Split 1 or 2 sides of spareribs down the middle and sprinkle liberally with salt and freshly ground black pepper. Place the ribs on the rack of a broiling pan and roast for 30 minutes at 350°. Turn the ribs and bake 30 minutes longer. Serve with braised Brussels sprouts.

Pigs' Feet St. Menehould

Although you may find it takes a bit of work to eat these delicious morsels, they are well worth it. When eating them, one must remove all the little foot bones to get at the edible parts. However, if you like foods that are gelatinous to the bite, you will love these. They are crisp and delicious and go well with crisp French fries.

Makes 4 servings

4 large or 8 small meaty pigs' feet

COURT BOUILLON
2 cups water
2 cups dry white wine
1 onion stuck with 2 cloves
1 carrot
1 celery rib

1 bay leaf
2 or 3 cloves garlic
A few leaves of sage
2 teaspoons salt
½ teaspoon freshly ground black pepper

FOR BROILING THE FEET
2 to 3 cups toasted bread crumbs

⅓ cup melted butter or pork fat

Wash the feet well and wrap tightly in several thicknesses of cheesecloth, muslin, or an old pillowcase, which prevents the skin from breaking as they cook. Tie securely. Bring the court bouillon ingredients to a boil in a large pan, add the feet, and simmer until very tender, about 2½ to 3½ hours. Cool in the bouillon.

Remove wrappings, roll the feet in toasted crumbs, dribble melted butter or fat over them, and brown either under the broiler, 5 inches from the heat, or in a 475° oven, turning them several times, until brown and crisp. Serve with a well-flavored vinaigrette sauce or a sauce diable (see page 74 or 533), French-fried potatoes and a bowl of watercress.

¶**Pickled Pigs' Feet.** Have the feet split. Wrap and cook in the court bouillon; remove. When cool enough to handle, discard wrappings and place feet in a jar with 2 sliced onions, salt and pepper to taste. Heat enough white wine vinegar or cider vinegar to cover the feet. Pour over feet and refrigerate several days before eating.

¶**Jellied Pigs' Feet.** For this dish, it is not necessary to wrap the feet. Simmer them in the court bouillon until tender, then remove. When cool enough to handle, remove and discard bones. Cut meat and slice in small pieces; place in a large casserole. Cook the broth down until reduced by one-third. Strain broth and ladle enough over the feet to cover. Cool, then chill until set. Slice and eat cold with pickles and salad.

¶**Jellied Pigs' Feet and Hocks.** Cook pigs' hocks in the court bouillon with the feet until tender, then follow preceding recipe.

Head Cheese

A very old traditional European recipe that has become part of the ethnic cooking patterns of this country through the German immigrants and French Canadians in New England. Delicious in summer or as part of an hors d'oeuvre selection.

Makes about 20 servings

1 pig's head	2 pigs' tongues
3 pig's feet	Salt

COURT BOUILLON

2 onions	2 sprigs thyme or 1 teaspoon dried
2 carrots	thyme
2 leeks	2 sprigs parsley
2 cloves garlic	8 peppercorns, crushed
2 bay leaves	4 tablespoons wine vinegar

FOR THE JELLIED STOCK

2 cups dry white wine	2 pinches (about ¼ teaspoon) quatre
Salt	épice seasoning (see page 536)
Lemon juice to taste	

Have the head sawed into four by the butcher so it will fit into a large pan. Reserve the brain and cook as for calf's brains (see page 449) for another meal. Soak the head in water to cover with 1 tablespoon salt for 2 hours. Then discard the water, put all the court bouillon ingredients in a pan with the head and the pig's feet, tightly wrapped in cheesecloth, according to directions on page 429. The pig's feet are to add gelatin to the stock, and after cooking they may be used in any of the ways recommended for pig's feet (see page 430). Add fresh water to cover and bring slowly to a boil. Skim off the scum, cover pan tightly with the lid, and simmer as gently as possible for 5 hours. The meat is cooked when it drops easily from the bone. Meanwhile, cook the tongues separately in salted water or court bouillon according to directions for beef tongue on page 456, for about 45 to 50 minutes or until tender.

Drain the head and feet and measure the liquid. Put 6 cups of strained liquid in a pan with the white wine and boil down to 4 cups. Taste, then season with salt and lemon juice.

Pick out the meat from the head, discarding bones and vegetables. Chop the meat into small dice by hand or in a food processor (do not put through a meat grinder). Season the meat with the spice seasoning, add it to the reduced bouillon-wine mixture, and simmer slowly for 20 minutes. Taste again for seasoning and put aside to cool. As it cools, taste again and adjust seasoning. Put a layer of chopped meat in two 9-by-5-by-3-inch loaf pans that have been rinsed with cold water. Arrange whole tongues on top, add another meat layer, then ladle in bouillon to cover the meat completely, and chill until set. To serve, unmold onto a platter and serve sliced rather thick, either plain or with sauce vinaigrette.

Roast Spareribs with Sautéed Lentils

Makes 4 to 6 servings

2 sides (4 pounds) country spareribs
Salt, freshly ground black pepper
2 cups quick-cooking lentils
1 onion stuck with 2 cloves
1 bay leaf

½ pound slab bacon, cut into
    small dice
1 cup finely chopped onion
2 cloves garlic, finely chopped
¼ cup chopped parsley

Lay the spareribs on a rack in a broiling pan, sprinkle lightly with salt and pepper, and roast in a 350° oven for 30 minutes. Turn, salt and pepper the other side, and roast for a further 30 minutes.

While the spareribs are roasting, cook the lentils. Put them in a saucepan with water to cover, the clove-stuck onion, and bay leaf. Simmer until just tender, about 25 to 30 minutes, adding a little salt after the first 15 minutes. Be careful not to overcook or they will become mushy. Drain well.

Cook the bacon in a heavy skillet until the fat is rendered, remove excess fat, add the chopped onion and garlic, and sauté lightly until just limp and golden. Add the drained lentils and toss well together, being careful not to break up the lentils. Taste and add freshly ground black pepper (you will probably not need salt) and the parsley. Serve with the spareribs.

¶**Glazed Spareribs.** Melt 1 cup orange marmalade and mix with 1 tablespoon Dijon mustard, 1 tablespoon lemon juice, and 1 tablespoon Worcestershire sauce. Brush spareribs with mixture frequently during roasting, until well glazed. Serve with rice.

NOTE: If quick-cooking lentils are not available, use regular lentils and cook according to directions on the package.

Cecilia Chiang's Red-Cooked Pork Shoulder

A very old Chinese dish which was prepared for me in her home by Cecilia Chiang, the owner of the Mandarin Restaurant on the West Coast. I like to serve this with rice and cooked mustard greens tossed with butter.

Makes 6 servings

*1 whole pork shoulder, 5 to 6 pounds,
    bone and skin left on*
¼ cup dry sherry

5 or 6 thin slices fresh ginger
1¼ cups soy sauce
⅓ cup sugar (preferably rock sugar)

Wash the pork and make a few slashes with a knife on the side of the meat where there is no skin to allow the sauce to penetrate more easily during the cooking. Place the pork in a heavy medium-sized pot and add enough water to cover. Cover the pot and bring to a boil over high heat. When the water boils, skim off all the scum, then add the dry sherry and the fresh ginger. Cover, turn heat to low, and simmer the pork for 1 hour. Drain off one-third of the liquid and add the soy sauce to the pot. Simmer for another 1½ hours, then add the sugar (rock sugar will give the skin a more glazed appearance). Cook for a further 30 minutes, basting the skin often with the hot sauce. To test for tenderness, pierce the meat with a fork or chopstick. If it penetrates easily, the meat is done. If not, cook a little longer. Serve the shoulder and the sauce in a deep bowl and slice the meat thin. Serve with the sauce.

Braised Pigs' Hocks

An inexpensive and much neglected part of the pig, the hocks are meaty, flavorful, with a luscious gelatinous texture. You will notice there is no salt in this recipe—the flavors of the meat, garlic, and vegetables come through with a kind of undisguised purity that is exciting to the palate. Try it this way, then add seasonings if you feel the dish needs them.

Makes 6 servings

6 meaty pigs' hocks, washed	1 tablespoon chopped fresh dill or
2 onions, sliced	1 teaspoon dried dill
12 cloves garlic, unpeeled	1½ cups dry white wine
1 rib fennel	

Arrange the pigs' hocks in a braising pan on a bed of the sliced onions, garlic, fennel, and dill. Pour over the white wine. Cover and braise in a 300° oven for 1½ hours, then reduce the heat to 250°, and cook for a further 1½ hours, or until tender. Serve with plain boiled potatoes or with crusty French bread and a salad.

¶**Pigs' Hocks with Sauerkraut.** Braise the hocks with sauerkraut, enough white wine to cover the sauerkraut, and freshly ground black pepper. Omit the onions and fennel and add a few caraway seeds instead of the dill.

¶**Marinated Pigs' Hocks.** The meat of cold hocks may be cut away from the bone and marinated in a good vinaigrette dressing, to which add 2 tablespoons chopped onion or shallot, 2 teaspoons capers, and 2 tablespoons chopped parsley. Marinate for several hours before serving.

Italian Sausage

I've often said that I'd be perfectly happy eating nothing but sausages, and I find making them almost as much fun. As it is becoming well-nigh impossible to get decent sausage meat these days, you'll find it a satisfying and engrossing pursuit. There's no end to the sausages you can make at home by experimenting with different mixtures of meat and seasonings, but probably the simplest and tastiest to start with are the Italian link sausages. I like the meat coarsely ground or chopped, so if you use a food processor, be careful not to grind the mixture too fine.

Makes 2 pounds

2 *pounds pork with 30 percent fresh*
    white pork fat (from the loin or
    belly, fatback, or leaf lard from
    the kidneys)
4 *garlic cloves, very finely chopped*

2 *teaspoons crushed dried basil*
1 *tablespoon salt*
1 *teaspoon freshly ground black pepper*
1½ *teaspoons crushed anise seed*

Either grind the pork coarse in a meat grinder, chop it coarse by hand with a large, heavy chef's knife, or use a food processor, turning it off and on quickly, so the meat isn't reduced to mush. Mix the pork thoroughly with the seasonings, using your hands. To check for seasoning, form 1 tablespoon of the mixture into a tiny patty and sauté it in 1 tablespoon butter until thoroughly cooked through (never taste raw pork; it's very dangerous), then taste and adjust the seasonings if necessary.

You can either form the sausage meat into cakes or force it loosely into casings for link sausages, using either natural hog intestines or the edible plastic kind. (Ask your local butcher where he buys his casings, or look in the yellow pages of the telephone directory under "Sausage Casings.")

Casings, especially the natural ones which are sold packed in salt, should be cleaned before stuffing. Slip one end of the casing over the faucet and let cold water run through, then dry and cut the casings into lengths of 4 or 5 feet.

There are various ways to stuff the casings. If you own an electric meat grinder with a stuffing attachment, you can grind the meat and seasonings and fill the casings in one operation. Otherwise, you can use a commercial sausage stuffer (one type, sold by various kitchen shops across the country, is about 2½ feet long and resembles a huge hypodermic needle with a plunger for forcing the meat into the casings), a large funnel, or a pastry bag without a tube. Tie one open end of the casing tightly with string and slip the other end over the tube of the grinder, stuffer, or funnel, or the opening of the pastry bag.

You should gauge the amount of stuffing forced into the casing for each sausage so as to get an even shape and size. Force the meat mixture down toward the tied end with the plunger or by working it down with your hand, and when you have one complete sausage about 4 inches long, either twist the casing twice to make a separation, or tie it off firmly with thin white cotton string. Continue until you have used all your meat mixture, unless you want to save some for patties. Homemade sausages or patties can be kept for 3 months in the freezer.

¶**Old-Fashioned Sausage.** To the pork add 1 tablespoon salt, 1 to 2 teaspoons freshly ground black pepper, and 2 teaspoons ground sage.

¶Hot Sausage. To the pork add 1 tablespoon salt, 1 to 2 teaspoons freshly ground black pepper, ½ teaspoon crushed anise seed, 1 teaspoon paprika, ½ teaspoon crushed dried basil, and 3 or 4 good dashes Tabasco.

¶Pork and Veal Sausage. Combine the pork with 1 pound coarsely ground veal (leg or shoulder), 6 finely chopped shallots, 1½ teaspoons crushed fennel seeds, 1 teaspoon crumbled dried sage, 1 teaspoon dried thyme, 1 tablespoon salt, and 2 teaspoons freshly ground black pepper.

Link Sausages

To cook link sausages, prick the skins well with a fork, put in a skillet with water to cover, bring to a boil, reduce the heat, and poach 1 minute. (This initial blanching draws out the excess fat and heats the sausages through so they take less time to cook.) Drain off the water and continue to cook over medium-low heat, or in a 350° oven, until brown, about 15 to 20 minutes. Or prick the skins again and brown under the broiler.

Sausage Cakes

Form the sausage meat into 3-, 4-, or 5-ounce cakes, making them rather flat and round or oval. Broil slowly about 5 inches from the heat until cooked through and browned, or sauté in 2 tablespoons butter and 2 tablespoons oil until cooked through and lightly browned, turning frequently.

Broiled Sausage Balls

Mold the sausage meat into balls about 5 to 6 ounces each and wrap each one loosely in foil. Broil over charcoal or under the broiler, turning twice, for about 20 minutes, or until cooked through. To serve, split the balls in half and serve in the foil with sauce diable (see page 533), crisp French fries, and watercress.

Sausage en Brioche

I find that Italian cotechino or the garlic sausage from a French butcher shop is best for this dish. Failing these, you could use a Polish kielbasa or a bologna (this does not need cooking, just heating and skinning). Although this is usually served in French restaurants as a first course with a hot potato salad (see page 95), it is sufficiently hearty, with potato salad or Spicy Coleslaw (see page 91), to make a main course for lunch or supper. You can also make individual sausages in brioche, using knockwurst or large frankfurters.

Makes 6 to 8 servings

1 large garlic sausage, cotechino, or   *1 egg beaten with 2 tablespoons water*
kielbasa
1 recipe Brioche Bread (see page 477)
refrigerated for second rising

Poach the sausage in water to cover for 30 minutes. Drain. When cool enough to handle, peel off the skin.

Remove the brioche dough from the refrigerator and punch it down, then turn out onto a floured board and roll out into a rectangle about ⅓ inch thick and large enough to envelop the sausage completely. Place the cooled, peeled sausage in the middle of the dough, fold each end of the dough over the ends of the sausage, then bring up the sides of the dough to overlap, forming a neat seam. (Do not cover the sausage too tightly; the dough should be slightly loose.) Press the seam to seal well.

Place the brioche-wrapped sausage on a buttered baking sheet, seam side down, and let rise in a warm place for 15 minutes. Preheat the oven to 375°. Brush the surface of the risen dough with the egg mixture and bake in the center of the oven for about 35 to 40 minutes, or until the crust is nicely browned and puffed. Remove from the oven and let stand a few minutes, then remove to a serving board by sliding two large spatulas under the brioche. Slice thick and serve with hot potato salad or coleslaw.

¶**Sausage en Brioche with Mustard.** Spread the surface of the dough with Dijon or German mustard before wrapping the sausage.

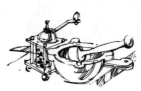

Ham

Baked Ham en Croûte

There are plenty of versions of ham en croûte, in puff pastry, in brioche dough, in a rich pastry crust—but this is something different, because after baking the ham you throw away the crust. It's not a waste; the crust is merely intended to be a container and the Madeira in it gives flavor, juiciness, and delicate texture to the ham. This works well with country hams or the tenderized hams sold in supermarkets.

Makes 16 to 20 servings

1 ready-to-eat (fully cooked) ham or a country ham, about 10 to 12 pounds
1½ cups brown sugar

6 tablespoons Dijon mustard
¼ teaspoon cinnamon or ground cloves (optional)

CRUST
4 cups flour
2 teaspoons salt
4 ounces lard

1⅓ cups Madeira, port, or sherry (preferably Madeira)

If you are using aged country ham, soak it in clear water for 24 hours before baking. After soaking, scrape off any little spots of mold there may be on the ham. Supermarket hams do not need soaking. With a sharp knife, loosen the skin on the ham, run your fingers between skin and fat and pull off the skin. If there is an excess of fat, trim off a little, but not too much, as this helps keep the ham moist during baking. Mix the brown sugar and mustard to a paste, adding the cinnamon or cloves, if desired. Rub the paste well into the ham fat and let rest while making the crust.

Put the flour in a bowl with the salt and cut in the lard, or crumble it in with your fingertips, until the mixture resembles coarse cornmeal. Mix in the Madeira and just enough water to make a firm pastry, like a good pie crust. It must roll out easily and yet not be flimsy. Refrigerate the dough for 10 minutes, then roll it out about ¾ inch thick, following in free form the conical shape of the ham. Roll the pastry over the rolling pin, carefully lift it up, and drape it over the ham so it hangs down about two-thirds of the way around. Cup your hands around the ham, fitting the pastry around the shank end, and press it into the flesh. Then press pastry into sides of ham, all the way around. The top and two-thirds of the sides should be completely covered.

Place ham on a rack in a roasting pan and bake at 400° for 1 hour. Reduce heat to 325° and continue baking for a further 1 hour and 10 minutes to 1 hour and 20 minutes, according to weight.

Remove the baked ham and let it rest for 15 to 20 minutes, then remove the hard crust; you may have to crack it with a mallet and remove in 2 or 3 pieces. This is for a hot ham. If you wish to serve it cold, cool in the crust before removing the pastry. Serve hot with a spinach ring or timbale (see page 263), cold with potato salad, and have a variety of mustards and perhaps some freshly made cornbread.

Braised Ham Chablisienne

Most European recipes for hot ham call for the ham to be braised rather than baked. The ham is then often served with a sauce, for which the wine from the braising supplies part of the liquid. The ham may be braised on a mirepoix or bed of vegetables, or just with wine, either of which makes for moist and deliciously flavorful meat. Slice the ham fairly thin and accompany with tiny new potatoes, boiled and sprinkled with parsley, and salad with some spinach leaves in it. Leftover ham can be served cold, with a mustard mayonnaise (see page 76).

Makes 16 or more servings

4 carrots, coarsely chopped
2 large onions, coarsely chopped
1 rib celery, coarsely chopped
1 teaspoon thyme
1 bay leaf

1 ready-to-eat 10-pound ham, skin
   removed
1 bottle French Chablis or similar
   very dry white wine

SAUCE
1 cup stock from the braised ham
4 tablespoons butter
4 tablespoons flour
1 cup dry white wine

3 tablespoons tomato paste
Salt, freshly ground black pepper
2 egg yolks
1 cup heavy cream

Make a bed of the chopped vegetables, thyme, and bay leaf in a deep roasting or baking pan. Place the ham on the vegetables, fat side down. Add the Chablis. Cover the pan with foil and braise the ham in a 350° oven for 2 to 2½ hours.

Remove ham and keep warm while making the sauce. Pour off ham stock from the pan and remove excess fat. Measure 1 cup of the ham stock. Melt the butter in a saucepan, blend in the flour, and cook slightly, then stir in the ham stock and white wine, and cook, stirring, until thickened. Mix in the tomato paste and seasonings to taste. Beat the egg yolks and cream, add a little of the hot sauce, then blend into the remainder of sauce in the pan. Cook gently (do not boil) until smooth and thickened. Serve sauce with the ham.

¶**Ham Braised in Madeira.** After skinning the ham, rub the fat with 2 tablespoons granulated sugar and 2 tablespoons Dijon mustard. Put the ham in the pan and pour over it 2 cups Madeira. Cover with foil and braise. Combine ¼ cup liquid from the pan with ¼ cup Madeira and 1½ cups brown sauce (see page 533). Bring to a boil, lower heat, and simmer 4 minutes. Add 2 finely chopped truffles, if you wish, and heat through. Serve sauce with the ham. You may use a rich, rather sweet sherry, port, Jamaica rum, or cognac instead of the Madeira. This calls for spinach, either *en branche* or chopped and seasoned with garlic, olive oil, and a dash or two of nutmeg.

Boiled Ham and Cabbage

A hearty peasant dish, similar to a pot-au-feu or a boiled dinner. Save the ham broth and use it as stock for split pea or lentil soup.

Makes 8 to 10 servings

½ ready-to-eat ham, weighing about 6 to 8 pounds, or a smoked picnic shoulder
1 onion, stuck with 2 cloves

1 bay leaf
½ cup wine vinegar
1 teaspoon mustard seed

ACCOMPANYING VEGETABLES
1 carrot per serving
1 turnip per serving
1 potato per serving

1 head cabbage
Butter
Salt, freshly ground black pepper

Put the ham in a deep pot with water to cover, the onion, bay leaf, vinegar, and mustard seed. Bring to a boil, lower the heat, and simmer for about 18 minutes per pound. Half an hour before the ham is done, add the carrots and turnips to the pot, halving them if they are large. Boil the potatoes separately in their jackets. Wash the cabbage, cut it into quarters or sixths, and cook in boiling salted water until done but still crisp, about 10 to 12 minutes. Drain well, dress with butter, and season to taste with salt and pepper. Serve the ham and vegetables with a variety of mustards. Crisp cornbread or the chili bread from *Beard on Bread* is an admirable accompaniment.

Leftover Ham

Ham that has been boiled, baked, or braised has innumerable uses, so there need never be any problem about what to do with leftovers. You can use it in a soufflé, mousse, pâté, soup, salad, pasta sauce, sandwich, stuffing. You can grind it and make deviled ham, ham loaf, or ham balls, or just cut it in thin, even slices, reheat in white wine to cover, and serve with a sauce or on top of choucroute garnie, along with the other pork products that go with this great dish. A slice of reheated ham can be a base for sweetbreads or brains, poached eggs, or many other foods, ad infinitum.

Broiled Ham Slice

These recipes are for ham slices cut from the leg, which supermarkets call "ham steaks," a term I happen to dislike.

Makes 3 to 4 servings

Slash the fat around the edges of a 1½-inch-thick slice of ready-to-eat country ham or tenderized ham to prevent its curling. Broil on a greased rack 3 inches from the heat, turning once during the cooking. Allow about 8 minutes' total broiling time.

¶**Ham Slice Glazed with Honey and Mustard.** Brush before broiling with 1 part honey to 2 parts Dijon mustard. Brush once or twice with mixture during broiling.

¶**Barbecued Ham Slice.** Baste during broiling with your favorite barbecue sauce.

¶**Ham Slice Glazed with Maple Syrup.** Brush during broiling with maple syrup.

¶**Ham Slice Broiled with Soy and Mustard.** Brush during broiling with a mixture of soy sauce and dry mustard.

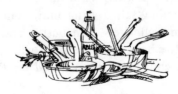

Baked Ham Slice in Red Wine

Makes 3 to 4 servings

Slash the fat on a ham slice 1½ to 2 inches thick and spread both sides with Dijon mustard. Place in a shallow baking dish, sprinkle with freshly ground black pepper, and add red wine to cover. Bake in a 350° oven for 35 minutes, basting several times during the cooking. Serve with polenta and puréed spinach (see pages 300 and 173).

¶**Ham Slice Baked in Champagne.** Put a 2-inch-thick ham slice in a baking dish with champagne to cover. Marinate several hours, turning once. Bake in a 375° oven for 35 minutes, sprinkle lightly with sugar, and put under the broiler to glaze. Serve with tiny new potatoes, tossed in melted butter and parsley, and an orange and onion salad.

¶**Ham Slice Floridian.** Put a 2-inch-thick ham slice in a baking dish with orange juice to cover. Bake in a 375° oven for 35 minutes, basting once or twice. Arrange ⅔ cup orange sections on the ham, sprinkle lightly with sugar and a touch of cinnamon, and put under the broiler to glaze. Serve with crusty French bread and sautéed zucchini (see page 175).

¶**Ham Slice Arthoise.** Arrange a 2-inch-thick ham slice in a baking dish and spread with purée of foie gras or good liver pâté. Top and surround with sliced sautéed mushrooms (see page 154). Pour ¾ cup Madeira over the ham and bake in a 350° oven for 10 minutes, then add ¼ cup more Madeira, bake 10 minutes, baste, and bake 10 minutes more, or until tender. Serve with Barley Casserole with Almonds (see page 296) and a green salad.

Fried Ham Slice with Red-Eye Gravy

This is the famous Southern way of treating a ham slice, which for frying should be only ½ inch thick. Southerners prefer their country ham sawed straight across the leg, so you have a piece of ham with the little round leg bone in the center and a rim of fat on the outside. Trim off most of the fat, and slash the remaining fat around the edges. Heat a large iron skillet to medium hot and rub it with a bit of the trimmed ham fat. Put in the ham slice and cook slowly for about 10 minutes, turning it several times, until cooked through and crisp on the edges. Remove the ham from the skillet and pour in ⅔ to ¾ cup hot water. Let it simmer for 3 minutes, stirring to lift the reddish-brown glaze from the pan (this is what makes it red-eye gravy). Spoon the gravy over the ham, to be mopped up with hot biscuits, or spoon it directly over hot biscuits or grits.

¶**Variation.** Some traditional recipes call for a cup of black coffee to be added to the pan instead of water.

Venison

Out in the woods, and even in the suburbs, wild deer are making a comeback, to the point of overpopulation in some areas not an hour's drive from Manhattan. But right here in town, commercially raised venison is quite easy to get and very reliable. How you cook it depends on the age of the animal and the cut of meat. The saddle, loin, tenderloin, leg, steaks, and chops cut from a young animal which has been hung for the proper length of time are usually tender enough to roast, broil, or sauté. The meat of older animals should definitely be given a good long soaking in a marinade to tenderize and flavor it. The tougher cuts from the shoulder, shank, and breast are best if used for stew or ground.

The following marinade is an excellent one. The meat should be allowed to soak for at least several hours, preferably for 2 days or more, in a cool place. Turn it frequently.

Marinade for Venison

1 bottle red wine	3 onions, sliced
1 cup wine vinegar	3 carrots, sliced
3 cloves	3 cloves garlic, crushed
1 teaspoon coarsely crushed peppercorns	2 bay leaves, crushed 1 sprig thyme
1½ tablespoons salt	1 cup olive oil

Combine all ingredients and use to marinate venison.

Marinated Roast Leg of Venison

Makes 8 to 10 servings

1 leg venison	1 tablespoon tomato sauce
2 cups strained marinade	1 teaspoon freshly ground black pepper
Fat salt pork	½ cup cream
Butter or oil	Salt to taste
4 tablespoons flour	

Soak a leg of venison in the marinade for 2 days. Remove and dry well. Venison is not well marbled, and it needs the addition of fat to tenderize the meat. Lard it with strips of fat salt pork, either with a larding needle (for description of larding technique, see page 375) or by making deep incisions in the meat with the point of a small sharp knife and pushing the salt pork into them. Rub the leg well with butter or oil, arrange on a rack in a roasting pan, and roast in a 375° oven from 1½ to 2 hours, or until the internal temperature registers 125° (for rare) on a meat thermometer, basting frequently with melted butter or oil.

Transfer the roast to a hot platter and let it rest 10 to 12 minutes before carving. Remove most of fat from roasting pan, leaving about 4 tablespoons. Mix in the flour and then add the strained marinade. Cook, stirring, until thickened, then stir in the tomato sauce, freshly ground black pepper, and cream. Taste and add salt. Simmer until well blended. Serve the venison with this sauce, roast potatoes, and cauliflower with browned butter.

Roast Saddle of Venison

A saddle of venison makes an impressive roast, which should always be served rare. Carve it in long, thin slices the length of the saddle, parallel to the bone, and don't forget to remove the tender little fillets and slice them as well. If the saddle comes from a very young animal, it will not need marinating. A saddle from an older animal should be rubbed with oil and marinated for several days before roasting. Serve the saddle with a purée of chestnuts or sweet potatoes and buttered Brussels sprouts.

Makes 4 to 6 servings, according to size of saddle

1 saddle young venison	¼ cup red wine
1 teaspoon freshly ground black pepper	1½ cups broth (venison, beef, or
1½ teaspoons salt	chicken)
1 teaspoon thyme	Beurre manié (see page 536)
6 tablespoons softened butter	½ cup Madeira
¼ cup melted butter	2 tablespoons chopped parsley

Rub the saddle well with pepper, salt, thyme, and softened butter. Arrange on a rack in a shallow pan and roast at 450° for 30 minutes, then reduce heat to 400° and continue roasting for 15 minutes longer, or until internal temperature registers 125° for rare. Baste occasionally with the melted butter and red wine, mixed. When done, transfer to a hot platter and let stand 10 minutes before carving, while you make the sauce.

Rinse the roasting pan with the broth, bring to a boil and thicken with small balls of beurre manié. Add the Madeira, and simmer 5 minutes. Taste and correct the seasoning. Add the parsley and serve with the venison.

Helmut Ripperberger's Roast Loin of Venison

For this you need a loin that has hung for several weeks. The marinade, a different one, with juniper berries, is used to make a wonderful sauce for the meat. Serve the roast with puréed chestnuts and braised Brussels sprouts.

Makes 2 to 4 servings, according to size of loin

MARINADE

1 pint wine vinegar	2 carrots, thinly sliced
1 pint red wine	1 lemon, thinly sliced
2 bay leaves	1 tablespoon juniper berries
6 shallots	1 teaspoon freshly ground black pepper
Loin of venison	Salt, freshly ground black pepper
6 strips thick bacon about ¼ inch wide	1 cup sour cream
¼ pound butter	

Combine the marinade ingredients. Add the venison and marinate for 2 to 3 hours, turning frequently. Remove and wipe dry. Lard the loin with the strips of bacon and arrange it on a rack in a roasting pan. Spread the top of the meat with butter, and melt the remaining butter for basting. Roast in a 450° oven for 30 to 45 minutes, depending on size, or until the internal temperature registers 125° on a meat thermometer. Baste frequently with melted butter and some of the marinade.

Remove the loin to a hot platter while making the sauce. Strain the marinade. Skim the excess fat from the pan juices, add 1 cup of the strained marinade and cook it down to ½ cup by rapid boiling. Add salt and pepper to taste. Remove pan from heat, stir in the sour cream, and heat through; do not boil. Correct seasoning and serve with the venison.

Broiled Venison Steaks

If these are from a young and tender animal that has been properly hung for 2 or 3 weeks, they will require no marinating. Have them cut thick—1 to 1½ inches. Press coarsely ground black pepper and coarse salt into the flesh and broil close to the broiling unit, turning once, for about 4 to 5 minutes a side, or 3 minutes if you like extremely rare meat. Serve with a purée of chestnuts and diced turnips tossed in butter.

¶Broiled Venison Steaks with Seasoned Butter. Put on a heatproof platter 2 tablespoons finely chopped shallot and 6 tablespoons butter. Heat in the oven until butter melts. Add a few dashes of Tabasco and a sprinkling of salt. Put the steaks on the butter and put another pat of butter on top. Turn in the seasoned butter several times. Carve in strips and serve with the hot butter and crisp fried potatoes.

¶Sautéed Venison Steaks. Heat a mixture of half butter and half oil in a heavy skillet and sauté the venison as you would a strip steak, for about 6 minutes a side, until nicely browned, turning frequently. Serve with sautéed potatoes (see page 171) and a green salad. If you like, flame the steaks with cognac before serving.

¶Peppered Venison Steaks. Push a layer of coarsely crushed or ground black peppercorns into each side of the steaks and leave at room temperature for 15 minutes. Season lightly with salt and sauté as before. Flame with cognac before serving and stir sour cream or yogurt into the pan juices to make a sauce for the steaks.

Venison Kebabs

For kebabs, the meat should come from the loin or leg of a young and tender animal that has been well hung. The marinade is typical of India and Pakistan. Serve the kebabs with rice pilaf.

Makes 4 to 6 servings

2 to 3 pounds venison, cut in 2-inch
  cubes
½ cup oil
½ cup lemon juice
2 teaspoons turmeric
½ teaspoon chopped hot chili pepper

¼ teaspoon Tabasco
1 teaspoon salt
Beef fat
Small pieces of onion (optional)
Olive oil

Marinate the venison in a mixture of the oil, lemon juice, turmeric, chili, Tabasco, and salt for several hours. Thread meat on skewers alternately with small pieces of beef fat and, if desired, onion. Brush well with olive oil and broil about 4 inches from the broiling unit or over hot coals, turning them several times and basting them frequently with the marinade, until done to taste, about 8 to 9 minutes for medium rare.

Venison Pot Roast

A tough piece of venison from an older animal is best pot roasted. You may marinate it if you wish, but as it is going to be cooked in wine this is not essential. You should, however, lard it well with strips of salt pork to add some lubrication to the dry meat, and give it more flavor by first soaking the strips for an hour or two in cognac or bourbon.

Makes 8 to 10 servings

5-pound piece of boned venison leg or
  shoulder, securely tied
8 strips salt pork, soaked in
  ½ cup cognac
¼ cup oil
2 teaspoons thyme
1 cut clove of garlic
1 teaspoon salt
1 teaspoon freshly ground black pepper

3 to 4 tablespoons rendered beef suet
1 onion, stuck with 2 cloves
2 carrots, halved
3 cloves garlic
1 leek
1 bay leaf
2 cups red wine
Beurre manié (see page 536)

Lard the venison with the salt pork strips, using a larding needle (see page 375 for technique). Rub well with oil, 1 teaspoon thyme, garlic, salt, and pepper. Heat the beef fat in a deep braising pan, add the venison and brown on all sides over fairly high heat or brown under the broiler. Add the onion, carrots, garlic, leek, bay leaf, remaining teaspoon thyme, and red wine. Bring to a boil, reduce heat and simmer 2½ to 3 hours, or until tender. Transfer the meat to a warm platter. Add enough beurre manié to the sauce to thicken lightly. Serve this pot roast with macaroni and dress it with the sauce, as you would a daube.

Venison Hamburgers

While tough old venison makes an acceptable stew or pot roast, it is my belief that, if the meat is fresh, it is best ground with a small amount of beef fat and used for hamburgers. Venison hamburgers and venison chili are fine ways to use up some of the less desirable parts of the animal. You can sauté the hamburgers or broil outdoors on the charcoal grill. Serve these with crisp fried onion rings and either baked potatoes or sautéed mushrooms (see page 154).

Makes 4 servings

2 pounds venison, ground with about
    20 percent beef fat
2 teaspoons coarse salt

1 teaspoon freshly ground black pepper
2 tablespoons butter
2 tablespoons oil

Mix the venison with salt and pepper and form into 4 large patties, or 8 small patties if you don't like large burgers. For rare burgers, make the patties thick, for medium rare rather thinner. Heat the butter and oil in a heavy skillet, add the patties, and sauté over fairly high heat for about 5 minutes, until nicely browned. Turn and brown for 5 minutes on the second side. This will give you rare burgers. Small patties will only take 3 minutes on a side.

¶Venison Hamburgers Flambé. Flame the burgers with ¼ cup warmed cognac or bourbon before removing from the pan. Pour pan juices over them.

¶Herbed Venison Hamburgers. Add ½ teaspoon crushed dried rosemary, thyme, or summer savory with the salt and pepper.

¶Venison Hamburgers with Garlic and Chives. Add 2 finely chopped garlic cloves, 1 tablespoon chopped chives, and 2 dashes Tabasco to the meat mixture. After sautéing, remove burgers to a hot platter, rinse the pan with ¼ cup red wine, cook down a little over high heat, and pour over the burgers.

Venison Chili

A pleasant variation on beef chili. Serve with pinto or kidney beans and rice. This also makes a tasty sauce for hot dogs: top each frankfurter with a spoonful or two of chili and a spoonful of chopped raw onion and put in toasted bun.

Makes 4 to 6 servings

4 large onions, finely chopped
2 cloves garlic, finely chopped
½ cup vegetable oil
2 pounds venison, ground
2 tablespoons chili powder
1 teaspoon ground coriander

½ teaspoon ground cumin
Dash of Tabasco
1 cup beer
½ cup tomato paste
1½ teaspoons salt

Sauté the onion and garlic in the oil in a large pot until limp and golden. Add the ground venison and cook through, breaking it up with a fork. Add the remaining ingredients, mix well, reduce the heat, and simmer for 45 minutes to 1 hour, adding more beer if mixture gets too dry. Taste and correct seasoning until rich in flavor and well thickened.

Offal

Originally the word *offal* meant something to be thrown away. Thank heavens today we no longer look upon offal or the innards of an animal with such disdain. Quite the contrary, most of us treasure all those choice, succulent morsels that add so much versatility to our table.

Nowadays I notice brains and sweetbreads are much more readily available in our supermarkets. Sometimes they have been frozen and thawed, but don't be afraid of that; it doesn't hurt them. However, if you're in any doubt about whether these perishable innards have been resting in the supermarket display case too long, simply unwrap and sniff them. I like to soak, trim, and blanch them as soon as I get them home (though one remarkable sweetbread recipe here does skip this step). Once prepared, they can be refrigerated overnight and very quickly turned into all sorts of delicate and sophisticated dishes.

Calves' liver has become a very expensive delicacy these days, although, as it is a rich meat with no waste, a little goes a long way. A quarter to a half pound is ample for a serving, depending on the style of preparation. Lambs' liver, if you can find it, is a good substitute for calves' liver and less costly. Cheapest of all is beef liver. While not as delicate in flavor and texture, beef liver, especially baby beef liver, which is now generally available, can be pretty palatable if not overcooked. (I don't recommend it for broiling.) Pork liver, which is very strong and rich in flavor, may be sautéed, although it is more often used in pâtés. Liver should be cooked rare. When it is overdone it loses texture and becomes very dull.

Tongue, whether smoked, pickled or fresh, needs careful trimming and thorough cooking. The cured variety particularly makes a durable refrigerator resource; the scraps are wonderful additives for aspics and pâtés, delicious in a herring salad, and, of course, there is nothing like a good tongue sandwich.

Kidneys, which are comparatively inexpensive in our markets, vary a great deal according to the animal from which they come. Gastronomically, the veal kidney is considered the prize, particularly if the calf has been milk fed. Lamb and pork kidneys have a very strong flavor that some people find unpleasant. I find that if you soak them in milk before cooking, it removes some of the blood and the kidney taste and makes them sweeter and more palatable. Veal kidneys seldom need soaking. As kidneys are now sold divested of all their fat, they need lubrication while roasting. Here in this chapter I have a number of recipes that I find simple to prepare, varied in flavor, and very adaptable to almost any kind of meal. If you love kidneys as I do, you might check out *Theory & Practice* for several quite different recipes: steak and kidney pie (and pudding), fritto misto, and liver bourguignon, for example.

I've always had a fondness for hearts and you'll find a delicious recipe for braising them. But avoid beef hearts—for me they are too coarse and indelicate.

I have given tripe much fuller treatment here than most cookbooks do, because it is a resource too long neglected by home cooks. A century ago, it was immensely popular in this country, and seems to be making a comeback with the new interest in French peasant cooking, in the form of tripes à la mode de Caen. But there's so much more you can do with tripe. As my recipes show, you can bake it, simmer it, broil it, or stir-fry it. It's inexpensive; several of the recipes are easily reheated or frozen; and finally, it's delicious.

Parboiled or Poached Brains

It is a good idea to do this preliminary step ahead of time—even the night before or the morning of the day you plan to serve them so that the brains can firm up and will hold their shape better.

Wash the brains well and soak in ice water for 30 minutes. Very carefully peel off the covering membrane and any remaining threads of blood. Put the brains in a pan, cover with lightly salted, acidulated water (1 tablespoon lemon juice or vinegar to each pint of water) or a court bouillon (made with the salted, acidulated water and a few peppercorns, a sprig of parsley, and an onion stuck with 2 cloves). Bring slowly to a boil, reduce heat and simmer gently for 15 minutes. Immediately remove the brains and put in a bowl of ice water to stop them from cooking further and to firm the texture. Drain and dry, put on a plate, and cover with wax paper. Put another plate on top so the brains will become firm and compact as they cool. Chill until ready to use.

One pair of calfs' brains, those most readily available, serves two. The small lamb's brains, if you find them in your market, serve one.

Sautéed Brains

Parboil the brains as in preceding recipe. Drain and dry. Dip them in flour, then in beaten egg, and then in freshly made bread crumbs. Sauté quickly in hot butter until golden brown on both sides. Season with salt and pepper and serve with lemon wedges.

¶**Sautéed Marinated Brains.** Parboil the brains. Cool and cut in thick slices. Marinate for several hours in a mixture of ½ cup olive oil, 3 tablespoons lemon juice, ¼ teaspoon Tabasco, 1 teaspoon salt, and 1 tablespoon each chopped parsley and chopped chives. Remove from marinade, dip in flour, beaten egg, and fresh bread crumbs, and sauté in hot oil until golden brown.

¶**Brains au Beurre Noir.** Parboil the brains, dip in flour, and sauté quickly in hot butter until golden brown. Remove and keep warm. Add to the pan 6 tablespoons butter and cook until it is a deep amber color. Add ¼ cup chopped shallots, then add 3 tablespoons white wine vinegar or lemon juice, 3 tablespoons capers, 2 tablespoons chopped parsley, and freshly ground black pepper to taste. Pour this sauce over the sautéed brains and serve.

Broiled Brains

Dip the parboiled brains in melted butter and then in fresh bread crumbs. Broil just until the coating is browned and crisp, turning once. Serve with beurre noir (see preceding recipe).

Fried Brains

Cut the cooled parboiled brains into thick slices. Dip the slices in flour and beer batter (see page 188) and fry in deep fat, heated to 375°, until golden brown, about 4 minutes. Drain on paper towels. Serve with fried parsley and lemon wedges.

Sautéed Liver with Bacon

Makes 4 servings

1½ to 2 pounds liver (calves', lambs',
    baby beef, or pork), sliced ½ inch
    thick (about 3 slices per serving)
½ cup flour

3 tablespoons butter
3 tablespoons oil
Salt, freshly ground black pepper
8 to 12 slices bacon, cooked until crisp

Lightly flour the liver slices and brown quickly on both sides in the hot butter and oil. Never overcook liver; it should be pink inside. Sprinkle with salt and pepper and serve with the crisp bacon slices and, if you wish, boiled new potatoes.

¶Sautéed Liver with Onions. Sauté 3 onions, sliced, in 4 tablespoons butter over medium heat, stirring frequently. When lightly colored and soft add 1½ tablespoons vinegar and mix well. Serve on top of the sautéed liver.

¶Liver Sautéed with Shallots and Madeira. Sauté finely chopped shallots in the butter and oil until limp. Add floured liver and sauté. Season; add ¼ cup Madeira and ¼ cup chopped parsley. Turn the liver once in the sauce. Transfer the liver to a platter and pour the sauce over it.

¶Sautéed Liver with Avocado. Peel 2 avocados and cut in quarters. Flour lightly and sprinkle with salt. Sauté avocado in butter for about half a minute per side and arrange on plates with the sautéed liver. To pan in which liver cooked add the juice of ½ lemon, 1 tablespoon chopped chives, and 4 tablespoons butter. Stir until butter is light brown, and pour over liver and avocado. Garnish with crisp bacon.

¶Sautéed Liver with Mustard Sauce. After removing liver, deglaze pan with ¼ cup dry white wine. Blend in 2 tablespoons Dijon mustard. Remove from heat and add ½ cup yogurt, stirring until warmed throughout. Pour sauce over the liver.

¶**Deviled Liver.** After removing liver, add to pan 1 tablespoon Dijon mustard, 1 tablespoon Worcestershire sauce, and a dash of Tabasco. Blend with pan juices and pour over liver.

Liver Venetian Style

This is one of the great, simple dishes of the Italian cuisine.

Makes 4 servings

1 pound calves' liver, sliced ¼ inch thick
3 tablespoons olive oil

2 cups thinly sliced onions
Salt, freshly ground black pepper
1 tablespoon wine vinegar

Trim off the skin around the liver slices, remove any pieces of gristly tube, and cut liver into strips about 1 inch wide. Heat the oil in a large skillet, add the onions, and sauté until limp and delicately browned. Remove and keep warm. Turn the heat high. Add more oil to the pan if the onions have absorbed most of it. When the oil is hot, sauté the liver strips very quickly on each side for about a minute, until the liver loses its raw look. Season with salt and pepper to taste, return onions to the pan, and toss with liver strips just long enough to reheat, then add 1 tablespoon wine vinegar and shake the pan thoroughly to distribute the flavor. Serve at once.

¶**Liver Julienne.** (Called in Switzerland "Suri Leberle.") Cut calves' or lambs' liver into strips about ⅜ inch wide and toss lightly in flour seasoned with salt and pepper. Sauté ½ cup finely chopped green onions in 4 tablespoons butter for 1 minute, add liver, and brown quickly on all sides. Remove to a hot platter and deglaze the pan with ½ cup dry white wine and 1 tablespoon wine vinegar. Remove from heat and mix in ¾ cup sour cream or yogurt and return to the heat just long enough to heat through, but do not allow it to boil. Stir in 3 tablespoons chopped parsley or dill and pour the sauce over the liver.

Roast Whole Liver

If you can afford it, this is a different and special way to present liver. Serve with Béarnaise sauce (see page 532), parsleyed potatoes and a purée of broccoli (see page 129).

Makes 8 servings

4- to 5-pound whole calf's liver, rolled *Freshly ground black pepper*
    and tied   *2 tablespoons chopped parsley*
1½ pounds good bacon   *1 clove garlic, finely chopped*

Put the liver on a rack in a shallow roasting pan and cover it completely with the bacon strips, which will provide all the lubrication needed. Roast in a 375° oven, allowing 15 minutes a pound. Transfer the liver to a platter and remove the bacon strips, which may be served around the liver. Sprinkle the liver with pepper and a mixture of the parsley and garlic. Slice medium thick.

Kidneys "on the Half Shell"

Makes 4 servings

4 veal kidneys or 12 lamb kidneys   *Salt, freshly ground black pepper*
Milk   *Tabasco*
4 to 6 slices bacon

Trim the kidneys of membrane and snip out the hard white core of tubes at the top with scissors. Cover with milk and leave to soak for 1 hour (you may not find this step necessary with veal kidneys if they are very fresh). Drain and dry. Preheat the oven to 475°.

Wrap each veal kidney in a bacon slice (for the smaller lamb kidneys, cut the slices in two) and put in a shallow baking pan. Roast for 10 to 12 minutes, or till done according to your taste, turning once. Remove to a hot platter, cut the veal kidneys in half and season with salt, pepper, and a dash of Tabasco, and serve with the bacon, if you wish. These are good with crisp shoestring potatoes and a watercress salad.

¶**Kidneys Flambé.** After halving the kidneys, put them on a flameproof platter and flambé them with 3 tablespoons warmed cognac. Salt and pepper to taste. Serve on hot plates and spoon the juices from the platter over them. Serve with herbed rice.

¶**Kidneys with Mushrooms.** While the kidneys are roasting, sauté 2 tablespoons chopped shallot or green onion and ½ pound sliced mushrooms in 6 tablespoons butter. Season with salt, pepper, and 1 tablespoon Dijon mustard, and mix into the pan juices ¾ cup heavy cream, sour cream, or yogurt. When kidneys are cooked, put them on a flameproof platter and flambé with 3 tablespoons warmed gin. Slice thin and add to the sauce along with the juices from the platter. Heat through quickly and serve garnished with parsley and the bacon.

Lamb Kidneys en Brochette

A good way to broil kidneys is to skewer them, which makes them easy to turn and simple to serve. Brushing them with a coating of Dijon mustard not only flavors them but also keeps them from hardening and toughening. Veal kidneys can be cooked this way, but as they are larger than lamb kidneys, allow only 1 per person. Nice accompaniments are shoestring potatoes or French-fried eggplant and a watercress salad or tomatoes vinaigrette. Or you can serve the kidneys on crisp buttered toast.

Makes 4 servings

12 *lamb kidneys*	4 *slices bacon*
Milk for soaking	*Melted butter*
2 *tablespoons Dijon mustard*	*Salt, freshly ground black pepper*

Remove membrane from kidneys, split in two lengthwise and snip out hard core of fat and white tubes. Soak in milk to cover for 1 hour. Drain and dry. Preheat the broiler.

Brush the kidneys well with the mustard and arrange on 4 skewers with the bacon, weaving it in and out between the kidneys. Brush kidneys with melted butter and broil for 5 minutes, turning once. Serve on hot plates, sprinkling them with salt and pepper.

¶Broiled Kidneys and Sweetbreads. Blanch a pair of sweetbreads and cool them on a plate, weighted down, until firm. Cut sweetbreads and kidneys into 1½-inch cubes and alternate on skewers. Brush well with lemon juice and melted butter, and broil. Season and serve with melted butter and lemon wedges.

¶Broiled Kidneys and Sweetbreads Flambé. After broiling, arrange on a heatproof platter and flambé with ¼ cup warmed cognac.

¶Broiled Kidneys and Mushrooms. Alternate halved kidneys with mushroom caps, brush well with melted butter, and broil. Serve with rice.

¶Broiled Kidneys, Mushrooms, and Bacon. Weave slices of bacon on skewers between kidneys and mushroom caps, and broil.

¶Broiled Kidneys with Herb Butter. Split kidneys almost all the way through. Put in the split: butter creamed with chopped parsley, scallions, and lemon juice (for 12 to 16 kidneys, use ¼ pound butter, ¼ cup each chopped parsley and scallions, 2 teaspoons lemon juice). Wrap each stuffed kidney in a half slice of partially cooked bacon, arrange on skewers, and broil until bacon is crisp and kidneys cooked through, but still pink on the inside.

¶**Broiled Deviled Kidneys.** Split 12 kidneys and spread flat. Cover cut surfaces with a mixture of ¼ pound butter creamed with ¼ cup chopped green onion, 1 finely chopped garlic clove, 2 teaspoons Dijon mustard, 2 teaspoons lemon juice, a dash of Tabasco and ½ teaspoon freshly ground black pepper. Arrange on a baking sheet and broil, spread side up, for 5 to 7 minutes. Serve on toast with the pan drippings poured over the kidneys.

Kidney Sauté Flambé

Makes 4 servings

8 lamb kidneys
Milk
4 tablespoons clarified butter
½ teaspoon salt

Freshly ground black pepper
½ cup cognac or bourbon
½ cup heavy cream
GARNISH: *Chopped parsley*

Soak the kidneys in enough milk to cover for 1 to 1½ hours. Remove the kidneys from the milk, cut them in half, and remove the core of fat and white tubes with a sharp knife or scissors. Place the kidneys on absorbent paper until ready to cook.

Melt the butter in a heavy skillet over high heat—do not burn the butter. Add the kidneys, toss well, and sauté for approximately 4 to 5 minutes. Add salt and pepper. Remove the skillet from the heat, add the cognac or bourbon, and flambé. When the flame has died down, remove the kidneys to a hot plate. Stir in the cream and reduce slightly over high heat. Pour the sauce over the kidneys, garnish with parsley and serve immediately.

¶**Deviled Kidney Sauté.** Combine 2 teaspoons Dijon mustard, 1½ teaspoons Worcestershire sauce, and a dash of Tabasco with the kidneys and sauté as above. Remove the kidneys and sauce and rinse the pan with ¼ cup bourbon. Pour over the kidneys and serve.

NOTE: Pork kidneys may be used, or veal kidneys if cut into thick slices.

Braised Veal Hearts

Little veal hearts braise beautifully, as do the smaller lamb hearts. This is, to me, the best way to treat this part of the animal, as it needs the addition of flavor and moisture. Serve with a little of the braising vegetables on top, boiled potatoes, and a salad.

Makes 4 servings

2 veal hearts
¼ cup flour
4 tablespoons butter
4 tablespoons oil or unsalted margarine
2 large onions, thinly sliced

2 carrots, shredded
6 cloves garlic, unpeeled
1 white turnip, shredded
Salt, freshly ground black pepper
½ cup dry white wine

Wash and dry the hearts and trim away the fatty covering. Cut in slices 1 inch thick, crosswise. Lightly flour the slices and sauté in the butter and oil or margarine until lightly browned. Make a bed of the onion, carrot, garlic, and turnip in a braising pan. Lay the heart slices on top, sprinkle with salt and pepper, and add the wine. Cover tightly and braise in a 350° oven for 1½ hours.

¶**Braised Lamb Hearts.** Allow 1 heart per serving. Leave whole and braise as for veal hearts.

Tongue

Beef tongue is sold various ways—fresh, smoked, and corned or pickled. Fresh tongue, while not as easy to find as the smoked variety, makes an excellent and rather different meat dish when boiled and served with various sauces, or in the style of a pot-au-feu. Whether you boil a fresh, smoked, or pickled tongue, the method is the same, although the salt would be omitted with smoked tongue. Tongues weigh from 3½ to 5 pounds, and, as they are practically all meat except for the root end, will make from 6 to 10 servings, according to size.

Beef Tongue with Provençal Tomato Sauce

Good with rice or boiled potatoes and a purée of spinach.

Makes 8 servings

4- to 5-pound fresh beef tongue
1 onion stuck with 2 cloves
2 cloves garlic
1 tablespoon salt
1½ teaspoons dried basil

½ teaspoon freshly ground black pepper
Tomato sauce (see page 534)
24 soft black olives, pitted
GARNISH: Chopped parsley

Put the tongue in a pot with cold water to cover, and add the onion, garlic, salt, basil, and pepper. Bring to a boil and boil 5 minutes, skimming off the scum. Reduce the heat, cover, and simmer for approximately 45 minutes a pound, until tender. Remove from the pan. Reserve 1 cup of the strained broth. When cool enough to handle, peel off the skin, loosening it with a knife and pulling it off with your fingers, and trim off the root end.

In a large pan heat together the tomato sauce and olives, add the tongue and the reserved cup of tongue broth. Simmer 20 minutes, turning the tongue once. Arrange on a platter with the sauce poured around it, and garnish with chopped parsley.

¶**Philip Brown's Tongue with Chicken Liver Sauce.** For the sauce, sauté ½ pound chicken livers in 4 tablespoons butter. Remove from the pan and chop coarsely. Add to the pan ½ pound sautéed sliced mushrooms and toss in the pan juices. Sprinkle with 3 tablespoons flour and stir in 1½ cups chicken (see page 529) or tongue broth. Cook until sauce is thickened. Add ⅓ cup Madeira and the chopped livers, and season to taste with salt, pepper, and nutmeg. Slice the cooked tongue and arrange in an ovenproof dish. Cover with the sauce and heat in a 300° oven for 30 minutes.

¶**Tongue with Madeira Sauce.** Reserve 1 cup broth from the cooked tongue. Make a white sauce with 2 tablespoons butter, 2 tablespoons flour, and the tongue broth, then stir in ½ cup currant jelly, ½ cup Madeira, ⅓ cup raisins, ⅓ cup finely chopped almonds, and simmer for 3 minutes. Reheat the tongue in the sauce. Serve tongue sliced, with the sauce, buttered noodles, and spinach *en branche.*

¶**Tongue with Spinach.** Slice the cooked tongue thin and arrange around a mound of puréed spinach (see page 173) garnished with thinly sliced onion rings and a grating of nutmeg. Serve with grated horseradish mixed with sour cream and a touch of lemon juice, and parsleyed boiled potatoes.

¶**Tongue Pot-au-Feu.** When boiling the tongue, use 1 teaspoon thyme instead of basil, and add to the pan 2 leeks, 1 carrot, 1 rib celery, and 1 bay leaf. Cook as before. One hour before it is done, add to the pot 6 medium-size onions, cook for 40 minutes, then add 6 small white turnips, 6 more leeks, and 6 more carrots. Cook until tongue and vegetables are tender. Skin and trim tongue, return to the broth to reheat, then serve on a platter, sliced and surrounded by the onions, leeks, and carrots. With this have potatoes boiled separately in their jackets, grated fresh horseradish and mustard, or horseradish-mustard-sour-cream sauce.

Lambs' Tongues Poulette

Lambs' tongues have a more delicate flavor than beef tongue and are especially good with a creamy sauce poulette, boiled potatoes, and a green salad, or pickled, with a green salad and potato salad or rice salad (see pages 93–96) as a light luncheon dish. Allow 2 or 3 of these tiny tongues per person. The larger veal tongues can be treated in the same way, but take about an hour longer to cook.

Makes 4 servings

8 to 12 lambs' tongues
1 onion stuck with 2 cloves
1 bay leaf
1 carrot

1 or 2 slices lemon
1 rib celery
1 teaspoon salt
1 teaspoon freshly ground black pepper

SAUCE POULETTE
3 tablespoons butter
3 tablespoons flour
1½ cups broth from the tongues

Juice of 1 lemon
2 egg yolks
Salt, freshly ground black pepper

Put the tongues in a pan with the onion, bay leaf, carrot, lemon, celery, salt, pepper, and water to cover. Bring to a boil, skim off the scum, then reduce the heat and simmer until tender when tested, about 30 to 45 minutes. Remove tongues from the broth, and when cool enough to handle, skin and trim them. Strain the broth and reserve 1½ cups for the sauce. Return the rest to the pan and put in the skinned tongues, to keep warm.

Melt the butter in a saucepan, blend in the flour and cook a few minutes, stirring, then mix in the reserved broth. Cook and stir until the sauce thickens, then add the lemon juice. Lightly beat the egg yolks and blend with a little of the hot sauce, then stir into the sauce in the pan. Cook gently, stirring until thickened. Do not allow to boil. Add salt and pepper to taste and a little more lemon juice, if needed. Split the tongues in two lengthwise and serve with the sauce.

¶**Lambs' Tongues with Tomato Sauce.** Cut the tongues in half and reheat in tomato sauce (see page 534).

¶**Lambs' Tongues Vinaigrette.** Serve the tongues cold with a mustard vinaigrette (see page 74) or sauce Gribiche (see page 535), a garnish of sliced hard-boiled eggs, and a potato salad (see pages 93–96).

¶**Pickled Lambs' Tongues.** Boil, skin, and trim 12 to 18 lambs' tongues.

Place in a large jar with 1 thinly sliced onion, 8 peppercorns, 1 garlic clove, 1 bay leaf, and a sprig of fresh tarragon or 1 teaspoon dried tarragon. Cover with a light white wine vinegar or Japanese rice wine vinegar or half vinegar and half dry white wine. Cover and refrigerate. These will keep 2 or 3 weeks under refrigeration. Serve with a potato, rice, or sauerkraut salad.

Tripes à la Mode de Caen
(Tripe in the Style of Caen)

One of the many classic French ways of cooking this excellent, inexpensive, but much neglected part of the steer. The long, slow cooking with onions, aromatic herbs, suet, and pig's feet gives this dish its luscious, savory quality. It is worth making a large quantity, and serving to tripe lovers, or else freeze the leftovers for another day. Boiled potatoes are the traditional accompaniment.

Makes 10 servings

2 pounds onions, sliced
5 pounds honeycomb tripe, cut into
    2-inch squares
2 pig's feet, split
1 pound beef suet, diced
Bouquet garni of 1 leek, 1 sprig thyme,
    1 bay leaf, 1 onion stuck with 2
    cloves, tied in cheesecloth

2 teaspoons salt
1 teaspoon freshly ground black pepper
¼ cup Calvados or applejack
1 cup dry white wine or dry (not sweet)
    cider

Arrange a layer of half the sliced onion in a large 8-quart casserole with a tight-fitting lid, follow with a layer of one-third of the tripe, then the pig's feet, half the suet, the remaining onion and another third of the tripe, the bouquet garni and the remaining tripe. Top with the remaining suet, season with the salt and pepper, and pour on the Calvados, wine, and just enough water to cover the ingredients. Put a piece of heavy aluminum foil over the casserole and cover with the lid (this creates an airtight seal so no steam can escape).

Cook in a 250° oven for 8 hours. Uncover, skim off the excess fat on top, remove the bouquet garni and take out the pig's feet. Remove meat from the feet and return it to the casserole. Correct the seasoning. Serve in soup plates with boiled potatoes.

¶Tripe with Red Wine. Instead of the Calvados and white wine, use ¼ cup cognac and 1 cup full-bodied red wine.

Tripe Niçoise

Another superb French way with tripe. The flavors of tomato and rosemary spell Provence. This improves if reheated and served the next day, and also freezes well.

Makes 4 servings

¼ cup olive oil
4 medium-size onions, sliced
1 pound firm ripe tomatoes, peeled,
    seeded, and chopped
½ teaspoon thyme
½ teaspoon rosemary
Salt and freshly ground black pepper
    to taste

2 cups dry rosé wine, preferably a
    Provençal rosé
1 pig's foot, split
2 pounds honeycomb tripe, cut into
    1-by-3-inch strips
¼ cup grated Parmesan cheese

Heat the olive oil in a deep pot and sauté the onions until limp. Add the tomatoes, herbs, and salt and pepper. Blend well. Add the wine, pig's foot, and tripe. Mix all the ingredients well, cover, and simmer over low heat for 2½ to 3 hours. Remove the pig's foot, take off the meat, and add to the tripe. Correct the seasoning and arrange on a hot platter. Sprinkle with the cheese.

Menudo

A traditional Mexican way with tripe, much favored for a morning-after breakfast. Although the beneficial effects on a hangover are doubtful, it's an excellent hearty dish for a New Year buffet or a Sunday supper.

Makes 8 servings

4 pounds honeycomb tripe, cut in
    1-inch squares
2 pig's feet
1 onion stuck with 2 cloves
4 garlic cloves
GARNISH: Chopped green onions, chopped peeled green chilies, chopped cilantro

1 tablespoon oregano
2 teaspoons coriander seed, crushed
Salt, freshly ground black pepper
3 cups canned whole hominy, drained

Put the tripe, pig's feet, onion, garlic, oregano, and coriander seed in a large casserole with salt and pepper to taste and water to cover. Bring to a boil on top of the stove. Cover, and cook in a 300° oven for 4 to 5 hours, or until tripe is thoroughly tender. Remove the pig's feet, take the meat from the bones, and replace meat in the casserole. Add the hominy and simmer for 30 minutes in the oven or on top of the stove. Serve in deep plates or bowls, topped with the garnish of green onions, chilies, and cilantro.

Tablier de Sapeur

Tablier de Sapeur, meaning workman's apron, is native to the Lyonnaise district—a great *specialité* of the restaurant La Voûte, where the chef-proprietor, Lea, has prepared it for years.

Makes 6 servings

4 pounds honeycomb tripe, cleaned
    and parboiled
1 bottle Pouilly Fuissé or other dry
    white wine
3 tablespoons lemon juice
½ cup plus 2 tablespoons peanut oil
1 tablespoon Dijon mustard
Salt, freshly ground black pepper

2 eggs
¼ cup cold water
2 cups fresh bread crumbs,
    approximately
6 to 8 tablespoons butter, melted
Sauce Gribiche (see page 535) or
    tartare (page 77)

Cut the tripe into 2-inch squares. Place in a large pot and cook in water to cover until tender, approximately 1½ hours. Drain.

In a bowl large enough to accommodate the tripe, mix the ingredients for the marinade—wine, lemon juice, ½ cup peanut oil, mustard, and salt and pepper to taste. Put the tripe in the marinade and marinate for about 3 hours. Drain well. Beat the eggs, 2 tablespoons oil, the cold water, and a dash of salt and pepper together in a bowl. Dip the pieces of tripe in the egg mixture and then roll in soft bread crumbs. Put the melted butter in a broiling pan. Arrange the pieces of tripe on the broiling pan and broil for approximately 5 minutes on each side or until delicately brown. Serve with sauce Gribiche or tartare.

Cecilia Chiang's Tripe with Gizzards

In Cecilia Chiang's restaurant, The Mandarin, in San Francisco, this dish is called Black and White to suggest the contrast between the color and texture of the gizzards and the tripe.

Makes 4 servings

½ pound honeycomb tripe
1 teaspoon baking soda
3 green onions, or scallions, shredded
(white part only)
1 tablespoon dry sherry
¾ teaspoon Oriental sesame-seed oil
1 teaspoon vinegar
1 teaspoon salt

2 tablespoons chopped fresh coriander
(cilantro)
1 teaspoon cornstarch
1 tablespoon cold water
½ pound chicken gizzards
1 quart chicken broth (see page 529)
2 tablespoons vegetable oil
1 large garlic clove, sliced

Cut the tripe into 1½-by-2-inch pieces and score in a crisscross pattern with a knife. Put the tripe in a bowl with water to cover and the baking soda. Soak overnight, then drain.

In a bowl, combine the scallion, sherry, sesame oil, vinegar, salt, coriander, and cornstarch mixed well with 1 tablespoon water. Mix all ingredients thoroughly.

Trim and rinse the chicken gizzards and score them in a crisscross pattern. Bring the chicken broth to a simmer in a pan, add the drained tripe and gizzards, and poach gently for 5 to 6 minutes. Remove tripe and gizzards from broth.

Heat the oil in a wok or a large skillet that has been heated over a high flame, add the sliced garlic, and stir-fry for 1 minute, then add the scallion-sherry mixture from the bowl, the tripe, and gizzards, and stir-fry briskly over high heat for 2 minutes. Serve at once with steamed rice.

Blanching Sweetbreads

The sweetbreads most often found in our markets come from the thymus gland of a calf, although occasionally you can find lamb or beef sweetbreads. Sweetbreads are very delicate and need to be soaked in ice water and blanched or parboiled before they can be trimmed of the covering membrane and connecting tubes; this is usually done before the final broiling, sautéing, or braising process. If they are to be sliced, they should be weighted down until cold to make them firmer.

Soak the sweetbreads in ice water for 30 minutes. Put in a pan with water to cover with ½ teaspoon salt and 1 tablespoon lemon juice, bring to a boil, reduce the heat, and simmer gently for 10 minutes. Remove and immediately plunge into ice water to stop them from cooking further. When cool enough to handle, peel off the covering membrane and trim away the connecting tubes and any particles of fat. A pair of sweetbreads will serve 2 or 3, according to the style of preparation.

Sweetbreads Albert

This was an invention of the late Albert Stockli while he was executive chef of the Four Seasons Restaurant in New York. The sweetbreads are not blanched and cleaned in the usual way, but braised, then trimmed, and the trimmings used for the sauce. Serve with rice and salad.

Makes 8 servings

3 tablespoons oil
1 leek, well washed, cut in fine
    julienne strips
3 ribs celery, cut in fine julienne strips
2 small carrots, peeled and cut in fine
    julienne strips
1 green pepper, seeded, and cut in fine
    julienne strips

6 shallots, very finely chopped
Salt, freshly ground black pepper
2 cups dry white wine
4 pairs sweetbreads
1 tablespoon cornstarch
1 tablespoon cold water
3 egg yolks
Juice of 1 lemon

GARNISH: 1 tablespoon chopped parsley

Heat the oil in a skillet, and cook the leek, celery, carrots, green pepper, and shallots until lightly colored. Arrange them in a layer in a braising pan, season with salt and pepper to taste, and add 1 cup of wine. Arrange the sweetbreads on the vegetables, cover the pan, and simmer over low heat for 30 minutes. Remove the sweetbreads and cool them between wet towels. Drain the vegetables, reserving both vegetables and liquid.

Measure 1 cup of the liquid, add the remaining cup of wine, and place in a saucepan over moderate heat. Mix the cornstarch with 1 tablespoon cold water and blend into the liquid. Simmer until slightly thickened.

Meanwhile, clean the sweetbreads. Add membranes, tubes, and other trimmings to the vegetables. Purée vegetables and trimmings in an electric blender or food processor and add to the thickened liquid. Beat the egg yolks lightly, stir a little of the hot sauce into them, then return to the pan, and cook slowly, stirring constantly, until the sauce thickens. Do not let it boil. Add the lemon juice, taste, and correct the seasoning.

Slice the sweetbreads ½ inch thick and put them on a hot platter in a 250° oven for a few minutes to heat through. Pour some of the sauce over them and serve the rest separately in a bowl. Garnish with chopped parsley.

Sweetbreads Panné

One of the simplest and best ways to prepare sweetbreads is to panné them
—which means they are coated with flour, egg, and bread crumbs, then
sautéed.

Makes 4 servings

2 pairs sweetbreads, blanched and
  trimmed
½ cup flour
2 eggs, lightly beaten

1½ cups fresh bread crumbs
4 tablespoons butter
2 tablespoons oil
Salt, freshly ground black pepper

GARNISH: Chopped parsley, lemon wedges

After blanching and trimming the sweetbreads, put them on a baking sheet,
cover with wax paper, put a board on top and weigh down with cans. Leave
for 2 hours, then remove. Cut into serving-size pieces just before cooking.

Coat the pieces lightly with flour, then dip in the egg and roll in the
bread crumbs. Heat the butter and oil in a heavy skillet, add the sweetbreads, and sauté over medium-high heat until nicely browned on both
sides. Season to taste with salt and pepper as they sauté. Remove to a hot
platter and serve sprinkled with parsley and with lemon wedges to squeeze
over the sweetbreads.

¶Sweetbreads Panné with Cream. Remove sweetbreads from skillet. Pour
off any excess fat. Deglaze pan with ¼ cup dry white wine, then pour in
1 cup heavy cream, and let it reduce until slightly thickened. Season with
freshly ground black pepper and pour over the sweetbreads.

¶Sweetbreads Panné with Mustard. Before flouring the sweetbreads, brush
them heavily with about ½ jar Dijon mustard.

Broiled Sweetbreads

Dip blanched and trimmed sweetbreads into heavy cream, then into beaten
egg, then roll in fresh bread crumbs. Broil slowly about 5 inches from the
heat until the crumbs brown, turning once. Serve with lemon wedges, or
with hollandaise or Béarnaise sauce (see page 532).

¶Sweetbreads Milanese. Dip sweetbreads in melted butter, then in a mixture of equal parts bread crumbs and grated Parmesan cheese, and broil.
Serve with lemon wedges.

¶**Herbed Sweetbreads.** Dip sweetbreads into melted butter and then into herbed crumbs (to 1½ cups bread crumbs add 1 tablespoon each chopped parsley, chives, and tarragon). Broil as above. Excellent served with a piquant mustard sauce.

Sweetbreads, Kidneys, and Sausages

This rather unusual combination makes an excellent brunch or luncheon dish.

Makes 6 servings

1 pound small pork sausages	*¼ cup cognac, warmed*
1 pair sweetbreads, blanched and	*¼ cup Madeira*
trimmed	*1½ cups beef stock (see page 530)*
3 veal kidneys, trimmed	*Beurre manié (see page 536)*
6 shallots, finely chopped	*1 tablespoon chopped parsley*
4 tablespoons butter	*6 patty shells, from a bakery or frozen,*
2 tablespoons oil	*heated*
Salt, freshly ground black pepper	*6 sautéed mushroom caps*
½ teaspoon dried tarragon	

Cut the sausages in small pieces and blanch in a skillet for 3 minutes in boiling water. Pour off water and let the sausages brown slowly until just cooked through. Cut the sweetbreads in small pieces. Slice the kidneys thin. Sauté the shallots in half the butter and oil until translucent, about 3 minutes, then add the sweetbreads and sauté for 4 to 5 minutes, shaking the pan to cook them evenly. Season with salt and pepper to taste and the tarragon. Remove sweetbreads, add the remaining butter and oil, and sauté kidneys quickly; do not overcook. Season with salt and pepper and flame with the warmed cognac. Combine the Madeira and beef stock and cook down until reduced to one-third; thicken with beurre manié. Combine this sauce with the kidneys, sweetbreads, sausages, and shallots, and correct the seasoning. Reheat to the boiling point and sprinkle with the parsley.

Serve in the heated patty shells (if frozen shells are used, follow package directions for baking) and top each one with a sautéed mushroom cap. Serve at once.

Breads and Cookies

All my life I've relished good bread and loved the resilience of dough in my hands, the relaxed rhythm of kneading, the fragrance of baking, the beautiful even-grained cross-section of a well-risen loaf. Now-adays my ideal day begins in my Greenwich Village garden, with the little fountain splashing among the flowers, an amazing number of birds in full voice, and the distant sounds of a great city waking up. I carry out a tray with a steaming pot of tea, curls of fresh butter, and a couple of thick golden slices of homemade toast to munch slowly.

For more and more people, I find, real bread is a part of life, one offering tremendous reward for

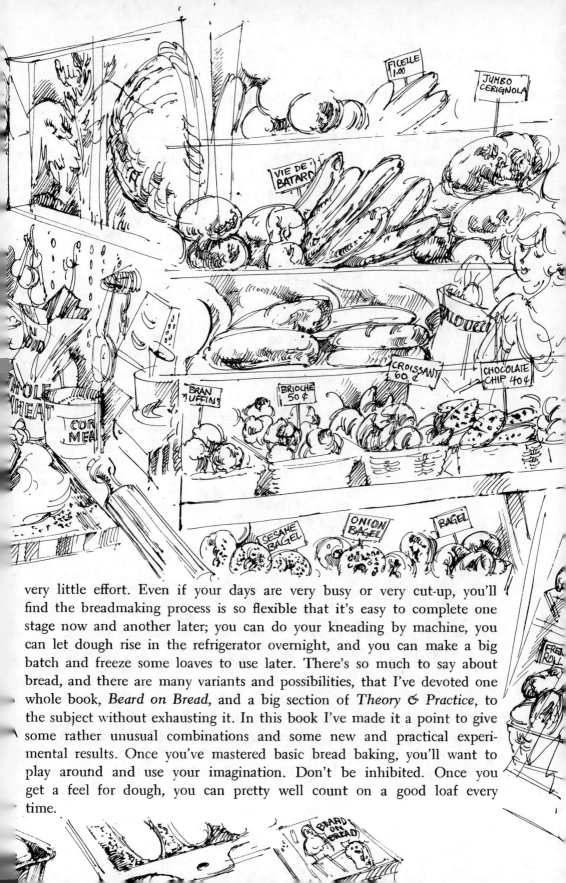

very little effort. Even if your days are very busy or very cut-up, you'll find the breadmaking process is so flexible that it's easy to complete one stage now and another later; you can do your kneading by machine, you can let dough rise in the refrigerator overnight, and you can make a big batch and freeze some loaves to use later. There's so much to say about bread, and there are many variants and possibilities, that I've devoted one whole book, *Beard on Bread*, and a big section of *Theory & Practice*, to the subject without exhausting it. In this book I've made it a point to give some rather unusual combinations and some new and practical experimental results. Once you've mastered basic bread baking, you'll want to play around and use your imagination. Don't be inhibited. Once you get a feel for dough, you can pretty well count on a good loaf every time.

BREADS AND COOKIES

Basic white bread

Pullman loaf or
   pain de mie

Dark rye bread

Pumpernickel bread

Polygrained bread
   with cornmeal
   with walnuts
   with garlic and dill

Egg bagels
   with onions
   with sesame seeds
   with poppy seeds

Gruyère garlic bread

Carrot bread

Raisin bread

Hard rolls

Breakfast baps

Brioche bread

Brioches à tête

Mrs. Maynard's cinnamon
   rolls

Lenten buns

Crumpets

Cottage cheese bread

Nut rum bread

Mealy bread

Whole-wheat bran muffins

Knusper brote

Tuiles

Soft almond cookies

Almond cookies

Cornmeal butter wafers
   with sesame

Chinese chews

Lace cookies

Ginger cakes

Oatmeal carrot cookies

Vadis bars

Lemon meringue bars

Chocolate macaroons

Gino's macaroons

Florentines

"Monster" peanut butter
   cookies

Meringue kisses

Linzer bars

Blond brownies

Sugar cookies

Apple pancakes

Brambles

Basic White Bread

Makes 1 large loaf or 2 smaller 8-inch loaves

1 package (1 tablespoon) active dry
   yeast
½ cup water (110° to 115°,
   approximately)
2 teaspoons granulated sugar
1½ cups plain yogurt (110° to 115°,
   approximately)

3¾ to 4 cups all-purpose flour
1 tablespoon salt
1½ to 2 tablespoons softened butter
1 egg white, beaten with 2 tablespoons
   cold water

Add the yeast to the warm water, along with the sugar, and stir well until the yeast is completely dissolved and starts to swell and bubble. Place the yogurt in a bowl. Stir in about 1½ cups of the flour with a wooden spoon. Add the yeast mixture, salt, and remaining flour, 1 cup at a time. Remove the dough to a floured board and knead, adding more flour as necessary if it gets sticky, until it is supple, satiny, and no longer sticky. Butter a bowl and place the dough in it, turning to coat all sides with the fat. Cover and allow to rise in a warm, draft-free spot until doubled in bulk, about 1½ to 2 hours.

Deflate the dough by punching it firmly 2 or 3 times, return to the floured board, and knead 4 to 5 minutes more. Divide into 2 equal parts and shape into loaves the size of your pans, or make 1 large loaf for a large pan. Place in buttered pans, cover lightly with a towel, and let rise again until doubled in bulk. Make 3 or 4 slashes across the loaves with a sharp knife and brush with lightly beaten egg white and water. Bake in a 400° oven for 40 to 45 minutes, or until the bread sounds hollow when tapped with the knuckles. Remove the loaves from the pans and put them in the oven for a few minutes longer to become crisped.

Pullman Loaf or Pain de Mie

Makes 1 large loaf or 2 smaller 8-inch loaves

2 packages (2 tablespoons) active dry yeast
1½ cups warm water
2 teaspoons sugar

6½ cups all-purpose flour
1 tablespoon plus 2 teaspoons coarse salt
1½ sticks (¾ cup) sweet butter

In a large bowl, dissolve the yeast in ¾ cup of the warm water with the sugar, and let stand until it starts to swell and bubble. In another bowl, combine 6 cups of the flour with the salt, then—using two knives—cut the butter into the flour and salt, being careful not to overwork it. (Or, using your hands, squeeze pieces of the butter into the flour very carefully.) Add this flour-and-butter mixture to the dissolved yeast, mixing it gently with one hand only, and add the remaining water to create a stiff, sticky dough. Turn the dough out onto a floured board and work it hard for a good 10 minutes: slap it, beat it, punch it, and give it a thorough kneading. When finally smooth, let it rest for a few minutes, then shape into a ball. Place the ball of dough in a well-buttered bowl and turn to coat the surface. Cover and let rise in a warm, draft-free spot for 1½ hours.

Punch the dough down, let it rest for 3 to 4 minutes, then turn it out and knead again vigorously for 3 to 4 minutes. Shape into a ball and put back in the buttered bowl to rise again, for from 45 minutes to 1 hour. Punch the dough down and let it rest another 3 or 4 minutes. Knead a third time and then shape carefully into a loaf to fit a well-buttered 13½-

by-4-by-3¾-inch pan or two 8½-by-4½-by-2½-inch pans. Let rise, covered, until almost double in bulk, approximately 1 hour. For this bread, the pans must be covered during baking so the bread remains compact and square-shaped. If you are using a pullman tin (the bread pan specifically designed for pain de mie), butter the inside of the lid. Otherwise use foil, well buttered, with a weight placed on top large enough to cover the baking tin (or a buttered cookie sheet with a weight on top would also do), and place in a preheated 400° oven. Immediately turn the heat down to 375°. After 30 minutes turn the tin on one side for 5 minutes and then on the other side for 5 minutes; it is all right to remove your improvised lid and weights at this point; the bread will be solid enough. Set it upright again and re-move the lid if you are using a pullman tin; the bread should have risen to the top of the pan.

Continue to bake until it is a golden color, which will take about an additional 12 to 15 minutes. Turn the loaf out of the pan and put it directly on the rack of the oven to bake for a few minutes longer, until the bread is a beautiful color and sounds hollow when tapped with the knuckles. Let it cool thoroughly on a rack before slicing.

Dark Rye Bread

Makes 1 eight-inch loaf

¼ cup warm water (110° to 115°)
1 package (1 tablespoon) active dry
    yeast
1 teaspoon sugar
¾ cup milk, warmed to lukewarm
¼ cup light or dark molasses

1 tablespoon melted butter
1 teaspoon salt
1 tablespoon caraway seeds (optional)
2 cups all-purpose flour
1½ cups rye flour
Ice water

Pour warm water into a large bowl; add yeast and sugar; stir until dissolved. Cover and set aside until mixture has swelled slightly and has surface bubbles—about 5 minutes.

Blend in milk, molasses, butter, salt, and, if you like, caraway seeds. Stir in 1 cup all-purpose flour, ½ cup at a time. Next, stir in all the rye flour, ½ cup at a time. Then beat vigorously until dough is smooth and elastic. Stir in most of remaining flour to make a stiff dough.

Turn out onto a heavily floured board. Knead until dough is not sticky —smooth and satiny—about 8 to 10 minutes. Add more flour while knead-ing, if necessary. Put dough in greased bowl; grease top lightly. Cover bowl and set in warm place to rise until almost doubled in bulk (about 1½ to 2 hours).

Punch down, turn out onto a lightly floured board, knead slightly and form into a loaf.

Put the loaf into a greased bread pan. Let the dough rise in a warm, draft-free place until almost doubled in bulk (1½ to 2 hours). Bake at 425° for 10 minutes, brush with ice water, lower the temperature to 350°, and continue baking for approximately 40 to 45 minutes until the bread has turned almost mahogany on top. Turn the loaf out of the pan and put directly on the rack of the oven if you want it very crusty. Let cool on a rack.

Pumpernickel Bread

Makes 2 large loaves

1 cup cornmeal
1½ cups boiling water
½ cup beer
2 packages (2 tablespoons) active dry
    yeast
1 tablespoon sugar
½ cup warm water

2 cups pumpernickel flour
3 tablespoons cocoa
2 tablespoons salt
2 tablespoons oil
3½ to 4 cups all-purpose flour
    (approximately)

Combine the cornmeal with the boiling water, mix well, and add the beer. Let the mixture rest until it comes to room temperature (put your finger in to make sure). Dissolve the yeast and sugar in the warm water and let stand until it swells. Put the cornmeal mixture in the bowl of an electric mixer with a dough hook attachment, and add the pumpernickel flour, cocoa, salt, oil, and yeast mixture. With the mixer on at its lowest speed, knead the dough until well combined. Gradually add the all-purpose flour, ½ cup at a time, until you have a firm, evenly textured dough.

Remove the dough to a floured work surface and shape it into a ball. Clean your bowl, butter it, and then place the dough in it, turning to coat all sides. Cover with a towel and let rise in a warm, draft-free spot, until doubled in bulk.

Punch the dough down, let it rest for 2 or 3 minutes, then knead by hand this time for a good 5 minutes. Shape the dough into 2 free-form loaves and place on a baking sheet dusted with cornmeal, and let rise, covered, until double in bulk. Bake the loaves at 425° for about 10 minutes, then reduce the heat to 350° and continue to bake for an additional 40 to 50 minutes. When done, the loaves will have a dark crust and will sound hollow when tapped on the top and bottom with the knuckles. Remove from the oven and cool thoroughly on racks before slicing.

Polygrained Bread

Makes 2 loaves

1 cup boiling water
1 cup rolled oats
1 cup cracked wheat
2 packages (2 tablespoons) active dry
    yeast
1 tablespoon brown sugar

½ cup warm water
2 teaspoons salt
1 cup yogurt
2 tablespoons olive oil
2 to 3 cups all-purpose flour

Pour the boiling water over the rolled oats and cracked wheat in a large mixing bowl. Set aside and allow to cool. Dissolve the yeast with the sugar in the warm water. Add the yeast to the oats and cracked wheat when cool enough to stick a finger in and hold it there comfortably. Add the salt, yogurt, olive oil, and 2 cups of the flour, and mix well. Turn out onto a floured board and knead, adding additional flour, until you have a smooth dough. Clean the bowl, butter it well, return the dough to it, and turn to coat the surface evenly. Let rise, covered lightly with a towel, until double in bulk, about 1½ hours. Punch the dough down and let it rise again. Form the dough into 2 loaves, place in greased pans, and let rise again. Bake in a 400° oven for 1 hour.

¶**Polygrained Bread with Cornmeal.** Use 1 cup coarse cornmeal instead of the rolled oats.

¶**Polygrained Bread with Walnuts.** Add 1 cup chopped walnuts to the bread mixture.

¶**Polygrained Bread with Garlic and Dill.** Add 3 garlic cloves, finely chopped, and 2 tablespoons chopped fresh dill or 2 teaspoons dried dill weed.

Egg Bagels

These ethnic rolls, distinctive in their shape and twice cooked—once in water, once in the oven—are eternally popular.

Makes 16 bagels

1 package (1 tablespoon) active dry
    yeast
1 cup warm water (110° to 115°)
1 tablespoon sugar
2 teaspoons kosher salt

3½ to 4 cups hard-wheat flour
2 eggs
1½ tablespoons vegetable oil
1 egg yolk
2 tablespoons water

Dissolve yeast in mixing bowl with the warm water and sugar. Add salt, 1 cup flour, 2 eggs, and oil. Add remaining flour to make a firm dough. Knead the dough until smooth and elastic, about 10 to 15 minutes. Place in a greased bowl, cover, and let rise until double in bulk, about 30 to 45 minutes.

Punch down dough and divide into 16 equal parts. Shape each part into a smooth ball, punch hole in center with floured finger and pull gently to enlarge the hole and make a uniform shape. Let rise 20 minutes. Preheat oven to 375°.

Heat approximately 4 quarts water to barely simmer in a large pot. Put the bagels in the simmering water, 4 at a time, and simmer about 7 minutes, turning once. Remove from water, brush with 1 egg yolk beaten with 2 tablespoons water, place on a greased baking sheet, and bake for 30 to 35 minutes or until golden brown.

¶Egg Bagels with Onions. Sauté 1 medium-size onion, finely chopped, in 3 tablespoons butter until translucent. Brush the onion mixture over the bagels before placing in the oven.

¶Egg Bagels with Sesame Seeds. Spread a layer of sesame seeds on a plate and before baking carefully press the tops of the bagels into the seeds so that they adhere to the surface.

¶Egg Bagels with Poppy Seeds. Follow same procedure as for sesame seeds.

Gruyère Garlic Bread

Makes 1 loaf

1 package (1 tablespoon) active dry
   yeast
1 tablespoon sugar
1½ cups warm water
1 tablespoon salt
2 tablespoons finely chopped garlic

3 to 4 cups all-purpose flour
½ teaspoon pepper
¾ cup grated Gruyère cheese
Butter or oil
1 egg white
1 tablespoon water

Dissolve the yeast with the sugar in the warm water. Combine the salt, garlic, and 2 cups of the flour. Add the yeast mixture, blend well, and add enough flour to make a manageable dough. Turn the dough out onto a lightly floured surface and knead for a few minutes. Sprinkle the pepper over the dough and knead for another minute. Add the cheese and knead again until the dough is smooth and elastic.

Clean the bowl, butter it well, return the ball of dough to it, and turn to coat the surface evenly. Cover with a towel, place in a warm spot, and let double in bulk (about 1 hour). Punch the dough down, shape free form in a round or oval loaf, and allow to rise again, covered lightly, until double in bulk. Lightly brush the top with egg white beaten with 1 table-spoon water. Bake in a 350° oven for 40 to 50 minutes, or until done.

Carrot Bread

Makes 1 or 2 loaves

½ cup vegetable oil
½ cup sugar
1½ cups grated carrot
1 egg
1 teaspoon salt
3½ cups unbleached flour
1 cup graham flour
½ teaspoon nutmeg
1 teaspoon cinnamon

½ cup chopped candied fruits and
   raisins
1 package (1 tablespoon) active dry
   yeast
1 teaspoon sugar
¾ cup warm water
1 tablespoon each honey and water
Cracked sunflower seeds

In a large mixing bowl, combine the oil, sugar, grated carrot, egg, and salt, then add the flours, spices, and fruits and raisins, and mix thoroughly.

Dissolve the yeast with the sugar in the warm water, and add to the carrot mixture. Lightly knead into a soft dough. Clean the bowl, butter it well, return the dough to the bowl, and turn to cover the surface evenly with the butter. Cover the dough and let it rise in a warm place until doubled in bulk, about 1 hour and 15 minutes. Punch the dough down, then let it rest for 10 minutes. Meanwhile, preheat the oven to 400°.

Turn the dough out onto a lightly floured work surface and form into 1 or 2 loaves, depending on the size of your pans. Brush the tops of the loaves with a mixture of honey and water, and sprinkle with cracked sun-flower seeds. Let the loaves rise in the pans for 10 minutes. Bake for 15 minutes at 400°, then lower the heat to 375° and bake 40 to 50 minutes longer.

Raisin Bread

Makes 2 loaves

1½ cups sultana raisins
¾ cup sherry or cognac
   (approximately)

1 package (1 tablespoon) active dry
   yeast
2 cups lukewarm milk

⅓ cup sugar
1 tablespoon salt
3 tablespoons butter
5 to 6 cups all-purpose flour
Melted butter

½ teaspoon ground mace
2 teaspoons grated fresh orange rind
1 egg yolk, beaten with 2 tablespoons
  cream

Plump the raisins overnight in enough sherry or cognac to barely cover.

In a large bowl, dissolve the yeast in ¼ cup of the warm milk. Add the remaining warm milk, sugar, salt, and butter. Then, using one hand or a heavy wooden spoon, gradually stir in enough flour to make a stiff dough. Turn out onto a floured work surface and knead for about 10 minutes, until smooth, elastic, and glossy. Clean the bowl, butter it well, return the dough to it, and turn to coat the surface with butter. Cover and set in a warm, draft-free spot to rise until doubled in bulk—about 1½ to 2 hours.

Punch the dough down and knead for 3 minutes. Return it to the bowl and let rise again for 30 minutes. Divide the dough into 2 equal pieces and roll each out into a rectangle about 7 by 20 inches. Brush with melted butter. Drain the raisins and mix with the mace and orange rind. Sprinkle over the dough and roll each rectangle up tightly, tucking the ends under. Fit the roll, seam side down, in 2 well-buttered 8-by-4-by-2-inch loaf pans. Cover the loaves and let rise in a warm spot until the dough just shows above the tops of the pans, approximately 45 minutes. Brush with the egg-yolk-and-cream wash and bake in a preheated 400° oven for 10 minutes, then reduce the heat to 350° and continue baking for 20 to 30 minutes, or until the loaves sound hollow when tapped on top and bottom. If necessary, return the loaves to the oven rack without their pans to brown the bottom crusts.

Hard Rolls

Makes about 24 rolls

2 packages (2 tablespoons) active dry
  yeast
1 teaspoon granulated sugar
2 cups warm water (100° to 115°,
  approximately)
1 tablespoon kosher salt

1 cup gluten flour
4 to 5 cups soft-wheat flour (available
  in health-food stores)
Cornmeal
⅔ cup ice water mixed with
  1 tablespoon salt

Combine the yeast with sugar and warm water in a large bowl and let stand until it starts to swell. Mix the salt with the gluten flour and add to the yeast mixture. Add the remaining soft-wheat flour, 1 cup at a time, until you have a firm dough. Remove to a lightly floured board and knead until no longer sticky, about 10 minutes, adding flour as necessary. Place in an oiled bowl and turn to coat the surface of the dough. Cover and let rise in a cool place for about 2 hours, or until doubled in bulk.

Punch down the dough. Turn out on a floured board and knead for about 2 minutes. Cut the dough into 24 pieces and form into balls. Place on a baking sheet that has been sprinkled with cornmeal. Slash the tops of the rolls. Cover, and let rise until doubled, approximately 30 minutes.

Place 4 small custard cups filled with boiling water on the corners of your oven rack. Preheat the oven to 400°. Place the baking sheet on the rack and bake for 25 to 30 minutes, brushing rolls with the salted ice water every 5 minutes during baking, until rolls are nicely browned and sound hollow when tapped. Remove to a rack to cool.

Breakfast Baps

Baps are a rather light roll, usually baked fresh and served for breakfast in Scotland. Somewhat oval in shape and delicious with butter and marmalade, they may also be used successfully as hamburger buns, split and filled with a freshly cooked hamburger and condiments.

Makes 16 rolls

3 packages (3 tablespoons) active dry yeast	¼ cup lard
	1 teaspoon sugar
Warm water	½ cup milk
3½ cups all-purpose flour	½ cup hot water
2 teaspoons salt	

Barely cover the yeast with warm water and let stand in a warm place for 5 minutes. Mix the flour and salt and rub in the lard. Add the sugar to the yeast, then add to the milk and water. Pour this into the flour mixture and blend to a soft dough with a wooden spoon. Cover and let rise in a warm place until double in bulk—about 1 hour.

Turn out onto a floured board and knead until you have a smooth ball of dough. Cut this into 16 pieces, work each into a ball, and place on a greased baking sheet to rise in a warm place for 20 minutes. Bake for about 15 minutes in a preheated 400° oven.

Brioche

Brioche dough is light and spongy in texture, less firm than most bread doughs, and needs to be handled rather differently. When you form brioche dough into traditional shapes (requiring special fluted brioche tins) such as brioches à tête, the familiar large or small brioches with a little topknot used in the recipes for Brioche Bohémienne (see page 26) and Brioche with ham (see page 27), or roll it out for Coulibiac (see page 214) or Sausage en Brioche (see page 436), the dough should rise once at room temperature and a second time under refrigeration, to give a firmer, more workable quality. When making a brioche loaf, refrigeration is not necessary. After the first rising, the dough can be arranged in the buttered loaf pan and given the second rising in the pan. Brioche bread makes wonderful breakfast toast and delicious little sandwiches.

The following recipe may be baked as loaves or rolled out like pastry and used to wrap Sausage en Brioche. Double the recipe for the coulibiac of salmon.

Brioche Bread

Makes 2 loaves

1½ packages (1½ tablespoons) active
    dry yeast
2 tablespoons sugar
½ cup warm water (110° to 115°)
1 cup unsalted butter, melted
1½ teaspoons salt

4 cups all-purpose flour
4 eggs
Egg wash (1 egg yolk beaten with
    ¼ cup light cream or evaporated
    milk)

Combine the yeast, sugar, and water in a cup measure and allow to proof (it is proofed when it begins to swell and bubble). Mix the melted butter and salt. Combine the flour, eggs, melted butter, and yeast mixture in a large bowl and beat with your hand until well combined and smooth. Butter a second large bowl, put the dough in it and turn it around so the surface is lightly coated with butter. Cover with a dish towel and put in a warm, draft-free place to rise until light and doubled in bulk, about 1 to 1½ hours.

Punch down the risen dough with your fist and divide it in half. Butter two 8-by-4-by-2-inch loaf pans. Form the dough into loaves and put in the pans. Cover with a towel and let rise a second time until doubled in bulk, about 1 hour. Preheat the oven to 400°.

Brush the risen loaves with the egg wash. Bake in the center of the oven for about 30 minutes, or until the loaves are a deep golden brown and, when removed from the pans, sound hollow when rapped on the bottom with the knuckles. If not quite ready, return loaves to the pans and bake another few minutes. Cool on a rack.

Brioches à Tete

Makes 12 large brioches or 24 small

After the dough has had one rising, deflate it by punching it down. Remove from the bowl and knead it for about 3 minutes. Return to the bowl, cover tightly with foil or plastic wrap, and refrigerate for several hours or overnight.

When ready to bake, punch down the dough, beat by hand for 2 minutes, and turn out onto a heavily floured board. Divide it into 2 portions, 1 portion 3 times as large as the other.

Butter 12 large brioche tins or 24 small. Divide the larger portion of the dough into 12 pieces of equal size and form into balls. Put a ball of dough into each tin—it should fill it by two-thirds. Form the remaining portion of dough into 12 roughly pear-shaped pieces. Poke your floured finger into the top of each large dough ball in its tin, making an indentation about an inch deep. Brush the holes and the tapered ends of the smaller pieces of dough with cold water, and gently press the tapered ends into the indentations so they are well rooted (these will form the classic topknots).

Cover the pans lightly with a towel and let the brioches rise until a little more than doubled in bulk. Brush lightly with egg wash. Bake in a preheated 375° oven for about 20 minutes, until delicately brown. To test for doneness, insert a toothpick in the center of a brioche; it should come out clean. The brioches will also shrink very slightly from the edges of the pans.

Mrs. Maynard's Cinnamon Rolls

You will find that this dough is extremely soft. It is wise to begin the kneading with the aid of a dough scraper, which looks something like a paint spatula, until you have a slightly firm dough.

Makes 12 rolls

3 packages (3 tablespoons) active dry
    yeast
2 teaspoons sugar
1 cup warm water
½ cup softened butter
½ cup sugar
2 teaspoons salt

3 eggs
3 to 4 cups all-purpose flour
3 tablespoons melted butter
3 tablespoons sugar mixed with
    1 tablespoon cinnamon
1 cup golden raisins soaked in rum
½ cup chopped pecans

ICING
1 cup powdered sugar

1 to 2 tablespoons water

Dissolve the yeast and the 2 teaspoons sugar in the warm water. Stir, and let stand 15 minutes.

Using an electric mixer, if you wish, cream together thoroughly the softened butter, ½ cup sugar, and salt, then add the well-beaten eggs. Add the yeast mixture and blend well. Add enough flour, mixing it in thoroughly, so that the dough is not sticky. Cover the bowl, put it in a warm place, and let the dough rise until double in bulk.

Punch the dough down and roll it into a rectangle about ¼ inch thick. Spread with the melted butter and sprinkle with the cinnamon-sugar mixture. Drain the raisins, distribute them evenly over the top, and sprinkle with the chopped pecans. Roll up the rectangle lengthwise so that you end up with a long cylinder. Cut the cylinder into 1½-inch slices and place them on a buttered cookie sheet, not touching. Cover with a towel and let rise again for 30 minutes.

Bake the rolls in a preheated 350° oven for 20 to 30 minutes, or until they are nicely browned. Mix the powdered sugar and water into a thick paste and spread on top of the hot rolls.

Lenten Buns

Makes 12 to 14 buns

2 packages (2 tablespoons) active dry
    yeast
1¾ cups milk
¼ pound unsalted butter
1 teaspoon salt
¾ cup sugar
¼ teaspoon ground cardamom

3¾ cups all-purpose flour
1 egg, beaten
1 pint heavy cream, whipped
1 cup almond paste
Confectioners' sugar
3 cups hot milk

Sprinkle the yeast into a mixing bowl and cream with a few spoonfuls of milk. Melt the butter, add the remaining milk, and heat until lukewarm, about 95°. Pour the melted fat and milk mixture onto the yeast and stir in the salt, sugar, ground cardamom, and 2 cups flour. Gradually work in the remaining flour and knead the dough until it is smooth and shiny, about 4 minutes only. Do not overknead. Put the dough in a greased bowl, cover with a cloth, and allow to rise until doubled in bulk.

Punch the dough down and knead on a board. If the dough seems too loose, work in some additional flour. Form into 5" buns, and put them on well-greased cookie sheets. Leave to rise for 45 minutes, then brush the tops of the buns with beaten egg, which gives a shiny finish. Bake in a preheated 425° oven for about 8 to 10 minutes.

Allow the baked buns to cool slightly, then cut in half sideways and pick out the soft insides. Mix these soft crumbs with whipped cream. Line the bottom of each bun with almond paste, add the crumb-cream mixture, and replace the tops of the buns. Sprinkle the tops with sifted confectioners' sugar. To serve, put buns in soup plates, pour hot milk over them, and eat while hot.

Crumpets

Makes 8 to 10 crumpets

½ cup milk
½ cup boiling water
1 package (1 tablespoon) active dry
    yeast
1 teaspoon granulated sugar
1½ teaspoons salt

1¾ cups sifted all-purpose flour
¼ cup plus 2 tablespoons warm water
    (110° to 115°)
¼ teaspoon baking soda, dissolved in
    1 tablespoon hot water

Combine the milk and boiling water and cool to lukewarm. Add the yeast and sugar and allow to proof. Blend the salt and the sifted flour, combine with the yeast mixture and the remaining warm water and beat thoroughly for several minutes with a wooden spoon or with your hand. Let the batter rise in a warm place until almost doubled in bulk and rather bubbly. Add the dissolved soda and beat into the batter. Allow to rise again until doubled in bulk.

Into buttered rings placed on a moderately hot griddle spoon the batter to a depth of about ½ inch. Cook until dry and bubbly on top. Remove the rings, turn the crumpets, and brown lightly on the other side. Let cool. To serve, toast and flood with butter.

Cottage Cheese Bread

Makes 2 loaves

1 package (1 tablespoon) active dry
    yeast
¼ cup warm water
8 ounces cream-style cottage cheese
    (at room temperature)
½ cup butter, softened

2 tablespoons sugar
1 teaspoon salt
¼ teaspoon baking soda
1 well-beaten egg
2½ to 3 cups unbleached white flour

In a large bowl, dissolve the yeast in the warm water. Add all the other ingredients and mix until well blended. Turn out onto a floured board and knead the dough for 10 minutes. Clean the bowl, butter it well, return the dough to it, and turn to coat the surface evenly. Cover the dough with a cloth and let rise in a warm place until doubled in bulk—about 1¼ hours. Punch the dough down and let it rest for 10 minutes. Turn out onto a floured board and shape into 2 loaves. Place the loaves in greased bread pans. Let rise again, covered, for about 30 minutes. Bake in a preheated 350° oven for about 40 minutes.

Nut Rum Bread

Makes 1 loaf

4 tablespoons butter, softened
3 tablespoons brown sugar
2 eggs, lightly beaten
1½ cups all-purpose white flour
1½ cups whole-wheat flour
1 tablespoon baking powder

½ teaspoon salt
1¼ cups milk
½ cup dark rum
1 teaspoon vanilla
½ cup golden raisins
1 cup walnuts, coarsely chopped

Cream the butter and sugar until smooth, add the eggs, and beat well. Add the white and whole-wheat flours, baking powder, salt, milk, rum, and vanilla. Stir briefly to moisten the dry ingredients and stir in the raisins and walnuts. Spoon into a buttered 8½-by-4½-by-2½-inch loaf pan and bake in a preheated 375° oven for 50 to 60 minutes, or until a straw comes out clean when inserted in the center. Remove the loaf from the oven and turn out onto a rack to cool.

Mealy Bread

Makes 1 loaf

½ cup rolled oats
½ cup yellow cornmeal
¼ cup honey
1½ cups boiling water
1½ cups white flour
½ cup whole-wheat flour

2 teaspoons baking powder
½ teaspoon baking soda
1½ teaspoons salt
¾ cup yogurt
3 tablespoons melted butter
2 eggs, slightly beaten

In a large bowl, combine the oats, cornmeal, and honey; with a whisk, briskly stir in the boiling water until the mixture is smooth. Set aside and let stand for 15 minutes.

Add the white and whole-wheat flours, baking powder, baking soda, and salt to the oat mixture. Briskly stir in the yogurt, butter, and eggs, mixing only to moisten all the dry ingredients. Spoon the batter into a buttered pan and bake in a preheated 375° oven for 50 to 60 minutes, or until a straw comes out dry when inserted in the center of the loaf. Remove from the oven, turn onto a rack, and cool.

Whole-Wheat Bran Muffins

Makes 12 medium-size muffins

1 cup bran
½ cup whole-wheat flour
½ cup all-purpose white flour
1 teaspoon baking soda
¼ teaspoon baking powder

½ teaspoon salt
2 tablespoons butter, melted
2 tablespoons honey
1 cup buttermilk
2 eggs, separated

Preheat the oven to 375°. Butter the muffin pans or line with paper cups.

Combine the bran, whole-wheat and white flours, baking soda, baking powder, and salt in a bowl. Stir to mix.

Mix together the melted butter, honey, buttermilk, and 2 slightly beaten egg yolks. Beat the egg whites until stiff but not dry. Add the mixed liquid ingredients to the dry ingredients and stir only until dry ingredients are moistened. Fold the egg whites into the mixture. Fill the muffin pans two-thirds full. Bake for 15 to 20 minutes, or until the centers are dry when a toothpick is inserted.

Knusper Brote

This is a traditional German recipe highly reminiscent in flavor of some of the coffee cakes of Western Europe, which are sometimes flat and crisp (you'll note no baking powder or yeast is used). It keeps very well if stored in an airtight tin.

Makes 30 to 32 squares

1 cup butter
¾ cup sugar
2½ cups all-purpose flour
1 teaspoon milk
1 teaspoon cinnamon

1 egg, beaten
1 cup sliced blanched almonds
Crystallized sugar (available from
   bakers' and confectioners' supply
   shops)

Cream the butter and sugar in the bowl of an electric mixer until light and fluffy. Stir in the flour, milk, and cinnamon to make a rather firm batter. Butter a 15½-by-10½-inch baking sheet and press the batter into the pan. Brush with beaten egg and sprinkle with the sliced almonds and crystallized sugar. Bake in a 350° oven for approximately 30 minutes or until golden brown. Remove from oven and cut into rectangles 1½ by 2 inches while still warm. When cool remove from pan.

Cookies

Like bread baking, cookie baking can vary a great deal. You can take one recipe and do it two or three different ways by adding different flavorings, adding more flour, more egg, or more liquid, and find that you are achieving a much different cookie every time. Cookies now have taken on an enormous importance all through the country. There are cookie shops, there are cookies on wheels, and there are cookies to be found in the most incredible locations. People seem to be cookie mad! But I am still convinced that a good, simple, homemade cookie is far preferable to all the store-bought cookies one can find.

Tuiles

A classic French almond cookie that takes its name from its shape, similar to curved terra-cotta roof tiles. It is delicate and crisp, a lovely partner for sherbet. You'll sometimes find it made in a very large size. Be sure to shape the cookies while they are hot and pliable.

Makes about 2 dozen cookies

6 tablespoons butter, softened
½ cup sugar
2 egg whites

⅓ cup sifted all-purpose flour
Pinch of salt
1 cup sliced almonds

Cream the butter and sugar together until well blended. Stir in the egg whites, flour, salt, and nuts. Butter a heavy cookie sheet and drop the batter by teaspoonfuls 1½ inches apart, leaving enough room to allow them to spread. Bake in a 400° oven for about 10 minutes, or until golden brown around the edges and slightly yellow in the center. Remove the cookies from the sheet with a spatula and press them onto a rolling pin while still hot. Leave for a few minutes and remove to a cake rack to cool completely.

Soft Almond Cookies

The following two recipes are from the Near East, where almonds are much used in cooking. While they have a certain similarity, the first—which is dipped into syrup—is the more characteristic and unusual.

Makes about 30 cookies

1¼ pounds blanched almonds
1 cup sugar

SYRUP
½ cup sugar
1½ cups water

1 tablespoon grated lemon zest
2 eggs

1 tablespoon orange-flower water
Confectioners' sugar

Pulverize the almonds in a blender or food processor, then place in a bowl. Add the sugar and grated lemon zest, and stir until thoroughly mixed. Make a well in the center, drop in the eggs, and stir until the batter is completely smooth. Divide the batter in half and roll each half on a well-floured surface into a cylinder about 18 inches long and 1½ inches in diameter. (Flour your hands frequently as you roll the dough.) Flatten the cylinders into oblongs about 2 inches wide and cut diagonally into 1½-inch slices. Dust them with flour and place about an inch apart on ungreased baking sheets. Bake in a preheated 350° oven for about 15 minutes. Cool on wire racks.

Prepare the syrup by boiling the sugar and water together in a saucepan for about 10 minutes. Let cool, then add the orange-flower water. Dip the cookies into the syrup, then roll in confectioners' sugar.

Almond Cookies

Makes about 30 cookies

1¼ cups sugar
2 cups flour
¼ teaspoon salt
½ pound chilled unsalted butter

1 egg yolk
1 teaspoon vanilla
1 egg white, lightly beaten
¼ cup finely chopped almonds

Combine 1 cup of the sugar, the flour, and salt in a mixing bowl. Cut the butter into ½-inch bits. Work the butter into the flour with your fingers until it is the consistency of coarse meal. Stir in the egg yolk and vanilla, and form the dough into a ball. Chill 1 hour.

Form the dough into 2-inch fingers and cut these into ½-inch pieces. Place 2 inches apart on a well-buttered cookie sheet, and flatten each piece with the palm of your hand.

Brush the tops of the cookies with the lightly beaten egg white and sprinkle with a mixture of the remaining ¼ cup sugar and the finely chopped almonds. Bake in a preheated 350° oven for 10 minutes.

Cornmeal Butter Wafers

A distinctive cookie with a nice lemony flavor and a crunchiness imparted by the cornmeal. Very easy to make.

Makes about 24 cookies

½ pound (2 sticks) unsalted butter,
    softened
1 cup sugar
2 egg yolks

1 teaspoon grated lemon zest
1½ cups all-purpose flour
1 cup yellow cornmeal

Combine the butter and sugar and beat until light and well blended. Add the yolks and mix well, then stir in the lemon zest, flour, and cornmeal, blending thoroughly. Chill the dough until firm. It may then be rolled into a long cylinder and cut into ¼-inch rounds, or rolled out and cut into different shapes. Arrange the cookies on ungreased baking sheets and bake in a 350° oven for 10 to 12 minutes.

¶**Sesame Butter Wafers.** Instead of the cornmeal, use 1¼ cups toasted sesame seeds and add ½ teaspoon Oriental sesame oil.

Chinese Chews

I have no idea why these are called Chinese Chews, but I've been making them for over 15 years and I've yet to find anyone who doesn't find the combination of flavors irresistible.

Makes about 30 cookies

2 cups plus 2 tablespoons all-purpose flour

½ pound (1 cup) unsalted butter
1 cup brown sugar (light or dark)

TOPPING
1½ cups brown sugar (light or dark)
¼ teaspoon salt
1 cup coarsely chopped pecans

2 eggs
1 teaspoon vanilla
½ teaspoon baking powder

Mix 2 cups of the flour, the butter, and 1 cup of the sugar until crumbly, and spread this in a shallow 8-by-16-inch baking pan. Bake in a 300° oven for 10 minutes, then remove from oven.

Beat the ingredients for the topping together and spread the mixture evenly over the prepared crumb crust. Return to the oven and bake until light brown, about 30 to 40 minutes. Cool. Cut into fingers.

Lace Cookies

A traditional oatmeal cookie that has been popular for generations.

Makes about 30 cookies

1½ cups uncooked oatmeal
1½ cups light-brown sugar
2 tablespoons flour
½ teaspoon salt

⅔ cup unsalted butter, melted
1 egg, slightly beaten
½ teaspoon vanilla

Mix the oatmeal, brown sugar, flour, and salt in a bowl. Stir in the melted butter, then add the egg and vanilla, and combine well. Drop the batter by half-teaspoonfuls, about 2 inches apart, on ungreased cookie sheets. Bake in a 350° oven until lightly browned—about 5 minutes. Cool slightly and remove the cookies from the baking sheet with a spatula as soon as they are firm. If they become too firm and tend to break before you have lifted them from the baking sheet, return them to the oven for a minute to soften in the heat again.

Ginger Cakes

The smooth texture of these cookies with a hot overtone of ginger is rather like a ginger shortbread. Use the shortbread technique of pressing the mixture into the pan with your fingers.

Makes about 50 cookies

2 cups sifted all-purpose flour
1 cup brown sugar, firmly packed
1 tablespoon ground ginger

1 teaspoon baking soda
½ pound (1 cup) unsalted butter

Mix the flour, sugar, ginger, and baking soda thoroughly, then combine with the butter, cut into small pieces, until the mixture is well blended and crumbly. Place a ½-inch thickness of the mixture in square 8-inch layer-cake pans, pressing it down in the pan with your fingers. Bake in a 325° oven for 45 minutes to 1 hour, until lightly browned. While the cake is still warm, cut it into finger-shaped pieces about 1 inch wide. Remove the pieces with a spatula and, when cool, store in covered tins.

Oatmeal Carrot Cookies

Makes 24 cookies

¾ cup butter
¾ cup sugar
1 cup grated raw carrot
1 egg
1 to 2 teaspoons lemon zest

1¼ cups sifted all-purpose flour
½ teaspoon salt
2 teaspoons baking powder
1 cup rolled oats

Cream the butter, cream in the sugar, beat in the carrot and egg, and blend well. Mix in the zest and the flour, salt, and baking powder sifted together. Stir in the rolled oats. Place about 1 teaspoonful of dough on a greased teaspoon and push off with the back of another onto a well-oiled or buttered baking pan or sheet. Continue with all the dough. Bake in a preheated 375° oven 10 to 12 minutes or until the cookies are a delicate brown around the edges. Loosen from the pan while still warm, cool on a rack, and store in airtight containers. These freeze well, as does the unbaked dough.

Vadis Bars

This cookie recipe came from a pastry chef at the Quo Vadis Restaurant in New York City many years ago. It makes a lot of cookies, but they keep well when stored in tins, and the sweet-toothed really go for them.

Makes 140 bars

4 cups sifted all-purpose flour
6 tablespoons sugar
¾ pound (1½ cups) unsalted butter,
    softened

1 teaspoon salt
4 teaspoons grated lemon zest
6 hard-boiled egg yolks, mashed
4 raw egg yolks

BUTTER CRUNCH TOPPING
2 cups granulated sugar
2 teaspoons lemon juice
½ cup heavy cream
½ pound (1 cup) unsalted butter

3 cups blanched and sliced toasted
    almonds or filberts
2 teaspoons vanilla

Place the flour in a bowl, make a well in the center, and add all the remaining ingredients to the well except the topping ingredients. With the fingertips, make a paste of the center ingredients, then gradually incorporate the flour to form a smooth, firm ball of dough. Work quickly so the butter does not become oily. When the sides of the bowl are left clean, wrap the dough in wax paper and chill until it is firm enough to roll.

Roll out the dough between sheets of wax paper into a rectangle about 11 by 16 inches, and press this into a lightly greased 11-by-16-inch jelly-roll pan. Prick well with a fork, and chill.

Meanwhile, make the butter crunch topping. Combine the sugar and lemon juice in a heavy saucepan or skillet. Stir over low heat until the sugar is completely melted and golden brown, then add the cream and butter, and let the mixture boil. (At first the sugar will harden, but it will soon melt and blend with the liquid.) Stir until smooth. Stir in the nuts and set the mixture aside to cool. Just before using, stir in the vanilla.

Remove the dough from the refrigerator and bake it in a 350° oven for about 45 minutes, or until almost completely baked. Remove from the oven and spread with the topping. Return to the oven, placing the pan on a high rack, and bake 10 to 15 minutes longer, or until the top is bubbling. Remove from the oven and cool slightly before cutting into very small bars with a greased knife.

Lemon Meringue Bars

This rather rich cookie, good with tea or with ice cream, is not difficult to make.

Makes about 2 dozen bars

¼ pound (½ cup) unsalted butter,
    softened
½ cup confectioners' sugar
2 egg yolks
1 cup sifted flour

¼ teaspoon salt
2 teaspoons grated lemon zest
2 egg whites
½ cup granulated sugar
1 tablespoon lemon juice

Put together in a bowl the butter, confectioners' sugar, egg yolks, flour, salt, and lemon zest. Knead with the hands until the mixture is smooth and the color evenly distributed. Spread in a 10-inch square or 10-by-12-inch un-greased pan, and bake at 350 degrees for 10 minutes. Remove from the oven and allow to cool while making meringue.

    Beat egg whites until stiff. Add sugar gradually. Add lemon juice, and beat until the meringue stands in peaks. Spread meringue on the dough and return to the oven for 20 to 25 minutes, or until nicely browned. Cool and cut into bars.

Chocolate Macaroons

Makes approximately 12 macaroons

½ pound almond paste
4 ounces semisweet chocolate, melted
½ cup sugar (to be used if almond
    paste has not been sweetened)

3 to 4 egg whites

Combine almond paste and chocolate and mix until well blended. Blend in sugar if needed. Add only enough egg white to make a thick paste. Put into a pastry bag fitted with a No. 6 tip. Onto a buttered baking sheet that has been covered with parchment paper squeeze 3-inch rounds. Bake in a 350° oven for 20 minutes, or until firm.

Gino's Macaroons

Makes 20 macaroons

8 ounces almond paste
7 tablespoons superfine sugar
¼ cup confectioners' sugar

⅓ cup egg whites
Grated rind of 1 lemon or orange
Granulated sugar

Line an ungreased baking sheet with kitchen parchment. Break the almond paste in pieces and put in the food processor or blender. Blend until smooth, then add the sugars and mix until thoroughly blended, about 1 minute. Transfer the almond-paste mixture to a mixer and gradually beat in the egg whites to make a soft but firm paste. Mix in the lemon or orange rind. Beat at high speed for 3 minutes.

Put mixture into a pastry bag fitted with a No. 7 metal tube and form into 1½-inch rounds on the parchment, 1½ inches apart. Or use a teaspoon and drop the mixture on the parchment, spreading to 1½ inches in diameter. Brush the tops with a pastry brush dampened with cold water, then sprinkle them lightly with granulated sugar. Bake in a 350° oven for 30 minutes, or until lightly browned. These can be stored in an airtight tin at room temperature for up to 6 months.

Florentines

Makes approximately 18

3½ ounces candied orange peel, finely
    chopped
5 ounces blanched almonds, finely
    chopped
1½ ounces slivered almonds
⅓ cup pastry flour

3 tablespoons butter
¾ cup heavy cream
¾ cup sugar
2 tablespoons corn syrup
½ teaspoon vanilla
7 ounces semisweet chocolate

Combine the candied peel and nuts in a bowl and toss with the flour. Reserve.

Place the butter, cream, sugar, and corn syrup in a heavy saucepan and bring to a boil over moderate heat, stirring constantly, until it reaches 240° on a candy thermometer. Remove from heat and stir in the reserved dry ingredients and vanilla. Batter should be soft and kept warm. If it should become too firm stir in a few more drops of heavy cream or milk.

Grease 6 three-inch tartlet rings with butter. Line a baking sheet with parchment paper and place the rings on the parchment paper. Drop 1 tablespoon of batter in the center of each ring. Spread the batter with the back of a spoon and bake in a preheated 350° oven for 10 minutes. Remove from oven, remove the rings, and allow to cool completely.

Melt the chocolate over hot water. Spread the chocolate over the bottom side of each florentine with a spatula and allow to cool until the chocolate is hard.

NOTE: These may be stored in plastic bags or a cookie jar. Do not put them in the refrigerator.

"Monster" Peanut Butter Cookies

I've always had great fun baking outsize cookies as big as a small plate. This recipe makes about a dozen 6-inch cookies, but you can increase the number by doubling or tripling the ingredients. You may use any favorite recipe for oatmeal, chocolate chip, or sugar cookies. Just follow the rule of using ⅓ cup dough for each cookie.

Makes 12 six-inch cookies

1 cup (½ pound) butter	1 cup smooth or chunky peanut butter
1 cup sugar	2½ cups flour

Cream together the butter and sugar until light and fluffy, then add the peanut butter and the flour. When well mixed, scoop up ⅓-cup measures of the mixture and place on a well-buttered cookie sheet, being sure to leave lots of room between the mounds. When all the dough has been used, dip the bottom of a 9-inch pie plate in sugar and press the mounds firmly, flattening them to 6-inch circles. Bake in a preheated 375° oven for 15 minutes. Remove the cookies from the oven but leave them on the cookie sheets for at least 5 minutes before lifting them with a spatula. This is essential, as they are thin.

Meringue Kisses

A very popular type of meringue in America is kisses—little drop-type cookies that may be flavored with vanilla, cocoa, spices, or chocolate bits. Crisp on the outside while moistly crunchy inside, kisses are one of the most delicious and palate-pleasing of cookies.

Makes 18

3 egg whites
½ teaspoon cream of tartar
Pinch of salt

1 cup superfine sugar
1 tablespoon rum or brandy flavoring,
    or vanilla

Beat the egg whites in an electric mixer with whisk attachment until foamy. Add the cream of tartar and salt and beat until fluffy, but not at all dry. Be careful not to overbeat them at this point. Gradually add the superfine sugar, 3 or 4 tablespoons at a time, beating well after each addition. When half the sugar has been added, beat in the flavoring or vanilla. Continue beating until the sugar is completely dissolved and the meringue stands in stiff, upright, glossy peaks.

Have ready 2 Teflon-coated baking sheets, or baking sheets lined with cooking parchment. Push the meringue mixture from the tip of one teaspoon with the back of another onto the baking sheets in small mounds, leaving at least an inch between the mounds. Bake in a preheated 275° oven for about 20 minutes, or until they are set and very lightly colored. Remove from the oven and cool slightly. Remove the meringues from the baking sheet to a rack to cool completely before storing them in airtight containers between sheets of wax paper or foil.

Linzer Bars

Makes about 30 bars

½ cup unsalted butter
½ cup each brown and white sugar
1 cup chopped almonds or filberts, or
    a combination of both, toasted
1 egg, lightly beaten
1½ cups all-purpose flour
1 teaspoon baking powder

1 teaspoon cinnamon
¼ teaspoon ground cloves
¼ teaspoon mace
1 tablespoon cocoa
Grated rind of 1 lemon
1 cup raspberry jam

Cream the butter and sugar until light and fluffy. Beat in the nuts and egg.

Sift the dry ingredients together and add to the butter-and-sugar mixture. Press two-thirds of the dough into a 4½-by-13-inch flan ring or 8-inch baking pan. Combine the lemon rind with the raspberry jam and spread over the dough.

Roll out the remaining dough between 2 pieces of wax paper to a thickness of about ¼ inch. Refrigerate for 30 minutes. Remove from the refrigerator and cut the rolled dough into ½-inch strips and place diagonally over the raspberry jam, creating a lattice top. Bake in a preheated 375° oven for 30 minutes. Cool. Cut into narrow wedges or 1½-inch squares.

Blond Brownies

Makes about 24 brownies

½ cup butter
5 ounces white chocolate
2 cups sugar
2 eggs
1 teaspoon vanilla

1 cup sifted all-purpose flour
½ teaspoon salt
1 cup coarsely chopped walnuts,
    macadamia nuts, or pecans

Melt the butter and chocolate in a saucepan (1½ to 2 quarts) over low heat. Remove from the heat, stir well, then stir in the sugar and beat in the eggs and vanilla. Quickly stir in the flour, salt, and nuts to just lightly mix. Spread in a well-greased 8-by-10-inch or 9-by-12-inch baking pan. Bake at 325°, 35 minutes for the smaller pan, 30 for the larger. Do not overbake, or they will lose their nice chewy texture. Remove the pan to a rack to cool. While still slightly warm, cut into squares with a greased knife.

Sugar Cookies

Makes about 48

½ cup unsalted butter
1 cup sugar
2 eggs
1¼ teaspoons vanilla

2½ cups sifted all-purpose flour
2 teaspoons baking powder
½ teaspoon salt

Cream the butter and cream in the sugar until fluffy, then beat in the eggs and vanilla. Add the flour sifted with the baking powder and salt. Blend well. Chill the dough for easier handling; if you are in a hurry, spread it out on aluminum foil in 2 portions, wrap, and place in the freezer for 10 to 30 minutes. Use only half the dough at a time for rolling and cutting. Roll between sheets of wax paper to ¼ to ⅓ inch thick. Peel off the wax paper: peel it off the top of the rolled dough, flop the dough over onto a lightly sugared board, and peel off the other sheet.

Cut the cookies with a sugared 3-inch cutter. Lift with a spatula onto a lightly buttered baking sheet. Allow about 1 inch between them for expansion. Sprinkle the cookies with sugar, preferably coarsely granulated white sugar. Bake in a preheated 375° oven 8 to 10 minutes, or until very lightly browned around the edges. Loosen from the pan while still quite warm. When they have cooled on a rack to room temperature, store in airtight containers.

Apple Pancakes

1 cup all-purpose flour
¼ teaspoon salt
1½ teaspoons baking powder
½ cup milk

1 egg
1 tablespoon melted butter
½ teaspoon vanilla
1¼ cups homemade applesauce

Sift the dry ingredients together in a mixing bowl. Stir in the milk, egg, butter, vanilla, and applesauce. Beat well, then spoon the batter onto a hot greased griddle, making cakes about 4 inches in diameter. When the edges are lightly browned, turn and bake on the second side. Serve as a dessert, with warmed honey or with melted apple jelly and whipped cream.

Brambles

1 recipe lard pie crust for a 2-crust pie
  (see page 509)
1 cup raisins
1 lemon
1 egg

1 cup sugar
Pinch of salt
1 egg yolk
2 tablespoons cream

Roll pie dough to ⅛ inch thick; cut into 4-inch rounds. Put the raisins and lemon through a food grinder or food processor. Combine them with the egg, sugar, and salt. Place a spoonful of this mixture in the center of each round, fold over to make a half moon, seal edges with water, and pinch edges with fork. Place on an ungreased cookie sheet. Brush with egg yolk mixed with 2 tablespoons cream just before baking. Bake in a preheated 375° oven until brown—about 20 minutes.

Desserts

A few of the recipes here are monumentally rich and luscious, especially the cheesecakes, the voluptuous Sharlotka, and the chocolate cakes, which I lovingly dedicate to those friends for whom a day without chocolate is a day lost. But these are things I taste only in tiny servings, if at all, as others might nibble a candy. I don't cook them for my own use at home, and I think they're best enjoyed separate from a good meal—at midnight, for instance, with a dessert wine, or in the afternoon with tea or coffee.

To me the best desserts are light, sort of transparent, in that they don't obliterate the dishes that preceded them. Fruit is my usual choice—but not with cheese necessarily (I like the two tastes separate). Today it's hard to buy the zesty old-fashioned apples that were a commonplace of my Oregon boyhood. Transport and storage take their toll. You can't realistically ask a big market to give you a gold-and-amber Comice pear just at its peak of honeyed ripeness, or

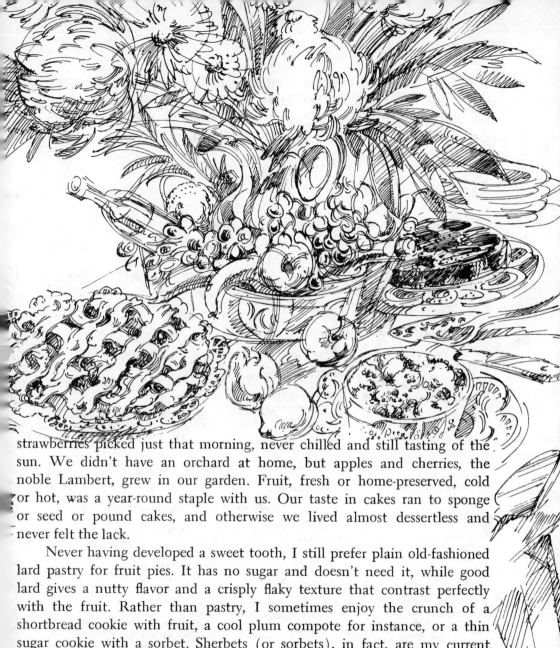

strawberries picked just that morning, never chilled and still tasting of the sun. We didn't have an orchard at home, but apples and cherries, the noble Lambert, grew in our garden. Fruit, fresh or home-preserved, cold or hot, was a year-round staple with us. Our taste in cakes ran to sponge or seed or pound cakes, and otherwise we lived almost dessertless and never felt the lack.

Never having developed a sweet tooth, I still prefer plain old-fashioned lard pastry for fruit pies. It has no sugar and doesn't need it, while good lard gives a nutty flavor and a crisply flaky texture that contrast perfectly with the fruit. Rather than pastry, I sometimes enjoy the crunch of a shortbread cookie with fruit, a cool plum compote for instance, or a thin sugar cookie with a sorbet. Sherbets (or sorbets), in fact, are my current favorites, and here I'm giving you the results of a long series of recent experiments. Their very light texture and intense flavor are refreshing after a hearty dinner, and I enjoy their brilliant color. Sometimes I serve a selection, all together in a deep crystal dish.

Appearance is important to me, with desserts in particular; for instance, I like to serve pots de crème in majolica cups, with very small spoons for slow savoring. Or I'll scatter a few tiny sprigs of mint over a bowl of raspberries, for their fragrance as well as their color. But I would never decorate a cake with sugar roses. Food should look like food. Plates

497

and bowls should be beautiful in themselves—I love porcelain in bold shapes and exciting colors—but when you serve, think of enhancement, not distraction. And that's really the point, for me, in choosing what to have for dessert. It shouldn't wipe out your memory of a good meal, it should enhance it.

DESSERTS

Simple syrup (for sherbets)

Apricot sherbet
  prune sherbet

Red-wine-pear sherbet
  white-wine-pear sherbet

Champagne sherbet

Peach sherbet
  orange
  grapefruit
  pineapple
  ginger and lime
  strawberry
  apple
  melon
  lichee
  lime and tea
  cranberry

Praline ice cream

Raisin and chestnut ice
  cream
  ginger and macadamia
  nut ice cream

Caramel ice cream

Brown bread ice cream

Cassis ice cream

Fruits (poached in heavy
  syrup, poached in
  light syrup, raw,
  canned)

Chocolate sauce

Cognac sauce

Brown sugar rum sauce

Butterscotch sauce

Apple pie (including lard
    pie crust)
  rhubarb pie

Nutted pumpkin pie

Pineapple and apricot tart
  (including pâte
  sucrée)

Pear and chocolate tart

The Coach House quince
  tart

Tarte tatin

Thin pear tart

Compote of dried fruits
  with cognac
  with rum

Strawberries Teresa
  glazed rhubarb

Gooseberry fool
  strawberry fool
  raspberry fool
  rhubarb fool
  fruit fool with yogurt

Chocolate ring

French chocolate cake

Austrian chocolate cake

Chocolate tweed cake

Sponge cake with apricot
  glaze

Orange and almond cake

Don Farmer's fresh apple
    cake
  fresh pear cake

Chocolate cheesecake

Hazelnut cheesecake

Sour cream cheesecake

Pound cake
  with citron
  with spices

Sharlotka

Bread-and-butter pudding
  with raisins
  with rum
  with French bread
  buttered-cake pudding

Apple tapioca
  with apples and pears
  or quince

Vanilla pots de crème
  with praline

Chocolate pots de crème

Sherbets

The vogue for simple food has increased the popularity—which was never minimal—of the mouth-tingling sherbets and sorbets and the related water ices. One of the great advantages of these desserts is that they may be quickly prepared before dinner, put in the freezer, and removed just long enough before serving to restore them to the softish texture at which they taste best—about half an hour in the refrigerator. Sherbets are easy to make from puréed fresh, canned, or dried fruits and fruit juices, and the variations of the theme are practically endless. You can freeze sherbet in an electric or hand-operated ice-cream freezer, turning it until just softly frozen (not as hard as ice cream); in the small electric sorbetières that fit into a freezer or freezing compartment; or in ice-cube trays. If frozen in trays, sherbet should be removed when mushy and partly frozen and beaten until smooth—for best results, 2 or 3 times during the freezing process.

Simple Syrup

This basic mixture of sugar and water cooked to a syrup serves two purposes—to sweeten the sherbet and to give it smoothness of texture. The usual ratio is 2 parts sugar to 1 part water, or slightly less sugar if you prefer—depending on your taste and the natural sweetness of the fruit purée. If you use canned fruits in syrup or poach the fruit in sugared liquid before puréing, the syrup from the can or the poaching liquid can take the place of the syrup. The usual proportion is 3 cups purée to 1 cup syrup; see details on pages 505–507.

Apricot Sherbet

Makes 6 servings

1 pound dried apricots
2 cups sugar
1 cup water

2 tablespoons cognac, apricot liqueur,
   or kirsch

Soak the apricots in water to cover for 2 hours. Drain. Make a simple syrup with the sugar and water, see above. Add the apricots to the syrup and cook for 10 minutes. Purée until smooth in a blender or food processor, or put through a food mill. Stir in the cognac, liqueur, or kirsch.

If you have an electric or hand-operated ice-cream freezer, churn the sherbet in the freezer, packed with ice and coarse salt, until the mixture is just softly frozen; it should not be hard. Otherwise, pour the mixture into ice trays and put in the freezer until partially frozen. Remove, turn the sherbet into a bowl, and beat thoroughly with a whisk or a heavy fork until smooth, then return to the trays and freeze. Repeat this process once or twice, then freeze the sherbet until firm but not hard.

¶**Prune Sherbet.** Use 1 pound dried, pitted prunes instead of the apricots. Flavor with ⅓ cup Madeira or sherry, and the juice of 1 lemon.

Red Wine–Pear Sherbet

Makes 1 quart

2½ cups red wine
1½ cups sugar
1 lemon slice, plus 1 tablespoon juice

6 pears
4 tablespoons eau-de-vie de poire

Combine wine, sugar, and lemon in a heavy pan and bring to a boil, stirring until the sugar dissolves. Peel, core, and halve the pears, dropping each peeled half into a bowl of water acidulated with 1 tablespoon lemon juice to prevent discoloring. Reduce the heat so the syrup is simmering. Drain the pears, add them to the simmering liquid, and poach, turning them once, for 10 minutes, or until just tender when pierced with a fork, but not overdone (the time depends on the size and firmness of the pears). Purée the pears until smooth in a blender or food processor. Combine with ½ cup of the wine syrup and the eau-de-vie. Freeze as for apricot sherbet (see preceding recipe).

¶**White Wine-Pear Sherbet.** Use 2½ cups dry white wine instead of the red wine.

Champagne Sherbet

Makes 6 to 8 servings

1 cup sugar
4 cups water
1 bottle brut champagne

Juice of 1½ oranges
Grated rind of 1 orange

Combine the sugar and water in a saucepan and bring to a rolling boil. Boil for 6 minutes. Add the champagne and heat to evaporate the alcohol. Remove from the heat and stir in the orange juice and rind. Cool, then freeze as for apricot sherbet (see above).

Peach Sherbet

Makes 1 quart

*3 cups peach purée, made with
approximately 7 or 8 fresh peaches
or drained canned peaches
(reserve syrup)*

*1 cup simple syrup (see page 499)
3 tablespoons bourbon, brandy, or
framboise*

If using fresh peaches, peel, cut them in half and core. Purée the fresh or canned peaches in a blender or food processor until smooth. Combine the purée with the simple syrup and bourbon. (If using canned peaches, use syrup from the can instead of simple syrup.) Freeze as for apricot sherbet (see page 500).

¶**Orange Sherbet.** Combine 3 cups fresh orange juice, 1 cup simple syrup, and flavor with 3 tablespoons Grand Marnier or Cointreau.

For a cream sherbet use 2 cups orange juice, ½ cup simple syrup, and 1 cup heavy cream, lightly whipped. Freeze.

¶**Grapefruit Sherbet.** Follow the recipe for orange sherbet, using 1 cup grapefruit juice and 2 cups orange juice (or use 3 cups grapefruit juice), and omit the liqueur. Freeze.

¶**Pineapple Sherbet.** Peel 1 very ripe pineapple, cut it into fingers, and process it to make 3 cups purée. Combine with 1 cup simple syrup and flavor with 3 tablespoons kirsch or rum. Freeze.

For a cream sherbet, use 2 cups pineapple purée sweetened with ½ cup simple syrup, 1 cup heavy cream, lightly whipped, and 1 cup yogurt.

¶**Ginger and Lime Sherbet.** Combine 2½ cups lime juice, 1½ cups simple syrup, ⅓ cup preserved ginger, cut into julienne strips, and 3 tablespoons of the syrup from the preserved ginger. Freeze.

¶**Strawberry Sherbet.** Use 3 pints fresh strawberries or 3 packages frozen to make 3 cups purée. Combine with ½ cup simple syrup, ½ cup orange juice, 3 tablespoons lemon juice, and ¼ cup Grand Marnier. Freeze.

¶**Apple Sherbet.** Peel and core 5 Golden Delicious or McIntosh apples and purée in a blender or food processor. You should have 2¾ cups purée. Combine with 1 cup simple syrup, ¼ teaspoon nutmeg, and ⅓ cup Calvados. Freeze. For a more textured sherbet, add ¼ cup finely chopped apple to the purée.

¶**Melon Sherbet.** Peel, seed, and quarter a melon (honeydew, Cranshaw, Hand melon, or Spanish melon) and purée in a blender or food processor.

You will need 3½ cups purée. Combine with ½ cup simple syrup, 2 tablespoons lemon juice, and 3 tablespoons port wine. Freeze.

For a cream sherbet, use 2¾ cups melon purée, ¼ cup simple syrup and 1 cup heavy cream, lightly whipped. Freeze.

¶**Lichee Sherbet.** Purée 2 eleven-ounce cans lichees with their syrup in a blender or food processor. Add 2 tablespoons lemon juice. Freeze.

¶**Lime and Tea Sherbet.** Combine 2 cups strong tea (preferably an English tea, although for a flavor variation you could use the same amount of Earl Grey, jasmine, or mint tea) with 1 cup lime juice and 1 cup simple syrup. Freeze.

¶**Cranberry Sherbet.** Purée 3 cups fresh cranberries, cooked until just soft, and 1 small navel orange, quartered with the peel on, in a food processor or blender until smooth. Combine with 1 cup simple syrup and 3 tablespoons bourbon or Grand Marnier. Freeze.

Ice Creams

Also growing in popularity, like sherbets, are the homemade ice creams, rich in butterfat. Small specialty ice cream shops are doing spectacular business, but you'll find making ice cream at home is both easy and rewarding, thanks to modern ice cream freezers. These range in size from 1 quart to 2 gallons and in type from compact little units that plug into an electrical outlet and are placed in the freezing compartment of a refrigerator to a very expensive Italian ice cream maker that works on freon tubes instead of the customary ice-and-salt mixture.

The two types of ice creams are those with a custard base, smooth, rich, and good for holding in the freezer, and the more delicate but definitely more caloric French or Philadelphia ice creams made entirely from cream and flavorings.

Praline Ice Cream

Makes about 2 quarts

6 egg yolks
1 cup sugar
⅛ teaspoon salt
2 cups milk

4 cups heavy cream
⅔ cup praline powder (see page 518)
2 tablespoons vanilla

Combine the yolks, sugar, and salt in a heavy 3-quart pan and beat until pale and creamy. Meanwhile, in another pan scald the milk and cream and slowly add to the yolk mixture. Cook over medium heat or in a double boiler until the mixture coats the spoon, but be careful not to heat it too much or it will curdle. If it does curdle, add a few tablespoons of boiling water and beat like crazy. Beat in the praline powder and vanilla. Cool the mixture and pour it into your ice cream maker or freezer, filling three-quarters full to allow for expansion, and freeze. Serve with chopped praline on top if you like.

Raisin and Chestnut Ice Cream

Makes about 2 quarts

6 egg yolks
1 cup sugar
⅛ teaspoon salt
2 cups milk
4 cups (1 quart) heavy cream
1½ to 2 tablespoons vanilla extract, or
    2½ inches vanilla bean

1 cup raisins, soaked in Scotch to
    cover until plump
½ cup finely chopped freshly cooked or
    canned chestnuts

Combine egg yolks, sugar, and salt in a heavy 3-quart enameled cast-iron saucepan or the top of a double boiler, and beat together with a wire whisk, hand or electric beater, or wooden spatula until well mixed, pale, and creamy. Meanwhile, in another pan, heat the milk to the boiling point. Mix the hot milk into the egg mixture, stirring constantly. Cook over medium heat or hot water (if using the double boiler), stirring constantly, until the custard is thick enough to lightly coat a wooden spatula or a spoon. Remove from the heat and cool. Strain the custard into a bowl. Stir in the heavy cream, vanilla extract (or slit the vanilla bean and scrape the tiny seeds into the custard), drained raisins, and finally the chopped chestnuts. Pour the mixture into the can of an ice cream freezer, filling it about three-quarters full to allow for expansion, put in the dasher, cover the can tightly with the lid, and freeze the ice cream until set.

¶**Ginger and Macadamia Nut Ice Cream.** Flavor the custard-cream mixture with 2 teaspoons vanilla and ¼ teaspoon ground ginger. Pour the mixture into the freezer and half freeze. Then add coarsely chopped preserved ginger and syrup from a 10-ounce jar (1 cup ginger, ½ cup syrup) and 1 cup coarsely chopped toasted macadamia nuts. Continue freezing until set.

Caramel Ice Cream

Makes 1 quart

CARAMEL SYRUP

1 cup sugar

1 cup boiling water

FOR THE CUSTARD (SAUCE ANGLAISE)

4 cups heavy cream
½ cup sugar
6 lightly beaten egg yolks
Pinch of salt

1 teaspoon vanilla extract
¾ cup caramel syrup

Toasted almonds

Cook the sugar in a heavy metal skillet until it melts and becomes golden. Carefully add the boiling water, standing back to make sure the caramel does not splash on you. Stir until the caramel is dissolved, then bring to a boil and cook 9 to 10 minutes, until it becomes a rich, thick caramel syrup.

Scald the heavy cream in a heavy saucepan, and add the sugar, mixing thoroughly. Pour this very slowly over the lightly beaten egg yolks, stirring constantly. Pour into a saucepan and cook over medium heat, stirring, until thickened. Add a pinch of salt, vanilla extract, and ¾ cup of the caramel syrup. Blend thoroughly, then pour into the ice-cream-freezer can and freeze. Serve with remaining caramel syrup and toasted almonds on top.

Brown Bread Ice Cream

Makes 1½ quarts

1½ cups dried whole-wheat
    bread crumbs
6 cups heavy cream

1¼ cups sugar
¼ teaspoon salt
4 teaspoons vanilla

Soak the crumbs in 4 cups of the heavy cream for 15 minutes. Add the sugar, salt, vanilla, and remaining 2 cups of cream. Chill. Freeze in a hand-cranked or electric ice cream freezer.

Cassis Ice Cream

Makes 8 servings

2 cups black currant preserves
1 cup crème de cassis liqueur
Juice of 1 lemon
½ teaspoon vanilla

2 cups light cream
2 cups heavy cream
⅛ teaspoon salt

Purée the preserves by putting them through a fine sieve, or purée in a blender or food processor with some of the crème de cassis. Add lemon juice, remaining crème de cassis, and vanilla. Mix the light and heavy cream together, add salt, and stir in the currant purée. Pour into an ice cream freezer packed with ice and rock salt and freeze.

Poached Fruits

I have always been extremely fond of poached fruits, either hot or cold, for desserts. Naturally each fruit requires a different cooking time, so I've given you a time chart here for the various poachable fruits and the type of syrup that should be used.

To make the syrup, put sugar and water in a heavy pan and bring to a boil, stirring until the sugar dissolves, then cook at a low boil for 10 minutes. Cool syrup before adding to purée and freezing.

Fruits

FRUIT	TIME	SERVE WITH
Fruits to be poached in a heavy syrup, made with 2 cups sugar to 1 cup water		
Kiwi	3–4 minutes	Heavy cream or sauce anglaise (see page 504)
Gooseberries	Until soft	Sauce anglaise (see page 504)
Kumquats	20 minutes	Plain or with mixed fruit
Blueberries	5–6 minutes	Heavy cream, kirsch, or mirabelle
Blackberries (a rose geranium leaf may be added to the syrup)	5–6 minutes	Heavy cream, crème fraîche, blackberry brandy
Strawberries	2 minutes	Kirsch, heavy cream, yogurt
Pineapple (peeled, cored, and sliced)	5–6 minutes	Rum, framboise
Fruits to be poached in a light syrup, made with 1 cup sugar to 1 cup water		
Lichee nuts, shelled	3 minutes	Serve plain
Rhubarb (green tops removed, stalks cut into 1-inch slices)	5 minutes	Heavy cream, yogurt, sauce anglaise (see page 504)

FRUIT	TIME	SERVE WITH
Cherries	10 minutes	Kirsch, cognac
Quince	20–25 minutes	Heavy cream, Calvados
Pineapple (peeled, cored and sliced)	5–6 minutes	Rum, framboise
Dried figs	15–20 minutes	Yogurt, heavy cream, crème fraîche, cognac
Dried prunes	15 minutes	Heavy cream, crème fraîche
Fresh prunes, halved and pitted	12 minutes	Heavy cream, crème fraîche
Plums	15 minutes	Mirabelle, cognac, port
Peaches, halved and pitted	10–15 minutes	Bourbon, brandy, framboise
Pears (may be poached in red wine or port)	20 minutes (or until tender)	Brandy, cassis, eau-de-vie de poire
Fresh apricots	10 minutes	Kirsch, brandy, apricot brandy
Dried apricots	15–20 minutes	Rum, apricot liqueur
Apples (peeled and sliced)	10–15 minutes	Calvados, brandy, sauce anglaise (see page 504)
Oranges (peeled and sliced thick)	35–40 minutes	Cointreau, Grand Marnier

FRUIT	SERVE WITH
Raw fruit	
Apples	Serve with cheese: Cheddar, fontina, or blue
Peaches	Brandy, framboise, maple syrup, kirsch, brown sugar and cream
Blueberries	Maple syrup and heavy cream, yogurt
Strawberries	Confectioners' sugar, orange juice, port, kirsch, framboise, Grand Marnier, whipped cream, sugar and cream, yogurt, crème fraîche
Bananas, sliced	Rum, or combine with other fruits such as strawberries, lichees, pineapple
Grapes	Yogurt and brown sugar
Raspberries	Kirsch, heavy cream, yogurt
Blackberries	Heavy cream, yogurt

FRUIT	SERVE WITH
Persimmons	Kirsch
Mangoes	Serve plain
Papaya	Lime juice
Pears	Cognac. Serve with fontina, Gorgonzola or other blue, Gruyère, goat cheese

Canned fruit

Nectar peaches	Serve plain
Bartlett pear halves	Cognac, sauce anglaise, chocolate sauce
Apricots	Toasted almonds and heavy cream
Cherries	Kirsch, cognac, cherry heering
Lichees	Bourbon

Sauces

Chocolate Sauce

Makes 1¼ cups

12 ounces semisweet chocolate
2 ounces unsweetened chocolate

½ pint heavy cream
2 tablespoons cognac or Grand Marnier

In top of double boiler, melt the chocolate over hot water. Stir in heavy cream gradually, stirring constantly, then add the cognac or Grand Marnier.

Cognac Sauce

This sauce adds great contrast to steamed puddings and very rich desserts. It is one of the sauces used for the traditional Christmas pudding.

Makes 2 cups

6 tablespoons butter
⅔ cup confectioners' sugar
2 egg yolks

¾ cup heavy cream
3 tablespoons cognac or brandy

Cream the butter with the sugar until the mixture is light and fluffy. Beat in the egg yolks, one at a time. Pour the mixture into a heavy-bottomed saucepan and stir in the cream. Place over medium-low heat and cook, stirring constantly, until the mixture coats a wooden spoon. As soon as the mixture coats the spoon, remove it from the heat and pour into a bowl. Flavor with the cognac or brandy.

Brown Sugar Rum Sauce

This sauce complements cooked fruits and baked and steamed puddings.

Makes 1 cup

½ cup brown sugar
½ cup water, plus 2 tablespoons
Pinch of salt

½ teaspoon cornstarch
¼ cup dark rum

Put the brown sugar and ½ cup of water in a saucepan with the salt. Bring to a boil and cook for 3 to 4 minutes. Blend the cornstarch with 2 tablespoons more water and stir it into the brown sugar mix, stirring and cooking until the mixture thickens. Remove from heat and add the dark rum.

Butterscotch Sauce

This is lusciously good with ice cream and cake-based puddings, like cottage pudding. A sprinkling of toasted almonds is delicious with it.

Makes 1 cup

1 cup brown sugar
¼ cup butter
¼ cup heavy cream

Pinch of salt
1 teaspoon vanilla extract

Mix the sugar, butter, cream, and salt together in a heavy-bottomed saucepan. Cook gently over low heat for 30 to 45 minutes or until rich and mellow. Remove from heat and add the vanilla.

Pies and Tarts

Apple Pie

The old-fashioned method of using lard in pie crust instead of butter is one I favor, as the result is much flakier and tenderer. The purer the lard, the better. If you can, buy leaf lard (pork kidney fat); this is the best lard you can use. Cut up a 3- or 4-pound piece of the leaf lard and render it (let it melt slowly) in a shallow pan in a 300° oven, pouring off the fat as it melts and transferring it to a jar. When all the fat is rendered and only the crispy bits of crackling remain, chill the fat in the refrigerator until firm and set.

Makes 1 nine-inch pie

LARD PIE CRUST
2½ cups all-purpose flour   ¾ cup lard
½ teaspoon salt   6 to 7 tablespoons cold water

FILLING
8 tart apples, cored, peeled, and cut   ¼ teaspoon nutmeg
    into ½-inch-thick slices   ⅓ cup bread crumbs (optional)
1 cup granulated sugar   4 tablespoons unsalted butter
2 tablespoons lemon juice   Egg wash (1 egg beaten with 1
2 tablespoons vanilla extract   tablespoon cream)

To make the pastry, mix the flour and salt in a bowl and cut in the lard
with 2 knives or a pastry blender. Combine lightly just until the mixture
resembles coarse cornmeal; the texture will not be uniform but will contain
crumbs and bits and pieces. Sprinkle water over the flour mixture, a
tablespoon at a time, and mix lightly with a fork, using only enough water
so the pastry holds together when pressed lightly into a ball. Refrigerate
30 minutes or more.

Preheat the oven to 425°. Combine the apples, sugar, lemon juice,
vanilla, and nutmeg in a bowl, and toss well.

Divide the chilled dough into 2 balls. Roll out one to make a bottom
crust 2 inches larger than a 9-inch pie pan. Ease it into the pan, fitting it
in loosely but firmly. Sprinkle the bottom of the pie shell with bread
crumbs. Fill the crust generously with the apple mixture, spooning it in
with a slotted spoon so as to drain off excess liquid which would otherwise
make the crust soggy. Dot layers of apple with the butter, cut into small
pieces. Roll out the remaining pastry for the top crust. Brush the rim of
the pie shell with cold water, put on the top crust, and trim, seal, and
crimp the edges. Prick in several places with a fork or cut vents in the
crust to allow the steam to escape. Brush with egg wash and bake at 425°
for 45 minutes, or until the crust is nicely browned and the pie is baked
through.

¶Rhubarb Pie. Mix 4 cups rhubarb stalks cut into ½- to ¾-inch pieces
with 1½ cups sugar, 3 tablespoons arrowroot, ¼ teaspoon salt, and 1
teaspoon grated orange rind. Turn into the prepared pastry-lined pan. Dot
with butter. Trim the edge of the pastry and moisten it. Top with remaining pastry, trim the edge, and crimp the top and bottom edges together.
Cut slits in the top for steam to escape. Bake at 450° 15 minutes, reduce
the heat to 350°, and bake about 25 to 30 minutes longer. Cool on a rack.
Serve warm or cold.

Nutted Pumpkin Pie

Makes 1 nine-inch pie

1¾ cups strained pumpkin
1 cup brown sugar
1½ cups heavy cream
½ cup bourbon
6 eggs, lightly beaten
2 teaspoons cinnamon
½ teaspoon mace

½ teaspoon ground cloves
1½ teaspoons ground ginger
¼ teaspoon salt
½ cup chopped toasted almonds or
    hazelnuts
½ recipe for lard pie pastry crust
    (see preceding recipe)

Combine all the ingredients except pastry in the order given. Turn into a prepared 9-inch pastry-lined pan. Bake in a 375° oven for 35 minutes or until the filling is set. Cool on a rack.

Pineapple and Apricot Tart

Makes 6 servings

PÂTE SUCRÉE
1 cup all-purpose flour
6 tablespoons frozen butter, cut in
    1-tablespoon pieces
2 tablespoons sugar

1 egg yolk
1 tablespoon cold water
⅛ teaspoon salt

FILLING
1 small pineapple, or 1 large can sliced
    pineapple
12 to 15 apricots, or 1 large can apricots
2 cups sugar (if making syrup)
1 cup water (if making syrup)

10-ounce jar apricot preserves,
    preferably without pectin
2 tablespoons bourbon
Whipped cream (optional)

Place the flour in the beaker of the food processor. Add the butter, sugar, egg yolk, water, and salt to the beaker. Process, turning on and off rapidly, for 5 seconds. Continue processing until a ball of dough forms on the blades. Chill until ready to use.

If using fresh pineapples and apricots, poach them in a simple syrup of 2 cups sugar to 1 cup water (see page 499). First, peel the pineapple and cut into slices, removing the core. Halve the apricots and remove the pits. Bring the sugar and water to a boil and add the pineapple slices. Poach until just tender. Poach the apricot halves in the same manner. Cool and reserve.

Remove the pastry from the refrigerator, roll it out, and fit into an 8- or 9-inch flan ring set on a cookie sheet. Preheat the oven to 425°. Prick the bottom of the shell, then line it with foil or wax paper and weight it down with raw rice or beans. Bake the shell for 14 to 16 minutes, until the bottom is set and the edges lightly browned.

After the initial baking, remove the shell from the oven, remove the lining, and return to the oven for 2 minutes. This seals the bottom and prevents a soggy crust. Remove to a wire rack to cool.

Put the apricot preserves into a small, heavy saucepan and stir over medium heat until the preserves come to a boil. Reduce the heat and cook for 2 minutes, stirring, until liquid. Add the bourbon and cool.

Brush the bottom of the tart shell with the apricot glaze and arrange slices of pineapple over the glaze. Arrange the halved apricots on top of the pineapple and mask the entire tart with the remaining apricot glaze. Serve with whipped cream if you desire.

Pear and Chocolate Tart

Makes 8 servings

1 recipe pâte sucrée (see preceding recipe)
2 cups water
1 cup sugar
1-inch piece vanilla bean or 1 teaspoon vanilla extract

APRICOT GLAZE
1-pound jar apricot preserves (preferably without pectin)

4 to 6 pears, peeled, halved, and cored (a small melon-ball cutter may be used to remove cores)
6 squares (6 ounces) semisweet chocolate
2 tablespoons butter

2 tablespoons cognac

Roll out the pastry and fit into a 9-inch flan ring set on a cookie sheet. Prick bottom of pastry, line with foil, and weight down with beans or rice. Bake in a 375° oven for 20 minutes. Remove foil and beans and cool shell.

Meanwhile, bring the water, sugar, and vanilla to a boil in a heavy skillet, and cook for 5 minutes to make a syrup. Poach the pears in the syrup until just cooked through but still firm. Do not overcook. Cool in the syrup, remove, and drain them on paper towels. (The syrup may be reserved for poaching other fruits.)

Melt chocolate and butter in a small saucepan over low heat, or in a low-temperature oven. Brush the bottom of the flan shell with the chocolate mixture and let it cool. Arrange the poached pear halves in the flan shell and prepare apricot glaze.

Melt the apricot preserves in a pan and bring to a boil, stir in the cognac, and boil down for 2 minutes. Brush the hot glaze over the pears. Leave to cool before serving.

The Coach House Quince Tart

Makes 12 servings

PASTRY

2½ cups flour
½ pound unsalted butter, softened
2 tablespoons sugar

3 egg yolks
½ teaspoon cinnamon
Grated zest of 1 lemon

FILLING

6 large quince
3 cups water
3 cups sugar
Juice of 1 lemon, strained

1 stick cinnamon
2 whole cloves
2 tablespoons chopped almonds,
  roasted lightly

HAND METHOD FOR PASTRY: Place the flour in a large bowl. Make a well and add the butter, cut into small pieces, sugar, egg yolks, cinnamon, and lemon zest. Knead well until well mixed and the dough forms a ball. Chill until firm.

FOOD PROCESSOR METHOD: Put the flour, sugar, cinnamon, and lemon zest in the work bowl, add the butter, and process until the mixture is the consistency of cornmeal. Then add the egg yolks and process until the dough forms a ball. Chill until firm.

For the filling, peel and core the quince, saving the seeds. Cut the quince into julienne strips. Meanwhile, in a heavy skillet or enamel pan, boil together the water, sugar, and lemon juice, then add the strips of quince along with the cinnamon, cloves, and quince seeds tied in a cheesecloth bag. The pectin in the seeds acts as a thickener. Bring the mixture to a boil, lower the heat, and simmer for 1½ hours, or until the juice is thickened. Stir the mixture from time to time, being careful that it doesn't stick or burn. Discard the bag with the seeds and spices and let the mixture cool. (At this point the filling can be poured into sterilized glass jars and sealed with paraffin, if you wish to use it for preserves rather than a tart filling.)

Preheat the oven to 375°. Roll out two-thirds of the pastry between 2 pieces of wax paper, and fit into a 12-inch round cake or quiche pan with a removable bottom. Bake for 10 minutes.

Fill the shell with the quince mixture, and use the remaining pastry to make a latticework top. Place the tart in the oven and bake for 20 to 30 minutes, or until the pastry is golden brown and the preserves are bubbling. Remove the tart from the oven and sprinkle the almonds on top. Let cool at least 2 to 3 hours, or overnight, but do not refrigerate. Serve with whipped cream, crème fraîche (see page 548), sour cream, or vanilla ice cream.

Tarte Tatin

Makes 1 ten-inch tart

CORNMEAL PASTRY
1 cup flour
½ cup cornmeal
½ teaspoon salt

½ cup shortening
¼ cup water

APPLE FILLING
½ to ¾ cup sugar plus 2 or 3
  tablespoons
5 to 8 apples, cored, peeled, and cut
  in quarters or sixths

4 to 6 tablespoons sweet butter,
  cut in tiny pieces
Nutmeg or cinnamon (optional)

Combine flour, cornmeal, salt in a bowl, add the shortening and cut into flour mixture until it looks like coarse meal. Sprinkle the water over, and stir with a fork. Pat into a ball and wrap in wax paper. Refrigerate until ready to use.

Melt ½ to ¾ cup sugar, depending on how sour your apples are, in a heavy iron or aluminum 8- or 9-inch skillet over medium heat until it turns a delicate brown. Remove pan from heat. Arrange the apples on the melted sugar and mound up in the center. Sprinkle them with 2 to 3 tablespoons sugar, and dot with butter. If you wish, sprinkle with a few grains of nutmeg or cinnamon.

Carefully roll out the chilled pastry to a size that will fit inside the skillet. Lay it over the apples, tucking it down inside the skillet. Make about 3 holes in the top with a skewer or sharp knife. Bake in a 350° oven from 1 to 1½ hours, until the crust is brown and firm to the touch and the apples possibly bubbling up a bit around the edge. Remove from the oven and let it stand 2 minutes, then run a sharp knife around the edge of the tart and invert it onto a plate rather larger than the skillet. Do this quickly and deftly so the apples don't fall off. Should they shift position, push them back into place with a spatula. Cut into wedges and serve warm or tepid.

Thin Pear Tart

Makes 1 ten-inch tart

½ recipe basic lard pie crust
  (see page 509)
5 or 6 firm ripe pears, cored, peeled,
  and thinly sliced

Granulated sugar
1 tablespoon vanilla extract
3 tablespoons unsalted butter
Confectioners' sugar

Preheat the oven to 425°. Roll out the pastry and fit into a 10-inch round flan ring, placed on a baking sheet. Arrange the sliced pears on the pastry, sprinkle with granulated sugar and vanilla extract and dot with butter. Bake for 30 minutes or until nicely brown. Remove from the oven and sprinkle with confectioners' sugar, then place under the broiler just long enough to glaze the top—watch carefully so that the top does not burn.

Compote of Dried Fruits

While dried fruits are hardly inexpensive these days, they do make a most delicious compote at times when fresh fruits are not at their best and ripest. I like to use a mixture of dried fruits, but you may use just 2 or 3, according to preference, increasing the amounts accordingly.

Makes 8 servings

½ pound each dried prunes, apricots, peaches, figs
3 to 4 cups water
6 thin slices lemon, seeds removed
1½ cups sugar

¼ to ⅓ cup bourbon
2 cups sour cream, heavy cream, or whipped cream, or a mixture of ½ whipped cream and ½ yogurt

Put the fruits in a 4-quart saucepan, cover with water, and bring to a boil. Add the lemon slices and sugar, reduce heat, and simmer fruits for 15 to 20 minutes, or until puffed. Add the bourbon. Turn off heat and let the fruit remain in the pan for a few minutes to absorb the flavor of the spirit. Transfer to a serving dish and allow to cool slightly. Serve with desired type of cream.

¶**Dried Fruit Compote with Cognac.** Substitute cognac for the bourbon.

¶**Dried Fruit Compote with Rum.** Substitute dark rum for the bourbon.

Strawberries Teresa

Makes 6 to 8 servings

4 cups sugar
1 cup water

1 quart strawberries
¼ cup rum

Boil 2 cups sugar and water in a saucepan until the syrup spins a thread, 232° on a candy thermometer. Add remaining 2 cups sugar and strawberries. Watch carefully, and the minute the berries start to boil, time them, giving them about 18 minutes. Shake the pan back and forth—do not stir. Cool the berries slightly, add the rum, and refrigerate overnight. They are best eaten cool, not chilled, with freshly made brioche or light hot biscuits and cream—either sour cream, whipped cream, or very thick heavy cream.

¶Glazed Rhubarb. Trim rhubarb, cut in 2-inch pieces, and blanch in boiling water for 1 minute. Remove and dry. Add to the 232° syrup and cook 3 minutes. Cool.

Fruit Fool

One of the simplest and loveliest of all summer fruit desserts is the English fool, merely a purée of berries with lightly whipped heavy cream stirred into it in a marbleized design, which looks quite beautiful served in a glass bowl. Traditionally, this was made with tart gooseberries, which are often hard to find these days, but if you do find them, or can grow them, here is the basic recipe. Rhubarb, strawberries, and raspberries also make delicious fools. You can use frozen raspberries, which need no sweetening.

Gooseberry Fool

Makes 4 servings

1 pound hard green gooseberries   1 cup heavy cream
¾ cup sugar

Cook the gooseberries and sugar over very low heat until they are quite soft—you may need to add a few drops of water to start the sugar melting. When they are very soft and mushy, put them through the finest screen of a food mill or force them through a sieve. Taste to see if they are sweet enough; if not, add a little more sugar or sugar syrup to the purée. Let the purée get quite cold, then lightly whip the cream and fold it into the purée with a rubber spatula. Chill until very cold. Serve in small glass bowls with thin crisp cookies, shortbread fingers, or thin slices of pound cake.

¶Strawberry Fool. Hull 1 to 1½ pints ripe strawberries and sieve them (there is no need to cook them). Stir about ½ cup sugar (or to taste) into the purée, and add a drop or two of lemon juice to accent the flavor. Combine with the whipped cream.

¶**Raspberry Fool.** Substitute 1 pound ripe raspberries for the strawberries. If using frozen raspberries, pour off some of the syrup from 4 packages thawed raspberries. Sieve 3 cups of the raspberries—they need no sweetening; just add lemon juice to taste.

¶**Rhubarb Fool.** Cook 1 pound rhubarb cut in ½-inch pieces with 1 cup sugar over very low heat until it is quite soft. Proceed as for gooseberry fool.

¶**Fruit Fool with Yogurt.** For a low-calorie version, use 1½ cups yogurt instead of the whipped cream. You may find this needs additional sugaring of the berries, unless you like a tarter fool.

Chocolate Desserts

It would be impossible to estimate the number of chocolate freaks in this country, but to many people a day without chocolate is a day lost. For those to whom chocolate desserts are close to a passion, I've chosen one of the more luscious examples, a type of soufflé. Then in the cake section that follows, you'll find several good rich chocolate cakes—a French, an Austrian, and a tweedy American cake as well as a splendid chocolate cheesecake.

Chocolate Ring

Another easy dessert for chocolate lovers.

Makes 6 servings

8 ounces semisweet chocolate bits
½ pound butter
2 teaspoons vegetable shortening
1⅛ cups sugar

8 eggs, separated
1 teaspoon vanilla extract
¼ teaspoon salt

Melt the chocolate with the butter and vegetable shortening in the top of a double boiler over hot water. Stir in the sugar and remove from the heat. Beat in the egg yolks and vanilla and cool the mixture for a few minutes. Beat the egg whites with the salt until stiff but not dry. Turn the chocolate mixture into a bowl and fold in the whites. Pour into a buttered and sugared 8-cup ring mold, and bake in a 300° oven for 2 to 2½ hours. Serve warm with whipped cream.

Cakes

French Chocolate Cake

This chocolate cake is very rich and gooey, and the center will appear to be undercooked. Don't worry, that's how it's meant to be—hence the soft texture and exceptional flavor. The cake both refrigerates and freezes perfectly, but should be brought to room temperature before serving so the glaze will become shiny again. It will be easier to cut if refrigerated before serving.

Makes 8 to 10 servings

¼ pound (1 stick) butter, softened
1½ cups (6 ounces) blanched almonds
   or filberts
¾ cup chocolate pieces or 4 ounces
   semisweet chocolate

⅔ cup sugar
3 eggs
Grated rind of 1 large orange
¼ cup very fine bread crumbs (about
   1 slice firm white bread)

GLAZE
2 ounces (2 squares) unsweetened
   chocolate

¼ cup butter, softened and cut up
2 teaspoons honey

GARNISH: Toasted slivered almonds or whole filberts

Use some of the butter to butter the bottom and sides of an 8-inch round cake pan. Line the bottom with kitchen parchment or wax paper; if you use wax paper, butter it too.

Grind the nuts as fine as possible in a food processor or blender. Melt the chocolate for the cake in a double boiler over hot—not boiling—water. Cream the remaining softened butter with an electric beater or in an electric mixer until very soft and light. Add the sugar gradually, beating constantly. When all the sugar has been added, add the eggs, one at a time, beating well after each addition. At this point the batter will look curdled, but it will all come together when the remaining ingredients are added. Stir in the melted chocolate, ground nuts, orange rind, and bread crumbs thoroughly with a rubber spatula. Pour the batter into the prepared pan and bake in a preheated 375° oven for 25 minutes. Cool the cake on a rack for about 30 minutes, then run a spatula around the edge and turn it out onto a cake rack. Remove and discard the paper. Cool completely before glazing.

For the glaze, combine the chocolate, butter, and honey in the top of a double boiler, and let the mixture melt over hot water. Take the pan off the heat and beat the chocolate mixture until cold and beginning to thicken. Place the cooled cake on a rack over wax paper and pour the glaze over it. Tip the cake so the glaze runs evenly over the top and down the sides. Smooth the sides, if necessary, with a metal spatula. Garland the rim of the cake with the nuts, placed fairly close together.

Austrian Chocolate Cake

This is somewhere between a cake and a pudding, heavy and rich, with an unbelievably unctuous texture, and wonderful after a light main course.

Makes 10 servings

2 cups milk
1½ cups sugar
½ pound butter
½ pound unsweetened chocolate

4 eggs, separated
2⅓ cups sifted cake flour
2 teaspoons baking powder

PRALINE POWDER
1 cup sugar
½ cup almonds, toasted and finely
    chopped

½ cup filberts, toasted and finely
    chopped

PRALINE BUTTER CREAM
¼ pound (1 stick) butter, softened
1 cup praline powder (recipe above)

¼ cup confectioners' sugar
GARNISH: Toasted almond halves

Combine the milk, sugar, butter, and chocolate, and bring to the boiling point over medium heat. Let cool slightly, and beat in the egg yolks and the flour sifted with the baking powder. Beat for 5 minutes by hand, or 2 minutes with an electric beater at medium speed. Beat the egg whites until stiff but not dry, and fold them into the chocolate mixture. Pour into a well-buttered 10-inch ring mold. Bake in a 325° oven for 50 minutes. This should not be baked until dry and too firm—it should be rather moist in the center when it is removed from the oven. Let the cake cool for 15 minutes in the mold before turning it out.

To make the praline powder, melt the sugar in a heavy 10-inch pan, and when it is melted and lightly colored, add the finely chopped nuts. Pour into a buttered flat pan to cool. When cool and set, crush to a powder with a rolling pin or in a food processor.

For the praline butter cream, cream the butter in an electric mixer and gradually work in the praline powder and the sugar, beating until smooth and creamy. Cut the cake in half horizontally and spread with the butter cream. Put the halves back together and decorate the top of the cake with the toasted almond halves.

Chocolate Tweed Cake

The old American custom of incorporating potatoes into a cake to give it a different texture and a certain lightness can be updated by using instant mashed potatoes. This cake gets its unusual name from the speckled, tweedy look given by chocolate that has been grated on the shredding side of a grater.

Makes 12 servings

Instant mashed potatoes (the amount
    for 2 servings)
¾ cup (6 ounces) soft butter or
    margarine
2¼ cups sugar
3 eggs
1¾ cups all-purpose flour, unsifted
2 teaspoons baking powder

1 teaspoon salt
½ teaspoon cream of tartar
½ teaspoon ground cloves
½ teaspoon ground nutmeg
1½ teaspoons ground cinnamon
½ cup milk
2 ounces unsweetened chocolate,
    shredded on a grater

GLAZE
2 cups unsifted confectioners' sugar
    beaten with 3 tablespoons water

Prepare the mashed potatoes, using the liquid called for on the package but omitting the butter and salt. Let cool. Beat the butter and sugar together until creamy. Beat in the potatoes and then the eggs, one at a time, until fluffy. Sift the flour with the baking powder, salt, cream of tartar, and spices. Add the flour mixture and the milk alternately to the potato mixture, blending after each addition. Stir in the chocolate. Spoon the batter into a greased and floured 10-inch tube pan with a removable bottom or a 9-by-13-inch baking pan.

Bake in a 350° oven for 1 hour and 15 minutes (or 50 minutes for the baking pan), or until a wooden pick inserted in the center comes out clean. Cool the cake for 10 minutes. Loosen the tube cake from the pan sides with a knife, lift the cake out by pushing up the removable bottom, then loosen the cake bottom. Turn out onto a rack and drizzle with glaze. Or spread glaze over warm cake in the baking pan. Cool.

Sponge Cake with Apricot Glaze

A simple light sponge cake makes a very pleasing dessert, either plain with fruit or ices, or bathed in an apricot glaze, which makes it rather special.

Makes 8 servings

1¼ cups sifted cake flour
1½ cups sugar
½ teaspoon salt
½ teaspoon baking powder
½ cup egg yolks (6 or more, depending on size)
¼ cup cold orange juice

1 teaspoon vanilla
½ teaspoon almond extract or 1 tablespoon grated orange rind
½ cup egg whites (about 4, depending on size)
¼ teaspoon cream of tartar

APRICOT GLAZE
1 cup sieved apricot jam
2 to 4 tablespoons cognac, kirsch, or applejack (optional)

Sift the flour with 1 cup of the sugar, the salt, and the baking powder. If using an electric mixer, sift into the small bowl. Add the egg yolks, orange juice, and flavorings, but do not stir the mixture at this time. Put the egg whites in the large bowl of the mixer, or into a good-sized mixing bowl, and beat them until fluffy. Add the cream of tartar and continue beating, then gradually beat in the remaining ½ cup sugar and continue beating until very stiff peaks are formed. With a rotary beater or the electric mixer on low speed, beat the flour, egg yolk, and flavoring mixture until well blended, about 1 minute. Gently fold—do not stir—this mixture, about a quarter at a time, into the egg whites. When the batter is smooth, turn into an ungreased 10-inch tube pan. Bake in a preheated 350° oven for 40 to 50 minutes. If the cake springs back when pressed lightly in the center, it is done. It should also have begun to shrink from the sides of the pan. Immediately invert it and allow it to cool before removing it from the pan. Heat the sieved apricot jam in a saucepan until boiling. Stir in the preferred flavoring, if used, and pour the hot glaze over the cake.

Orange and Almond Cake

A very unusual cake from the Middle East with a moist, dense consistency that makes an utterly delicious dessert. It will not rise very much, and you may wonder if it will ever bake firm. Don't worry, it will.

Makes 8 servings

2 large oranges (preferably the
    seedless navels)
6 eggs
1½ cups ground almonds

Pinch of salt
1 cup sugar
1 teaspoon baking powder

GARNISH: *Thin slices of peeled orange sprinkled with confectioners' sugar and a
touch of cinnamon, or fresh raspberries. Serve with whipped cream.*

Wash the oranges and boil them in water to cover, without peeling, until very soft, about 30 minutes. Drain, cool, cut into quarters, and remove the seeds, if any. Process the oranges to a fairly fine purée in a blender or food processor or by putting them through a meat grinder. Don't make it too fine. The little bits of skin, which will not be at all bitter after the long boiling, are pleasant to bite on. Beat the eggs in a bowl until thick, then add the ground almonds, salt, sugar, baking powder, and orange purée, and mix well. Pour into a deep 9-inch cake pan that has been buttered and floured, and bake in a 400° oven for 1 hour or longer, until firm to the touch when pressed with the tip of your finger. Remove the pan to a rack, allow the cake to cool, then turn it out of the pan onto a serving dish. Serve garnished with orange slices or berries, and whipped cream.

Don Farmer's Fresh Apple Cake

With the crunch of the raw apple and an almost puddinglike texture and spiciness, this has a distinction not often found in cakes.

Makes 12 servings

1½ cups vegetable oil
2 cups sugar
3 eggs
3 cups all-purpose flour
1 teaspoon baking soda
2 teaspoons cinnamon
½ teaspoon nutmeg

½ teaspoon salt
3 cups diced tart raw apples (preferably
    Pippins or Greenings)
1 cup black walnut or regular walnut
    meats
2 teaspoons vanilla extract

GLAZE
2 tablespoons butter
2 tablespoons brown sugar
2 tablespoons granulated sugar

2 tablespoons heavy cream mixed with
    ¼ teaspoon vanilla extract

Combine the oil and sugar in a bowl or the bowl of an electric mixer. Blend very well. Add the eggs, one at a time, beating well after each addition. Sift together the flour, baking soda, cinnamon, nutmeg, and salt. Sift these into the oil-egg mixture and combine thoroughly. Add the diced raw apples and the walnuts. Mix well with a spoon or spatula, then add the vanilla. Pour the batter into a buttered and floured 9- or 10-inch tube pan. Bake in a 325° oven for 1¼ hours, or until the cake tests done when pierced with a skewer or toothpick. Remove from the oven and let rest in the pan while you prepare the glaze.

For the glaze, melt the butter, sugars, and heavy cream mixed with vanilla in a heavy pan. Boil for 1 minute. Remove from the heat and spoon over the warm cake. Let it cool in the pan before removing.

¶**Fresh Pear Cake.** Instead of apples, use 3 cups firm Anjou or Bartlett pears. Proceed as above.

Chocolate Cheesecake

Alice Petersen, long the food editor of the New York *Daily News*, perfected this cheesecake, which is almost overpoweringly rich. It's well worth the trouble to shop the health-food stores for a light, natural cream cheese without additives when you make cheesecake, as the gummy commercial, supermarket version is a travesty.

Makes 8 servings

CRUST
2 cups graham-cracker crumbs
¼ cup sugar

½ cup (4 ounces) butter, melted

FILLING
4 eggs, separated
⅔ cup sugar
1 pound cream cheese, cut into cubes
2 six-ounce packages semisweet
    chocolate bits

½ cup hot strong coffee
2 tablespoons dark rum
1 teaspoon vanilla extract
⅛ teaspoon salt

TOPPING
½ cup heavy cream

2 tablespoons sugar

GARNISH: *Chocolate curls*

Preheat the oven to 350°. Butter the bottom and sides of a 9-inch spring-form pan. Blend crust ingredients in a bowl and pat the crumb mixture onto the bottom and sides of the pan. Set aside while preparing the filling.

Beat the egg yolks and ⅓ cup sugar in an electric mixer until thick and lemon-colored. Beat in the cream cheese and continue beating until smooth. Melt the chocolate bits in the top of a double boiler over hot but not boiling water and blend in the hot coffee, rum, vanilla, and salt. Beat this mixture into the cream cheese mixture.

Beat the egg whites until they hold soft peaks, then gradually beat in the remaining ⅓ cup sugar until you have a rather stiff meringue mixture, with glossy, upright peaks. Fold this gently into the chocolate mixture and pour into the prepared crumb crust. Bake at 350° for 1 hour. Turn the oven off, but leave the cake inside until it is completely cooled. Remove the cake to a rack. When ready to serve, carefully remove the sides of the springform pan.

Whip the cream, flavoring it with the sugar. Spread the whipped cream on the cheesecake and decorate with chocolate curls, shaved from a block of chocolate with a heavy knife. To facilitate making the shavings, either slightly warm the chocolate or dip the knife in hot water.

Hazelnut Cheesecake

The nuts give a pleasing crunchiness to the smooth texture of the cheesecake. To prevent the cake mixture from leaking from the springform pan, cover the outside of the pan with heavy aluminum foil. The cake will also cool more slowly and will be less likely to crack.

Makes 8 servings

1½ cups hazelnuts, blanched	*1¾ cups sugar*
2 pounds cream cheese, at room	*4 eggs*
temperature	*⅓ cup graham-cracker crumbs*

Butter the bottom and sides of an 8-inch springform pan, 3 inches deep, and set aside. Arrange the rack on which the cake will bake one-third up from the bottom of the oven, which has been preheated to 350°.

Spread the hazelnuts in a shallow pan and bake for about 15 minutes, stirring them occasionally, until lightly browned. Cool the nuts, then grind them in a blender or food processor. It doesn't matter if they are not evenly ground.

Place the cheese in the large bowl of an electric mixer and beat at medium speed until absolutely smooth. During the beating stop the machine occasionally and scrape the sides and bottom of the bowl with a rubber spatula to keep the cheese evenly blended. When smooth, beat in the sugar, and mix well. Then add the eggs, one at a time, being careful not to beat any more than necessary to thoroughly mix all the ingredients. Stir in the nuts with a rubber spatula.

Pour the batter into the prepared springform pan and level the top by briskly rotating the pan, first in one direction, then in the other. Cover the outside with heavy aluminum foil to prevent leakage. Place the springform pan inside another larger pan, so that the cake pan does not touch the sides, but no more than 3 inches deep (a roasting pan is a good choice). Pour 1½ inches of hot water into the larger pan, place in the oven, and bake for 1½ hours, or until the top is a rich, golden brown and feels dry to the touch. The cake should still be soft inside. Remove the cheesecake pan from the water bath and place on a rack for a few hours, until completely cool. Do not cool the cake in the refrigerator. When cool, remove the sides of the springform pan very carefully, and sprinkle the top of the cake with the graham-cracker crumbs.

Sour Cream Cheesecake

Makes 8 servings

3 eight-ounce packages cream cheese,
    cut into cubes
1¼ cups sugar
6 eggs, separated
1 pint sour cream

⅓ cup flour, sifted
2 teaspoons vanilla extract
Grated zest of 1 lemon
Juice of 1 lemon

CRUST
2 cups graham cracker crumbs
¼ cup sugar

6 tablespoons butter

GARNISH: *Confectioners' sugar (optional)*

Beat the cheese until soft and creamy. Add the sugar and mix thoroughly. Blend in the egg yolks one at a time until well blended. Add the sour cream, flour, vanilla, and lemon zest and juice, and mix well. Beat the egg whites until stiff but not dry. Stir one-third of the whites into the cheese mixture, then fold in the remaining whites very gently.

Mix 1½ cups of the crumbs with the sugar and butter, and use this to line the bottom and sides of a 10-inch springform pan. Pour the cheese mixture into the prepared crust and bake in a preheated 350° oven for 1 hour. Turn off the heat and allow the cheesecake to remain in the oven for an additional hour. Remove to a rack and cool to room temperature. Sprinkle the remaining ½ cup crumbs on top of the cake. Chill overnight. Dust with confectioners' sugar just before serving, if desired.

Pound Cake

Makes one 9-inch loaf

3 cups sifted all-purpose flour
1 teaspoon baking powder
Large pinch of salt
1 pound unsalted butter, softened

1¾ cups granulated sugar
7 extra-large or 8 large eggs, separated
2 tablespoons cognac
1 tablespoon grated lemon zest

Sift the flour onto wax paper, then spoon it gently into a measuring cup. Spoon it back into the sifter, add the baking powder and salt, and sift twice more, each time spooning it very lightly into the measuring cup.

In a large bowl, cream the butter with a wooden spoon or a hand mixer until it is very light and fluffy. Then beat in ¾ cup of the sugar. Beat in the egg yolks until the mixture is light and lemon-colored, then add the cognac and lemon zest. Gradually fold in the sifted flour mixture. In a separate bowl, beat the egg whites until they hold soft peaks, then very gradually beat in the remaining 1 cup sugar—about 2 tablespoons at a time—beating thoroughly after each addition. Gently fold the whites into the batter until completely smooth, being careful not to overmix.

Pour the batter into a buttered and floured 9-by-5-by-3-inch loaf pan, and bake in a preheated 350° oven for 1 hour. Test with a cake tester to see that it is thoroughly baked. The edges of the cake should begin to pull away from the sides of the pan. Remove cake from the oven and cool on a rack for at least 12 to 15 minutes. A few more minutes won't hurt. Loosen the sides very gently with a spatula and invert the cake onto the rack to finish cooling completely.

¶**Pound Cake with Citron.** Place thin strips of citron on top just before baking.

¶**Pound Cake with Spices.** Blend into the batter one or more of the following: 2 tablespoons caraway seeds, 1 teaspoon mace, 1 tablespoon nutmeg, or 1½ teaspoons ground ginger.

Puddings and Custards

Sharlotka

This moist and flavorful Polish pudding is best made with black bread, although store-bought pumpernickel will serve. A lovely and economical winter dessert, it might be served instead of the customary Christmas pudding.

Makes 6 to 8 servings

1 loaf stale dark bread, preferably
    Jewish-style pumpernickel
¼ *pound butter*
½ *cup sugar*
½ *cup red wine*
1 *teaspoon lemon juice*
1 *teaspoon grated orange zest*

Pinch of salt
½ *teaspoon vanilla extract*
10 *Pippin apples, or other tart cooking*
    apples, peeled, cored, and cut
    into eighths
2 *teaspoons cinnamon*
1 *cup tart jelly, melted*

Remove the crusts from the bread and crumble the bread into tiny pieces. Melt the butter in a skillet and fry the crumbs lightly. Remove from the heat and mix in the sugar, wine, lemon juice, orange zest, and salt. Add the vanilla and mix well. Cook the apples in very little water until they just turn soft, but don't let them get mushy. Butter a 2-quart mold and sprinkle it lightly with some of the crumb mixture, then alternate layers of crumbs and apples, sprinkling each apple layer with cinnamon. Cover the last layer of apples with the jelly, and top this with the remaining crumbs. Bake in a 350° oven for 1 hour. Serve at once.

Bread-and-Butter Pudding

This traditional, perfectly plain baked custard is a great favorite of mine— and of many others.

Makes 4 to 6 servings

10 *thin slices white bread, crusts*
    removed, buttered on one side
4 *large eggs*
½ *cup sugar*

Pinch of salt
4 *cups milk, or half milk and half cream*
Sherry-flavored whipped cream
    (optional)

Butter a 2-quart baking dish well. Arrange the slices of bread, buttered sides down, in the dish. In a mixing bowl, lightly beat the eggs and add the sugar, salt, and milk. Heat the mixture slightly, strain it over the bread slices, and allow to stand for 30 minutes so the bread absorbs the liquid. Cover the dish with foil, place it in a larger baking pan, and add enough water to the large dish to come halfway up the sides of the pudding dish. Place in a 325° oven and bake for 30 minutes. Remove the foil and bake for 30 minutes more, or until the top of the custard is a delicate golden brown. Remove from the oven and chill the pudding. Serve it with sherry-flavored whipped cream, if desired.

¶**Bread-and-Butter Pudding with Raisins.** Plump ¾ cup raisins in sherry or cognac to cover. Drain the raisins and sprinkle them between the slices of bread.

¶**Bread-and-Butter Pudding with Rum.** Flavor the custard with 2 tablespoons Jamaica rum, and use rum in the whipped cream instead of sherry.

¶**French-Bread-and-Butter Pudding.** Instead of other white bread, use 14 thin slices of French bread, buttered on one side. Float the slices on top of the custard, buttered side up, instead of arranging them in the baking dish.

¶**Buttered-Cake Pudding.** Instead of the white bread, use buttered thin slices of stale sponge cake or pound cake. Arrange, buttered side down, and proceed as in basic recipe.

Apple Tapioca

Often damned, this rather gelatinous pudding is sometimes referred to as fish eyes. To those who, like me, love it, it is indeed a treat.

Makes 6 servings

¾ cup small pearl tapioca
2 cups boiling water
½ teaspoon salt
1 cup sugar
6 tart apples, peeled and thinly sliced

1 teaspoon vanilla extract
2 tablespoons plus butter
½ cup fresh bread crumbs (preferably
  pumpernickel or whole wheat)
⅓ cup brown sugar, firmly packed

Soak the tapioca in water to cover for 2 hours. Drain. Put the tapioca in the top of a double boiler over simmering water and add the boiling water and salt. Cover and cook until tapioca is transparent, approximately 50 minutes.

Place the sugar in a heavy iron skillet over moderate heat and caramelize. Add the sliced apples and cook until the apples are soft. Stir in the vanilla and butter.

Alternate layers of apples and tapioca in a buttered 9-by-7-inch baking dish, ending with apples. Combine the bread crumbs with the brown sugar and sprinkle over the top. Dot with butter and bake for 30 minutes in a preheated 350° oven. Serve hot with heavy cream or ice cream.

¶**Tapioca with Apples and Pears (or Quince).** Use half apples and half pears (or half apples and canned quince).

Vanilla Pots de Crème

Makes 6 to 8 servings

3 cups heavy cream
3 tablespoons granulated sugar

6 egg yolks
1 teaspoon vanilla extract

Heat heavy cream with granulated sugar in the top of an enamel double boiler over boiling water. Beat the egg yolks until lemony in color. Add the hot cream gradually to the eggs, stirring well; then flavor with vanilla. Strain into 6 to 8 small custard cups. If you have little cream pots with covers, so much the better.

Put the cups or pots in a pan of hot water and place in a preheated 325° oven to bake slowly until an inserted knife comes out clean, about 25 to 30 minutes. Be careful not to overcook. Cool, and then place in refrigerator. Serve well chilled in the cups in which they were baked.

¶**Pots de Crème with Praline.** After custard is partially set, sprinkle ¼ cup praline powder (see page 518) over the top.

Chocolate Pots de Crème

Makes 6 to 8 servings

2 cups heavy cream
¼ cup granulated sugar
1⅓ cups semisweet chocolate morsels

6 egg yolks
1 teaspoon vanilla extract

Put heavy cream in top of a double boiler. Add granulated sugar. Place over boiling water and scald (i.e., heat almost to boiling). Remove from heat and add the semisweet chocolate morsels and stir until completely melted. Beat egg yolks and gradually beat them into the hot chocolate cream. Place top of double boiler over boiling water again and cook, stirring constantly, until well thickened, about 3 minutes. Remove from fire, stir in vanilla, and then pour into 6 or 8 small custard cups (½-cup size). When cool, place in refrigerator to chill before serving.

Basic Stocks and Sauces

Chicken Stock or Broth

Makes 2½ quarts

2 pounds chicken gizzards
2 pounds chicken necks and backs
1 onion, peeled and stuck with 3 cloves
1 leek, well washed and trimmed
1 carrot, scraped
2 garlic cloves, peeled

1 bay leaf
1 sprig parsley
1 teaspoon dried thyme
6 peppercorns
3 quarts water
1 tablespoon salt

Put the chicken pieces, vegetables, garlic, herbs, peppercorns, and water in a deep 8-quart pot and bring to a boil. After 5 minutes, skim off the scum that forms on the surface, using a wire skimmer or a large spoon. Continue to boil rapidly for 15 minutes, skimming, then reduce the heat. Cover the pot and simmer for 2 to 2½ hours. Season with salt to taste. Strain the stock through a sieve lined with several thicknesses of cheesecloth into a large bowl and cool thoroughly in the refrigerator. Save the gizzards (they are good eating) and discard the other chicken parts and vegetables. When the stock is cold, remove the layer of fat that has formed on the surface.

Beef Stock or Broth

Makes 2½ to 3 quarts

2 to 3 pounds bones (beef, beef
    marrow, veal)
All-purpose flour
5-pound piece shin of beef
1 large onion, peeled and stuck with
    2 cloves
1 carrot, scraped

1 leek, well washed and trimmed
1 white turnip, peeled
2 garlic cloves, peeled
1 bay leaf
1 sprig of parsley
1 teaspoon dried thyme
1 tablespoon salt

Dust the bones with flour and place on a broiling rack. Place under a broiler or in a 500° oven, turning once, until nicely browned. Put the bones and remaining ingredients in a stock pot with water to cover. Bring the water to a boil over high heat and boil for 5 minutes, skimming off the scum that rises to the surface. Reduce heat until water just simmers; cover the pot and cook for 3 hours. The meat from the shin bone can be used as you would boiled beef; test after 2 to 2½ hours and fish out when tender. Remove the pot from the heat and strain the broth into a large bowl through a sieve lined with several thicknesses of cheesecloth, and chill overnight. The next day, remove the layer of fat on the top; put the broth in a large pot, uncovered, and simmer very slowly for 3 to 4 hours to concentrate and reduce the stock. Strain again; refrigerate or freeze.

Fish Stock

If you can't buy fish bones and heads, use an inexpensive bony white fish such as whiting or catfish but not an oily fish. I like to add salt to taste after the stock has cooked, as the fish throws off a good deal of natural salt. Stock may be frozen until needed.

Makes 6 cups

2 pounds fish bones and heads or
    2 pounds bony fish
3 cups water
3 cups dry white wine
1 lemon slice

1 small onion, stuck with 2 cloves
1 teaspoon fennel seeds
4 sprigs parsley
6 crushed peppercorns
Salt

Wash fish well and remove gills from heads. Combine in a pan with all other ingredients except salt. Bring to a boil. Reduce heat to a simmer and simmer 20 to 30 minutes. Strain. Taste and add salt as needed.

Béchamel Sauce

Makes 1 cup sauce

2 tablespoons unsalted butter *1 cup heated milk*
2 tablespoons all-purpose flour *Salt, freshly ground black pepper*

Melt the butter over low heat in a heavy-bottomed 1½-quart saucepan. Mix the flour into the melted butter and cook slowly, stirring all the time, for 2 to 3 minutes, or until the roux of butter and flour is well blended. Gradually stir in the hot milk. Increase the heat to medium and cook, stirring all the time, until the sauce is smooth, thick, and at the boiling point. Let the sauce simmer, stirring, for 3 or 4 minutes, then season to taste with salt and pepper.

If you are not using the sauce right away, butter a piece of waxed paper large enough to fit inside the pan and lay it on the surface of the sauce, buttered side down, to prevent a skin from forming.

¶**Mustard Sauce.** Stir 2 tablespoons Dijon mustard into the finished sauce. Simmer for 2 to 3 minutes. This makes a fairly hot sauce. For a milder sauce, add less mustard.

¶**Sauce Mornay.** Stir ¼ to ½ cup grated Parmesan cheese into the finished sauce, and add 1 or 2 tablespoons butter, depending on how rich you want it, 1 tablespoon at a time. Simmer 3 or 4 minutes.

¶**Creamy Cheese Sauce.** When sauce has thickened, add ½ cup heavy cream and simmer, stirring occasionally. Then add ¼ to ½ cup grated Parmesan or Gruyère cheese and, if you wish, a dash of Tabasco.

¶**Egg Sauce.** Add 2 coarsely chopped hard-boiled eggs to the finished sauce.

¶**Parsley Sauce.** Add ½ cup finely chopped parsley to the finished sauce.

¶**Caper Sauce.** Add 1 to 2 tablespoons capers, according to your taste, to the finished sauce.

Curry Sauce

This is a simple French type of curry sauce.

Makes 1 cup sauce

1 small onion, finely chopped
2 tablespoons clarified butter
2 teaspoons good curry powder

1 cup béchamel sauce (see preceding
* recipe)*

Sauté the onion in clarified butter with the curry (this is to remove the raw taste of the curry). When the onion is tender and the curry well combined, fold into the béchamel sauce. If a more intense flavor is desired, add finely chopped dried red pepper or Tabasco to taste.

Hollandaise Sauce

Makes 1 cup sauce

3 egg yolks
½ teaspoon salt
Pinch of cayenne pepper or dash of
* Tabasco*

1 tablespoon lemon juice
8 tablespoons (1 stick) butter, cut into
* small pieces*

Put the egg yolks, salt, pepper or Tabasco, and lemon juice in a small pan over low heat. Beat with a wire whisk until the eggs and seasonings are well blended and the egg yolks have thickened to the consistency of heavy cream. Add the butter piece by piece until it has been absorbed by the eggs. The sauce should be of a consistency that coats the whisk heavily.

¶**Béarnaise Sauce.** Combine 4 or 5 chopped shallots or scallions with 2 tablespoons chopped fresh tarragon or 2 teaspoons dried tarragon and ½ cup dry white wine, and reduce until the mixture is practically a glaze. Fold into 1 cup finished hollandaise.

¶**Maltaise Sauce.** Add 2 teaspoons grated orange zest and 1 tablespoon orange juice to 1 cup finished hollandaise.

¶**Anchovy-Flavored Hollandaise.** Add 4 finely chopped anchovies or 2 teaspoons anchovy paste to 1 cup finished hollandaise.

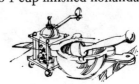

Quick Brown Sauce

This is an easy, economical brown sauce, not as time-consuming as the classic version. It will keep in the refrigerator for a week or two.

Makes 4 cups

1 slice ham, cut ½ inch thick (fat removed) and diced
2 onions, sliced
2 carrots, sliced
2 tablespoons unsalted butter
1 quart beef stock (see page 530)
½ bay leaf
1 sprig fresh thyme or ¼ teaspoon dried thyme
1 large ripe tomato, peeled, seeded, and chopped, or 1 tablespoon tomato paste
Salt, freshly ground black pepper
½ cup red wine (optional)
Beurre manié (optional; see page 536)

Sauté the ham, onion, and carrot in the butter until the onion is brown. Slowly mix in the beef stock. Add the bay leaf and thyme. Simmer gently for 1 hour, uncovered, then add the tomato or tomato paste, salt and pepper to taste, and, if you like, the wine. Simmer for a further ½ hour, then strain through a sieve. If the sauce does not seem thick enough, boil down to the required consistency or thicken with beurre manié.

¶**Madeira Brown Sauce.** Add Madeira to taste to the finished sauce.

¶**Mushroom Brown Sauce.** Add Madeira or dry sherry to taste and about ½ cup duxelles (see page 535) to the finished sauce.

¶**Sauce Diable.** Sauté 4 to 6 shallots or scallions in 3 tablespoons butter and add 1 cup of the brown sauce. Season with ½ teaspoon freshly ground black pepper, 1 teaspoon hot mustard (dry or Dijon), and ¼ to ½ teaspoon Tabasco, according to your palate, plus 1 teaspoon fresh lemon juice. Simmer 3 or 4 minutes to amalgamate the flavors; correct the seasoning.

¶**Bordelaise Sauce.** Reduce by one half 1 cup red wine (preferably a Bordeaux or an American Cabernet Sauvignon). Add 6 shallots or scallions which have been lightly sautéed in 3 tablespoons butter. Combine with 1 cup brown sauce.

¶**Bordelaise Sauce with Poached Beef Marrow.** Have the butcher saw through marrow bones to make 3 or 4 pieces. Remove the marrow from the bone and slice into ¼-inch slices. Poach in simmering water or stock until just translucent—about 2 to 3 minutes.

White Wine Sauce

Makes 2 cups

3 tablespoons butter
3 tablespoons flour
1 cup fish stock
¼ cup dry white wine

Salt, freshly ground black pepper
½ cup heavy cream blended with
    2 egg yolks

Melt the butter in a saucepan, stir in the flour, and cook gently over medium heat until the roux is golden and bubbling. Mix in the fish stock and wine, and cook, stirring constantly, until thickened and smooth. Season to taste with salt and freshly ground black pepper. Pour a little of the hot sauce into the egg yolk and cream mixture, and stir. Add this to the sauce in the pan and cook gently, over low heat, until thickened, but do not allow the sauce to overheat or boil or the eggs will curdle.

Fresh Tomato Sauce

Makes 2 cups

¼ cup olive oil
¼ cup finely chopped shallots
2 large cloves garlic, finely minced—
    or left whole if you wish
2 cups tomato pulp (fresh tomatoes,
    peeled, seeded, and chopped), or
    2 cups canned Italian plum
    tomatoes, drained and broken up
    with a fork

1 tablespoon fresh basil, or 1 teaspoon
    dried basil, or ½ teaspoon mixed
    dried herbs, such as a prepared
    Provençal or Italian seasoning
Salt and freshly ground black pepper
    to taste

Heat the olive oil in a saucepan, add the shallots and garlic, and sauté gently, without browning, for about 2 minutes. Add the fresh tomato pulp, or the canned tomatoes, and the seasonings. Simmer for about 10 minutes, until the sauce thickens slightly and reduces to about 2 cups. Taste and correct seasoning.

Garlic Purée

A Provençal recipe that I have taught for years in my classes is chicken braised with 40 cloves of garlic (page 323). While this may sound like an incredible amount, the long slow cooking reduces the cloves to a butter-soft smoothness and a delicate flavor that has to be tasted to be believed. Along with the chicken you eat the garlic spread on bread like butter, and one day it occurred to me that it would be a smart idea to make a purée of garlic and keep it on hand as a flavoring for stews and sautés, to mix into vegetables or a salad dressing, or to serve on toast as an hors d'oeuvre. On another occasion, I made a sublime sauce for roast lamb by combining equal quantities of the garlic purée and crème fraîche (page 448), combined with some of the degreased lamb pan juices and a little seasoning.

Makes 1 to 1½ pints

2 dozen heads of garlic
Salt

2 to 3 tablespoons olive oil

Separate the heads into cloves, leave the cloves in their papery husks, and simmer in a pan of water seasoned with 1 teaspoon salt for 30 to 40 minutes, or until very, very soft. Drain, then put through a food mill to extract the soft pulp from the skins. Season the purée with a touch of salt and mix in the oil. Put in a jar and refrigerate until needed. It will last several weeks, or longer if you cover the top with a thin film of olive oil.

Sauce Gribiche

Makes about 2 cups

3 hard-boiled eggs
1 teaspoon dry mustard
1 teaspoon salt
½ teaspoon freshly ground black pepper
1 cup olive oil
1 tablespoon wine vinegar

1 tablespoon finely chopped dill pickle
1 teaspoon finely chopped capers
2 tablespoons finely chopped mixed
   herbs (chives, parsley, chervil,
   tarragon)

Remove the egg yolks and crush with a fork. Mix with the mustard, salt, and pepper. Gradually stir in the oil. When it is all absorbed, add the vinegar, finely chopped egg whites, pickle, capers, and herbs. Let stand for 1 hour or more to blend the flavors.

Duxelles

Makes 3 cups

2 pounds mushrooms
½ pound unsalted butter

1 shallot or garlic clove, finely chopped
Salt, freshly ground black pepper

Wipe mushrooms with a damp towel. Chop very fine, stems and all, then put the chopped mushrooms in a linen towel or dish towel and squeeze all the moisture out of them (squeeze liquid into a bowl and add to soups or stews). Melt the butter in a heavy iron skillet, add the mushrooms and shallot or garlic, and cook very slowly, over low heat, stirring occasionally, until reduced to a thick, dark paste. Season to taste with salt and pepper. This will keep for a week in the refrigerator, or may be frozen.

Beurre Manié

Beurre manié is a mixture of butter and flour that may be used to thicken sauces and stews at the end of the cooking time. As in the case of a roux, 2 tablespoons flour will thicken 1 cup liquid.

Blend soft unsalted butter and all-purpose flour together with your fingertips in the proportions of 2 tablespoons flour to 1 tablespoon butter. Then roll into tiny balls about the size of a green pea.

To thicken liquid, turn heat to low under the pan and sprinkle beurre manié balls, a few at a time, over the surface, stirring them in vigorously with a wooden spatula to avoid lumping. The liquid must not be too hot, certainly not boiling. Add only as many balls as needed to thicken the sauce—underestimate, as you can always add more. Continue to stir and cook until the liquid thickens and becomes smooth. If it should lump, rub it through a fine strainer.

Quatre Épices

1 ⅛ cups ground white pepper   *3 ½ tablespoons ground nutmeg*
3 ½ tablespoons ground ginger   *1 ½ tablespoons ground cloves*

Combine all spices in a small bowl and mix well. Store in a sealed jar.

Tarragon Butter

This may be made ahead and stored in the refrigerator until ready to use.

Makes 6 tablespoons

6 tablespoons unsalted butter   *2 tablespoons chopped fresh tarragon*
1 teaspoon salt   *or 1 ½ teaspoons crushed dried*
½ teaspoon freshly ground black pepper   *tarragon*

Mix the butter, salt, pepper, and tarragon in a bowl, mashing them well together with a wooden spoon or working them with your hands, until thoroughly mixed.

Other flavored butters may be prepared in the same manner and used for various dishes. You may double or triple quantities if desired.

¶**Dill Butter.** Substitute 2 tablespoons fresh dill weed or 1½ teaspoons dried dill weed for the tarragon. Proceed as for the above recipe.

¶**Garlic Butter.** Use 2 teaspoons fresh, minced garlic (or to taste) instead of the tarragon. Proceed as for the above recipe.

¶**Rosemary Butter.** Substitute 1½ teaspoons dried rosemary (best crushed in a small mortar and pestle) or 2 tablespoons fresh rosemary for the tarragon. Proceed as for the above recipe.

¶**Caraway Butter.** Substitute 1 to 1½ teaspoons crushed caraway seeds for the tarragon. Proceed as for the above recipe.

¶**Chili Butter.** Substitute 1 tablespoon finely chopped peeled green chilies (or to taste) or 1 to 2 teaspoons chili powder for the tarragon. Proceed as for the above recipe.

¶**Orange Butter.** Substitute 1 tablespoon finely grated orange zest for the tarragon. Proceed as for the above recipe, omitting the pepper.

Concordance

All references to *T & P*
are for *James Beard's Theory & Practice of Good Cooking.*

APPLES. For cooking, one needs tart apples. On the East Coast I shop for Greenings or Granny Smiths, which are firm, of a good texture, and highly satisfactory. In other parts of the country I buy Pippins in the spring, Gravensteins in the early fall. Both are flavorful, with a good bouquet and excellent texture. Many authorities recommend Golden Delicious and Rome Beauties, but I find they don't cook as well. There are a lot of good basic apple recipes in *T & P*—and here you'll find an excellent apple pie (page 508), as well as tarte tatin (page 513). For eating apples, McIntosh and Delicious are the most generally available year round, but look for other firm, juicy varieties, particularly in farm markets in the fall.

APRICOTS. One of our finest fruits when fully ripe. They should be tender to the touch, sweet to the tongue, and full of flavor, but are seldom found that way in the markets today because they are picked too green. You may be better off using dried apricots and reconstituting them by bringing them to a boil in water and letting them stand. They have a fine flavor. For an excellent apricot sherbet, see page 499. A good brand of canned apricots can be substituted in some dishes.

ARTICHOKES. See page 119 for preparation, cooking, and serving of artichokes.

ASPARAGUS. See page 123 for remarks about fresh asparagus. Frozen asparagus is limp, tasteless, and not worth buying. Canned asparagus tastes like an entirely different vegetable—either you enjoy it as a salad or you hate it.

AVOCADOS. One of the pleasantest fruits we have, in season most of the year. There are many varieties, of which the russety-green-skinned California, or Calavo, is probably the best. A ripe avocado will be yielding to the touch, soft but not mushy, with buttery-tender green flesh. If the flesh is dark or brown, the avocado is overripe. If firm when bought, avocados will ripen if left in a dark place for a day or two. Avocados are usually served in their natural state, peeled and cut up in salads, split and stuffed with seafood or other salads (see salad chapter), mashed with a fork or in a blender to a soft purée (see guacamole, *T & P*, page 337), or blended in cold soups (see *T & P*, page 341). They may also be stuffed and baked. In Central and South America they are blended with sugar and lime juice for a dessert. When cut and exposed to air, avocados discolor quickly, so serve as soon as possible after cutting. To keep a leftover piece, rub cut surfaces with lemon juice and cover tightly with plastic wrap. Some say that leaving the pit in puréed avocado prevents discoloration.

BAKING POWDER. In the markets today you are likely to find only baking powder marked "double-acting." This means that the baking powder acts twice—when it is first mixed into the batter and again after the cake goes into the warm oven. Some home bakers were distressed recently to learn that the famous old-fashioned Royal baking powder is no longer being manufactured, owing to the rising cost of cream of tartar. They claim that the chemical double-acting powders leave a slightly bitter aftertaste. If you want to pay the price, you can make your own natural mixture by combining 2 parts cream of tartar to 1 part baking soda (bicarbonate of soda); don't try to store it, though, because it won't keep well.

In a recent test we found that 1 teaspoon of double-acting baking powder worked as the equal of 2 teaspoons of the Royal baking powder. Directions on a tin of double-acting baking powder recommend 1 teaspoon for each cup of flour (for Royal, or for your own homemade equivalent, simply double the amount—2 teaspoons to 1 cup of flour). Exceptions to the double-acting formula: mixtures containing fruits such as raisins or made with heavy flours like whole wheat, cornmeal, or bran require 1½ teaspoons per cup of flour; in recipes calling for more than 3 eggs, use ½ teaspoon less for each extra egg.

BAKING SODA. Baking soda or bicarbonate of soda is another leavening agent, mostly used for doughs mixed with sour milk, buttermilk, orange juice, and molasses, which have a rather high acid content. It is a valuable leavener, but take care not to use too much or it will adversely affect the taste and color of the finished product.

BANANAS. Considered a great source of potassium, if that means anything to you and your diet. Never refrigerate bananas. If you buy them yellow and firm, they will ripen quite quickly at room temperature. The riper they become, the more brown-speckled the skin and the more intense the flavor. For desserts, bananas are used whole, sliced, or puréed. There are recipes in *Theory & Practice* for broiled, baked, and sautéed bananas, as well as for banana ice cream. In season all year, widely available.

BARLEY. The round and rather slippery grain of a cereal grass. It is little used in this country, save as an ingredient in certain soups, and I think this a great pity. Pearl barley, the whole grain, has a most distinctive flavor and texture when cooked, and a barley casserole (see page 295) is a most agreeable substitute for rice or wild rice with poultry and game. Other forms of barley are barley meal, which may be added to breads or made into a mush, somewhat like polenta; and barley flour, which makes one of my favorite breads. Pearl barley is pretty generally available, but barley meal and flour are more difficult to find. Look for them in health-food stores and stores that specialize in cereal products, or order them by mail from mills that sell a range of meals and flours.

BEANS
One of America's great gifts to the world. Always plentiful, both fresh and dried.
Green beans. (See page 125 for remarks on fresh beans.) Frozen green beans are acceptable, and canned ones, rinsed off, are possible in a pinch.
Wax beans. Pale-yellow version of the green bean. Cook in the same way.
Lima beans. Shell and cook in boiling salted water to cover until tender, from 10 to 20 minutes, according to size. Drain and dress with butter, or serve in a béchamel sauce.
Fava beans or broad beans. Rather like a lima bean, but with a thicker, fleshier pod, varying in size from half an inch to an inch in diameter. Often found in Italian markets, occasionally in supermarkets. Shell and cook in boiling salted water to cover until just tender, about 10 to 20 minutes, according to size. Cool slightly, slip off the heavy skin, and serve with butter, or with oil, garlic, and a touch of lemon juice.
Shell or cranberry beans. For description and recipes, see page 127.
    The above kinds of shell beans may be combined with fresh, frozen, or canned corn kernels and butter to make different versions of succotash. Use equal amounts of each vegetable and enough butter to coat them well.
Dried beans. All dried beans require either overnight soaking or the following quick treatment. Cover the beans with enough water to come 1 inch above the top, bring to a boil, and boil 2 minutes. Turn off the heat and let stand in the water for 1 hour—no longer. Add salt, seasonings, extra water, if needed, bring to a boil again, and simmer until just tender, but not mushy. Drain and use for various recipes, such as those on pages 303–309, or with pasta (page 286), or in salad.

BEETS. One of the few vegetables that is equally good canned or fresh. Fresh beets bought in the market should be small and firm (larger ones tend to be woody and tasteless), with the tops still on. (For cooking beet tops, see "Greens Primarily for Cooking.") Never peel fresh beets before cooking, or they'll bleed to death. Cut off the stem an inch above the bulb and leave the roots on. Boil in salted water to cover until tender. Small beets will take 25 to 30 minutes, larger ones 35 to 40 minutes. Drain and cool a little until you can peel them by slipping off the skins. Leave whole if small, or slice or cut into thin julienne strips. Serve hot with butter or cold in salads, especially salads of slightly bitter greens such as endive or chicory that welcome the sweetness of the beet. Tiny baby beets take less cooking time and are usually served whole. To bake beets— my preferred method incidentally—see page 128.

BLACKBERRIES. The little wild blackberries that trail through the woods are full of flavor, though hard to pick, and make delicious pies, jams, and jellies. Large cultivated blackberries are somewhat seedy but heavenly with sugar and cream, baked in pies, or puréed for sauce.

BLUEBERRIES. It is hard to differentiate between wild huckleberries and wild blueberries. I think the wild huckleberries gathered in hilly or mountainous regions have greater flavor and bouquet. Wonderful for pies, preserves, and syrups. Wild blueberries can often be found in country markets in the summer. Cultivated blueberries, the kind sold in supermarkets, are much larger and should be relished with sugar and heavy cream, sour cream, or yogurt; stewed; or baked in pies, muffins, and pancakes. Buy only firm berries. Look below the top level of the basket. Both blueberries and huckleberries freeze successfully. Do not wash. Freeze in the basket, just as they are, wrapped in foil or plastic wrap. That way they hold their color and shape.

BROCCOLI. In season most of the year. Don't be deceived just because it looks green. If the stems are thick and woody and the buds beginning to open, it is old. Look for tender young buds, tiny and tightly packed. To cook, see page 129, also good chilled in salads. Frozen broccoli, if not overcooked, merely blanched briefly in boiling water, is quite acceptable.

BROCCOLI RABE. For description of this more vigorously flavored member of the broccoli family and recipes, see page 130.

BRUSSELS SPROUTS. For notes on fresh Brussels sprouts, see page 131. Small frozen Brussels sprouts are good if blanched briefly in boiling salted water. They need minimum cooking. Canned ones are to be avoided at all costs.

BUCKWHEAT. A grain plant native to Siberia but widely cultivated in other parts of the world, including Europe and America, it gives us buckwheat flour and buckwheat groats or kasha, the hulled kernels of the grain. The flour is used for buckwheat cakes, breads, and the little Russian blini (see page 40), so delectable with caviar, sour cream, and lots of melted butter. Kasha (see page 296), while less familiar to us than bulghur or rice, is very popular with Jewish people of Russian or Polish ancestry and a staple of the Russian cuisine. It has a delicious crunchiness when cooked that makes it an excellent alternative to other starches with chicken or meat dishes that have sauces or gravies. Buckwheat flour and groats are sold in health-food stores or may be ordered by mail from mills in various parts of the country.

BUTTER

Salt butter. Comes in ¼-pound sticks, 1- and 2-pound blocks, and sometimes in tubs, to be sold by the pound. Even though the salt does help to preserve the flavor and quality, it is highly possible and fairly common to find strong-tasting, even rancid salt butter in stores. Buy in small quantities and, if the butter doesn't taste right, switch to another brand. If you buy in quantity, freeze the butter you are not using immediately.

Unsalted butter. Commonly referred to as sweet butter, it is more perishable than salt butter, but more delicate in flavor and by far the more desirable for cooking, especially for baking. Keep butter you are using in a covered container in the refrigerator away from strong-flavored foods, or it will absorb the flavors very quickly. Freeze what you aren't using. One uses sweet butter for flavor, so keep it pure.

Clarified butter. Something you make, rather than buy. Melt sweet butter in a heavy pan over low heat, to prevent it from browning. The white froth that rises to the top should be skimmed off with a spoon, and the clear yellow "clarified" liquid butter carefully poured off into a container, leaving the white curdlike dregs in the pan. Clarified butter will remain fresh for 2 or 3 weeks, so you may make it in quantity and use as needed. Use it for sautéing when you need high heat, and for delicate cakes such as génoise.

CABBAGES. You'll often find in the markets not only the familiar green-to-white cabbages, but also red cabbages and the curly-leafed savoy cabbages, which have a looser head. Both the green and red cabbages should have firm heads and fresh, unwilted leaves. The leaves of savoy cabbages should be crisp and deep green. Heads vary from 1 to 5 pounds. If you use only part, cover the rest tightly with plastic wrap and refrigerate. Trim off the stalk and any discolored or limp outer leaves. Cut into wedges, remove the hard core with a large sharp knife, and shred. Soak the shreds well in cold water for an hour to crisp. Drain well for coleslaw (pages 89–92). To cook, see recipes pages 133–135. Raw cabbage is used for other salads as well as coleslaw, with red and green sometimes combined for color.

CARROTS. For best flavor, look for small young carrots, either those sold in bunches with the feathery tops on, or the packaged small California carrots. Old carrots have a woody core. Large carrots, which are what you find most of the time, should be soaked in water before preparing, to crisp them. To cook, see page 137. Carrots, of course, are delicious eaten raw, crisp, and chilled. Canned carrots are not very good—and why use them when carrots come fresh in the market all year?

CAULIFLOWER. Flowerets may be used raw as a vegetable hors d'oeuvre, with a dip. Frozen cauliflower is acceptable, but I don't really recommend it.

CELERIAC. For description and recipes, see pages 140–142. Celeriac may be peeled raw (rub with lemon to prevent discoloring), cut into very fine julienne, and mixed with mustard mayonnaise for celery root rémoulade, a fine hors d'oeuvre.

CELERY. Buy the green or Pascal celery; it is tastier and crisper. Wash well to get rid of dirt at the base of the ribs and trim off the bottom and leafy tops (save tops for flavoring soups or stocks, or use in salads). Remove the coarse outer ribs; use for stock or mirepoix for braised meat. Celery, to my mind, is better sautéed (see page 140) than boiled. The inner ribs, known as the heart, are delicious split and braised (see page 168, *T & P*). The tiny leafy ribs in the center are good as a raw vegetable hors d'oeuvre or in salads. Canned celery hearts are quite acceptable for braising and need only to be heated through.

CHEESE

Among the enormous and constantly growing range of cheeses in the market today are some old faithfuls we cannot cook without. Cheese, whether for cooking, eating, or both, should be kept in the refrigerator (the warmer, not the colder part) tightly covered in plastic wrap or foil, or in plastic bags. If a cheese is to be eaten, remove and bring to room temperature an hour before serving.

Cheddar. This firm cheese can be white or orange, sharp, medium sharp, or bland. Sharp is best for cooking. A good Canadian, English, or American Cheddar from the Northeast or Northwest is fine, but be sure it is natural Cheddar, please, not processed. Buy aged Cheddar—it has the most flavor. Cheddar keeps well, and if you buy a whole wheel, it will last you several months. Grate or shred for soufflés, cheese sauce, omelets, or as a topping for baked dishes, or use for toasted cheese sandwiches and Welsh rarebit. And, of course, eat with salad or fruit, especially apples.

Cottage cheese. In its many variations, the fresh soft cheese favored by dieters. Try to find a natural cottage cheese, without preservatives (health-food stores have them). **Ricotta,** a very soft, light, and creamy fresh cheese, is mostly used for Italian dishes such as lasagne and cannelloni, for cheesecake or cheese pie and other desserts.

Cream cheese. Soft fresh cheese mixed with cream to a smooth consistency, for cheesecakes, cheese pie, coeur à la crème (see *T & P*, page 350), salad dressings. It is bland and very receptive to strong flavorings such as chives, onions, and anchovies. Eat it with lox and bagels, fruit, or with preserves for breakfast or tea. May be bought by the package or the pound—if you use a great deal, there are 3-pound blocks. The packaged cream cheese sold in supermarkets contains vegetable gum, and the texture leaves much to be desired. Whipping it with a little heavy or sour cream improves both texture and flavor.

Gruyère. A cooking and table cheese with a fine-grained, rather firm texture and a few holes or eyes. Nutty aroma and flavor. Not to be confused with **Emmenthaler,** a similar Swiss cheese that has much larger eyes. The best comes from Switzerland, other versions from France, Austria, and Finland. Sold by the piece. Never buy the processed Gruyère in small, foil-wrapped triangles—it will not do the job at all. Used extensively in cooking because of its superb melting qualities. The only suitable cheese for fondue, and perfect for topping casseroles and gratinéed dishes, such as onion soup, for soufflés, quiches, and other custardy dishes. A salad of Gruyère and olives makes a lovely summer lunch. Also to be eaten with salad and fruit, especially pears. Keeps well, wrapped in foil or plastic. Should a slight mold form, cut it off; it will not affect the cheese. **Monterey Jack.** A California-born cheese, smooth, semisoft, creamy, and excellent for melting. Much used on the West Coast for Mexican-style dishes, such as chilies rellenos. Most Monterey Jack has an extremely bland taste, which has made it popular for sandwiches, cheeseburgers, and some baked dishes. Sometimes used for pizza, like **mozzarella,** although I feel it does not have the quality of the Italian mozzarella, a super melting cheese which in its best version comes in bell-shaped pieces. Absolute hell to slice but essential for pizza, lasagne, eggplant Parmigiana, and veal Parmigiana. **Parmesan or Parmigiana.** A rock-hard, very pungent, sharp, and slightly salty grating cheese, the very essence of Italian cooking. The ground domestic version of Parmesan sold in jars is third rate and should be shunned save for emergencies. Imported Italian Parmesan, sold by the piece and, in some cheese stores, grated, is very expensive. Don't buy more than you need. Keeps well wrapped in foil or plastic, and may be grated in the food processor or blender or on the finest side of a hand grater. Used more extensively than almost any other cheese, as a topping for pasta and gratinéed dishes, for soufflés, quiches, and other egg and cheese dishes, for mornay sauce (see page 531), risotto (see page 291), and gnocchi. A less costly substitute for Parmesan is **asiago,** a hard Italian skim-milk cheese with a sharp, piquant flavor. Some good asiago is made here.

CHERRIES. For cooking, buy the tart Kentish or pie cherries, or the Montmorency. They are best for poaching, pies, or as a garnish for meats and poultry. The large, lusciously sweet Bings and Lamberts are used for open-face tarts and other desserts and, of course, eaten raw.

CHICKEN
Fresh chickens are infinitely preferable to frozen. Some are of higher quality than others. In the San Francisco area, look for the fresh-killed Petaluma chickens. On the East Coast the Perdue chickens from the Delmarva Peninsula have a considerable reputation. If chicken is wrapped in polyethylene, remove it. Wrap loosely in waxed paper and refrigerate. Use fresh chicken within 3 days. Estimate about ¾ pound of chicken per serving, to allow for the bone.
Broiling chickens. Small birds, weighing 1½ to 2½ pounds, should be split in two lengthwise by you or your butcher. Be sure to cut out the backbone (see illustration in *T & P,* page 183) and the part that goes over the fence last so

the broiler will lie flat in the pan. Marinate before broiling, if you wish, in red wine, oil, and garlic, or in teriyaki marinade (page 366). Or push flavored butter under the skin (see page 318).

Frying chickens. Weighing 3 to 3½ pounds, these fowl represent by far the largest part of all chicken production. Though plentiful, the way they are raised and fed affects the flavor and texture, so shop around until you find those most satisfactory to your palate. Use for fried chicken, for sautés, for fricassees, or for braised dishes such as coq au vin (see page 325 and *T & P*, page 163). Whole fryers may be roasted (see *T & P*, page 83, for a basic roasting recipe), or poached. If, like me, you are a lover of dark meat, you'll buy your frying and sautéing chicken in parts and get only drumsticks and thighs. The chicken-in-parts business has done us all a great service. The breasts may be boned and sautéed (see *T & P*, pages 185–87); fried my favorite way; pan-fried; deep-fried; or poached, chilled, and glazed with aspic. The less expensive wings and thighs can be used for sautés, fricassees, and casseroles. For recipes in which frying chicken can be used, see pages 321–328.

Poaching chickens. The mature, fairly good-sized hens or stewing fowls that once gave rich flavor to our chicken stock are now very hard to find. If you do run across them in the market, remember they have worked hard for a living producing eggs and need long, slow cooking to achieve tenderness. The poached flesh is excellent for chicken hash, creamed chicken, and chicken à la king. Usually an economical buy. Nowadays we are more often forced to buy expensive roasting chicken for stock and poached chicken dishes.

Roasting chickens. Usually run 4 to 5 pounds. They should be plump and tender with a good amount, but not an overabundance, of fat. It is difficult in most parts of the country to find roasters larger than 5 pounds, but occasionally you can find them in the frozen-poultry section, or frozen 8- to 9-pound capons (the desexed male birds), which are expensive but beautifully meaty and tender. Chickens may be roasted stuffed or unstuffed (see *T & P*, pages 83 and 85) or roasted and flamed (page 316).

Squab chickens. Tiny birds weighing about 1 pound. Once quite common but now hard to find outside specialty markets. Serve 1 to a person. They can be sautéed or split and broiled (see page 337) or stuffed and roasted (see *T & P*, page 87).

CHICKPEAS. Also known as *garbanzos* in Spanish and *ceci* in Italian. This legume is used extensively in the cuisines of Mediterranean and Asian countries, Mexico and other parts of Latin America. In certain parts of North Africa, raw chickpeas are roasted, salted, and eaten as a crunchy snack. Here we buy them dried or canned. Dried chickpeas should be soaked overnight and then cooked like dried beans—brought to a boil in water to cover, boiled 2 minutes, left to stand for 1 hour off the heat, and then cooked until soft, about 1½ to 1¾ hours, depending on their age and hardness. However, if you don't want to cook them from scratch, the canned product is inexpensive and excellent.

Cooked or canned chickpeas make an absolutely delicious purée (see page 309) that to my mind is superior to chestnut purée with game or roast meats and poultry—and certainly cheaper. You'll find most people haven't the faintest idea what it is when they taste it, so you can have a little fun making them guess.

CHOCOLATE. There's a good deal of artificial chocolate in the markets today, so be careful to read the label. Most recipes call for unsweetened or semisweet chocolate, and occasionally for sweet. Shop around for uncommon brands (some kitchenware shops carry good imported cooking chocolate) and make a taste comparison with the supermarket variety—there is often a vast difference. To melt chocolate, put it in the top of a double boiler over hot water, or in a pan set in a second pan of hot water, or in a dish in a 300° oven. If it seems to tighten up when melted, stir in a small amount (1 to 2 tablespoons) of vegetable shortening to reliquefy. Chocolate keeps well, if tightly covered with plastic wrap. If it "blooms" (gets dusty-looking on the outside), that is because of exposure to air; it doesn't mean the chocolate is stale.

CORN. Naturally, the shorter the time from field to pot, the better the eating. Whenever possible, buy corn freshly picked from the farm and cook as soon as you can. However, the corn on the cob sold in markets nowadays has been specially chilled after picking to keep the kernels moist and juicy and prevent starch from forming. It is also much easier to find the desirable white ears than before. Never buy corn with coarse, dry kernels. To check, peel down the husk and silk at the top (you can also spot any worm damage). To my way of thinking, corn on the cob should be put into cold water, just brought to a boil, without cooking further, and served at once with lots of butter, salt, and pepper. For other new ways with corn, see pages 142–144. Both frozen and canned whole-kernel corn are most acceptable and can be used in many dishes.

CORNMEAL. There are two grades of cornmeal, one quite coarse, the other rather fine. The coarse is best for polenta (page 300) and cornmeal mush (see *T & P*, page 50) and the fine for muffins and cornbread (see *T & P*, page 278). Also excellent used like bread crumbs for breading sautéed fish, or for thickening casseroles.

CRACKED WHEAT. A coarsely ground wheat, sold in health-food stores and in Middle Eastern stores, usually under the names bulghur or burghul. A nutritious alternative to rice, with a nutty texture and flavor. Fine-grade cracked wheat is best for uncooked dishes for which the grain is merely soaked, such as tabbouleh (see *T & P*, page 337) and kibbeh (see *T & P*, page 341), medium and coarse grades for pilaf (see *T & P*, page 49) and cooked dishes. Also used in porridge, and, in small amounts, in some breads, as a substitute for other ingredients.

CREAM

Natural cream that is really thick and rich is almost impossible to find. Dairies in various parts of the country differ greatly in what they have to offer. The kinds most commonly found in the supermarkets are:

Half and half. Supposedly half cream and half milk, but more like very rich milk. Can be used in coffee, for hot chocolate, some soups and sauces, and with some fruits.

Light cream or coffee cream. Called one or the other, depending on which part of the country you are in. A very light cream with a lower butterfat content than heavy cream, which means it will not whip. Works well in sauces and soups and with fruits.

Heavy cream or whipping cream. Although the butterfat content varies somewhat from one area to another, this is the heaviest cream available, and may be whipped and used as a topping for desserts, or in mousses and other chilled or frozen desserts, such as orange Bavarian cream (see *T & P*, page 359). Unwhipped, it is often added to soups and sauces as an enrichment.

Sour cream. A cultivated product, rather thick in texture and slightly acid in flavor. Sometimes good on fruits and baked potatoes and in some soups, and good mixed half and half with mayonnaise for salads or coleslaw; it is also less rich if cut with yogurt. Traditional in Central European and Russian cooking, including such recipes as beef Stroganoff. If used in sauces, it should be stirred in slowly and with great care, and never allowed to come to the boiling point, or it will break and curdle.

Sterilized cream. A specially treated heavy cream found in some communities. Sterilization is supposed to give it a longer shelf-life and stability. I have found that if sterilized cream is bought in quart containers and kept for several days before using it whips quite well, almost as well as heavy cream, but others have reported that they find it totally unsatisfactory as a substitute. Best try it out for yourself.

Crème fraîche. Another cultivated cream only recently produced in this country and close to the famous French cream of the same name. It can be purchased at relatively few specialty shops throughout the United States and is undeniably expensive. High in butterfat, it makes a beautiful topping for fruits and desserts, and adds new quality to many sauces. It may be stirred into sauces such as béchamel, suprême, and sauces for braised veal or fish, as an additional thickener. For a homemade approximation of crème fraîche: Combine 1 cup heavy cream and 2 tablespoons buttermilk or sour cream in a jar. Cover and shake the jar, as if you were shaking a cocktail, for 2 minutes. Let the jar stand at room temperature for at least 8 hours or overnight, until the cream has thickened. This crème fraîche will keep under refrigeration for at least one week.

CUCUMBERS. In addition to the types and cooking methods on page 145, there is also the pale-yellow lemon cucumber, found in parts of the West—small, round, crunchy, never bitter, and delicious in salads.

Ducks. Except for cities such as New York, San Francisco, and Los Angeles, where there are Chinese neighborhoods and markets, ducks are, alas, available only in the frozen state. In Chinese markets you can always buy fresh-killed ducks, often with the feet and heads on, and in certain country areas you may find a farmer who raises ducks and will sell them to you live, or freshly killed. Otherwise, you'll just have to make do with frozen duck, which should be thawed before use either in the refrigerator, still wrapped, for 1 or 1½ days; or at room temperature 4 to 5 hours; or in cool water 2 to 3 hours. Thawed ducks are pretty wet. Dry them well inside and out by rolling them in and stuffing them with paper towels. If you have an electric fan, blow it on the duck for a little while to help dry it out. Ducks vary in weight from 5 to 8 pounds. Long Island ducks, the ones most widely available, have a thick layer of fat under the skin and not very much meat, so a 5-pound duck will serve 4 only scantily. It is not too extravagant to gauge half a duck per person, whether you roast it, braise it, or use it for kebabs (see recipes pages 338–340) or broil it (see *T & P*, page 117). This is not true of ducks raised for Chinese markets, which have a different structure, less fat, and more breast and leg meat. Be sure to prick the skin of Long Island ducks well during roasting or broiling to let the fat drain out, and don't, whatever you do, overcook the meat, or it will be dry and tasteless. Don't discard the duck liver, either. This is a great delicacy. If you don't cook it with the duck, accumulate livers in the freezer until you have enough for a pâté or terrine, or some other duck liver dish.

Wild duck is a very different bird, with no thick layer of fat. While the breast is usually well-meated, the legs and thighs are less tender. Roast it, spit it, broil it, make a salmi (see recipes, pages 342–345), but don't overcook. Wild ducks are really hell to pluck. Try to find an accommodating butcher or, if you live in a community where duck hunting is common, someone who makes a business of plucking ducks during the season. Wild ducks weigh only from 1 to 2 pounds. A small duck, such as teal, will serve 1; a larger duck 2.

Eggplants. For selection, preparation, and cooking, see pages 146–148. Other eggplant recipes in *Theory and Practice* include broiled eggplant (page 132), French fried (page 228), and baked stuffed (page 293).

Eggs. For the most part, the eggs we buy are produced in vast quantities on poultry ranches, graded, packed, and shipped to market. In country districts, or in some markets and health-food stores, you will be able to buy eggs from free-range (as opposed to battery-fed) hens. These tend to be richer in flavor and darker in yolk—and more expensive. Egg sizes range from the very small pullet eggs, not widely available, to small, medium, large, extra-large, and jumbo, based on minimum weight per dozen according to U.S. Department of Agriculture standards, and grades AA and A to B and C (B and C are seldom seen in markets; the usual grade is A). Despite what some people may tell you, there is absolutely no difference, in flavor or nutrition, between white eggs and brown eggs. Pick the color that appeals to you. Unless a recipe specifies a certain size of egg, you can take it for granted that it should be the large size. Naturally, the fresher the egg when you use it, the better. It has been my experience that most supermarkets have a quick turnover of eggs, more so than the neighborhood grocery store, where they may be left on the shelf for a longer time. Store eggs in the refrigerator, but don't let them hang around for months, getting stale and absorbing food odors and flavors. Buy them by the half dozen and use them up, unless you are a great egg eater.

For most recipes, it is better to remove the eggs from the refrigerator 30 minutes to an hour before using, to come to room temperature. Room-temperature eggs beat better and have greater volume. For mayonnaise, there's the likelihood that the sauce will curdle unless the egg yolks and oil are the same temperature. When separating eggs, be careful not to get whites in the yolks or vice versa, especially important for soufflés, where the oiliness of the yolks can prevent the whites' beating to their greatest volume (see *T & P*, page 247, for separating technique). If you need only whites for a recipe, store the yolks in a tightly covered jar in the refrigerator, or freeze them, first labeling the jar so you know how many are in the container. Egg whites freeze well. Put them in 1-cup or 1½-cup containers (8 to 11 egg whites, or 12 to 14 egg yolks, according to size, equal 1 cup). Use the egg whites for meringues (see *T & P*, page 290), certain cakes such as angel food, or for clarifying stock (see *T & P*, page 24). Use the egg yolks for emulsified sauces such as mayonnaise (page 76, or for more detailed instructions see *T & P*, page 314), hollandaise, and Béarnaise (see page 532 or more detailed instructions in *T & P*, pages 311–13); to enrich sauces (see *T & P*, page 305); and in rich custards such as pots de crème (page 528) or crème brûlée (see *T & P*, page 137). For scrambling and omelets, beat eggs with a little water to lighten them.

FENNEL. For description and cooking, see page 149. The bulb may also be halved or quartered and braised (see *T & P*, page 167); poached à la Grecque (see *T & P*, page 60); or sliced and used raw, like celery, in salads and as a vegetable hors d'oeuvre. Wild fennel grows quite tall and the long stalks are dried and used as a flavoring.

FIDDLEHEAD FERNS. For description and cooking, see page 148.

FISH

We are blessed in this country in having many varieties of fish that are caught along our shores and in our waters. Although it is harder to get a good selection of fish in the interior sections of the country than along the coastal regions, you should always be able to find some of the more popular prolific types, either fresh or frozen, and, of course, the ubiquitous fish fillets. Whole fish should look and smell fresh and have bright eyes, shiny scales, and flesh that springs back when pressed with a finger. After buying, wrap fish in wax paper or place in a covered dish and refrigerate. Cook as soon as possible. Estimate ⅓ to ½ pound boneless fish per serving or 1 pound of whole fish, to allow for head, tail, and bone.

Blowfish. Sometimes called the *puffer* or *globe fish.* This unique fish can suck in water and air and enlarge itself until it is almost balloonlike. But only the meat around the spine is eaten—and that is what we call *sea squab.* In eastern markets you will see the prepared fish looking something like a large chicken drumstick from which the skin has been removed. It is delicious eating but no longer as inexpensive as it once was. I find it's excellent sautéed simply or broiled or deep-fried. You don't see it often in our markets, and when you do, you should quickly avail yourself of the opportunity to buy it.

Bluefish. One of the most plentiful fish along the Atlantic coast, a very popular sporting fish, and a commercial fish as well. It is to my mind very oily, and I must confess I don't like it much. However, it is enormously popular with many people and it does have a pleasant flavor; it's best prepared in the simplest way, broiled on a bed of dried herbs—perhaps thyme or wild fennel; it can also be sautéed or baked.

Cod. A fish with rather coarse white flesh, less expensive than many others and a familiar sight in our markets, especially on the East Coast. Fresh cod can be bought whole, in steaks, and in fillets. Whole cod run from 5 or 6 pounds to large specimens of 30 or 40 pounds. Cod may be poached, broiled, baked, and sautéed, and is excellent cold. **Salt cod** is much used all over the world, especially by the Italians and Portuguese. To prepare the hard, dried, salted fillets, see page 243. Use creamed or gratin; in codfish cakes; in soufflés; in a salad with potatoes, onions, and vinaigrette sauce; or in other codfish dishes. Particularly good is a brandade of cod. For recipes see pages 243–245.

EELS. Erroneously called freshwater fish by most French authorities, they are both freshwater and marine and range in size from 1½ to 7 feet although the average size will probably run 4 to 5 feet. All the European and American eels are born in the same place, a deep spot in the ocean south of Bermuda. From there they migrate to localities previously frequented by their parents—European eels go to Europe, and American eels to America. They ascend the freshwater streams, stay for a while, and then return to the spawning grounds in the Atlantic.

Haddock. Another coarse-textured fish, similar to cod, with excellent flavor. At its best poached or baked whole. Fillets must be handled carefully as they tend to break easily. Poach, broil, sauté, or bake them in aluminum-foil packages. Haddock takes kindly to strong flavors, such as onion, garlic, and tomato mixtures. **Smoked haddock,** commonly known as *finnan haddie,* is a great breakfast favorite. Poach in milk and serve with parsley butter or béchamel sauce, or broil. Also good flaked and used for fish cakes and soufflés, like salt cod. Smoked haddock makes a delicious mousse (see page 9).

Halibut. A white-fleshed fish with a rather coarse texture and a pleasant but slightly bland flavor, which, to my mind, needs dressing up. It is very friendly to strong seasonings such as garlic, onion, capers, to herbs like rosemary and thyme, to olive oil and tomato sauce, and is excellent prepared in the Italian manner. Halibut comes in sizes from 6 to 8 pounds (known as chicken halibut), up to 100 pounds or more. Usually cut into steaks. Steaks from halibut, cut

1 to 2 inches thick, may be poached (page 202), baked (page 208), or broiled (see page 206). Leftover halibut is delicious cold with vinaigrette sauce or mustard mayonnaise.

Herring. One of the most plentiful fish to be found but not popular in its fresh state. However, cured, pickled, smoked, all the other herrings are enormously in demand for delicatessen food. I find fresh herring to be most delicious and pleasant when lightly sautéed or baked, or spiced and eaten for an hors d'oeuvre; see pages 6–7 for a number of recipes. Herring roe also is delicious when poached or sautéed. In some parts of New England the herring run in the spring will overflow streams and attract huge numbers of people to bail them in. They are not as numerous on the West Coast as they are on the East, although cured herring is widely fancied there, as well as on the East Coast.

Red snapper. Found on both the Pacific and Atlantic coasts and in the Gulf of Mexico. The eastern snapper, quite a different fish from the western species, is a delicate white fish with a brilliant red skin; it is delicious broiled or poached, or prepared in many different ways as one would prepare flounder or sole. The fish comes in many different sizes and weights—some as much as 3 to 4 feet long, weighing up to 30 pounds, although most of them we get in the market nowadays are about 10 to 14 inches long and will weigh 3 to 5 pounds. The Pacific Coast snapper is not nearly as delicate or as useful as the eastern. There are also some other snappers that are found in the Gulf—mainly yellowtail and gray snapper, mutton fish, and the school master. All these are quite good eating but don't compete with the basic red snapper.

Salmon. A splendid though expensive fish caught on the Pacific and Atlantic coasts. In fairly good supply throughout the country, either fresh or frozen. Fresh salmon in season is extraordinarily good, with rich but delicate flesh. When it is not available, frozen is quite acceptable. Whole salmon or large cuts of salmon may be poached (page 200, or *T & P*, page 35), and served hot with hollandaise, cold with mayonnaise, or glazed with aspic. They can also be stuffed and baked, like other large fish. Salmon steaks are good almost any way —poached, broiled (page 206), sautéed (see *T & P*, page 198), or baked. One of the more unusual ways to prepare salmon is to pickle it with salt and sugar for the Scandinavian *gravad laks* (see *T & P*, page 345). Salmon smokes and cans extremely well. The best and most expensive smoked salmon comes from Scotland and Nova Scotia. The less-expensive lox is much saltier, and though it can be used like better-grade smoked salmon, it is more at home with bagels and cream cheese, scrambled eggs, or steamed over potatoes. Smoked salmon is a very elegant first course, sliced paper thin and dressed with oil, lemon juice, capers, and freshly ground pepper, but try it sometime slivered in a risotto (see *T & P*, page 48) or a quiche. Both choice and inferior cuts of salmon are canned, so shop carefully. Only the best grades are worth the money canned salmon costs these days.

Shad. On both coasts, the harbinger of spring. The season starts around January with shad from Florida and works up the coast to New York, Massachusetts,

Connecticut, finishing off in May or early June. On the West Coast, where this lovely fish was transplanted into the Columbia River from the East Coast to benefit people who missed it, shad appears in April or May, and has a rather short season. For many the choice roe is the only part of the shad that is eaten because people feel the fish itself is too bony. This is nonsense, since the shad you buy today in most fish markets has been expertly boned. Very few fish have its delicate, delicious flavor and very few seafoods can compete with shad roe when perfectly cooked—one of the great delicacies of the world. In my opinion it should be smothered in butter and not broiled or fried as many cooks do it. If it is really steamed in butter, it is tender, delicious, and needs only a few drops of lemon to make it sublime.

Smelts. Sometimes called the king of small fish, smelts have a distant relationship to salmon, and their spawning habits are somewhat the same. One extremely oily type of smelt from the West Coast used to be called from time to time the *candle fish* because the smelt was dried, had a wick implanted in it and was used for light. Smelt have a run in the spring but they also may be fished the year round with less ease. They're quite silvery in their color and have a very simple backbone, which is easily removed if you wish to sauté them boneless. However, if you are going to deep-fry or broil them it is best to leave that backbone in. Smelt are also delicious when spiced and baked in a rather sweet-and-sour court bouillon and served cold.

Striped bass. One of the greatest eating fish we have. Commercially fished in the East and a sports fish on the West Coast, striped bass weigh from 3½ to 12 or 15 pounds. Most often cooked whole, either poached (page 200) or stuffed and baked (see *T & P*, page 297). The boned fillets may be broiled (see page 196) or poached in a court bouillon or in water and white wine (see *T & P*, page 36). Serve in the bouillon, or with a sauce made from the reduced poaching stock, or chill and glaze with aspic.

Sturgeon are found on both the East and West coasts, around New England and the Carolinas and Florida, and throughout California, Oregon, and Washington. They also, from time to time, will return to the Great Lakes, where they used to be very prominently active members of the fish family. Naturally, when one thinks of sturgeon one immediately associates it with caviar and nowadays we are producing some extraordinarily fine caviar, especially from the Oregon and California roes; some of it is challenging the Iranian and the Russian. However, many people forget that sturgeon itself is a most delicious and useful fish. It braises particularly well, it broils extremely well, and it will take to a sauté meunière when cut into steaks. It has a lovely texture and delicious flavor, and it is a fish to seek out. In California it is only a game fish.

Tilefish is found in the deep waters off Nova Scotia, southern Florida, the Gulf of Mexico, and all the way from the state of Washington to Baja California on the West Coast. It's a brilliant-colored, stout-bodied fish with sort of a greenish back touched with gold, and it grows to as much as 50 pounds, although the average 6- to 8-pounder is what we find in our markets. The meat has a delicious flavor that slightly resembles a lobster, and it is very firm in its meat and extremely tender. It's often used for sashimi because of its firm quality and its delicate flavor. Sometimes on the West Coast you will find it has a rather bitter flavor, not as sweet and delicate as our eastern variety. Tilefish poaches beautifully, it broils magnificently, and it tastes good cold.

Trout. An adaptable fish with delicate flesh. Large trout may be prepared like salmon. The small trout, usually served whole, with head and tail on, are handy little fish, for one is usually just enough for a serving. Brook trout, speckled (mountain) trout, and the frozen rainbow trout widely available throughout the country can be cooked in all manner of ways—poached, sautéed (see *T & P*, page 197), French-fried, stuffed and baked, broiled (page 212), or poached, chilled, and glazed with aspic. Live trout, fresh from the stream or the tank, may be tossed straight into the pot and cooked *au bleu* (the skin turns blue and the fish curls up).

Fish fillets. Fillets comprise the major part of the fish bought in this country, no doubt because they are easy to prepare and satisfy those who shun fish with bones. Fillets come both fresh and frozen, varying from ⅓ to 1½ or 2 inches in thickness, depending on the type and size of fish they are taken from. A tremendous amount of fish is filleted—cod, haddock, flounder, sole, snapper, ocean perch, and many others. More often than not, the fish from which the fillets come is not identified, but try to find out, for some have a poorer taste and texture than others. The finest fillets are from members of the flounder family of flat fish found on both coasts. This includes gray sole, lemon sole, rex sole, and petrale sole, for there is no true sole in this country. Most "fillets of sole" are really flounder, for at this point the words have become interchangeable in our shopping language. The most expensive, delicate, and fragile fillets are lemon sole. They break easily and are best poached (see *T & P*, page 36) or marinated for seviche (see *T & P*, page 344). Don't attempt to fry them. Fillets of petrale sole and flounder can be stuffed and rolled for paupiettes; flounder or haddock fillets can be deep-fried (see *T & P*, page 225). Flounder can be baked, broiled, sautéed, or fried. Haddock, cod, and ocean perch, coarser in texture, lend themselves to any style of cooking. Ocean perch are the cheapest and most widely available of all the frozen fillets. Bland in flavor, they cry out for sauces, stuffings, and strong seasonings.

Flour

There are many different types of flour on the market today, some generally available, others mainly sold by mail or in health-food stores. Always use the flour specified in a recipe, if it is a type other than all-purpose. Substitutions can ruin a recipe.

All-purpose flour. The most commonly used flour for cooking, for everything from sauces to cakes and cookies. It is a mixture of hard-wheat (high-gluten) and soft-wheat (low-gluten) flours and now comes both bleached and unbleached. I much prefer the unbleached, which retains more of the natural qualities and nutrition of the wheat, for breadmaking.

Cake flour. Cake flour, made from soft wheat, is fine and soft and may contain cornstarch. At one time much used for the kind of cakes popular in the earlier part of the century, but now less frequently called for.

Hard-wheat flour. A high-gluten flour used for certain breads. It makes a loaf with a firmer, tougher texture, similar to French and Italian breads. Sold in many health-food stores and by mail from mills. Use only if specified in a recipe.

Instant flour. Very fine, powdery, pretreated all-purpose flour sold under various brand names. Good for thickening sauces and gravies, as it does not lump. Preferred by some people for making puff pastry.

Self-rising flour. Flour to which baking powder and salt have been added. Much used in the South. Use only in recipes calling for this type of flour, such as certain cakes and quick breads. Because it contains baking powder which with age loses its leavening power, self-rising flour does not have a long shelf life.

Stone-ground flours. Flours from mills that grind the old-fashioned way, with millstones, rather than with modern steel rollers. They do not keep as well as commercial all-purpose flour and should be stored in a cool place or the refrigerator.

Whole-wheat or graham flour. Not two different flours, but the same thing. Whole-wheat flour comes in a number of different grinds, some coarser than others. There is also a finely ground whole-wheat pastry flour, made from soft wheat, sold in health-food stores. Whole-wheat flour is a whole-kernel flour that still retains the wheat germ, which white flour does not.

FROGS' LEGS. These vary in size from tiny to huge, depending on the size of the frog. I prefer them small; they are more delicate and look more appetizing. The flesh is tender and white and rather resembles the white meat of chicken. The usual way of cooking frogs' legs is to sauté them in olive oil, often with garlic and parsley, in the French manner (see page 241). I like to soak them in milk first for about 1 hour, then dry them on a towel, roll them in flour, and sauté them in a combination of olive oil and butter. But they may also be poached and served with a sauce poulette, or breaded and deep-fried (called "roadhouse style" on Middle Western restaurant menus). I also like them cold with a rémoulade or vinaigrette sauce. Until recently frogs' legs were plentiful in this country, but I'm told they are becoming scarcer and scarcer, although I still seem to hear as many frogs croaking as ever I did. They have to be ordered specially through better fish markets; they're apt to be brought in from California, Louisiana, or Florida, and many are shipped frozen from Japan. They usually come skinned and cleaned and tied in bunches of a dozen. If you buy them frozen, let them thaw before cooking. Allow about 12 small frogs' legs per person.

GEESE. Geese, for the most part, come to the market frozen. At holiday time you may find fresh-killed ones. Geese weigh from 5 to 20 pounds and are the bearers of a good deal of fat. The packaged, frozen geese are usually smaller, more compact birds. A 6-pound goose will serve 4. An 8-pound goose will serve

6 to 8. Geese are good stuffed with an apple and apricot stuffing (page 340), or a fruit, crumb, and chestnut stuffing (see *T & P*, page 93). Goose fat is useful in many types of cooking, particularly for sautéing potatoes.

GINGER. In its various forms, a spicy, sometimes fiery, accent for dishes—a major spice. Ground ginger, the least pungent, goes into spice cakes and gingerbread, and a touch adds an interesting fillip to codfish cakes. Fresh ginger root, subtler in flavor, enhances many marinades, such as teriyaki (see page 366) and most Oriental dishes. Look for young, plump, juicy ginger root. As it ages, it dries out and becomes woody, stringy, and much hotter. Ginger root can be kept for quite a long time in the refrigerator if peeled and put into a small jar of vodka. The vodka, tasteless itself, takes on a spicy ginger flavor and can be used for seasoning. If you cut a piece of ginger root, wrap it tightly in plastic wrap and refrigerate. Candied ginger can often be substituted for ginger root if the sugar is washed off. Finely chopped, it is good for such things as teriyaki marinade, fruit compotes, and syrups. Preserved ginger, in syrup, can also be used for fruit compotes and for ginger-flavored sherbet and ice cream (see page 503 or *T & P*, page 371). Avoid dried ginger root, sometimes found in jars on the spice shelves of supermarkets—it is virtually useless.

GREENS FOR SALADS
Wash and dry thoroughly before using, wrap loosely in paper towels, put into a plastic bag, and refrigerate. Before washing head lettuce, such as Boston, cut out core. Hold head, core side up, under running water; leaves will then separate easily. Salad dryers with a centrifugal action are good for all but very delicate Bibb lettuce, which bruises easily. Use faded outer leaves of lettuce in stuffings for turkey, chicken, and meat to add moisture and texture.

Bibb lettuce. Small tender head lettuce with very crisp leaves. Soak and rinse well to get rid of sand and dirt that cling to the leaves. The small leaves should be left whole.

Boston or butter lettuce. Pale-green, deliciously tender head lettuce. Use in salads or as a garnish. Small leaves may be left whole, the larger ones broken with the fingers. Add coarse outer leaves, not good for salads, to soup stocks. Whole heads may be braised (see *T & P*, page 168).

Chicory. Sometimes called *curly endive.* A robust, crisp salad green with a slightly bitter tang. Best combined with other greens. Use the feathery leaves for garnishing. May be braised.

Dandelion greens. Commercially grown or wild dandelion leaves are excellent in salads, with a refreshingly bitter taste. Use alone or with other greens. Pick wild dandelions before the flowers form, dig up the root, and use the tender inner leaves.

Endive, also called Belgian or French endive (true name, witloof chicory). A small elongated lettuce with a tight head, blanched for marketing and carefully packed, so it requires little cleaning. Usually it is sufficient to wipe it off with a damp cloth and remove any discolored outer leaves. Crisp in texture with a delicately bitter flavor. One of the choicest and most expensive salad greens. However, the heads have no waste and go a long way. Use leaves whole, shred, or cut into julienne strips or rings. The sweetness of chopped beets is almost a must with endive salads. Separated leaves may be stuffed with various hors d'oeuvre mixtures. Braises or sautés beautifully.

Escarole. Rather coarse-leafed, slightly bitter green. Preferably, use only the tender greeny-yellow inner leaves for salads. Outer leaves may be added to soup. May be braised.

Field salad, corn salad, lamb's lettuce. A less common type of green with small tongue-shaped leaves, usually sold with roots attached. Flavor is tangy and "wild." Best combined with blander greens. Difficult to find, except in eastern markets in fall and winter.

Iceberg lettuce. Many people damn it, but when broken up (not cut) it adds good flavor and a wonderfully crisp texture to a salad, with other greens. Keeps longer than other lettuce.

Leaf lettuce. Lettuce with loose leaves that do not form a head but branch from the stalk. Comes in various colors—green, red, and coppery brown—and is sold under such names as salad bowl, oak leaf, ruby. The curly, fringed leaves are very decorative and add great color to mixed salads. Wash, dry, and use immediately, as leaves wilt quickly.

Romaine or cos lettuce. Head lettuce with long, crisp leaves shading from bright green to yellow. Excellent texture and flavor. Recommended for salads that need a lot of tossing, such as Caesar, as it does not wilt. Break large leaves into pieces, leave small ones whole. Coarse outer leaves may be added to soups or shredded, blanched, drained, and added to a cheese soufflé mixture, to give a crunchy texture.

Rugula or arugula. Small, flat-leafed greens with a bitter, slightly peppery flavor and rather coarse texture. Extremely popular for salads. Usually sold with the roots on. Wash thoroughly. Known in English as rocket, it is easy to grow from seed.

Sprouts. Bean sprouts, alfalfa sprouts, and other sprouted seeds make a wonderfully fresh, crunchy addition to a mixed green salad. When you buy them, check to see that they have not sat around too long and turned brown and slightly slimy—sprouts sold in plastic bags can deteriorate fairly quickly. It's easy and much cheaper to buy the seeds at a health-food store or by mail from a house that sells seeds and grains and sprout them yourself. There's a special sprouter you can buy, or you can make your own.

Watercress. Sold in bunches. Look for those with crisp, bright green leaves, not limp or yellowed. The small leaves have a refreshing bite and are usually mixed with other greens in salads. Watercress wilts quickly when dressed. A big bowl of plain watercress is good to munch on with steaks or chops. Or roll sprigs in buttered soft white homemade bread for a lovely sandwich.

Greens primarily for cooking

The leafy green tops of beets and turnips, mustard greens, collards, kale, spinach, Swiss and rhubarb chard, and dandelion greens are all good cooked. For some of my favorite recipes, see pages 149–152.

Beet greens. Wash, put into a heavy pan with just the water clinging to the leaves. Sprinkle lightly with salt. Cover and cook over medium heat about 5 minutes or until just wilted—the leaves will lose most of their water, reduce in bulk, and become limp. Turn once or twice with a wooden spoon or spatula so top leaves fall to the bottom during cooking. If water evaporates too fast and leaves show signs of sticking, add a very little boiling water. Drain, leave whole or chop, dress with butter, and serve with lemon wedges. Very tiny, young, and tender beet greens may be mixed raw in a salad with other greens.

Chard. Swiss chard has green leaves and long white ribs. The less common rhubarb chard, more often found on the West Coast than the East, has red ribs and reddish-green leaves. Cook the leaves like beet greens, about 10 minutes. Or sauté in oil, like mustard greens. Cook the white or red ribs as a separate vegetable, like asparagus, in boiling salted water to cover until just tender. Serve hot with melted butter or hollandaise, or cold with a vinaigrette sauce.

Collards. Unlike most other greens, collards are best cooked in the southern way, for 2 hours in water to cover with a piece of ham or bacon. Drain and serve.

Dandelion greens. Delicious sautéed with bacon. Fry squares of bacon in a heavy skillet until the fat has been drawn out, add the washed and dried dandelion greens, and toss in the fat with the bacon, a little chopped garlic, finely chopped fresh mint, and a touch of wine vinegar until wilted, about 5 minutes.

Kale. A heavy, coarse green with curly leaves. Best cooked like collards, for 1 hour. Drain and serve.

Mustard greens. Pungent, flavorful greens beloved of the Chinese, the French, and Southerners. I like to chop them coarsely and sauté in olive oil (about 4 tablespoons or just enough to cover the bottom of a heavy skillet) with a clove of garlic in the Italian manner. Cover the pan and cook for 10 minutes, or until wilted, shaking the pan occasionally to keep the greens from sticking.

Sorrel. Also known as *sourgrass*, for its strong, sour taste. This perennial is easy to cultivate and grows for 9 or 10 months of the year in many parts of the country. Oddly enough, it is seldom seen in produce markets, apart from those specializing in a wide range of vegetables, probably because sorrel is not as popular or as widely used here as it is in Europe. (There is also a wild version, sheep sorrel, that grows as a weed in many gardens and in the countryside.) Sorrel wilts down very quickly and needs minimum cooking time. It can be made into a purée or a soup (see page 52), or combined in purées with other greens, such as spinach, watercress, mustard greens, and chard greens where a little of that distinctive sour taste adds an intriguing note. As sorrel turns brownish when cooked, it looks more appetizing when mixed with greens that hold their color. A few tender green leaves are refreshing in a mixed green salad, but don't overdo them. If you can't find fresh sorrel, it can be bought in jars under the Yiddish name *chav* or *schav*.

Spinach. A very versatile vegetable, with many uses in cooking. Prewashed spinach packaged in bags is not a good buy; it is damp, has many small broken leaves and a lot of waste. Whenever possible, buy fresh, loose spinach with crisp, undamaged leaves. Wash well in several changes of water to remove all the sand, and pull off the heavy stems. May be cooked in just the water that clings to the leaves, like beet greens, for about 5 minutes until wilted, or sautéed in oil (see *T & P*, page 210). Plainly cooked spinach may be puréed (try combining it with a purée of cooked watercress) or drained very well and chopped fine to use in spinach roll (see *T & P*, page 250), soufflés, crêpes, stuffings, quiche, or omelet fillings. Frozen spinach is an acceptable substitute, but it holds a great deal of water and yields less than fresh. Tender young spinach leaves can be tossed into a salad with other greens. The large leaves, stronger in flavor and coarser in texture, are best used alone for spinach salads (see pages 79–80). **Turnip greens.** Cook like mustard greens, for 10 minutes.

HERBS

With the vastly increased use of fresh herbs in cooking, herb-growing has become more popular in this country, and it is easier than ever before to find herbs, both cut and potted, in vegetable stores and supermarkets. There is no doubt that the herbs you grow and dry yourself are vastly superior to the packaged ones. If you do buy dried herbs, shop around for a good brand. Some companies powder their herbs too much. Look for large leaves with a strong perfume, such as the dried herbs from Provence, sold in many specialty shops. Dried herbs lose their potency very fast. Always keep them in a dark place, away from heat, and replace them frequently. Most dried herbs are improved by crushing, either in a mortar and pestle or in the palm of your hand with your thumb, before being added to a dish. Soaking them in a little wine also helps to release the flavor. When substituting dried herbs for fresh, the standard ratio is 1 teaspoon dried herb for 1 tablespoon chopped fresh herb. Some of the more essential kitchen herbs are:

Basil. The sweet basil used for cooking (there are also ornamental basils) is an annual that grows abundantly, with a deliciously pungent leaf. There are two types: the large-leafed basil and the tiny-leafed bush basil. Basil is the definitive herb for tomatoes, whether they are sliced as a salad, turned into tomato sauce, or used for a sautéed zucchini or salade Niçoise. Ground with oil, garlic, and pine nuts, it makes that most glorious of pasta sauces—the Italian pesto (see page 281). Chopped fresh basil leaves or the whole tiny leaves give lovely flavor to a green salad. Basil is easy to grow on your windowsill.

Bay leaf. The dried leaf of the bay tree is essential in a bouquet garni and for flavoring stocks, court bouillon, marinades for game and meat, stews, and many meat dishes. It can also impart an unusual and interesting flavor to custard and some sauces. The imported Mediterranean bay leaf has a better and more lasting flavor than the California floral bay.

Bouquet garni. Not a single herb, but a little bundle of herbs that flavor stocks and stews. Bay leaf, thyme, and parsley are the usual assortment, tied with string to a rib of celery or a leek which hold them firmly together so the bouquet can be easily removed after cooking. Or the flavorings, perhaps with the addition of an onion and a clove or two, may be tied in a cheesecloth bag. Sometimes a sprig of rosemary is included.

Chives. This slender green member of the onion family is one of the favorite herbs for salads, sauces, or garnishes for soups and vegetable dishes and is part of the classic fines herbes trio for an omelet. Often mixed into cream cheese or cottage cheese, or the horseradish cream that goes with roast beef. Chives should be finely cut, not chopped, as their moist tubular stalks bruise easily. A hardy perennial for garden or flowerpot.

Coriander. Also known as *Chinese parsley* and, in Spanish, *cilantro.* Fresh coriander has pale-green leaves, rather like those of Italian parsley. Much used in Chinese, Indian, and Latin-American cooking, coriander has had quite a vogue in the last few years, although some people find the strange, strong, distinctive flavor unpalatable. This is one herb you either love or loathe. Guacamole (see *T & P*, page 337) and seviche (see *T & P*, page 344) are dishes that depend for their flavor on freshly chopped coriander, which is more often sprinkled over food as a seasoning and garnish than cooked in a dish. But try it in an American dish like chicken salad (page 99), and see what it does. Chinese and Spanish American markets always have coriander, but now you find it in some vegetable markets, especially on the West Coast. This is an herb that is always sold with the roots on. Do not remove. To keep, wrap, roots and all, in damp paper towels and store in a plastic bag or a covered glass jar in the refrigerator. Do not wash until ready to use. Coriander is easy to grow, but goes to seed quickly in hot weather. The dried seeds, which have an entirely different flavor, are much used in curries, and are excellent with pork and chicken.

Dill. Very popular in Scandinavian, Russian, and Central European cookery. The dill sold in markets is mostly raised in hothouses. The branches are about 8 inches long, extremely feathery, and highly aromatic. Garden dill goes to seed fast, especially in the summer. Dried dill seeds are a standby for pickles—in fact, for most of us, our first acquaintance with dill was the ubiquitous dill pickle. Finely chopped fresh dill leaves are good with fish, veal, chicken, vegetables such as sauerkraut, cabbage, and boiled new potatoes, in cucumber salad, sour-cream sauces, and soups. A whole bunch of dill is part of the curing ingredients for the Scandinavian *gravad laks* (see *T & P*, page 345). In most cases, dried dill weed, although not as flavorful as fresh dill, is an acceptable substitute.

Mint. Popularized by the English in the form of mint sauce (see *T & P*, page 71) with roast lamb, which to my mind smothers the good flavor of the meat, mint, both fresh and dried, is used with great imagination in Middle Eastern dishes such as tabbouleh (see *T & P*, page 337) and yogurt soup (see page 57). Mint is chopped and added as a flavoring and a garnish, rather than cooked. Use it in some salads, with cooked dandelion greens, on new potatoes and peas —and don't forget one of its most important roles, crushed in a mint julep. I like to use it in unusual ways, such as with sardines, or pepper vinaigrette. Can be bought in markets across the country and is an easily grown perennial— beware, it spreads like mad.

Parsley. Probably the most widely used of all fresh herbs—and the most easily available. There are 2 kinds, the familiar curly parsley that garnishes practically every platter, and the Italian flat-leaf parsley, not as useful as a garnish (it wilts easily) but infinitely better for cooking, with a subtler, more refined flavor. Curly parsley is delicious fried in hot fat (see *T & P*, page 226) as a garnish for fish. Parsley belongs in a bouquet garni, in stocks, soups, stews, almost everything from salads to a chicken sauté. Parsley butter, like other herb or flavored butters (see *T & P*, page 111), can be made in quantity, frozen, and put on cooked vegetables, a broiled steak, or broiled fish. Parsley keeps well in a plastic bag in the vegetable compartment of the refrigerator. A sturdy biennial; it will flourish in the garden for 2 years, then disappear. To make fried parsley: Rinse and dry thoroughly 2 cups parsley sprigs. Drop them into deep hot fat (370 to 375°). Fry not more than 1 minute. Remove and dry on absorbent paper. The parsley should retain its color and develop a unique flavor and texture.

Rosemary. A marvelously fragrant perennial that grows wild in great bushes in Europe, especially the South of France. Quite easy to grow and very ornamental, but best potted in cold climates as it cannot survive an icy winter. The sweet-and-bitter pungency of rosemary does marvels for roast lamb, beef, chicken, and turkey, but it is a powerful herb and must be handled with caution and never overused. The needlelike leaves are as good dried as fresh (or even better), but must be crushed before using.

Sage. This may well have been the herb that traveled the covered-wagon trail in the days when pork and game were the mainstay of our diet and usually seasoned with sage. Nowadays dried sage is most often used in sausage and in poultry stuffings, but a little can enhance pork, duck, goose, and some beef dishes. Use sage with discretion; it can be unpleasant if overdone.

Tarragon. One of the most highly prized members of the family of herbs, French tarragon being considered the choicest. The pungent but light anise flavor of the long pointed leaves is highly complementary to sautéed chicken or rabbit, roast chicken, veal, fish, poultry stuffings, and egg dishes. A lovely salad herb, and the essential flavoring for Béarnaise sauce (see page 532). Always cut, rather than chop, the leaves. Tarragon is a perennial, usually grown from plants rather than seeds. After a few years, it will lose its flavor and have to be replaced.

Thyme. Next to parsley, the most useful of the kitchen herbs for stocks, soups, stews, marinades, bouquet garni, poultry stuffings, brown sauce, braised dishes, and roasts. There are very few savory dishes that can't benefit from a touch of thyme, including beefsteak and kidney pudding. There are various kinds of thyme, all easily grown as perennials in the garden or in pots. English and French thyme, very similar in flavor, are preferred for cooking. Lemon thyme has a distinct and pleasant lemony tang.

HOMINY. Corn kernels treated with lye and steamed until the skins come off and the kernels are puffed and look like white popcorn. Whole hominy is a much neglected vegetable, excellent cooked in butter and combined with sour cream and green chilies, or served with bacon and gravy. Available both dried and canned. Hominy grits is a cereal made from ground dried hominy. As served in the South, on the breakfast plate, it pleases me not. I prefer, after cooking it, to combine it with butter, garlic, and grated cheese, and bake it as an accompaniment to entrées, or to mold the hominy, then slice and sauté it until crisp in butter or bacon fat, to be served with game birds or chicken.

HORSERADISH. A pungent root that carries a tremendously hot message. Freshly grated and combined with vinegar, or with sour cream or whipped cream, it is one of the greatest accompaniments for hot or cold roast or boiled beef. Also good with steak, ham, oysters, smoked trout. Excellent combined with applesauce and served with roast pork. Widely available ready-prepared in jars, but best if you buy the root and grate it fresh. Country markets and stores in Jewish neighborhoods often carry horseradish root.

JERUSALEM ARTICHOKES. See page 121 for description and recipes.

KIWI FRUIT. Sometimes called the *Chinese gooseberry* because it was a native of China before being introduced into New Zealand, where the name was changed. This fruit can be found most of the year in fruit markets. The oval fruit has a soft, slightly rough brown skin and brilliant green flesh with dark flecks around the core that look like eyelashes. When sliced crosswise, this makes a pretty pattern, hence the widespread use of kiwi fruit as a decoration for tarts, sorbets, and other desserts by pastry chefs and practitioners of the nouvelle cuisine. Frankly, I think that kiwi fruit have very little flavor and have become overused by fancy chefs, to the point of boredom, but this is the decade of the kiwi fruit and I am in the minority.

KOHLRABI. A small pale-green, slightly knobby, turnip-shaped vegetable. Sometimes called cabbage turnip but with the virtues of neither. Not one of my favorites. Both tops and bulbs may be eaten. The root bulb is the better part. Buy small or medium-size kohlrabi. Remove tops, peel bulb, and slice thin. Put in a pan with a small quantity of salted water, cover, and steam gently until tender, about 25 minutes. Drain, dress with butter, and season with salt and pepper to taste.

LARD. Lard, the rendered fat of the pig, has fallen from favor since we have become so accustomed to using vegetable shortening. However, good lard, especially the pure and delicate leaf lard rendered from kidney fat, is excellent for baking, frying, and sautéing. See page 508 for rendering. Pastry made with leaf lard is even shorter than pastry made with butter (see page 509). An interesting fat for the kitchen. If you have never used it, I would advise you to experiment a little bit.

LEMONS. Brilliant yellow citrus fruit, irreplaceable in cooking. Fresh lemons, available all year, easily outdistance the artificial lemon juice and flavorings. The juice is an essential flavoring for hollandaise (see page 532), mayonnaise (page 76), egg-lemon soup (see *T & P*, page 320), for pies, soufflés, cakes, ice cream, and sherbet (see *T & P*, page 374). A squeeze of lemon in the butter for vegetables gives a zesty tang. In marinades for meat, game, or fish, the acidity of lemon juice is a tenderizer. Lemon juice or a cut lemon rubbed in the cavity of poultry or game birds freshens the meat and improves the taste. Lemon is used widely as a garnish and condiment for caviar, fish, all shellfish, veal, and beef. The lemon zest, the yellow part of the rind, is added to many dishes, from frozen lemon mousse to Viennese goulash, and it is an important part of the Italian garnish called *gremolata* (see page 416). To remove zest without pith, use a special tool called a zester, or a grater, or strip it off with a potato peeler and shred fine with a knife.

LENTILS. The seeds of a shrubby plant, these are an ancient food mentioned in the Bible as the "mess of pottage" eaten by Esau and one of our most valuable legumes. Various kinds of lentils are sold in 1-pound packages or in bulk. There are the tiny green ones from the Auvergne in France, the red Egyptian lentils, and the larger brown lentils from Oregon, Washington, and Colorado, which you find in every supermarket. Lentils need very little cooking time, only about 15 to 25 minutes if you use the quick-cooking American type. Apart from lentil soup, this tasty little legume is mostly overlooked. I like to serve them sautéed or as a purée (see page 310) with game, pork, or beef; make a salad of them; or use them in casseroles. There is also a version of the French cassoulet in which lentils replace the usual white beans.

LICHEES OR LICHEE NUTS. A delicacy that for centuries was exclusively Chinese. Inside the fragile, nubby reddish-brown shell of a fresh lichee is a delicate white fruit with an exotic, slightly acid flavor and a pit of varying size. The Chinese dry lichees in the shell and the shrunken fruit then becomes rather like a large raisin. I grew up on dried lichees and found them a fascinating sweet to nibble on. Later I encountered the fresh lichees, which are now one of my preferred fruits. Lichees grow on fairly low trees and are picked in clusters with stems and leaves, the way they are usually sold, although you can also find them separate, off the stem. If you can't find the fresh fruit, canned lichees in syrup are very good and make a most delectable sherbet (see page 502). Although China used to be the main supplier of this luscious fruit, they are now grown in Florida, California, Hawaii, and Jamaica.

LIMES. Like the lemon, the green-skinned, green-fleshed lime is immensely valuable in cooking, for baking, marinades, as a flavoring for chicken, duck, or fish. Lime juice "cooks" raw fish for seviche (see *T & P*, page 344). Tough of skin, the lime is best juiced with a small metal hand squeezer of the type used in bars.

MANDARINS. The mandarin, which originated in China, is a type of small orange with a soft, loose skin that peels easily. Tangerines belong to this family, as do satsumas, the type of mandarin orange found in cans, and hybrids such as the tangelo (a grapefruit-tangerine cross) and the temple orange (an orange-tangerine cross). Mandarin oranges and tangerines have a bouquet and flavor slightly different from a true orange and are excellent eating fruits. Mandarins make delicious sherbet. Tangerines can be made into preserves and chutneys, and the sections are often used in salads. As with other fruit, pick tangerines and mandarins that are heavy in the hand, which means they are full of juice.

MANGOES. A tropical and subtropical fruit, these were once so rare and precious that Queen Victoria is said to have offered a peerage to the man who brought her a ripe mango. Now they are grown in the West Indies, Hawaii, and Florida, and are a fairly common sight in produce markets from January through August. There are several varieties. Those from the West Indies and Hawaii are rather flat and oval, with a red-tinged yellow skin. The two varieties cultivated in Florida are rounder and slightly tapering, with a rosy skin and more delicate flesh. I find them easier to peel and slice than the others. While I adore the spicily exotic flavor and aroma of a ripe mango, it is not the easiest fruit to eat gracefully because of the way the rather stringy flesh clings to the large flat seed. Slice it down the two widest sides, not too near the seed, and you will have most of the edible flesh, with a little remaining on the two narrow edges. To eat a mango with decorum and without bathing yourself in the juice, try the Indonesian trick of slicing off the sides and then scoring the flesh length-wise and crosswise down to the skin. Push the skin upward from the back and the little cubes of flesh will pop up and can be bitten off neatly. When you buy mangoes, be sure the skin is fully colored, not green, and that the fruit is soft to the touch. Mangoes combine well with other fruits in a compote and can be turned into a glorious sherbet or ice cream—when the fresh fruit are not in season, mango slices or purée canned in syrup can be substituted.

MEAT

We have two categories of markets where we buy meats. One is the rapidly vanishing small private butcher, who cuts meats to order, and the other is the supermarket, which deals primarily with packaged, ready-cut meats, although many supermarkets do have butchers on the premises who will, on request, cut meat for you and order special cuts and variety meats.

To buy packaged meats requires a working knowledge of the cuts most suitable for the various cooking processes and the difference between the more expensive and less expensive cuts (for instance, if you are making braised beef, you have a choice between the very lean top or bottom round and the fatter but less costly chuck). Once you know your cuts, you can start experimenting and use parts of the animal you never thought of before.

When buying meat cuts with a good deal of bone, estimate 1 pound per person; for cuts with a small amount of bone, ½ to ¾ pound. And for bone-less beef, 8 ounces is a generous serving, 5 to 6 ounces normal.

I personally feel that uncooked meat should be kept in the refrigerator no longer than 4 or 5 days. It should not be wrapped airtight, but have an opening at the end so the meat can breathe. Ground meat is best cooked the day of purchase because bacteria grow easily. Certainly it should never be kept in the refrigerator for more than 24 hours. Wrap like other meat. The freezer can be a great boon. When there are specials on meat, you can stock up on various cuts and later refer to them as you would a library of books, knowing there is always something to cook in an emergency. I find the commercially flash-frozen meats to be equally as good as fresh, but on the other hand I have eaten a good deal of meat that has lost its savor and texture because it was carelessly wrapped and tossed into the freezer. If you freeze meat, wrap it well and tightly and store at a temperature of 0° or below.

BEEF

Certainly more beef is consumed in the United States than any other meat and, because of the diversity of cuts and names, it is the most difficult and tricky to shop for. Beef is sold by U.S. Department of Agriculture grades, of which the finest is Prime. Prime beef is from grain-fed steers, well marbled with little flecks of fat that break down in the cooking and lubricate the flesh, and therefore very tender. While most Prime beef goes to restaurants, a certain amount can be found in markets. Choice, the most generally available grade, has less marbling of fat in the meat. A change in grading made in the mid-seventies has allowed a higher percentage of grass-feeding. Grass-fed beef has less fat content, is more chewy, and requires longer cooking to become tender, so one must be doubly careful these days when buying and cooking Choice beef. Examine it carefully. Grain-fed beef will have a little more fat on it and more marbling in the lean. Unfortunately, there is no chart that gives you cooking times for grass-fed vs. grain-fed beef—it's something you have to find out by experiment. Some people prefer the chewier texture of grass-fed beef, claiming it has a better flavor, but this is a matter of palate, and palate is a very personal thing. Decide for yourself. The other, lesser grades are Good, less tender and with less fat; and Commercial, used almost entirely for sausage-making and for adding to other products. You seldom come across these grades, but if you do, this is meat to use only for soup or stock.

If you follow the drawing just inside the back cover of this book, you will learn a great deal about beef cuts and how to cook them. We will start at the head, wherein lies the **tongue**, excellent boiled and served hot with a sauce, cold in a salad, or thinly sliced for sandwiches. Then we go to the **shoulder or chuck** section. The individual chuck cuts are blade cut, arm cut, and cross cut. They may be bought bone in or boned and are braised, stewed, pot roasted, and ground for hamburger. Cuts with a lot of bone can be used for stock and the boiled meat saved for hash. The rack of the **rib** section, from which we get rib roasts, usually contains 7 ribs. The 3 closest to the chuck are the least desirable because of excess fat. The next 4 ribs are the choicest and usually sell for a premium price. Most roasts for home use are cut short and the cut-off rib ends, known as **short ribs,** are sold separately for braising, or to be marinated and barbecued. A rib steak or boneless rib eye steak cut from the ribs can be broiled or sautéed—pick one that is not too fatty. Under the rib cage is the **heart,** which can be stuffed and braised, or cut up and stewed. Stuffed heart is pretty good eating, but I prefer to use the smaller, tenderer veal or pork hearts.

Next to the rib is the **loin,** first the short loin, which furnishes the most expensive steaks, and then the sirloin. Lining the bone is the tenderloin or fillet, a boneless, fat-covered strip of meat that rates as the most expensive of all cuts but has practically no waste when trimmed. With the tiny tip removed it becomes a luxury roast that needs to be barded with fat or marinated before roasting. Beef fillet is exceedingly tender but, for my taste, greatly in need of flavor enhancing. The fillet is also cut into steaks for sautéing or broiling. A châteaubriand is cut on the diagonal from the thickest part. Smaller steaks cut an inch or more thick are known as fillet steaks or tournedos. The most misunderstood term of all, *filet mignon*, rightly refers only to the tip of the fillet, a part that is usually sliced fairly thin, pounded and flattened, or cut into cubes and broiled *en brochette*. Steaks cut from the smaller end of the loin, nearest the ribs, are first the club steak, which has none of the tenderloin; then the T-bone, which has a small amount of tenderloin. The porterhouse, a real luxury steak with a T-shaped bone, cut from the large end of the loin next to the sirloin, is the best cut. If the entire top loin section is boned out, with the fillet removed, it is sold as a shell roast, or cut into steaks known variously as *shell steaks, top loin* or *strip steaks, club steaks, sirloin strip, faux filet, New York* or *Kansas City cut*, according to the part of the country you are in. This is the best cut for a sautéed steak. Supermarkets often offer whole or half shells as specials.

The sirloin, which lies between the porterhouse and the rump, is not quite as tender because it includes the hip, a working part of the animal, but it is still excellent eating. Sirloin steaks contain different sizes and shapes of marrowbone and are known as *pinbone* (nearest the porterhouse), *flat-bone, round-bone*, and *wedge-bone* sirloin steaks. They are good buys and should be broiled. Top sirloin steaks are cut from the largest part of the sirloin, a continuation of the top loin. The sirloin tip, a triangular, boneless piece trimmed from the base of the sirloin (technically, it is the part of the round nearest the sirloin), is usually sold as a roast or cut into steaks for sautéing or cubes for shashlik and kebabs. It costs less than the better-known cuts though; naturally, it isn't as tender.

Next comes the **rump,** sold as a roast or as steaks. Many people prefer the chewier but good-flavored rump to the tenderer cuts. The **round,** the meat from the hind leg, is divided into the top round, bottom round, and eye of the rump, the top being the choicest quality. Though less tender than loin or rump, top round may be roasted if barded with fat, cooked quickly to the rare stage—this is the cut sold as roast beef in delicatessens—but it is more often braised. Ground round, especially top round, makes good, lean hamburger (see page 382).

The leg bone contains a great deal of marrow. Sometimes it is sold with the knuckle for soup bones, or it may be sawed into pieces and used for marrow-bones and pot-au-feu (see *T & P*, page 25). **Oxtail** is a very bony cut that yields a thick, gelatinous, flavorful broth, and is excellent braised.

Below the loin and the ribs are two pieces of rather flat, long-grained meat. The one closest to the loin is the **flank.** Flank steak, formerly considered only worthy of braising, makes perfect London broil (see *T & P*, page 112), especially if marinated first, then cooked very fast and close to the heat; a teriyaki marinade is particularly good. Next to the flank is the **plate,** a less tender cut often used for boiling in conjunction with other cuts. Then comes **brisket,** much favored for boiled beef. There is a fairly heavy coating of fat on either side, but the meat itself is juicy and full of flavor. Brisket is good braised and is considered the best cut for corned beef (see *T & P*, page 18). When you are shopping, look for "corned beef brisket" on the package. "Corned beef rump" is less good but acceptable, but do not buy "corned beef spiced," which is highly spiced and has liquid in the bag. Kosher corned beef is always a good buy. Now we come to the **shank** or shin of beef, the lower part of the fore or hind leg, cut in crosswise pieces. It has a great deal of gelatinous fiber and is an excellent cut for soup or stock, less tender than brisket for boiled beef, but very flavorful.

The other variety meats and lesser-known cuts that are found in certain markets should not be ignored. They are usually a good buy. **Skirt steak,** for instance, similar in texture to flank, is very often rolled up and braised. Or, if you care to try, marinate and broil it like flank. Butcher's tenderloin is a small tender piece of beef from below the tenderloin, by the kidneys, also known as hang tenderloin. It's unlikely that you'll find it, as there's only one to an animal, but if you do, it is tender and can be broiled or sautéed. Butt is a triangular piece of meat found between the sirloin and the short loin. One end is very tender and can be broiled; the other is much less so and should be braised or boiled. If it isn't labeled, ask your butcher to identify it. **Beef kidneys** are larger and less tender than veal or lamb kidneys. Never try to boil or sauté them, only braise. I always soak them in milk for 2 hours before using them, to draw out some of their strong flavor. **Beef liver** used to be extremely coarse and heavy and was shunned by most people. Now, with smaller cattle and shorter grazing and fattening times, beef liver is much more acceptable. Best braised or simmered in wine, but may be sautéed if it is sliced very thin and cooked very quickly (see *T & P*, page 180). **Tripe,** the lining of the stomach, varies in texture from that of a Turkish towel to a large honeycomb. Honeycomb tripe is considered the best. Tripe is partially cooked before being sold, and proper cooking time depends on how much processing it has had; the only way to tell when it is tender is to taste. For tripe recipes, see pages 459–461. **Testicles** have a rich, heavy flavor and are regarded by some people as a great delicacy. They must be peeled and sliced before being broiled or sautéed.

LAMB

Good lamb with pinkish-red flesh and rather flaky, creamy-colored fat is available in markets throughout the country, especially on the East and West coasts, where most of the lamb is eaten. Yearling lamb, approximately 1 year old, is what one generally finds. Younger, smaller lamb, known as spring lamb, is available at certain times of year. A very small number of butcher shops, mostly those with a clientele of European origin, will have for about 2 weeks of the year baby lamb so tiny that a whole lamb may serve only 3 or 4 people. This, naturally, is a great delicacy and expensive. Mostly we must content ourselves with yearling.

In some areas and markets you may be able to buy the head, which should be split and either roasted or braised. **Lambs' brains,** while less well known than calves' brains, are equally good and may be prepared in the same ways, as may the very small **tongues,** which, if properly seasoned, make tasty and inexpensive morsels. Pickled lambs' tongues, sold in jars, are very popular in America.

Neck is a good cut for stews and similar dishes. Sometimes it is included with the **shoulder,** a cut usually boned, rolled, and tied for roasting, braising, or poaching. Many people consider roast shoulder of spring lamb to have an even more delicious flavor than the leg. Shoulder chops are extremely bony, but well flavored. Don't try to sauté them; broil or braise. The **rib** section is used in a variety of ways. The whole rack of ribs is a popular roast (sometimes 2 racks are tied together to make a crown roast), see page 387. The ribs are cut into thick chops—when the rib bones are scraped to look fancy, they are known as frenched chops. Rib chops can be broiled or braised. For a special dinner, the eye section may be removed from the rack, cut into thick slices, known as medallions, and sautéed. Next to the ribs is the **loin,** the choicest part of the lamb. Here, as in beef, the bone becomes a T-bone, with meat on both sides of the bone: the tiny tenderloin, which is hardly ever removed, and the top loin. This part of the lamb is sometimes cut as a double loin, known as a saddle, and sometimes tied with the kidneys in. A whole saddle and the 2 legs as one piece are called a baron and are sometimes roasted for a large dinner party. Loin chops are broiled or braised, like rib chops. Lamb kidneys are delicious; for recipes, see pages 453–455.

The most commonly used cut of lamb is the leg, which can weigh anywhere from 4½ to 9 pounds, according to the size of the animal. In many markets you can buy half a leg, either the shank (leg) end or the sirloin or butt end, the part that is next to the loin. For roasting, I prefer not to have the shank bone cracked or the little sirloin chops removed, as is so often done. A good butcher will remove the fell, the thin papery covering, from the leg. If he doesn't, remove it yourself. A leg may be roasted; braised; poached; or boned, butterflied, and broiled (see recipe in *T & P,* page 120); or sliced for lamb steaks. Boned and cubed leg of lamb is the standard cut for shish kebab (see *T & P,* page 123), and the ground meat (or ground shoulder) make the Middle Eastern dish kibbeh (see *T & P,* page 341). For recipes in this book see pages 385–400.

Lambs' **liver,** while as delicate as calves' liver, is less appreciated and therefore less expensive. Cook in the same ways—sauté, broil, or roast whole. The humblest of the cuts is the **breast.** If not too fatty, it may be broiled to crispness over charcoal or under the broiler and makes delicious eating, almost like spare ribs. In some markets, the breast is cut into 1- or 1½-inch strips and sold as lamb riblets. Broil in the same way. The breast may also be braised, stewed, or poached and deviled (see *T & P,* page 196) and stuffed (page 393). The front legs of the lamb are usually cut short and sold as **shanks.** When braised, the meat is chewy and moist (page 399). Lamb's **sweetbreads** from the neck, near the shank, are less common than calves' sweetbreads, and lend themselves to the same styles of cooking. Tiny, tender lamb hearts may be cubed and broiled like kebabs, or braised. Lastly, let us not forget the **testicles,** which are highly prized by some people, especially the Basque sheepherders, who sauté or fry them.

PORK

The pig is by far my favorite meat-yielding animal, for he is edible from snout to tail and provides an enormous variety of eating. Unfortunately, like many humans, the pig has been put on a diet within the last 10 years—and we have suffered because of it. The meat is less streaked with fat and less juicy and tender than before. Let's hope that the streamlined porker will not last forever.

We start with the **head,** the basis of head cheese, a highly gelatinous mixture of bits and pieces of meat from that area, which is one of our more popular cold cuts. The **tongue** is of medium size, and 1 person could eat 1 or possibly 2 at a sitting. Tongue is often braised, sometimes boiled with sauerkraut. The **brains,** less often seen than calves' brains, may be prepared in the same way. **Pigs' ears** have a chewy, gelatinous texture for which one has to develop a taste. I like them parboiled, crumbed, and either sautéed or fried, or stuffed and braised.

Behind the head comes the **shoulder** and **fatback,** the plain white fat sold for larding meat, for barding, and for lining molds for pâtés. Below the fatback and before the loin comes the **shoulder butt,** used fresh for braising, roasting, and boiling, and also one of the choicest smoked cuts. Adjoining it is a very fatty square piece at the end of the head known as a **jowl butt** or pig's jowl, mostly smoked like bacon and extensively used in southern cooking—in boiled dishes, boiled with greens, or occasionally sliced and fried.

The **loin** is one of the choicest cuts. It extends from the shoulder to the ham and includes the rib and loin sections and the tenderloin. Rib chops are smaller and less choice than the loin chops, which contain a good piece of the tenderloin and are sautéed (see pages 425–426), and braised. **Loin chops** cut extra thick are often split and stuffed before braising. In certain parts of the country or in pork stores, the succulent little tenderloin is removed and sold separately for sautéing, braising, or broiling. The loin is the most popular roast (see pages 417–419), and the best for roasting is the **center cut,** which contains part of the rib and part of the loin. It is also the most costly. The two end cuts of the loin are the blade end or rib end (sometimes cut into pieces and sold as thick, meaty country-style ribs) and the sirloin end, the part next to the ham. The loin cuts may be roasted with the bone, or boned, rolled, and tied. For a crown roast, 2 loin roasts are tied together. Boned loin is also good for braising. Below the loin, more or less in the center of the pig but extending right through, is the side pork or siding, which is boned from the rib cage and smoked for **bacon** or salted for salt pork. Some is put down in a brine, or pickle, and sold as pickled pork. The **spareribs** themselves are roasted (see *T & P*, page 84), braised, or broiled. The **heart** is mostly stuffed and braised. The **tail** is a much neglected little delicacy that is sometimes cut deep into the animal, poached, and barbecued, or cut short only with a small bit of bone and boiled with sauerkraut, collards, or other greens.

The hind legs of the pig are sold as fresh hams or smoked hams, either whole or separated into the butt end, that closest to the loin, and the shank end, closest to the foot. I prefer the shank end; it slices better. Fresh ham takes to roasting (see pages 421–422) or to braising. Steaks from ½ inch to 2 inches thick may be cut from the leg and boiled, sautéed, or braised. **Pork kidneys,** though rather hard to find, are tender and sweet and, to my taste, quite as good as other kidneys. Soak in milk for an hour before cooking. **Pork liver** can be sautéed, but is more often ground for pâtés and terrines because of its high fat content and excellent flavor. The front section of the pig includes the **shoulder** and **butt.** The small **picnic shoulder,** which is cut deep into the shoulder, around and down to the front foot, in the shape of a ham, is often smoked and sold as a picnic ham. It is also excellent fresh, braised, boiled, or roasted. You often see picnic shoulder and picnic ham in supermarket ads. While they have a different bone structure from ham and are less simple to carve, the meat is well flavored and they are good, economical buys. If the picnic shoulder is short cut, a piece of the leg about 2 or 3 inches long is removed. This is the **hock,** which contains some very edible meat covered by a thin layer of fat and skin. When boiled or braised (see *T & P*, page 161), hocks make a delectable dish, and the gelatin in the skin helps to thicken the liquid. Pork hocks are often lightly smoked and may be treated like smoked ham and served hot or cold. In some markets you will find **pigs' feet,** cut long or short. Italian and Chinese markets cut them deep enough to include the hock; others cut them short, about 4 to 6 inches. Around holiday time you might see in Italian markets a specialty called *zampone,* which is the entire picnic shoulder, hock, and foot boned and stuffed with sausage meat. It is excellent poached. Pork meat and other bits of the pig are, of course, turned into various kinds of sausage. Even the blood goes into the making of blood sausage.

Ham. There was a time when there were as many different country hams as there are states in the Union, but things have changed. Now the majority of hams we find in the market are what are known as ready-to-eat hams, very lightly cured and bland in taste. Although they are labeled ready-to-eat, this merely means that they have been heated during the curing and smoking process to a high enough internal temperature to make them safe for consumption. But they still need the benefit of cooking. I usually bake these hams for 10 to 15 minutes a pound in a 350° oven, basting them with a little red or white wine, cider, or ginger ale to add flavor. (I would avoid, if I were you, that famous southern recipe that calls for basting ham with Coca-Cola.) Country hams are still available by mail from smokehouses in certain states such as Kentucky, Vermont, Virginia, and New York. These are more heavily cured and smoked, and far more delicious. Basically, the difference between these hams and the supermarket hams is that they often need soaking and are then boiled or baked slowly in a covered pan (see *T & P*, page 79) and sometimes glazed before serving. They should be cooked according to the directions that come with them. You can often buy slices of country ham from these mail-order smokehouses. Broil, like ham slices (see page 440), or cook in a heavy skillet and eat for breakfast with eggs, fried potatoes, and red-eye gravy made from the pan drippings. A good ham will keep for several weeks in the refrigerator. Eat it cold or use in casseroles, soufflé, quiches, and ham mousse.

One of the world's greatest hams is Smithfield ham, a Virginia ham with a special cure that may be made only in the county of the same name. Heavily cured and quite salty, it is usually eaten cold, in paper-thin slices. The taste is quite similar to that of Chinese ham, and practically all Chinese restaurants use Smithfield ham in their dishes. Canned hams are, to me, the least interesting in flavor of all the hams, but some people find them extremely practical to have on hand. Be sure to prepare according to the directions given on the can.

Veal

The best veal, which exists in this country in exceedingly small quantities, is ivory colored, an indication that it has been specially raised (see page 400). Most supermarkets in major cities carry premium veal, although across the country a good deal of the veal sold in supermarkets is a reddish-pink and is really baby beef. In the last 10 years, better meat markets have been carrying milk-fed veal from calves up to 6 months of age. It is tender and pale, admittedly costly but worth the money. Because of its youth, veal has very little fat and needs some moisture in cooking. Usually it is better braised than roasted or broiled. This is also one of the most gelatinous of the meat animals, and the bones and bony cuts are ideal for stocks, aspics, and meat jellies.

The head, while difficult to get in this country, is a great delicacy; in France it is boiled and served as *tête de veau vinaigrette*. The small and extremely tender **tongue** is delectable braised, especially in the Italian manner, with tomato sauce, and is often incorporated into terrines and pâtés. **Calves' brains,** by far the best of the animal brains, are usually blanched about 15 minutes in slightly acidulated water, then sautéed, but they are also extremely good poached, sliced, and served cold with vinaigrette sauce.

Bony veal **neck** is used extensively for stock (see *T & P*, page 24). The pieces of meat from the bones make lovely jellied veal. Veal **shoulder** is generally boned and braised (see *T & P*, page 145). Eat hot or press under a heavy weight and serve cold, with the natural jelly around it. Use boned, cubed shoulder meat for stews and braised dishes. Shoulder chops, while not the most desirable, braise successfully. I don't recommend sautéing them. Veal **loin** and **saddle** (the saddle comprises the 2 loins and part of the legs) is the tenderest part of the animal. A rolled and tied saddle, boned or bone in, sometimes with the kidneys included, is a luxurious and spectacular roast for a special dinner party. A roast of rib chops is called a rack. A loin may be roasted whole, with or without the bone, or cut into thick chops for sautéing or braising (pages 411–412). If the chops are broiled, baste well with butter or oil to prevent the meat from drying out. The **kidneys** are very delicate and lend themselves to broiling, braising, and sautéing. Never overcook or they will toughen. Kidneys should still be slightly pink in the center. Certain butchers will prepare **rump** of veal as a roast. While not all markets carry this, it is worth a try.

The **leg** is prepared in many different ways. It may be roasted (usually after being boned and tied), or braised, or sliced into veal cutlets. Steaks may be cut across the leg, either bone out or with the tiny round bone left in. Smaller, thinner pieces of veal leg, cut as scaloppine or veal scallops and pounded thin, are usually sautéed (pages 406–408) or braised as veal birds (pages 409–410), although they are occasionally deep-fried, as wiener schnitzel (see *T & P*, page 227). The **breast,** boned or bone in, is an excellent cut for roasting (page 413) and stuffing and braising (see *T & P*, page 148) and for stews. There's a famous Italian dish, *cima di vitello,* for which the stuffed breast is wrapped in a cloth and poached, then braised and eaten cold. The breast meat has a rather long grain and an interesting texture. The bones from both the leg and the breast are much valued for stocks, as is the highly gelatinous **knuckle.** The **shank,** which adjoins the breast, is commonly braised for such dishes as the Italian *ossi buchi* (page 416), or it may be used, like the neck, for jellied veal, once a very popular American summer dish. Although **calves' feet** are pretty hard to come by these days, if you find them they make a delicious dish when poached and served with a sauce poulette, hollandaise, or Béarnaise. Highly gelatinous, the feet are much sought after for stock.

Calves' liver and **sweetbreads** are the most delicious and prized of all. Veal sweetbreads may be blanched in boiling water for 12 minutes. They are then plunged into ice water, and when cool enough to handle, excess fatty pieces are removed. Sweetbreads are often placed in between 2 plates and weighed down before cooking. The liver may be sliced thick and broiled rare (see *T & P*, page 121); sliced thin and sautéed quickly (pages 451–452); rolled, tied, barded with bacon, and roasted rare, to be served with mustard sauce; or cut into pieces and deep-fried, along with kidneys, brains, and thin pieces of veal, for an Italian *fritto misto* (see *T & P*, page 221). Veal hearts, which weigh about a pound, lend themselves to braising (page 455). Ground veal goes into certain sausages, such as bockwurst and bratwurst, and is important in the making of pâtés and terrines. Because of its lack of fat, it makes a very dry meat loaf unless combined with fattier meats such as pork and beef.

Melons

Some of the members of this large family are seasonal. Others, like cantaloupes, are widely grown and can be found in the markets throughout the year. Melons are one of the hardest fruits to pick out. If you have a trustworthy fruit dealer, ask him to select a melon for you; he should know more about judging ripeness than you. If the melon you buy is less than ripe, leave it at room temperature until it ripens. A ripe melon will keep for a week in the refrigerator, 2 to 4 days if cut and tightly covered with plastic wrap. Leave the seeds in a cut piece; it helps to keep the flesh moist.

Cantaloupes. Small melons with webbed skin and orange flesh. Extremely sweet and pungent at their best, tasteless at their worst. While not as desirable as other melons, cantaloupes are the most easily found. Halve and eat for breakfast, as a dessert, or cut into balls for a fruit compote.

Casabas. White-fleshed melons, extremely sweet when ripe, undistinguished when not. Serve like cantaloupes, or as a first course, with prosciutto or Virginia ham and a little pepper.

Cranshaws or Crenshaws. Yellow-skinned with pinky-orange flesh, these are probably the most delicious of all melons when fully ripe, with an intoxicating bouquet. Enjoy them as they come, unsullied by sugar or liqueurs, or eat as a first course with prosciutto or Virginia ham.

Hand melons. Named for the man who created this strain, Hand melons have a beautiful perfume, even before they are cut, and a superb flavor. Raised in relatively few parts of the country, so one must search them out. Do not chill. Eat at the peak, as soon as possible. Fine for breakfast, dessert, or as a first course with ham.

Honeydews. White-skinned, green-fleshed melons that 9 times out of 10 are quite dull. The tenth time they can come right out and surprise you. Good used in combination with other varieties in a melon-ball compote.

Persian melons. Large russet-colored, orange-fleshed melons with a breathtaking flavor and bouquet when fully ripe. In the market in the fall, all too briefly. Serve cool, not chilled, with a tiny touch of sugar if you wish, nothing more.

Spanish melons. Between a Cranshaw and a casaba. Extraordinarily sweet and pungent melons that come late in the fall and last into the winter.

Watermelons. Round or oblong in shape, brilliant green on the outside and pure watermelon pink on the inside, these are the quintessential American melons, with a luscious, liquid sweetness that is positively addictive. Pick one up and thump it with your knuckles. If it sounds hollow and resounding, it is probably full of juice. Best eaten very cold on a hot day. Good for sherbet. The leftover rind makes highly prized watermelon pickles. To gild the lily (or watermelon), fill it with liquor for drunken watermelon (see *T & P*, page 350).

Mushrooms. Cultivated mushrooms with firm, snowy-white caps are available year round. They need no peeling and usually no washing—just a wipe with a damp cloth. Should mushrooms look dusty or dirty, toss under running water in a colander and dry well before cooking. Sauté sliced or whole mushrooms quickly over fairly high heat in butter, or butter and oil, seasoning them with salt and pepper. Use alone, or combine with other vegetables. Cook mushrooms soon after buying; they discolor and shrivel if stored more than a few days. Discolored mushrooms (often sold off at a lower price in markets) may be made into duxelles, a delicious mushroom paste (see page 535). Add some to scrambled eggs, omelets, vegetables, sauces, stuffings, or spread on toast as an appetizer with drinks. Use raw firm white mushroom caps for salads, sauté (page 154), broil (see *T & P*, page 131), or cook à la Grecque (see *T & P*, page 60).

Dried mushrooms, imported from Europe and the Orient, are usually wild, not cultivated, varieties, with totally different tastes. Soak in warm water, or in wine, to rehydrate, then drain, and chop or slice. They don't have the texture of fresh mushrooms but bring delicious flavor to stews, soups, and certain meat dishes.

MUSTARD. A universal and widely used spice of varying degrees of hotness and pungency. Available in two forms: dry mustard or mustard powder and prepared mustard of different types, strengths, and flavors. Most of the good prepared mustards, like the Dijon mustards, come from France. Some contain coarsely ground mustard seeds; others are perfumed with herbs such as tarragon, dill, or thyme, spiced with green peppercorns, or mixed with wine. These mustards are delicious with meats, in certain sauces, and for dishes where mustard is the main flavoring, like the classic French *lapin à la moutarde*. Sometimes kidneys or liver are coated with mustard before being broiled. German mustards mostly ally a little sweetness to their bite and are excellent with pork, ham, and sausage dishes. American mustards are the mildest, with a sweet-sour flavor, and are good mainly for hot dogs, hence the popular name, "ball-park mustard." Use dry or prepared mustards to flavor sauces, dressings, mayonnaise.

NECTARINES. Fruits that look like fuzzless peaches, with golden flesh and a lovely aroma that sometimes belies their flavor and ripeness. Look for well-fleshed fruits, not too hard, or they will take a long time to ripen. Best eaten as a dessert fruit, with no accompaniments.

NUTS

Today, most nuts sold for cooking purposes, such as baking, stuffings, and garnishing, are already shelled. They come either whole and blanched (with the skins removed) or unblanched, sliced, chopped, or broken into pieces. In supermarkets, nuts are sold in glassine or cellophane bags or vacuum cans, but if you use a lot of nuts and can locate a store where they are sold in bulk, you can save an amazing amount of money. Why pay for packaging? Bulk nuts (or any nuts apart from those in the shell or in sealed vacuum tins) keep better if put in plastic bags and stored in the freezer. Exposure to heat turns the oil in nuts rancid. Distributors of nuts always keep them at freezing temperatures because they hold better, so unless you are using them right away I strongly recommend that you store them in the freezer. Thaw at room temperature before using. You can chop whole nuts by hand with a chef's knife, but it is infinitely faster and easier to chop or grind them in a food processor or blender, if you own one.

Almonds. The nuts we use most in cooking and as a garnish for sautéed and broiled fish and vegetables—either the long Jordan almonds or the California almonds, which are interchangeable. You can buy almonds unblanched or blanched and whole, thinly sliced, slivered, or chopped, and toasted. To blanch almonds in the skin, plunge them into boiling water, remove after 30 seconds, and when cool, rub the skins off between thumb and forefinger. Unless a recipe requires pure white, blanched almonds, I think a little toasting for 10 minutes or so in a 350° oven, either before or after cutting, improves the flavor of almonds—and most other nuts. Should a dish require a strong almond flavor, intensify it with 1 or 2 drops of almond extract.

Brazil nuts. These very large nuts are sold whole or sliced, and semi-blanched (with part of the brown skin on). Blanch if you wish. To slice them yourself, soak whole nuts in boiling water for 30 minutes to soften them up. Also improved by toasting at 350° for 15 to 20 minutes.

Filberts or hazelnuts (two names, but the same nut). These have heavy skins, and I strongly advise blanching them, or rubbing them vigorously between Turkish towels—it is amazing how much skin will come off. Available whole, sliced, or chopped, and also improved by a slight toasting.

Lichee nuts. See page 563.

Peanuts. Need no blanching since the skins rub off easily. Unless you buy raw peanuts, they are already roasted and need no further toasting. Be careful when chopping them in a blender or food processor not to overdo it, or they will turn into peanut butter. If that should happen, add a little salt and oil and enjoy your own good homemade product.

Pecans. Sold halved or chopped. They do not blanch well because of their crinkly contours. A strong-flavored nut, seldom in need of toasting. Excellent for pies, cakes, cookies, or in dishes such as celery and pecan ring (see *T & P*, page 294).

Pine nuts. The tiny kernels of certain pine cones, they are probably the least known of all nuts. There are two varieties. The thin, tapering pignolia nut is sold shelled and blanched. A very oily, delicately flavored nut, it is improved by toasting for 10 minutes at 350°. The harder-to-find Indian pine nuts of the Southwest are more the shape of a coffee bean and have to be shelled. They have a slightly more piny flavor, but may be used in the same ways, in stuffings for poultry (see *T & P*, page 89) and vegetables (see *T & P*, page 293), and in casseroles and various other dishes.

Pistachio nuts. The most distinctive because instead of being white-meated, like other nuts, they are pale to medium green in their natural state (avoid those that have been dyed red). More often used for decoration, because of their lovely color, than as an ingredient, although there are several cakes and a pistachio bread that include them in the batter. When bought shelled, they are usually salted, but the small amount of salt can usually be rubbed off and what remains is hardly noticeable. Pistachios are fairly easy to shell, because the nuts crack on one side during the roasting process. Extremely expensive but cheaper bought in bulk.

Walnuts. There are two varieties. The glorious American black walnut is practically unobtainable. If you are fortunate enough to find any, use them for black-walnut cake or to dress sautéed fish (see *T & P,* page 198), for they are as delicious as they are precious. The English walnut, grown extensively in California, is the common type. Usually bought shelled, in halves or broken into pieces. Like pecans, the contours of walnuts make them hard to blanch, but it can be done. Toasting at 350° for 15 to 20 minutes gives walnuts a different and better flavor. Next to almonds, the most popular nut for pastries, breads, cakes, cookies, and as a garnish for vegetables such as zucchini (page 175) and fish. Salted and toasted they are a popular and addictive snack or cocktail nibble.

OIL. A kitchen staple that varies enormously in quality, taste, and price. The finest oil, to my mind, is olive oil. One finds 8 or 10 different qualities, from the very rich first pressing, called "virgin olive oil," down to the low-quality oil made from the final pressing of fruit and cracked pits. The best and most flavorful, fruity olive oil comes from Provence, in the South of France. After this I would rate the better Italian and Greek oils and then the Spanish and North African. Buy the best you can afford and store it carefully. Olive oil should not be kept in the refrigerator (when refrigerated it turns thick and cloudy); if the weather is warm or the oil is left open for a long time, it can turn rancid, so buy in small quantities unless you are a liberal user. The vegetable oils (corn, cottonseed, soybean, peanut) are mostly flavorless and odorless—to my mind too tasteless for salads, but practical, inexpensive, and highly efficient for deep-frying, sautéing, mayonnaise, marinades, and general cooking. Peanut oil is my preference. Two other oils which have come into great favor in the last few years are safflower and sunflower oil. Both are very light, flavorless, and acceptable for frying, sautéing, baking, and certain pastries.

OKRA. See page 156.

ONIONS

The members of this family see more service in the kitchen than any other vegetable. They range from the dry yellow, white, and red onions to small brown shallots, green onions, leeks, garlic, and chives. When bought, dry onions, garlic, and shallots should be hard and firm, with no soft spots or green sprouting tops. Buy as needed and store in a cool, dry place. Refrigerate green onions, leeks, and chives.

Yellow globe onions. Sometimes called Spanish onions. General-purpose onions with brownish-yellow skin, either large or medium size. Excellent raw, baked, boiled, braised (see *T & P,* page 171), French-fried (see *T & P,* page 222), or in soup (see *T & P,* page 39). Used in many dishes, chopped or sliced.

Large white onions. Sometimes called Bermuda onions, though they no longer come from that island. Mild and sweet, excellent French-fried or for salads. Sweet white onions, namely Walla Walla sweets and Maui sweets, are superb in salads or sandwiches, or sliced in vinaigrette sauce.

Small white onions. About 1½ to 2 inches in diameter. Fairly mild. Excellent whole in stews and braised dishes, such as coq au vin (see page 325 and *T & P*, page 163), and boeuf à la mode (see *T & P*, page 154) or Beef in Red Burgundy (page 368). Smaller ones may be prepared à la Grecque (see *T & P*, page 60). If dropped into boiling water for 1 to 2 minutes, the skins will peel off easily. Canned white onions are acceptable, if not overcooked.

Pearl onions or pickling onions. Very tiny white onions, usually pickled but also good for garnishing dishes.

Red or Italian onions. Exceptionally sweet and decorative onions, delicious raw in sandwiches and salads.

Green onions. Also called **scallions** and, in some parts of the country, **shallots,** which they are not. Fresh young onions with a white bulb and leafy green top, harvested while immature. Those with thin white bulbs are to be preferred to the rounder, thicker ones. Trim off the root end, all but an inch or two of the green tops, and the outer layer of skin before using. To cook, see page 160, or page 60 of *T & P* for an à la Grecque recipe. Chop and sauté for use in various dishes. May be used in place of shallots. Eat raw in vegetable hors d'oeuvre and salads.

Leeks. Somewhat similar in appearance to green onions, but much larger, with darker, coarser green tops. Known in France as "poor man's asparagus," but expensive here and often hard to find. To prepare and cook, see page 152. Widely used as a flavoring, an aromatic vegetable in soups, stews, and braised dishes, traditional in pot-au-feu. Good poached à la Grecque (see *T & P*, page 60), braised, or broiled and served with vinaigrette sauce.

Shallots. Sometimes called the aristocrat of the onion family, these small bulbs of cloves covered with papery brown skin have a subtle flavor, more pungent than onion, more delicate than garlic. A little goes quite a long way. Chopped and sautéed, they are an important flavoring for many dishes, from sauces such as Béarnaise, Bordelaise, and diable (see pages 532 and 533) to sautéed chicken. Much used in French cooking. Hard to find in stores, but available by mail order. Packaged freeze-dried shallots are more easily found, although not as desirable.

Garlic. The most pungent member of the family. Widely used in soups, sauces, salads, braised dishes, sautés, and as a seasoning for roasts, such as leg of lamb or pork loin. Always use cloves of garlic, never garlic powder or garlic salt, which have an ersatz flavor. Look for full, firm, heavy heads and buy garlic loose, not packaged in the cardboard boxes sold in supermarkets—the packaged kind is frequently old and stale. Buy only as much as needed and use quickly. To peel, either drop in boiling water for 5 seconds to loosen the skin, or bruise the clove slightly with the flat of a large knife blade, which splits the skin. Chopping garlic with a touch of salt prevents it from sticking to the knife blade. In sautéing, do not let garlic brown or burn or it will turn bitter. Garlic cloves cooked whole in their husks, either in liquid or in a sauté, add flavor but lose their strong pungency and become delicate, mild, and buttery-soft. Squeeze the garlic out of the husk after cooking.

Chives. Herbs that are also members of the onion family, with a delicate onion flavor. Sold cut or in pots—the more you cut chives, the better they grow. The blue chive flowers have an intense onion flavor and can be tossed in salads. Chop chives and use in fines herbes mixtures for omelets, in scrambled eggs, cold soups, salads, herbed mayonnaise, and dressings, on sliced tomatoes, or anywhere their bright color and zippy flavor are appropriate.

ORANGES. Smooth-skinned Florida oranges, the Spanish or Valencia type, are most favored for juice. The temple orange, which has a more textured skin, is preferable for eating or slicing. California oranges, mostly navel oranges, have a more brilliant color than the Valencias and usually a thicker, pithier skin. They are better for slicing, sectioning, and general cooking, extremely good for candying and glazing, or for eating out of hand. Try to find oranges that are not waxed. Pick those that are not overripe or scarred and do not have soft spots. They should be firm and heavy in the hand, which means that they are full of juice (this applies to all citrus fruits). Team oranges with onions for a salad. Use the juice and/or grated rind as a flavoring for soufflés, sauces, glazes, frozen desserts, Bavarian cream (see *T & P*, page 359), and as the fruit for open-face tarts. Section or slice oranges for fruit salads, compotes.

PAPAYAS. A tropical fruit with brilliant orange flesh, round black seeds, and an extremely delicate, unusual flavor and texture. Known as pawpaw in the West Indies, where it is also cooked, when green and unripe, as a vegetable. Fully ripened, soft-skinned papayas are the best buy. Serve chilled, halved, and seeded, with a wedge of lime, or as a first course with prosciutto, like melon. Delicious in fruit salads or, puréed in a blender or food processor, for ice cream and sherbet.

PAPRIKA. Paprika can easily fool you—it looks like red pepper, but it's not. Nor was it created to garnish food and look pretty, as some people think. Paprika is a spice in its own right. The finest comes from Hungary, where it is much used in dishes such as paprikash and goulash, in sauces, and in salad dressings. There is also a paprika from Spain, coarser in texture and flavor, that I favor a great deal for Spanish recipes. The spice is ground from a variety of capsicum peppers, some of which are sweet, others hot—in some cases, almost as hot as cayenne pepper, from another capsicum variety. A very perishable, heat-sensitive spice, paprika should be kept in a tin, never a glass bottle or shaker, preferably in the refrigerator. If you are purchasing paprika in bulk from a specialty food shop, you may be asked if you want the sweet or the hot variety—sweet paprika is what is called for in most recipes, unless otherwise specified.

PARSNIPS. See page 161.

PASTA. Pasta is one of the 3 or 4 most popular foods in existence, and as versatile as any single food can be. The Chinese had noodles; the Italians perfected pasta. In one form or another it has gone the rounds of most of the major Eastern and Western countries. Nothing takes more readily to seasonings and flavorings, and it can be anything from a first course or main dish, with a sauce, to a salad, a soup, or a dessert. Nowadays, with the aid of an electric or hand-operated pasta machine, it's easy to make your own pasta fresh, dry it briefly, and cook it right away (see page 276). Fresh pasta takes only a few minutes to cook, much less than the commercial, dried type. You can also, in some cities, buy pasta from shops that make it fresh. There are many, many brands of dried pasta, and you should shop around until you find one to your liking—the imported Italian pasta is usually the best, and of the American brands I prefer Buitoni.

In dried pastas, we have the various round, straight ones, starting with the very small spaghettini, usually listed on the package as spaghettini #2, which can be used generally with any type of the spaghetti sauces, from the simplest of all, which is just melted butter and grated cheese. Then you have larger spaghetti and macaroni of various sizes and shapes, from the small elbow macaroni to larger, straight macaroni to the huge ziti. Pasta comes in dozens of other shapes; some are like little seashells (conchiglie) or butterflies (farfalle). The cooking time for dried pastas varies according to shape and size. Naturally, the thin spaghettini cooks faster than the large macaroni and the small seashells faster than the large ones. This is something you gauge from the package directions and your own experience and preference—whether you like your pasta cooked to the traditional Italian al dente stage, still firm to the bite, or cooked to a mushy paste. Pasta should always be cooked in a large pot in ample amounts of salted water kept at a rolling boil throughout the cooking period. After 6 minutes, taste often until it reaches the degree of doneness you prefer. Drain at once. If you wish, you may rinse the pasta with hot or cold water and then with hot water again. If you are going to serve the pasta on individual plates, toss it with a spoonful or two of oil first so it doesn't stick together, then add the sauce. However, I have come to like the modern Italian way of saucing pasta, in which the cooked pasta is marinated in the hot sauce for 2 or 3 minutes and tossed well with 2 forks so that it becomes imbued with the flavors. Pasta is usually served with grated Parmesan, Romano, or asiago cheese, save for seafood pastas and one or two others that are best without it—though that, too, is a matter of personal taste.

PEACHES. The sweet, tender, and perishable peaches that used to abound in our markets have been almost ruined by modern growing and shipping practices. Now peaches may look beautiful, but they are hard-hearted under the skin. Naturally, try to find soft-fleshed ones. Take advantage of the 2 to 3 weeks when local tree-ripened peaches may be found. Early white peaches, if you can find them, are pure nectar. Simply chill and slice; eat with sugar and cream. The later, golden-fleshed peaches are good this way, too, or with a raspberry purée (see *T & P*, page 348). They are superb in ice cream (see *T & P*, page 372), and for preserves or pies. Peaches may be broiled (see *T & P*, page 134), baked, or poached (see *T & P*, page 61) with the addition of a little lemon, vanilla, or bourbon for flavoring, and make a great dessert. Poaching is a good way to treat hard peaches. For certain cooked dishes, such as roast duck with peaches (see *T & P*, page 95), a firm canned variety may replace the fresh.

PEARS. Like peaches, pears for the market are picked too green and are artificially ripened. They never approach the lusciousness of tree-ripened fruit. If you find pears that are soft and ripe to the touch, rush them home and eat them at once. The Bartlett or Williams pear, bell-shaped and yellow, is the earliest, on the market from July to November. At its best, it has an indescribable perfume and wonderful flavor and texture and is delicious eaten raw or poached. The small sweet brown Seckel, good for eating, pickling, and cooking, arrives in September. The later, winter pears are the chunky green or greenish-yellow Anjou; the Bosc, brown or russet color with a tapering neck; the large Comice, yellow or greeny-yellow, splashed with red; and the brown Winter Nelis, all artificially ripened. However, all these pears poach extremely well (see *T & P*, page 62), and most of them bake well. Baked pears are usually not peeled, just halved, cored, and baked with brown sugar and a clove or two for about an hour in a 325° oven. The result, when cloaked in heavy cream, is pretty spectacular. Pears make interesting tarts (see page 513) and fritters (see *T & P*, page 223), and are good sautéed (see *T & P*, page 214). They are very friendly to cheese—Roquefort, Brie, Camembert, and practically all of the fine cheeses are good companions for pears.

PEAS

Green peas. For fresh peas, see page 163. This is one vegetable that freezes well. Often frozen peas are better than fresh. Choose the tiny frozen peas and never follow the package directions or you will have stewed peas. Merely heat them through with butter to keep that nice crisp freshness.

Snow peas. Once a delicacy confined to Chinese restaurants, these edible-pod peas are becoming more generally available. Buy very young, when the pods are flat and the peas undeveloped. Test by breaking one. It should snap easily and have no strings down the sides. To cook, trim the ends and boil in salted water to cover for just a minute, until merely blanched, so they stay crisp. Drain and toss with butter. Or sauté sliced mushroom caps in butter, cut snow peas into julienne strips, and toss with the mushrooms for less than a minute, until they turn bright green. Add more butter, season with salt and pepper, and serve. They may also be cut into julienne strips, tossed quickly in butter, and added to lamb or beef stew at the last minute, as a garnish. Frozen snow peas are passable, but they lack the delicious crispness of the fresh.

Sugar snap peas. These are a new variety of edible-pod pea developed fairly recently in Idaho and California. They are similar to snow peas, but the pod is rounder, fuller, and a more brilliant green, with fully formed peas inside. These crunchy pods are delicious eaten raw, with a snap one finds in no other vegetable. If you cook them, remove the strings and give them minimum time—like snow peas, they cook in nothing flat. Sugar snaps are becoming a more familiar sight in better vegetable markets and are easy to grow if you have a garden. Be sure to pick them when they are young and tender.

PEPPER

Pepper is a funny spice, really three spices in one, each with a different flavor. Peppercorns are the berries of the tropical *Piper nigrum* vine and no relation to the vegetable capsicum pepper.

Black peppercorns. The dried berries—the ones we use most generally. They are sold whole, to be ground in a pepper mill, or cracked or ground by spice companies. As with other spices, best ground fresh.

White peppercorns. The black peppercorns minus the wrinkled black outer layer—and minus much of the flavor. Some people feel it is more refined to use white pepper in a white sauce or dish so that you don't have black specks. To me white pepper is unpleasant, acrid, and lacking in flavor. Forget niceties—who cares if there are a few flecks of black in a white sauce? It's the taste that counts. To make aromatic pepper: grind a mixture of 3 parts black peppercorns, 2 parts white peppercorns (in this case the white is traditional, but you can use extra black), and 1 part allspice berries.

Green peppercorns. The fresh immature berries, imported preserved in brine or frozen, are soft in texture, with an extremely pungent and exciting flavor, totally different from dried peppercorns. They have been on the market less than 15 years and are our newest flavor. Very perishable, they should be used quickly, made into green peppercorn butter (see page 318) and frozen, or put into a small jar, covered with water, and frozen. Use crushed green peppercorns in sauces and butter to serve with meat, poultry, and fish, as a replacement for crushed black peppercorns in such dishes as broiled peppered duckling (see *T & P*, page 118) or steak au poivre (see *T & P*, page 176).

Cayenne pepper. Not ground from peppercorns but from the capsicum pepper (see next entry).

PEPPERS

Sweet or bell peppers. Members of the capsicum genus; come in green, red, and yellow. The red and yellow peppers are ripe versions of the green. Look for firm, shapely peppers without soft or discolored spots or wrinkled skins. Remove stem end, seeds, and white ribs, and slice into strips or rings, or chop, for salads, sautés, cooked dishes. Personally, I feel that if peppers are to be served cooked, they should be broiled until the thin, indigestible skin chars and can be scraped off (see page 165, and the recipes that follow).

Pimientos. Another type of sweet red capsicum pepper, available skinned, cored, processed, and packed in jars or cans. Very mild in flavor. Use for color in salads and as a garnish.

Hot chili peppers. There are many different varieties with varying degrees of heat. These are also members of the capsicum genus. When preparing chilies for cooking, remove all the tiny seeds that hold the heat. Wash hands well after handling; the juice from chilies is highly irritating to the skin and eyes.

Tabasco is a hot, pungent liquid pepper sauce made from small, fiery red Tabasco chilies packed into barrels, sealed with salt, aged 3 years, then mixed with vinegar and bottled. A most valuable product for cooking. Use as a substitute for cayenne pepper, in sauces such as hollandaise and in egg dishes. I always add a dash of Tabasco to scrambled eggs.

PERSIMMONS. These brilliant orange fruit with smooth skin that we get from October almost until Christmas are easy to spot in the markets because of their glowing color and the way they are packed, each in its own little container within the crate. There are two kinds of cultivated persimmon, the bright orange type, slightly pointed at one end, which is the leading variety, and the flatter Japanese persimmon. In many areas of this country you also find tiny native persimmons growing wild that are gathered when they are dead-ripe and fall from the tree. Persimmon pudding, made with the puréed pulp of wild persimmons mixed with flour, milk, sugar, and spices is a Midwestern specialty. Although there is nothing more lusciously sweet than the flesh of persimmons, they should not be eaten until they are yieldingly soft and ripe, which is something you can't tell by the color of the skin, only by touch. An unripe persimmon is very astringent and mouth-puckering. While I am hopelessly addicted to eating persimmons just as they are, you can make them into a superb sherbet or ice cream, too.

PHEASANT. One of our finest game birds. Raised extensively on game farms and always available. There was a time when pheasant and other game were not considered to be edible until they had been hung in the barn or a tree long enough to become quite green and odoriferous. They were then referred to as "high," which they certainly were. We have, thank heavens, graduated from this barbaric custom. Pheasant must be cooked in such a way that the breast meat is kept moist, otherwise it becomes dry and unpalatable. For roast pheasant, bacon or barding fat is usually draped over the breast as protection and lubrication. Young tender pheasant may be sautéed like chicken or broiled, while older pheasants are best braised or fricasseed. For recipes see pages 352–356.

PINEAPPLES. One of the Western Hemisphere's great food gifts to the world and long a symbol of hospitality. There are several varieties, from the very small sugar pineapples, about 4 to 6 inches long, to the conical Brazilian pineapples (said to be the original fruit) that run 12 to 14 inches. Pineapples are in the market all year, brought in from Hawaii, Mexico, Honduras, the Dominican Republic, and Costa Rica. To test for ripeness, lift the fruit to see if it is heavy with juice, press the skin at the bottom to see if it is soft, and smell it—there should be a full, fruity fragrance. Some say that if a center frond pulls out easily the fruit is ripe. Avoid fruit that looks old or dry or has brown leaves.

Large pineapples are a better buy, as there is proportionally more edible flesh. To peel a pineapple, slice off the bottom and leafy top and cut away the rind with a sharp knife, removing the little eyes with the knife point. Cut into fingers or crosswise slices and remove the core. There is a special cutter, resembling a wheel, that simultaneously cores pineapple and cuts it into fingers. Unless you are fortunate enough to get a fully ripened, sweet fruit, it will usually need sugaring to taste. Pineapple may be broiled and sautéed, but to my mind it is best served raw and very cold, with some added flavor, such as a sprinkling of rum, kirsch, or framboise (white alcohol made from raspberries). For buffet presentation, cut off the top, remove the flesh with a small ball cutter, sugar it, and return to the shell, either alone or with other fruits, and chill before serving. Canned pineapple is one of the more successful canned fruits.

PLUMS. In the summer, plums are in season through July, August, and September in at least 10 to 12 different colors, shapes, and flavors. The most common are the tender-skinned, yellow-fleshed red plums that must be eaten very ripe or they are sour to the tongue. They are followed by the Japanese plum or greengage, with greeny-yellow skin and yellow flesh, excellent for tarts, pies, stewed plums, and preserves. Then come the large yellow plums, good for eating raw, for baking, or for poaching, like pears and peaches, in a red-wine syrup or a plain syrup flavored with liqueur. Greengage and yellow plums have a delicious sweetness. The last plum of the season is the small blue-black Italian prune plum. Rich in flavor and high in natural sugar, with a pit that separates easily from the firm flesh, this is the kind dried for prunes. It is also a perfect cooking plum for tarts and kuchen, preserves, puddings, baking, and poaching. Extremely good if flavored with a little cinnamon or a little plum brandy or cognac. All plums should be soft to the touch; prune plums will be a little firmer than others. If hard when bought, they can be ripened in a plastic bag in a dark place.

POMEGRANATES. A subtropical fruit with a long history that supposedly originated in Persia. Now widely cultivated in California, they are fairly plentiful in markets from late fall until December. The fruit is about the size of an apple with a glossy hard red or purplish-red skin and lives up to its name (pomegranate means apple with many seeds) by being loaded with edible seeds in brilliant red pulp capsules that have a tart-sweet taste. The Mexicans use these jewel-like seeds to garnish dishes, and a few scattered over a green salad add a dash of color and an intriguing flavor. Eating a pomegranate is rather a production, as you have to strip the spongy outer membrane from the pulpy seeds or squeeze them to extract the juice. Pomegranate juice is sold bottled and also made into grenadine, the red syrup used in mixed drinks.

POTATOES
It was once possible to have a pretty good working knowledge of the different varieties of potato and to choose the best for each cooking purpose. Now, with

the standardization of agricultural produce, potatoes have become anonymous. We get simply—potatoes. All we can determine about them is that they come from Idaho, or Maine, or Oregon, or California. There are 2 basic types, mealy and waxy. Waxy potatoes hold together better when boiled and sliced and are preferable for potato salad, sautéed potatoes and hash browns (see page 170). Mealy potatoes are best for baking and roasting, and are also good for boiling. Either type may be French-fried (see *T & P*, page 229).

The **brown-skinned Idaho** is our most dependable potato. Grown in lava soil, it is extremely mealy and bakes perfectly. May also be boiled, French-fried, or used for potatoes Anna (see *T & P*, page 238) or a gratin (page 169). The **russet** potato, very like the Idaho, and the round white Oregon potato can be used in the same ways. **Maine** potatoes, available in the early part of the year, are semiwaxy and best boiled. The widely available **California Long White** I find variable in quality. Carefully boiled in its skin, it remains firm and waxy, excellent for potato salad and sautéed potatoes. It may also be baked or French-fried. The small round so-called **new potato** (not really new, but dug before it reaches maturity) is a waxy type available almost all year, ideal for boiling or steaming whole. Do not peel. Scrub well, then cut a little belly band of skin from around the center to keep it from bursting. Slightly undercook; it should be firm and crisp. Use for hot potato salad as one of the accompanying vegetables for any kind of boiled beef or stew. When buying potatoes, reject those that are soft, have wrinkled, scarred, or green-tinged skins (caused by exposure to the light), and sprouting eyes. Store in a cool, dry, well-ventilated cellar or cabinet, away from the light.

To bake potatoes (see page 168), just scrub well and leave in their jackets. I like the skins crisp, so I don't rub them with fat, and I never, ever bake them in foil, which makes the skins soggy. To boil, either peel or leave the skins on (they hold together better for slicing), put into a deep saucepan with salted water to cover, put on the lid, and boil until tender when pierced with a knife, about 20 to 25 minutes, according to size and whether they are left whole or cut into pieces. After boiling, drain, return to the pan, and let dry out over heat, covered, shaking the pan so they don't stick. To steam, put into an adjustable vegetable steamer in a deep pan with just enough water to come almost to the bottom of the steamer. Bring to a boil, cover, and steam until tender—slightly longer than for boiling.

QUAIL. These delicate little game birds are expensive luxuries, except in parts of the country where quail shooting is a major sport. Quail are raised on game farms, and may be bought fresh or frozen. Frozen quail are quite plentiful. Quail lend themselves to roasting, broiling like squab, and sautéing. One of my favorite methods is to remove the breasts and sauté them quickly (see *T & P*, page 191), using the less meaty legs and carcass for broth and soups. They are also delicious roasted and braised (pages 349–351). Whole roasted or broiled quail should be eaten with the fingers and, to my mind, they are not for company but for the family.

QUINCE. Rather like large, slightly misshapen apples with a pale-yellow skin, these are one of our oldest known fruits. But, alas, they seem to have gone out of fashion. There was a time when people planted a couple of quince trees in their gardens as a novelty and a change from other fruits, but that doesn't seem to happen any more. You may find quince in the markets from about October to December. They are in limited supply and fairly expensive, but if you haven't tried them you are missing out on a different and flavorful part of the fruit spectrum. Quince are too hard and tart to eat raw and must be poached or baked to bring out the perfume and flavor—poached quince make one of the best tarts I have ever tasted (see page 512). If you are poaching quince or making quince jelly, a heavenly preserve, tie the pectin-rich seeds in a cheese-cloth bag and cook them with the fruit to take advantage of their gelatinous quality (in the old days, quince seeds were used in hair fixatives). Another form of prepared quince of which I am very fond is the dense sweet-tart quince paste that comes canned from Spain and Mexico. In Latin American countries it is often served with a bland cheese, as a dessert, but I also like it as an accompaniment to the spicy Moroccan meat dish, kadjemoula (see page 397).

RABBIT. I'm always astounded by the number of people who say they don't like or have never eaten rabbit. They are to be pitied. I find this delicate, flavorful meat to be almost as useful as chicken. Commercially raised rabbits are available throughout the country, fresh and frozen. Fresh rabbits are usually sold skinned and cut up, if you so require. Or you may buy them whole and disjoint them yourself (see page 357). Frozen rabbits have been cut up and packaged. Wild rabbits, spoils of the hunter, must, of course, be skinned and cleaned. Young tender rabbits may be sautéed like chicken; older rabbits and wild rabbits are better braised or stewed.

RASPBERRIES. Perhaps the most luscious and, in some ways, the most glamorous of all the fruits. These brilliant red thimble-shaped berries are in the market for 8 to 10 months—at staggering prices. No other berry comes close to them in flavor, and raspberry jam is probably the most popular of all preserves. Apart from jam-making, it would be a crime to cook raspberries. Eat them raw, with or without sugar, with cream or crème fraîche, flavored with a little liqueur, if you like. Use them whole in little raspberry tarts. Purée them for raspberry fool (see page 516) or to spoon as a sauce over other fruits, such as strawberries, peaches, and pineapples.

RHUBARB. Long before supermarkets existed, rhubarb was the first fruit of the spring season, and a tonic, too, in the form of the rhubarb and soda given to children as a blood purifier. Nowadays the light-pink hothouse rhubarb appears on the market in January and lasts through most of the year. It is milder in flavor than the later, dark-red field-grown or garden rhubarb, with its coarse leaves and tart taste. Botanically a vegetable, but always used as a fruit, rhubarb is fragile and needs very little cooking, but a good deal of sweetening. Only the red stalks are used; the leaves contain too much oxalic acid and should not be eaten. Buy crisp, firm, tender stalks, wash, trim off leaves and base, and cut them into 3-inch lengths. Blanch in boiling water for 1 minute, then drop into a simple syrup and poach until just tender. Or place in a casserole or baking dish with sugar to taste and perhaps a little grated orange rind, cover, and bake in a 350° oven for 12 to 15 minutes. The fault with most rhubarb is that, over-cooked to a stringy pulp, it is not the firm, interesting fruit it can and should be. Rhubarb makes excellent pies (in the old days, it was known as pie plant); see page 509. Poached, puréed, and mixed with heavy cream, it becomes a delicious rhubarb fool.

RICE

Probably the most universally used of all the starches, yielding only to the potato in this country. Rice comes in two versions, long grain and short grain, and various types, and may be bought both loose and packaged. I like to use **long-grain rice** for boiling, pilafs, and most recipes where rice is needed, such as stuffings, salads, casseroles, the Spanish paella and arroz con pollo, and for egg-lemon soup (see *T & P*, page 320). **Short-grain rice** is better for puddings. **Converted or parboiled rice** works well steamed according to the directions on the package. **Precooked or instant rice** needs no cooking; it is just mixed with boiling water and left to stand, covered, for 5 minutes, until it swells. **Brown rice,** unpolished rice with merely the husk removed, is treated like long-grain rice but will take longer to cook—40 to 50 minutes. **Arborio or Italian short-grain rice,** with a plump starchy grain, is the classic rice for risotto (see page 291 and *T & P*, page 47), although I find long-grain rice works almost as well, if carefully cooked. One of the very few rices that still needs washing and soaking is the Indian **Basmati rice,** used in Indian cooking and also for Middle Eastern dishes such as *chello*. Rice expands considerably in cooking—1 cup of raw rice makes 3 cups cooked (converted rice somewhat less).

Wild rice. Not a rice but the seed of an aquatic grass that grows in the lake areas of Wisconsin, Minnesota, and other states. It is now being cultivated successfully, and I find the cultivated product superior, more uniform in size and somewhat better in flavor. Although wild rice has always been extremely expensive, it is in great demand both here and in Europe and is served a good deal (to excess, in my opinion) with game, poultry, and roast meats, and as a stuffing for birds. I find it pleasant to eat on occasion but boring if you have it too often. You can save a little money by ordering wild rice by mail from the source, rather than buying it packaged in a store. Or you may stretch it by combining it with long-grain rice. Wild rice is usually steamed (see page 294), and served with butter. Sautéed mushrooms, onions, and nuts are good additions.

ROCK CORNISH HENS. Small birds, weighing about 1 pound, a cross between a chicken and a game hen. Until recently, available mostly frozen, either stuffed or unstuffed, and while not too flavorful, popular because they were inexpensive, quick cooking, and the right size for an individual serving. Now available fresh, in larger sizes, and fattened properly, they are one of the more rewarding birds on the market, with delicate meat. Cook like squab chicken: roast, stuffed or unstuffed, at 400° for 35 to 40 minutes. Or you can broil or poach them (see page 336). Good hot or cold. If you don't find fresh Rock Cornish hens in your market, request them.

SALSIFY. This long, tapered, thin vegetable with rather brownish-black skin was tops in favor through the Victorian and Edwardian eras but seems to have lost caste in the last few years. To me it is one of the pleasantest winter vegetables. It should be steamed or boiled (see recipes, page 171). Oddly it is far more popular on the Pacific Coast than in the East, I find; there it is served very often with game, beef, and lamb. Sometimes it is called oyster plant, and some folk, notably Mrs. Rorer, felt it had the taste of oysters. Alas, I don't find that so.

SALT

Salt, which comes from salt flats formed by evaporated sea water and from land deposits of rock or crystalline salt, has always been considered to be the most basic and necessary of all seasonings. Salt is one of the oldest known methods of preserving or curing meat and fish, especially beef, ham, and cod. Salt is used to "cook" the Scandinavian cured salmon called *gravad laks* (see T & P, page 345). There are several kinds of salt on the market, of different strengths and types.

Ordinary table salt. Often mixed with magnesium or sodium carbonate to make it flow more easily, table salt is fine and quite intense in flavor. Use it with care.

Kosher salt. Coarser in texture and less salty in flavor, I consider this preferable for both cooking and the table. It is pure salt, with no additives.

Malden salt. This salt from England and other sea salts have large crystals and must be ground in a salt mill. They are expensive and are mostly used as table salt.

Ice-cream salt or rock salt. Used in ice-cream freezers or as a bed on which clams or oysters on the half shell are broiled or roasted. It has the coarsest crystals.

SAUSAGES

A favorite subject of mine. I adore them, especially with sauerkraut. You'll find it's not hard to make your own (see page 433). There are hundreds of varieties of sausage, but the following are some you find most often in supermarkets, pork butchers', and sausage shops. If you can shop around in ethnic markets, you'll find many more.

Blood sausages. There are two kinds. One, known in French as **boudin noir** or in German as **blutwurst,** is made with pigs' blood, meal, and coarse pieces of pork. Traditionally broiled and served with potatoes and applesauce. The other, known as blood-and-tongue sausages, is a dried, ready-to-eat blood sausage inlaid with pieces of tongue and fat, usually sliced and served cold.

Bockwurst. A German veal sausage, flavored with chives. Generally available in the spring. Poach or broil. Serve with mashed potatoes or sauerkraut, or for breakfast with scrambled eggs.

Bologna. The most common of the ready-to-eat sausages, served cold and thinly sliced. The American version of this Italian sausage is made with pork and beef, and is very bland.

Bratwurst. A veal and pork or pork sausage, rather bland, with an herby flavor, popular in German and Swiss cuisine. Readily available and delicious broiled and served with sauerkraut or sautéed onions. **Weisswurst** is very similar.

Chorizo. A sausage of coarsely cut pork colored with paprika, slightly piquant, and much used in Spanish dishes, such as paella, and in Mexican cooking. Can be bought fresh or dried. May be poached, sautéed, or broiled. Available in some supermarkets, in Spanish American markets, and imported, canned in lard, from Spain.

Cotechino. A large Italian sausage that should be poached before using.

Frankfurters. Our beloved hot dogs. The best are made from beef, the lesser quality from a variety of meats and innards. Their flavor ranges from very bland to very spicy. Look for all-beef kosher frankfurters and those known as "specials," which cost more but are better flavored and better eating. Heat through in water, or broil. **Knockwurst** are similar but thicker and heavier—4 to the pound as against 7 or 8 to the pound for frankfurters. Again, the all-beef are best.

Italian link sausages. Coarsely ground fresh pork sausages, either sweet or hot— the latter are spicily seasoned with very hot pepper. Much used in Italian cooking, with pasta, cooked with green peppers, or served with polenta. Good with eggs, or in a casserole with lentils (see *T & P*, page 295). Parboil sausages first to draw out excess fat. Place in a skillet with cold water to cover, bring to a boil for 1 minute, drain, then sauté or broil (page 435).

Kielbasa. A large, highly seasoned Polish sausage, widely available. Sold as long sausages or as rings. Some are fresh and should be poached or broiled; other types are dried and can be eaten cold, or heated. See page 29 for a delicious appetizer of kielbasa and croissants.

Mortadella. An enormous dried sausage, similar to bologna but larded with fat pork. Should be sliced very thin. Sometimes served wrapped around a bread-stick as an hors d'oeuvre.

Pork sausages. The familiar link sausage or sausage meat we buy or make. May be finely or coarsely chopped with varied seasonings, mostly sage, but also thyme, garlic, coriander, chives, and anise. Treat link sausages like Italian link sausages. Form sausage meat into flat cakes and sauté gently until cooked through and crisp on the outside.

Salami. There are a dozen different varieties of salami, from the very dry Italian Genoa salami containing peppercorns and garlic to salamis seasoned with paprika and other spices. Taste and decide which of the many are for you. May be bought sliced, but I prefer to buy a piece and slice my own.

SHELLFISH

Clams. Found in great variety along our shores. The two East Coast species are the soft-shell or long-neck clams, usually steamed, and the hard-shell, known in New England as quahogs, that come in three sizes: the largest, used for chowder; the smaller, littlenecks and cherrystones, eaten raw on the half shell, baked (see page 14), broiled (see *T & P*, pages 135 and 136), or added to seafood stews and similar dishes. On the West Coast one finds both hard-shell clams and the soft-shell razor clams of Oregon and Washington. The long, meaty razor clams are sautéed, deep-fried, scalloped, made into chowder and fritters. All clams need to be scrubbed well and soaked in cold water to remove the sand inside the shells. Raw clams—one of my dislikes—are best served very cold, on the half shell like oysters, with nothing but lemon juice and freshly ground pepper. Red cocktail sauce ruins the flavor. Steam clams in a half inch of water or wine from 5 to 10 minutes, until the shells open. Discard any with closed shells. The resulting broth may be sipped with the clams or used as the liquid for a seafood sauce. If you live near the shore, gather your own clams if possible —a sport I loved to indulge in as a child. Clams can be minced and used for fritters, quiches, or clam sauce for pasta (see page 283). Canned minced clams are extremely good and may be substituted for fresh.

Crabs. We have wonderful crabs in this country. From the West Coast comes the enormous **Alaska king crab**, shipped frozen. Carefully thawed, the coarse but flavorful meat is good for cooked dishes such as crab soufflé and deviled crab, but is not as successful in salads. The huge, meaty legs may be split and broiled. **Dungeness crab,** caught from California to Alaska, is to me the most distinctive of all. The legs are meaty, the lump crabmeat deliciously sweet. On its native coast, it is usually sold precooked and served cracked with mayonnaise, in salads, deviled crab, and other dishes. It is sheer, unadulterated crab heaven. Available flash-frozen in other parts of the country.

Next to Dungeness, my favorite is **Florida backfin lump crabmeat** (backfin meat is the choicest), sold cleaned, shelled, and chilled, in pound cans. It is extremely meaty and well-flavored and perfect for salads, sautéed, or in cooked dishes. The **stone crab** of Florida, unique because only the large claw is sold (the crab is returned to the water to grow another claw), has a coarser texture, but is considered a great delicacy, hot with melted butter or cold with mayonnaise. **Virginia, Carolina, and Maryland backfin lump crabmeat** is equal to Florida, though in short supply and therefore expensive. It may be used in the same ways or made into such regional specialties as crab cakes and crab Imperial. Also sold refrigerated, in cans. Recently some eastern markets have been receiving refrigerated **Maine crabmeat** of excellent quality. The legs are small, the meat delicate and sweet, perfect for crab salad or cocktail. When buying crabmeat, estimate 1 pound for 3 to 4 servings. Occasionally you will find **live blue crabs** in eastern markets. They may be boiled (allow 8 minutes a pound), cleaned, and eaten from the shell. The delicious little **soft-shell crabs,** found in the markets at certain times of the year, are merely blue crabs that have molted and are growing a new shell. The small ones are best; larger ones develop a coarse shell. Two or three of these babies make a serving. Soft-shell crabs are best sautéed (see *T & P*, page 200), but can also be broiled (see page 239) or deep-fried. They are eaten in their entirety, shell and all, and rate as one of the great American delicacies. If you buy them live and uncleaned, either have the fish market kill and clean them for you (or follow the directions in *T & P*, page 200).

Crayfish. After having almost disappeared from our waters, crayfish have now become an industry. California, Minnesota, Wisconsin, and Louisiana are producing excellent crayfish in quantity and shipping them around the country. Cook crayfish in a highly seasoned, spicy court bouillon or *à la nage* (see *T & P*, page 37)—nothing is more fun than a feast of beer and freshly boiled crayfish, eaten from the shell with your fingers. Or shell them and use for salads or in various seafood dishes, like other shellfish.

Lobsters. The Atlantic lobster, mostly found off Long Island, Massachusetts, Maine, and on up into Canada, is one of our great delicacies. Store-bought lobsters, kept on beds of seaweed or in salt-water tanks, lack the quality of those taken fresh from the ocean, on their native shore, but that is what most of us must settle for. You can also have live lobsters shipped by air from Maine lobster farms—at a price. Lobsters are sold both live and cooked, and vary in size from babies of 1 pound or less, known as chicken lobsters, up to giants of 25 to 30 pounds. Smaller lobsters are better eating. The average 1- to 2-pounder, boiled or broiled, is considered a serving for 1. For cooking, buy only lively lobsters. Have the fish merchant lift one so you can see how active it is. There are dozens of ways to prepare lobster but, to me, the simplest and by far the best is boiling (see *T & P*, page 38). Serve hot with melted butter or cold with mayonnaise. Fresh or frozen lobster meat, though horrendously expensive, goes quite a long way in salads, seafood combinations, and other cooked dishes; see pages 109–111 and 235–237 for new recipes. Canned lobster is not bad, but the taste is not the same as the fresh.

In the South and on the West Coast one gets **small rock lobsters,** sometimes live but more often cooked. These are really members of the crayfish family, without the big claws of the true lobster. They have good flavor and may be used for salads and cooked dishes. Then we have **frozen rock lobster tails** from various parts of the world, such as Spain, South Africa, and India. They vary in size from ¼ or ½ pound up to 3 or 4 pounds. Some of the larger ones can be quite tough, so check the weight before buying. Thaw and boil or broil, following directions on the package, and use like lobster in salads and main dishes.

Mussels. A delicious bivalve with a tapering bluish-black shell. Although mussels abound in our waters, they are much neglected, possibly because they are at times subject to a disease called "red tide" and, therefore, particularly on the West Coast, are unavailable at times. Consult your local fisheries before gathering them; those you buy in the markets are perfectly safe. Mussels must be carefully cleaned (see directions on page 41 in *T & P*). They are usually sold by the quart (a quart will serve 2) and range in size from about 1½ inches to almost 6 inches long. Small ones are the choicest. May be eaten raw, like clams, but are more usually steamed in water or white wine until the shells open and served in their lovely broth, or used in seafood stews and paella. Eat from the shell or remove and use in soup, pasta (see page 283), salads, and as a cold hors d'oeuvre (pages 13–14). They're a tremendously addictive delicacy.

Oysters. There are three species of American oysters: the eastern, the large Pacific or Japanese oyster, and the tiny coppery Olympia. The Olympia, native to the Northwest and seldom seen in the East, is to me the most distinguished. We get oysters from Canada, from Cape Cod, Long Island, Chesapeake Bay, the Gulf of Mexico, and the waters off Oregon and Washington. In the 19th and early 20th century they were shipped by train in barrels and kept very well. According to the locale, they differ in size, flavor, and texture and carry a local name, such as the Blue Point of Long Island or the Chincoteague of Chesapeake Bay. Sold in the shell or on the half shell by the dozen, freshly shucked (shelled) by the pint or quart, and in jars especially treated so they will keep under refrigeration. Freshly opened raw oysters are perishable and should be eaten right away. To serve raw, open the shells with an oyster knife (or have the fish dealer do it for you), loosen the oyster from its lower shell, and serve it that way—resting on the half shell. Count on at least half a dozen raw oysters per person, or about ½ pint shucked oysters, if they are to be cooked. Oysters may be broiled (see *T & P*, page 135), baked or scalloped, fried, added to beefsteak and kidney pie (see *T & P*, page 270), or simmered in soups and stews just until the edges curl—they must never be overcooked. See pages 229–231 for new ideas.

Scallops. Scallops are so pretty in their shells with the little white round muscle and the red comma of roe, the way they are sold in Europe, that it's a pity we can't buy them that way. Here only the shelled white muscle is marketed. The large, rather coarse sea scallops, sometimes as much as an inch thick and 2 inches in diameter, are shucked and frozen at sea. The tiny sweet and delicate bay scallops in coastal waters are by far the greater delicacy. Though sometimes frozen, they can usually be bought fresh. Bay scallops are delicious marinated in lime juice for seviche (see *T & P*, page 344) or even eaten raw. All scallops, whether broiled (see *T & P*, page 129), sautéed, poached, or deep-fried, should be cooked very quickly, otherwise they toughen and become tasteless. One pound of scallops will serve 2 or 3.

Shrimp. Shrimp come in all sizes, from the tiny Pacific, Alaskan, and Maine shrimp, perfect for salads, shrimp cocktail, or potted shrimp, to the medium-sized pink-shelled Florida shrimp and the very large gray-green Gulf shrimp. Occasionally you see enormous shrimp from the Indian Ocean weighing as much as a quarter of a pound apiece. I find the medium size best for most general cooking, such as sautéing and frying, for shrimp casseroles and other dishes, and for eating cold as appetizers or in salads. The very large ones are fine for broiling or for butterflied shrimp. One pound of shrimp serves 2 as a main course. You can buy raw shrimp in the shell, cooked shrimp in the shell or shelled, and quick-frozen shrimp both raw and cooked. Most ready-cooked shrimp are **so** overdone they are mushy and tasteless (and canned shrimp are not worth buying). If possible, buy fresh raw shrimp and cook them yourself. There's no need to remove the black vein from raw or cooked shrimp, except for aesthetic reasons. To do so, cut the shell along the back with sharp-pointed scissors, and remove the vein. The shrimp are then easier to shell, before or after cooking. I don't think it makes one whit of difference whether you cook shrimp in or out of the shell. The important thing is to cook them in well-salted water or court bouillon or *à la nage* (see *T & P*, page 37), to give them flavor. Bring the liquid to a boil, add the shrimp, and, timing from the moment the water returns to a boil, cook from 3 to 4 minutes, according to size, never more. Drain at once; they overcook if left in the water. Serve cold shrimp as an appetizer with lemon, mayonnaise, or rémoulade sauce, but never, please, with that overpowering red menace known as cocktail sauce if you value their sweet and delicate flavor.

SHORTENING. Hydrogenated vegetable fats used for baking and deep-frying, but not something I use very often. Whenever you find the term "shortening" in a recipe, it simply means any cooking fat. Butter can always be substituted.

SPICES

There are two important things to remember about spices. (1) Buy in small quantities only as needed and don't buy every spice you see. (2) Don't keep spices too long. The principal spices you need for general cooking, apart from peppercorns, which are discussed on page 581, are **cloves, cinnamon, ginger** (see page 556), and **nutmeg.** Also useful to have on hand are **anise seed, allspice, caraway seed,** and **mace.** Commercially ground spices deteriorate very quickly and lose their brightness, bouquet, and pungency. I grind most of my spices as I need them, using a small electric coffee mill that I keep just for that purpose. It even grinds cinnamon bark. Spices may be ground in a mortar and pestle, but it is an arduous job and the results are never as even and fine. If you don't want to grind spices, buy them ground, in small amounts, from a spice store (many sell by mail) and discard them when they lose their freshness. Nutmeg should always be bought whole and freshly grated; the little tin nutmeg grater of classic design costs only a dollar or so. Spices are for use, not for show. Keep them away from heat and light, in the dark of a kitchen cabinet, not in pretty jars on open shelves.

SQUAB. Young domesticated pigeons, weighing about ¾ to 1 pound. Usually bought cleaned and ready for the oven. The meat is darkish and flavorful. Squab may be roasted like squab chickens (see *T & P*, page 87) or sautéed (page 337). I like to stuff them with fresh herbs, garlic, and a tiny onion, and roast them in a baking dish with bacon over the breasts for 40 to 45 minutes at 400°. Or they may be split down the back, flattened with a blow of the fist, and broiled on both sides, like chicken. Squab, like quail, should be regarded as finger food. They are ideal birds for picnics if roasted or broiled the day before.

SQUASH

Despite the fact that many squash are in the market all year round, they are commonly referred to as summer squash and winter squash. Summer squash are the soft-shelled types which are eaten at an immature stage: zucchini, yellow straightneck and crookneck, the round, scalloped-edge pattypans or cymling squash. Winter squash, the large mature types with hard shells, are acorn, buttercup or turban, butternut, banana, and Hubbard.

Summer squash. At their best when very young and small. Unfortunately, too often they are allowed to grow until they are oversized and watery, with hard, inedible seeds. Look for small, firm, unblemished squash. Never boil until mushy or they'll taste as interesting as old dishrags. Steam them quickly in a very small amount of salted water or, preferably, in butter, until tender-crisp. Summer squash need no peeling or seeding. Leave them whole if really tiny, otherwise quarter, or slice, or cut into strips, toss in butter in a skillet or sauté pan, sprinkle with salt, cover, and steam over low heat until just tender. If the squash are rather large, you can eliminate some of their water by first blanching them briefly in boiling water.

Zucchini particularly are good sliced or shredded, salted to draw out the liquid, drained, and sautéed (see pages 175 and 176). They may also be French-fried, cooked à la Grecque, or eaten raw in salads or as a vegetable hors d'oeuvre. Large zucchini may be hollowed out, stuffed, and baked like eggplant (see *T & P,* page 293).

Winter squash. Once one of our standard cold-weather vegetables. We used to store the huge Hubbards in the barn, chop them into pieces with a hatchet, then seed them and bake them in the shell with butter or bacon fat. Or we might steam them, scrape out the pulp, and whip it up with butter and a little nutmeg or cinnamon. In some parts of the country you can sometimes find Hubbard and banana squash in the markets in the fall, chopped up and ready to cook. Mostly it is the small, round, green-skinned acorn and turban squash and the pale-skinned cylindrical butternut, available most of the year, that appear in the markets. When buying winter squash, gauge ¾ to 1 pound per serving. Choose squash with firm, hard shells and no mildewed or decayed parts. To bake hard-shelled squash, halve small types like acorn, turban, and butternut; large ones should be cut into big pieces. Remove seeds and strings. Butter well or add bacon fat or bacon. Bake in a 350° oven until tender, 50 minutes to 1 hour for smaller squash. Hubbards will take from 1 to 1¼ hours. Serve small squash in the shell with salt, pepper, and other seasonings, such as nutmeg and ginger. Acorn squash can also be spread with butter and sprinkled with brown sugar before baking, or stuffed with well-seasoned sausage meat, or baked with bacon, maple syrup, nutmeg, and cinnamon. Winter squash may also be steamed in the shell, scooped out, and mashed. Butternut, often sold peeled, cut into long pieces, and packaged, can be cut up, steamed, and mashed. Puréed cooked squash makes a delicious soufflé and, like pumpkin, a damned good pie. **Pumpkin,** incidentally, is not just for jack-o'-lanterns on Halloween and for Thanksgiving pumpkin pie. Halved, seeded, and baked like Hubbard squash from 45 minutes to 2 hours, according to size, it makes an excellent vegetable. Puréed, it can be turned into one of the world's most luscious and creamy soups.

Squid. Squid belong to the family of mollusks, but have no outer shell, only a thin bladelike bone inside the tubular body. With their grayish skin, beady eyes, and long tentacles, squid look like smaller, elongated octopuses, which may be the reason they are unfairly shunned. Most people don't like the look of them, don't know how to prepare them, and seem to be afraid to try them— a great pity, for the flesh is delicious if not overcooked. Squid need careful cleaning and should be skinned before cooking. Remove the head and pull out the pulpy intestines. Remove the thin, transparent, bladelike bone, leaving the tubular body in one piece. If the recipe calls for the tentacles, which are just below the eyes, cut them off and reserve them. Also reserve the sac of inky fluid if this is needed; otherwise discard it. Peel off the thin grayish skin covering the outside of the body. The cleaned body may be stuffed and braised, sliced and sautéed, cooked in rice with its own black ink, cut into rings, floured, and deep-fried, along with the tentacles, or used in a fish stew or paella. Squid are plentiful and inexpensive and should be used more often than they are.

Strawberries. Strawberries were once a great seasonal delight, heralded in summer with strawberry socials. Now we have them the year round, but unfortunately some are bred more for beauty than for taste. One has to be careful about buying, especially in the winter. Don't let your eyes fool your palate. Snitching and tasting one is kind of hard to do in today's markets, but you *can* feel and smell the berries. They should feel ripe but not mushy, and have a good fragrance. Be sure to check the box to make sure there are no rotten ones hidden on the bottom. Strawberries vary in shape and size from plump and rounded to long and pointed to enormous bulbous berries cut and sold with the long stem intact, perfect for dipping into sugar and eating by hand. Wild strawberries, tiny and deliciously sweet, may be picked in the summer all over the country, but are seldom seen in markets. Eaten with cream, with raspberry purée (see *T & P,* page 347), or in strawberries Romanov (see *T & P,* page 346), a pint of strawberries will serve 2. Or stretch them in a tart (see *T & P,* page 262), shortcake, sherbet (page 501), or ice cream.

Suet. Suet, or beef kidney fat, was once quite common in this country for cooking, especially for the traditional steamed puddings, most of which are English or early American in origin. Finely chopped suet makes an interesting and different pastry for meat pies and turnovers, and it is a necessity for beefsteak and kidney pudding (see *T & P,* page 30). If rendered until melted in a heavy skillet on top of the stove, it adds great flavor to a steak sautéed in the

French manner. Rendered suet or rendered beef fat trimmed from steak are marvelous for French-fried or home-fried potatoes.

SWEET POTATOES. An elongated tuber with an orange or reddish skin, resembling a potato, but not as thick. There are two types, the moist-fleshed orange sweet potato, often called a yam (although the true yam belongs to another family entirely), and the dry and mealy sweet potato, which is smaller and has yellowish flesh. Bake (about 1 hour) or boil (30 to 40 minutes until tender) in the jacket, like potatoes. May be mashed or puréed, and used in casseroles, as a pie filling, sliced and sautéed, or peeled, cut into strips, and deep-fried like French fries.

TOMATOES. One of the most versatile and popular of all our fruits, but seldom as good as they might be. We find in our markets the small, round, generally unripe "cannon-ball" tomatoes, sold in plastic containers, which for my money are not worth buying; the very large beefsteaks, best sliced as a salad; the firm red, vine-ripened tomatoes that come in summer and have a superior texture and flavor; and the tiny cherry tomatoes, once laudable, but now grown more for shelf life than for flavor. In country districts you may find seasonal yellow tomatoes, less acid than the red, and delicious for salads. Pale hard tomatoes can be ripened by keeping them in a dark place in a brown paper or plastic bag. Use only firm, ripe tomatoes for broiling, sautéing, or tomato salads. For cooking, tomatoes should be peeled and seeded. Drop in boiling water for half a minute to loosen the skin. Cut out core at stem end, peel, cut in half crosswise, and squeeze in your fist to force out the seeds. Or quarter and scoop out the seeds with your finger. Unless tomatoes are fully ripe, canned peeled Italian plum tomatoes or solid-pack tomatoes are a better buy for cooking. Other canned forms of tomato are tomato purée, often used as part of the liquid in braised dishes, and concentrated tomato paste, used to intensify tomato flavor in dishes such as tomato sauce.

TURKEY. What used to be the great Thanksgiving treat is now one of our more common and inexpensive foods, plentiful throughout the year. Turkeys nowadays are bred to grow firmer, larger breasts, much to the dismay of those who prefer the dark meat. Fortunately, one may buy turkey in parts, fresh or frozen, so dark-meat lovers can feast on legs and thighs. Turkey breasts of varying sizes are an excellent buy, as they are practically solid meat. Roast them or use for a variety of dishes, such as turkey salad, turkey tonnato (see page 332), and escalopes of turkey (sliced thin, like veal scaloppine; see page 406). It has become increasingly difficult, although not impossible, to find fresh-killed, hand-plucked turkeys. While they are more expensive, I happen to feel that they are superior enough to the frozen birds to warrant the higher price. What we mostly see in the markets are frozen turkeys of various types, chiefly what are called "self-basting" turkeys. This means that the breast has been injected with fat, either butter, vegetable oil, or vegetable fat, to lubricate the breast meat during roasting and keep it moist. You can, of course, also buy frozen turkeys that are not self-basting. Don't go by the packer's directions for roasting or you will get overcooked white meat. Frozen, stuffed self-basting turkeys need to be roasted with great care and attention. While whole turkeys are most often roasted (see *T & P*, page 89), they may also be braised or poached. They vary in size from very small, around 5 pounds, up to 30 and 35 pounds. Buy according to how much you and your family like turkey, for there are bound to be leftovers and it's silly to buy more than you can use. An 8-pound turkey will serve 4, with ample leftovers; a 10-pounder will serve 6, with leftovers; and a 12- to 14-pounder will serve 8 to 10. Today we can buy turkey parts which lend themselves to some new ideas (pages 329–335).

While the chances of getting a tough, scrawny bird are almost nil these days, I find that, despite the so-called improvements, these perfect-looking birds have less of the real turkey flavor. **Wild turkeys** or domesticated wild turkeys, available from specialty markets in some cities, while not as beautifully structured, have a remarkably good flavor, reminiscent of old-time turkeys.

TURNIPS. There are two types of turnips in our markets, the small purple-topped white ones and the huge yellow rutabagas, available all winter. White turnips are at their best when young and very small, about egg size. Peel, slice, and cook in boiling salted water to cover until just tender. Combine with carrots or celery, or purée and mix with puréed carrot. Also good braised, or parboiled and sautéed (see *T & P*, page 211). Use turnips as an accompanying vegetable for roasts or in the mirepoix for braised meats. When buying rutabagas, look for the small or medium size. Large ones are often pithy and spongy. Rutabagas, like many vegetables, are coated with wax. Peel carefully. Cut into pieces, steam, or boil in salted water to cover until tender. Mash with plenty of butter and freshly ground pepper. Mashed rutabagas are extremely good with mushroom duxelles swirled into them (see page 187), excellent baked in a casserole with eggs, crumbs, and onions. I also like to cut white turnips and rutabagas into julienne strips, blanch them, and sauté with julienne strips of broccoli stalks (see Three-Vegetable Sauté, *T & P*, page 212).

VANILLA. Probably the most popular and widely used flavoring for cakes, cookies, puddings, custards, and creams such as crème anglaise (see *T & P*, page 309), ice cream (see *T & P*, pages 370 and 371), poached peaches (see *T & P*, page 61), and other desserts. Use only vanilla beans or pure vanilla extract, made from vanilla beans soaked in alcohol. Artificial vanilla, known as vanillin, has only the smell and not the rich taste of the real thing. The thin, long, dark-brown vanilla bean, though expensive, will give you a lot of mileage. Put into a jar of sugar, vanilla beans aromatize the sugar and give it a permanent delicate flavor. For a fine homemade vanilla extract, slit 4 or 5 beans, put into a pint bottle of cognac or vodka, and after 2 weeks it's ready to use. Or slit an inch of vanilla bean and scrape the tiny, flavorful black seeds into custard, an ice cream mixture, or a cake or pudding batter. Single vanilla beans packaged in glass tubes can be found in supermarkets, but the finest, moist and almost overpowering in flavor, are sold in bulk by bakers' supply houses. Also check your local spice store.

VENISON. The meat from the wild deer, considered a very great delicacy. If you shoot a deer, unless you are a very deft butcher and have a great deal of freezing and refrigeration space, make a deal with a butcher in your neighborhood who will skin it, cut it up into proper pieces, and wrap it and age it for you. By far the greatest dish from the deer is the liver, which must be eaten within a few hours of its kill. It has a superb flavor; it's best when cut paper thin, sautéed quickly in butter, and served forth with bacon. One liver is worth ten carcasses of venison. The other cuts depend on the youth of the animal. The tenderloin, the rack, some steaks can be exquisitely done. The saddle is greatly prized as a dish for a celebration meal, and the haunch and the other parts of the venison are used for marinating and braising and stewing, and for hamburgers, which are excellent, for sausages, and for mincemeat. For recipes see pages 442–448.

Naturally, being a game animal, venison is not marketable, although one finds in certain metropolitan centers imported venison or reindeer which is available during certain months of the year and may be prepared according to any of the recipes given for venison.

VINEGAR. In salad making, remember the old adage "A spendthrift for oil, a miser for vinegar." Vinegar should never overpower. The recent vogue in French cooking for chicken, rabbit, and game birds with a vinegar sauce is, to my palate, more fashionable than delicious. Traditionally, in many Western and Oriental countries, vinegar and sugar are combined in sweet-and-sour dishes, such as sauerbraten and sweet-and-sour pork. And, of course, vinegar and sugar go together in pickling. Vinegar alone is for vinaigrette sauce and salad dressings, marinades, and court bouillon, and a touch is essential in mayonnaise (page 76). If you can beg or borrow a "mother," the natural yeast culture that, put into leftover wine, turns it into vinegar, it is easy to make your own. Otherwise, buy the best wine vinegar you can, either white or red. Should you want a tarragon or basil flavor, steep fresh herbs in the vinegar for a week or two. For general cooking purposes, use wine or cider vinegar. For salads, use wine vinegars, rice wine vinegar, sherry vinegar, fruit vinegars, herb-flavored vinegars. For pickling and preserving, use cider vinegar or distilled white vinegar.

YAMS. Often confused with the orange-fleshed sweet potato, commonly known as the Louisiana yam. The true yam is an entirely different tuber, most often seen in West Indian markets. The flesh is white or yellow and the texture rather like a potato. Boil or bake in the jacket, like potatoes. Peel, slice, and dress with butter, or purée.

YEAST. Sold commercially in two forms: granular yeast in packages and jars and fresh yeast in cakes. Both are standardized for our baking convenience and are equally efficient. Granular yeast is stocked by every supermarket, but in many communities fresh yeast is hard to find. One may have to beg a 1-pound brick of it from a friendly baker. A pound of yeast will keep for several months if you cut it into small pieces (enough for one batch of bread at a time), wrap it tightly in foil or plastic wrap, and store it in the freezer. Just remove as needed and place in warm water to proof (the foaming and swelling that prove the yeast is still active). Granular yeast dissolves best in lukewarm water (110° to 115°) with the addition of a tiny bit of sugar to make it proof faster. Fresh yeast, on the other hand, must not be put in water over 95°, or the delicate organism that causes fermentation and makes the bread rise will be killed. The best way to make sure the water is the right temperature is to test it with a very sensitive meat thermometer, the kind that registers from 0° to 220°, but soon you will get the feel for the appropriate temperature when you simply test it on your wrist.

Index

acorn squash, 177, 593
  baked, 180, 593; bacon
    and garlic, 180; maple
    sugar and bacon, 180
  cream soup, 57
  stuffed, 593
  see also squash, winter
aïoli, 203
allspice, 592
almonds, 575; to blanch,
    575; to toast, 575
  barley and mushroom
    casserole, 296
  beef and pork chili, 381
  cookies, 485; soft, 484–5
  orange cake, 520–1
  praline powder, 518
  with rice, 289; pilaf and
    raisins, 291
  in salad, 79
  tuiles, 484
anchovies, 5
  butter, 15
  hollandaise, 532
  leg of lamb, weeping,
    389
  mayonnaise, 77
  and olive stuffing for veal
    birds, 409
  with peppers, 5; eggs and

anchovies *(cont.)*
  tomatoes, 6; raisins,
    36; shallots and
    parsley, 6; tuna, 6;
    vinaigrette with
    mozzarella and
    tomatoes, 167
  pot roast, 377
  rabbit provençal, 356–
    357
  in salad, 79; crab, with
    cucumber and onion,
    111
  sauce, 391; raisin and
    pine nut, 281
  tapenade, 35–6
  with tomatoes, 6
  with tuna and artichoke
    hearts, 10
  with tuna and hard-
    boiled egg, 10
anglaise, sauce, 504
anise seed, 592
anticuchos, 31
  with chicken hearts, 31
apples, 539; kinds, 539
  cake, Don Farmer's
    fresh, 521–2
  horseradish applesauce,
    422

apples *(cont.)*
  pancakes, 494
  pie, 509
  poached, 506
  raw, as dessert, 506
  in salad: grapefruit, 98;
    tuna, 113
  sautéed slices, for pork
    crown roast stuffing,
    420
  sharlotka, 525–6
  sherbet, 501
  tapioca, 527; and pear,
    527; and quince, 527
  tarte Tatin, 513
  vichyssoise, 55
apricots, 539
  canned, as dessert, 507
  dried, compote, 514
  jam or preserves, glaze,
    510, 511, 520
  and pineapple tart, 510–
    511
  poached, 506
  sherbet, 499–500
artichokes (globe
    artichokes), 119, 120
  boiled, 119
  bottoms, 120; French-
    fried, 187; mixed

599

artichokes (cont.)
vegetable sauté, 189–190
cold, 120; stuffed with seafood, 121
frittata, 259
hearts: French-fried, 187; in salad, 78; with tuna, 10
microwave-cooked, 120
mixed vegetable sauté, 189–90
serving suggestions, 120
soup, 53
steamed, 120
stuffed, 121; ham or prosciutto, 121; shrimp, 121
artichokes, Jerusalem, see Jerusalem artichokes
arugula (rugula; rocket), 557
asiago, 545
asparagus, 123, 540; doneness, testing for, 39, 123
in ambush, 40
Belgian, 40
boiled, 123
canned, 540
Dutch, 40
French-fried, 187
Italian-style, 39
microwave-cooked, 123
minute, 124–5
with prosciutto, 32
purée, with poached eggs, 252
raw, 124
sauces and dressings, 124
steamed, 123
tips: mixed vegetable sauté, 189–90; omelet, 256; with risotto, 293
turkey divan, 332
Austrian chocolate cake, 518–19
avocados, 540; to prevent discoloring, 540
crab salad, with onion, 111; and radish, 112
and liver, sautéed, 451
lobster salad, with onion, 110
scallop salad with chili, 109; and sauce Gribiche, 109
shrimp salad, 112; and papaya, 98

avocados (cont.)
stuffed: chicken, ham, and cheese, 37; chili, hot, 37; crabmeat, 37; diced avocado and Russian dressing, 37; seviche, 37; shrimp, 37; tapenade, 36
-yogurt sauce or dressing, 75

bacon, 570
onion and spinach frittata, 259
in salad, 79
bagels, egg, 472–3
with onions, 473
with poppy seeds, 473
with sesame seeds, 473
baking powder, 540
homemade, 540
baking soda, 540
Balilla (N.Y.C.), 258
bananas, 540–1
raw, as dessert, 506
banana squash, see squash, winter
baps, breakfast, 476
barding, 569
barley, 274, 541
and mushroom casserole, 295–6; almonds, 296; celery and water chestnuts, 296; chicken gizzards, 296
basil, 559; to keep, 282
pesto, 281–2; with walnuts, 282
in salad, 78
timbales, 263
bass, see sea bass; striped bass
bay leaf, 559
beans, 274, 541
black, 274; soup, 61–2; with sour cream, 307–308; sour cream, cheese, and bacon, 308
cannellini, puréed, with Madeira, 304
dried, 274, 541; to cook, 541
and lamb shanks, 399–400
pasta with beans, 286–7
pinto: cowpuncher beans, 308; Nevada chili beans, 308

beans (cont.)
succotash, 541
see also chickpeas; lentils
beans, cranberry (shell beans), 127
with bacon, 127
boiled, 127
cold, with vinaigrette, and onion, 127
beans, fava (broad beans), 541
beans, green, 125, 541
and almonds, toasted, 126
chicken and crabmeat salad, 106–7
chicken and potato salad, 103
cold: dilled vinaigrette, 126; mustard-flavored mayonnaise, 126; shallots and green olives, 126; walnut oil, 126
duck and foie gras salad, 106
French-fried, 187
with garlic and pine nuts, 126
with herbs, fresh, 126
mixed vegetable sauté, 189–90
with onion rings, 126
quick-boiled, 125–6
with risotto, 293
tomatoes stuffed with, 89
beans, kidney, 308
and sauerkraut salad, 93
with sausages, 307
Vanessi special, with rice, 260
beans, lima, 541
cassoulet, 305–6; with codfish, 306–7; duck legs, roasted, 306; lamb, cooked, 306; lamb and pork, cooked, 306
succotash, 541
beans, wax (yellow), 127, 187, 541
beans, white, 274, 308
cassoulet, 304–5
with cognac, 303; ham and sausage, 303
lamb shanks, 399–400
purée, 303–4
bean sprouts, see sprouts

Béarnaise sauce, 532
Beaucaire, salade, 88
béchamel sauce, 531
   as thickener, 54
   variations, 202, 531, 532
beef, 363–4, 565–7;
   boneless, serving
      portion, 564; grades,
      565
   birds, 373–4; ham and
      onion stuffing, 374;
      stuffings, 409–10
   bollito misto, 372–3
   bourguignon (in red
      Burgundy), 368–9;
      instant, 370–1
   in brain sauce, 285
   braised, with sautéed
      peppers, 165
   brioche bohémienne, 26–
      27
   chili, with pork, 381;
      beer, 381; nuts, 381;
      olives, 381
   chili con carne, 380
   corned beef, 567
   curried, and tomato
      sauce, 279
   daube, 377–8; aixoise,
      378; niçoise, 379;
      provençale, 378;
      provençale, with tripe,
      378
   fillet, Elizabeth David's
      stuffed, 367
   frankfurters, see
      frankfurters
   hamburger, basic
      sautéed, 382; au poivre,
      382; cheese, 382; chili,
      383; eggplant, 383;
      flambé, 383; garlic and
      pine nuts, 382–3;
      herbs, 383; onions,
      broiled, 159; onions,
      steamed, 382; onions
      and cream, 383; red
      wine, 383; serving
      suggestions, 383;
      Welsh rarebit, 269
   heart, 449, 566;
      anticuchos, 31
   herring salad, 7
   kadjemoula, 397–8
   kidneys, 567
   liver, 448, 567; meat loaf,
      384; sautéed, 451–2
   marrow, poached, in
      Bordelaise sauce, 533

beef (cont.)
   meat loaf, old-fashioned,
      364, 383–4; beef liver,
      384; chilied, 385;
      clams, minced, 384;
      eggs, hard-boiled, 384;
      ham, 384; olives, 384
   on a string (à la ficelle),
      369–70
   oxtail, 567; consomme,
      43, 48–9, 567; gratin,
      49; and vegetable
      soup, 49–50
   peppers stuffed with,
      167
   pot roast, 375–6;
      anchovied, 377;
      Flemish, 377; leftover,
      with ratatouille, 377;
      Madeira and turnips,
      376; marinated, 376;
      Mexican, 377;
      tomatoes, 376
   roast, 364–6; escabeche,
      16; and Manka's
      babies, 267
   roast fillet, 364; flambé,
      365; flambé, with
      truffle and chicken
      liver stuffing, 365–6;
      glazed, 366; marinated,
      366; slices with
      poached eggs, 252;
      spiced, 365
   salad: hearty, 105;
      hearty, with tarragon
      vinaigrette, 105;
      hussar, 105–6
   sausages, see sausages,
      meat
   scallops bluegrass, 371
   short ribs, braised, 379–
      380; chili, 380;
      onions, 380; tomatoes,
      380
   steak, broiled: cuts, 364;
      formula for cooking
      time, 364
   stew with sautéed
      peppers, 165
   stock, 530
   Stroganoff, 372
   suet, 594–5
   testicles, 567
   and tomato sauce, 284
   tongue, see tongue
   tournedos: Argentina,
      368; Béarnaise, 368;
      Bordelaise, 367–8;

beef (cont.)
   marinated, 368;
      onions, 368; sherry,
      368
   tripe, see tripe
   Vanessi special, 260
beer batter, 187, 188
beets, 541–2
   baked, 129
   boiled, 542
   borsch, 50
   cold, vinaigrette, 128
   dill, 128
   greens, 128, 150, 558; in
      salad, 558; wilted,
      150, 558
   old-fashioned pickled
      eggs, 250–1
   with onion and chopped
      tarragon, 128
   with onion and orange,
      128
   purée: with carrots, 137;
      with poached eggs,
      252
   salad: with greens, 78,
      544, 559, 560;
      marinated mushrooms,
      86
   soup, cold, 56
   with yogurt, 128
Belgian asparagus, 40
bell peppers, see peppers,
      sweet or bell
beurre blanc, 201
beurre manié, 536
Bibb lettuce, 556
   mushroom salad, 82; with
      crab, 82
   vintner's salad, 81
billi bi, 66
Billy's coleslaw, 90–1
   with seafood, 90–1
Le Bistrôt (Mougins,
      France), 19
black beans, see beans,
      black
blackberries, 542
   poached, 505
   raw, as dessert, 506
blini:
   buckwheat, 40–1
   carrot, 41
blood sausages, 570, 587
blowfish (puffer;
      globefish), 551
blueberries, 542
   poached, 505
   raw, as dessert, 506

bluefish, 551
    broiled fillets, 196–7;
        variations, 197–8
    broiled steaks, 206
    sautéed fillets, 199
boar, mock, 422
bockwurst, 587–8
boiled dressing, 94
bollito misto, 372–3
bologna, 588
Bordelaise sauce, 533
    with poached beef
        marrow, 533
borsch, 50
bouillabaisse, 220–1
boula-boula, 47
bouquet garni, 560
brains, 448
    au beurre noir, 450
    broiled, 450
    calves', 450, 571;
        Gribeche, 15; minina,
        261
    escabeche, 16
    fried, 451
    lambs', 450, 568
    parboiled or poached,
        449
    pork, 569
    sauce, 284; and lasagne,
        285; with meat, 285;
        and tomato, 284
    sautéed, 450 marinated,
        450
    with scrambled eggs,
        254
brambles, 494
brandade (of cold), 244–5
    eggs Benedictine, 252
    fritters, 245
    and mashed potatoes,
        245
    portugaise, 245
    tart, 245
bran muffins, whole-wheat,
    482
bratwurst, 572, 588
Brazil nuts, 575
bread, 466–7
    bagels, egg, 472–3; with
        onions, 473; poppy
        seeds, 473; sesame
        seeds, 473
    baps, breakfast, 476
    buns, Lenten, 479–80
    carrot, 474
    cottage cheese, 481
    croutons, 78
    crumpets, 480

bread (cont.)
    Gruyère garlic, 473–4
    knusper brote, 483
    mealy, 482
    muffins, whole-wheat
        bran, 482
    nut rum, 481
    polygrained, 472;
        cornmeal; 472; garlic
        and dill, 472; walnuts,
        472
    pullman loaf (pain de
        mie), 469–70
    pumpernickel, 471
    raisin, 474–5
    rolls: hard, 475–6; Mrs.
        Maynard's cinnnamon,
        478–9
    rye, dark, 470–1
    sharlotka, 525–6
    white, basic, 468–9
    see also brioche
bread-and-butter pudding,
    526
    French, 527
    with raisins, 527
    with rum, 527
breading, cornmeal, 547
brioche, 477
    à tête, 478
    bohémienne, 26–7
    bread, 477–8
    coulibiac in, 214–15;
        with rice, 215
    with ham, 27–8
    pork liver pâté in, 23–4
    sausage en, 28–9
broccoli, 128–9, 542; to
    buy, 128, 542
    with black butter, 129
    boiled, 129
    crumbed, 130
    flowerets, 189–90;
        French-fried, 187;
        steamed, 129
    frozen, 542
    with garlic and parsley,
        129
    julienne, sautéed with
        cucumbers, 146
    with maltaise sauce, 129
    purée, 129; with poached
        egg, 252
    timbales, 263
    turkey divan, 332
broccoli rabe, 130
    cold, vinaigrette, 130
    purée, 130; with cheese
        and Manka's babies,

broccoli rabe (cont.)
    267; with poached
        egg, 252
    steamed, 130
broth, see stock and broth
Brown, Philip:
    duck kebabs, 340
    romaine soufflé, 150–1
    tongue with chicken liver
        sauce, 457
brown bread ice cream,
    504
brownies, blond, 493
brown sauce, quick, 533
    variations, 533
brown sugar rum sauce,
    508
Brussels sprouts, 131, 542;
    to buy, 131
    braised, with chestnuts,
        for pork crown roast
        stuffing, 420
    with chestnuts, 131
    cold, with mustard
        mayonnaise, 132
    crisp-cooked, 131
    French-fried, 187
    frozen, 542
    microwave-cooked, 132
    mixed vegetable sauté,
        189–90
    with mushroom caps,
        sautéed, 131
    with Parmesan cheese,
        131
    with shallots, 131
buckwheat, 274, 542–3
    blini, 40–1
    groats (kasha), 296,
        542–3; giblets,
        sautéed, 296;
        mushrooms, 296
bulghur, see cracked
    wheat
Burgundian mustard, 421
butter, 543
    anchovy, 15
    beurre: blanc, 201;
        manié, 536
    caraway, 537
    chili, 537
    clarified, 543
    cream frosting, 518
    curry, 233, 234
    dill, 537
    garlic, 20, 537; parsley,
        336
    herbed, 198
    lemon, 197; parsley, 231

butter *(cont.)*
  orange, 537
  pepper, green, 142
  peppercorn, green, 318
  roquefort stuffing, 402
  rosemary, 537
  salt, 543
  tarragon, 536–7
  unsalted (sweet), 543
  white butter sauce, 201
buttercup squash, *see*
  turban squash
butternut squash, 177, 179,
  593–4
  baked, 179, 593
  cream soup, 57
  spiced, 177
  see also squash, winter
butterscotch sauce, 508

cabbage, 132, 543; to buy,
  543
  braised, 133; with heavy
    cream, 134; with
    vinegar and dill, 133
  French-fried strips, 187
  goloubtzys (choux
    farcis), 136
  and ham, boiled, 439
  lemon, 134
  mixed vegetable sauté,
    189–90
  with partridge, braised,
    and sausage, 348–9
  red, 132, 543; braised,
    with apples and wine,
    135; braised, with
    apples and raisins, 135
  salad, 543; spicy
    Szechuan, 84
  savoy, 132, 543; whole
    stuffed, 134–5; whole
    stuffed, in chicken
    broth, 136; whole
    stuffed, with tomato
    sauce, 135
  steamed, 133; vinaigrette,
    133
  stuffed, 132
  see also coleslaw;
    sauerkraut
Caesar salad, 85–6
cakes:
  apple, Don Farmer's
    fresh, 521–2
  buttered-cake pudding,
    527
  cheesecake: chocolate,

cakes *(cont.)*
  522–3; hazlenut, 523–
    524; sour cream, 524
  chocolate: Austrian, 518–
    519; French, 517–18;
    tweed, 519
  flour, 555
  orange and almond,
    520–1
  pear, fresh, 522
  pound, 525; with citron,
    525; with spices, 525
  sponge, with apricot
    glaze, 520
calves' brains, 450, 571
  Gribiche, 15
  minina, 261
calves' feet, 572
calves' liver, 448, 572
  julienne, 452
  roast whole, 452–3
  sautéed, 451–2
  Venetian style, 452
calves' sweetbreads, *see*
  sweetbreads
cantaloupes, 573
  with prosciutto, 32
capers:
  in salad, 79
  sauce, 531
caponata, 34
  with tuna, 35
caramel ice cream, 504
caraway seed, 592
  butter, 537
carrots, 136, 543
  blini, 41
  boiled, 137
  bollito misto, 372–3
  bread, 474
  with cognac, 137
  coleslaw: with peppers,
    90; radishes, 90
  glazed, 137
  with herbs, fresh, 137
  mixed vegetable sauté,
    189–90
  oatmeal carrot cookies,
    487–8
  purée: with beets, 137;
    parsley, 137; parsnips,
    137; potatoes, 137
  with rum, 137
  vichyssoise, 55
casabas, 573
cassis ice cream, 504–5
cassoulet, 304–5
  with codfish, 306–7
  with limas, 305–6; duck

cassoulet *(cont.)*
  legs, roasted, 306;
  lamb, cooked, 306;
  lamb and pork, cooked,
    306
Castilian mussel soup, 65
cauliflower, 137–8, 544; to
  buy, 137–8
  with Béarnaise sauce, 138
  with black butter and
    capers, 138
  boiled, 138
  with cheese sauce, 138
  cold, sauces and
    dressings, 139
  with curry sauce, 139
  flowerets, 546; French-
    fried, 187; mixed
    vegetable sauté, 189–
    190
  with Gruyère cheese, 138
  on ham, with cheese
    sauce, 139
  microwave-cooked, 139
  with mornay sauce, 138
  with olive oil and garlic,
    138
  with Parmesan cheese,
    138
  purée, 139; with cheese
    sauce, 139; olive oil
    and garlic, 139;
    parsley, 139
caviar:
  with potatoes, 38
  and sour cream omelet,
    256
  vichyssoise, 55
cayenne pepper, 581
celeriac, *see* celery root
celery, 140, 544
  sauté, 140
  wilted salad, 82
celery root (celeriac), 140,
  544; to prevent
    discoloring, 544
  baked stuffed, 141–2
  boiled, 141
  with cheese, 141
  with maltaise sauce, 141
  and potatoes, baked, 141
cèpes à la Bordelaise, 155–
  156
champagne sherbet, 500
chard, 150, 558
  lentil soup, with lemon,
    59
  tian, 191; with noodles,
    191; with rice, 191

chav, *see* sorrel
Cheddar cheese, 544
  soup, 69; with olives, 69
  Welsh rarebit, 269;
    variations, 269
cheese, 246–7, 544–5; to
    keep, 544
  creamy sauce, 531
  with hamburgers, 382
  omelet, 256
  with rice, 289
  in salad, 79
  soufflé in pastry, 265;
    with whole eggs, 265
  soufflé with zucchini
    blossoms, 177
  and vegetables, 116
cheesecake:
  chocolate, 522–3
  hazlenut, 523–4
  sour cream, 524
cherries, 545
  canned, as dessert, 507
  poached, 505
  sauce, for roast duck,
    338–9
chestnuts:
  and Brussels sprouts, 131;
    braised, for pork crown
    roast stuffing, 420
  purée: and braised
    chestnuts, for lamb
    crown roast stuffing,
    388; for pork crown
    roast stuffing, 420
  and raisin ice cream,
    503
Chiang, Cecilia:
  red-cooked pork shoulder,
    432
  tripe with gizzards, 461–
    462
chicken, 312–13, 545–6
  avocado with ham and
    cheese, 37
  bollito misto, 372–3
  boned breasts poached in
    tomato sauce, 328;
    with basil and hot
    peppers, 328
  in brain sauce, 285
  braised, with ham
    stuffing, 318; mustard
    and cream sauce, 318–
    319
  broiling chickens, 545–6
  coq au vin, quick, 325
  and curry omelet, 257
  escabeche, 16

chicken *(cont.)*
  with forty cloves of garlic,
    323–4
  frying chickens, 546
  gizzards: barley and
    mushroom casserole,
    296; with tripe,
    Cecilia Chiang's, 461–
    462
  gizzards and hearts,
    sautéed, 326–7; with
    Madeira, 327;
    mushrooms and sour
    cream, 327
  gizzards, hearts, and
    livers, sautéed, 327;
    with kasha, 296
  hearts: anticuchos, 31; en
    brochette, 31
  hearts and livers en
    brochette, 30–1;
    Béarnaise sauce, 31;
    scrambled eggs, 31
  legs, sautéed: paprika,
    sour cream, and lemon
    rind, 326; walnuts,
    326; yogurt and red
    peppers, 326
  in lettuce leaves, 29–30
  livers: and ham, pâté,
    22; sauce, for tongue,
    457; and truffle
    stuffing, for beef fillet,
    365–6; *see also*
    gizzards; hearts *above*
  minina, 261
  in Moroccan style, with
    pickled lemons and
    olives, 322–3
  mustard, 327–8
  paella, 293–4
  pan-fried, 322; with
    cream, 322
  parts, 320
  pâté, rolled, 21–2
  peppers stuffed with, 167
  piquant broiled halves,
    327
  poached, 319; with garlic,
    319; hollandaise, 320;
    onion-rice sauce, 320;
    vegetables, 319
  poaching chickens, 546
  with risotto, 292
  roast: flamed with
    Armagnac, 316; flamed
    with Calvados, 316–7;
    flamed with cognac,
    315–17; flamed with

chicken *(cont.)*
  whisky, 317; green
    peppercorn butter,
    318; Picasso, 317;
    sarthoise, 317; sautéed
    peppers, 165
  roasting chickens, 546
  salad: bean and
    crabmeat, 106–7; bean
    and potato, 103; ,
    coriander, fresh, 100–
    101; lobster and celery,
    110; olive sauce, 101–
    102; and rice, 102; and
    seafood, 102
  salad, basic, 99–100; with
    celery, 100; with celery,
    tomatoes stuffed with,
    89; celery and grapes,
    100; with macadamia
    nuts, 100; with
    macadamia nuts,
    tomatoes stuffed with,
    89; with sweetbreads,
    100; tomatoes stuffed
    with, 89
  sauté basquaise, 325
  sauté with herbs, 324–
    325; with lemon, 325;
    onion, garlic, and
    tomato, 325; onions
    and chilies, 325; with
    vinegar, 325
  southern-fried, 321–2;
    with cinnamon or
    paprika, 322; with
    rosemary, 322
  squab chickens, 337, 546
  stock, 529
  strips and rice, 328
  timbales, 263
  and tomato sauce, 284
  in yogurt, 328–9
chickpeas (ceci; garbanzos),
    274; 546–7
  purée, 309, 547; with
    Madeira, 309
chicory (curly endive), 556
  and beet salad, 542
  grapefruit and apple
    salad, 98
  wilted, 150
Child, Julia, 125
chili con carne, 380
chili peppers, hot, 165, 582
  beef chili, 380; with
    avocado, 37
  beef and pork chili, 381;
    with beer, 381; with

chili peppers (cont.)
  nuts, 381; with olives,
    381
  butter, 537
  chicken breasts poached
    in tomato sauce, 328
  corn-chili soufflé, 302–3
  with hamburgers, 383
  hominy casserole, 297–8
  with huevos rancheros,
    253
  meat loaf, 385
  omelet, 256
  with rice pilaf, 291
  sauce piquante, 299
  with short ribs, braised,
    380
  turkey chili, 333–4
  turkey wings piquant,
    335
  venison chili, 447–8
Chinese chews, 486
Chinese parsley, see
    coriander
chives, 560, 576, 578
  coleslaw, quick-chopped,
    90
  green rice, 289
  in salad, 78, 578
chocolate, 516, 547; to
    keep, 547; to melt, 547
  blond brownies, 493
  cake, Austrian, 518–19;
    French, 517–18;
    tweed, 519
  cheesecake, 522–3
  curls, for garnish, 523
  glaze, 517–18
  macaroons, 489
  and pear tart, 511
  pots de crème, 528
  ring, 516
  sauce, 507
chorizo, 588
  paella, 293–4
Chuck's baked shrimp,
    234–5
cider, dry, 211
cider vinegar, 74, 597
cilantro, see coriander
cima di vitello, 572
cinnamon, 592
  rolls, Mrs. Maynard's,
    478–9
cioppino, 222
  with clams, 222
  with mussels, 222
clams, 589; to clean, 589
  with anchovy butter, 15

clams (cont.)
  au gratin, 14
  bisque, 64
  bouillabaisse, 220–1
  Casino, 15
  cioppino, 222
  curried seafood with rice
    pilaf, 225–6
  deviled, 239
  hash, 227
  Hellenic seafood stew,
    219–20
  herbed, 15
  marinière, 225
  minced, and sour cream
    roll, 264
  paella, 293–4
  pie, 228–9
  provençal, 15
  risotto with shellfish, 292
  sautéed, 227–8; mustard
    and Worcestershire
    sauce, 228; tarragon,
    228; white wine, 228
  scalloped, 228
  soup, 48
  steamed, 591
  and tomato sauce, 283
cloves, 594
The Coach House
    Restaurant (N.Y.C.):
  black bean soup, 61–2
  crabmeat and prosciutto,
    33
  quince tart, 512
  tripe soup, 42, 62–3
cod, 551
  baked, niçoise, 208
  balls, 244
  bouillabaisse, 220–1
  broiled fillets, 196–7;
    variations, 197–8
  broiled steaks, 206
  cakes, 244; with ginger,
    244; with onions, 244
  cotriade, 223
  curried seafood with rice
    pilaf, 225–6
  escabeche, 16
  fillets, 554
  salad, 107–8
  salt cod, 243, 551; au
    gratin, 244; béchamel,
    244; mornay, 244;
    poached, 243; with
    polenta, 301; raïto, 245
  sautéed fillets, 199
  see also brandade (of
    cod)

cognac sauce, 507
coleslaw, 89
  Billy's, 90–1; with
    seafood, 90–1
  hot slaw, 91–2; with red
    slaw, 92; with red
    slaw and crisp duck
    skin, 92
  pepper slaw, 92
  quick chopped, 90;
    carrots and peppers,
    90; carrots and
    radishes, 90; crabmeat,
    90; dilled, 90; green
    onions or chives, 90;
    mustard mayonnaise,
    90; shrimp, 90; tuna,
    90; yogurt mayonnaise,
    90
  sauerkraut slaw, 93
  spicy, 91
collards, 150, 558
  tian of mixed greens,
    152
cookies, 483
  almond, 485; soft,
    484–5
  blond brownies, 493
  butter wafers: cornmeal,
    485–6; sesame, 486
  Chinese chews, 486
  chocolate macaroons,
    489
  Florentines, 490–1
  ginger cakes, 487
  Gino's macaroons, 490
  lace, 486–7
  lemon meringue bars,
    489
  Linzer bars, 492
  meringue kisses, 491–2
  oatmeal carrot, 487–8
  outsize, 491
  peanut butter,
    "monster," 491
  sugar, 493
  tuiles, 484
  Vadis bars, 488–9
coq au vin, quick, 325
coquilles St. Jacques, lo-cal,
    241
coriander (Chinese
    parsley; cilantro), 560
  in salad, 78, 100; with
    chicken, 100–1
corn, 142, 547; to buy,
    547
  with bacon crumbs and
    butter, 142

corn (cont.)
with basil, fresh, 143
with herb mayonnaise,
142
microwave-cooked, 143
with mustard
mayonnaise, 142
off the cob, with cream,
143
and okra, 156–7
oysters, 143–4
and peppers, sweet:
green pepper butter,
142; and onion,
sautéed, 166; stuffed,
167
pudding, 144; with
bacon, 144
raw, with cream, 143
with rémoulade sauce,
142
and salad of marinated
vegetables and noodles,
87
skillet-boiled, 142
soufflé: with chili, 302–
303; with cornmeal,
302
and sour cream roll, 264
and squash soup, 51;
puréed, 51
succotash, 541
tomatoes baked and
stuffed with, 182–3
cornmeal, 274, 299–300,
547
butter wafers, 485–6
gnocchi, 301
mush, 300
pastry, for tarte Tatin,
513
polygrained bread, 472
soufflé, 302; corn-chili,
302–3; Parmesan
cheese, 302; whole-
kernel corn, 302
as thickening, 547
see also polenta
corn oil, 576
corn salad, see field salad
cotechino, 588
bollito misto, 372–3
cassoulet, 304–5
partridge, braised, with
cabbage, 348–9
pheasant, braised, with
sauerkraut, 353–4
sausage en brioche, 436;
with mustard, 436

cotriade, 223
cottage cheese, 544
bread, 481
cottonseed oil, 576
coulibiac, 214–15
with rice, 215
court bouillon:
for brains, 450
for fish, white wine, 203
head cheese, 430–1
for pigs' feet, 429
couscous, 298–9
leftover, serving
suggestions, 299
couscousier (and
substitute), 298
cowpuncher beans, 308
crabs, 589–90; kinds, 589–
90
and avocado, 37
bouillabaisse, 220–1
cioppino, 222
cocotte of seafood
Manzanilla, 218–19
coleslaw: Billy's, 90–1;
quick chopped, 90
deviled, 239
jambalaya, 232
Parisienne, 238
and prosciutto, 33
salad: Bibb lettuce, 82;
chicken, 102; chicken
and bean, 106–7;
papaya and shrimp,
99; and rice, tomatoes
stuffed with, 89
salad with onion and
egg, 111; avocado, 111;
cucumber and
anchovies, 111; radish,
111
salad with Oriental
vegetables, 111–2;
avocado, onion, and
radish, 112; carrot,
onion, and celery, 112;
cucumber, anchovies,
and onion, 112
seafood sausages, French,
218
soft-shell, 589–90;
broiled, 239–40
soufflé, 238; in pastry,
265
in sour cream with
mushrooms, 18
with tapenade
mayonnaise, 36
timbales, 263

cracked wheat (bulghur),
547
pilaf, 290–1
with pine nuts, for lamb
crown roast stuffing,
387
cranberry beans, see
beans, cranberry
cranberry sherbet, 502
Cranshaws (Crenshaws),
573
with prosciutto, 32
sherbet, 501–2
crayfish, 590
cream, 548
crème fraîche, 402, 548
and vegetables, 116
see also sour cream
cream cheese, 544
pastry, 216
cream puff pastry, 268
crème fraîche, 402, 548
crêpes:
savory, 265–6
trout, sautéed, in, 212–13
croutons, 78
crumbs:
brown bread ice cream,
504
as thickener, 43
crumpets, 480
cucumbers, 144, 548
cream vegetable soup,
basic, 52–4
poached, 145
salad, 78; Greek, 87;
Greek, with radishes
and capers, 87;
spinach, 80; Turkish,
83–4
sautéed: with cream,
145; with julienne of
broccoli, 146; with
mushrooms, 145; with
snow peas, 146; with
yogurt, 145
steamed, 145; with
herbs, 145
tomatoes stuffed with
smothered cucumbers,
88–9
cullen skink, 68
Cunningham, Marion:
minestrone, 60–1
curry:
beef and tomato sauce,
279
butter, 233, 234
and chicken omelet, 257

curry (cont.)
  sauce, 532; sautéed, sole
    fillets, 200
  seafood with rice pilaf,
    225–6

dandelion greens:
  salad, 556
  sautéed, with bacon, 558
  tian of mixed greens,
    152; and bacon, 152
daube, 377–8
  beef: aixoise, 378;
    niçoise, 379;
    provençale, 378;
    provençale, with tripe,
    378
  lamb, 377–8, 394–5
  veal, 414
David, Elizabeth:
  poached fish fillets with
    garlic mayonnaise,
    202
  stuffed fillet of beef,
    367
Dekking, Max:
  hussar salad, 105
diable, sauce, 533
Diat, Louis:
  vichyssoise, 54–5, 152
diet dishes:
  artichokes with vinegar,
    120
  coleslaw, 89
  coquilles St. Jacques, 241
  fruit fool with yogurt,
    516
  onions, 158
  pesto, 282
  salad dressings, 75, 77–8
  spaghetti squash as pasta
    substitute, 177
  vegetables, dressings, 124
dill, 560
  butter, 537
  in salad, 78
  sauce, 202
duck, 313, 549
  frozen, 549
  kebabs, 340; flamed, 340
  liver, 549; with shirred
    eggs, 251
  roast, 338; with cherries,
    338–9; with green
    olives, 339; wild rice
    and mushrooms, 295
  roasted legs, cassoulet
    with limas, 306

duck (cont.)
  salad: bean and foie gras,
    106; and olives, 104;
    and orange, 104
  skin, 338; hot slaw with
    red slaw, 92; salad
    garnish, 104
  in white wine, 339
duck, wild, 314, 342, 549
  broiled, 344; flambé, 345;
    with soy sauce, 345;
    teriyaki, 345
  favorite Oregon, 343
  roast, rare, 342; with
    juniper berries, 342;
    with olives, 342–3
  roasted stuffed, 343–4;
    southern-French-style,
    344
  salmi of, 345
  spitted flamed, 343
  stock, 345
Dumas, Alexandre:
  potato salad, 95
Dutch asparagus, 40
duxelles, 535-6
  brown sauce, 533
  omelet, 256
  roulade of veal Île-de-
    France, 405
  with rutabagas, 187
  with scrambled eggs in a
    tart shell, 254
  and tomato sauce, 284
  with wild rice, 295

eels, 209–10, 551; to skin
    and clean, 210
  cotriade, 223
  Flemish green, 210
  matelote, from
    Normandy, 211
eggplant, 146, 549; to buy,
    146
  caponata, 34; with tuna,
    35
  casserole, 147
  French-fried, 187
  with hamburgers, 383
  imam bayildi, 147
  mixed vegetable sauté,
    189–90
  purée, 33–4
  ratatouille, 190; eggs,
    poached, and cheese,
    191; fennel, 191; leeks,
    191; mushrooms, 191;
    spicy, 191

eggplant (cont.)
  roast shoulder of lamb
    and tomato, 392
  sautéed, 146–7; with
    bacon, 147; in
    cornmeal, 147; and
    onions, 147; with
    Parmesan cheese, 147;
    with tomato sauce,
    147; tomato slices,
    broiled or sautéed, 147
eggs, 246–7, 549–50; to
    freeze or store, 550; to
    separate, 550; whites,
    550; yolks, 550
  bagels, 472–3; with
    onions, 473; with
    poppy seeds, 473; with
    sesame seeds, 473
  Belgian asparagus, 40
  Benedict, 252
  Benedictine, 252
  Dutch asparagus, 40
  frittata, 258; variations,
    258–60
  hard-boiled: asparagus
    Italian-style, 39; meat
    loaf, 384; old-fashioned
    pickled, 250–1; in
    onion sauce, 249; with
    peppers, anchovies,
    and tomatoes, 6; with
    tapenade, 36; with
    tuna, 10
  huevos rancheros, 253;
    with jalapeño peppers,
    253; with tortillas, 253
  meurette, 253
  minina, 261
  mollet, pasta with, 285
  omelet, basic, 255–6;
    cold layered, 257–8;
    fillings, 256–7
  pasta, rich, 277
  Peruvian, 261–2
  pipérade basquaise,
    255
  poached, 252; with pâté,
    252; ratatouille and
    cheese, 191; roast fillet,
    252; sausage, 252;
    spinach, 252; stewed
    tomatoes, 181; vege-
    table purée, 252;
    Welsh rarebit, 269
  sauce, 531
  Scotch, 250
  scrambled, 253–4; with
    alfalfa sprouts, 254;

eggs (cont.)
    brains, 254; chicken
        hearts and livers en
        brochette, 31; duxelles
        in a tart shell, 254;
        lamb kidneys, 254;
        mozzarella, 254;
        peppers, roasted, 254;
        prosciutto, 254;
        tomatoes, 254;
        zucchini blossoms, 176
    shirred, 251; duck livers
        and Madeira, 251;
        Gruyère cheese, 251;
        ham, 251; pesto, 251;
        spinach purée, 251
    soufflés, rolled, 263–4
    soufflés in pastry, 264–5
    stuffed: with sardines,
        250; special, 249–50
    timbales, 262–3; fillings,
        263
elderberry blossoms, deep-
    fried, 188
Emmenthaler, 246, 545
    Swiss cheese salad, 270
endive (Belgian or French;
    witloof chicory), 556–
    557
    roast chicken sarthoise,
        317
    salad with beets, 542,
        557
    turkey divan, 332
escabeche, 15–7
escarole, 557
    tian of mixed greens and
        bacon, 152
    wilted, 150

Farmer, Don:
    fresh apple cake, 521–2
farmer's omelet, 256
fat:
    barding, 569
    goose, 556
    lard and pork fat, 321,
        417, 497, 508, 562,
        569
    larding and lardoons,
        375, 569
    shortening, 592
    suet, 594–5
fava beans (broad beans),
    541
fennel, 149, 550
    ratatouille, 191
    in salad, 550

fennel (cont.)
    and sardine sauce, 280
    tuna salad, with onion,
        avocado, and egg, 113
    vegetable and olive salad
        with mustard-yogurt
        dressing, 84–5; blue or
        Gruyère cheese, 85
fiddlehead ferns, 148
    batter-dipped, 148
    boiled, 148
    cold, 149
field salad (corn salad;
    lamb's lettuce), 557
figs:
    dried: compote, 514;
        poached, 506; raisin
        and pine nut sauce,
        281
    with prosciutto, 32
filberts, see hazelnuts
finnan haddie, 551
    cullen skink, 68
    mousse, 9
    omelet, 256
    Scotch vichyssoise, 68
fish and seafood, 192–4,
    550–4, 589–92; to buy,
    550, cooking time,
    determination of, 196
    à l'Américaine, 223–4
    avocado with seviche, 37
    bouillabaisse, 220–1,
    cioppino, 222; with
        mussels, 222; with
        oysters, 222
    cocotte Manzanilla, 218–
        219
    cold, sauces for, 194
    cornmeal breading, 547
    court bouillon, white
        wine, 203
    curried seafood with rice
        pilaf, 225–6
    en brochette, 218
    essence de poisson, 45
    fillets, 196, 554;
        escabeche, 15–6;
        frozen, 196; poached,
        with garlic mayon-
        naise, 202–3; with
        tapenade, 36
    fillets, broiled, 196–7
        with almonds, 197;
        bacon and green
        onions, 198; bread
        crumbs, 198; cheese,
        198; herbed butter,
        197–8; leftover,

fish (cont.)
    marinated, 198; lemon
        butter, 197; peanuts,
        197; provençal, 198;
        white wine and garlic,
        198; white wine and
        herbs, 198
    fillets, sautéed, 199; curry
        sauce, 200; walnut-
        breaded, 199
    and garlic, 194, 206
    hash, 206
    Hellenic seafood stew,
        219–20
    Marseilles soup, 67
    with mint, 19–20
    mousse, 9–10
    poached, 200–1; dill
        sauce, 202; egg sauce,
        202; green mayonnaise,
        202; parsley sauce, 202;
        white butter sauce,
        201–2; white wine
        sauce, 202; yogurt-herb
        sauce, 202
    with risotto, 292
    salad, 108; and chicken,
        102; tomatoes stuffed
        with, 89; yogurt
        dressing, 108
    sausages, 194; French,
        217–18; French, with
        crab, 218; French, with
        shrimp, 218; oyster,
        231
    seafood soup, 45
    solianka, 221–2; with dill,
        222
    steaks, broiled, 206
    stock, 530
Flemish green eel, 210
Flemish leek pie, 267–8
Flemish pot roast, 377
Florence fennel, see fennel
Florentines, 490–1
flounder:
    bouillabaisse, 220–1
    escabeche, 16
    fillets, 556; broiled, 196–
        197; broiled, variations,
        197–8; poached, with
        garlic mayonnaise,
        202–3; sautéed, 199;
        sautéed, with curry
        sauce, 200; sautéed,
        walnut-breaded,
        199
    salad, 108; yogurt
        dressing, 108

flour, 554–5
  all-purpose, 554
  barley, 541
  beurre manié, 536
  buckwheat, 542, 543
  cake, 555
  hard-wheat, 555
  instant, 555
  self-rising, 555
  stone-ground, 555
  as thickener, 555
  whole-wheat (graham),
    555
flower blossoms, deep-fried,
  188
fontina, 246
fool, 515
  gooseberry, 515
  raspberry, 516
  rhubarb, 516
  strawberry, 515
  with yogurt, 516
frankfurters, 588
  onion and pepper frittata,
    259
  roast goose with
    sauerkraut, 341
  and sauerkraut salad, 93
  sausage en brioche, 436;
    with mustard, 436
  venison chili, 447–8
freezers:
  ice cream, 502
  sherbet, 499
French-bread-and-butter
  pudding, 527
French chocolate cake,
  517–18
frittata, 258
  bean sprouts and pork,
    259–60
  onion: and artichoke,
    259; frankfurter or
    sausage, 259; ham and
    potato, 259; spinach,
    259; spinach and
    bacon, 259; tomato,
    259; zucchini, 258–9;
    zucchini with
    prosciutto, 259
  Vanessi special, 260;
    beans and rice, 260;
    ham, 260; spinach, 260
frogs' legs, 555
  batter-fried, 243
  deep-fried, 243
  deviled, 242
  fines herbes, 242
  Italian style, 242

frogs' legs (cont.)
  niçoise, 242
  provençal, 242
  sautéed, 241–2
  southern-fried, 242; with
    Madeira sauce, 242
fruit:
  canned, as dessert, 507
  dried, compote, 514; with
    cognac, 514; with rum,
    514
  fools, 515–6
  pies, 508–10
  poached in syrup, 505–6
  with prosciutto, 32
  raw, as dessert, 506–7
  and rice salad, 97
  tarts, 510–14

game, see individual listings
garbanzos, see chickpeas
garbure basquaise, 59–60
  gratiné, 60
  with pigs' knuckles, 60
garlic, 576, 577–8; to buy,
  577; to peel, 577
  aïoli, 203
  butter, 20, 537; parsley,
    336
  and fish, 194, 206
  purée, 534–5
  vinaigrette, 74; with
    herbs, processor,
    74–5
garlic sausage:
  cassoulet, 304–5; limas
    and roasted duck legs,
    306
  homemade, 434
  partridge, braised, with
    cabbage, 348–9
  pheasant, braised, with
    sauerkraut, 353–4
  sausage en brioche, 436;
    with mustard, 436
ginger, 556, 592; root, to
    keep, 556
  cakes, 487
  and lime sherbet, 501
  and macadamia nut ice
    cream, 503
  -pumpkin soup, 57
Gino's macaroons, 490
globe fish, see blowfish
gnocchi:
  cornmeal, 301
  with pesto, 281
goloubtzys, 136

goose, 313, 555–6
  frozen, 340
  rillettes, 26
  roast: apple and apricot
    stuffing, 340–1;
    sauerkraut, 341; wild
    rice and mushrooms,
    295
goose, wild:
  gumbo, 346
  roast, 346
gooseberries:
  fool, 515
  poached, 505
gougères, 268
goujonettes of sole, 19
  in beer batter, 19
goulash, pork:
  and sauerkraut, 427–8
  and veal, 428
grapefruit:
  and apple salad, 98
  sherbet, 501
grapes, 506
Greek salad, 87
  with cucumber, 87;
    radishes and capers, 87
green beans, see beans,
  green
green mayonnaise, 77
green rice, 289
greens (for cooking), 149–
  150, 558–9
  tian, 152; and bacon, 152
  wilted, 150
greens (for salad), 77–8,
  556–7
  vintner's salad, 81
green sauce, 372, 373
gremolata, 416
Gribiche, sauce, 535
Gruyère cheese, 246, 544–
  545
  avocado with chicken,
    ham, and cheese, 37
  creamy cheese sauce,
    531
  garlic bread, 473–4
  gougères, 268
  Malakoff, 268–9
  in salad, 79
  soup, 68–9

haddock, 551
  fillets, 551, 554; broiled,
    196–7; broiled,
    variations, 197–8;
    poached, with garlic

haddock *(cont.)*
mayonnaise, 202–3;
sautéed, 199
smoked (finnan haddie),
551; cullen skink, 68;
mousse, 9; omelet, 256;
Scotch vichyssoise, 68
steaks: baked, niçoise,
208; broiled, 206
halibut, 551–2
bouillabaisse, 220–1
salad, 108; yogurt
dressing, 108
seafood en brochette, 218
steaks: baked, niçoise,
208; broiled, 206
ham, 570–1
artichokes stuffed with,
121
avocado with chicken and
cheese, 37
baked, 571; en croûte,
437–8
boiled, and cabbage,
439
braised: chablisienne,
438–9; Madeira, 439
brioche filled with, 27–8
canned, 571
chicken, braised, stuffed
with, 318; mustard and
cream sauce, 318–19
country, 570, 571
eggs Benedict, 252
farmer's omelet, 256
Flemish leek pie, 267–8
frittata, 260; onion and
potato, 259
leftover, serving
suggestions, 440
and Manka's babies, 267
meat loaf, 384
omelette savoyarde, 256
and onion stuffing, for
beef birds, 374
with prosciutto, 32
ready-to-eat, 570–1
with shirred eggs, 251
slice, baked: arthoise,
441; in champagne,
441; Floridian, 441; in
red wine, 441
slice, broiled, 440;
barbecued, 440; glazed
with honey and
mustard, 440; glazed
with maple syrup, 440;
soy and mustard, 440;
slice, fried, with red-eye

ham *(cont.)*
gravy, 441–2; variation,
442
Smithfield, 571
soufflé in pastry, 265
timbales, 263
and tomato sauce, 283
Vanessi special, 260
veal birds stuffed with,
409
Virginia, 571; with
asparagus, 32; with
fruit, 32; spinach and
rosemary sauce, 279–
280
white beans with cognac
and sausage, 303
with wild rice, 295
see also prosciutto
ham, fresh, *see* pork, leg
hamburgers, beef, *see* beef,
hamburgers
hamburgers, venison, 447
herbed, 447
Hand melons, 573
sherbet, 501–2
hazelnut oil, 74
hazelnuts (filberts), 415,
575
cheesecake, 523–4
praline powder, 518
head cheese, 430–1, 569
hearts, 449
beef, 449, 566;
anticuchos, 31
chicken: anticuchos, 31;
en brochette, 31; and
gizzards, sautéed, 326–
327; gizzards and livers,
sautéed, 296, 327; and
livers en brochette,
30–1
lamb, 569; braised, 456
pork, 570
veal, 572; braised, 455–6
Hellenic seafood stew, 219–
220
herbs, 559–61; to buy, 559;
to keep, 559; ratio of
dried to fresh,
559
butter, 198
green mayonnaise, 77
green rice, 289
green sauce, 372, 373
pâté, 24–5
with rice, 289
in salad, 78
vinaigrette, 74; with

herbs *(cont.)*
garlic, processor, 74–5
yogurt-herb sauce, 202
herring, 6–7, 552
kipper mousse, 10
Madeira, 7
marinated, 7
mustard, 7
pickled, 7
rollmops, 8
salad, 7; tomatoes
stuffed with, 89
in sour cream, 7
hollandaise sauce, 532
anchovy-flavored, 532
hominy, 297, 562
casserole, 297–8
sautéed, with cream,
297
honeydews, 573
with prosciutto, 32
sherbet, 501–2
horseradish, 562
applesauce, 422
cream, 9
Hubbard squash, 117, 178–
179, 593
baked, 178–9, 593; with
bacon, 179; with
brown sugar, 179
cream soup, 57
spiced, 177
steamed, 593
see also squash, winter
huevos rancheros, 253
with jalapeño peppers,
253
with tortillas, 253
hussar salad, 105–6

ice cream, 502; freezers, 502
brown bread, 504
caramel, 504
cassis, 504–5
praline, 502–3
raisin and chestnut, 503
imam bayildi, 147–8
Isbel, Tom:
parsley salad, 80–1
Italian link sausages, 433–4,
588; to cook, 435
cassoulet with limas,
305–6
hot, 435
old-fashioned, 434
paella, 293—4
with peppers, sautéed,
166

Italian link sausages *(cont.)*
 with polenta, 300
 and veal, 435
Italian-style asparagus, 39

Jerusalem artichokes (sun
 chokes), 121–2
 buttered, 122
 cream vegetable soup,
  basic, 52–4
 purée, 122
 vinaigrette, 122

kadjemoula, 397–8
kale, 150, 558
kasha, *see* buckwheat,
 groats
kidney beans, *see* beans,
 kidney
kidneys, 449
 beef, 567
 lamb, 449, 568; omelets,
  256; and roast saddle
  of mutton, 398–9;
  sauté flambé, 455; with
  scrambled eggs, 254
 lamb or veal: broiled
  deviled, 455; deviled
  sauté, 455
 lamb or veal en brochette,
  454; herb butter, 454;
  mushrooms, 454;
  mushrooms and bacon,
  454; sweetbreads, 454;
  sweetbreads flambé,
  454
 lamb or veal "on the half
  shell," 453; flambé,
  453; mushrooms, 453
 pork, 449, 570; deviled
  sauté, 455; sauté
  flambé, 455
 veal, 449, 572; sweet-
  breads and sausages,
  465; *see also* lamb or
  veal *above*
kielbasa, 588
 cassoulet, 304–5; limas
  and cooked lamb, 306
 with kidney beans, 307
 partridge, braised, with
  cabbage, 348–9
 sausage and croissant, 29
 sausage en brioche, 436;
  with mustard, 436

kipper mousse, 10
kiwi fruit, 562
 poached, 505
knockwurst, 590
 onion and pepper frittata,
  259
 and sauerkraut salad, 93
 sausage en brioche, 436;
  with mustard, 436
Knopf, Mildred, 168
knusper brote, 483
kohlrabi, 562
 mixed vegetable sauté,
  189–90
kosher salt, 587
kumquats, poached, 505

lace cookies, 486–7
Lady Curzon soup, 46–7
lamb, 385, 568–9
 blanquette of, 396–7
 brains, 450, 568
 breast, braised stuffed,
  393–4
 cassoulet, 304–5; with
  limas, 306; with limas
  and pork, 306
 couscous, 298
 crown roast, 387;
  stuffings, 387–8
 en daube, 394–5
 hearts, 569; braised, 456
 kadjemoula, 397–8
 kidneys, 449, 568; broiled
  deviled, 455; deviled
  sauté, 455; omelets,
  256; and roast saddle
  of mutton, 398–9;
  sauté flambé, 455; with
  scrambled eggs, 254
 kidneys en brochette,
  454; herb butter, 454;
  mushrooms, 454;
  mushrooms and bacon,
  454; sweetbreads, 454;
  sweetbreads flambé,
  454
 kidneys "on the half
  shell," 453; flambé,
  453; mushrooms, 453
 leg, 568
 leg, roast, 568; mock
  venison, 389;
  provençal, 388;
  provençal No. 2, 388;
  shallots, 388; spoon,
  389–90; Swedish, 389;
  weeping, 389; weeping,

lamb *(cont.)*
 with anchovies, 389
 with lentils, braised, 310–
  311
 liver, 448, 569; julienne,
  452; sautéed, 451–2
 mutton, roast saddle of,
  398–9
 Navarin, 396–7
 on a string (à la ficelle),
  390–1
 rack, roast, 385–6;
  persillé, 386–7; Quo
  Vadis, 387
 shanks, 569; with beans,
  399–400; onions and
  beer, 400; with
  ratatouille, 400
 shoulder, roast, 391–2;
  with cream, 392;
  eggplant and tomato,
  392
 stock, 396–7
 sweetbreads, *see* sweetbreads
 testicles, 569
 tongues, 458, 568;
  pickled, 458–9;
  poulette, 458; with
  tomato sauce, 458;
  vinaigrette, 458
lamb's lettuce, *see* field
 salad
lard, 321, 562; to render,
 508
 pastry, 497, 562
 pie crust, 508
larding, 569
 lardoons, cognac-soaked,
  375
lasagne with brain sauce,
 285
leeks, 152–3, 576, 577; to
 clean, 152–3
 bollito misto, 372–3
 braised, 153
 microwave-cooked, 153
 mixed vegetable sauté,
  189–90
 pie, Flemish, 267–8
 purée, 154
 ratatouille, 191
 steamed, 153
 vinaigrette, 154
 vichyssoise, 54–5;
  variations, 55
lemons, 563
 butter, 197; parsley, 231
 meringue bars, 489

lemons (cont.)
  pickled, 323
  vinaigrette, processor, 75
  zest, 563
Lenten buns, 479–80
lentils, 309, 563
  braised, with lamb, 310–
    311
  buttered, 310
  herbed, 310
  puréed, 310
  sautéed, 310; with onion,
    bacon, parsley, for pork
    crown roast stuffing,
    420; with roast
    spareribs, 431–2
  soup, 58; with chard and
    lemon, 59; with
    cotechino, 59; with
    cream, 58; with
    frankfurters or knock-
    wurst, 58; with ham,
    58
lettuce, 556, 557
  mixed vegetable sauté,
    189–90
  romaine soufflé, Philip
    Brown's, 150–1
  in salad, 77, 556, 557
  timbales, 262–3
  wilted, 150
  see also Bibb lettuce;
    endive
Lianides, Leon:
  black bean soup, 61–2
  tripe soup, 42, 62–3
lichee nuts, 563
  canned, as dessert, 507
  poached, 505
  sherbet, 502
lima beans, see beans, lima
limes, 563
  and ginger sherbet,
    501
  and tea sherbet, 502
Linzer bars, 492
liver, 448
  beef, 448, 567; meat loaf,
    384
  calves', 448, 572;
    julienne, 452; roast
    whole, 452–3;
    Venetian style, 452
  chicken, see chicken,
    livers
  duck, 549; with shirred
    eggs, 251
  lambs', 448, 569;
    julienne, 452

liver (cont.)
  pork, 448, 570; meat loaf,
    384; pâté in brioche,
    23–4
  sautéed: with avocado,
    451; with bacon, 451;
    deviled, 452; with
    mustard sauce, 451;
    with onions, 451; with
    shallots and Madeira,
    451
  venison, 597
lobster, 590
  Billy's coleslaw, 90–1
  bouillabaisse, 220–1
  Hellenic seafood stew,
    219–20
  Napoule, 236–7
  risotto with shellfish, 292
  salad: avocado and onion,
    110; chicken, 102;
    chicken and celery,
    110; cucumber and
    egg, 110; mayonnaise,
    109; potato and onion,
    109; tomatoes and
    green onion, 111
  sausage: fish, 194; French
    seafood, 217–18
  seafood à l'Américaine,
    223–4
  soufflé, 237
  stuffed baked, 235–6
  with tapenade mayon-
    naise, 36
  timbales, 263
Louis dressing, 77
lovage, 78
lox, 554
  marinated, 8

macadamia nuts:
  and ginger ice cream, 503
  in salad, 79; chicken,
    100; chicken, in stuffed
    tomatoes, 89; turkey,
    100; veal, 100
macaroni with beans, 286–7
macaroons:
  chocolate, 489
  Gino's, 490
mace, 592
mackerel:
  cotriade, 223
  escabeche, 17
  fillets: broiled, 196–7;
    broiled, variations,
    197–8; sautéed, 199

Madeira brown sauce, 533
Madeira herring, 7
Malakoff, 268–9
Malden salt, 587
maltaise sauce 532
The Mandarin (San
    Francisco):
  red-cooked pork shoulder,
    432
  tripe with gizzards, 461–
    462
mandarins, 564
mangoes, 507, 564
Manka's babies, 266–7
  with broccoli rabe and
    cheese, 267
  with ham, 267
  with roast beef, 267
  with spinach and cheese,
    267
  with strawberries and
    yogurt, 267
marrow:
  poached in Bordelaise
    sauce, 533
  soufflé in pastry, 264–5
Marseilles fish soup, 67
Maynard, Mrs.: cinnamon
    rolls, 478–9
mayonnaise, 76
  anchovy, 77
  blender method, 76
  food processor method,
    76
  garlic (aïoli), 203
  green, 77
  Louis dressing, 77
  mustard, 76, 90
  rémoulade sauce, 77
  tapenade, 36
  tartare sauce, 77
  yogurt, 76, 90
mealy bread, 482
meat, 358–60, 564–72
  barding, 569
  bollito misto, 372–3
  cuts, 564
  to freeze, 565
  frozen, 565
  ground, 565
  larding, 375, 569
  uncooked, to keep, 565
meat loaf, old-fashioned,
    364, 383–4
  with beef livers, 384
  chilied, 385
  with clams, minced, 384
  with eggs, hard-boiled,
    384

meat loaf (cont.)
  with ham, 384
  with olives, 384
Meerson, Mary, 358–9
melons, 573; to keep, 573
  with prosciutto, 32
  sherbet, 501–2
menudo, 460–1
meringue kisses, 491–2
Mexican pot roast, 377
minestrone, Marion
    Cunningham's, 60–1;
    with chickpeas or
    kidney beans, 61; with
    ham, 61; with sausage,
    61
minina, 261
mint, 560–1
Monterey Jack cheese,
    545
mornay, sauce, 531
mortadella, 588
mousse:
  haddock, smoked, 9
  kipper, 10
  sardine, 10
  trout, smoked, 10
mozzarella, 246, 545
  with scrambled eggs, 254
  with tomatoes, 79; baked,
    stuffed, 182; and
    peppers vinaigrette,
    167
mushrooms, 154, 573–4
  and barley casserole, 295–
    296; almonds, 296;
    celery and water
    chestnuts, 296; chicken
    gizzards, 296
  brown sauce, 533
  cèpes à la Bordelaise,
    155–6
  dried, 574
  duxelles, 535–6; brown
    sauce, 535; omelet,
    256; roulade of veal
    Île-de-France, 405;
    rutabagas, 187;
    scrambled eggs in a
    tart shell, 254; tomato
    sauce, 284; wild rice,
    295
  French-fried, 187
  as garnish, 154
  with kasha, 296
  mixed vegetable sauté,
    189–90
  pasta with spinach, 286;
    Parmesan cheese, 286

mushrooms (cont.)
  pâté, 35
  with pork chops, sautéed,
    425
  ratatouille, 191
  in salad, 78; marinated
    mushrooms and beets,
    86; spinach, 82
  sautéed, 154–5; with
    bacon bits, 155; with
    buttered peas, 164;
    with fresh herbs and
    cream, 155; with heavy
    cream, 155; with
    noodles, for pork
    crown roast stuffing,
    420; pork crown roast
    stuffing, 420; with sour
    cream, 155; with
    yogurt, 155
  sautéed caps: with
    Brussels sprouts, 131;
    with cucumbers,
    sautéed, 145; with
    herbs, for lamb crown
    roast stuffing, 388;
    stuffed with snails, 21
  and sour cream roll, 264
  stems, uses for, 154
mussels, 590–1; to clean,
    224
  billi bi, 66
  bouillabaisse, 220–1
  Castilian soup, 65
  cioppino, 222
  curried seafood with rice
    pilaf, 225–6
  with garlic butter, 14
  Hiely, 13
  marinière, 224; with
    cream, 225; with garlic,
    224; with tomatoes,
    225
  paella, 293–4
  The Palace mussel soup,
    65–6
  provençal, 13–14
  rémoulade, 14
  risotto with shellfish, 292
  salad, 14
  and tomato sauce, 283
mustard, 574
  Burgundian, 421
  chicken, 327–8
  herring, 7
  mayonnaise, 76, 90
  rabbit, with turnips, 357
  sauce, 531
  tapenade, 36

mustard (cont.)
  vinaigrette, 74
  -yogurt dressing, 85
mustard greens, 558
  braised, 151
  purée, with poached egg,
    252
  sautéed, 558
  soup, 50–1
  tian of mixed greens,
    152; and bacon, 152
  wilted, 150, 558

Nassikas, Jim:
  rich egg pasta, 277
nasturtium leaves, 93
Navarin, 396–7
nectarines, 574
Nevada chili beans, 308
noodles:
  homemade (fettucini),
    276
  and salad of marinated
    vegetables, 86–7; with
    corn, 87; with foie
    gras, 87; with
    tomatoes, 87
  with tian, 191
nutmeg, 592
nuts, 574–6; to buy, 574;
    to keep, 574
  with rice, 289
  rum bread, 481
  in salad, 79
  as thickener, 43

oatmeal carrot cookies,
    487–8
ocean perch fillets, 554
  broiled, 196–7; variations,
    197–8
  sautéed, 199
offal, 448–9
oils, 74, 576
okra, 156
  and corn, 156–7
  French-fried, 188
  steamed, 156; with butter
    and lemon, 156; with
    garlic-anchovy butter,
    156; with garlic and
    oil, 156
  vinaigrette, 156
olive oil, 74, 576; to keep,
    576
olives:
  beef and pork chili, 381

olives (cont.)
  with duck, 339; salad,
    104
  with meat loaf, 384
  in salad, 79
  sauce, 101–2
  tapenade, 35–6
  and vegetable salad with
    mustard-yogurt
    dressing, 84; blue
    cheese or Gruyère
    cheese, 85
omelet, basic, 255–6
  asparagus, 256
  caviar and sour cream,
    256
  cheese, 256
  chicken and curry, 257
  chili, 256
  cold layered, 257–8
  duxelles, 256
  farmer's, 256
  finnan haddie, 256
  lamb kidneys, 256
  salmon, smoked, 256
  shrimp, 257
  spinach, 256
  tomato, fresh, 256
  zucchini blossom, 176
omelette savoyarde, 256
onions, 157, 576–8; to buy,
    576; to keep, 157, 576;
    to peel, 157
  and baked beets: with
    orange, 128, with
    tarragon, 128
  boiled, 157–8
  bollito misto, 372–3
  braised, 159; with
    Parmesan cheese, 159;
    pasta sauce, 280; with
    sherry, bourbon, or
    Madeira, 159–60
  broiled slices, 159; with
    cheese, 159; with
    hamburgers, 159
  brown onion skins, uses
    for, 157
  buttered, 158; with
    nutmeg, 158
  with cheese sauce, 158
  with cream sauce, 158
  eggplant casserole, 147
  fried, 158; caramelized,
    158; dieter's, 158
  frittata: and artichoke,
    259; ham and potato,
    259; pepper and
    frankfurter or sausage,

onions (cont.)
  259; spinach, 259;
    spinach and bacon,
    259; tomato, 259;
    zucchini, 258–9;
    zucchini and pro-
    sciutto, 259
  gratin, 39
  green (scallions), 157,
    576, 577; anchovies
    and parsley, 6; boiled,
    160; coleslaw, quick
    chopped, 90; French-
    fried, 187; green rice,
    289; hollandaise sauce,
    160; mornay sauce,
    160; peas, buttered,
    164; vinaigrette, 74;
    wild rice with pine
    nuts, 295
  with hamburgers, 159,
    382, 383
  old-fashioned pickled
    eggs, 250–1
  orange and shrimp salad,
    99
  pearl (or pickling), 577;
    and buttered peas, 164
  with pork chops, sautéed,
    425
  ratatouille, 190; with
    eggs, poached, and
    cheese, 191; fennel,
    191; leeks, 191; mush-
    rooms, 191; spicy, 191
  red or Italian, 577
  -rice sauce, 320
  rice with pine nuts, 289–
    290
  in salad, 78
  sautéed: and sautéed
    eggplant, 147; rings
    with sautéed peppers,
    165
  with short ribs, braised,
    380
  stuffed, 160
  with tomato sauce, 158
  white, large, 577
  white, small, 577; à la
    Grecque, 38–9; boiled,
    157–8; gratin, 39;
    mixed vegetable sauté,
    189–90; monégasque,
    39; to peel, 157
  with wild rice and bacon,
    295
  yellow globe (Spanish),
    576; oxtail gratin, 49

onions (cont.)
  see also chives; garlic;
    leeks; shallots
oranges, 578; to buy, 578
  and almond cake, 520–1
  and baked beets, with
    onion, 128
  butter, 537
  poached, 506
  salad: and duck, 104;
    fruit and rice, 97;
    onion and shrimp, 99;
    radish, 97–8
  sauce, for partridge, 347
  sherbet, 501
Oregon duck, a favorite,
    343
Oregon potato salad, old-
    fashioned, 93–4
Oregon veal birds, 410
ossi buchi, 416, 572
  with prosciutto and black
    olives, 416
Owen, Jeanne, 313
oxttail, 567
  consomme, 48–9; as
    thickener, 43, 567
  gratin, 49
  and vegetable soup, 49
oyster plant, see salsify
oysters, 591
  bisque, 63–4
  cioppino, 222
  fried, 230–1
  loaves, 231
  on the half shell, baked
    with shrimp sauce,
    229–30
  roast quail with, 350
  sausages, 231
  stuffed, 230

paella, 293–4
pain de mie, 469–70
The Palace (N.Y.C.):
  mussel soup, 65–6
palm, hearts of:
  and potato salad, 96
  with veal chops, 412
pancakes:
  apple, 494
  blini: buckwheat, 40–1;
    carrot, 41
  zucchini, 175–6; with
    cheese, 176
papayas (pawpaw), 578
  avocado and shrimp, 98
  with prosciutto, 32

papayas (cont.)
  raw, as dessert, 507
  shrimp and crab salad,
    99
paprika, 578; to keep, 578
Parmesan (Parmigiana),
    246–7, 545
  creamy cheese sauce, 531
  mornay, sauce, 531
parsley, 561
  with anchovies and
    shallots, 6
  butter: garlic, 336;
    lemon, 231
  fried, 561
  Italian, 561; pesto, 282
  in salad, 78; Tom Isbel's,
    80–1
  sauce, 531
parsley, Chinese, see
    coriander
parsnips, 161; to buy, 161
  cream vegetable soup,
    basic, 52–4
  French-fried: in beer
    batter, 189; in egg
    crumb, 162
  glazed, 161
  puréed, 162; with carrots,
    137; patties, 162; with
    potatoes, 162
  sautéed, 161
  steamed, 161
partridge, 346–7
  braised, with cabbage and
    sausage, 348–9
  roast, 347; with orange
    sauce, 347
pasta, 272–3, 579; to cook,
    278–9; 579
  asciutta rustica, 287
  with beans, 286–7
  with eggs mollet, 285
  homemade: to cook, 278;
    egg, rich, 277; food
    processor method, 277;
    hand method, 276; to
    roll and cut, 277–8;
    spinach, 277; tomato,
    277
  spaghetti squash as diet
    substitute, 177
  with spinach and mush-
    rooms, 286; and
    Parmesan cheese, 286
pasta sauces, 278
  to serve, 579
  see also sauces and
    dressings

pastry:
  cornmeal, 513
  cream puff (pâte à
    choux), 268
  crust, cheesecake, 522,
    524
  pâte sucrée, 510
  pie crust, lard, 509
  tart, 512; rich, 264–5
pâté:
  chicken, rolled, 21–2
  chicken livers and ham,
    22
  goose rillettes, 26
  herbed, 24–5
  liver, special stuffed eggs,
    249–50
  mushroom, 35
  pork liver in brioche, 23
  pork rillettes, 25–6
  rabbit, 22–3
  salmon, 11; and pike, 12
  sturgeon, smoked, 11
  truffled rillettes, 26
  tuna, 11
pâte à choux, 268
pâte sucrée, 510
pawpaw, see papayas
peaches, 579–80
  canned, as dessert, 507
  dried, compote, 514
  poached, 506, 580
  raw, as dessert, 506
  sherbet, 501
peanut butter cookies,
    "monster," 491
peanut oil, 576
peanuts, 575
  in salad, 79
  with winter squash, 178
pears, 580; kinds, 580
  and apple tapioca, 527
  baked, 58
  cake, fresh, 522
  canned Bartlett, as
    dessert, 507
  and chocolate tart, 511
  poached, 506
  with prosciutto, 32
  raw, as dessert, 507
  sherbet: red wine, 500;
    white wine, 500
  tart, thin, 513–14
peas, green, 163, 580; to
    buy, 163
  boiled, 163
  boula-boula, 47
  buttered: with green
    onions, 164; with

peas, green (cont.)
  herbs, 163; with
    mushrooms, 164; with
    pearl onions, 164
  with heavy cream, 164;
    and herbs, 164
  mixed vegetable sauté,
    189–90
  with prosciutto and
    cream sauce, 285
  puréed, 164
  and rice pilaf, 291
  risotto with, 293
  salad, 83
  soup, cold minted, 55–6
peas, snow, 163, 580
  French-fried, 187
  sautéed with cucumbers,
    146
peas, sugar snap, 163, 580–
    581
  French-fried, 187
  mixed vegetable sauté,
    189–90
pecans, 575
  with rice, 289
  with winter squash and
    ginger, 178
Pennsylvania Dutch
    tomatoes, 184
pepper (peppercorns), 581
  green peppercorn butter,
    318
pepper, cayenne, 581
peppers, chili, see chili
    peppers, hot
peppers, sweet or bell, 164–
    165, 581; to peel, 165
  with anchovies, 5; eggs
    and tomatoes, 6;
    raisins, 36; shallots and
    parsley, 6; tuna, 6
  butter, for corn, 142
  chicken legs and yogurt,
    326
  coleslaw, with carrots, 90
  eggplant casserole, 147
  French-fried, 187
  mixed vegetable sauté,
    189–90
  pipérade basquaise, 255
  ratatouille, 190; eggs,
    poached, and cheese,
    191; fennel, 191; leeks,
    191; mushrooms, 191;
    spicy, 191
  in salad, 78
  sautéed in butter, 166;
    with corn kernels, 166;

peppers, sweet or bell (cont.)
  with Italian sausages,
    166; with pork chops,
    166
  sautéed in olive oil, 165;
    with braised beef, 165;
    with onion rings, 165;
    with pasta, 166; with
    roast chicken, 165
  with scrambled eggs, 254
  slaw, 92
  stuffed, 167; with corn
    kernels, 167; with
    leftover meat, 167
  vinaigrette, 166–7;
    anchovies, 167; mint,
    167; mozzarella and
    tomatoes, 167
Persian melons, 573
persimmons, 507, 582
Peruvian eggs, 261–2
pesto, 281–2
  diet, 282
  with parsley, 282
  with walnuts, 282
Petersen, Alice:
  chocolate cheesecake,
    522–3
pheasant, 352, 582
  braised, with sauerkraut,
    353–4
  broiled, 356: with
    tarragon butter, 356
  fricassee, 353
  roast, Pompadour, 352
  sautéed, 354–5; Calvados
    and apples, 355; white
    wine and tarragon,
    355
pie:
  apple, 509
  nutted pumpkin, 510
  rhubarb, 509
pie crust, lard, 508, 509
pigeon, see squab
pike:
  poached, with white
    butter sauce, 201–2
  and salmon pâté, 12
pilaf:
  bulghur (cracked wheat),
    290–1; pine nuts, for
    lamb crown roast
    stuffing, 387
  rice, 290–1; curried
    seafood, 225–6; green
    chilies, 291; nuts and
    raisins, 291; peas, 291;
    sautéed lamb kidneys,

pilaf (cont.)
  for lamb crown roast
    stuffing, 387
pimientos, 581
pineapples, 582–3; to buy,
    582; to peel, 583
  and apricot tart, 510–11
  fruit and rice salad, 97
  poached, 505, 506
  with prosciutto, 32
  sherbet, 501
pine nuts, 575
  and raisin sauce, 281;
    with anchovies, 281;
    with figs, 281
  rice with onions, 289–90
  in salad, 79
  wild rice with green
    onions, 295
pinto beans, see beans,
    dried
pipérade basquaise, 255
piquante, sauce, 299
pistachio nuts, 575–6
pizza, deep-dish, 270
plums, 583
  poached, 506
polenta, 274, 300
  cakes, 301
  with fontina cheese, 300
  with salt cod, 301
  with sausages, 300
  with spinach, 300–1
polygrained bread, 472
  with cornmeal, 472
  with garlic and dill, 472
  with walnuts, 472
pomegranates, 583
poppy-seed dressing, 97
pork, 416–17, 569–71;
    cooking temperature,
    417
  bacon, see bacon
  and bean sprouts frittata,
    259–60
  and beef chili, 381, with
    beer, 381; nuts, 381;
    olives, 381
  bollito misto, 372–3
  brains, 569
  cassoulet, 304–5; limas
    and lamb, 306
  chicken pâté, rolled, 21–
    22
  chops, 421, 425, 569;
    charcutière, 426;
    grilled, with sautéed
    peppers, 166; Mexican
    style, 425–6

pork (cont.)
  chops, sautéed: with
    mushrooms, 425; with
    onions, 425; with
    sauerkraut, 426
  chops, stuffed, 426–7;
    onion and herb, 427;
    pork and onion, 424
  crown roast, 419–20,
    570; stuffings, 420
  drunken, 422
  fat, 417, 569; barding,
    569; lard, 321, 497,
    508, 562; larding, 375,
    569
  goulash: and sauerkraut,
    427–8; and veal, 428
  ham, see ham
  ham, fresh, see leg below
  head cheese, 430–1, 569
  heart, 570
  kidneys, 449, 570; deviled
    sauté, 455; sauté
    flambé, 455
  leg (fresh ham), 570
  leg (fresh ham), roast:
    with Burgundian
    mustard, 421; drunken,
    422; Italian boned
    stuffed, 422; Norman
    style, 421–2; taste like
    wild boar, 422
  liver, 448, 570; meat loaf,
    384; pâté in brioche,
    23–4; sautéed, 451–2
  loin, 569–70
  loin, roast, 417–18; 571;
    coriander and fennel,
    419; flambé, 418;
    garlic, 418; green
    peppercorn butter,
    419; marinated
    Oriental style, 418;
    marinated Oriental
    and glazed, 418;
    orange glazed, 418–19;
    prune stuffed, 419;
    prune stuffed with
    potatoes and onions,
    419; rosemary, 418;
    smoked, 420–1
  meat loaf, old-fashioned,
    364, 383–4; chilied,
    385; clams, minced,
    384; eggs, hard-boiled,
    384; ham, 384; liver,
    384; olives, 384
  peppers stuffed with,
    167

pork *(cont.)*
  pig, roast suckling: with
    aïoli, 424; pistachio-
    rice stuffing, 423–4
  pigs' ears, 569
  pigs' feet, 429, 570
  pigs' feet St. Menehould,
    429; jellied, 430;
    pickled, 430
  pigs' hocks, 570; braised,
    433; braised, with
    sauerkraut, 433; jellied,
    430; marinated, 433
  pig's jowl, 569
  rillettes, 25–6; truffled,
    26
  salad, 99–100
  sausages, 570, 587, 588;
    homemade, en brioche,
    28–9; with sweetbreads
    and kidneys, 465; *see
    also* Italian link
    sausages; sausages,
    meat
  shoulder: Cecilia
    Chiang's red-cooked,
    432; roast, with apples
    and onions, 422–3
  spareribs, 570
  spareribs, baked with
    sauerkraut, apples, and
    potatoes, 428; dill,
    429; onions, 429
  spareribs, roast: glazed,
    432; plain, 429;
    sautéed lentils, 431–2
  tongue, 569
  tonnato, 403
  and turkey, veal birds
    stuffed with, 409
  zampone, 570
port wine sauce, 26–7
potatoes, 167–8, 583–4; to
  buy, 584; to keep,
  584; kinds, 584
  baked, 168, 584; with
    beef drippings, 168;
    with caviar, 38; with
    yogurt, 168
  boiled, 584
  and celery root, baked,
    141
  disgustingly rich potatoes,
    168–9
  duchesse, 170
  farmer's omelet, 256
  French-fried, 188–9
  German-fried, 170
  gratin, 169

potatoes *(cont.)*
  ham and onion frittata,
    259
  hash brown, 170
  leg of lamb, weeping,
    389; with anchovies,
    389
  mashed, 169; parsley or
    chives, 169; yellow
    turnips (rutabagas),
    170
  mashed, instant:
    chocolate tweed cake,
    519; as thickener, 53,
    54
  new, 584; baked, 168;
    with caviar, 38; mixed
    vegetable sauté, 189–
    190
  with pesto, 281
  puréed: with carrots,
    137; with parsnips, 162
  roesti, 171
  salad, 93; Alexandre
    Dumas, 95; boiled
    dressing, 94; chicken
    and bean, 103; French
    hot, 95; hearts of
    palm, 96; old-fashioned
    Oregon, 93–4
  sautéed in beef suet, 171
  skins, twice-baked, 38,
    168
  steamed, 584
  vichyssoise, 54–5;
    variations, 55
pots de crème:
  chocolate, 528
  vanilla, 528; with praline,
    528
poulette, sauce, 458
poultry, 312–14
pound cake, 525
  buttered-cake pudding,
    527
  with citron, 525
  with spices, 525
praline:
  butter cream, 518
  ice cream, 502–3
  powder, 518
prosciutto:
  artichokes stuffed with,
    121
  with asparagus, 32
  chicken pâté, rolled, 21–
    22
  and crabmeat, 33
  with fruit, 32

prosciutto *(cont.)*
  onion and zucchini
    frittata, 259
  peas and cream sauce,
    285
  saltimbocca, 408; with
    mozzarella cheese,
    408
  with scrambled eggs, 254
prunes:
  dried, compote, 514
  poached, 506
  sherbet, 500
  stuffing, for roast pork
    loin, 419
puffer, *see* blowfish
pullman loaf, 469–70
pumpernickel bread, 471
pumpkin, 594
  cream vegetable soup,
    basic, 52–4
  -ginger soup, 57
  pie, nutted, 510
purple cauliflower (purple
    broccoli), 138

quail, 349, 584
  braised, with white wine,
    351
  roast, 349–50; with
    duxelles, 350; with
    mustard, 350; with
    oysters, 350; on
    scrapple, 350; with
    tarragon, 350; in vine
    leaves, 350
  sautéed, 350–1; with
    juniper berries, 351;
    with shallots and
    mushrooms, 351
  Scotch eggs, 250
quatre épices, 536
quince, 585
  and apple tapioca, 527
  poached, 506
  tart, The Coach House,
    512
Quo Vadis Restaurant
  (N.Y.C.):
  rack of lamb, 387
  Vadis bars, 488–9

rabbit, 314, 357, 585
  mustard, with turnips,
    356
  pâté, 22–3
  provençal, 356–7

radishes:
  coleslaw with carrots, 90
  with crab salad, 111
  mixed vegetable sauté,
    189–90
  and orange salad, 97–8
raisins:
  bread, 474–5
  and chestnut ice cream,
    503
  and pine nut sauce, 281;
    with anchovies, 281;
    with figs, 281
raïto, 245
rape (broccoli rape), see
    broccoli rabe
raspberries, 585
  fool, 516
  raw, as dessert, 506
ratatouille, 190
  with eggs, poached, and
    cheese, 191
  with fennel, 191
  and lamb shanks, 400
  with leeks, 191
  with mushrooms, 191
  and pot roast, leftover,
    377
  spicy, 191
red snapper, 552
  broiled fillets, 196–7;
    variations, 197–8
  poached, with various
    sauces, 200–2
  sautéed fillets, 199
red wine-pear sherbet, 500
reindeer, 599
rémoulade sauce, 77
Renggli, Seppi:
  roast duck, 338
Rhode, William, 54–5
rhubarb, 585–6
  fool, 516
  glazed, with strawberries
    Teresa, 515
  pie, 509
  poached, 506
rhubarb chard, 558
rice, 288–9, 586
  with cheese, 289
  and chicken salad, 102
  green, 289
  with herbs, 289
  with nuts, 289
  -onion sauce, for poached
    chicken, 320
  with onions and pine
    nuts, 289–90
  Oriental fried, 290

rice (cont.)
  paella, 293–4
  pilaf, 290–1; curried
    seafood, 225–6; green
    chilies, 291; nuts and
    raisins, 291; peas, 291;
    sautéed lamb kidneys,
    for lamb crown roast
    stuffing, 387
    -pistachio stuffing, for
    roast suckling pig, 424
  risotto, 291–2; variations,
    292–3
  saffron-flavored, 289
  salad, basic, 96; and
    crab, tomatoes stuffed
    with, 89
  with tian, 191
  Vanessi special, with
    beans, 260
rice, wild, 294, 586
  basic, 294–5; bacon and
    onion, 295; duck or
    goose fat and mush-
    rooms, 295; duxelles,
    295; green onions and
    pine nuts, 295; ham,
    295; walnuts, 295
rice vinegar, 74
ricotta, 544
rillettes:
  goose, 26
  pork, 25–6
  truffled, 26
Ripperberger, Helmut:
  roast loin of venison,
    444–5
risotto, 291–2
  alla milanese, 292
  with asparagus tips, 293
  with cherry tomatoes,
    293
  with chicken, 292
  with green beans, 293
  with green peas, 293
  with shellfish, 292
  with shrimp, raw, 292
  with white truffles, 292
Rock Cornish hens, 313,
    335, 586–7
  à la crème, 337
  broiled: garlic-parsley
    butter, 336; rosemary
    butter, 336; tarragon
    butter, 336
  poached, 336
  roast, stuffed, 335; garlic,
    336; herbs, 336;
    tarragon, 335

Rock Cornish hens (cont.)
  sautéed, with bacon, 337
  spatchcocked, 337
rocket (rugula; arugula),
    557
Rockey, Mrs.: shad roe,
    211–12
rockfish, see striped bass
rock salt, 587
roesti, 171
Rojas-Lombardi, Felipe:
  Peruvian eggs, 261–2
rollmops, 8
rolls:
  baps, breakfast, 476
  cinnamon, Mrs.
    Maynard's, 478–9
  hard, 475–6
romaine (cos lettuce), 557
  mixed vegetable sauté,
    189–90
  soufflé, Philip Brown's
    150–1
roquefort-butter stuffing,
    402
rose geranium, 505
rosemary, 561
  butter, 537
rouille, 67
rugula (arugula; rocket),
    557
rum and brown sugar sauce,
    508
Russian dressing, 37
rutabagas (yellow turnips),
    185, 596
  buttered, 186
  cream vegetable soup,
    basic, 52–4
  with duxelles, 187
  with Madeira or sherry,
    187
  mashed, 186–7
  and mashed potatoes, 187
  puréed, with poached
    eggs, 252
  with yogurt, 186
rye bread, dark, 470–1

sablefish:
  bouillabaisse, 220–1
  broiled steaks, 206
safflower oil, 576
sage, 561
salad, 70–2
  additions to, 78–9
  as first course, serving
    portion, 99

salad *(cont.)*
  greens, 77–8, 556–7
  herbs, 78
salad dressings, *see* sauces
    and dressings
salami, 589
  onion, pepper frittata, 259
salmi, *see* duck, wild
salmon, 193, 552
  broiled fillets, 196–7;
    variations, 197–8
  broiled steaks, 206
  cheeks, sautéed, 216
  coulibiac, 214–15; with
    rice, 215
  escabeche, 16
  lox, 554; marinated, 8
  pâté, 11; with pike, 12
  poached: salad, 107; with
    various sauces, 200–2
  sautéed fillets, 199
  scalloped, 215
  smoked, 552; fish sausage,
    194; marinated, 8;
    omelet, 256; rolls with
    horseradish cream, 9;
    sour cream roll, 263–4
  solianka, 221–2; with dill,
    222
  tart, 216–7
  tartare, 12–13
  turban of sole
    mousseline, 204–5
salsify (oyster plant), 171,
    587
  boiled, 171–2
  cream vegetable soup,
    basic, 52–4
  French-fried, 187
  with mornay sauce, 172
  sautéed, 172
  with shallots and lemons,
    172
salt, 587
saltimbocca, 408
  with mozzarella cheese,
    408
sardines:
  baked spiced, 214
  cotriade, 223
  eggs stuffed with, 250
  and fennel sauce, 280
  fried, 213; with garlic
    and parsley, 213
  with mint, 19–20
  mousse, 10
  skewered, 213
sauces and dressings:
  aïoli, 203

sauces and dressings *(cont.)*
  à l'Américaine, 223, 237
  anchovy, 391;
    hollandaise, 532;
    mayonnaise, 77
  anglaise, 504
  avocado-yogurt, 75
  Béarnaise, 532
  béchamel, 531; variations,
    531
  boiled dressing, 94
  Bordelaise, 533; with
    poached beef marrow,
    533
  brains, 284; with meat,
    285; and tomato,
    284
  brown, quick, 533;
    variations, 533
  brown sugar rum, 508
  butterscotch, 508
  caper, 531
  cheese, creamy, 531
  cherries, 338–9
  chicken livers, 457
  chocolate, 507
  cognac, 507
  curried beef and tomato,
    279
  curry, 532
  diable, 533
  diet, 75, 77–8, 282
  dill, 202
  egg, 533
  garlic: mayonnaise
    (aïoli), 203; purée,
    534–5; vinaigrette, 74;
    vinaigrette, with herbs,
    74–5
  green, 372, 373;
    mayonnaise, 77
  Gribiche, 535
  hollandaise, 532;
    anchovy, 532
  horseradish cream, 9
  Louis dressing, 77
  maltaise, 129, 532
  mayonnaise, 76; anchovy,
    77; blender method,
    76; food processor
    method, 76; garlic
    (aïoli), 203; green, 77;
    mustard, 76, 90;
    tapenade, 36; yogurt,
    76, 90
  mornay, 531
  mustard, 531; Burgun-
    dian, 421; mayonnaise,
    76, 90; tapenade, 36;

sauces and dressings *(cont.)*
  vinaigrette, 74; yogurt,
    85
  olive, 101–2
  onions, braised, 280
  orange, 347
  parsley, 531
  pasta, 278, 581
  peppers, sautéed, 166
  pesto, 281–2; diet, 282;
    with parsley, 282; with
    walnuts, 282
  piquante, 299
  poppy-seed, 97
  port wine, 26–7
  poulette, 458
  prosciutto, peas, and
    cream, 285
  raisin and pine nut, 281;
    with anchovies, 281;
    with figs, 281
  rémoulade, 77
  Russian dressing, 37
  sardine and fennel, 280
  sesame oil and soy, 84
  soy dressing, 79;
    vinaigrette, hot, 104
  tapenade, 35–6; mayon-
    naise, 36; mustard, 36
  tarragon vinaigrette, 105
  tartare, 77
  tomato, fresh, 534; and
    brains, 284; with
    duxelles, 284
  tomato, light, 282–3; and
    beef, 284; and brains,
    284; and chicken, 284;
    and clams, 283; and
    ham, 283; and mussels,
    283; and turkey, 284;
    and veal, 284
  tuna (tonnato), 403;
    with yogurt and
    mayonnaise, 403
  vinaigrette: basic, 74;
    garlic, 74; garlic-herb,
    processor, 74–5; herb,
    74; lemon, processor,
    75; mustard, 74;
    shallot (or green
    onion), 74; and soy,
    hot, 104; tarragon, 105
  Virginia ham, spinach,
    and rosemary, 279–80
  white butter (beurre
    blanc), 201
  white wine, 534
  yogurt, 108; avocado, 75;
    dieter's, 75; herb, 202;

sauces and dressings (cont.)
    mayonnaise, 76, 90;
    mustard, 85
sauerkraut:
    with goose, roast, 341
    with pheasant, braised,
        353–4
    with pigs' hocks, braised,
        433
    with pork chops, sautéed,
        426
    and pork goulash, 427–8
    salad, 92–3; with beans,
        93; with knockwurst
        or frankfurters, 93;
        with tomatoes, 93
    slaw, 93
    spareribs baked with
        apples and potatoes,
        428; dill, 429; onions,
        429
sausages, meat, 587–8;
    casings, 434; kinds,
        587–8; to stuff, 434
    acorn squash stuffed with,
        593
    blood, 570, 587
    bollito misto, 372–3
    broiled balls, 435
    cakes, 435; with poached
        eggs, 252
    cassoulet, 304–5; limas
        and lamb, 306; limas,
        lamb, and pork, 306;
        limas and roasted duck
        legs, 306
    and croissants, 29,
    en brioche: homemade,
        28–9; store-bought,
        436; with mustard,
        436
    hot, 435
    link, to cook, 435
    old-fashioned, 434
    paella, 293–4
    partridge, braised, with
        cabbage, 348–9
    with peppers, sautéed,
        166
    peppers stuffed with,
        167
    pheasant, braised, with
        sauerkraut, 353–4
    with polenta, 300
    pork, 570, 587, 588
    with sweetbreads and
        kidneys, 465
    veal, 435, 572, 587–8
    veal birds provençal, 410

sausages, meat (cont.)
    white beans with cognac
        and ham, 303
    see also individual kinds
sausages, seafood:
    fish, 194
    French, 217–18; crab,
        218; shrimp, 218
    oyster, 231
savory crêpes, 265–6
scallions, see onions, green
scallops, 591
    avocado with seviche, 37
    chili soup, 65
    cocotte of seafood
        Manzanilla, 218–19
    coquilles St. Jacques,
        lo-cal, 241
    curried soup, 64–5
    fish sausage, 194
    poached, 240–1; with
        heavy cream and
        tarragon, 241
    provençal, 240
    risotto with shellfish, 292
    salad, with chili: and
        avocado, 109; avocado
        and sauce Gribiche,
        109; tomato and egg,
        109
    salad, marinated, 110;
        with potato and onion,
        110; tomatoes stuffed
        with, 89
    sautéed, 240
    seafood à l'Américaine,
        223–4
    seafood en brochette,
        218
    in sour cream with
        mushrooms, 18
    soused, 17
Scotch eggs, 250
    quail, 250
Scotch vichyssoise, 68
sea bass:
    broiled fillets, 196–7;
        variations, 197–8
    broiled steaks, 206
    cioppino, 222
    poached, with various
        sauces, 200–2
    poached fillets, with
        garlic mayonnaise,
        202–3
    salad, 108; yogurt
        dressing, 108
    sautéed fillets, 199
seafood, see fish and seafood

sea squab, see blowfish
sesame butter wafers, 486
sesame oil and soy
    dressing, 84
seviche and avocado, 37
shad, 208, 552–3
    baked stuffed, 208–9
    broiled fillets, 196–7;
        variations, 197–8
    roe: Mrs. Rockey's, 211–
        212; poached in
        butter, 209
    sautéed fillets, 199
shallots, 576, 577
    with Brussels sprouts,
        131
    in salad, 78
    sweet peppers with
        anchovies and parsley,
        6
    vinaigrette, 74
sharlotka, 525–6
shell beans, see beans,
    cranberry
shellfish, see fish and
    seafood
sherbet (sorbet), 497, 499;
    to freeze, 499
    apple, 501
    apricot, 499–500
    champagne, 500
    cranberry, 502
    ginger and lime, 501
    grapefruit, 501
    lichee, 502
    lime and tea, 502
    melon, 501–2
    orange, 501
    peach, 501
    pineapple, 501
    prune, 500
    red-wine-pear, 500
    strawberry, 501
    syrup, simple, 499
    white-wine-pear, 500
shortening, 592
shrimp, 591–2
    artichokes stuffed with,
        121
    avocado stuffed with, 37
    Chuck's baked, 234–5
    cioppino, 222
    cocotte of seafood
        Manzanilla, 218–19
    coleslaw: Billy's, 90–1;
        quick chopped, 90
    curried seafood, 225
    with curry butter, 233–4
    with dill butter, 234

shrimp *(cont.)*
  Floridian en papillote,
    234
  Hellenic seafood stew,
    219–20
  jambalaya, 232
  Kiev, 18
  loaf, 235
  omelet, 257
  on a stick, 232–3
  paella, 293–4
  salad: avocado, 112;
    chicken, 102; cucum-
    ber and tarragon, 112;
    olives and eggs, 112;
    orange and onion, 99;
    papaya and avocado,
    98; papaya and crab,
    99
  sautéed, with pesto, 281
  seafood à l'Américaine,
    223–4
  seafood sausages, French,
    218
  soup, 64
  sour cream with mush-
    rooms, 17–18
  soused, 17; with
    tarragon, 17;
  with tapenade mayon-
    naise, 36
  timbales, 263
  turban of sole with
    shrimp mousseline,
    205
Sicilian veal roll, 404–5
  cold, 405
  with omelet stuffing, 405
slaw, *see* coleslaw
smelts, 553
  baked spiced, 214
  fried, 213; garlic and
    parsley, 213
  with mint, 19–20
  skewered, 213
snails, 20
  with garlic butter, 20–1;
    mushroom caps, 21
snapper, 552
  bouillabaisse, 220–1
  see also red snapper
snow peas, *see* peas, snow
sole, 556
  bouillabaisse, 220–1
  broiled fillets, 196–7;
    variations, 197–8
  escabeche, 16
  goujonettes, 19; in beer
    batter, 19

sole *(cont.)*
  Marseilles fish soup, 67
  poached fillets: with
    garlic mayonnaise,
    202–3; in vermouth,
    203–4; in whisky, with
    caviar, 204
  salad, 108; yogurt
    dressing, 108
  sautéed fillets, 199; with
    curry sauce, 200;
    walnut-breaded, 199
  seafood à l'Américaine,
    223–4
  turban, mousseline, 204–
    205; individual, 205;
    with shrimp, 205
solianka, 221–2
  with dill, 222
sorbet, *see* sherbet
sorrel (sourgrass), 558–9
  roulade of veal Île-de-
    France, 405; with
    duxelles, 405
  soup, 52; with crème
    fraîche, 52; with
    yogurt, 52
soufflés:
  basic mixture, 265
  cheese, with zucchini
    blossoms, 177
  cornmeal, 302; with
    Parmesan cheese, 302;
    with whole-kernel
    corn, 302
  crab, 238
  lobster, 237
  romaine, 150–1
  winter squash, 178
soufflés in pastry:
  cheese, 265; with whole
    eggs, 265
  crabmeat, 265
  ham, 265
  marrow, 264–5
  spinach, 265
soups, 42–3
  thickeners, 42, 53, 54
sour cream, 548
  and caviar omelet, 256
  cheesecake, 524
  and corn roll, 264
  and minced clam roll,
    264
  and mushroom roll,
    264
  and salmon roll, 263–4
sourgrass, *see* sorrel
soybean oil, 578

soy dressing, 79
  and sesame oil, 84
  vinaigrette, hot, 104
spaghetti squash, 177
  boiled, with pasta sauce,
    177
Spanish melons, 573
  sherbet, 501–2
spätzle, 288
  with heavy cream, 288
spices, 592; to buy and
    keep, 592
  quatre épices, 536
spinach, 150, 172, 559
  cream soup, 54
  with eggs, poached, 252
  French-fried, 187
  lentil soup with spinach
    and lemon, 59
  and Manka's babies with
    cheese, 267
  mixed vegetable sauté,
    189–90
  mussels Hiely, 13
  omelet, 256
  and onion frittata, 259;
    with bacon, 259
  pasta, homemade, 277
  pasta with mushrooms,
    286; and Parmesan
    cheese, 286
  pâté, herbed, 24–5
  with polenta, 300–1
  purée, 173; with poached
    egg, 252; with shirred
    eggs, 251; with tongue,
    457
  roulade of veal Île-de-
    France, 405; with
    duxelles, 405
  salad, 79, 561; with
    bacon, 79; with cucum-
    ber, 80; with mush-
    rooms, 78, 82; and
    tongue, 104; tongue,
    with hot soy vinai-
    grette, 104; wilted, 80
  sardines with mint, 19–
    20
  soufflé in pastry, 265
  tian, 191; with noodles,
    191; with rice, 191
  timbales, 263
  tossed, 173; almonds and
    garlic, 173; bacon bits,
    173; tomatoes, 173
  turkey divan, 332
  Vanessi special, 260;
    with ground beef, 260

spinach *(cont.)*
  wilted, 172; garlic and
    oil, 173; hard-boiled
    egg, 173; nutmeg, 173
split-pea soup, 58
sponge cake:
  with apricot glaze, 520
  buttered-cake pudding,
    527
sprouts, 557
  and pork frittata, 259–60
  with scrambled eggs, 254
squab, 314, 592–3
  à la crème, 337
  in lettuce leaves, 30
  sautéed, with bacon, 337
  spatchcocked, 337
squab chickens, 337, 546
squash, 177, 593–4
  summer, 174, 593; and
    corn soup, 51; puréed,
    and corn soup, 51;
    cream vegetable soup,
    basic, 52–4; sautéed,
    174; steamed, 174;
    steamed, with oil,
    herbs, and garlic, 174
  winter, 177, 593–4;
    baked, 593; baked
    acorn or turban, 180,
    593; baked butternut,
    179, 593; baked
    Hubbard, 178–9, 593;
    with black walnuts,
    178; cream soup, 57;
    cream vegetable soup,
    basic, 52–4; with
    peanuts, 178; with
    pecans and ginger, 178;
    with raw zucchini, 178;
    soufflé, 178; spiced,
    177; steamed, 593
  see also zucchini
squid, 594
stock and broth:
  beef, 530
  chicken, 529
  duck, wild, 345
  essence de poisson, 45
  fish, 530
  lamb, 396–7
  oxtail, 43, 48–9, 567
  veal, 397
  vegetable, 44–5
Stockli, Albert:
  sweetbreads Albert, 463
strawberries, 594; to buy,
    594
  fool, 515

strawberries *(cont.)*
  fruit and rice salad, 97
  Manka's babies and
    yogurt, 267
  poached, 505
  raw, as dessert, 506
  sherbet, 501
  Teresa, 514–15; with
    glazed rhubarb, 515
striped bass (rockfish), 553
  bouillabaisse, 220–1
  broiled fillets, 196–7;
    variations, 197–8
  broiled steaks, 206
  cioppino, 222
  poached, with various
    sauces, 200–2
  poached fillets, with
    garlic mayonnaise,
    202–3
  salad, 108; yogurt
    dressing, 108
  sautéed fillets, 199
  tartare, 13
sturgeon, 553
  broiled steaks, 206
  coulibiac, 214–15; with
    rice, 215
  seafood en brochette, 218
  smoked, pâté, 11
  tartare, 13
suet, 594–5
sugar cookies, 493
sugar snap peas, *see* peas,
    sugar snap
sun chokes, *see* Jerusalem
    artichokes
sunflower oil, 576
Swedish leg of lamb, 389
sweetbreads, 448, 462;
    blanched, 462
  Albert, 463
  broiled, 464
  calves', 462, 572
  and chicken salad, 100
  escabeche, 16
  herbed, 465
  and kidneys: en
    brochette, 454; en
    brochette flambé, 454;
    with sausages, 465
  lambs', 462, 569
  milanese, 464
  panné, 464; with cream,
    464; with mustard,
    464
  and turkey salad, 100
sweet potatoes, 595
  French-fried, 189

Swiss chard, *see* chard
Swiss cheese salad, 270
swordfish:
  baked steak, 207
  bouillabaisse, 220–1
  broiled steak: garlic and
    olives, 207; marinated,
    207; pepper, 207;
    rosemary, 207
syrup:
  caramel, 504
  for poached fruit, 505–6
  simple, for sherbet, 499
Szechuan salad, spicy, 84

Tabasco, 582
tablier de sapeur, 461
tangelos, 564
tangerines, 564
tapenade, 35–6
  with avocado, 36
  with hard-boiled eggs, 36
  mayonnaise, 36; with
    seafood, 36
  with mustard, 36
  tomatoes stuffed with, 36
tapioca, apple, 527
  and pear, 527
  and quince, 527
tarragon, 561
  butter, 536–7
  in salad, 78
  vinaigrette, 105
tartare sauce, 77
tarte Tatin, 513
tart pastry, rich, 264–5
tarts:
  brandade, 245
  pear, thin, 513–14
  pear and chocolate, 511
  pineapple and apricot,
    510–11
  quince, The Coach
    House, 512
  tarte Tatin, 513
  tuna, 226–7
tea and lime sherbet, 502
teriyaki, marinade, 345,
    366, 368
testicles:
  beef, 567
  lamb, 569
thickeners:
  aïoli, 202
  béchamel, 54
  beurre manié, 536
  cornmeal, 547
  crumbs, 43

thickeners (cont.)
 flour, 555
 nuts, 43
 oxtail stock, 43, 567
 potato, instant mashed,
  53, 54
 vegetables, puréed, 43
thyme, 561
tian, 191
 of mixed greens, 152; and
  bacon, 152
 with noodles, 191
 with rice, 191
tilefish, 553–4
 baked steak niçoise, 208
 broiled steaks, 206
 seafood à l'Américaine,
  223–4
timbales:
 basil, 263
 broccoli, 263
 chicken, 263
 crabmeat, 263
 ham, 263
 lettuce, 262–3
 lobster, 263
 shrimp, 263
 spinach, 263
 watercress, 263
tomatoes, 180, 595; to peel,
  595; to ripen, 595; to
  seed, 595
 with anchovies, 6; sweet
  peppers and eggs, 6
 baked: Greek, 183;
  stuffed with corn, 182–
  183; stuffed with
  mozzarella, 182
 broiled: with garlic and
  spices, 183; herbed,
  183; with pesto, 183;
  with sautéed eggplant,
  147
 canned, 180, 595
 caponata, 34; with tuna,
  35
 cherry, 78, 595; with
  risotto, 293; steamed,
  184–5; steamed peeled,
  185; stuffed with
  tapenade, 36
 eggplant casserole, 147
 fried green, with cream,
  184
 lamb, roast shoulder, and
  eggplant, 392
 mixed vegetable sauté,
  189–90
 omelet, 256

tomatoes (cont.)
 and onion frittata, 259
 pasta, food processor
  method, 277
 Pennsylvania Dutch, 184
 with peppers vinaigrette
  and mozzarella, 167
 pipérade basquaise, 255
 primavera, 11
 ratatouille, 190; with
  eggs, poached, and
  cheese, 191; fennel,
  191; leeks, 191; mush-
  rooms, 191; spicy, 191
 salad, 78; Greek, 87;
  marinated vegetables
  and noodles, 87; and
  mozzarella, 79; and
  sauerkraut, 93
 sauce, fresh, 534; brain
  sauce, 284; duxelles,
  284; provençal, with
  beef tongue, 456–7
 sauce, light, 282–3; and
  beef, 284; brains, 284;
  chicken, 284; clams,
  283; ham, 283;
  mussels, 283; turkey,
  284; veal, 284
 sauce, with pesto, 281
 sauce and curried beef,
  279
 sautéed, 184; with sautéed
  eggplant
 scalloped: canned, 182;
  fresh, 181–2
 with scrambled eggs, 254
 with short ribs, braised,
  380
 soup, fresh, 46; with
  orange juice, 46; purée,
  46
 with spinach, tossed, 173
 stewed, 180–1; with
  basil, 181; chilies, 181;
  eggs, poached, 181;
  garlic and lemon zest,
  181; onion, 181
 stuffed: with crab and
  rice salad, 89; cucum-
  bers, smothered, 88–9;
  fish salad, 89; green
  beans, 89; herring
  salad, 89; scallop salad,
  89; tuna, 10; tuna and
  onions, 10
 stuffed with basic chicken
  salad, 89 and celery,
  89; macadamia nuts, 89

tongue, 449
 beef, 456, 565: bollito
  misto, 372–3; chicken
  liver sauce, Philip
  Brown's, 457; esca-
  beche, 16; Madeira
  sauce, 457; pot-au-feu,
  457; provençal tomato
  sauce, 456–7; spinach,
  457
 and herring salad, 7
 and horseradish, veal
  birds stuffed with,
  409–10
 lambs', 458; 568; pickled,
  458–5; poulette, 458;
  tomato sauce, 458;
  vinaigrette, 458
 pork, 569
 and spinach salad, 104;
  hot soy vinaigrette,
  104
 veal, 571; bollito, misto,
  372–3; pickled, 458–9;
  poulette, 458; tomato
  sauce, 458; vinaigrette,
  458
tripe, 449, 567
 à la mode de Caen, 459;
  with red wine, 459
 with daube provençale,
  378
 with gizzards, Cecilia
  Chiang's, 461–2
 menudo, 460–1
 niçoise, 460
 soup, The Coach House,
  42, 62–3
 tablier de sapeur, 461
trout, 554
 broiled, 212
 broiled fillets, 196–7;
  variations, 197–8
 salad, 108; yogurt
  dressing, 108
 sautéed, 199; in crêpes,
  212–13
 smoked, mousse, 10
truffles:
 and chicken liver stuffing,
  for fillet of beef, 365–
  366
 rillettes, 26
 with risotto, 292
tuiles, 484
tuna, 10
 with anchovies and
  peppers, 6
 with artichoke hearts, 10

tuna (cont.)
 broiled steaks, 206
 with caponata, 35
 coleslaw, quick chopped,
  90
 coulibiac, 214–15; with
  rice, 215
 with egg, hard-boiled, 10
 pâté, 11
 salad, with apple, 113
 salad, with onion,
  avocado, and egg, 113;
  fennel, 113; tomatoes,
  113
 sauce (tonnato): for
  pork loin, 403; for
  turkey, 332; for veal,
  402–3; for veal, with
  yogurt and mayon-
  naise, 403
 tart, 226–7
 tartare, 13
 with tomatoes, 10; and
  onions, 10; primavera,
  11
turban (or buttercup)
 squash, 177, 593
 baked, 180, 593; bacon
  and garlic, 180; maple
  sugar and bacon, 180
 see also squash, winter
turkey, 313, 595–6
 bollito misto, 372–3
 in brain sauce, 285
 breast, roast, 329–30;
  cold, variations, 330;
  deviled, 330; hot,
  variations, 330
 breast, sautéed, pappa-
  gallo, 330–1
 casserole, 333
 chili, 333–4
 divan, 332; with aspara-
  gus, 332; with endive,
  332; with spinach, 332
 drumsticks, deviled, 334
 in lettuce leaves, 29–30
 parts, 329; to thaw, 329
 and pork, veal birds
  stuffed with, 409
 salad: and chutney, 103;
  chutney, with foie
  gras, 103; hot, 332
 salad, basic, 99–100;
  celery, 100; celery and
  grapes, 100; maca-
  damia nuts, 100; sweet-
  breads, 100
 saltimbocca, 331

turkey (cont.)
 and tomato sauce, 294
 tonnato, 332
 wings, braised, 334–5;
  piquant, 335;
  provençal, 335
turkey, wild, 596
Turkish cucumber salad,
 83–4
turnips, 185, 596
 buttered, 186; with
  mushrooms, 186
 gratin, 186
 greens, wilted, 150, 559
 with mustard rabbit, 357
 raw, salad or crudité, 187
 vichyssoise, 55
 see also rutabagas
turtle soup:
 boula-boula, 47
 Lady Curzon, 46–7

S.S. United States:
 baked potatoes with
  caviar, 38

Vadis bars, 488–9
Vanessi special, 260
 with beans and rice, 260
 with ham, 260
 with spinach, 260
vanilla, 596–7
 extract, homemade, 596
 pots de crème, 528; with
  praline powder, 528
veal, 400–1; 571–2
 birds: with ham, 409;
  olive-anchovy stuffing,
  409; Oregon, 410;
  provençal, 410; tongue
  and horseradish, 409–
  410; turkey and pork,
  409
 blanquette of, 397
 in brain sauce, 286
 chops: broiled, 412
 chops sautéed with
  cream, 411; hearts of
  palm, 412; mushrooms,
  412; onion sauce,
  411–2
 en daube, 414
 hearts, 572; braised, 455–
  456
 kidneys, 449, 572; broiled
  deviled, 455; deviled
  sauté, 455; sauté

veal (cont.)
 flambé, 455; sweet-
  breads and sausages,
  465
 kidneys en brochette,
  454; herb butter, 454;
  mushrooms, 454;
  mushrooms and bacon,
  454; sweetbreads, 454;
  sweetbreads flambé,
  454
 kidneys "on the half
  shell," 453; flambé,
  453; mushrooms, 453
 meat loaf, old-fashioned,
  364, 383–4; beef liver,
  384; chilied, 385; with
  clams, minced, 384;
  eggs, hard-boiled, 384;
  ham, 384; olives, 384
 "minced," with cream,
  410–11; mustard sauce,
  411; onions and
  mushrooms, 411
 ossi buchi, 416, 572;
  with prosciutto and
  black olives, 416
 paillard of, 413
 and pork goulash, 428
 ragout, 415–16
 roast, with roquefort-
  butter stuffing, 401–2
 roast breast, 413–14
 roll, Sicilian, 404–5;
  cold, 405; omelet
  stuffing, 405
 roulade Île-de-France,
  405; with duxelles, 405
 salad, 99–100; herring, 7;
  macadamia nuts, 100
 saltimbocca, 408;
  mozzarella cheese, 408
 sausages, 435, 572, 587–
  588
 scallops, 401, 406;
  almonds, 407; cognac,
  407; cream, 407; herbs,
  407; Lafayette, 407–8;
  lemon, 406; lemon and
  Parmesan cheese,
  406–7; Marsala, 407;
  piquant, 408; port, 407;
  sherry, 407; smitaine,
  407; white wine,
  407
 shanks, braised, with
  tomatoes and sausages,
  414–15
 stock, 397

veal (cont.)
  sweetbreads, 572
  and tomato sauce, 284
  tongue, 571; bollito
    misto, 372–3; pickled,
    458–9; poulette, 458;
    tomato sauce, 458;
    vinaigrette, 458
  with tuna sauce (ton-
    nato), 402–3; yogurt
    and mayonnaise, 403
vegetables, 114–16; cooking
  time, 115
  à la Grecque, with lobster
    Napoule, 236
  beer batter, 187, 188
  bollito misto, 372–3
  broth, 44–5
  cream soup, basic, 52–4
  French-fried, 187–8
  mixed sauté, 189–90
  and oxtail soup, 49–50
  puréed: with poached
    eggs, 252; as thickener
    for soups, 43
  salad of marinated
    vegetables and noodles,
    86–7; with corn, 87;
    with foie gras, 87; with
    tomatoes, 87
  salad of vegetables and
    olives with mustard-
    yogurt dressing, 84;
    and blue cheese, 85;
    and Gruyère cheese, 85
venison, 362, 597
  broiled steaks, 445;
    seasoned butter, 445
  chili, 447–8
  hamburgers, 447; flambé,
    447; garlic and chives,
    447; herbed, 447
  kebabs, 445–6
  liver, 597
  marinade, 442, 444
  pot roast, 446
  roast: leg, marinated,
    443; loin, Helmut
    Ripperberger's, 444–5;
    saddle, 443–4
  sautéed steaks, 445;
    peppered, 445
venison, mock, 389
vichyssoise, 54–5
  apple, 55
  carrot, 55
  caviar, 55
  Scotch, 68

vichyssoise (cont.)
  turnip, 55
  watercress, 55
vinaigrette sauce:
  basic, 74
  garlic, 74
  garlic-herb, processor,
    74–5
  herb, 74
  lemon, processor, 75
  mustard, 74
  shallot (or green onion),
    74
  and soy, hot, 104
  tarragon, 105
vinegar, 73–4, 597
vintner's salad, 81
La Voûte (Lyons):
  tablier de sapeur, 461

walnut oil, 74
walnuts, 576
  black, 576; with winter
    squash, 178
  bread: nut rum, 481;
    polygrained, 472
  pesto, 282
  with rice, 289
  with rice, wild, 295
  in salad, 79
  toasted, 576
  zucchini, sautéed, 175
watercress, 557
  Chinese style soup, 56–7
  cream soup, 54
  cream vegetable soup,
    basic, 52–4
  timbales, 263
  vichyssoise, 55
  wilted, 150
watermelons, 573
weisswurst, 588
Welsh rarebit, 269
  with hamburger, 269
  with poached egg, 269
  with tomato juice, 269
white butter sauce, 201
whitefish:
  broiled fillets, 196–7;
    variations, 197–8
  poached, with various
    sauces, 200–2
  sautéed fillets, 199
white wine:
  court bouillon, 203
  pear sherbet, 500
  sauce, 534

Williams, Chuck:
  baked shrimp, 234–5
wine vinegar, 74, 597

yams, 595, 597
yeast, 597–8; fresh, to keep,
  598; to proof, 598
yellow turnips, see ruta-
  bagas
yogurt:
  dressing or sauce, 108;
    avocado, 75; dieter's,
    75; -herb, 202; mayon-
    naise, 76, 90; mustard,
    85
  soup: cold minted, 57–8;
    cold minted pea, 55–6;
    and sorrel, 52
  Turkish cucumber salad,
    83–4

zampone, 570
zester, 563
zucchini, 174, 593
  à la Grecque, with
    lobster Napoule, 236
  blossoms, 176
  blossoms, deep-fried or
    sautéed, 176; cheese
    soufflé, 177; omelet,
    176; with scrambled
    eggs, 176
  cream vegetable soup,
    basic, 52–4
  French-fried, 188
  mixed vegetable sauté,
    189–90
  and onion frittata, 258–
    259; with prosciutto,
    259
  pancake, 175–6; with
    cheese, 176
  ratatouille, 190; with
    eggs, poached, and
    cheese, 191; fennel,
    191; leeks, 191; mush-
    rooms, 191; spicy, 191
  raw, with puréed winter
    squash, 178
  sautéed, 175; garlic and
    herbs, 175; shallots,
    175; walnuts, 175
  shredded, sautéed, 175;
    pesto, 281
  tian, 191; with noodles,
    191, with rice, 191

Conversions

Equivalent Imperial and Metric Measurements

American cooks use standard containers, the 8-ounce cup and a table-spoon that takes exactly 16 level fillings to fill that cup level. Measuring by cup makes it very difficult to give weight equivalents, as a cup of densely packed butter will weigh considerably more than a cup of flour. The easiest way therefore to deal with cup measurements in recipes is to take the amount by volume rather than by weight. Thus the equation reads:

$$1 \text{ cup} = 240 \text{ ml} = 8 \text{ fl. oz.} \qquad \tfrac{1}{2} \text{ cup} = 120 \text{ ml} = 4 \text{ fl. oz.}$$

It is possible to buy a set of American cup measures in major stores around the world.

In the States, butter is often measured in sticks. One stick is the equivalent of 8 tablespoons. One tablespoon of butter is therefore the equivalent to ¹/₂ ounce/14 grams.

Solid Measures

U.S. and Imperial Measures Metric Measures

OUNCES	POUNDS	GRAMS	KILOS
1		28	
2		56	
3 ¹/₂		100	
4	¹/₄	112	
5		140	
6		168	
8	¹/₂	225	
9		250	¹/₄
12	³/₄	340	
16	1	450	
18		500	¹/₂
20	1 ¹/₄	560	
24	1 ¹/₂	675	
27		750	³/₄
28	1 ³/₄	780	
32	2	900	
36	2 ¹/₄	1000	1
40	2 ¹/₂	1100	
48	3	1350	
54		1500	1 ¹/₂
64	4	1800	
72	4 ¹/₂	2000	2
80	5	2250	2 ¹/₄
90		2500	2 ¹/₂
100	6	2800	2 ³/₄

Liquid Measures

Fluid ounces	U.S. Measures	Imperial measures	Milliliters
	1 TSP	1 TSP	5
	2 TSP	1 DESSERT SPOON	10
1/2	1 TBS	1 TBS	14
1	2 TBS	2 TBS	28
2	1/4 CUP	4 TBS	56
4	1/2 CUP		110
5		1/4 PINT OR 1 GILL	140
6	3/4 CUP		170
8	1 CUP		225
9			250 OR 1/4 LITER
10	1 1/4 CUPS	1/2 PINT	280
12	1 1/2 CUPS		340
15		3/4 PINT	420
16	2 CUPS		450
18	2 1/4 CUPS		500 OR 1/2 LITER
20	2 1/2 CUPS	1 PINT	560
24	3 CUPS		675
25		1 1/4 PINTS	700
27	3 1/2 CUPS		750
30	3 3/4 CUPS	1 1/2 PINTS	840
32	4 CUPS OR 1 QUART		900
35		1 3/4 PINTS	980
36	4 1/2 CUPS		1000 OR 1 LITER
40	5 CUPS	2 PINTS OR 1 QUART	1120
48	6 CUPS		1350
50		2 1/2 PINTS	1400
60	7 1/2 CUPS	3 PINTS	1680
64	8 CUPS OR 2 QUARTS		1800
72	9 CUPS		2000 OR 2 LITERS
80	10 CUPS	4 PINTS	2250
96	12 CUPS OR 3 QUARTS		2700
100		5 PINTS	2800

Suggested Equivalents and Substitutes for Ingredients

all-purpose flour—plain flour
arugula—rocket
beet—beetroot
bell peppers—fleshy peppers
bouillon cubes—stock cubes
coarse salt—kitchen salt
confectioner's sugar—icing sugar
cornstarch—cornflour
eggplant—aubergine
fava beans—broadbeans
flat-leaf parsley—continental parsley
granulated sugar—caster sugar
green grapes—white grapes
romaine—cos lettuce
scallion—spring onion
sour cherry—morello cherry
squash—courgettes or marrow
tomato paste—tomato concentrate
unbleached flour—strong, white flour
vanilla bean—vanilla pod
zest—rind
zucchini—courettes
heavy cream—double cream
baking sheet—oven tray
cheesecloth—muslin
parchment paper—greaseproof paper
plastic wrap—cling film

Oven Temperature Equivalents

Fahrenheit	Celsius	Gas Mark	Description
225	110	1/4	COOL
250	130	1/2	
275	140	1	VERY SLOW
300	150	2	
325	170	3	SLOW
350	180	4	MODERATE
375	190	5	
400	200	6	MODERATELY HOT
425	220	7	FAIRLY HOT
450	230	8	HOT
475	240	9	VERY HOT
500	250	10	EXTREMELY HOT

Any broiling recipes can be used with the grill of the oven, but beware of high-temperature grills.